501

MOST NOTORIOUS CRIMES

501
MOST NOTORIOUS CRIMES

PAUL DONNELLEY

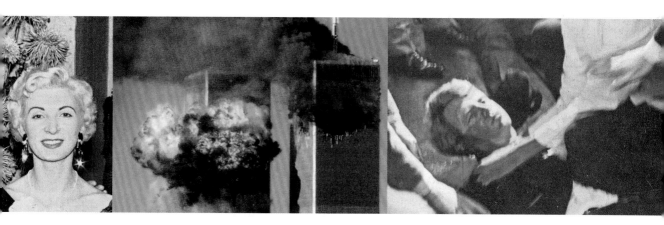

Bounty Books

501 MOST NOTORIOUS CRIMES
PAUL DONNELLEY

**In loving memory of Jeremy Beadle (1948-2008)
mentor, counsellor, true crime aficionado and
always a friend in need**.

Publisher: Polly Manguel
Project Editor: Emma Beare
Editor: Jane Birch
Designer: Ron Callow/Design 23
Picture Researcher: Emma O'Neill
Production Manager: Neil Randles
Production Assistant: Gemma Seddon

First published in Great Britain in 2009 by Bounty Books,
a division of Octopus Publishing Group Limited
Reprinted 2011

This paperback version published in 2013 by Bounty Books,
a division of Octopus Publishing Group Limited,
Endeavour House, 189 Shaftesbury Avenue, London WC2H 8JY
www.octopusbooks.co.uk
Reprinted 2014

An Hachette UK Company
www.hachette.co.uk

A CIP catalogue record is available from the British Library

ISBN: 978-0-753725-98-6

Printed and bound in China

Please note: Warning! As one would expect from a book on this subject some of the material
contained within is graphic and explicit. Please do not read if this is likely to cause offence.

Contents

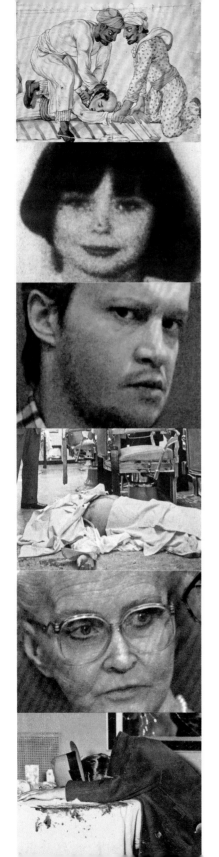

Introduction

Every day we open our newspapers, turn on the television and radio or log on to the internet and we are assailed with tales of malfeasance and misdemeanour. Some are instantly forgettable while others remain in the memory due to their sheer horror. This book lists more than five hundred of the most horrific, gruesome, memorable crimes ever committed. It features serial killers, cannibals, rapists, robbers, burglars, muggers, forgers, pirates, gangsters, cop killers, kidnappers and plain old murderers. It shows man's (and woman's) inhumanity to man, his ingenuity when it comes to thinking up ever more devious crimes and also his stupidity when he gets caught.

Some of the crimes in this book can be written off as youthful folly, while others are perpetrated by hardened criminals and by the simply insane – who can imagine dating a mad woman (Knight) who killed her boyfriend and intended to serve up his remains as dinner for his children? Or the old aged pensioner (Fish) who raped and murdered his victim before stewing her with carrots and onions and eating her?

Some of the stories feature miscarriages of justice (Hauptmann) and others that were assumed to be until proven to be a safe conviction by modern technology (Hanratty).

It contains tales of great robberies (Blood) and ones that didn't go quite according to plan (Great Train Robbery).

Clifford Irving probably thought he was on safe ground when he proposed to a publisher the "autobiography" of the notoriously reclusive billionaire Howard Hughes. How could he know that Hughes would break his self-imposed silence to give a press conference, albeit only over the telephone?

You think the toyboy phenomenon started in the 1980s with the likes of Britt Ekland taking younger lovers? Wrong. Alma Rattenbury was sharing her bed with a teenager in 1930s Bournemouth – only for it all come to a tragic end when the toyboy bashed in the husband's head with a mallet. Or did he?

One thing that struck me during the writing of this book was how young some of the criminals were or how much of their lives they wasted behind bars. Honour among thieves there may well be, but stupidity among criminals seems to be a more accurate maxim. If there is a moral to this book it is simple – crime doesn't pay (except when it does).

Acknowledgments

This is the first major book I have written without being able to call upon the sagacity, advice and good humour of Jeremy Beadle. His death on the evening of Wednesday 30 January 2008 at the ridiculously early age of 59 robbed television of one of its most experienced performers, true crime writing and the world of oddities of a knowledgeable and generous benefactor and many people – myself included – of a very good friend. I knew Jeremy for almost thirty years – I was a teenager when we first spoke – and in that time he was always my first port of call for advice on my career, to discuss a new book or just for a chat. I miss him.

My second debt goes to Ian Harrison, an extremely talented writer, whose life has taken him in a different direction. The law's gain is a loss for all those who enjoy good books. Ian compiled the original list that formed the basis of the 501 crimes herein before generously passing the project onto me.

To write this book I used my own extensive crime library and also called upon the unpublished research I have done over many years. I prevailed upon the good natures of many people and for their help I would like to thank: Mel Ayton; Ellen Carmody of the Notre Dame De Sion School; the late George Carpozi, Jr. (1920-1999); Gavin Fuller of the Telegraph Media Group; the late Joe Gaute (1904-1991); Barry A. Kemelhor; Sally Morgan; James Morton; Howard Sounes; the late Professor Keith Simpson (1907-1985); James Steen; Mitchell Symons; Liz Williams, Nicola Wilson, and of course, my beloved Karima without whom none of this would be possible.

Paul Donnelley
www.pauldonnelley.com

TREASON, OUTLAWRY, PIRACY, ANARCHY, RIOTING & TERRORISM

David III (aka Dafydd ap Gruffydd)

"The last survivor of a family of traitors"

WHERE:
Shrewsbury, England
WHEN:
Saturday 2 October 1283
THE AFTERMATH:
Dafydd's body parts were sent to four English cities for display while his head joined that of his brother, Llywelyn, on top of the Tower of London, where the skulls were still visible many years later. The final insult was that in 1301 Edward invested his own son, Edward II, with the title Prince of Wales.

A prisoner being drawn and quartered.

THE CRIME: As well as being the first nobleman in England to be hanged, drawn and quartered, Dafydd was also the last native Prince of Wales. Born on 11 July 1238, he was the son of Llewelyn ap Gruffydd. For several years Dafydd fought alongside the English King Edward I against his elder brother Llywelyn ap Gruffydd. Eventually he turned against the King and, on the death of his brother on 11 December 1282, he styled himself "Prince of Wales and Lord of Snowdon" and assumed leadership of the Welsh fight against Edward. After Dafydd's inevitable capture, on 22 June 1283, his punishment was specifically devised to be harsher than any previous form of capital punishment with the intention of eliminating further Welsh resistance.

Edward had already had Dafydd's young sons incarcerated for life in Bristol Castle and his daughters sent to a nunnery in England, and now summoned all the English nobles to Shrewsbury for the trial of "the last survivor of a family of traitors". Before a court overseen by John de Vaux, Dafydd was sentenced to death for treason. The punishment was meted out in four stages: he was dragged through the streets of Shrewsbury to the scaffold; he was hanged for the murder of Fulk Trigald and others; he was disembowelled and his entrails burnt because the murders had been committed during the Lord's passion; and finally, for plotting the king's death, he was beheaded and his body was quartered. Geoffrey of Shrewsbury was paid 20 shillings to perform the ghastly ritual.

Sir William Wallace rejecting English proposals.

William Wallace

"Guardian of Scotland and Leader of its Armies"

THE CRIME: The first to have his head adorn the ramparts of London Bridge as a warning to other wrongdoers was William Wallace. Despite some reports that he was a petty criminal, nothing is known for certain about Wallace before 1297.

In May of that year he killed William Heselrig, the Sheriff of Lanark. Six months later, on 11 September, his army beat the English at the Battle of Stirling Bridge. Wallace was afterwards named "Guardian of Scotland and Leader of its Armies". Wallace was defeated at the Battle of Falkirk on 22 July 1298 and fled to France, returning in 1303. On 5 August 1305 he was captured after Scot, John de Menteith, handed him over. On 22 August 1305, William Wallace was brought to London.

WHERE:
London, England
WHEN:
Monday 23 August 1305
THE AFTERMATH:
Early the next morning he was taken to Westminster Hall where, to fulfil his boast that one day he would wear a crown in Westminster, a laurel crown was mockingly placed on his head. As an outlawed thief, the law allowed him no defence; his trial and judgement were mere formalities and the sentence was carried out immediately. He was stripped naked then drawn on a hurdle by two horses to the gallows at Smoothfield (today King Street in Smithfield). Along the way he was pelted with offal, garbage and dung and struck with whips and cudgels by the bloodthirsty Londoners. Still naked, he mounted the scaffold and was hanged by a halter but let down still alive. Next his genitals were cut off and then a deep gash made in his belly; the executioner then ripped out his intestines, liver, and lungs, holding each aloft for the crowd to see before consigning them to the fire before Wallace's eyes. Then the executioner reached into the chest cavity to tear out Wallace's still beating heart. Finally, mercifully, his head was cut off and his trunk cut into four pieces. His head was dipped in pitch to delay putrefaction then spiked and placed upon the ramparts of London Bridge. His quarters were later displayed at various towns: his right arm above the bridge at Newcastle-upon-Tyne; his left arm at Stirling; his right leg at Berwick and his left leg at Perth. The total cost of the butchery was 61 shillings and ten pence.
YOU SHOULD KNOW:
Ironically Wallace, the name of Scotland's greatest patriot, originally meant "Welshman".

Anne Boleyn faints as an angry Henry VIII looks on.

WHERE:
Tower Hill, London, England
WHEN:
11am Friday 19 May 1536
THE AFTERMATH:
Anne was sentenced "to be burned alive or beheaded, at the King's pleasure". The king chose beheading but, as Anne had suffered a morbid fear of the axe since childhood, she begged to die by the sword – a request Henry granted. A highly skilled French executioner was bought over from Calais. He was paid 100 French crowns (about £23), which included payment for a tight-fitting black suit and a high horn-shaped hat attached to a half mask, which covered the upper part of his face. Just after 11am, Anne arrived at the straw-laden scaffold and removed her grey damask cloak to reveal a red underskirt. Her famous long black hair was held in place by a black cap, which was removed and replaced by a white one. She prayed, declared her loyalty to Henry and was then blindfolded with a linen handkerchief. She knelt and, as she did so, the executioner silently drew the sword from where he had hidden it from her view under the straw. He signalled to his assistant to approach Anne who, hearing the footsteps, turned towards the sound. As she turned the sword swept down and with one clean stroke severed her head. With blood gushing everywhere the executioner held the head high and witnesses saw that Anne's eyes and lips were still moving convulsively. Her remains were placed in an old arrow chest and buried under the altar of the Chapel Royal of Peter ad Vincula within the Tower walls.
YOU SHOULD KNOW:
If Henry's charges of adultery had failed, Anne would still have lost her head. Henry planned to use the fact that she had six fingers on one hand and a third nipple as proof she was a witch.

Anne Boleyn

"Burned alive or beheaded, at the King's pleasure"

THE CRIME: The last person to be executed by the sword in England was also responsible for the formation of the Church of England. King Henry VIII was married to Catherine of Aragon, his late brother's fiancée, when he fell in love with Anne Boleyn, having already had an affair with her sister Mary. Henry tried to persuade Pope Clement VII to annul his marriage to Catherine but the pope refused and rather than abiding by the papal ruling, Henry split from Rome. Henry's project to divorce Catherine was known as "the king's great matter". Henry secretly married Anne, who was pregnant, on 25 January 1533 (although historian David Starkey reports the couple first married on 14 November 1532). On 10 April Thomas Cranmer, the Archbishop of Canterbury, declared Henry's marriage to Catherine void and in July Henry was excommunicated. On 7 September 1533 Anne gave birth to the future Queen Elizabeth I. Henry tired of Anne when she was unable to provide him with a male heir. To rid himself of Anne, she was condemned on trumped-up charges of adultery and treason.

Anthony Babington

"Spare me, Lord Jesus"

THE CRIME: In January 1586 Mary, Queen of Scots, was confined to Chartley Hall, a manor house belonging to the Earl of Essex in Staffordshire, under the supervision of Sir Amyas Paulet. That year a plot was hatched to assassinate Queen Elizabeth I and liberate Mary. The conspirators – young, well-bred and Catholic – hoped it would lead to the restoration of Catholicism in England. Anthony Babington, a wealthy leading conspirator, met the Catholic priest John Ballard who told him that the leaders of the Catholic League in France had been asked by the pope to lead an invasion force into England. Babington was unsure how much of this information was true. Ballard told him that former soldier John Savage would assassinate the queen. Babington was introduced to Savage after he had recruited a small band of conspirators. They included Thomas Salisbury, Edward Abington, Chidiock Tichborne, Charles Tilney, Edward Windsor and Robert Barnewell. Five more – Edward Jones, Henry Donne, Robert Gage, John Travers and John Charnock – joined the plot later.

As with many plots there was a double agent in the camp. In this case it was Gilbert Gifford who was working for Sir Francis Walshingham. Gifford intercepted letters to and from Mary and passed them to Walsingham for decryption. The conspirators met on 7 June 1586 to outline their plans. Babington said, "We seemed to stand in a dilemma… On the one side the magistrates here would take aways our lives … and on the other side the straunger shoulde invade and bring [our country] into servitude to foreigners." On 6 July Babington wrote to Mary pledging his devotion. Eleven days later, Mary replied, thanking Babington and urging him to act soon.

WHERE:
London, England
WHEN:
Tuesday 7 June 1586
THE AFTERMATH:
Babington fled in August 1586, after Ballard was arrested, and hid in St John's Wood, London. He was arrested in Harrow, Middlesex. All of the conspirators confessed after being interrogated. Seven defendants were arraigned before the judges on 13 and 14 September. Ballard, Babington, Barnewell, Donne, Salisbury, and Tichborne then all pleaded guilty to conspiring to free Mary and alter religion, but not guilty to planning to kill the queen. Told that they could not plead in different ways to separate charges, all except Tichborne changed their pleas to guilty. All were condemned to die traitors' deaths. On 15 September the remaining seven were arraigned. On 20 September the first seven conspirators, led by Ballard and Babington, were executed. They were hanged for a short time, cut down while they were still alive, and then castrated and disembowelled. Babington cried, '"*Parce mihi, domine Jesus*" ("Spare me, Lord Jesus"). The remaining seven were executed the following day but were disembowelled only after death. Mary, Queen of Scots was beheaded on 8 February 1587.

Portrait of Mary, Queen of Scots

Guy Fawkes

"Remember, remember the fifth of November"

WHERE:
Houses of Parliament, London,
England
WHEN:
Midnight Tuesday 5 November 1605
THE AFTERMATH:
Fawkes was arrested, taken to the
Tower of London and tortured. The
conspirators were arrested, apart
from Catesby who was shot evading
capture. On 27 January 1606 at
Westminster Hall the conspirators
were tried. All pleaded guilty apart
from Sir Everard Digby. The plotters
were hanged, drawn and quartered
on 30 and 31 January. Henry Garnet,
the priest who had heard confession
from several of the conspirators, was
executed on 3 May 1606 at St Paul's
Cathedral. The Houses of Parliament
are still searched by the Yeomen of
the Guard before the State
Opening every year.
YOU SHOULD KNOW:
Guy Fawkes escaped being drawn
and quartered alive by jumping from
the gallows and breaking his neck.

*The Gunpowder Plot
conspirators, including
Guy Fawkes*

THE CRIME: In May 1604 Robert Catesby rented rooms adjacent to
the House of Lords as the beginning of a plot to kill King James I of
England and install Elizabeth, his nine-year-old daughter, on the
throne. His conspirators included Thomas Winter, Robert Winter,
John Wright, Christopher Wright, Robert Keyes, Sir Thomas Percy,
Lord John Grant, Sir Ambrose Rokewood, Sir Everard Digby, Sir
Francis Tresham, Thomas Bates (Catesby's servant) and Guido
Fawkes, an explosives expert.

Robert Catesby confessed the plot to his priest Oswald Tesimond
who told his colleague, the principal Jesuit of England, Father Henry
Garnet. The plot had to be delayed because the Black Plague arrived
in London in the summer of 1604 and the opening of Parliament was
put off until 3 October 1605. The conspirators learned that the lease
on a cellar under the House of Lords was up and Thomas Percy took
it on. By March 1605 barrels of gunpowder had been put into the
cellar. In May the conspirators left London for the country or to
travel abroad, arranging to return in September. However, the
opening of Parliament was postponed again.

Sir Francis Tresham was recruited to help finance the plot but he
wrote to his brother-in-law Lord Monteagle to warn him not to
attend the opening of Parliament: "I would advise you as you tender
your life to devise some excuse to shift of your attendance at this
parliament for god and man hath concurred to punish the
wickedness of this time... retire youre self into youre control where
you may expect the event in saftey for though there be no appearance
of any stir yet i say they shall receive a terrible blow this parliament
and yet they shall not see who hurts them." Monteagle gave the note
to Robert Cecil, 1st Earl of Salisbury, the Secretary of State. At
midnight on 5 November a party of armed men discovered Fawkes
guarding 20 barrels of gunpowder.

14

Captain Kidd

"Pursue and seize the said Kidd and his accomplices"

THE CRIME: One of history's most infamous pirates, William Kidd was born about 1645, probably at Dundee in Scotland, and was the son of a Presbyterian minister.

He took to the sea but little is known of his life before 1689 when he served with an Anglo-French pirate vessel that sailed the Caribbean, docking at Nevis. The crew mutinied and renamed the ship the *Blessed William*, with Kidd as captain. The governor of Nevis, Christopher Codrington, hired the *Blessed William* as part of a small fleet to protect the island from the French. Since he did not pay them, the fleet made their money from looting. They attacked the French island of Mariegalante, looting goods to the value of £2,000.

In December 1695 Kidd was hired to attack any French ships and all English ships that associated with pirates. This was the voyage that made Kidd's reputation. He bought a new ship, the *Adventure Galley*, which had 34 cannons, oars, and 150 crew, personally selected by Kidd. In September 1696, Kidd set sail for the Cape of Good Hope. The ship began to leak and many of the crew suffered from cholera. It was on this voyage that Kidd first became a pirate, attacking a Mughal convoy. The pirate ships that Kidd thought would offer him rich pickings did not materialize and many of his crew deserted. On 30 January 1698, sailing under a French flag, Kidd captured the 400-ton *Cara Merchant* and its cargo of gold, silver, silks, muslins and satins. When news reached the Admiralty, word went out to 'pursue and seize the said Kidd and his accomplices'.

Engraving of Captain Kidd hanging in chains

WHERE:
Caribbean Sea
WHEN:
Sunday 30 January 1698
THE AFTERMATH:
Captain Kidd sailed to New York where he was arrested on 6 July 1699 and placed in solitary confinement. A year later, Kidd was extradited to England to be questioned by Parliament but the pirate refused to name names. He believed that his silence would lead his former allies to help him. It did not happened and he was sent to Newgate Prison. He was not allowed a lawyer when he came to trial on five charges of piracy on the high seas and the murder of one of his men (William Moore on 30 October 1697). Found guilty, he was hanged on 23 May 1701 at Wapping in London. During the execution, the hangman's rope broke and Kidd was hanged on the second attempt. His body was gibbeted – left to hang for 20 years in an iron cage over the Thames – as a warning to other would-be pirates.
YOU SHOULD KNOW:
While imprisoned in Newgate, Kidd wrote several letters to King William III, begging for clemency.

Rob Roy

"I was on top of my bussines"

THE CRIME: Rob Roy, the Scottish Robin Hood, was born as Robert MacGregor at Glengyle, northwest of Loch Katrine. He was baptized on 7 March 1671. He became known as Rob Roy (from the Gaelic, meaning 'Red Robert') because of his ginger hair. He became a cattle rustler and extortionist at an early age and his father took an active part in the Jacobite rising of 1689 led by Viscount Dundee to support the Stuart King James who had been deposed by William of Orange. His father was jailed for treason.

Rob Roy became a successful businessman but in the autumn of 1711 he overextended himself and defaulted on a loan. Rob was appalled that "when I was on top of my bussines [sic]" action would be taken that might "brake my credit". In June 1712 James Graham, 1st Duke of Montrose, one of his creditors, denounced Rob as a bankrupt and offered a reward for his capture. Rob fled to a remote area of the highlands. From there he seized all the boats on Loch Lomond, slaughtered a herd of Montrose's deer and supplied military intelligence to the Hanoverian Duke of Argyll. He encouraged Montrose's tenants not to pay their rent and in January 1716 occupied Falkland Palace, which he plundered. In June he was charged *in absentia* with high treason. In November he kidnapped one of Montrose's aides and demanded the cancellation of all his debts. The demand was unrealistic and he freed his hostage after two weeks. On 3 June 1717 Rob surrendered to the Duke of Atholl. However, Rob believed he had been tricked on and on 5 June he escaped from Atholl's prison at Logierait.

On 25 June he issued his Declaration of Rob Roy to all true lovers of honour and honesty in which he claimed that he was the victim of political conspiracy. The next month he returned to his thieving ways and he threatened arson if Montrose built barracks at Inversnaid. In January 1719 a reward of £200 was offered for his capture. In March 1720 he attacked and wounded a party of soldiers.

*Rob Roy engaged in
a sword fight.*

Blackbeard

"If I don't shoot one or two crewmen now and then, they'd forget who I am"

THE CRIME: Little is known about one of the most notorious pirates of the early 18th century. Blackbeard's real name may have been Edward Teach and he was born about 1680, possibly at Bristol, England. He went to sea when still young and served during the War of the Spanish Succession. It was after the war ended in 1713 that Blackbeard turned to piracy.

Refusing a royal pardon, he took over a ship, *Le Concorde* that had belonged to fellow pirate, Benjamin Hornigold. Blackbeard renamed it *Queen Anne's Revenge*. Despite reports of Blackbeard stealing food, liquor, water supplies, weaponry and valuables from other ships, there are no accounts of him killing anyone.

Terrorizing his crew was another matter. One tale has him shooting his first mate: "If I don't shoot one or two crewmen now and then, they'd forget who I am." Another has him locking the crew and himself below decks and starting a fire to see how long they could survive. Blackbeard was the last to emerge, roaring: "Damn ye, ye yellow-bellied sapsuckers! I'm a better man than all ye milksops put together!" In May 1718 Blackbeard sailed with four ships into the mouth of Charleston harbour in South Carolina. He blockaded the harbour, robbing any ship that tried to enter or leave. Blackbeard held one crew ransom for a chest of medicines and when it was delivered he released his hostages, minus their clothes. Shortly after making good his escape, Blackbeard scuttled two of his own ships at Topsail Inlet. Views vary as to whether this was an accident or a deliberate attempt to downsize his crew and outlay.

The capture of the pirate, Blackbeard

WHERE:
Charleston harbour,
South Carolina, USA
WHEN:
May 1718
THE AFTERMATH:
In 1718 Blackbeard was pardoned at Bath, North Carolina, and retired to live off his ill-gotten gain. However, Governor Alexander Spotswood of Virginia did not believe that Blackbeard's retirement was genuine. He hired Lieutenant Robert Maynard £100 to kill Blackbeard. On 21 November Maynard and his men discovered Blackbeard and his crew in a North Carolina inlet. Early the next morning, Maynard began to chase Blackbeard and a battle ensued. Blackbeard and Maynard engaged in hand-to-hand combat and Maynard shot the pirate. He was supposedly shot five times and stabbed more than 20 before he died from blood loss. Maynard then cut off his head and hung it from his bow. It was then placed on a pike on the north shore of the Hampton River in Virginia, at a place now called Teach's Point.
YOU SHOULD KNOW:
Legend has it that when Blackbeard's headless body was thrown overboard it swam seven times around his ship before sinking.

Black Bart

"It was better being a commander than a common Man"

WHERE:
Off the Brazilian coast
WHEN:
July 1719
THE AFTERMATH:
To prevent his body being abused or displayed *post mortem*, the crew threw it overboard. It was never found.
YOU SHOULD KNOW:
The nickname Black Bart was never used during John Roberts's lifetime.

THE CRIME: Born as John Roberts on 17 May 1682 at Casnewydd-Bach, Pembrokeshire, Wales, Black Bart became one of the most notorious pirates to sail the Americas and West Africa. He was 13 when he made his first sea voyage and in June 1719 pirates captured his ship and he was press-ganged into joining them. Quickly, he fell in with them saying, "A merry life and a short one shall be my motto."

He became captain after the original captain Howell Davis was shot dead. He accepted: "It was better being a commander than a common Man." His first voyage was revenge on the people who had killed Howell Davis and then in July 1719 he sailed for Brazil where he began his full-time piratical career, during which time he was estimated to have captured 470 ships. One ship had aboard 40,000 gold moidors and jewellery for the King of Portugal.

In February 1720 the French pirate Montigny la Palisse joined Bart and the authorities in Barbados sent two armed ships to stop the pirates. In the encounter, the French pirate ship fled and Bart's ship suffered damage. Bart swore vengeance against Barbados and Martinique, who had also sent ships to hunt him. He then sailed north to Newfoundland. On 21 June he attacked Trepassey harbour and captured 22 ships. The next month, he captured another ten ships and then headed for the West Indies with la Palisse who had rejoined them. In late October Bart captured 15 more ships in three days. His actions virtually brought trade in

Bartholomew Roberts was said to have taken more than 400 vessels.

the West Indies to a halt. On 5 February three of Bart's ships were involved in a skirmish with HMS *Swallow* that left ten pirates dead. Five days later, in another encounter with the *Swallow,* the end came. Black Bart, dressed in his best clothes was killed by grapeshot cannon fire, which struck him in the throat while he stood on the deck.

Boston Tea Party

Three-quarters of the tea sold in America was smuggled into the country

The Sons of Liberty throw the tea into Boston Harbour.

THE CRIME: In 1763 King George III needed to raise money after heavy losses in the French and Indian War and imposed hefty taxes on his American colonies. On 22 March 1765 the Stamp Act was passed followed, two years later on 2 July 1767, by the Townsend Acts and the Boston Massacre on 5 March 1770 (in which five civilians were killed by British soldiers). The colonists claimed that they were not obliged to pay the new tariffs because they had no representation in Britain. Parliament agreed to withdraw the taxes but not the one imposed on tea. By 1773 the British East India Company had large stocks of tea that they were unable to sell and were facing bankruptcy. The government came to the aid of the East India Company and exempted it from taxes that the Americans still had to pay. This allowed them to undersell the American tea sellers and create a monopoly.

It was this reduction in tax and the consequent cheap British tea that precipitated the Boston Tea Party. Three-quarters of the tea sold in America was smuggled into the country. When the first shipments of tea arrived in New York and Philadelphia the Americans refused to allow the ships to dock. Three ships did manage to dock in Boston with the help of armed British vessels. One ship captain agreed to return to England but was prevented from doing so by the authorities. On the evening of 16 December, three groups of 50 men – the self-proclaimed Sons of Liberty – marched down to Griffin's Wharf and boarded the three ships. By 9pm they had broken open 342 crates of tea and dumped the contents into Boston Harbour.

WHERE:
Griffin's Wharf, Boston, Massachusetts, USA

WHEN:
Thursday 16 December 1773

THE AFTERMATH:
After destroying the tea the men washed and tidied up after themselves and the next day sent a man to repair a padlock that had been broken. It was then noted that large amounts of tea were floating on the water and, to prevent it being recovered, several small boats were rowed out and the tea hit with oars and paddles until it was waterlogged. When the Bostonians refused to pay for the tea they had ruined the British closed the port. They also introduced the Restraining Acts in 1774, which led to the American Revolution. However, not everyone was enamoured of the Tea Party – George Washington thought it would incur serious retaliations and Benjamin Franklin believed that the partygoers should reimburse the East India Company for their lost tea.

Captain Bligh is cast adrift in a small boat.

WHERE:
Pacific Ocean
WHEN:
5.20am Tuesday 28 April 1789
THE AFTERMATH:
Eighteen members of the crew remained loyal to Bligh (four more were forced to stay behind because there was no room in the boat) and they sailed for six weeks and 5,823 km (3,618 mi) before landing at Timor and safety on 14 June 1789. Upon his return to England on 14 March 1790, Bligh was exonerated of any blame. In 1805 he was appointed Captain General and Governor of New South Wales at a salary of £2,000 a year. In February 1806 he sailed to Australia. He faced another mutiny – the so-called Rum Rebellion – in New South Wales on 26 January 1808. He was found by the mutineers cowering under a feather bed in a back room of the gubernatorial mansion and was imprisoned until March 1810. Released, he sailed for London on 27 April 1810 where he died of cancer on 7 December 1817. The mutineers arrived at Pitcairn Island on 15 January 1790 where they burnt the *Bounty*. Soon tensions grew between the mutineers and the Tahitians they had taken with them. The Tahitians killed five of the mutineers, including Fletcher Christian. Another mutineer committed suicide in 1798. John Adams was the last mutineer to die, passing away in 1829.
YOU SHOULD KNOW:
The *Bounty*'s captain was nicknamed "Breadfruit Bligh" because of the purpose of the voyage.

Mutiny on the *Bounty*

A "cowardly rascal"

THE CRIME: The most famous mutiny in the world occurred in the Pacific Ocean in the spring of 1789. On 23 December 1787 HMS *Bounty* had set sail for Tahiti to collect breadfruit under the captaincy of Lieutenant William Bligh, aged 35. Ten months later, it docked at its destination, 43,000 km (26,718 mi) from home.

The *Bounty* stayed for six months to allow the breadfruit to grow and become sturdy enough for the long voyage home. During that time the crew enjoyed the delights of fresh food, sunshine, beautiful scenery and local hospitality. When the *Bounty* sailed on 6 April the crew was not in a good mood. Bligh exacerbated their anger by accusing his friend and highly-strung first mate Fletcher Christian of being a "cowardly rascal" and stealing coconuts. Bligh had cut the crew's rations and flogged crew members on the slightest pretext.

Three weeks later the crew, led by Christian, mutinied. They burst into Bligh's cabin and dragged him, clad in his nightshirt, onto the deck where he was tied to the mast.

Cato Street Conspiracy

"An overt act of treasonable conspiracy"

THE CRIME: In 1820 an attempt was made to murder the British cabinet and Prime Minister Lord Liverpool by members of the Spencean Philanthropists. On 16 August 1819 around 60,000 people gathered in Manchester to protest about lack of parliamentary enfranchisement. The local magistrates ordered the militia to break up the meeting. The cavalry charged, resulting in the deaths of 15 people and around 500 were injured. On 30 December Parliament passed the Six Acts, which banned any similar meeting as "an overt act of treasonable conspiracy". It was these two events that precipitated the Spencean Philanthropists to act.

They intended to introduce a Committee of Public Safety that would institute a revolution. One of the group, George Edwards, suggested using the instability after the death of King George III to put their plan into action. They intended to murder the cabinet while they dined at the house of Lord Harrowby, Lord President of the Council. Leading conspirator Arthur Thistlewood believed that the public would rally to their cause after the deaths and began to recruit new members. He soon had 27 new members on his side.

Conspirator William Davidson, a former employee of Lord Harrowby, went to his former master's house to discover more details about the dinner. He was told that Harrowby was not home but when Davidson told Thistlewood this, Thistlewood insisted the attack should begin at once.

The conspirators met at a rented house in Cato Street, just off the Edgware Road. Thistlewood had appointed George Edwards as his second-in-command but was unaware that Edwards was a double agent. George Edwards was keeping the Home Office informed of all the conspirators' plans. At 7.30pm on 23 February 1820 the Bow Street Runners raided the Cato Street headquarters. In the mêlée Thistlewood killed policeman Richard Smithers. All the conspirators were either arrested then or captured later.

WHERE:
Cato Street, London, England
WHEN:
7.30pm Wednesday 23 February 1820
THE AFTERMATH:
At the trial the defence successfully prevented the testimony of John Edwards but the prosecution persuaded Robert Adams and John Monument to testify against their former colleagues. On 28 April the accused were convicted of high treason. John Brunt, William Davidson, James Ings, Arthur Thistlewood and Richard Tidd were hanged at Newgate Prison on 1 May 1820. Charles Cooper, Richard Bradburn, John Harrison, James Wilson and John Strange were transported.

Bow Street runners raid the Cato Street headquarters.

Henry Plummer

"Give me two hours and a horse, I'll bring back my weight in gold"

WHERE:
Bannack, USA
WHEN:
Sunday 24 May 1863
THE AFTERMATH:
At 10pm on 10 January 1864 the controversial Montana Vigilantes, armed with revolvers, rifles and shotguns, arrived at Plummer's cabin where he lay ill. They blackmailed him into leaving the safety of his home by threatening to lynch a robbery suspect in custody. Plummer stepped outside and it was reported that he said, "Give me two hours and a horse, I'll bring back my weight in gold." Vigilantes surrounded him and marched him to the pine gallows up the gulch. They provided no drop, but tied his hands, slipped a noose over his head, and gradually hoisted him until he slowly strangled to death. Teacher and editor Thomas Dimsdale who in 1866 wrote a book entitled *The Vigilantes Of Montana* said that Plummer had been a "very demon" who headed a group that murdered more than 100 people. However, recent research has suggested that fewer than ten people were killed and that Plummer may have been completely innocent.

THE CRIME: Born William Henry Handy Plumer in Addison, Maine on 6 July 1837 (some sources say 1832), Henry Plummer became marshal and city manager of Nevada City in May 1856 (changing the spelling of his name at the same time). "He was not only prompt and energetic," citizens noted, but "when opposed in the performance of his official duties, he became as bold and determined as a lion."

He was re-elected the following year and began an affair with Lucy Vedder, a married woman. When her violent husband John Vedder found out, Plummer killed him on 26 September 1857. After two trials, Plummer was sentenced to ten years in San Quentin but was released in 1859, ill with consumption. He killed another man but was acquitted on grounds of self-defence. He joined a gang of road agents, tried to rob a Wells Fargo bullion express and was told to leave the state. In 1862 the soft-spoken Plummer moved to Bannack, Montana where gold had been discovered. He was elected sheriff on 24 May 1863. "No man," a *Sacramento Union* reporter said, "stands higher in the estimation of the community than Henry Plummer."

However, Plummer broke the law as often as he upheld it and crime increased in Bannack. That winter the stage was robbed twice, a man was murdered and an attempted robbery of more than $75,000 in gold dust from a freight caravan disturbed the peace. In late December 1863 a group of men calling themselves the Vigilance Committee formed in nearby Virginia City to take matters into their own hands.

Henry Plummer

Captain Thunderbolt

Mary Ann swam across shark-infested waters to rescue her husband

THE CRIME: Frederick Wordsworth Ward was born at Wilberforce, New South Wales, Australia probably on 15 May 1833. He was the youngest of ten children of a convict transported in 1815.

He began working with horses honestly before he was tempted to join his elder brother William in a plot to steal and sell them. Caught, he was sentenced to ten years' hard labour at Cockatoo Island prison in Sydney. On 1 July 1860 he was freed having served four years and went to his mother's home at Cooyal Station near Mudgee. That same year "he met and fell in love with a remarkably beautiful half-caste woman known as Mary Ann Bugg". They married, her second marriage, in 1860. As part of his release he had to report to a police station and one day in September 1861 he borrowed a horse and rode to Mudgee. On arrival he discovered his probation had been rescinded and he was accused of stealing the horse he was riding. He was returned to prison to complete his sentence with a punitive four years added to his tariff. A fortnight later on 26 October 1861, Mary Ann gave birth to their first child, Marina Emily.

On 11 September 1863 Mary Ann swam across the shark-infested waters surrounding Cockatoo Island, laden down with jail-breaking tools, to rescue her husband. Ward, Mary Ann and another prisoner, Fred Britten, swam back to freedom. A reward of £50 was offered for their capture. Over the next six and a half years, the couple – he was known by then as Captain Thunderbolt – perpetrated more than 200 crimes in northern New South Wales. Their villainy included stealing horses and highway robbery. The first robbery was on 21 December 1863 when Ward held up the toll bar house at Campbell's Hill between Rutherford and Maitland. In March 1864 the police arrested Mary Ann but her husband staged a daring rescue mission. However, she was soon again arrested and convicted under the Vagrancy Act.

Sentenced to six months inprisonment, Mary Ann was released after two months because she was pregnant. On 25 March 1866 she was again arrested and sentenced to another six months inprisonment for vagrancy. Released, she was again arrested on 6 January 1867. While incarcerated, her husband committed a robbery while drunk.

Captain Thunderbolt's grave at Uralla in New South Wales

WHERE:
Cockatoo Island, Sydney, New South Wales, Australia
WHEN:
Friday 11 September 1863
THE AFTERMATH:
Mary Ann died on 17 November 1867 from "acute inflammation of the lungs". On 25 May 1870, Ward committed two robberies and one of his victims went to the police. Senior Constable John Mulhall and Constable Alexander Walker set off in search of Captain Thunderbolt. A fight ensued between Ward and Constable Walker during which the policeman shot Ward in the chest. He died early the next day. Constable Walker received a £400 reward and promotion.
YOU SHOULD KNOW:
Captain Thunderbolt rarely shot at his police pursuers and usually had just one bullet in his gun. He preferred using the speed of his horse to get him out of trouble.

Cole
Younger

Bob
Younger
(rear)

Jesse
James

Frank
James

The James Boys and the Younger Brothers

WHERE:
First National Bank, Northfield,
Minnesota, USA
WHEN:
Thursday 7 September 1876
THE AFTERMATH:
Jesse went back to his wicked ways
in 1879, forming a new gang but it
soon disintegrated. Jesse trusted just
two men: his brother Frank and
Charley Ford. Charley Ford and his
brother Bob moved in with Jesse and
his family. Bob Ford had been
negotiating to capture Jesse and
claim the $5,000 reward. However,
on the morning of 3 April 1882 while
Jesse stood on a chair to do the
dusting, Bob Ford shot him in the
back. One obituary described Jesse
as "the most renowned murderer
and robber of his age". Six months
later, Frank James surrendered.
YOU SHOULD KNOW:
During one train robbery, the gang
examined the hands of the
passengers so that working men
would not be robbed.

Jesse James

"The most renowned murderer and robber of his age"

THE CRIME: Jesse Woodson James was born on 5 September 1847 in Clay County, Missouri, USA, the son of a Baptist minister. In 1864 he joined a guerrilla outfit led by "Bloody Bill" Anderson but was wounded in the chest when they met a Union patrol. His cousin, Zerelda Mimms, tended him and they married nine years later on 24 April 1874.

It seems likely that James took part in the first armed bank robbery in the United States in peacetime. On 13 February 1866 the Clay County Savings Association in Liberty, Missouri, was robbed. However, some believe that James was too ill to participate. In 1869 Jesse and his brother Frank robbed the Daviess County Savings Association in Gallatin, Missouri. The following year, Jesse began his PR campaign, writing to the *Liberty Tribune* claiming that he was being persecuted because of his political beliefs, not his criminal behaviour. Over the next ten years, Jesse James often appeared in the press with testimonials from public and politicians sympathetic to the South.

On 21 July 1873, having joined up with the Younger brothers, Jesse began robbing trains, stealing $3,000 from the Rock Island train in Adair, Iowa. During a robbery in 1874 a press release, exaggerating the height of the outlaws, was handed to passengers to give to the media. Jesse did his best to portray himself and his gang as modern-day Robin Hoods. On 26 January 1875 detectives from the Pinkerton Agency raided the James home and in the rumpus Jesse's nine-year-old brother was killed. Politics became a major tenet of the James legend: Republicans blamed Democrats for supporting banditry while Democrats condemned Republicans for slandering the James brothers. In September 1876 the James-Younger gang robbed the First National Bank of Northfield, Minnesota. It was a disaster – three robbers were killed, and three Younger brothers were wounded and captured. Only Jesse and Frank James remained at liberty.

*Jesse and Frank James seated in front
of some of the Younger brothers.*

Ned Kelly

"What's the use of a watch to a dead man?"

THE CRIME: Edward "Ned" Kelly was born at Beveridge, Victoria, Australia on 3 June 1854, the son of a villain who had been deported from Great Britain. He entered the family trade at an early age, being arrested at the age of 14 for attacking a Chinese pig farmer. Kelly spent ten days in prison before the charge was dropped. In 1869 he was again arrested, this time for being an accomplice of bushranger Harry Power, and was released without charge. In 1870 he received six months' hard labour for assault and sending an obscene letter. Three weeks after he was released, he was back in trouble for assaulting a policeman and being in possession of stolen property. Kelly was sentenced to three years' imprisonment.

On his release, he joined his stepfather George King in rustling cattle. On 25 October 1878 a police posse set out to capture Kelly. They camped at Stringybark Creek where they were spied by Kelly and his brother Dan. The Kellys approached the camp and ordered the police to surrender. Constable McIntyre did so but Constable Lonigan drew his pistol and Ned Kelly shot him dead. As other police arrived, Ned Kelly murdered Constable Scanlon and Sergeant Kennedy while Constable McIntyre escaped unharmed in the mêlée. As they fled, Ned Kelly stole Sergeant Kennedy's gold fob watch and later remarked, "What's the use of a watch to a dead man?"

WHERE:
Stringybark Creek, Victoria, Australia
WHEN:
Friday 25 October 1878
THE AFTERMATH:
In response to the triple murder, Victoria's parliament passed the Felons' Apprehension Act which allowed anyone to shoot members of the Kelly gang. On 10 December 1878, the gang robbed the National Bank at Euroa of £2,000. On 10 February 1879 they robbed the bank at Jerilderie, New South Wales. On 27 June 1880 they arrived in Glenrowan and donned the homemade armour – probably made from parts of a plough – that was to become famous. Early the next day Kellly left the Glenrowan Inn where he had been holed up and began a gun battle with the police. The bullets bounced off his armour but his legs were unprotected and so the police shot him in the legs. The rest of the gang perished in the hotel; Joe Byrne from loss of blood after being shot and Dan Kelly and Steve Hart committed suicide. Ned Kelly was hanged on 11 November 1880 at Melbourne Gaol for the murder of Constable Lonigan.
YOU SHOULD KNOW:
More than 30,000 people signed a petition asking for clemency for Ned Kelly.

Ned Kelly, in his homemade armour, surrounded by police

Billy the Kid

"It was a game for two, and I got there first"

THE CRIME: Legend has it that Billy the Kid killed 21 men, one for each year of his life, but the truth is that he was probably responsible for just four. Born in 1859 probably at New York City, his real name may have been Henry McCarty and he used the aliases Henry Antrim and William H. Bonney. In April 1875 he was arrested for stealing cheese and again on 24 September for stealing clothes and a gun. He escaped from jail via the chimney and became a ranch hand. In 1876 he moved to Arizona and became a horse thief.

On 17 August 1877 he shot Frank "Windy" Cahill during an argument. Witnesses later claimed that the Kid had acted in self-defence but, fearful for his life, he fled to New Mexico Territory where he became a cattle rustler and took to calling himself Willam H. Bonney. In the winter of 1877–78 Bonney became involved in the Lincoln County War, a conflict between town businessmen and local ranchers. In March 1879 Bonney met Lew Wallace, the Governor of the New Mexico Territory, with a view to seeking an amnesty for his part in the Lincoln County War. Bonney agreed to testify and spend a short time in jail in return for the amnesty. However, John Dolan, the district attorney, ignored Governor Wallace's instructions and Bonney was forced to escape.

He lived on his wits and in January 1880 he killed Joe Grant during a fight in a Fort Sumner saloon. He later said, "It was a game for two, and I got there first." In November 1880 barman and former buffalo hunter Pat Garrett was elected as sheriff of Lincoln County. In December he announced his intention to capture Billy the Kid and claimed the $500 reward. On 19 December one of Bonney's friends Tom O'Folliard was killed in an ambush at Fort Sumner. Four days later, another friend a cattle rustler named Charlie Bowdre was mistaken for Bonney and killed. Bonney was captured and taken to Las Vegas where he wrote to Lew Wallace seeking clemency but received no reply.

A poster (real or fake?) offering a reward for the capture of Billy the Kid.

Belle Starr

"I am a friend to any brave and gallant outlaw"

THE CRIME: The outlaw was born Myra Belle Shirley at Carthage, Missouri, USA on 5 February 1848. The daughter of a wealthy publican, she married Jim Reed, a horse thief, in 1868 and had two children.

In April 1874 Jim Reed robbed a stagecoach, and Belle Starr was charged as an accessory (although the charges were later dropped). Four months later, on 6 August 1874, a deputy sheriff killed Reed near Paris, Texas. In 1878 she moved in with Bruce Younger whose relations rode with Jesse James (see page 24). On 5 June 1880 she married Samuel Starr, a Cherokee Indian.

Three years later, both were convicted of horse theft and were given a year in prison by Isaac "Hanging Judge" Parker at Fort Smith, Arkansas. They served nine months. After being released they continued to rustle cattle and steal horses. Lack of evidence prevented her prosecution and she denied culpability in interviews, telling one reporter on 7 June 1886, "Next to a fine horse I admire a fine pistol. You can just say that I am a friend to any brave and gallant outlaw." Samuel Starr was killed in a gunfight on 17 December 1886 and in July 1887 Red Indian Bill "Jim" July, 15 years Belle Starr's junior, moved in with her.

A fully-loaded Belle Starr

WHERE:
Fort Smith, Arkansas, USA
WHEN:
1883
THE AFTERMATH:
On 3 February 1889, two days before her 41st birthday, Belle Starr was shot and killed in an ambush near her home in Youngers' Bend, Indian Territory (now Oklahoma). The identity of her murderer remains unknown. Sharecropper Edgar J. Watson, an escaped murderer from Florida, was tried for her murder, but was acquitted. He died in 1910. Another suspect was her son James Edwin (Edward) with whom she was said to have had an incestuous relationship. He became a bootlegger and died in a saloon fight in 1896. Her daughter, Pearl, became a prostitute in Fort Smith and died in 1925.

The bomb went off and the shooting began.

WHERE:
Haymarket Square, Randolph Street, Chicago, Illinois, USA
WHEN:
Tuesday 4 May 1886
THE AFTERMATH:
The trial began on 21 June and the prosecution claimed that whoever threw the bomb had been encouraged to do so by the defendants, even though no one suggested any of them had been responsible for the blast. Defence lawyer William Foster said, "If these men are to be tried... for advocating doctrines opposed to our ideas of propriety, there is no use for me to argue the case. Let the Sheriff go and erect a scaffold... and let us stop this farce now." On 19 August 1886 the jury found August Spies, Michael Schwab, Samuel Fielden, Albert R. Parsons, Adolph Fischer, George Engel and Louis Lingg, guilty of murder. All of them were sentenced to death. Oscar W. Neebe was found guilty of murder and sentenced to 15 years in jail. On 10 November 1887, Louis Lingg committed suicide in his cell and the sentences of Fielden and Schwab were commuted to life in prison. The next day Spies, Parsons, Fischer and Engel were hanged. The site of the incident was designated as a Chicago Landmark on 25 March 1992.

The Haymarket Affair

"Let the Sheriff go and erect a scaffold... and let us stop this farce now"

THE CRIME: In October 1884 the American Federation of Organized Trades and Labor Unions declared that from 1 May 1886 the working day would constitute eight hours. Unions decided to strike on that day in support of the new measure and thousands took to the streets in major American cities. On 3 May six workers were shot and killed outside the McCormick Harvesting Machine Company plant at a meeting addressed by upholsterer and anarchist August Spies. Anarchists called for a rally the next day in protest with leaflets urging, "Workingmen Arm Yourselves and Appear in Full Force!" Spies refused to speak unless those words were removed and a new leaflet was issued.

As a light rain fell on the evening of 4 May, the rally began. A large crowd listened to Spies while a group of policemen watched him. The last speaker finished at 10.30pm, at which time the police moved in to break up the rally.

A pipe bomb was thrown and exploded, killing policeman Mathias J. Degan. The police began shooting and some workers returned fire. The incident was over in fewer than five minutes but eight police lay dead and 60 injured (most probably hit by their own comrades). An unknown number of protesters were also injured and probably four killed. Eight anarchists were arrested and went on trial.

Butch Cassidy & the Sundance Kid

Butch Cassidy became disenchanted with robbery and began rustling again

THE CRIME: Butch Cassidy was born as Robert LeRoy Parker in Beaver, Utah, on 13 April 1866, one of ten children. He adopted the name Butch Cassidy aged 16 after meeting cowboy, Mike Cassidy, and becoming a cattle rustler. Butch took over Mike Cassidy's small gang when Mike Cassidy shot a Wyoming rancher. In early 1887 Cassidy met Bill and Tom McCarty and joined their gang. On 3 November 1887 Cassidy and the McCarty gang robbed the Denver and Rio Grande Express near Grand Junction, Colorado. The guard refused to open the safe and Bill McCarty threatened to shoot him but the gang members voted not to kill the man so the gang moved off without making a cent. Butch Cassidy became disenchanted with robbery and began rustling again. On 30 March 1889 Cassidy and the McCartys robbed the First National Bank of Denver of $20,000. On 24 June the gang robbed a bank in Telluride, Colorado of $10,500. In both robberies the gang never fired a shot.

A huge posse was raised so Cassidy went into hiding and took honest employment. However, he ended up in jail after punching a drunk and being convicted of disturbing the peace. On his release he became an extortionist with Al Hainer. If ranchers did not pay up, the two rustled their cattle. They were caught and on 15 July 1894 were sentenced to two years in jail. On 19 January 1896 Cassidy was released and went to the Colorado hideout known as the Hole in the Wall. There he linked up with the Wild Bunch (see page 30). With them, he organized bank robberies, scouting ahead to ensure the success of each plan. Over the next few years Cassidy and his new sidekick, the Sundance Kid, robbed several trains, netting more than $100,000.

WHERE:
Denver and Rio Grande Express, near Grand Junction, Colorado, USA
WHEN:
Thursday 3 November 1887
THE AFTERMATH:
What happened to Butch Cassidy and the Sundance Kid remains a mystery. They travelled to Fort Worth, Texas where the Sundance Kid hooked up with a woman named Etta Place and all three moved on to New York. Next stop was Bolivia where, in spring 1908, they were cornered after a robbery and shot. Some stories say both were killed, others that Sundance was mortally wounded and Cassidy finished him off before escaping with the loot. Butch Cassidy supposedly made it back to the States where he died on 20 July 1937, 1943 or 1944 (depending on the source).
YOU SHOULD KNOW:
During his period of honest employment in the late 1880s, he became a butcher in Rock Springs, Wyoming where he was given the nickname Butch.

From left to right, standing: Willam Carver, Harvey 'Kid Curry' Logan. Seated: Harry 'Sundance Kid' Langbaugh, Ben 'The Tall Texan' Kilpatrick, Robert LeRoy 'Butch Cassidy' Parker

Wild Bunch (aka the Hole in the Wall Gang)

"A man with that kind of nerve deserves not to be shot"

WHERE:
Wilcox, Wyoming, USA
WHEN:
Friday 2 June 1899
THE AFTERMATH:
Cassidy decided that the gang should split up to avoid capture. He, the Sundance Kid and Ben Kilpatrick headed for the Hole in the Wall while the others, Harvey and Lonnie Logan and Elzy Lay, were surrounded by a posse near Teapot Creek, Wyoming on 5 June. Harvey Logan shot Sheriff Joe Hazen as the posse charged their position. The killing temporarily disunited the posse and the three gang members escaped. Lonnie Logan was killed aged 29 by a posse 28 February 1900 in Dodson, Missouri. Harvey Logan committed suicide near Glenwood Springs, Colorado, on 8 June 1904, the day after he had robbed a bank and found jut a few dollars in the safe. Elzy Lay was arrested in August 1899 and, on 10 October, jailed for life. He was pardoned on 10 January 1906 and turned away from his criminal past. He died on 10 November 1934 at Los Angeles.
YOU SHOULD KNOW:
Kid Curry in the Wild Bunch was nothing like the charming, affable, good-looking bank robber of the same name in the television show, *Alias Smith & Jones*. The real Kid Curry was a small, dark-eyed killer.

THE CRIME: The Wild Bunch consisted of a group of outlaws that included the Logan brothers, Harvey (known as Kid Curry) and Lonnie. On 27 June 1897, with Butch Cassidy (see page 29), they robbed the bank at Belle Fourche, South Dakota, of $5,000. Two years later, on 2 June 1899, the Wild Bunch, Cassidy and the Sundance Kid robbed the Union Pacific's Overland Flyer at Wilcox, Wyoming. They stopped the train and Cassidy ordered the engineer, W.R. Jones, to uncouple the express car but he refused so Harvey Logan pistol-whipped him. Gang member William Elsworth "Elzy" Lay jumped into the cab and drove the train forward over a bridge but the gang had forgotten that they had dynamited the bridge. When the train came to rest they ordered the guard to open the express car door but he refused shouting, "Come in and get me", so the gang placed a stick of dynamite against the door and the carriage was blown apart. The guard survived but Harvey Logan put his six-gun next to the man's head, saying, "This damned fellow is going to hell." Butch Cassidy intervened, "Now Harvey, a man with that kind of nerve deserves not to be shot." The gang collected more than $30,000 in bank notes and securities, which had been scattered by the explosion. The railway hired the Pinkerton Detective Agency to track down the robbers.

The posse that captured the Wild Bunch aboard a Union Pacific train.

Siege of Sidney Street

"Who let 'em in?"

The Scots Guards and police await their orders to close in on 100 Sidney Street.

THE CRIME: The early 20th century saw an influx of immigrants from Russia and the Balkans to Britain. The government encouraged the eastern Europeans to come, much to the consternation of the indigenous population.

Crime levels began to rise among the immigrants and a group of Latvian anarchists under the leadership of Peter Piatkow – known as Peter the Painter – attempted a wages snatch at Schnurmann's rubber factory on Chestnut Road in London on 23 January 1909, an incident that became known as the Tottenham Outrage. On 16 December 1910 the gang killed three policemen – Sergeant Robert Bentley, 40, PC Walter Choate, 32, and Sergeant Charles Tucker, 46 – in a jewellery robbery.

A large manhunt resulted in several of the gang being arrested and an informant told police on New Year's Day 1911 that other members of the gang were hiding at 100 Sidney Street. By 2am on 3 January 200 policemen surrounded the house and cordoned off the street. The gang had more and better weapons than the police and a contingent of Scots Guards was called from the Tower of London, the first time armed soldiers had been seen on the streets of the capital since Bloody Sunday in 1887.

When Home Secretary Winston Churchill heard that the military had been summoned, he was in the bath. He quickly dressed himself and hastened along to Sidney Street where he was met by chants from the crowd of "Who let 'em in?" He suggested that the house should be bombarded and then stormed by police and the army. This suggestion was not acted upon, however, as smoke began billowing from the top floor of the house. Churchill refused to let the fire brigade in to extinguish the flames. In a few minutes the upper floors collapsed.

WHERE:
100 Sidney Street, East London, England
WHEN:
2am Tuesday 3 January 1911
THE AFTERMATH:
When the police entered the building they found the charred remains of Fritz Svaars and William Sokolow. Of Peter the Painter there was no sign. Churchill found himself heavily criticized for his role in the siege. The police later captured five more members of the gang but their prosecution was bungled and they were acquitted.

Sir Henry Wilson

"You may kill my body, my Lord, but my spirit you will never kill"

THE CRIME: Born on 5 May 1864 at Currygrane, Ballinalee, County Longford in Ireland, Sir Henry Hughes Wilson joined the Army in 1884 and won the DSO during the Boer War. In 1910, he became Director of Military Operations at the War Office. Four years later, his career stuttered when he refused to authorize the use of troops against Ulster Unionists opponents of Third Irish Home Rule Bill in the Curragh Mutiny. On 18 February 1918, he was promoted to Chief of the Imperial General Staff. Lloyd George thought Wilson "had undoubtedly the nimblest intelligence amongst the soldiers of high degree". On 3 July 1919, he was further promoted becoming Field Marshal, awarded $10,000 by Parliament and made a baronet.

When he retired from the Army in February 1922, he became MP for North Down. On 22 June 1922, he dedicated a memorial at Liverpool Street Station, London, to those who had fallen in the First World War. Then he and Lady Wilson caught a taxi back to their home at 36 Eaton Place in Belgravia. As Sir Henry paid the cab driver, Reginald Dunne and Joseph O'Sullivan, two members of the IRA, shot him in the back four times. The two murderers then fled and were chased by PC March whom they shot in the stomach and PC Sayer who was shot in the leg. The police finally cornered the two men, saving them from a lynching.

Sir Henry Wilson was given a state funeral.

WHERE:
36 Eaton Place, London, England
WHEN:
Thursday 22 June 1922
THE AFTERMATH:
The murderers were tried at the Old Bailey on 18 July 1922 and found guilty after a trial lasting just three hours. As sentence of death was passed, O'Sullivan said, "You may kill my body, my Lord, but my spirit you will never kill." They were hanged on 10 August 1922 at Wandsworth Prison. The murder of Sir Henry was ordered by Michael Collins. Sir Henry was given a state funeral and buried in the crypt of St Paul's Cathedral on 26 June 1922.

Adolph Hitler and the Munich Beer Hall Putsch

"Hatred grew in me, hatred for those... Miserable and degenerate criminals!"

THE CRIME: The First World War defeat of his country lit a fire in Adolf Hitler: "In these nights hatred grew in me, hatred for those responsible for this deed...Miserable and degenerate criminals!" In March 1920 Hitler became active in the German Workers' Party. On 11 July 1921 he resigned from the party knowing that his popularity meant it would collapse without him. When he was asked to return, he agreed but on condition that he was in charge. On 29 July 1921 Hitler was introduced as Führer of the National Socialist Party and he changed the name of the party to the National Socialist German Workers' Party.

On 8 November 1923 Hitler awoke with a sore head and a toothache but refused aides' suggestions that he see a doctor and dentist, saying that he was too busy. That day, he attempted to seize power in the Munich "Beer Hall Putsch". Around 3,000 gathered in the Bürgerbräukeller to listen to a speech by Gustav Ritter von Kahr, the state commissioner of Bavaria. At 8.30pm, as von Kahr spoke, around 600 storm troopers surrounded the hall. Hitler walked up the aisle of the hall and jumped on a chair. He fired a shot in the air and shouted, "The Bavarian government and the government at Berlin are hereby deposed. A new government will be formed at once."

Hitler took von Kahr and other dignitaries into a side room and told them that he and the war hero General Erich Ludendorff would form a new administration. By early the next morning, Hitler began to realize that his plot may not be successful. At 11am, with Ludendorff, Herman Goering and Julius Streicher, he began a demonstration moving towards the centre of Munich. When the 3,000 protesters reached their destination at 12.20pm, 100 armed policemen met them. Hitler ordered the police to lay down their weapons. They responded by opening fire. In seconds, 16 Nazis and three policemen were dead. Goering was shot in the thigh and Hitler fled in a car. Three days later, Hitler was arrested and charged with treason.

WHERE:
Bürgerbräukeller, Munich, Germany
WHEN:
8.30pm Thursday 8 November 1923
THE AFTERMATH:
On 26 February 1924, the trial opened at the Infantry Officers' School in Munich. Virtually all the judges had sympathy for Hitler and the other ten defendants. By the time closing arguments were made on 27 March millions of Germans supported Hitler. The verdict was delivered on 1 April 1924. Ludendorff, unsurprisingly, was acquitted but the others were found guilty. Hitler was sentenced to five years in prison, with the possibility of parole after six months.

The principle collaborators. From left to right: Heinz Pernet, Friedrich Weber, Wilhelm Frick, Hermann Kriebel, Erich Ludendorff, Adolf Hitler, Wilhelm Brückner, Ernst Röhm and Robert Wagner

Reichstag Fire

"This fire will be a beacon to lead Germany into communism for years to come"

WHERE:
Reichstag, Berlin, Germany
WHEN:
10pm Monday 27 February 1933
THE AFTERMATH:
Marinus van der Lubbe was beheaded in a Leipzig prison yard on 10 January 1934, three days before his 25th birthday. Such is the passage of history that authors come to very different conclusions about him. One says that he was "three-quarters blind, quite mad and incapable of coordinated movements" while another insists that he was of "above average intelligence". In 1981, a West Berlin court posthumously overturned the 1933 verdict and declared van der Lubbe not guilty. Torgler joined the Nazi Propaganda Ministry in June 1940. After the war Dimitrov returned to Bulgaria to head the Communist party there and, on 22 November 1946, succeeded Kimon Georgiev as prime minister. In 1948 he was removed from power as a result of his lax adherence to the Kremlin. Dimitrov died on 2 July 1949 in the Barvikha sanatorium near Moscow, amid rumours that he had been poisoned. Seventy years on, historians are still debating the origins of the Reichstag fire. Some, including Alan Bullock and William L. Shirer, believe that, despite the court case, the Nazis burned down the parliament building so that Hitler could consolidate his hold on power. However, Fritz Tobias wrote a detailed account of the event, which came to the conclusion that van der Lubbe was the sole arsonist. Yet in June 1931 Hitler had given an interview to Richard Breitling, the editor of *Leipziger Neueste Nachrichten* giving two reasons in favour of burning down the building. The first was aesthetic and the second that the Reichstag represented the degenerate bourgeoisie and the deluded working class.

The Reichstag in flames

THE CRIME: Adolf Hitler had come to power on 30 January 1933. Less than four weeks later, at 10pm on 27 February 1933, the authorities were informed that the Reichstag – the German parliament building – was ablaze. At the time industrialist Carl Duisberg said, "This fire will be a beacon to lead all Germany into the hands of communism for years to come." In fact, the communists suffered because of the fire. By 11.30pm, the conflagration had been extinguished.

German police arrested a 24-year-old Dutch communist, Marinus van der Lubbe, who claimed that he alone had started the fire. Ernst Torgler was also arrested, as were three Bulgarian communists, Georgi Mikhailovich Dimitrov, Blagoi Popov and Vasily Tanev. Their trial began at Leipzig on 21 September 1933 and ended exactly three months later. Van der Lubbe was brought into the courtroom in chains while the other four defendants were unfettered. Van der Lubbe was found guilty of high treason, insurrectionary arson and attempted common arson. The other four men were acquitted.

John Dillinger sits handcuffed to Deputy Chief Carroll Holby, beside attorney Joseph Ryan.

John Dillinger

"Betrayed by a woman dressed all in red"

THE CRIME: John Dillinger's name lives in the annals of American crime but in fact he had a very brief criminal career. In September 1924 Dillinger and his friend Ed Singleton stole $555 from a grocer's in Mooresville, Indiana, USA. When caught, Singleton pleaded not guilty and was sent down for two years while Dillinger pled guilty and was sent to Michigan City State Prison for 10–20 years. He was released on parole on 22 May 1933 and began robbing banks. In January 1934 he murdered a policeman during a $20,376 raid on the First National Bank in East Chicago, an action that led to him becoming public enemy number one. Ten days later in Tucson, Arizona he was arrested and, after being extradited to Indiana, sentenced to 20 years in prison.

He escaped two weeks later by brandishing a gun made of wood and covered in shoe polish. On the run, he grew a moustache, had plastic surgery and plunged his fingertips into acid to expunge his prints. On 31 March 1934 he narrowly escaped arrest in a shoot-out with the police in St Paul's, Minnesota after his landlord's wife tipped off the authorities. On 23 April he murdered two more policemen and injured five as he escaped another ambush.

WHERE:
First National Bank, 720 Chicago Avenue, Chicago, Indiana, USA
WHEN:
Monday 15 January 1934
THE AFTERMATH:
On Sunday 22 July 1934 Dillinger, his girlfriend Polly Hamilton and her friend a prostitute called Anna Sag went to the Biograph Theatre in Chicago to see the Clark Gable film *Manhattan Melodrama*. Sage had been persuaded by the law to befriend the killer and that night she wore a bright orange dress (although history has referred to it as a red dress, even in a poem about the event: "I was a good fellow most people said/Betrayed by a woman dressed all in red") so that she would be instantly recognizable to the police. As the trio left the venue, the FBI were waiting and as Dillinger made to run, they opened fire hitting him three times and killing him. At the time Dillinger was wanted for 16 murders.

The cottage where Fred and Ma Barker were slain after a four-hour gun battle.

Barker-Karpis Gang

Ma and Fred were shot to death after a four-hour gun battle

WHERE:
St Paul, Minnesota, USA
WHEN:
8.30am Wednesday 17 January 1934
THE AFTERMATH:
Doc was captured on 8 January 1935 and on 13 January 1939 guards killed him during an attempted escape from Alcatraz. On 16 January 1935 Ma and Fred were shot to death after a four-hour gun battle at a cottage at Lake Weir, Florida. Karpis told FBI chief J. Edgar Hoover that he intended to kill him the way the bureau had killed Ma and Fred. Hoover personally arrested Karpis on 1 May 1936. Karpis was sentenced to life imprisonment at Alcatraz in August 1936. In April 1962 he was transferred to McNeil Island Penitentiary in Washington state. Karpis was released on parole in 1969 and deported to Canada. He wrote two books of memoirs and died in Spain on 26 August 1979.
YOU SHOULD KNOW:
When Hoover arrested Karpis none of the agents had handcuffs so the villain had to be restrained by a G-man's tie.

THE CRIME: Born on 10 August 1907 as Alvin Karpowicz in Montreal, Canada, Alvin Karpis became known as Creepy because of his smile. He began his criminal career aged ten, working with gamblers, bootleggers and pimps. In 1926 he was jailed for ten years at the State Industrial Reformatory in Hutchinson, Kansas, for attempted burglary. He escaped with another convict, Lawrence Devol, and for a year the two carried out a crime wave until Devol was re-arrested. Karpis was arrested when he tried to steal a car and was sent back to the State Industrial Reformatory before being transferred to the Kansas State Penitentiary in Lansing, where he met Fred Barker who had been jailed for burgling a bank.

Barker was one of Ma Barker's notorious bank-robbing, murdering sons – the others were Herman, Lloyd and Arthur or "Doc". In January 1922 Lloyd was sentenced to 25 years in prison for stealing mail. Doc had murdered a watchman on 16 August 1921 and was sentenced to life imprisonment in February 1922. On 29 August 1927 Herman committed suicide at Wichita, Kansas after being stopped at police roadblock. On 30 March 1931 Fred was released and teamed up with Karpis to form the Karpis-Barker Gang. They were ruthless, killing anyone who got in their way. On 10 September 1932 Doc was released from prison and he joined his brother's gang.

On 15 June 1933 they kidnapped wealthy brewer, William Hamm, from outside his home in St Paul, Minnesota. He was ransomed for $100,000 and released unharmed. The success encouraged them to a second kidnapping and at 8.30am on 17 January 1934 they abducted Edward George Bremer, the president of the Commercial State Bank in St Paul, Minnesota, as he went to work. Mr Bremer was released on 7 February after a ransom of $200,000 was paid. Mr Bremer's father was a friend of president Franklin D. Roosevelt and he encouraged the FBI to step up the prosecution of "public enemies".

Bonnie & Clyde

"This old world is made sweeter by the lives of folks like you"

THE CRIME: The Texas Rattlesnake and Suicide Sal, aka Bonnie Parker and Clyde Barrow, were not lovers on a romantic, albeit criminal, spree across America as the myth has it. For a start, he was homosexual. The gruesome twosome met in January 1930. The next month Barrow was jailed but Parker smuggled a gun into the prison and he escaped on 11 March. He was recaptured a week later and spent the next two years inside. He was released on 2 February 1932 and the pair began the killing orgy that left 13 people dead. They also sent poetry about their exploits, written by Bonnie, to newspapers for publication.

The first victim was a shop owner in Hillsboro and after that Bonnie and Clyde indiscriminately killed anyone who got in their way. They escaped two police ambushes – one in Missouri on 19 July 1933 and another on a motorway near Sowers, Texas four months later on 22 December. 1933 was the year that the FBI took an interest in Parker and Barrow because they had driven a stolen car across state lines.

WHERE:
Route 154, Louisiana, USA
WHEN:
Wednesday 23 May 1934
THE AFTERMATH:
On 23 May 1934 as they returned to Black Lake, Louisiana, a third ambush was set. This time the police did not miss and a six-man posse waited for the pair's V-8 Ford sedan. The criminals died in a hail of bullets on Route 154 13 km (8 mi) south of Gibsland. Bonnie Parker, aged just 23, sustained more than 50 gunshot wounds and her sidekick, two years older, was hit 27 times. Soon souvenir hunters arrived and one even tried to hack off Clyde's ear. Bonnie's gravestone reads "This old world is made sweeter by the lives of folks like you". When he heard the news, John Dillinger (see page 35) was pleased – he thought the pair was "giving bank robbery a bad name".

Bonnie Parker and her partner Clyde Barrow clowning around with a shotgun.

Lord Haw-Haw

"Jairmany calling, Jairmany calling…"

WHERE:
Berlin, Germany
WHEN:
Wednesday 6 September 1939
THE AFTERMATH:
On 28 May 1945 Joyce and his wife were captured at Flensburg on the Danish–German border by a British naturalized German–Jewish soldier. Joyce's trial began at the Old Bailey on 17 September 1945. Joyce denied treason and, in truth, the British knew that being an American-born German citizen, he could not be guilty. At 3.37pm on 19 September 1945 the judge instructed the jury to find Joyce guilty, which they did at 4pm. Sentenced to death, Joyce was hanged by Albert Pierrepoint at Wandsworth Prison at 9pm on 3 January 1946. He was 39.

THE CRIME: Born in New York City on 24 April 1906, William Joyce moved to Galway in southern Ireland with his family in November 1909. He spent so much time with the Black and Tans and supposedly informed on a priest who was killed by them that the IRA reputedly ordered his assassination. On 8 December 1921 he escaped to England. He developed an interest in fascism and on 22 October 1924, while working as a steward at a Conservative Party meeting at Battersea, he was slashed across the face, leaving a large scar on his right cheek. On 6 July 1933 he lied on an application for a passport claiming that he had been born in Galway. It was a deception that would end on the gallows. On 17 August 1933 Joyce joined the British Union of Fascists and rose to become deputy to Sir Oswald Mosley. On 11 March 1937 the movement made him redundant to save costs after membership fell.

Joyce founded his own organization whose aim was to prevent war with Germany. On 27 August 1939 Joyce and his second wife arrived in the Fatherland. On 6 September 1939 he made his first, albeit anonymous, broadcast on German radio. Joyce soon became the best known of the treacherous broadcasters nicknamed Lord Haw-Haw. Lord Haw-Haw was the name given to several announcers on the Engligh-language programme broadcast by Nazi German radio to British and American audiences.

Joyce's nasal delivery, beginning "Jairmany calling, Jairmany calling" brought him the opprobrium of millions as he broadcast pro-German propaganda. He had become a German citizen on 26 September 1940. On 30 April 1945 – the day Hitler committed suicide – Joyce made his last broadcast drunk. He finished "You may not hear from me again for a few months – I say *Es lebe Deutschland. Heil Hitler* – and farewell."

Leader of the British Union of Fascists, Oswald Mosley with some of his members. William Joyce is on the far left.

38

George Metesky (aka the Mad Bomber of New York)

"Con Edison crooks – this is for you"

THE CRIME: For 16 years New Yorkers lived in fear of the Mad Bomber, a lunatic seeking revenge for an industrial accident by placing explosives in public places including phone boxes, public lavatories, cinemas, offices and celebrated locations such as Grand Central Station (five times), Pennsylvania Station (five times), Radio City Music Hall (three times), the New York Public Library (twice), the Port Authority Bus Terminal (twice) and the RCA Building. Of the 33 bombs planted by the Mad Bomber, 22 exploded injuring 15 people. He was finally caught through the letters he had sent to newspapers.

The first bomb was planted on 16 November 1940 on a windowsill at the Consolidated Edison power plant in Manhattan, where the accident had occurred nine years earlier on 5 September 1931. It was discovered before it could explode and came with a note bearing the legend, "Con Edison crooks – this is for you" and signed F.P. A second bomb also failed to go off in September 1941 at 4 Irving Place. In December 1941 the Bomber halted his campaign for the duration of the war for patriotic reasons.

The campaign again began in earnest on 29 March 1951 when a bomb went off at Grand Central Station and the public took notice. The bomber warned his victims and often wrote to newspapers but never revealed his motive. On 22 October 1951 the *New York Herald Tribune* received a message, "Bombs will continue until the Consolidated Edison Company is brought to justice for their dastardly acts against me. I have exhausted all other means. I intend with bombs to cause others to cry out for justice for me." again signed F.P.

The bombs continued in 1952 and in December the first person was injured when an explosive went off at Loew's cinema on Lexington Avenue. The police described the bomber in 1953 as a "publicity-seeking jerk". Three men were injured when a bomb went off in March 1954 and at Radio City Music Hall four people were hurt when the Bomber struck during a showing of Bing Crosby's film *White Christmas* on 7 November. On 3 December 1956 Police Commissioner Stephen P. Kennedy ordered the "greatest manhunt in the history of the Police Department".

George Metesky grins from behind the bars of Waterbury Jail.

WERE:
170 West 64th Street,
New York City, USA
WHEN:
Saturday 16 November 1940
THE AFTERMATH:
The Bomber was finally arrested on 21 January 1957 after one of the first instances of offender profiling and revealed to be George P. Metesky (b. 2 November 1903) of 17 Fourth Street, Waterbury. He told police, " I know why you fellows are here. You think I'm the Mad Bomber." He told them that F.P. stood for "Fair Play". On 18 April 1957 Metesky was found legally insane and committed to the Matteawan Hospital for the Criminally Insane at Beacon, New York. In 1973 he was moved to the Creedmoor Psychiatric Center and then released on 13 December 1973. He died at his home at Waterbury on 23 May 1994.
YOU SHOULD KNOW:
When bomb disposal experts searched locations for bombs, they looked for a sock because that was how Metesky carried them to the sites.

A German policeman checks out the nine members of the Red Army Faction.

Baader-Meinhof Gang

"You can't argue with people who made Auschwitz"

THE CRIME: The 60s was a time when young people rebelled against the established order, developing left-wing ideologies.

In West Germany the rebellion took the form of violence when Andreas Baader, Thorwald Proll, Horst Sohnlein and Gudrun Ensslin formed the Red Army Faction. Among their early actions were firebombing "capitalist" department stores in the spring of 1968. The four were sentenced to three years' imprisonment but were released under a political amnesty in June 1969. They were recalled to prisons in November but only Sohnlein acquiesced. The year before, the journalist Ulrika Meinhof had written a number of sympathetic articles about the group. She left her job in 1969 and began life as a terrorist. In 1972, the German government banned radicals from public sector jobs. Gudrun Ensslin raged, "They'll kill us all. This is the Auschwitz Generation. You can't argue with people who made Auschwitz."

The gang was arrested in June 1972. The West German establishment came down heavily on them and they were put into solitary confinement, denied visits and force fed when they went on hunger strike. On 9 May 1976 Meinhof committed suicide in her cell. Between May 1972 and October 1977 a second Red Army Faction committed new atrocities, bombing police stations and American army barracks and assassinating Siegfried Buback, the Federal Prosecutor General and his driver, while they waited at as traffic light on 7 April 1977. Between September and October 1977 – a time known as *Der Deutsche Herbst* (the German Autumn) – the Red Army Faction kidnapped Hans-Martin Schleyer, the president of the Association of German Industry on 5 September 1977 and hijacked a Lufthansa airliner bound for Frankfurt at Palma Airport, Mallorca on 13 October 1977.

WHERE:
West Germany
WHEN:
1968–1977
THE AFTERMATH:
For three days the plane flew around the world landing in Rome, Larnaca, Dubai and Aden where the pilot Captain Jurgen Schumann was tried before a "revolutionary council" and executed. The co-pilot flew to Mogadishu in Somalia where at 12.05am on 18 October 1977 all four hijackers were killed by GSG9, a branch of the German federal police. Baader and Ensslin were already in prison when they heard of the failed hijacking. That night Baader shot himself in his cell and Ensslin hanged herself. That same day his kidnappers shot Hans-Martin Schleyer.

Black September Olympic Massacre

"Money means nothing to us. Our lives mean nothing to us"

THE CRIME: The innocence of the Olympic Games was wrecked forever in 1972 in Munich, West Germany. At 4.30am on 5 September eight masked men broke into the Olympic Village and entered the Israeli athletes' quarters. They were members of Black September, a group with Palestinian sympathies who also wanted to see the overthrow of King Hussein of Jordan.

Two Israelis, wrestling coach Mosche Weinberger and weightlifter Josef Romano, fought back against the terrorists and were killed. Nine hostages were taken. The terrorists demanded that 234 Palestinians and non-Arabs should be freed from Egyptian prisons. They also wanted Andreas Baader and Ulrike Meinhof (see opposite) released. The West German authorities refused to free anyone, but instead offered vast amounts of money, only to be rebuffed, "Money means nothing to us. Our lives mean nothing to us."

On 5 September the terrorists demanded to be taken to Cairo and at 10.10pm two helicopters took them and their hostages to Füstenfeldbrück airfield. Snipers were sited around the area but were not given telescopic sights for their weaponry. A 727 aircraft waited to take the terrorists onto their journey, staffed by German police posing as cabin crew. As the helicopters hove into view the police aboard the aeroplane aborted their mission and left it empty.

WHERE:
Munich, West Germany
WHEN:
4.30am Tuesday 5–12.06am
Wednesday 6 September 1972
THE AFTERMATH:
As the terrorists reached the 727 and saw that it was empty, they realised that they had been double-crossed. At that moment the snipers opened fire, killing two terrorists but the rest made it to safety. The hostages were tied up and unable to move from the helicopters. In the confusion the West German police began shooting at their own snipers. At 12.06am on 6 September the terrorist began shooting the hostages. In all, 17 people died – 11 members of the Israeli team, one policeman and five hostages.

A member of the International Olympic Committee speaks with a masked Black September terrorist.

Ross McWhirter

"Liberty still has its vigilant defenders"

WHERE:
50 Village Road, Enfield,
Middlesex, England
WHEN:
6.50pm Thursday 27 November 1975

THE AFTERMATH:
On 6 December 1975, following a police chase through the streets of London, four IRA terrorists – including the two responsible for the death of Ross McWhirter – burst into the council flat home of John Matthews, 54, and his wife Sheila, 53. Thus began the Balcombe Street siege that was to last for six days. Detective Chief Superintendent Peter Imbert oversaw the police operation. At 2.54pm on 12 December, shortly after Mrs Matthews's negotiated release, police sent in hot sausages, Brussels sprouts and potatoes, peaches and cream. This was the first food the terrorists had eaten since the siege began. At 4.15pm, the terrorists agreed to surrender. One by one they left the flat with their hands in the air. The siege had lasted 138 hours. The gang members, Hugh Doherty, aged 27, Eddie Butler, 28, Harry Duggan, 25, and Martin O'Connell, 22, were given 47 life sentences at the Old Bailey in February 1977. All four men were released on 14 April 1999 under the Good Friday Agreement and were greeted as heroes by Martin McGuinness and Gerry Adams who, disgustingly, referred to them as "our Nelson Mandelas".

THE CRIME: Alan Ross and his twin Norris Dewar McWhirter created and edited *The Guinness Book of Records*. In 1974, IRA bombers were plaguing London and there had been 40 attacks in a year, including the accidental murder of cancer specialist Gordon Hamilton-Fairey in Campden Hill Square on the morning of 23 October 1975 (the car bomb was intended for his next door neighbour, the Tory MP Sir Hugh Fraser). Ross, of whom the *Daily Mirror* once said, "Liberty still has its vigilant defenders", decided to shame the Home Secretary and his advisors into taking action. He offered £50,000 to anyone who could give information that would lead to the capture of the Irish bombers.

Three weeks later, on 27 November, Ross and his wife, Rosemary, were intending to go to the theatre with some friends. Mrs McWhirter drove off to fill her car with petrol. As she returned home at 6.50pm, two men ambushed her and took her car keys. She ran to her front door to get help from her husband and rang the doorbell. As he opened the door, she pushed past him into the hallway and he stood outlined in the doorframe. An IRA gunman shot him in the body and then again in the head. Ross McWhirter was pronounced dead on arrival at Chase Farm Hospital. He was buried in an unmarked grave at Southgate Cemetery, North London.

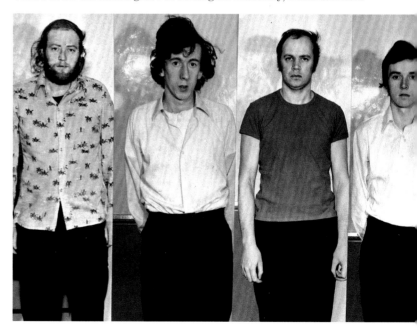

The Balcombe Street Gang. From left to right: Hugh Doherty, Martin O'Connell, Edward Butler and Harry Duggan

Carlos the Jackal

Carlos had been paid around $30 million for the hostages

Ilich Ramírez Sánchez, aka Carlos the Jackel

THE CRIME: Ilich Ramírez Sánchez was born on 12 October 1949 in Caracas, Venezuela, and joined the communist party in 1959. He became a guerrilla in January 1966 and later that year went to study at the London School of Economics. He enrolled at the Patrice Lumumba University in Moscow but was expelled in 1970.

He then joined a terrorist training camp run by the Popular Front for the Liberation of Palestine in Amman, Jordan, where he was given the nickname 'Carlos' to which was added 'Jackal' after the Frederick Forsyth thriller *The Day Of The Jackal* was found among his belongings (although reportedly the book belonged to someone else).

In 1973 he took part in the failed assassination attempt on Jewish businessman Joseph Sieff. In 1975 he tried to bring down two El Al airliners at Orly Airport near Paris on 13 January and 17 January with a rocket-propelled grenade launcher. On 27 June he shot two policemen as they tried to arrest him in Paris. Six months later, he led six people in an attack on Opec headquarters in Vienna. The gang took more than 60 hostages and demanded that the Austrian government broadcast a pro-Palestinian message on radio and television every two hours. After five days, the terrorists and 42 hostages were flown to Algiers, and then to Baghdad where 30 hostages were liberated. The plane flew to Tripoli where more hostages were freed, before returning to Algiers where the remaining hostages were set free. The terrorists were granted asylum in Algeria. It was later revealed that Carlos had been paid around $30 million for the hostages and it was alleged that he had kept most of it.

WHERE:
Vienna, Austria
WHEN:
Saturday 20 December 1975
THE AFTERMATH:
Carlos was arrested in September 1976 in Yugoslavia and then flown to Baghdad. He formed the Organization of Arab Armed Struggle in Aden. They did not carry out any terrorist attacks until 1982 when they failed to destroy the Superphénix, a French nuclear power station. In September 1991 Carlos was expelled from Syria and moved to Khartoum. On 14 August 1994 he was flown to Paris and charged with the 1975 police murders. On 23 December 1997 he was jailed for life.

Israeli Foreign Minister, Yigal Allon, welcomes the pilot and passengers back to Tel Aviv.

Entebbe Raid

"I'm no Nazi … I am an idealist"

THE CRIME: At 12.30pm on 27 June 1976 Air France Flight 139, an Airbus A300 with 238 passengers and a crew of 12, originating at Ben Gurion International Airport, Tel Aviv, left Athens for Paris.

Shortly into the flight, two Palestinians from the Popular Front for the Liberation of Palestine, along with German terrorists Wilfried Böse and Brigitte Kuhlmann, hijacked the plane. The plane was diverted to Benghazi, Libya, and then at 3.15am on 28 June it landed at Entebbe Airport in Uganda, where the four hijackers were joined by three more. The hijackers demanded the release of 53 prisoners held in various jails worldwide and threatened to begin killing hostages from 1 July. The hijackers separated the passengers into Jews and gentiles and released all but 83 Israelis and French Jews.

One holocaust survivor showed Böse his concentration camp tattoo. "I'm no Nazi … I am an idealist," replied Böse. The entire crew refused to leave the Israeli and Jewish passengers and the hostages were moved to the transit hall of the airport, where they stayed for a week. On 3 July the Israel cabinet approved a rescue attempt. One hundred Israeli troops set out for Uganda, landing at 11pm. They immediately went into action, attacking the terminal building, shouting, "Get down!" in Hebrew and English.

French Jew Jean-Jacques Maimoni, 19, was accidentally killed by the Israelis, as were fellow hostages Pasco Cohen, 52, and 56-year-old Ida Borochovitch. Ten others were wounded in the shooting. The Israelis killed all the kidnappers. Yonatan Netanyahu was the only Israeli commando who died during the operation, although five were wounded.

WHERE:
Greek airspace
WHEN:
12.35pm Sunday 27 June 1976
THE AFTERMATH:
The entire event took just 35 minutes – the Israelis were airborne by 12.40am on 4 July. As the Israelis loaded the hostages onto their plane, Ugandan military personnel opened fire on them. Forty-five Ugandan soldiers were killed and 11 Ugandan Army Air Force MiG-17 fighter planes were destroyed. One hostage, Dora Bloch, 75, had been taken to Mulago Hospital in Kampala where two Ugandan army officers dragged her from her bed and killed her. The Ugandan government tried and failed to have Israel sanctioned at the United Nations.
YOU SHOULD KNOW:
The leader of the assault force, Lieutenant-Colonel Yonatan Netanyahu, the only Israeli to die, was the elder brother of Binyamin Netanyahu, Israel's Prime Minister from 1996–99.

Rex Cinema Fire

"The second-deadliest terrorist attack in modern history"

THE CRIME: The Rex cinema in a poor district of Iran called Abadan was a popular venue in the last days of the Shah. On a hot summer's day in 1978 Muslim militants set it ablaze, killing 422 patrons. They had gathered to watch a controversial anti-government film called *Gavaznha* (The Deer), starring Behrouz Vossoughi.

Police noticed smoke emanating from the cinema, which was on the upper storey of an office block. They radioed for help and were told not to let anyone leave the cinema until reinforcements arrived. They believed that they were preventing a small-time arsonist from escaping and did not realize the plan was to burn the whole building, so they padlocked the main door. By the time additional men arrived the building was engulfed. The fire brigade arrived twenty minutes after the start of the conflagration. Investigators thought that the Freon gas from the air-conditioning system had caused people to pass out before the fire reached them. One writer described the blaze as "the second-deadliest terrorist attack in modern history".

WHERE:
Abadan, Iran
WHEN:
Sunday 20 August 1978
THE AFTERMATH:
Initially, it was believed that the secret service of Mohammad Reza Shah Sazeman-e Ettelaat va Amniyat-e Keshvar (Savak) had been behind the fire to discredit radical Islamist revolutionaries who had attacked and burned cinemas in earlier protests. The cinema had been showing an anti-government film so it was a perfect opportunity to send a message to dissidents, it was alleged. The Shah replaced the prime minister with Jafar Sharif-Emami but he was deposed on 16 January 1979 and went into exile. The fundamentalists moved quickly to consolidate their position. On 21 February 1979 Captain Monir Taheri, a member of the Shah's army, was arrested at Mianeh and accused of being involved in the fire. There was no evidence to link the captain to the blaze but, nonetheless, he was found guilty and executed by firing squad two days later. It was later revealed that four Shiite revolutionaries loyal to the Ayatollah Khomeini started the fire. Public disquiet forced the authorities to open a trial and the Revolutionary Tribunal oversaw 17 court sessions that involved the trial of 26 individuals from 25 August until 4 September 1980. Five people, including the lone surviving arsonist Hossein Takializadeh (the others had died in the blaze), were put to death in public.

Workers search through the rubble of the Rex cinema.

US Embassy Siege

"Our opponents do not dare act against us"

WHERE:
Teheran, Iran
WHEN:
6.30am Sunday 4 November 1979
THE AFTERMATH:
President Carter agreed to unfreeze
Iranian assets and not to interfere
internally in Iran. The crisis and the
failed rescue mission was a blow to
his credibility and he lost the
November 1980 presidential election
to Ronald Reagan (see page 313). An
agreement, the Algiers Accords, was
signed on 19 January 1981 at Algeria.
The hostages were freed shortly
after President Reagan's inauguration
on 20 January 1981 and flown to
Algeria and then to Rhein-Main Air
Base in West Germany where
President Carter met them.
YOU SHOULD KNOW:
The plan to seize an embassy was
formulated by student Ebrahim
Asgharzadeh and four others in
September 1979. Two of those
present wanted to seize the Soviet
embassy but were overruled by the
other three. The original plan was "to
detain the diplomats for a few days,
maybe one week, but no more".

THE CRIME: In January 1979 the Shah of Iran was deposed and on 22 October he travelled to America for treatment for cancer. In Teheran the action infuriated Muslim students, several hundred of whom stormed the American embassy, taking 66 diplomats hostage. Six diplomats avoided capture and took refuge at the nearby Canadian and Swiss embassies for three months. Calling themelves the Muslim Student Followers of the Imam's Line, the terrorists demanded that the Shah and his wealth be returned to Iran. They were supported by the ayatollahs and much of the general public in Iran. Ayatollah Khomeini said, "This action has many benefits … This has united our people. Our opponents do not dare act against us."

On 14 November 1979 President Jimmy Carter froze $8 billion of Iranian assets in America. Thirteen black and female embassy staff were released. Another hostage, Vice Consul Richard Queen, 28, was released on 11 July 1980 after he was diagnosed with multiple sclerosis. It was to be the start of 444 days of captivity for the 52 remaining hostages. The White House Christmas tree in 1979 was left dark except for the star on the top.

The treatment meted out to the hostages was not always good – one man was handcuffed for 24 hours a day for a fortnight for insulting Ayatollah Khomeini. On 5 February 1980 the hostages were told to strip to their underwear and then subjected to a mock execution. On 24 April 1980 President Carter authorized a rescue mission, codenamed Operation Eagle Claw, but it was a disaster and eight soldiers died.

*Demonstrators on top of the
United States embassy burn the
Stars and Stripes.*

Iranian Embassy Siege

"They took the two terrorists, pushed them against the wall and shot them"

THE CRIME: To many Britons in the spring of 1980 Iran was a "far away country of which we knew little". There had been the news of the Shah's overthrow the previous year but it had not affected Britain directly.

That all changed when six men calling themselves the Democratic Revolutionary Movement for the Liberation of Arabistan captured the Iranian embassy in central London. They wanted autonomy for Khuzestan, a petrol-rich area in southern Iran. Then they demanded the freeing of 91 political prisoners. They took 26 hostages, including PC Trevor Lock who had been guarding the building, and two BBC employees. The BBC broadcast an appeal from the terrorists and they released five of their hostages.

At 7pm on Bank Holiday Monday 5 May 1980, the sixth day, the terrorists killed 28-year-old press attaché Abbas Lavasani, and threw his body outside. The Counter Revolutionary Warfare (CRW) wing of the SAS had been sent to the embassy on the first day. The five four-man teams had rehearsed the mission in a mock-up of the building in a nearby Army barracks. The SAS went into action at 7.23pm, 23 minutes after Mr Lavasani had been thrown from the building, with an explosive charge in the second floor stairwell at the rear of the building. At the same time the power to the building was cut and stun grenades thrown. Five of the six terrorists were killed in Operation Nimrod and 19 hostages were saved. A terrorist killed one hostage during the attack.

WHERE:
16 Princes Gate, London, England
WHEN:
11.30am Wednesday 30 April 1980
THE AFTERMATH:
The remaining terrorist, Fowzi Nejad, pretended to be a hostage and was taken outside. When the SAS realized their error one soldier wanted to take him back inside but the presence of the world's media stopped him. Two of the terrorists, Shai and Makki, had been persuaded to surrender by the hostages but were killed by the SAS. A hostage named Dadgar said, "They took the two terrorists, pushed them against the wall and shot them. They wanted to finish their story. That was their job… [they] certainly had no weapons in their hands at the time." A coroner's inquest cleared the SAS of any unlawful conduct. When Margaret and Denis Thatcher visited the SAS, Mr Thatcher "had a big grin on his face and said, 'You let one of the bastards live'." Fowzi Nejad was sentenced to life imprisonment. He was released in October 2008. He is still in Britain.
YOU SHOULD KNOW:
To cover the noise of the SAS preparations, the flight path into Heathrow was lowered and British Gas began drilling in a neighbouring street.

Two SAS officers guide one of the hostages to safety.

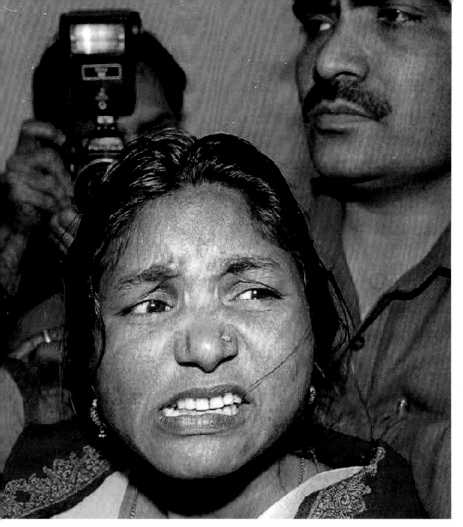

Phoolan Devi

The Bandit Queen

THE CRIME: Phoolan Devi, known as the Bandit Queen, was born on 10 August 1963 at Gorha Ka Purwa, Uttar Pradesh, India. Aged 11, she was married off to a much older man who, by one account, raped her before sending her back to her family. In the late 70s she was kidnapped by a gang of bandits (*Dacoits*) whose leader, Baboo, a member of the Thakur caste, was murdered by his deputy Vikram when he tried to rape Devi. She then married Vikram. When the *Dacoits* raided the village of her first husband she went along, stabbed him and left him to bleed to death.

Devi soon became an integral part of the gang, accompanying them on ransacking and kidnapping raids. An ex-convict, Shri Ram, joined the gang and tensions arose which, in September 1979, led to Shri Ram killing Vikram and kidnapping Devi, imprisoning her at Behmai where she was gang-raped. After three weeks, Devi managed to escape and, with some of Vikram's cohorts, formed a new gang, which committed violent robberies in north and central India, mainly targeting upper-caste people. On 14 February 1981 she returned to Behmai with her gang, all dressed in police uniforms. She demanded her kidnappers be produced and, when not all of them appeared, she ordered the murders of the Thakur caste men in the village – 22 in total. A massive manhunt was begun in the wake of the massacre but Devi was not found. In February 1983 the Gandhi government negotiated Devi's surrender. Three hundred policemen arrested her before a crowd of 10,000. Devi faced 48 charges but it was 11 years before she came to trial, spending the time in prison in ill health.

Phoolan Devi is freed after more than a decade behind bars.

WHERE:
Behmai, India
WHEN:
Saturday 14 February 1981
THE AFTERMATH:
Devi was released on parole in 1994, married Umaid Singh, her sister's husband, published her autobiography (despite being illiterate) and launched Eklavya Sena, an organization to teach the lower castes self-defence. In 1996 she was elected to serve in parliament. On 25 July 2001 she was shot dead outside her New Delhi home.
YOU SHOULD KNOW:
After every crime Devi visited a Durga temple and thanked the goddess for her safe return.

Enniskillen

"It's really desecrating the dead and a blot on mankind"

THE CRIME: It was Remembrance Sunday 1987 at the cenotaph in Enniskillen, the county town of County Fermanagh, when the IRA exploded a bomb without warning, causing the highest death toll in a terrorist attack in Northern Ireland for five years.

The bombing was co-ordinated by three IRA units and the bomb was put against the gable wall inside the town's Reading Rooms. Eleven Protestants were killed – Bertha Armstrong, 53, Edward Armstrong, an off-duty member of the Royal Ulster Constabulary, Wesley Armstrong, 62, Samuel Gault, 49, Jessie Johnston, 66, Kit Johnston, 70, John Megaw, 68, Agnes Mullan, 70, William Mullan, 72, Georgina Quinton, 72, and a nurse, Marie Wilson, 20. Sixty-three people, including 13 children, were injured in the atrocity, among them Ronnie Hill, the former headmaster of Enniskillen High School, who remained in a coma until his death on 28 December 2000.

Prime Minister, Margaret Thatcher, commented, "It's really desecrating the dead and a blot on mankind."

WHERE:
Enniskillen, County Fermanagh, Northern Ireland
WHEN:
10.43am Sunday 8 November 1987
THE AFTERMATH:
The bombing was regarded by many as tipping point in the Troubles, turning what little public support there was against the IRA. Tom King, the Secretary of State for Northern Ireland, denounced the bombing in the House of Commons and his Irish counterparts, Brian Lenihan in Dáil Éireann and Senator Maurice Manning, spoke of their revulsion. Gordon Wilson, father of victim Marie, became a peace campaigner. He said, "I bear no ill will. Dirty sort of talk is not going to bring her back to life. She was a great wee lassie." On Remembrance Day 1997, Gerry Adams, the leader of Sinn Féin, formally apologized for the bombing. The site of the bombing was rebuilt as a youth hostel, which was opened by President Bill Clinton in 2002.

The bomb scene in Enniskillen

Lockerbie Bombing

"Clipper 103 requesting oceanic clearance"

WHERE:
Airspace over Lockerbie, Scotland
WHEN:
7.02:46pm Wednesday
21 December 1988
THE AFTERMATH:
Two men accused of being Libyan
intelligence agents were eventually
charged with planting the bomb and
their trial began on 3 May 2000.
Abdelbaset ali Mohmed al-Megrahi
was jailed for life on Wednesday 31
January 2001 following an 84-day
trial under Scottish law, at Camp
Zeist in Holland. His alleged
accomplice, Al Amin Khalifa Fhimah,
was found not guilty. On 14 March
2002 Al Megrahi's appeal against
conviction was rejected. In 2005 a
former Scottish police chief came
forward to corroborate a statement
made in 2003 by a retired CIA officer,
claiming that the evidence against al-
Megrahi had been planted. A date for
a second appeal has yet to be set
and he remains in prison.
YOU SHOULD KNOW:
The FBI took 15,000 witness
statements during their joint
investigation with the Dumfries and
Galloway Constabulary.

THE CRIME: It was a small Scottish town 32 km (20 mi) from the England border and 121 km (75 mi) from Glasgow that became internationally known on Wednesday 21 December 1988. The wreckage of Pan Am Flight 103, a Boeing 747-121, named *Clipper Maid of the Seas*, landed there, following a terrorist bomb, 38 minutes after take-off.

Until the 11 September 2001 attacks (see page 56), the bombing of Flight 103 was the worst act of terrorism against Americans. Of the 270 victims (259 on the plane, 11 on the ground) from 21 nations, 189 were Americans. Eleven residents were killed in Sherwood Crescent, where the plane's wings and fuel tanks crashed, leaving a huge crater.

At just after 7pm, when Flight 103 was cruising at 9,500 m (31,000 ft) First Officer Ray Wagner spoke to Scottish Air Traffic Control, "Clipper 103 requesting oceanic clearance." Those were the last words heard from the plane. Eight seconds later the plane was disintegrating over a 1.85 nautical km (1 nautical mi) radius.

Forensic pathologist, Dr William G. Eckert, told police that he thought that the flight crew, some of the air hostesses, and 147 passengers survived the bomb blast and were killed only when the plane crashed. The police investigation that followed was the largest ever mounted in Scottish history and became a murder inquiry when evidence of a bomb was found.

The cockpit of Pan Am Flight 103 in a field outside Lockerbie

Rodney King Riots

"The men who beat Rodney King do not deserve to wear the uniform of the LAPD."

WHERE:
Lakeview Terrace, California, USA
WHEN:
Sunday 3 March 1991
THE AFTERMATH:
When news of the acquittal broke, Los Angeles was hit by a series of riots. It took the combined efforts of the police, army, marines and National Guard to restore order in the city, but not before 53 people were killed, 2,383 injured, 7,000 fires started and 3,100 firms damaged. Losses were estimated at almost £1 billion. On the third day of the rioting, 1 May 1992, King appeared on television to appeal for calm. "It's not right... it's not going to change anything. We'll get our justice... Please, we can get along here. We all can get along. I mean we're all stuck here for a while. Let's try to work it out." New charges were filed against the police and at a new trial Officer Laurence Powell and Sergeant Stacey Koon were found guilty while Timothy Wind and Theodore Briseno were acquitted of all charges. Powell and Koon were sentenced to 30 months in prison. King was awarded $3.8 million in a civil case. In May 1991 he was arrested on suspicion of trying to run over a policeman who had discovered him with a Hollywood transvestite prostitute. Two years later, he was admitted to rehabilitation for alcoholism. In July 1995 he was convicted of a hit-and-run assault on his wife and jailed for 90 days. On 27 August 2003 he was again arrested for speeding and crashed his car into a house, breaking his pelvis.

THE CRIME: On 3 March 1991 Rodney King, a black building site labourer, was speeding on his way home when four Los Angeles policemen – Laurence Powell, Timothy Wind, Theodore Briseno and Sergeant Stacey Koon – stopped him. They then administered a severe beating to King. The policemen later claimed that they believed that King was under the influence of phencyclidine (PCP). Later tests showed that his system was clear.

It was unfortunate for the policemen that George Holliday, who lived nearby, was videotaping the entire incident which ended up on television. The four policemen were charged with using excessive force but only Powell was convicted on 29 April 1992 when the jury, consisting of ten whites, one Asian and one Latino, delivered their verdict. Tom Bradley, the mayor of Los Angeles, was not satisfied with the result, saying, "The jury's verdict will not blind us to what we saw on that videotape. The men who beat Rodney King do not deserve to wear the uniform of the LAPD."

A video camera captured the scene where Rodney King was beaten by police officers.

52

Waco Siege

"That's them shooting, that's not us!"

THE CRIME: Founded in the 1930s in Los Angeles, the Branch Davidian Seventh Day Adventists were mostly unheard of until 1993 when they made front-page news all over the world. The group moved to Mount Carmel, 14.5 km (9 mi) from Waco, Texas. In 1990 they appointed a new leader, Vernon Wayne Howell, aka David Koresh.

Two years later, the Bureau of Alcohol, Tobacco and Firearms (BATF) was informed by Chief Deputy Daniel Weyenberg of the McLennan County Sheriff's Department that weaponry and explosives were being sent to Mount Carmel through UPS. At 9.30am on 28 February 1993 BATF tried to execute a search warrant on the premises but, as they did so, shots were fired. Four BATF agents – Steve Willis, Robert Williams, Todd McKeehan and Conway LeBleu – were killed and 16 wounded. As the first shots were unleashed, a Davidian dialled 911 and shouted, "That's them shooting, that's not us!" A cease fire was called at 11.30am but BATF spokesmen said that shots were fired intermittently throughout the day.

Thus began a siege that lasted 51 days and involved the BAFT, Texas Rangers, local police, FBI and Justice Department. From time to time Koresh let some of his people leave the compound, although it was believed that they had enough food to last out a siege of at least a year. Demands to end the standoff increased. Some advocated cutting off power and water while others suggested more direct action. Loud music was played outside the Branch Davidian compound in a bid to force them to leave. After discussion within factions of the FBI, water and power supplies to Mount Carmel were cut. Koresh claimed that he and the Branch Davidians were awaiting the impending Second Coming of Christ and had been ordered to stay where they were. Fearing another Jonestown (see page 217) mass suicide, Attorney-General Janet Reno allowed the FBI to mount an assault on the compound. It began just after 6am on 19 April 1993. CS gas was fired inside and met by shots from the Davidians. After six hours and much CS gas none of the Davidians had left. At 12.07pm flames were seen in the front of the building and then the fire spread quickly, engulfing the compound. All but nine people inside burned alive. David Koresh was pronounced dead at 3.45pm.

Smoke and flames consume the headquarters of the Branch Davidian compound during the FBI assault.

WHERE:
Mount Carmel, near Waco, Texas, USA
WHEN:
6.04am Monday 19 April 1993
THE AFTERMATH:
Debate still continues as to who or what started the fires. Ten survivors of the fire were indicted by a federal grand jury. Eight Davidians were convicted on firearms charges. On 12 May 1993 Texas authorities bulldozed the site.

The wanted poster of bin Laden issued by the FBI

Most Wanted Terrorists

MURDER OF U.S. NATIONALS OUTSIDE THE UNITED STATES;
CONSPIRACY TO MURDER U.S. NATIONALS OUTSIDE THE UNITED STATES;
ATTACK ON A FEDERAL FACILITY RESULTING IN DEATH

USAMA BIN LADEN

Aliases: Usama Bin Muhammad Bin Ladin, Shaykh Usama Bin Ladin, the Prince, the Emir, Abu Abdallah, Mujahid Shaykh, Hajj, the Director

DESCRIPTION

Date of Birth Used:	1957	Hair:	Brown
Place of Birth:	Saudi Arabia	Eyes:	Brown
Height:	6'4" to 6'6"	Sex:	Male
Weight:	Approximately 160 pounds	Complexion:	Olive
Build:	Thin	Citizenship:	Saudi Arabian
Language:	Arabic (probably Pashtu)		
Scars and Marks:	None known		
Remarks:	Bin Laden is believed to be in Afghanistan. He is left-handed and walks with a cane.		

CAUTION

USAMA BIN LADEN IS WANTED IN CONNECTION WITH THE AUGUST 7, 1998, BOMBINGS OF THE UNITED STATES EMBASSIES IN DAR ES SALAAM, TANZANIA, AND NAIROBI, KENYA. THESE ATTACKS KILLED OVER 200 PEOPLE. IN ADDITION, BIN LADEN IS A SUSPECT IN OTHER TERRORIST ATTACKS THROUGHOUT THE WORLD.

REWARD

The Rewards For Justice Program, United States Department of State, is offering a reward of up to $5 million for information leading directly to the apprehension or conviction of Usama Bin Laden. An additional $2 million is being offered through a program developed and funded by the Airline Pilots Association and the Air Transport Association.

SHOULD BE CONSIDERED ARMED AND DANGEROUS

IF YOU HAVE ANY INFORMATION CONCERNING THIS PERSON, PLEASE CONTACT YOUR LOCAL FBI OFFICE OR THE NEAREST AMERICAN EMBASSY OR CONSULATE.

www.fbi.gov

October 2001

WHERE:
Nairobi, Kenya; Dar es Salaam, Tanzania
WHEN:
10.30am Friday 7 August 1998 (Nairobi); 10.39am Friday 7 August 1998 (Dar es Salaam)
THE AFTERMATH:
In retaliation for the attacks President Bill Clinton ordered cruise missile strikes on targets in Sudan and Afghanistan in Operation Infinite Reach on 20 August. Meanwhile, the FBI began to investigate, along with help from the Kenyan and Tanzanian authorities. Twenty-one people were eventually indicted for their role in the bombings. Some are held at Guantanamo Bay while others are at liberty. In May 2001 Mohamed al-Owhali, a 24-year-old Saudi, Khalfan Khamis Mohamed, a 28-year-old from Tanzania, Mohamed Odeh, 36, from Jordan, and Wadih el Hage were convicted for their role in the bombings. They each got life without parole when they were sentenced on 18 October 2001. The sentencing marked the end of the only American prosecution to date involving members of al Qaeda. Another defendant, Ali Mohamed, pleaded guilty in 2000.
YOU SHOULD KNOW:
As a result of the bombings the FBI placed Osama bin Laden on its 'Ten Most Wanted' list.

East African Bombings

Around 212 people were killed, and an estimated 4,000 injured

THE CRIME: It was the simultaneous bombing of the American embassies in Dar es Salaam, Tanzania and Nairobi, Kenya that first brought the names of Osama bin Laden and al Qaeda to international attention. On an August morning suicide bombers parked lorries packed with explosives outside the embassy buildings and detonated them. The bombers began buying their supplies in May 1998 and Mohammed Odeh made both bombs, each weighing 907 kg (2,000 lb). In Nairobi, around 212 people were killed, and an estimated 4,000 injured; in Dar es Salaam, the attack killed at least 11 and wounded 85. Most of the injured and dead were locals and only a dozen Americans died in the carnage in Kenya. The bombs exploded on the eighth anniversary of American troops entering Saudi Arabia in the first Gulf war.

Omagh

"Appalling act of savagery and evil"

THE CRIME: On 10 April 1998 the Good Friday Agreement for peace in Northern Ireland was signed but the treaty did not please everyone.

Four months later, on 13 August, a maroon Vauxhall Cavalier was stolen from Carrickmacross, County Monaghan in Ireland. Two days later, three warning telephone calls were made in the morning, two to Ulster Television and one to the Samaritans. The first two claimed that a bomb was planted outside Omagh courthouse. That plan was changed when the bombers could not find a parking space and instead left the car filled with 227 kg (500 lb) of explosive outside Kell's draper's shop in Omagh town centre. Details of the calls were given to the Royal Ulster Constabulary who began to evacuate streets around the court building. They shepherded people towards the town centre, the very place where the bomb was now primed to go off. Shortly after 3pm it exploded, killing 29 people and injuring more than 220.

British Prime Minister Tony Blair called it an "appalling act of savagery and evil". Sinn Féin leader Martin McGuiness said, "This appalling act was carried out by those opposed to the peace process." However, that did not stop Sinn Féin initially refusing to help with any inquiry into the outrage. The Real IRA who had carried out the bombing denied misleading the police and said that civilians were not the targets.

WHERE:
Lower Market Street, Omagh, County Tyrone, Northern Ireland
WHEN:
3.10pm Saturday 15 August 1998
THE AFTERMATH:
Those injured by the carnage were taken to Tyrone County Hospital and the Erne Hospital on stretchers and on foot as well as in cars, buses and ambulances. Helicopters arrived to take the wounded to the Royal Victoria Hospital in Belfast and Altnagelvin Hospital in Derry. A week later, the Irish National Liberation Army called for a ceasefire and the Real IRA also halted its missions for a short time, apologizing for the attack on 18 August. On 22 September the RUC arrested 12 men in connection with the bombing and later freed them all without charge. Seven men were detained on 25 February 1999 and on 28 February County Louth builder and publican, Colm Murphy, was charged. He was convicted on 23 January 2002. He was sentenced to 14 years in prison but his conviction was deemed unsafe in January 2005 and a retrial ordered. His nephew Sean Hoey spent four years in prison on remand before being cleared of 56 charges of murder and terrorism on 20 December 2007.

Sean Hoey at his original trial in Belfast Crown Court

9/11

"Let's roll"

WHERE:
World Trade Center, New York;
Pentagon, Washington DC; Somerset
County, Pennsylvania, USA
WHEN:
Tuesday 11 September 2001
THE AFTERMATH:
As the events of the terrible day
were pieced together it became
apparent that 19 Muslim fanatics had
been responsible for the carnage.
The men were members of al-Qaeda,
a loosely linked grouping of terrorist
cells and funded by the Saudi
Arabian billionaire Osama bin Laden,
a former ally of America in the war
against the Soviet Union in
Afghanistan. On 20 September 2001
President George W. Bush declared a
war on terror. His staunchest
supporters were Prime Minister Tony
Blair of the United Kingdom and
Prime Minister Aznar of Spain. It was
to cost both men their jobs. Troops
invaded Afghanistan on 7 October
2001 to depose the Taliban who it
was believed had given succour to
al-Qaeda. On 19 March 2003 the
second Gulf War began, a conflict
that has left Iraq unstable. Its
president Saddam Hussein died on
the gallows on 30 December 2006.

THE CRIME: The day dawned like so many others in New York with busy New Yorkers bustling their way to work alongside tourists eager to see the sights. At airports across America people boarded aeroplanes for rendezvous with loved ones, for business meetings or holidays.

At 8.46:40am New York and the world changed forever. An American Airlines Boeing 767-223ER Flight 11 out of Boston and bound for Los Angeles International Airport, crashed into the northern facade of the North Tower (Tower 1) of the World Trade Center, the twin skyscrapers that had come to symbolize New York and America to the world. All 81 passengers and 11 crew died instantly. At first it was believed that a terrible accident had occurred but that belief was dispelled when a second airliner, United Airlines Flight 175, a Boeing 747-200ER, hove into view and headed for the southern facade of the South Tower (Tower 2) hitting at 9.03:11am. All 56 passengers and nine crew died. The horror was magnified because the incident was seen live on television.

Meanwhile, two more airliners had been hijacked and one was heading for the Pentagon and the other was believed to be making for the White House or the Capitol. President George W. Bush was not at Pennsylvania Avenue at the time. The Boeing 757 thought to be heading for the White House was United Airlines Flight 93 – 42 minutes late – bound for San Francisco out of Newark, New Jersey with 37 people on board. At 9.28am four Muslims took over the

plane. At 09.43:48am Todd Beamer, a 32-old-year-old salesman with a computer firm, used an airphone and gave "very calm" details of the terrible events to the airline's ground-based supervisor, Lisa D. Jefferson. At 9.36am the hijackers had taken the plane off its planned flight path and a minute later, at 9.37:46am, American Airlines Flight 77 ploughed into the Pentagon.

Through Mr Beamer's conversation with United Airlines base and other mobile calls the passengers aboard Flight 93 were aware that three other aircraft had crashed into iconic symbols on America's east coast. Mr Beamer and other men on the flight decided that they had to try and retake the plane. Mr Beamer and Miss Jefferson recited the Lord's Prayer together and then he spoke the 23rd Psalm. She then heard him say to other passengers, "Are you guys ready? Okay, let's roll." At 10.03:11am United Airlines Flight 93 crashed into a field near Shanksville in Stonycreek Township, Somerset County, Pennsylvania, about 240 km (150 mi) northwest of Washington, D.C.

Meanwhile, four minutes earlier, the South Tower had collapsed, followed 24 minutes later by the North Tower. At 5.20pm 7 World Trade Center, also known as the Salomon Brothers Building, also collapsed.

The official death toll that day varies, depending on which source you believe. It is believed to be more than 2,800, including 157 aboard the two aeroplanes that crashed into the World Trade Center; 64 on the plane that hit the Pentagon and that a further 125 died on the ground; 44 died in Pennsylvania on board the fourth plane; the Fire Department of New York recorded the deaths of 343 of its personnel while the New York Police Department lost 23.

Bush labelled Iran, North Korea and Iraq as the Axis of Evil. In May 2006, an incredible 42 per cent of polled Americans believed that their government and the 9/11 Commission hid crucial evidence or refused to investigate evidence that contradicted the official verdict of the events of 9/11.

YOU SHOULD KNOW:
The hijackers were Mohammed el-Amir Atta, Abdulaziz Alomari, Waleed M. al-Shehri, Wail al-Shehri, Satam al-Suqami (American Airlines Flight 11); Marwan al-Shehhi, Fayez Ahmed (aka Banihammad Fayez), Ahmed al-Ghamdi, Hamza al-Ghamdi, Mohaid al-Shehri (United Airlines Flight 175); Hani Hanjour, Khalid al-Midhar, Nawaf al-Hamzi, Salem al-Hamzi, Majed Moqed (American Airlines Flight 77); Saeed al-Ghamdi, Ziad Jarrah, Ahmed al-Nami and Ahmed al-Haznawi (United Airlines Flight 93).

United Airlines Flight 175 as it approaches, and then hits, the World Trade Center's South Tower.

Bali bombs

"You will be bombed just as you bomb"

THE CRIME:
Bali was a popular location for many tourists, especially Australians, but in 2002 that was changed by three bombs that killed 202 people including 164 foreign nationals (88 Australians, 26 British and seven Americans among the dead) and injured 209 more.

At 11.05pm a suicide bomber detonated his backpack bomb inside the Paddy's Pub nightclub. Unhurt clubbers rushed into the street but, fifteen seconds after the first bomb, another went off inside a white Mitsubishi van parked outside the Sari Club, opposite Paddy's Pub. The 1.143 tonne (1.125 ton) bomb, which was made from potassium chlorate, aluminium powder and sulphur left a crater 1 m (1 yd) deep and wrecked buildings in the vicinity. A third bomb, filled with human excreta, was detonated outside the United States consulate in Denpasar but caused little damage.

The local Sanglah hospital was unable to cope with the scale of the injured and some patients with particularly bad burns had to be flown to Darwin and Perth in Australia for treatment. Members of Jemaah Islamiyah, a violent Muslim group led by Abu Bakar Bashir, claimed responsibility for the outrage.

A week later, the television network al-Jazeera aired a message supposedly from Osama bin Laden saying the bombs were a response for America's war on terror and Australia's role in the liberation of East Timor: "You will be killed just as you kill, and will be bombed just as you bomb. Expect more that will further distress you."

WHERE:
Kuta, Bali, Indonesia
WHEN:
11.05pm Saturday 12 October 2002
THE AFTERMATH:
The police began their investigation and quickly arrested Amrozi Nurhasyim who was still in bed. Police found evidence linking him to bomb-making. He named six accomplices: Imam Samudra, Ali Imron, Idris, Abdul Ghani, Dul Matin and Umar Patek. In April 2003 Indonesian authorities charged Abu Bakar Bashir with treason. On 2 September Bashir was acquitted of treason but convicted of other charges and jailed for four years. On 21 December 2006 Indonesia's Supreme Court overturned Bashir's conviction. On 30 April 2003 Amrozi was tried and on 8 August he was found guilty and sentenced to death. As sentence was passed he smiled and gave a thumbs-up. Imam Samudra was sentenced to death on 10 September. Ali Gufron was sentenced to death on 1 October. At 12.15am on 9 November 2008, the three men were executed by firing squad on the island prison of Nusakambangan. The deaths resulted in rioting in Tenggulan, East Java.

Ali Gufron is escorted away by police after receiving the death penalty.

Madrid Bombs

"We are all Madrileños today"

THE CRIME: Within a three-minute period during rush hour in Madrid, ten bombs exploded around three railways stations – the main terminus of Atocha and two smaller ones, El Pozo and Santa Eugenia. The attacks killed 191 people and left 1,755 injured. Eyewitnesses reported pieces of train thrown into the air and bodies being trapped in twisted iron. Corpses lay on the tracks and the dazed and bloodied walking wounded had to step over them on their way to receive medical attention.

There had been no warning of the attack and every Spanish television station replaced its logo with the Spanish flag draped in black ribbons. The leader of the Catalan government Juan Maragall said, "We are all Madrileños today." The bombings were just three days before the general election in Spain and President Aznar's government, keen to downplay outside intervention, announced that Basque separatist group Euskadi Ta Askatasuna (Eta) had been responsible, even going so far as to arrange anti-Eta demonstrations on the streets the day after the bombing. The police found three more unexploded bombs and safely detonated them. With them was a mobile, which was linked to Jamal Zougam, a Moroccan with links to Abu Dahdah, a Muslim terrorist.

WHERE:
Atocha Railway Station,
Madrid, Spain
WHEN:
7.37am 11 March 2004
THE AFTERMATH:
On 13 March seven men suspected of helping the bombers were arrested. They were three Moroccans, two Indians and two Spaniards. Forensic examination showed that the bombs were unlike those normally used by Eta. The election went ahead and the Spanish people had their revenge for Aznar's lies and, many believed, his support of the Iraq War by voting him out and replacing his People's Party government with a socialist one led by José Luis Rodríguez Zapatero. He immediately promised to withdraw all Spanish troops from Iraq. On 18 March five more men, all but one Moroccan, were arrested. Yet more Moroccan links came on 22 March with more arrests. In April 2004, as the police went to arrest them, four more terrorists (three Moroccan) blew themselves up. Among them was Sarhane Ben Abdelmajid Fakhet, a Tunisian thought to be the main perpetrator of the Madrid atrocity. However, the Spanish judiciary declared that the bombers were a loose collection of Algerian, Syrian and Moroccan Muslims with no link to the non-existent al-Qaeda organization.

A CCTV shot shows a bomb exploding in Atocha station.

Beslan School Siege

"Weak people are beaten"

WHERE:
Beslan Number 1 School, Beslan,
North Ossetia-Alana, Russia
WHEN:
9.30am 1 September 2004
THE AFTERMATH:
At 3.15am on 4 September Putin
ordered the borders of North Ossetia
closed. The first funerals of the
victims took place the next day and
Putin defended the handling of the
siege saying, "Weak people are
beaten." On 17 September Chechen
terrorist Shamil Basayev claimed
responsibility for the school siege,
saying the dead hostage-takers were
in heaven and the killed children in
hell. On 26 May 2006 the only
surviving terrorist, Nur-Pashi Kulayev,
is jailed for life. On 10 July 2006
Shamil Basayev was killed in the
Russian republic of Ingushetia. The
official death toll stood at 355,
including 186 children.

THE CRIME: On a Wednesday in September 2004, the first day of the new school term, a group of 32 male and two female Chechen separatists broke into the Beslan Number 1 School yelling "Allah Akbar" and taking 1,128 people, including 777 pupils hostage. In the confusion, more than 50 people managed to escape.

To ensure the building was not stormed by police the terrorists put children at strategic points around the gymnasium where they held their victims. The siege was well organized. Disguised as workmen, the terrorists had hidden weapons and explosives in the school in July 2004. The terrorists ordered everyone to speak in Russian and when one man, named Ruslan Betrozov, stood to repeat the rules in the local language, a terrorist shot him in the head. At 1pm the terrorists demanded an end to the Second Chechen War and then they executed between 15 and 20 of the male hostages. At 3pm the two female terrorists died after exploding the bombs they had wrapped about their bodies. Five hours later, the terrorists told a *New York Times* journalist that they belonged to a militant organization called Riyadh al-Salihin, led by Chechen warlord Shamil Basayev. The siege went into a second day and the terrorists refused to allow any food or water into the gym. It was reported that the terrorists and hostages had to drink their own urine.

The Russian government, still with a Cold war mentality, claimed that there only 354 hostages and 15 terrorists. Russian President Vladimir Putin only made one public comment on the siege, to the fury of the terrorists and families of the hostages. The Russian authorities also lied, saying that the terrorists had made no demands. At 1.05pm on the third day two bombs went off in the gym, killing some hostages while others took the chance to try and escape. The terrorists opened fire on them. At 1.30pm the gym roof collapsed, killing more hostages. Ten minutes later, Russian forces moved in to end the siege. Some terrorists attempted to flee and five were killed.

Pandemonium ensued as hostages tried to escape and terrorists fought back, using them as human shields. By 3.15pm most of the hostage were freed but 15 or so terrorists were still at large. One, Nur-Pashi Kulayev, tried to pass himself off as a hostage and was almost lynched when he was recognized. At 9pm 646 people were admitted to hospital. Two hours later, the authorities reported that they had killed 27 terrorists.

Students gathered in the gym during the seige.

7/7

"They are trying to use the slaughter of innocent people to frighten us"

THE CRIME: 7 July 2005 witnessed the deadliest single act of terrorism in the United Kingdom since Lockerbie (see page 50), and the deadliest bombing in London since the Second World War.

At 8.50am on 7 July 2005 a bomb exploded on a packed underground train on the Circle Line about 100 m (328 ft) from Liverpool Street station as it headed for Aldgate. Within less than a minute, bombs also went off on an underground train which had just left Edgware Road and was heading for Paddington, and on a Piccadilly Line train, travelling between King's Cross St. Pancras and Russell Square. At 9.47am an explosion occurred in Tavistock Square on a number 30 double-decker bus, travelling from Marble Arch to Hackney Wick.

The bombings were the first to be perpetrated by suicide bombers in Western Europe. The Edgware Road bomber was Mohammad Sidique Khan, the ringleader and eldest, who killed six people; the Aldgate atrocity, which caused the deaths of seven, was carried out by Shehzad Tanweer; Germaine Maurice Lindsay was responsible for murdering 26 people on the Russell Square tube, and Hasib Mir Hussain carried a bomb that killed 13 people on the number 30 bus.

Earlier that day Khan, Tanweer, Lindsay and Hussain picked up their bombs from a house in the Burley area of Leeds and drove to Luton in a red Nissan Micra, hired a few days earlier by Khan. They boarded a train to King's Cross, arriving at 8.26am, before each went on their separate deadly missions. It is believed that Hussain had intended to get on to the Northern Line but discovered it was suspended that day due to a defective train at Balham. He was captured on CCTV on the concourse of King's Cross station after the other bombs had gone off, and mobile phone records indicated that he had tried to call the other bombers.

About 50 minutes after the other bombs had exploded, Hussain boarded the number 30 bus, and shortly thereafter detonated his bomb. The remnants of his skull, driving licence and credit cards were discovered in the wreckage of the bus in Tavistock Square.

Prime Minister Tony Blair said of the terrorists, "They are trying to use the slaughter of innocent people to frighten us… they should not and must not succeed."

WHERE:
London, England.
WHEN:
8.50am Thursday 7 July 2005
THE AFTERMATH:
In total 52 people were killed and more than 700 injured. A second plot failed on 21 July 2005 and the next day the police shot an innocent Brazilian electrician Jean Charles de Menezes by mistake.

The wreck of the number 30 double-decker bus in Tavistock Square

SWINDLES, HOAXES, FRAUD & CORRUPTION

Thomas Chatterton

"The Marvellous Boy"

WHERE:
Bristol, England
WHEN:
1764
THE AFTERMATH:
On the night of 24 August 1770
Chatterton died from an accidental
overdose of arsenic and laudanum.
Although for many years it is thought
that the 17-year-old committed
suicide, recent research shows that
is more likely that his death was an
accident caused by mixing the drugs
he took socially and those to get rid
of his venereal disease. The Rowley
poems were published in 1777 with
a new edition the following year
admitting the poems were
Chatterton's. Romantic and Pre-
Raphaelite poets added to the myth
of Chatterton, a boy genius who died
before he was a man.

The Death of Chatterton *by
Henry Wallis*

THE CRIME: Born at Pile Street School, Bristol, on 20 November 1752, poet and forger Thomas Chatterton's life was all too brief. Despite his later literary precocity, Chatterton was not a quick learner at school but he was not short of self-confidence, telling one friend, "My name will live 300 years." He began to write poetry, *Apostate Will, Sly Dick* and *A Hymn for Christmas Day* being among his earliest efforts.

One day he found a box of manuscripts that had belonged to his father and spent a great deal of time poring over the ancient screeds. He began telling people that among the treasures were the works of a monk, Thomas Rowley (*c.*1400–1470), a priest, poet, antiquarian, connoisseur, and the literary agent, biographer, and confidant of William Canynge, five-times mayor of Bristol. In 1764 Chatterton began to produce examples of 'Rowleyana' earning himself the sobriquet "the Marvellous Boy". According to Chatterton, "T. Rowleie was a Secular Priest of St John's, in this City. His Merit as a Biographer, Historiographer is great, as a Poet still greater: some of his Pieces would do honour to Pope." Chatterton, encouraged by the response, wrote to Horace Walpole on 25 March 1769 enclosing some of his poetry and Walpole was impressed but when Chatterton sent more denounced it as a forgery. Chatterton was furious but continued to write more 'Rowleyana' plus political letters, heroic satires and prose narratives.

By 1770 he had earned enough money to move to London to work as a writer. Chatterton left for the capital on 24 April 1770 but he had left his Rowleyan notebook in Bristol and couldn't write any more until it arrived in July. In June, the month he had seven pieces published, he moved into the garret of a Mrs Angell at 39 Brooke Street, Holborn. She ran a brothel and Chatterton slept with her and her prostitutes and caught a social disease.

William Henry Ireland

"When this solemn mockery is o'er"

THE CRIME: *Vortigern*, the Shakeperean play that never was, had its premiere (and indeed only performance) on 2 April 1796 at the Drury Lane Theatre, London. It was the work of forger William Henry Ireland, the son of bookseller, Samuel Ireland. Father and son visited Stratford the home of Samuel's idol, William Shakespeare, in 1793. There were rumours that William Henry may not have been Samuel's progeny and certainly the son believed that the father loved the bard more than him.

William came up with a plan to gain his father's attention and on 2 December 1794 he told Samuel that he had been given Shakespeareana by a man he would identify only as "Mr H". Samuel was intrigued and overjoyed especially when William Henry produced more of 'Shakespeare's' private papers, including apparently original transcripts of parts of *King Lear* and *Hamlet*. The items were put on display and some of the literary establishment, including Poet Laureate, Henry Pye, flocked to see them. James Boswell said, "I now kiss the invaluable relics of our bard to thank God that I have lived to see them."

Doubts began to arise as to the veracity of the items and by January 1796 the media began to trash Ireland's name and reputation. The previous year he had "discovered" a previously unseen five-act Shakespeare play. The play opened at the Drury Lane Theatre before 2,500 people and Acts I and II went well enough but after that the play began to unravel. In Act IV the actor Phillimore died too far upstage and became trapped under the safety curtain; a drunk tried to drag the unfortunate thespian off the stage.

It was in Act V when the lead actor John Kemble spoke the line "And when this solemn mockery is o'er" that the audience knew for sure what the doubters had believed. The house erupted and it took ten minutes for quiet at which time Kemble repeated the line. This was unprofessional and the theatre owner, Richard Brinsley Sheridan, disassociated himself from Kemble's performance.

WHERE:
Drury Lane Theatre, London, England
WHEN:
Saturday 2 April 1796
THE AFTERMATH:
William Henry confessed that all of the Shakespeareana was forged but Samuel refused to believe him and the two men never spoke again. Samuel died in July 1800. William Henry Ireland passed away almost 35 years later at Sussex Place, St George's-in-the-Fields, London, on 17 April 1835.
YOU SHOULD KNOW:
The bill matter for *Vortigern* identified the author as "W.H. Ireland" and not Shakespeare and was part of a double bill with a play called *The Grandmother*, a farce about an art scholar who was fooled by the resemblance between a girl and her ancestor.

William Henry Ireland

MacGregor is depicted here as a young soldier, in the uniform of the 57th Regiment of Foot.

Gregor MacGregor

For a few trinkets he bought 3.2 million hectares (8 million acres) of land

THE CRIME: Gregor MacGregor was born in Edinburgh on 24 December 1786 and joined the army in 1803. Two years later he bought a captaincy and married Maria Bowater. In 1810 he decided that he was not cut out for British military life after all and sold his commission. The next year his wife died and he sailed for Venezuela to join the struggle for independence from Spain. In 1812 he married Simón Bolívar's niece, Josefa Antonia Andrea Aristiguieta y Llovera. When the first Venezuelan republic collapsed the same year, MacGregor and his wife fled to Colombia and then on to Haiti. He participated when Bolívar recaptured Venezuela but was disappointed at his reward.

The two eventually fell out and in 1820 MacGregor travelled to the Mosquito Shore of what is now Honduras. For a few trinkets he bought 3.2 million hectares (8 million acres) of land from King George Frederick Augustus of the Mosquito Indians. Returning to England, he registered his land and began calling himself Gregor I, *Cacique* (or prince) of Poyais, the name he gave his fictional country. MacGregor even opened a legation and land office in London selling commissions in the non-existent Poyaisian navy and army, plus land in Poyais at three shillings and three pence an acre. He published leaflets extolling the greatness of Poyais and its capital St Josephs. The city supposedly had a bank, a cathedral and many beautiful public buildings. In 1822 MacGregor published a 350-page guidebook entitled *Sketch of the Mosquito Shore, including the Territory of Poyais, Descriptive of the Country.* As a result more than 200 people, mainly Scottish, invested in Poyais and embarked from London on 10 September 1822 and Leith on 22 January 1823. On arrival they found only swamps, jungles and disease.

In 1823 MacGregor launched a £200,000 Poyais bond on the Stock Exchange and raised £50,000 before his fraud was uncovered and in October he fled to Paris. In 1825 he sold 195,000 hectares (480,000 acres) of Poyais to a French trading company, which led to his imprisonment for fraud on 7 December 1825. He was tried on 6 April 1826 and acquitted on appeal on 14 July 1826. MacGregor returned to London and spent 12 years moving between London, Paris and Edinburgh selling Poyais land grants.

WHERE:
London, England
WHEN:
1820
THE AFTERMATH:
In 1838 following the death of his wife, MacGregor returned to Venezuela and resumed his position as a general becoming a respected, if not respectable, member of the community. He died peacefully in bed on 4 December 1845. The president and cabinet attended his military funeral.
YOU SHOULD KNOW:
Of the more than 200 people who sailed to Poyais in 1822–23, fewer than 50 survived to return to Britain.

Ann Carson

One of the most beautiful women in Pennsylvania

THE CRIME: Ann Carson (née Baker) was considered one of the most beautiful women in Pennsylvania during the early 19th century. In June 1801, two months before her 16th birthday, she married John Carson, a retired navy captain, twice her age. In 1810 his wanderlust returned and John Carson became the captain of a ship bound for China. Ann Carson rented a room in her house to Lieutenant Richard Smith of the 23rd Infantry and the pair became friendly. After two years, with no word from her husband, Ann assumed that he had been lost at sea and the friendship with Smith became a sexual affair, culminating in their marriage in 1812. Three years later, John Carson turned up and went to the Smith home to reclaim his wife. Ann was urged to return to her first husband but she had grown very fond of her second, younger husband. Things came to a head on 20 January 1816 during an argument in the parlour of the Smith home at Second and Dock streets. Smith shot and killed John Carson. Smith was convicted of murder and sentenced to death by hanging. Ann was acquitted of murder but jailed as an accessory.

Freed on a technicality, she asked newspaper editor John Binns to ask his friend, Pennsylvania Governor Simon Snyder, to pardon Smith but he refused. Carson then decided to kidnap Binns and hold him prisoner until the governor relented. But the men she hired to do this were unable to get close to Binns and the plan was abandoned. Ann Carson then made a plan to kidnap first Binns's son and then the governor's son. But both plans were thwarted and she fled. While she was on the run, Smith was hanged. She returned to Philadelphia where she became involved in counterfeiting. She hired a gang and they intended to launder a large number of counterfeit notes through Girard's bank but the forgeries were detected and the gang arrested. They went on trial on 2 July 1823 and were jailed.

WHERE:
Philadelphia, Pennsylvania, USA
WHEN:
1823
THE AFTERMATH:
Ann Carson was sent to the Walnut Street Prison in Philadelphia where she contracted typhoid fever while nursing other prisoners. She died on 27 April 1824, aged 38.

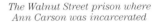

The Walnut Street prison where Ann Carson was incarcerated

Tichborne Claimant

"The pretty girls they'll always think, Of poor Roger's Wagga Wagga"

WHERE:
Paris, France
WHEN:
Thursday 10 January 1867
THE AFTERMATH:
The civil trial began on 11 May 1871 at the Court of Common Pleas. It lasted 103 days and collapsed on 6 March 1872. Orton was sent to Newgate prior to the criminal trial. He was released on bail from Newgate on 26 April 1872. The second trial opened on Wednesday 23 April 1873 and lasted 188 days, ending on 28 February 1874 at 12.35pm. It resulted in Orton being sentenced to 14 years' hard labour (two consecutive terms of seven years) for perjury. The jury retired for just 30 minutes in this, the longest British trial (a record held until 1996). The whole case spanned 827 days and cost £55,315. Doggerel of the time ran:
"When the jury said I was not Roger,
Oh! How the jury made me stagger,
The pretty girls they'll always think,
Of poor Roger's Wagga Wagga"
Arthur Orton was released from prison on 22 October 1884. Perhaps appropriately, he died on 1 April 1898, at his home in London. A plaque attached to his coffin bore the legend 'Sir Roger Charles Doughty Tichborne'.

THE CRIME: In 1853 Sir Roger Doughty Charles Tichborne, the 24-year-old heir to a rich estate, left his home to experience the world. The ship he was on sank in April 1854 and he was never seen again. His devoted French mother, Lady Henriette, refused to believe that he had died and began placing advertisements in newspapers worldwide, seeking information.

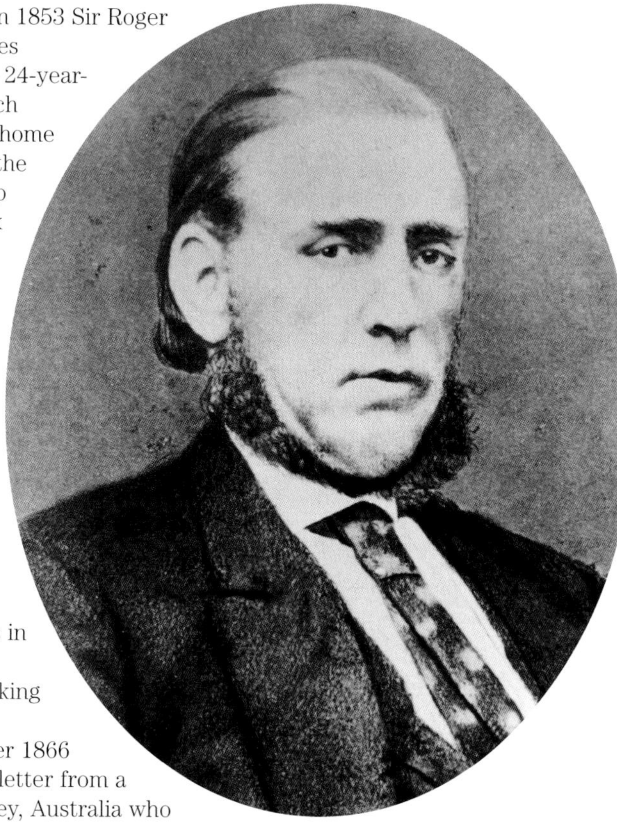

In November 1866 she received a letter from a lawyer in Sydney, Australia who said he had found her son. She sent money and the "son" arrived in London on a snowy 25 December 1866 and visited the family estate in Hampshire. On 10 January 1867 Henriette met her "son" in Paris where she lived, and embraced him. She gave him an allowance of £1,000 per annum. The locals in Hampshire accepted the man as Roger Tichborne, as did the family solicitor and his former Army colleagues in the 6th Dragoon Guards. Lady Tichborne died on 12 March 1868.

The trustees of the Tichborne estate doubted that this man was, in fact, Roger Tichborne and they had a point. The overweight claimant bore little resemblance to Tichborne and was, in fact, a butcher from Wagga Wagga, New South Wales, born in London and named Arthur Orton. Seeing the money slipping from his fingers, Orton had to sue to be recognised as the legitimate heir.

Butcher, Arthur Orton, who claimed to be Lady Henriette Tichborne's son, Sir Roger.

Thérèse Humbert

"Let us hope this gifted woman be spared"

THE CRIME: Thérèse Humbert was a born storyteller. She persuaded her friends that if they pooled their gems they could persuade eligible young men that they were wealthy and worth marrying. It worked for her and she married the son of the mayor of Toulouse who later became the French justice minister. In 1879 she claimed that she had helped an American millionaire, Robert Henry Crawford, and he had promised to reward her one day. In 1881 she said that she had received a letter saying that Crawford had died and had left her a large sum of money. Thérèse claimed that her safe contained four documents: Crawford's will leaving his money to her; a second will that left everything to Thérèse's younger sister, Marie, and to Crawford's nephews; the third document was a waiver from the nephews stating they would allow Thérèse to look after the money while the two wills were settled; and a fourth document in which the nephews agreed to forego any share in the money if they were paid FF6million. Thérèse borrowed large sums of money against the supposed inheritance of 6 million francs and moved to a large house on the Avenue de la Grande Armée in Paris with her husband. For the next 20 years, they lived a life of luxury and when the loans had to be repaid they simply borrowed more. Eventually, the bank asked what form the wealth in the safe took and Thérèse told them it was in government bonds. Deciding to do some checking, the authorities discovered that no such bonds had been purchased. The media, already sceptical, demanded that the safe be opened. In 1901 her creditors sued Thérèse realizing that the inheritance would never be able to cover her debts. In 1902 the court demanded that the safe be opened. When it was opened on 10 May it was found to contain about 5,000 francs worth of securities, an empty jewel box, a brick and an English halfpenny (although one rumour had it that it contained a trouser button). Many creditors were ruined and at least one committed suicide.

WHERE:
Paris, France
WHEN:
1881–1902
THE AFTERMATH:
Thérèse Humbert fled to Madrid two days before the safe was opened but was extradited in December 1902 and charged on 9 March 1903 with 257 counts of forgery and financial malfeasance. The media, among her severest critics, came over to her side. One newspaper reported, "Let us hope this gifted woman be spared." The trial opened on 8 August 1903 and a fortnight later Thérèse was sentenced to five years' hard labour. Her husband received the same sentence. Released from prison, Thérèse emigrated to America. She died in 1917 in Chicago.

Thérèse Humbert, who perpetuated large-scale fraud on the strength of a bogus inheritance.

James Addison Reavis

The Baron of Arizona

WHERE:
Arizona, USA
WHEN:
1883
THE AFTERMATH:
Reavis was released on 18 April 1898
and attempted to begin
developments in Arizona but no one
was interested. His wife also left him.
YOU SHOULD KNOW:
It was said that Reavis spent his last
days in public libraries reading
newspaper articles about his life. He
died on 20 November 1914.

THE CRIME: Born in 1843, James Addison Reavis was unusual in that he served in both armies during the American Civil War beginning with the Confederates and changing to the Union side when they fared better. In 1871 in St Louis he met Dr George Willing who had recently bought some Spanish deeds to American land from a Mexican, Miguel Peralta, for $1,000. Two years later, Reavis met the owners of the Southern Pacific Railway. He mentioned the Peralta deeds and they paid him $2,000 to find the deeds, realizing that it would allow them to extend their railway.

When Reavis located them he realized that they were worthless but, undeterred, he set about forging a history of the Peralta clan, beginning with Don Miguel, the first Baron Arizoniac who died when he was 116 and ending with Don Miguel Jr who lost the family fortune and had to sell to Dr Willing. In 1879, after failing to stake his claim in Tucson, Reavis went to San Francisco where he arranged backers, including William Randolph Hearst's father George. In March 1883 Reavis staked his claim for 47,000 sq km (18,750 sq mi), more than a tenth of what was soon to become the state of Arizona. In 1884 Reavis was exposed as a fraud and returned to California. Four years later, he returned to stake his claim once more, this time with a wife he claimed was Baroness Peralta, the great-granddaughter of Don Miguel, whom he had married on 31 December 1882. The next year on 12 October 1889, Royal Johnson, the surveyor-general, published his report, a document that was six years in the making, exposing Reavis as a fraud.

In 1893, Reavis filed his claim once more, this time in Santa Fe, New Mexico. He did not realize that the real Peraltas had founded the city and they claimed the deeds. On 3 June 1895 the land court finally heard the case of James Addison Peralta-Reavis, his wife Dona Sofia Loreta Micaela Reavis and Clinton F. Farrell (a Reavis financier who never appeared) vs. the United States of America. Reavis did not show up to court until day four and spent four days outlining his case. On 28 June 1895, the claim was ruled fictitious and fraudulent and the documents as clever forgeries. As he left the court, Reavis was arrested for fraud and spent a year in jail awaiting trial which took place on 27 June 1896. He was jailed for two years and fined $5,000.

A poster for a film made about the life of James Addison Reavis

Horatio Bottomley

"Sewing Mr Bottomley?" "No, reaping"

THE CRIME: Horatio Bottomley was orphaned when he was 4-years-old and, to combat his loneliness, developed a fantasy world, a world in which he lived all his life. He became a solicitor's clerk, then joined a firm of legal shorthand writers, rising to become a partner. He began publishing weekly reports of the doings of local councils and managed to con money out of his advertisers. By 1885, he owned the Catherine Street Publishing Association. Most businessmen are wary of splashing money they do not have on wild schemes but Bottomley was the opposite. In 1889 he floated the Hansard Publishing Union with £500,000 capital – more commonly known on the Stock Exchange as "Bottomley's swindle". In 1891, he filed for bankruptcy and was charged with conspiracy to defraud, but was acquitted. He then founded the Joint Stock Trust and Institute which he used to float the Western Australian gold mining companies he now promoted. In little over ten years he promoted nearly 50 companies with a total capital of over £20,000,000.

Bottomley liked to live beyond his means and he bought a villa in Monte Carlo, a country house in Sussex and a luxurious flat in Pall Mall. In 1898 he moved into horseracing, and also established a stable of mistresses. Between 1901 and 1905, 67 bankruptcy petitions and writs were filed against him.

In 1906 he was elected Liberal MP for Hackney South, his third attempt at getting into the House of Commons. He was not welcomed into the Commons and his maiden speech was heard in silence, though hard work and self-effacement did win him a few friends. The same year he became editor of his own weekly newspaper. *John Bull,* whose masthead claimed that it was written "without fear or favour, rancour or rant" was a success from its first issue in 1906. In 1909 he was successful in winning a fraud case lodged against him by the shareholders of the Joint Stock Trust and in 1910 he was re-elected twice as MP but his colleagues saw through him and he was treated as a pariah in the House.

In February 1912, the Prudential Assurance Company made a claim against him and Bottomley was forced into bankruptcy. He returned to Parliament in December 1918 as the independent member for Hackney South and the following year, raised £900,000 from readers of *John Bull* investing in government Victory Bonds – it was another scam. In March 1922 he was charged with fraudulent conversion and appeared at the Old Bailey. He pleaded "decidedly not guilty". The jury disagreed and he was found decidedly guilty on 23 out of 24 counts and sentenced to seven years' penal servitude. A prison visitor, chancing upon Bottomley working on mailbags, asked: "Ah, sewing Mr Bottomley?" to which he replied, "No, reaping."

Horatio Bottomley leaving the Old Bailey after a trial.

WHERE:
London, England.
WHEN:
1889–1922
THE AFTERMATH:
On 29 July 1927 Bottomley was released from Maidstone Prison after serving five years. He tried to start a new journal, *John Blunt*, and arranged a speaking tour. On 12 September 1932 he appeared at the Windmill Theatre, London in a variety show telling anecdotes to a puzzled crowd. After a few nights, he collapsed on stage with a heart attack. He died of a stroke at the Middlesex Hospital, London on 26 May 1933.

Sakigake Watanabe

His woman was a geisha and he became a criminal to fund her lifestyle

WHERE:
Fukue, Japan
WHEN:
1890
THE AFTERMATH:
Sakigake's father was sentenced to 18 months in jail for forgery and Sakigake was sent back to the Miike coalmine. The public rallied to 33-year-old Sakigake and he received a pardon late in 1892.

THE CRIME: Like many men, Sakigake Watanabe was in thrall to a woman. His woman was a geisha and he became a criminal to fund her lifestyle. He began to steal money from his employer and in 1880 he was caught and sentenced to life imprisonment with hard labour. Sakigake attempted to escape and, as a further punishment, he was sent to the Miike coalmine, a desolate place from which few ever returned.

Two years later, he managed to escape after hiding in a lavatory. Sakigake's father was a *petit fonctionnaire* in the government and he helped his son to arrange a new identity. Using the new name and credentials, Sakigake joined the civil service. He then applied for a job as a tax official and then a judicial clerk. In 1887 he had shown himself to be so proficient at the job that he was offered an assistant judgeship. The problem was that the job was in Nagasaki district, the very area where he had been sentenced. Throwing caution to the wind, Sakigake took the job. Again, he was excellent in the position and in 1890 was made up to be a full judge. He heard criminal cases and that became his downfall.

On 19 February 1891 he was recognized by the prosecuting counsel who had handled his embezzlement trial. Sakigake claimed that he was his own younger brother but, after five days of interrogation, he broke down and confessed.

Jabez Balfour

"You will never be able to shut out the cries of the widows and orphans you have ruined"

THE CRIME: Jabez Spencer Balfour's story was one of rags to riches and back to rags again. He was born at Marylebone, Middlesex, on 4 September 1843, the son of temperance workers. His star was soon in the ascendancy. He became Justice of the Peace, the first mayor of Croydon in Surrey (9 June 1883–1884) and Liberal MP for Tamworth (1880) and Burnley (1889).

He was also said to have created the snowballing technique whereby one company finances another when he set up the Liberator Building Society in 1868. He was on the point of appointment to the Cabinet when his empire collapsed and he was forced to flee the country. It was in the 1870s that Balfour's empire really expanded with the formation of numerous companies including the Lands Allotment Company, George Newman & Co, and Real Estates Co. In 1882 he founded London and General Bank which, among its other duties, laundered the cheques that he wrote for his other companies. Balfour became a public success and people clamoured to give him their money but he used the new money to pay dividends on the old investments. On 1 September 1892 London and General Bank cheques were returned unpaid and the next day the bank shuts its doors. The whole system crashed with one company after another ending in bankruptcy. Balfour owed £8 million.

WHERE:
England
WHEN:
Friday 2 September 1892
THE AFTERMATH:
Balfour resigned his set and fled the country, landing in Argentina in December 1892. Balfour made good his disappearance until he was recognized in the small town of Salta and arrested on 20 January 1894. On 10 April 1895 he was extradited and committed for trial at the Old Bailey on 17 May. He was convicted on 28 November 1895 and sentenced to 14 years' imprisonment. As Mr Justice Bruce sentenced Balfour, he said, "You will never be able to shut out the cries of the widows and orphans you have ruined." Balfour was released in 1906 and his memoirs appeared in the *Weekly Despatch*. He was attempting a comeback when he died on 23 February 1916 in a third-class smoking carriage on the London to Fishguard express.

Jabez Balfour in the cells at Bow Street police station after his arrest.

Cassie Chadwick

"The Queen of Ohio"

WHERE:
Cleveland, Ohio, USA
WHEN:
1897
THE AFTERMATH:
Leroy Chadwick divorced his wife and fled to Europe. On 10 March 1905 Cassie Chadwick was fined $70,000 and sentenced to 14 years in prison. She was sent to the State Penitentiary at Columbus, Ohio on 1 January 1906. She was not to serve her sentence;she died in prison on her 50th birthday.
YOU SHOULD KNOW:
When she was arrested in New York, Chadwick was sitting in bed wearing a money belt containing $100,000. Her mansion on Euclid Avenue, Cleveland was demolished and is now the site of the Liberty Hill Baptist Church.

THE CRIME: Cassie L. Chadwick was born Elizabeth Bigley in Eastwood, Canada on 10 October 1857. In 1879 she was arrested for forgery at Woodstock, Ontario, but was released after convincing authorities that she was insane. In 1882 she married Wallace Springsteen at Cleveland, Ohio, but the marriage ended after 11 days when he discovered her background. Five years later, as Madame Lydia DeVere, she became a clairvoyant and hypnotist. The lure of criminality was too much and in 1889 Cassie was jailed for nine and a half years for forgery. Paroled after four years, she opened a brothel and married a gullible, wealthy man, Dr Leroy Chadwick, in 1897.

That year she went to the home of multi-millionaire Andrew Carnegie with a lawyer called Dillon, a friend of her husband, who waited outside in the car while Cassie went in. She spent half an hour inside the mansion and, as she left, waved to a man who looked like Carnegie but was in fact his butler. Back in the car she conveniently dropped a piece of paper. When Dillon opened it, it turned out to be a promissory note of $2 million, bearing Carnegie's signature. Swearing Dillon to secrecy, Chadwick claimed to be the illegitimate daughter of the industrialist and philanthropist. It was not long before the word was out and banks fell over themselves to offer Cassie millions of dollars in loans – various estimates put the figure at between $10 and $20 million. Cassie spent the money as fast as it was offered, once spending $100,000 on a party. She bought so many jewels that she became known as "the Queen of Ohio". The edifice came tumbling down on 2 November 1904 when the H.B. Newton Bank of Boston called in a loan of $190,800 and Cassie was unable to repay the money. She was arrested at the Hotel Breslin in New York on 7 December 1904 and returned to Cleveland where she stood trial.

Jefferson Randolph "Soapy" Smith

"King of the Frontier Con Men"

Right: Jefferson "Soapy" Smith in the saloon he owned in Skagway, Alaska, shortly before his death

THE CRIME: Jefferson Randolph Smith was born in 1860 at Newnan, Georgia to a well-to-do family. Notwithstanding, he became a criminal known variously as "Soapy" (because of his most celebrated trick) or as the "King of the Frontier Con Men". The nickname Soapy came about through the Prize Package Soap Sell Swindle. Smith would hide

"Soapy" Smiths Saloon. no. 2. Skagway, Alaska.

Jeff "Soapy" Smith. Killed July 8th 1898.

Flashlight Pho

money up to the value of $100 under the labels of bars of soap and then sell the bars for $1 each. "Shills" (or accomplices) in the audience would buy the soap containing the money and then announce their finds thus encouraging the punters also to invest. Needless to say, the only money ever found was in the bars sold to the shills.

Smith was one of the most adroit con artists operating in America in the late 19th century. He was also – perhaps because of a guilty conscience – a generous contributor to charity. Smith operated out of Denver and Creede, Colorado from 1879 until 1896 and then from 1897–98 at Skagway, Alaska. In 1897 Skagway had a gold rush and Smith, ever keen to make an easy dollar, had his men (he called them his "lambs") set up a fake telegraph station to send telegrams, at $5 each, to the miners' homes. As the message was prepared the miner was pumped for information on his background and finances and then invited to play poker during which he would lose everything. To add insult to injury, the telegraph line did not reach Skagway until 1900.

WHERE:
Skagway, Alaska, USA
WHEN:
1897
THE AFTERMATH:
In 1898 the townspeople of Skagway tired of Smith and his men and a gang of vigilantes was formed to run them out of town. On 8 July 1898 a guard by the name of Frank Reid prevented Smith from entering the town. The two engaged in gunfire – Smith always carried two revolvers and a double-barrelled rifle – and Smith died of his wounds that night. Reid expired 12 days later.

YOU SHOULD KNOW:
A wake is held for Smith at Skagway each year on 8 July. Smith's motto was "Get it while the gettin's good." Frank Reid's tombstone bears the legend, "He gave his life for the Honor of Skagway". Nearby is the tombstone of a local prostitute whose reads, "She gave her Honor for the life of Skagway".

Wilhelm Voigt

"Lovable scoundrel"

WHERE:
Köpenick, Germany
WHEN:
Tuesday 16 October 1906
THE AFTERMATH:
The police and army launched
investigations in to what had
happened, although the public was
amused by the whole scam. On 26
October Voigt was arrested. On 1
December he was sentenced to four
years in prison for forgery,
impersonating an officer and
wrongful imprisonment. Kaiser
Wilhelm II is said to have called Voigt
a "lovable scoundrel" and pardoned
him on 16 August 1908. He died at
Luxembourg on 3 January 1922.
YOU SHOULD KNOW:
Voigt published his autobiography in
1909 but an American tour to
publicize it almost failed to
materialize when he was refused a
visa. Using his initiative, he entered
the USA via Canada.

THE CRIME: Germany in 1906 was
a militaristic place and the people
deferred to the army without
thought. This subservience gave
Wilhelm Voigt an idea. He had
been born at Tilsit, Prussia on 13
February 1849. He was 57-years-
old and had spent much of his life
in prison. His first spell behind
bars was when he was 14 and was
jailed for stealing. In 1891 he was
jailed for 15 years and finally
released on 12 February 1906.

On 24 August he was expelled
from Berlin as a vagrant. He did
not actually leave the city and one
day decided to go window-
shopping in Potsdam, near Berlin,
when he saw the smart uniform of
a captain in a second-hand shop.
The price tag was equal to a whole
week's wages but Voigt threw
caution to the wind and bought the
uniform. He went to a brewers'
exhibition and was pleasantly
surprised by the reaction he
received – admiring glances from ladies and stiff salutes from soldiers.

Then on 16 October 1906 he donned his uniform again and
marched to the local barracks where he stopped a group of soldiers
(some sources say a corporal and five grenadiers, others a sergeant
and four grenadiers) and ordered them to follow him. On the way
he ordered four (some say six) more soldiers to join his band and
took a train to Köpenick, east of Berlin. Once there he had the
treasurer, von Wiltberg, and burgomaster, Dr Georg Langerhans,
arrested by the soldiers for alleged fraud. Dr Langerhans, a reserve
soldier, asked to see the arrest warrant but Voigt said his authority
came from the men he commanded. The burgomaster was puzzled
as Voigt seemed a little old for duty and his cap badge was on
upside down. He nonetheless handed over 4002 marks and 37
pfennigs to Voigt who signed the receipt "Von Aloesam, Captain,
Guards Regiment". He then commandeered two carriages and had
the entire council sent to Berlin for questioning. Voigt then changed
into civilian clothes and fled.

Wilhelm Voigt

Serge Alexandre Stavisky

"The Minister of the Colonies was counselled… by Stavisky"

THE CRIME: Ukraine-born Stavisky began his nefarious activities in Russia in 1908 with fraud and swindling. Following one arrest, his father committed suicide from the shame. Prior to the outbreak of the First World War Stavisky moved to France where, legitimately, he worked as a singer, nightclub manager and then a gambler. Illegally, he sold drugs, committed armed robberies and confidence tricks. He moved to Bayonne where he was appointed the manager of a chain of pawnshops. He financed the shops by selling emeralds he claimed belonged to the late Empress of Germany. They turned out to be glass.

In addition, Stavisky issued millions of francs' worth of bonds claiming that they would be honoured by the City of Bayonne. Most of the bonds were bought by insurance companies acting on the advice of "the Minister of the Colonies, who was counselled by the Minister of Commerce, who was counselled by the Mayor of Bayonne who was counselled by Stavisky". Eventually, someone became suspicious and the police began to investigate the affairs of Stavisky. In 1927 he was arrested and charged with fraud but various legal contentions meant the trial was postponed and Stavisky was bailed 19 times. In December 1933 the authorities finally got their case in order but Stavisky fled to Chamonix where he died under mysterious circumstances on 8 January 1934. He had a gunshot wound to the head and it is uncertain whether he committed suicide or was killed by the police.

WHERE:
Bayonne, France
WHEN:
1908–1933
THE AFTERMATH:
Camille Chautemps, the Prime Minister, was made to resign in the wake of the scandal and Jean Chiappe, the Prefect of the Paris Police, was sacked by Edouard Daladier, Chautemps's successor. Riots broke out in Paris on the night of 6 February 1934 during which 14 people died at the hands of 800 police. Twenty of Stavisky's associates were arrested and tried, including his widow Arlette, in 1935. Twelve hundred pages of charges were levelled against them but in 1936 all were acquitted. Arlette Stavisky later spent eight weeks performing in a New York nightspot.

Serge Stavisky with his private secretary Gilbert Romgins

Piltdown Man

Evanthropus dawsoni

THE AFTERMATH:
A number of sceptics doubted the authenticity of Piltdown Man and they were right. No one, however, was allowed to test the skull until 1949 when Dr Kenneth Oakley, one of Woodward's successors, carried out tests. He pronounced that the skull was not half a million years old but only 50,000. He was wrong. In November 1953 a group of palaeontologists tested the skull and pronounced it a fake. The skull was indeed man but the teeth and jawbone came from an orang-utan whose teeth had been filed down. The skull had been stained to age it, then broken up and buried at Piltdown.

YOU SHOULD KNOW:
No one knows for certain who the forger was. The prime suspect is Charles Dawson but some suspect Sir Arthur Conan Doyle, the creator of Sherlock Holmes.

THE CRIME: In September 1912 a respected country lawyer by the name of Charles Dawson made a discovery that shocked science. He said that he had found a prehistoric humanoid skull in a gravel pit near Piltdown Common, Sussex, in southern England.

Dawson had been told that there were some valuable geological artefacts to be found and spent days burrowing in the pit. At first he found fossilized bone fragments then flint tools, fossilized teeth, and finally, the skull. He sent his findings to his friend, Dr Arthur Smith Woodward, of the British Museum. Woodward opened the package and was so excited that he rushed down to join his friend at the dig. The skull was final proof of Charles Darwin's 1859 Theory of Evolution. The two men sifted through the gravel and unearthed more finds. More experts were called in and they all agreed that Piltdown Man was the proof of the missing link between ape and man. The skull had an ape-like jaw and tiny brain area, but its teeth were worn down, the way that human teeth erode. The find was announced on 18 December 1912.

Woodward meticulously built a full head from the skull and fragments and named the find *Evanthropus dawsoni* – Dawson's Early Man. He said it was 500,000 years old. Geologists wanted Piltdown to be granted National Monument status. Dawson became a geological hero; Woodward wrote a book on the find and the British Museum displayed the skull. The local pub in Sussex changed its name from The Lamb to The Piltdown Man and the area became a popular tourist destination. Dawson continued to excavate the area and began building a second skull from his finds. Dawson died aged 52 in August 1916 and no further objects were found at Piltdown.

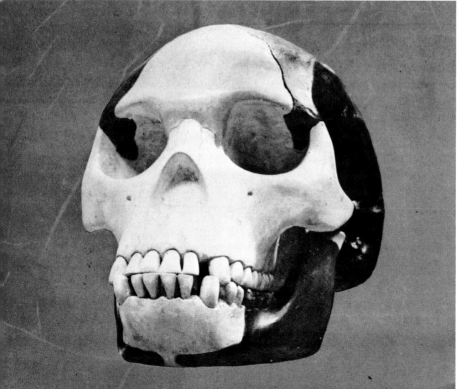

The reconstructed skull. The dark parts show the fragments found, the lighter parts are copies of the reverse side, and the rest are the result of conjecture.

Philip Musica

"My God, daddy, why did you do it?"

THE CRIME: Philip Musica was born in 1877, six years before his family emigrated to America from Italy. His life of crime began in earnest in 1909 when he bribed customs officials to misrepresent the weight of his imports. Some of those he had bribed were racked with remorse and confessed. Musica was sent to Elmira jail in New York in 1909 but President William Taft pardoned him after a few months.

His next venture – the United States Hair Company – began in October 1909 shortly after his release from jail and involved importing human hair from Italy to be made into wigs and hairpieces for ladies. Using false invoices, Musica was able to borrow $600,000 from banks before his calumny was discovered on 17 March 1913. To avoid arrest the whole family rushed to New Orleans where they boarded a ship bound for Honduras. However, before it left port, the police boarded the vessel on 20 March and arrested Philip, his brothers Arthur and George, and their 72-year-old father, Antonio.

Philip took the blame for the whole family and he was the only one jailed. In April he was sent to the Tombs Prison in New York where he became a warders' nark and was released in 1918. He joined the New York District Attorney's Office under the alias William Johnson. He charged William Randolph Hearst, the newspaper tycoon, with favouring Germany over the Allies in the First World War and later persuaded two Sing Sing convicts to give false testimony against Joseph Cohen when he was tried for the murder of Barnet Baff. In 1920, before sentence was passed, the deceit was discovered and Musica indicted but before he could be arrested, he fled. His next scam was portraying himself as Frank Costa, the co-owner of the Adelphi Pharmaceutical Manufacturing Company, a maker of hair tonic. Despite Prohibition, the company was able to purchase 19,000 litres (5,000 gallons) of alcohol every month to put into their hair tonics. Musica distilled this into cheap booze that he sold to speakeasies. The Musica family bought a successful drug company and Frank Costa became Frank Donald Coster and began to milk it for every dollar, issuing fake invoices and paying the money received into the family coffers.

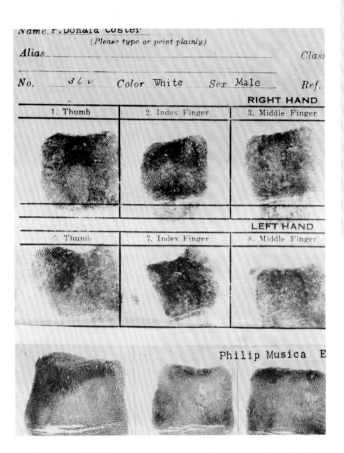

Fingerprints of Philip Musica

WHERE:
New York City, USA
WHEN:
March 1913
THE AFTERMATH:
The end came when Julian F. Thompson was hired in 1937 and he discovered that the company was built on nothing. The New York Stock Exchange suspended trading in the company in early December 1938. As an investigation began, Musica shot himself in the head in his Connecticut bathroom on 16 December 1938. He fell into the bathtub to avoid getting blood on a new carpet. His widow wailed, "My God, daddy, why did you do it?" for hours after his death.
YOU SHOULD KNOW:
As "Frank Donald Coster", Musica had an entry in *Who's Who In America* listing many phony qualifications including a Ph.D. and M.D. from the University of Heidelberg.

Maundy Gregory touted peerages and baronetcies.

Maundy Gregory

"What about a down payment of £2,000 or £3,000 on account?"

THE CRIME: Liberal Prime Minister David Lloyd George sold honours to finance his political aims and to ensure that the House of Lords was packed with his supporters. Arthur John Peter Michael Maundy Gregory, the son of a Southampton clergyman, saw what was happening and offered his services. Lloyd George hired Gregory to raise funds for his putative United Constitutional Party. Gregory set up an office near Downing Street and installed a commissionaire in a uniform very similar to those of government messengers. Gregory used bribery, flattery and gifts to learn who was in line for an honour and then wrote inviting them to dinner. For a sum, he told them, he could ensure that they received an appropriate honour – he charged £50,000 for a peerage, £35,000 for a baronetcy and £10,000 for a knighthood.

As news spread, various businessmen seeking honours approached him. Not all of them were honest – Richard Williamson received a CBE for "untiring work in connection with various charities". He was a Glasgow bookmaker with a criminal record. There were many other instances. Gregory earned about £1.2 million for the Liberal and later Tory parties – about £32 million at present values. He also earned about £3 million annually, enabling him to buy the Ambassador Club in 1927 and his own newspaper, which he used to spew anti-Bolshevik and anti-Semitic views. He also acquired *Burke's Landed Gentry* in 1929.

When Lloyd George's government lost power to the Conservatives they passed the Honours (Prevention of Abuses) Act on 7 August 1925, making the sale of honours illegal. In 1932 he began to offer papal honours after being received into the Church of Rome on 22 January. Edith Rosse, Gregory's long-term platonic companion (he was homosexual), died on 14 September of the same year at their London home. She left her entire estate, worth £18,000, to Gregory. He had her buried in an unsealed lead-lined coffin in a shallow grave in a cemetery next to the Thames, which meant that it often flooded.

On 23 January 1933 Gregory met Commander Edward W. Billyard-Leake and offered him a knighthood for £10,000. Commander Billyard-Leake went straight to Scotland Yard where he filed a complaint. He told Gregory that he "definitely [did] not wish to continue the matter" resulting in Gregory asking him to reconsider, asking for a payment of "£2,000 or £3,000 on account". Thirty-six hours later, on Saturday 4 February, Gregory was arrested at his home. The case opened at Bow Street Magistrates Court on 16 February and Attorney-General Sir Thomas Inskip prosecuted Gregory. It was the first trial under the new Act and Gregory was the first offender – he was eventually persuaded to plead guilty and was jailed for two months, fined £50 and ordered to pay an additional fifty guineas in costs.

WHERE:
38 Parliament Street, London, England
WHEN:
1918-1933
THE AFTERMATH:
On his release from Wormwood Scrubs on 12 April Gregory moved to France where, calling himself Sir Arthur Gregory, he lived on a pension of £2,000 per annum. On 28 April 1933 Edith Rosse's body was exhumed and examined at Paddington mortuary for evidence of poison but the waterlogged ground prevented any conclusion being reached. The celebrated pathologist Sir Bernard Spilsbury had been unable to find any cause of death when he performed the autopsy. Many police believed that Gregory had murdered her. In November 1940 the Germans arrested Gregory and put him in an internment camp at Drancy. He died on 28 September 1941 of heart failure.

Charles Ponzi

"The greatest Italian of them all"

THE CRIME: Born on 3 March 1882, Ponzi emigrated from Italy to the United States in 1901 and his first scam was quite small.

He learned that international postal reply coupons in some countries could be bought at below face value. If taken to the United States they could be resold at a profit of up to 50 per cent. He made $1,250 from his work. His next scam in June 1919 upped the stakes and offered investors a 50 per cent return on their money after three months, a period he later cut to 45 days after he began making $200,000 a day.

As people invested, Ponzi used that money to pay off his investors and also treated himself to a few gewgaws, including two dozen diamond stickpins, 48 Malacca canes with gold handles and 200 suits, plus a substantial portfolio of real estate. His clients labelled him "the greatest Italian of them all". On 26 July 1920 the *Boston Globe* published a story stating that Ponzi was not the clean-cut businessman he appeared to be and had served prison time in Canada for cheque frauds in 1905 and people-smuggling in Atlanta, Georgia in 1908. His scheme began to crumble especially when it became apparent that there were not enough international postal reply coupons in the world to meet his needs. The shortfall was reported to be between $5 million and $10 million.

WHERE:
Boston, Massachusetts, USA
WHEN:
June 1919
THE AFTERMATH:
Ponzi paid out $15 million of the $20 million he had taken and, on 1 November 1920, he pleaded guilty to mail fraud. He was sentenced to five years in federal prison, serving his term in Plymouth Prison. Ponzi was freed on appeal in 1925 but was soon arrested when he tried to con real estate investors. He was jailed again in 1926 for nine years for the new and old scams. On his release he moved to Brazil where he worked for an airline and ran a hot dog stall. He died in Rio de Janeiro on 18 January 1949.

Prison shots of Charles Ponzi

Black Sox Scandal

"Say it ain't so, Joe"

WHERE:
Comiskey Park, Chicago, Illinois;
Redland Field, Cincinnati, Ohio, USA
WHEN:
Wednesday 1 October 1919
THE AFTERMATH:
A Grand Jury investigated the series
in September 1920 and Comiskey
was forced to suspend the
suspected players. At the trial in the
summer of 1921 no one was
convicted, although the players were
later banned from baseball for life. As
"Shoeless Joe" Jackson left court
after the grand jury testimony a boy
approached him and asked, "It ain't
true, is it Joe?" to which he received
the rely, "I'm afraid it is." When the
encounter was reported in the
press the boy apparently said,
"Say it ain't so, Joe."

THE CRIME: For as long as people have played and bet on sports, others have tried to fix the outcome. In America after the First World War the government closed racetracks, forcing gamblers to bet on baseball instead. The best team was the Chicago White Sox owned by Charles A. Comiskey. The Sox finished 1919 with a record of 88–52 and a batting team average of .287. Their opponents in the World Series were the Cincinnati Reds. The team from Ohio were the underdogs, with some bookies offering odds of 5–1 on them winning. It would take a complete Chicago collapse for Cincinnati to have any chance of victory. Anyone betting on that stood to win big.

Chick Gandil was the Sox's first baseman and he was friendly with Boston bookie Joseph "Sport" Sullivan. Three weeks before the series the two men met in a Boston hotel room where Gandil offered the services of several of his teammates in 'throwing' the series in return for $80,000.

A few days later in a New York hotel room Gandil made the same deal with "Sleepy Bill" Burns, a retired pitcher turned oilman. Gandil recruited six colleagues but they lacked the financial clout to make a killing so they went to Arnold Rothstein (see page 327) who paid the money and also put $270,00 on Cincinnati to win.

The Sox traitors were Eddie Cicotte, Claude Williams, "Swede" Risberg, Fred McMullin, "Happy" Felsch, "Shoeless Joe" Jackson and "Buck" Weaver. The World Series opened on 1 October 1919 and Cicotte was paid $10,000 up front.

Cincinnati Reds won 9–1 and on the second day they won 4–2 and became favourites to win but many became suspicious. The White Sox won the third match 3–0 but the Reds triumphed 2–0 in the fourth game. Game five resulted in a 5–0 win for Cincinnati but the Sox won the sixth and seventh matches to make the tally 4–3 with two games to play. Arnold Rothstein became nervous and insisted the fix was complete in game eight.

*Frontpage headline of the
New York Times on 29
September 1920 describes the
Black Sox Scandal.*

Samuel Insull

Annual revenues reached nearly $40 million

THE CRIME: Samuel Insull was born in London on 11 November 1859. After school he became a clerk, before becoming Thomas Edison's secretary which necessitated a move to America in 1881. He was one of the founders of Edison General Electric, which later evolved into General Electric. In 1892 Insull left Edison General Electric to relocate to Illinois where he became president of Chicago Edison.

The company had a monopoly on supplying power to the city and by 1920 the company's 6,000 employees served around half a million customers and annual revenues reached nearly $40 million. Insull began to buy up parts of the city's utility infrastructure as well as its transport. There were some who believed that Insull was exploiting people though his company's monopoly. One of his main critics was Harold L. Ickes who, in 1933, became Secretary of the Interior in President Franklin D. Roosevelt's administration. Insull's holding company collapsed during the Great Depression, wiping out 600,000 shareholders' investments.

Samuel Insull refuses to tell of campaign donations to Frank L. Smith.

WHERE:
Chicago, Illinois, USA
WHEN:
1920
THE AFTERMATH:
Samuel Insull fled America for Greece but he was extradited to America where he stood trial on mail fraud and anti-trust charges. He was acquitted but, as a result, the government introduced the Public Utility Holding Company Act of 1935. He died of a heart attack at the Place de la Concorde station in Paris on 16 July 1938.

Victor Lustig

"I cannot understand honest men. They lead desperate lives full of boredom"

THE CRIME: In the summer of 1925 five businessmen received a letter from the Deputy Director General of the Ministry of Posts and Telegraphs asking to meet at the Hotel Crillon on the Place de la Concorde in Paris to discuss a government contract. When they arrived they met an impeccably dressed gentleman who announced that the government was to dismantle and sell the Eiffel Tower and he was authorized to offer them first refusal on the 6,350 tonnes (7,000 tons) of high-grade scrap iron.

WHERE:
Paris, France
WHEN:
1925
THE AFTERMATH:
Nine years later, in 1934, the FBI arrested Lustig on charges of counterfeiting. A day before he was due to go on trial, he escaped from the Federal House of Detention in New York, but was recaptured after 27 days on the run, in Pittsburgh. Lustig pleaded guilty at his trial and was sentenced to 20 years in Alcatraz. On 9 March 1947, he contracted pneumonia and died two days later at the Medical Center for Federal Prisoners in Springfield, Missouri.

YOU SHOULD KNOW:
Lustig once convinced Al Capone (see page 330) to invest $50,000 in a stock deal. Lustig kept the gangster's money in a safety deposit box for two months and then returned it to him, claiming that the deal had fallen through. Impressed with Lustig, Capone gave him $5,000, which had been Lustig's aim in the first place.

The Eiffel Tower had been built for the 1889 Paris Exposition, and was not intended to be permanent. It was to have been taken down in 1909 and moved elsewhere. The government official then took them on a tour of the landmark and decided that one of the men, André Poisson, a rough diamond who felt uncomfortable among the rich, was the most likely target. Back at the Hotel Crillon, the man from the ministry solicited a bribe from Poisson and a week later handed over a fine looking document, selling the Eiffel Tower in exchange for a large cheque. This was duly pocketed by "Count" Victor Lustig who, far from working for the French government, was a skilled conman. Victor Lustig was born in Bohemia on 4 January 1890 and was fluent in several languages. He counted on Poisson being too embarrassed to tell anyone, which he was, so two years later Lustig returned to Paris and pulled the same stunt again. This time his mark did go to the police and Lustig narrowly avoided arrest. He once said, "I cannot understand honest men. They lead desperate lives full of boredom."

Conman Victor Lustig

Harold G. Hoffman

"Never let any of your sons enter politics. It is a lousy game"

THE CRIME: Born in South Amboy, New Jersey, on 7 February 1896, Harold Giles Hoffman served in Company H, Third Regiment, New Jersey Infantry from 25 July 1917, rising to the rank of captain of the 114th Regiment Infantry. In 1920 he was appointed his home town's city treasurer. He represented, as a Republican, New Jersey's third congressional district in the United States House of Representatives, from 4 March 1927 until 3 March 1931. His daughter, Ada, wrote a campaign poem:

> "Lucky, plucky, happy fella,
> Once he's started, he won't stop.
> And he'll win this darned election,
> I should know – cause he's my Pop!"

Four years later on 15 January 1935, he was the Governor of New Jersey, a position he held until 18 January 1938. He also served simultaneously as the president of the South Amboy Trust Company. During his gubernatorial term, he was involved in at least two punch-ups with reporters including one with lightweight boxer, turned hack, Lou Angelo and falling out with his own party meant that he was not re-nominated for a second term in office.

It was not until 16 years after he left office that Hoffman's crimes came to light. On 18 March 1954 Governor Robert B. Meyner suspended Hoffman from his role as Employment Security Division Director after discovering a substantial amount of money had been embezzled from the state. It had been in the 1926 election that Hoffman first began to steal. He was promised $17,000 in campaign donations by Senator Hamilton Kean and duly spent that amount but when the pledge was made good he had only $2,500. Hoffman spent freely in Washington but left Congress to become Commissioner of Motor Vehicles in 1928. The job gave him access to public money. Every month, he would take up to $50,000, covering his tracks with forgeries, fake ledger statements and fund transfers.

WHERE:
New Jersey, USA
WHEN:
1928
THE AFTERMATH:
In May 1954 Hoffman wrote a letter to his daughter in an envelope bearing the legend, "Do not open until my death". In it, he confessed to stealing $300,000 from New Jersey. "It is a sad heritage I leave to Mother... and to you. But I pray it may be somewhat softened by the knowledge that I do love you all so much... Never let any of your sons enter politics. It is a lousy game. In order to be elected, you must necessarily accept favors from a large number of people. If you attempt to repay them after being elected to office, it becomes wrongdoing. If you don't, you are an ingrate." Before he could be tried he died of a heart attack while bending down to tie his shoelaces in a New York City hotel room on 4 June 1954.
YOU SHOULD KNOW:
On 16 October 1935 while governor, Hoffman carried out a secret visit to Bruno Hauptmann, the alleged kidnapper of the Lindbergh baby (see page 456) and afterwards encouraged the members of the New Jersey Court of Errors and Appeals to visit the prisoner because he had doubts as to Hauptmann's guilt. They ignored Hoffman's appeals.

Governor Hoffman conducts a class in financing.

Ivar Kreuger

"Match King"

THE CRIME: Known as the "Match King", Ivar Kreuger was an incredibly ruthless businessman. In 1907 he founded a match company and set out to build a monopoly. He did not just intimidate his opponents in the boardroom, he arranged for rival companies to have their supplies stopped or, worse, their employees beaten up. The First World War was good for his company, Svenska Tändsticks AB, and by 1928 Kreuger was responsible for 65 per cent of the world's supply of matches with factories in 34 countries and a huge headquarters in Stockholm. He lived a jet set lifestyle with fast cars and even faster women all over Europe.

Through his company Kreuger and Toll, founded in May 1908, he loaned money to poor countries. In return he had sole rights to manufacture and distribute matches in those countries. He loaned £15 million to France in 1927, £1 million to Greece in 1926, £7 million to Hungary in 1936 and £4 million to Yugoslavia in 1928 among many other imprests. In 1929 he became the major shareholder in the telephone firm, Ericsson, a gold mining company and a bank. In a methodology that would be repeated years later by companies such as Enron (see page 106), Kreuger reported vast profits for his companies when there were none and paid huge dividends using new investment or the finances of a newly acquired business. In 1929 he was said to be worth thirty billion krona and by 1931 he controlled more than 200 companies. In October 1929 Wall Street crashed and eventually it began to have an impact on Kreuger's business.

In 1931 the financial world was awash with rumours that all was not well in the Kreuger empire. He went to the Swedish banks to ask for a loan but was refused. The Bank of Sweden went further and demanded a complete set of accounts and also insisted that Kreuger return from America and meet the bank chairman personally.

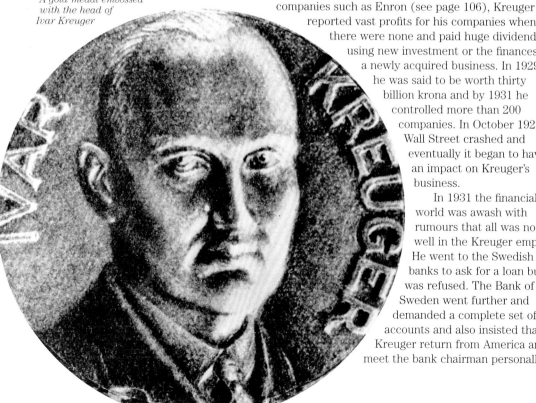

A gold medal embossed with the head of Ivar Kreuger

Joseph Weil, (aka the Yellow Kid)

"I never cheated an honest man, only rascals"

THE CRIME: Joseph Weil was one of America's most successful conmen, purported to have stolen more than $8 million. Born in Chicago, Illinois in 1875, he ran a pub, sold patent medicines that he claimed would eradicate tapeworm and worked at a racecourse. He also sold "miracle" spectacles for $3 having bought them by the dozen for 15¢ each. From 1903 he was known as The Yellow Kid, from the comic strip Hogan's Alley And The Yellow Kid.

He worked various cons with an ex-policeman Fred "The Deacon" Buckminster who arrested Weil and then let him go when Weil gave him $8,000 – his takings from a morning's cons. They ran a con whereby they sold dogs to unsuspecting punters making $5,000 a week for the mutts. The two men even went to the trouble of creating their own bank in Muncie, Indiana, with a branch and staff (hired from the ranks of prostitutes, bookies and other low lifes). They then fleeced a gullible millionaire into buying non-existent surplus government land that the bank had been authorized to sell. The set-up had cost Weill and Buckminster around $50,000 but they made seven times that amount on the deal. He was wont to say, "I never cheated an honest man, only rascals. They wanted something for nothing. I gave them nothing for something."

Weill may have been good at parting people from their money but he was not good at keeping it himself – he lost thousands on bad investments, gambling and women; the rest he wasted. After being released from one spell inside, he began selling magic pills that could turn water into petrol and sold stock in a non-existent copper mine. On 3 February 1934 he was arrested in Peoria, Illinois, with two suitcases marked "$200,000" and filled with newspaper cut into money shapes. Unfortunately, the police had taken him into custody before he had committed any crime and they had to let him go.

Joseph "The Yellow Kid" Weil seen at the age of 84.

WHERE:
Muncie, Indiana, USA
WHEN:
1930s
THE AFTERMATH:
Weil retired, living off his ill-gotten gains before writing his autobiography in 1948. He died in a Chicago nursing home in 1976 at the age of 100.
YOU SHOULD KNOW:
Weill spent ten years in prison and each time he was jailed his goods would be seized by a bailiff – his own brother.

Richard Whitney leaving Sing Sing prison after his release.

Richard Whitney

When he declared bankruptcy, he owed approximately $6.5 million

THE CRIME: Richard Whitney was born into a wealthy Boston, Massachusetts, family on 1 August 1888. In 1910 he moved to New York where he founded his own bond brokerage firm and, two years later, bought a seat on the New York Stock Exchange. In 1919 he joined the board of the Stock Exchange where he quickly became its vice-president and, in 1930, its president. His brother George was doing well at J.P. Morgan & Co where he was expected to succeed bank president, Thomas W. Lamont.

However, it became apparent that far from being a brilliant banker Richard Whitney was losing money hand over fist. He had speculated on a number of investments that had failed and was forced to borrow large sums of money from his brother and other wealthy friends. By 1931 Whitney was at least $2 million in debt, but he kept up his opulent lifestyle. If he couldn't borrow, he stole. Whitney took money from the New York Stock Exchange Gratuity Fund, the New York Yacht Club where he was the treasurer, plus an additional $800,000 of bonds from his father-in-law's estate. In 1935 he retired as president of the New York Stock Exchange but remained on the board of directors.

Han van Meegeren

"The painting in Goering's hands is not, as you assume, a Vermeer of Delft, but a Van Meegeren"

THE CRIME: Han van Meegeren was a genius artist but one who used his talents for forgery, rather than honestly. He perfected his technique of forging paintings by the great Dutch masters, including Vermeer and Frans Hals.

Van Meegeren was born on 10 October 1889 at Deventer, Overijssel, Holland, as Henricus Antonius van Meegeren. Raised a Catholic, he studied architecture at university because his father wanted him to but van Meegeren rebelled and became a painter. He began to adopt the styles of the Masters but critics lambasted his efforts, dashing his hopes. He decided he wanted revenge. He would paint a "Master", give it to a gallery and then wait for the critics to praise it before revealing his fraud. In 1936 he painted a "Vermeer", entitled *Christ And The Disciples At Emmaus* and then artificially aged it. The critics declared the work genuine and van Meegeren was delighted. The Boymans Museum of Rotterdam bought the painting for 520,000 guilders. Van Meegeren was doubly pleased – he had painted the forgery to hit back at his critics but now he could make money from his work.

By the time the Second World War began, van Meegeren had a nice income from his illegal sideline. In the summer of 1938 he had moved to Nice and bought a 12-bedroom estate at Les Arènes de Cimiez.

In 1943 he sold *Christ And The Adulteress* to a Nazi banker who then sold it on to Hermann Goering. It was a sale too far, one that would see him tried for collaborating at the end of the war.

WHERE:
Holland
WHEN:
1936
THE AFTERMATH:
On 29 May 1945 Han van Meegeren was arrested and charged with fraud and aiding and abetting the enemy. After three days in prison van Meegeren confessed that he had created the work of art. "The painting in Goering's hands is not, as you assume, a Vermeer of Delft, but a Van Meegeren. I painted the picture." To prove it he painted *Jesus Among The Doctors* and was released in early 1946. Nevertheless, he went on trial for forgery and fraud on 29 October 1947 in Room 4 of the Amsterdam Regional Court. On 12 November he was found guilty and sentenced to a year in jail. A fortnight later, he suffered a heart attack and was taken to Amsterdam's Valeriuskliniek hospital. He suffered a second coronary on 29 December and died at 5pm the next day, aged 58.

Van Meegeren with one of his "Masters"

Martin T. Manton

WHERE:
New YorkCity, USA
WHEN:
1939
THE AFTERMATH:
Manton served one year and seven months of his sentence before his release. He died at Fayetteville, Onondaga County, New York, on 18 November 1946. He was buried in the Immaculate Conception Cemetery in Fayetteville.

Manton, right, with his attorney James M. Noonan

"Defraud the United States of its right to have its legal functions exercised free from unlawful impairment"

THE CRIME: In 1939 Martin Thomas Manton was the senior judge of the US Circuit Court of Appeals for the Second Circuit, a position second only to that held by the members of the US Supreme Court. He had been appointed to the bench 21 years earlier, and had earned more than a million dollars from his law practice and real estate investments prior to his nomination by President Woodrow Wilson on 15 August 1916. Large, baldish and worldly, Manton was born on 2 August 1880 in New York. He lost much of his fortune in the Wall Street crash of 1929 and many believe that it was this that caused the Catholic judge to become crooked.

On 28 January 1939 the Department of Justice announced that it was investigating Manton for financial misdemeanours. District Attorney Thomas E. Dewey claimed that the judge had received more than $400,000 from litigants and provided details of six specific cases to US House Judiciary Committee. Manton told the press that he would issue a statement explaining his financial situation. The statement, released the next day, was a resignation letter. In April 1939, Manton was indicted for conspiring to influence, obstruct and impede justice and to "defraud the United States of its right to have its legal functions exercised free from unlawful impairment". Tried in May and June 1939 Manton was found guilty of conspiracy to obstruct the administration of justice and sentenced to two years' imprisonment and a $10,000 fine. He appealed but the sentence was upheld on 4 December 1939 before a specially constituted federal court.

Elmyr de Hory

He was imprisoned in a German concentration camp for being both a Jew and a homosexual

Elmyr de Hory with his forged Matisse

THE CRIME: As with many frauds, what is true and what fable is often difficult to ascertain.

Elmyr de Hory was born in 1906, probably as Elmyr Dory-Boutin, and claimed that his father was an Austro-Hungarian ambassador and his mother the scion of a banking family. In reality, it seems that de Hory had a comfortable middle-class upbringing but his parents divorced when he was 16 and he moved to Budapest where he lived a bohemian, gay life. At the age of 18, he enrolled in the Akademie Heinmann art school at Munich, Germany to study classical painting. On his return to Hungary he began an affair with a British journalist who turned out to be a spy. De Hory was jailed in the Carpathian Mountains and soon realized that he could improve his lot in prison by painting. He was released during the Second World War but re-imprisoned in a German concentration camp for being both a Jew and a homosexual. He was badly beaten up and one of his legs broken. Despite the disability, he managed to escape from a Berlin prison hospital. He returned to Hungary where he discovered that his parents were dead and their estate confiscated by the Nazis.

He made his way to France where he began to earn a living by forging art. His first forgery was a "Picasso", which he sold to a British friend who believed it was an original. De Hory did not copy paintings, but created "originals" in the style of the artist and then lied about their provenance. He met Jacques Chamberlin who became his dealer, selling de Hory's "Matisses", "Modiglianis" and "Renoirs" to galleries worldwide. The two men fell out when de Hory learned that Chamberlin was ripping him off by selling the paintings for more than he told de Hory. In 1947 de Hory visited the United States on a three-month visa and decided to stay. In 1955 one of his Matisse forgeries was sold to the Fogg Art Museum at Harvard University and an expert there identified it as a fake. De Hory fled to Mexico where the police accused him of murdering a gay tourist. He returned to America where he attempted suicide. Recovered, he began a relationship with Ferdinand Legros who became his dealer but, like Chamberlin before him, he too double-crossed de Hory.

WHERE:
France
WHEN:
1946
THE AFTERMATH:
In 1962 de Hory moved to Ibiza and made up with Legros who continued to sell his paintings, paying him a flat fee of $400 a month. In August 1968 a Spanish court convicted de Hory of being gay and mixing with criminals and sent him to prison for two months. He was released in October 1968 and expelled from Spain. He returned to Spain a year later a broken man. He committed suicide on 11 December 1976.
YOU SHOULD KNOW:
De Hory was the subject of a documentary by Orson Welles, *F For Fake*, and a biography, *Fake! The Story Of Elmyr de Hory The Greatest Art Forger Of Our Time*, by Clifford Irving who was himself a forger (see page 97).

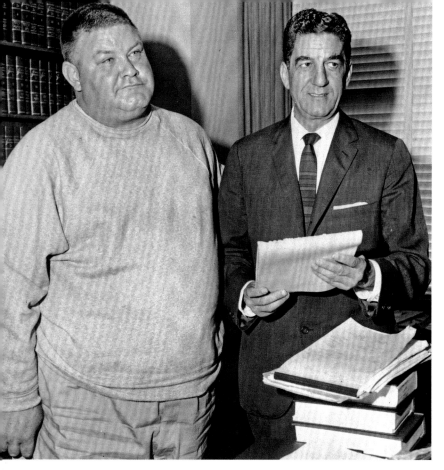

Demara, left, with Deputy D.A. Manley Bowler.

Ferdinand Waldo Demara

"Rascality, pure rascality"

THE CRIME: Ferdinand Waldo Demara, Jr was born at 40 Texas Avenue, Lawrence, Massachusetts at 7.30am on 21 December 1921. He wanted to become a priest, trying to enter a Trappist monastery on Rhode Island in 1935. Two further attempts at seminary life failed and in 1941 he joined the army.

It was in uniform that he began the career of impersonation that led to his being labelled "The Great Impostor". In 1942 he "borrowed" the life of his friend Anthony Ignolia and promptly went AWOL. Faking his suicide, he then became Robert Linton French, a doctor of philosophy. Caught, he served 18 months but, on his release, he continued to impersonate people.

Demara was variously a doctor of applied psychology, an editor, a cancer researcher, a biologist, a hospital orderly, a lawyer, a child-care expert, a Benedictine monk, a Trappist monk, an accountant, a warder in a maximum security prison, a civil engineer and a doctor.

It was during the Korean War that he had his most successful stint as an impostor in March 1951, when he passed himself off as Lieutenant-Surgeon Joseph Cyr of the Canadian Navy aboard HMCS *Cayuga*. Demara read medical textbooks before performing operations, some of them serious. Luckily, no one died as a result of Demara's surgeries. On one occasion he removed a bullet from within 2 cm (1 in) of the heart of a soldier and received a round of applause when he finished the operation.

The incident made the newspapers in Canada and one surprised reader was the mother of the real Dr Joseph Cyr. Demara was deported back to the States in January 1952. In 1956 he was jailed after being caught posing as Martin Godgart, a school teacher in Maine.

WHERE:
Sea of Japan
WHEN:
March 1951
THE AFTERMATH:
Demara was featured in a magazine article about his life, making it difficult to carry on his impostures. He died on 7 June 1982 of a heart attack caused by his diabetes. When asked why he did what he did since he did not make much money from his impostures, he replied, "Rascality, pure rascality."
YOU SHOULD KNOW:
The longest sentence served by Demara was 15 months.

Bernie Cornfeld

"Do you sincerely want to be rich?"

THE CRIME: Turkish-born Bernard Cornfeld did not look like a conman but he was; he did not look like a ladies' man but he was that, too – a remarkably successful one. One lover was the future madam to the stars Heidi Fleiss (see page 500) even though he was almost 40 years her senior. Other paramours included Victoria Principal and Alana Hamilton Stewart.

Cornfeld started the Investors' Overseas Service (IOS), an insurance and investment fund, which at one time controlled more than $1 billion in stocks and shares, in Paris in 1956 and then registered it in Panama. IOS salesmen – 10,000 of them – were encouraged to outdo each other and were paid handsomely for their efforts. High-earning salesmen would be rewarded with stays in top hotels in luxury resorts and the highest earning would be taken to Cornfeld's homes in Geneva, the French Riviera and Beverly Hills, where they could see how the boss lived, with his bevy of 20 bathing beauties and his stable of racehorses. Cornfeld's skill in moving IOS to Geneva in 1958 meant that, by using Switerland's secretive banking laws, he could circumvent laws in America and the UK designed to control investors in foreign companies.

American GIs based in Paris, charmed by his slogan "Do you sincerely want to be rich?", were Cornfield's first clients. Soon Cornfeld's stake in IOS was worth $100 milllion but, like all pyramid schemes, paying the commissions of the top people meant that those lower down the system had to work doubly hard to find new clients. IOS lasted five years before it imploded amid claims that assets had been mismanaged and that much of the wealth existed only on paper.

A meeting of shareholders on 9 May 1970 ended with Cornfeld – nicknamed "the Midas of Mutuals Funds" – being replaced as chairman and his shares dwindling in value to just $4 million. On 1 July he was voted off the board. The Swiss authorities began a fraud investigation into IOS and Cornfeld was arrested on 14 May 1973 in Geneva and accused of defrauding IOS investors. He was released on bail on 5 April 1974. His replacement as head of IOS was an American called Robert Lee Vesco but, just when it seemed he had rescued much of the company's money, he disappeared in April 1972.

WHERE:
22 Boulevard Flandrin, Paris, France; 119 Rue de Lausanne, Geneva, Switzerland
WHEN:
March 1956–Saturday 9 May 1970
THE AFTERMATH:
Robert Vesco fled from country to country, always keeping one step ahead of the authorities until he was jailed in Cuba. He died on 23 November 2007 of lung cancer in hospital at Havana. Bernie Cornfeld was found guilty of fraud in California in June 1978. He had been using a device to bypass paying for long-distance telephone calls and was sentenced to 90 days' imprisonment. However, a year later, Cornfeld went on trial in Geneva on 24 September 1979, accused of persuading IOS employees to buy stock in the company even though he knew it was on the verge of collapse. He was acquitted on 15 October 1979 after a Swiss jury deliberated for 50 minutes. He died of a cerebral aneurysm on 27 February 1995 at London's Chelsea and Westminster Hospital.

Cornfield at home in Belgravia, London after having bought his way out of jail in Switzerland.

Charles Van Doren

"I have deceived my friends and I had millions of them"

WHERE:
New York City, USA
WHEN:
Wednesday 28 November 1956
THE AFTERMATH:
NBC fired Van Doren and he was allowed to resign from Columbia University. However, his literary career flourished and he wrote several books. Now Van Doren is in his 80s and adjunct professor at the University of Connecticut.
YOU SHOULD KNOW:
Although his infamy stems from *Twenty-One*, Van Doren was originally asked to appear on *Tic-Tac-Dough*.

Charles Van Doren on Twenty-One, *trying to come up with the correct answer.*

THE CRIME: Television was still in its infancy in the 1950s but a number of quiz shows were popular with viewers, including *The $64,000 Question, The $64,000 Challenge, Twenty-One* and *High Finance*. For some time rumours had circulated that not all was well with the shows and that some had been fixed. The District Attorney of New York and a subcommittee of the House of Representatives set out to investigate.

The highest ratings shows in 1955 were *The $64,000 Question* and *The $64,000 Challenge* but when a good-looking young man called Charles Van Doren began appearing on *Twenty-One* on 28 November 1956, that show's ratings began to rise. Van Doren was the scion of a literary family and he was up against the nerdish Herbert Stempel. The two battled out for several weeks until Van Doren finally beat Stempel. He had banked $129,000 on 14 shows before he lost to Vivienne Nearing on 11 March 1957. Van Doren was then hired at $1,000 a week to present *Today* on NBC as a stand-in for David Garroway and offered a three-year contract. On 11 February 1957 he appeared on the cover of *Time*.

In August 1958 Van Doren was an English professor at Columbia University when Herbert Stempel went public with a claim that the show had been fixed. Van Doren emphatically denied the allegation. In January 1959, Frank Hogan, District Attorney of New York, convened a grand jury and called witnesses. Van Doren again denied all claims, as did other witnesses. Then the Special Subcommittee on Legislative Oversight of the House of Representatives also called witnesses.

NBC urged Van Doren to appear but he dropped out of public view for ten days. When he reappeared he travelled to Washington DC and on 2 November 1959 appeared before the committee whose chairman was Arkansas Democrat Oren Harris and confessed that "I have deceived my friends and I had millions of them." Van Doren revealed that he had finally begged the producers to let him lose because of the pressure he was under, winning each week.

Frank Abagnale

Catch Me If You Can

THE CRIME: Frank William Abagnale Jr was born at Bronxville, Westchester County, New York, on 27 April 1948 and became well known when Leonardo Di Caprio portrayed him in the film, *Catch Me if You Can*. Much of Abagnale's story is disputable by the very nature of his "profession". His earliest victim was his father, whom he defrauded of $3,400 by using his credit card. After his parents were divorced, Abagnale moved to New York. He stole more than $60,000 by writing his bank account number on pay-in slips, so when customers banked cheques the money went into Abagnale's account. He also conned people into believing that he was an airline pilot and flew free more than 250 times on Pan Am. Abagnale also claims to have forged a Columbia University sociology degree and taught for a term at Brigham Young University.

Abagnale at the premiere of the film Catch Me If You Can *in Los Angeles in 2002*

Next, calling himself Frank Conners, he worked as a paediatrician at an Atlanta, Georgia hospital. He then claimed that he genuinely passed the Bar exam of Louisiana and became a minion in the office of the state attorney general of Louisiana. He left after eight months. During the 1960s he was said to have passed $2.5 million in bad cheques in 26 countries.

In France in 1969 he was arrested for fraud and sentenced to a year in prison. He served six months of the sentence before he was freed and deported to Sweden. He then spent six months in a Malmö prison for cheque fraud before being deported back to his homeland where, in April 1971, he received a sentence of 12 years in the Federal Correction Institution at Petersburg, Virginia for multiple counts of forgery. He was released early in 1974 and later founded Abagnale & Associates, a company that advises financial institutions on their security. In 1980 he published his autobiography.

WHERE:
Worldwide
WHEN:
1960s
THE AFTERMATH:
Through his legitimate work, Abagnale is now said to be a millionaire and an adviser to the FBI.
YOU SHOULD KNOW:
Abagnale had a small part in the film of his life as a French policeman arresting Leonardo Di Caprio

Dr Emil Savundra

"I came here to cross swords with England's greatest swordsman"

Emil Savundra arrives at Ealing Magistrates Court.

WHERE:
London, England
WHEN:
Thursday 14 February 1963-Sunday
24 July 1966
THE AFTERMATH:
Savundra was released from prison
at 7.30am on a wet 4 October 1974,
having served six years, seven
months and three days of his ten-
year sentence. Savundra approached
the American government and
offered to sell them his wife's land in
Ceylon for $200,000,000 on condition
she was made Queen of North
Ceylon. Before the Americans could
turn down his offer, Savundra
suffered a heart attack at his home
in Ousely Road, Old Windsor on 21
December 1976 and was pronounced
dead on arrival at King Edward VII
Hospital. At the end of 1977 FAM's
creditors received a dividend of
30 pence in the pound.

THE CRIME: Emil Savundra was for much of his professional life a lucky man. He was a lover of Mandy Rice-Davies at the time of the Profumo affair (see page 494) but was only referred to in court as "the Indian doctor". He was freed from a five-year jail sentence in Belgium after only two months following the intervention of the Vatican. He described himself as "God's own lounge lizard turned swindler," adding, "I don't like work". Born as Michael Marion Emil Anacletus Savundranayagam in Ceylon on 6 July 1923, he had been involved in a number of shady businesses in China, Ghana and Belgium before he arrived in Britain in the 1950s. After discovering that anyone could become an insurance broker if they had £50,000, he founded Fire, Auto and Marine (FAM) in 1963. The company offered very attractive deals – premiums were half the cost of other insurance brokers. Savundra explained, "My methods are the most modern and cost-effective. Traditional insurance companies need to charge exorbitant fees because their out-of-date system loads them with big overheads and costs." Money began to pour in; by some estimates as much as £40,000 per week. The law dictates that an insurance company must have enough assets to meet claims but the money that came into FAM quickly left again via Savundra's wallet, buying him luxuries including a speedboat. It was two years after the formation of the company that money out began to exceed money in.

Initially, Savundra told his staff to limit payouts to £10,000 a week. The Board of Trade demanded to examine the company's books but Savundra fooled them by producing a fake document from Liechtenstein stating that FAM had more than £500,000 of government bonds. It only delayed the inevitable. As FAM collapsed so did Savundra, taken to hospital with a convenient heart attack. He fled to Switzerland and then on 9 July 1966 to Ceylon. On 24 July 1966 the company was wound up, leaving 400,000 motorists unprotected. In January 1967 Savundra unexpectedly returned to Englanda and went to the Labour Exchange on Regent's Park Road to sign on the dole. A week later, he received a writ from the Official Receiver for £386,534.

A comedy sketch on *The Frost Programme* about a thinly disguised Savundra prompted him to ask to appear on the programme. On the show Savundra said, "I am not going to cross swords with the peasants. I came here to cross swords with England's greatest swordsman." David Frost responded, "Nobody is a peasant. They are people who gave you money" with Savundra riposting, "They have given me nothing at all." He claimed he had no legal or moral responsibility to his former customers. A week later, he was arrested. Savundra went on trial on 10 January 1968 at the Old Bailey. The jury found him guilty and he was sentenced to eight years in prison and a £50,000 fine.

Clifford Irving

"Cliff lives in a world of fantasy"

THE CRIME: Billionaire Howard Hughes was an aviator, founder of Trans World Airlines, billionaire, film producer, owner of RKO Pictures, bra inventor and much more, but it is for his eccentricities that he is best known. Hughes became a paranoid recluse and little-known novelist Clifford Irving decided to take advantage of this.

In December 1970 he decided to write the "authorized" biography of Hughes. Irving forged a correspondence between himself and Hughes and presented it to publishing executives demanding $750,000. On 7 December 1971 McGraw-Hill announced the book would be published on 27 March 1972. Rosemont Enterprises Inc., Hughes's main company, denied the book was genuine. Irving explained that Hughes was so paranoid he had not even told his own men, an explanation that satisfied McGraw-Hill. Cheques were issued to an H.R. Hughes and deposited in an account at Credit Suisse, which had been opened by Irving's wife, Edith.

At 6.45pm on 7 January 1972, from the ninth floor suite of the Britannia Beach Hotel in Nassau, Hughes made his first public utterance in 15 years when he denounced the book as a fake in a phone link to journalists at the Sheraton Hotel in Los Angeles. It was when the Swiss banks broke their traditional vow of secrecy to reveal that H.R. Hughes was a woman (Helga Rosencrantz Hughes) that the plot quickly began to unravel. A friend of Irving's said, "Cliff lives in a world of fantasy." Hughes informed the IRS that he had not received any of the $750,000 advance and had no intention of paying tax on it. This caused the tax men to began an investigation. Signatures on the back of cashed cheques were re-examined. On 28 January 1972 Irving admitted that his wife was the mysterious H.R. Hughes.

WHERE:
New York City, USA
WHEN:
December 1970–1972
THE AFTERMATH:
On 7 February Irving and his wife took the Fifth Amendment before a grand jury in New York. During the hearings singer, Baroness Nina van Pallandt, revealed she had travelled to Mexico with Irving during the time he had said he was interviewing Hughes. On 16 June 1972, Judge John M. Cannella sentenced Edith to two years in prison, all but two months of which were suspended. She was then tried in Zurich and sentenced to a further two years' imprisonment. She was released on 5 May 1974. Irving was fined $10,000 and sentenced to 30 months. Upon his release in 1974, he got divorced and wrote the story of the hoax. In June 1975, he was declared bankrupt with assets of $410 and debts of $55 million.

Clifford Irving, right, and Richard Suskind, who co-wrote the autobiography, at work.

Watergate

"There will be no whitewash at the White House"

WHERE:
Watergate Hotel, 2600 Virginia
Avenue NW, Washington DC, USA
WHEN:
1.47am 17 June 1972

THE AFTERMATH:
In June 1973 a Senate Committee convened and the truth, including the revelation that Nixon taped all the Oval Office conversations, emerged. Grudgingly, and after losing a lengthy court battle, Nixon released the tapes – "There will be no whitewash at the White House" – but numerous transcripts were heavily edited and featured the words "Expletive deleted" as Nixon's foul language was censored. On 9 August 1974 Nixon resigned to avoid impeachment. Many of the revelations of the scandal came in the *Washington Post* and they were written by novice local reporters Bob Woodward and Carl Bernstein. They were helped by a secret source nicknamed *Deep Throat* after a porno movie of that name. On 31 May 2005, it was revealed that former FBI Deputy Director, W. Mark Felt, 91, was Deep Throat. He died at the age of 95 on 18 December 2008.

YOU SHOULD KNOW:
Curiously, an 18-minute gap appeared on a crucial tape discussing the break-in but, most incriminating, it failed to delete Nixon's demand on 23 June 1972 that the CIA be directed to interfere with the FBI's investigation into Watergate (known as 'The Smoking Gun" tape, it sealed the President's fate).

THE CRIME: Guard Frank Wills was doing his rounds in the Watergate hotel that served as headquarters of the Democratic Party when he became suspicious that someone had broken in. Wills called police after seeing that tape used to hold a door open had reappeared after he'd removed it during his earlier rounds. He called the police at 1.47am and at 2.30am they arrested five men who gave fake names. They had sophisticated spying equipment with them and one had a direct-line phone number for the White House. The next day, on holiday in Florida, President Nixon dismissed the incident as "a third-rate burglary". At Republican Party headquarters, an aide boasted of their own security in the hands of James W. McCord, a former CIA operative who at that moment was appearing in court – as one of the five Watergate burglars.

Alongside him were Frank Sturgis, Bernard Barker, Virgilio Gonzalez and Eugenio Martinez who had been hired by the White House and the Citizens' Committee to Re-elect the President (known as CREEP) to spy on their political enemies. It was imperative that the burglary was not linked to the White House in an election year and for five months the façade was maintained; Nixon was easily elected to a second term. The FBI investigated and linked the Watergate break-in to two White House officials, G. Gordon Liddy and E. Howard Hunt. In 1971 a newspaper had reported on Nixon's covert military operations in Vietnam and he was determined that the White House would stop such damaging information from getting out, so a group – nicknamed the Plumbers, because they would plug such "leaks" – was formed.

The White House pressurized McCord to plead guilty and to blame the CIA, and it was later learned that Nixon had approved the payment of as much as $1 million ("A million dollars? We could get that," he said) from CREEP campaign coffers to buy the burglars' silence. At the trial only McCord and Liddy pleaded guilty but Judge John Sirica postponed sentence for two months; McCord lost his nerve and revealed the depth of the conspiracy.

Richard Nixon announces his resignation on national television.

Rev Jim Bakker

"A cancer that needed to be excised from the body of Christ"

Tele-evangelist Jim Bakker

THE CRIME: Jim Bakker was a seemingly charming tele-evangelist who, with his permanently over made-up wife Tammy Faye, was the public face of the PTL Ministry. PTL stood for Praise The Lord or People That Love but wags suggested it really meant Pass the Loot, as the Bakkers earned a fortune from their religion.

One of their main rivals was a Southern fundamentalist firebrand named Jimmy Swaggart. Based in Baton Rouge, Louisiana, Jimmy Swaggart Ministries grossed about $140 million annually. In March 1987 it was revealed that Jim Bakker had, on 6 December 1980 in a Florida hotel room, had sex with (she says she was drugged and raped) a 21-year-old virgin by the name of Jessica Hahn and then had bought her silence with $265,000. Bakker, said Jessica Hahn, told her that by "helping the shepherd, you are helping the sheep" before having sex with her. Aftewards, Bakker's fellow evangelist John Wesley Fletcher also, according to Jessica, raped her. Bakker, far from accepting he had done wrong and going quietly, accused Swaggart of a "diabolical plot" to take over PTL, which included a satellite television network and a Christian theme park called Heritage USA. Swaggart hit back by claiming that the Bakker affair was "a cancer that needed to be excised from the body of Christ". Swaggart had reported the extra-marital activities of two preachers – Bakker and a New Orleans-based TV clergyman called Marvin Gorman – to the Assemblies of God in a bid to clean up the evangelist industry. Unbeknown to his congregation, Swaggart had himself been visiting a prostitute, Debra Murphee, in a New Orleans motel room. She adopted suggestive poses for him, which she was happy to do until he suggested her nine-year-old daughter join them. Murphee was so disgusted she went straight to the newspapers. In February 1988, Swaggart appeared on his own channel in tears confessing to his "moral sin" without specifying what it was.

In 1984 *The Charlotte Observer* began to investigate the goings-on at PTL. These included selling $1,000 lifetime memberships that entitled the purchaser to an annual three-night stay at Heritage USA. Bakker sold tens of thousands memberships but only one 500-room hotel was ever built. Much of the money went into Bakker's personal bank account. Bakker resigned on 19 March 1987 when the story of Jessica Hahn was made public. Jerry Falwell replaced Bakker at PTL and then raised $20 million to keep Heritage USA open. Falwell called Bakker "a liar, an embezzler, a sexual deviant and the greatest scab and cancer on the face of Christianity in 2,000 years of church history". On 6 May 1987 the Assemblies of God defrocked Bakker for his encounter with Jessica Hahn.

WHERE:
Sheraton Sand Key Resort, Clearwater Beach, Florida, USA
WHEN:
Saturday 6 December 1980
THE AFTERMATH:
On 21 September 1987 a federal grand jury convened in Charlotte to hear testimony in the allegations against Bakker. The first witness was Jessica Hahn. In 1988 Jim Bakker was indicted on eight counts of mail fraud, one count of conspiracy and 15 counts of wire fraud. On 5 October 1989 Bakker was found guilty on all 24 charges and sentenced to 45 years in federal prison and a $500,000 fine. Bakker appealed his sentence and in 1991 his 45-year sentence and fine were quashed. Instead, he was sentenced to 18 years in prison. He was paroled in 1993. Three years later Bakker wrote a book, *I Was Wrong*, in which he admitted that the first time he had read the Bible completely was in prison. In 2003 Bakker returned to broadcasting. He still owes the Internal Revenue Service about $6 million. He and Tammy Faye were divorced on 13 March 1992. She died at 4am on 20 July 2007 after an eleven-year battle with cancer. Heritage USA closed in 1989. Jessica Hahn posed topless for *Playboy* in November 1987 – for which she was supposedly paid $1 million. She posed naked for the magazine in 1988 and again in 1992.

The Stern *reporter Gerd Heidemann, right, who came up with the forged diaries.*

Hitler Diaries

"They're forgeries, pure and simple"

THE CRIME: In 1976 Gerd Heidemann was a reporter for the German magazine *Stern* and he was also in debt. He had just split from his third wife and had spent a fortune on a yacht that once belonged to Hermann Goering. His boss at *Stern* gave him permission to write a story about the vessel and Heidemann began research. He contacted Goering's daughter, Edda, and they began an affair. She introduced him to surviving Nazis and one gave him a book that told the story of Hitler's last days including a tale of how Hitler's archive had been destroyed. But what, wondered Heidemann, constituted the führer's archive?

In December 1980 he got his answer when he was told that a Stuttgart engineer held a volume of Hitler's personal diary. The engineer, who collected Nazi memorabilia, had got the 100-page volume from Konrad Kujau, an antiques dealer and painter. Kujau had more diaries. Edda Goering and the other high-ranking Nazis immediately discounted the authenticity of the diaries but Heidemann was undeterred. Gruner + Jahr, the owners of *Stern*, authorized him to offer five million deutschmarks for the 26 volumes of Hitler's diary. On 28 January 1981 Heidemann made a down payment for the diaries to Kujau with a suitcase full of cash. Three weeks later, on 17 February, Kujau delivered the first three volumes with the rest arriving piecemeal. The publishing executives were ecstatic and dreamed of the riches they would make from worldwide book deals.

On 1 June 1981 Heidemann reported that the price for each volume had increased by 25 per cent. On 22 August the 18th volume was delivered and the price doubled. In March 1982 Gruner + Jahr finally sent a page from the diary to be checked by experts. The first expert reported the diaries were genuine and a second and third expert concurred. By March 1983 the 58th volume had arrived and the bill was astronomical. Meanwhile, Heidemann was living a life of luxury but no one seemed to notice. Gruner + Jahr's agents offeried serialization deals and the bidding was fierce, but West German police had been asked to test the age of the paper and on 28 March reported that it was post-war. Historian Hugh Trevor-Roper authenticated the diaries for Rupert Murdoch and *The Sunday Times* published six pages of them on 24 April 1983.

WHERE:
Stuttgart, West Germany
WHEN:
Wednesday 28 January 1981
THE AFTERMATH:
Historians around the world dismissed the diaries as fakes. David Irving said, "They're forgeries, pure and simple." *Stern* executives offered the entire 60 volumes for analysis and on 1 May 1983 were shocked to be told that they were all fake. The paper contained chemicals that were unavailable before 1955. On 13 May 1983 Kujau was arrested. When told that Gruner + Jahr had paid 23 million deutschmarks for the diaries he revealed that he had only received five; Heidemann had siphoned off the other 18 million. Both men were sentenced to four and a half years in prison. Heidemann, now 76, is living alone in a cramped Hamburg apartment on £280 a month with £560,000 of debts. Kujau, who was born on 27 June 1938 died on 12 September 2000.

Robert Maxwell

"He is not...a person who can be relied upon to exercise proper stewardship of a publicly quoted company"

THE CRIME: Cap'n Bob and the Bouncing Czech were just two of the more printable nicknames for Ian Robert Maxwell (né Jan Ludwig Hoch, born on 10 June 1923). By dint of hard work and sheer bloodymindedness, he built up one of the biggest publishing companies in the world – only to die in mysterious circumstances and have it all come tumbling down, amid accusations of wholesale fraud and theft. It could have been all so different for the egotistical Maxwell whose aim in life was to get one over on fellow publishing tycoon, Rupert Murdoch.

Bob Maxwell founded Pergamon Press in the ashes of the Second World War where he had distinguished himself winning a Military Cross. He chose to live in Britain; a fact that he believed gave him some kind of special status. Printing scientific journals made Pergamon successful but the world of publishing was not enough for Maxwell and a Department of Trade Inquiry published on 13 July 1971 did not help. It decided that "he is not in our opinion a person who can be relied upon to exercise proper stewardship of a publicly quoted company".

In 1964 Maxwell had become a Labour MP but he lost his seat in 1970. On 13 July 1984 – to the consternation of many – he bought the British institution *The Daily Mirror*. Displaying an ego as vast as his enormous girth, he thought that *Mirror* readers would be interested in the doings of himself and his family – to such an extent that wags renamed the paper the *Daily Maxwell*. In 1969 Maxwell had attempted to buy *The News of the World* but had been thwarted by Rupert Murdoch. Maxwell now tried to use *The Mirror* to beat *The Sun*, Murdoch's best-selling tabloid. It was a battle that he was destined to lose.

Maxwell tried and failed to launch a London-based newspaper and did buy the *New York Daily News*. Regarded by many as something of a buffoon, he used the courts to silence his critics on a regular basis. No one, apart from the magazine *Private Eye,* ever questioned Maxwell's behaviour. Then on 5 November 1991, on board his $19 million yacht which was named after his youngest daughter Ghislaine, Maxwell went missing in the Canary Islands.

WHERE:
London, England
WHEN:
July 1984–November 1991
THE AFTERMATH:
Maxwell's body was found and taken to the Mount of Olives in Israel where it was buried amid much pomp. Then his empire began to unravel. It soon became clear that Maxwell had been not a munificent newspaper tycoon but a crook on a huge scale – the worst financial chicaner in post-war Britain. He had even stolen money – around £400 million – from Mirror Group Newspapers' pension fund, leaving many ex-employees destitute.

Would you trust this man with your pension?

Ivan Boesky

"Greed is all right... I think greed is healthy"

WHERE:
Fifth Avenue, New York City, USA
WHEN:
1986
THE AFTERMATH:
Ivan Boesky was fined $100 million and sentenced to three and a half years in Southern California's Lompoc Federal Prison Camp near Vandenberg Air Force Base, also known as Club Fed West. He served two years before being released, but was banned for life from working in the financial industry.

THE CRIME: Born on 6 March 1937 in Detroit, Michigan, the son of a Russian immigrant, Ivan Frederick Boesky was yet another financier unknown to the public until his public disgrace. He went to Wall Street in 1966 as a stock analyst. Nine years later, he started his own arbitrage firm with the help of his wife's family fortune. By the mid 1980s, working up to 20 hours a day at his desk in a white marble office on Manhattan's Fifth Avenue, he was worth an estimated $200 million.

Boesky made money from stock in firms that were about to be taken over which was legal as long as the buyout was public knowledge. However, there were so many instances of favourable dealing that insider trading could be the only explanation. Nearly 3,000 mergers and buyouts, worth more than $130 billion, occurred in 1986 alone. Boesky and others bought a large bloc of shares in Gulf+Western before rumours of a takeover bid drove up the price of that stock. On 14 November 1986 the Securities and Exchange Commission (SEC) charged Boesky with illegal stock manipulation based on insider information. The arbitrageur was banned from working in securities, fined $100 million and jailed.

He then co-operated with the SEC on a wide-ranging investigation into insider trading that led to the uncovering of the Guinness share fraud scandal (see page 105). He allowed inverstigators to tape his telephone conversations with junk bond dealers and takeover merchants and, in return, the SEC allowed him to sell compromised stocks before his crimes were made public, much to the annoyance of members of Congress and fellow dealers. Boesky said, "Greed is all right, by the way I think greed is healthy. You can be greedy and still feel good about yourself."

Ivan Boesky arrives at the Federal Court in New York.

Michael Milken

"The greatest criminal conspiracy the financial world has ever known"

THE CRIME: Born on Independence Day 1946 in Encino, California, Michael Robert Milken was unknown to the general public until 29 March 1989 when he faced 98 charges of racketeering, insider trading and securities fraud and, after plea bargaining, pleaded guilty to six although he was not guilty of insider trading. One critic described Milken's actions as "the greatest criminal conspiracy the financial world has ever known".

Milken began his career with Drexel Harriman Ripley in 1969. When the company merged with another, Milken persuaded his boss to allow him begin a high-yield bond-trading department. The gamble paid off and he moved into offices at 9560 Wilshire Boulevard in Beverly Hills where he worked long hours at an X-shaped desk. Milken attracted a number of high-profile clients to his company. He once said, "There is no shortage of capital; there is only a shortage of management talent."

In 1979 the Securities and Exchange Commission began to take an interest in Milken, whom they believed was behaving with a degree of illegality in his trades. Nothing happened until 1986 when arbitrageur Ivan Boesky (see opposite) pleaded guilty to securities fraud as part of a larger investigation into insider trading. United States Attorney for the Southern District of New York Rudolph Giuliani launched a criminal probe into Milken's activities and for two years Drexel insisted that there had been no illegal activities carried out. On 20 December 1989 Drexel's lawyers found suspicious activity in a section set up by Milken and the next day pleaded no contest to six counts of stock parking and stock manipulation.

Milken keeps his head down after a press conference in New York.

WHERE:
Beverly Hills, California, USA
WHEN:
1986
THE AFTERMATH:
Milken was jailed for ten years after pleading guilty to six securities and reporting violations on 24 April 1990 but served only 22 months (from March 1991 until January 1993) before he was freed. Not long after he declared that he had been diagnosed with terminal prostate cancer and given a year to 18 months to live. He was also fined $200 million and banned from working in the financial industry for life. In 1996 he launched computer technology and retraining company, Knowledge Universe.
YOU SHOULD KNOW:
The judge, Kimba Wood, who told Milken, "When a man of your power in the financial world... repeatedly conspires to violate, and violates, securities and tax business in order to achieve more power and wealth for himself... a significant prison term is required" was appointed to be Attorney General by Bill Clinton. However, she had to withdraw because she had given a job as nanny to an illegal alien.

Real estate queen Leona Helmsley leaving court.

Leona Helmsley

"Only the little people pay taxes"

THE CRIME: In the 1980s the world learned of hotel magnate Leona Helmsley, who was dubbed the Queen of Mean by the press because of her ruthlessness. Helmsley was born Lena Mindy Rosenthal on 4 July 1920 at Marbletown, Ulster County, New York, the daughter of a hatter. She worked hard to ensure that she was never poor like her father, often staying up until 3am to finish a deal when she began her career as an estate agent. By the time of her third marriage to landlord Harry Helmsley in 1972 she was the top estate agent in New York and reputedly worth $1 million. She took over the running of Harry Helmsley's property empire, which included 27 hotels and a number of skyscrapers, including the Empire State Building. On her birthday each year her husband would decorate the iconic building in red, white and blue lights.

Leona Helmsley introduced a clever marketing strategy of being a perfectionist: if she was one, then a stay at one of her hotels could be expected to be perfect also. It was a remarkably successful plan and businessmen and the rich began to stay regularly at Helmsley hotels.

If Leona Helmsley was a perfectionist, she expected her staff to be the same. Busboys, chambermaids, receptionists and even bodyguards were all terrified of her and tried their best to avoid her when she stalked the corridors looking for examples of sloppiness. The staff looked forward to the hour between 6.30am and 7.30am because they knew that was the only time she would not be on the prowl – that was the time she used the swimming pool in her penthouse at the Park Lane Hotel. The swimming pool attendants had to keep a platter of fresh seafood at each end of the pool and as she completed a lap they had to drop a shrimp into her open mouth as she called out, "Feed the fishy."

And then it all went wrong. Helmsley was investigated by the Internal Revenue Service who discovered that she had spent $8 million on her Connecticut home and claimed it against tax. On 14 April 1988 the Helmsleys were indicted on 188 charges. They managed to have the trial delayed until 26 June of the following year. On 12 July a former housekeeper at Dunellen Hall reported Leona Helmsley as saying in 1983 (although she denied having said it), "We don't pay taxes. Only the little people pay taxes."

On 30 August 1989 Leona Helmsley was found guilty of one count of conspiracy, three counts of tax evasion, three counts of filing false tax returns, ten counts of mail fraud and 16 counts of filing incorrect business tax returns. She was acquitted on a charge of extortion that would have led to life in prison. On 14 November she was sentenced to 16 years in prison (later reduced to four years after all but eight charges were dropped), 750 hours' community service and fined $7.75 million. She cried when the verdict was passed.

WHERE:
New York City and Greenwich, Connecticut, USA
WHEN:
Wednesday 30 August 1989
THE AFTERMATH:
Leona Helmsley went to a low-security prison in Danbury, Connecticut where she continued to behave as the Queen of Mean. She hired inmates to make her bed and one as a secretary. Rather than fulfil her community service in the cold climate of New York, Helmsley carried her out her punishment in the warm air of Phoenix, Arizona, having persuaded the judge that her 84-year-old husband would suffer in the Big Apple cold. She served 19 months with a further two under house arrest. Leona Helmsley died of congestive heart failure on Monday 20 August 2007. She was 87.

Guinness Share-trading Fraud

"Unjustifiable favours for friends and himself"

THE CRIME: As with the Michael Milken (see page 103) case, the Guinness scandal came to light after American trader Ivan Boesky (see page 102) tried to plea bargain his way out of trouble. The Guinness Four – Ernest Saunders, Gerald Ronson, Sir Jack Lyons and Anthony Parnes – attempted to manipulate the stock market on a massive scale to boost Guinness shares to enable a £2.7 billion takeover bid for Distillers, the Scottish drinks company. The board of directors of Distillers faced a hostile takeover bid and favoured the Guinness solution. Using $100 million raised by Guiness CEO, Ernest Saunders, Boesky invested it in shares to support the Guinness share price.

When questioned on other matters, Boesky mentioned the money and the American authorities passed the information on to the Department of Trade and Industry's corporate inspectorate. Further investigation revealed that Saunders had done other secret deals and had not informed the Guinness board of his actions. The company had paid £38 million to 11 companies in six countries to buy $300 million worth of Guinness stock. Bank Leu, Switzerland's oldest private bank, had bought half the stock. The four men were arrested and charged. In September 1990 all four were found guilty. Saunders was jailed for five years for false accounting, conspiracy, and theft. Lyons was fined £4 million for theft and stripped of his knighthood. Parnes was sent down for 30 months for false accounting and theft. Ronson was jailed for a year and fined £5 million for false accounting and theft. Ronson, Parnes and Lyons were also ordered to pay £440,000 in costs.

WHERE:
London, England
WHEN:
1990
THE AFTERMATH:
On 16 May 1991 the convicts appealed against their sentences. All the verdicts remained but Saunders's sentence was halved and Parnes's was reduced to 21 months. At a second appeal, the convictions were again upheld. Bank Leu was forced to merge with Crédit Suisse in 1990. The Guinness share price increased before the takeover. On 28 June 1991 Ernest Saunders was diagnosed with the incurable Alzheimer's disease and was released from prison. He has since made a full recovery.
YOU SHOULD KNOW:
In 1997 the Department of Trade and Industry published its report on the scandal. Of Saunders they said he did "unjustifiable favours for friends and himself".

Ernest Saunders, centre, during the share-trading fraud

Enron

"There is an appearance that you are hiding something."

WHERE:
USA
WHEN:
1990s–2 December 2001
THE AFTERMATH:
Kenneth Lay and Jeffrey Skilling went on trial in January 2006 for their part in the scandal. Both men were found guilty on 25 May 2006. Lay died of a heart attack on 5 July 2006, three months before he was due to be sentenced. Skilling was sentenced to 24 years and four months in federal prison on 23 October 2006.

Kenneth Lay remained tight-lipped during the trial.

THE CRIME: Most people had never heard of a company called Enron until it filed for bankruptcy at the end of 2001. It had been one of the world's leading utility companies, with 22,000 employees. Investors in the company had lost $60 billion. In the 1990s the financial press began writing stories, claiming that all might not be well with Enron and its accounting firm, Arthur Andersen. On 14 August 2001 the company's CEO Jeffrey Skilling resigned after just six months in the job, having sold 450,000 shares in the company. Chairman Kenneth Lay sought to reassure the markets that there was nothing amiss. However, the market was still not satisfied and began asking questions about Enron's finances, particularly the offshore businesses that allowed Enron bosses to move money around without paying tax or declaring its provenance.

After 9/11 Enron began selling off some of its less profitable arms and one commentator said that the "stock is trading under a cloud". On 17 October 2001 Enron announced third-quarter losses and five days later the share price fell $5.40 after the Securities and Exchange Commission announced it was investigating some suspicious deals. On 23 October Lay held a conference call to reassure investors but one said, "There is an appearance that you are hiding something." Two days later Lay sacked Andy Fastow, the CFO. On 2 November 2001 Enron borrowed another $1 billion. It was then revealed that Lay and other top executives had been selling hundreds of millions of dollars of stock in the run-up to the crisis. Enron employees lower down the scale found their pensions, which were linked to the value of company stock, virtually worthless. On 2 December 2001 Enron filed for Chapter 11 bankruptcy. The bankruptcy declaration also led to the dissolution of Arthur Andersen, which was found guilty in 2002 of obstruction for destroying Enron documents. The Supreme Court overturned the charge in 2005.

Nick Leeson

Rogue Trader

THE CRIME:
Anonymous traders trade millions each day on stock markets around the world. Their actions are, for the most part, unknown. That changed in 1995 when a derivatives trader by the name of Nick Leeson caused the collapse of Barings Bank, the oldest of the United Kingdom's investment banks.

Leeson was born in Watford, Hertfordshire on 25 February 1967 and joined Coutts & Co bank on leaving school. In 1992 he became general manager of a new operation in futures markets on the Singapore International Monetary Exchange for Barings Bank. At first all went well and Leeson made £10 million for his employer, earning a bonus of £130,000. Then things went disastrously wrong and Leeson tried to cover his tracks by using an error account (an account specifically set up to correct mistakes made in trading). At the end of 1992 the error account had lost £2 million. By the end of 1994 the figure stood at £208 million.

On 16 January 1995 Leeson gambled on the Nikkei Japanese stock market remaining relatively static. An earthquake hit Kobe the next day and the value of shares on the Japanese stock market plummeted. Leeson then bet on a recovery but the shares went lower still. On 23 February Leeson scribbled, "I'm sorry" on a piece of paper and fled the country. Three days later, the bank's losses stood at £827 million and it was declared insolvent. On 2 March 1995 Leeson was extradited from Germany and charged with fraud. On 2 December he was sentenced to six and a half years in Tanah Merah prison in Singapore.

Nick Leeson arrives in Singapore after being extradited from Germany.

WHERE:
Singapore
WHEN:
Thursday 23 February 1995
THE AFTERMATH:
In prison in 1996 Leeson wrote his autobiography *Rogue Trader*, later made into a film starring Ewan McGregor and Anna Friel. One reviewer described it as "a dreary book, written by a young man very taken with himself." Leeson was released from prison on 3 July 1999, suffering from colon cancer. On 26 April 2001 he was banned from driving for 30 months for being almost three times over the legal alcohol limit. He is presently CEO of Irish football club, Galway United.

Conrad Black

"Corporate kleptocracy"

WHERE:
England; USA
WHEN:
November 2003

THE AFTERMATH:
On 13 July 2007, after the jury deliberated for 12 days, Black was found guilty in Illinois US District Court of three counts of mail and wire fraud and one count of obstruction of justice and acquitted of nine other charges. A cheer went up in the *Daily Telegraph* newsroom when the conviction was announced. On 10 December he was sentenced to serve 78 months in federal prison, pay Hollinger $6.1 million and a fine of $125,000.

YOU SHOULD KNOW:
Barbara Amiel, Black's second wife, once famously said. "My extravagance knows no bounds." According to Hollinger expense accounts she had spent $2,463 on handbags, $2,785 on opera tickets, and $140 on "jogging attire".

THE CRIME: Born in Montreal, Quebec on 25 August 1944, Conrad Moffat Black was a right-wing newspaper proprietor and biographer. At one time he owned *The Daily Telegraph*, *The Sunday Telegraph* and *The Spectator* (UK), *Chicago Sun Times* (USA), *Jerusalem Post* (Israel), *National Post* (Canada), and more than 400 local newspapers in North America.

He bought his first newspaper in 1966, the *Eastern Townships Advertiser* in Quebec and five years later formed a holding company with two friends to buy more newspapers. The death of his father in 1976 and his subsequent inheritance allowed Black to become a major player in business. However, he gradually began to sell off interests in manufacturing, mining, retailing, banking and broadcasting and concentrate on newspapers. In 2008 Canadian author John Ralston Saul wrote, "Lord Black was never a real 'capitalist' because he never created wealth, only dismantled wealth… his career has been largely about stripping corporations. Destroying them."

In 1985 Black invested in the ailing Telegraph Group in Britain and in 1990 bought the *Jerusalem Post*. Black's company, Hollinger International, was listed on New York Stock Exchange in 1996. Seven years later shareholders began complaining that financial impropriety was taking place at the company, in particular compensation and fees paid directly and indirectly to Ravelston's (Black's personal holding company) and Black's associates. The complaints reached the United States Securities and Exchange Commission (SEC) and Black and his colleagues were accused of running a "corporate kleptocracy". In November 2003 Black resigned as CEO of Hollinger

International. In December he refused to answer questions about
business dealings before the SEC. In February 2004 he sold his
stake in Hollinger to David and Frederick Barclay but the sale was
prevented by a legal challenge. In February, 2004, Delaware judge
Leo E. Strine, Jr said, "Black breached his fiduciary and contractual
duties persistently and seriously… I found Black evasive and
unreliable." In November Black was charged with mail and wire
fraud and obstruction of justice. His trial began on 14 March 2007.

*Toppled media tycoon
Conrad Black leaves the
Dirksen Federal Court after
being arraigned.*

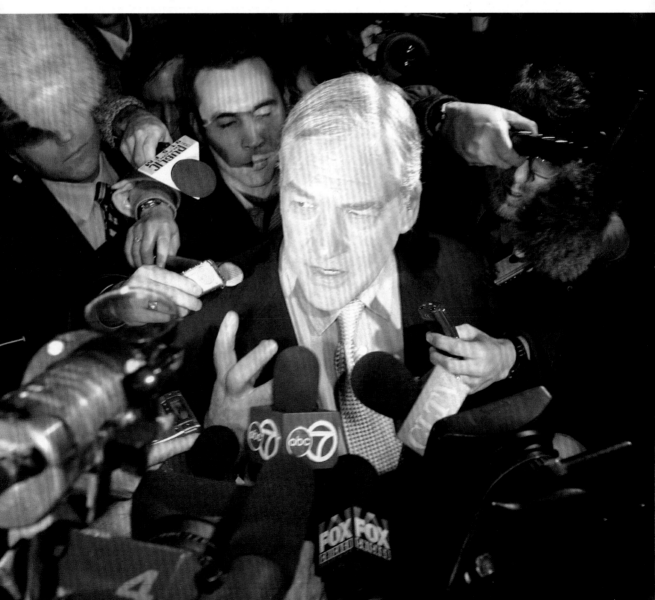

MURDERS

Cain

"Am I my brother's keeper?"

THE AFTERMATH:
At first Cain was pleased with what he had done saying, "I am free; surely the flocks of my brother fall into my hands." Then God asked Cain, "Where is your brother Abel?" to which he replied, "I don't know. Am I my brother's keeper?" God said, "What have you done? Your brother's blood cries out to me from the ground! So now you are cursed from the ground that opened its mouth to receive your brother's blood you have shed. If you work the land, it will never again give you its yield. You will be a restless wanderer on the earth." God placed a protective mark on Cain so that no one would kill him – "whoever kills Cain, vengeance shall be upon him sevenfold" – and Cain left with his wife and family and lived in the land of Nod, east of Eden. Cain later founded a city he called Enoch, after his son.

YOU SHOULD KNOW:
The Coptic Church celebrates Abel as a saint whose feast day is 28 December.

THE CRIME: Cain committed the world's first murder when he slew his brother Abel. The brothers were the first and second sons of Adam and Eve. Cain (original name Qayin) was a farmer who was jealous of Abel (Havel), a shepherd. Cain had offered to God some of his produce while Abel offered some of the firstborn of his flock and their fat portions. God accepted Abel's sacrifice but not Cain's, which infuriated the farmer. Cain suggested that he and Abel go for a walk in the fields where he murdered Abel. However, other non-Biblical theories posit that the brothers were due to marry twin sisters and Cain was jealous because Abel's girlfriend was prettier.

Cain Killing Abel by Bartolomeo Manfredi

John Billington

The Mayflower in Plymouth Harbour *by William Hassell*

"Justice rewarded him, the first murtherer [sic], with the deserved punishment of death"

THE CRIME: America's first recorded murderer travelled to the New World in December 1620 on the *Mayflower*, with his wife Eleanor or Ellen, and their two sons John and Francis, in an attempt to escape creditors. The Billingtons caused trouble among the 102 pilgrims on board the ship, with Billington, a thug from the slums of London, labelled a "foul-mouthed miscreant" and his sons troublemakers. The ship's captain Miles Standish ordered that Billington's feet and neck be bound after an attempted mutiny but it had no effect on him. In March 1621 Billington was convicted of contempt for insulting Captain Standish but escaped punishment after begging for mercy. Three years later he was part of a failed revolt against the Plymouth church but again escaped punishment. It was only a matter of time before serious trouble found John Billington and in September 1630 he got into an argument with fellow colonist John Newcomen, just 17 years old, that ended with Billington shooting Newcomen with a blunderbuss. "The poor fellow perceiving the intent of this Billington, his mortal enemy, sheltered himself behind trees as well as he could for a while; but the other, not being so ill a marksman as to miss his aim, made a shot at him, and struck him on the shoulder, with which he died soon after," wrote William Hubbard in *A General History of New England from the Discovery to MDCLXXX*, published in 1680.

WHERE:
Pilgrim Colony, Plymouth, Massachusetts, USA
WHEN:
September 1630
THE AFTERMATH:
Billington was tried by jury, hoping that "either for want of power to execute for capital offences, or for want of people to increase the Plantation, he should have his life spared; but justice otherwise determined, and rewarded him, the first murtherer [sic] of his neighbor [sic] there, with the deserved punishment of death, for a warning to others". He was hanged on Thursday 30 September 1630 and his corpse left to rot. His skull was nailed to a tree as a warning to others. His son John predeceased him. His other son, Francis, married Christian Penn Eaton, the widow of *Mayflower* passenger Francis Eaton. They had nine children who at one point were taken into care. Francis Billington died on 3 December 1684 at Middleboro, Massachusetts.

Mary Blandy

WHERE:
Henley-on-Thames, Oxfordshire,
England
WHEN:
Wednesday 14 August 1751

THE AFTERMATH:
Public opinion was divided on whether Mary was a calculating murderess or a "poor lovesick girl" in thrall to her older lover. Mary Blandy, protesting her innocence, was hanged outside Oxford Castle Prison at 9am on Easter Monday (6 April) 1752. Her last words were, as she ascended the scaffold, "Gentlemen, do not hang me too high for the sake of decency" and, as she stood there, "I am afraid I shall fall". She was buried with her parents in Henley parish church. William Cranstoun had fled to France in 1751 to avoid prosecution where he died of natural causes on 2 December 1752. He left his money to the wife and daughter he had once renounced.

Mary Blandy

"Do not hang me too high for the sake of decency,"

THE CRIME: Born about 1718 at Henley-on-Thames, Oxfordshire, Mary Blandy was an only child spoiled by her doting parents. It was said of her father that his "whole thoughts were bent to settle her advantageously in the world". He also let it be known that he was worth £10,000 when in fact he had less than £3,000. It is believed that he thought his daughter would attract a better class of suitor if she were a wealthy heiress since, although pleasant enough with nice manners, she was no great beauty. However, every boyfriend was put off because Mary's father refused to spend his "fortune" on her but promised to "leave her his All at his Death". The behaviour began to grate on Mary who grew to resent her father for ruining her happiness.

In the summer of 1746 a new suitor appeared in the form of Captain William Henry Cranstoun, the fifth and younger son of a Scottish laird. Mary was by this time in her late twenties and in danger of becoming an old maid, so she may have seen Cranstoun as her last chance of happiness even though he was short, cross-eyed, had a face that was badly pockmarked and was 20 years her senior. A further problem was that he was married and also had a daughter still in Scotland. He was, however, a serial flatterer and became interested in Mary, probably as much for her supposed fortune as herself.

When Francis Blandy discovered that his daughter's new boyfriend had a wife and child he forbade the relationship to continue. Cranstoun was not easily dissuaded and continued to court Mary, telling her that his marriage was illegal. In June 1751, Mary began – perhaps at Cranstoun's urging – to put arsenic into her father's tea and later his gruel. She called it a "love powder" and said that she hoped it would lessen his contempt for her boyfriend. Two months later Francis Blandy fell ill and, on 14 August 1751, he died. Almost immediately, Mary was arrested for murder. She had burned all the letters from Cranstoun but servants discovered one package containing arsenic and an incriminating letter to Cranstoun was intercepted. Her trial opened in the Divinity School at the Oxford Assizes on 3 March 1752 and family servants testified that Mary had called her father "a rogue, a villain, a toothless old dog" and said that she wanted him "dead and at Hell". A servant testified that Mary had told her father that she had been giving him arsenic but only "to make him love Cranstoun". Mary implored her father not to curse her and he replied, "My dear, how couldst thou think I could curse thee? No, I bless you, and hope God will bless thee and amend thy life". He then told her to keep quiet in case she said anything "to her own prejudice". The jury took just five minutes to pass a guilty verdict and the judge sentenced Mary to death. Her impending doom didn't hurt her appetite and she sat down to mutton chops and apple pie soon after the judge's sentence.

Laurence Shirley, Fourth Earl Ferrers

"Your time is come, you must die!"

THE CRIME: Laurence Shirley inherited the title of the fourth Earl Ferrers in 1745, following the death of his uncle, Henry, the third earl, who had been confined to a lunatic asylum. On 16 September 1752 he married Mary Meredith. They had no children and Ferrers locked Mary in his house at Staunton Harold in Leicestershire until a warrant was issued for her release. This was typical of Ferrers, who had a violent streak in him. He was also prone to paranoia and generally unbalanced behaviour. After one argument his family considered having him sectioned. Following his separation from his wife in 1758 Ferrers's estates were placed in the hands of trustees. A servant called John Johnson was appointed rent collector. Ferrers developed an irrational hatred of the man, believing that he had swindled him out of a lucrative coal-mining contract. On 18 January 1760 Ferrers made Johnson kneel before him and shouted, "Down on your other knee! Declare that you have acted against Lord Ferrers. Your time is come, you must die!" then shot him in the stomach. Johnson died 17 hours later at 9am on the following day.

WHERE:
Staunton Harold Hall, Leicestershire, England
WHEN:
Friday 18 January 1760
THE AFTERMATH:
Ferrers was apprehended as he tried to escape and on 13 February was cross-examined at the bar of the House of Lords before he was taken as a prisoner to the Tower of London. After two months and two days in the Tower, Ferrer's trial began on 16 April in Westminster Hall. His family urged him to claim that he was insane at the time of the crime. The following day the peers found Ferrers guilty of felony and murder and on 18 April the Keeper of the Great Seal, Robert, first Baron Henley, acting as Lord High Steward, sentenced him to death. He asked to be beheaded, as was his right as a nobleman, but was refused. Ferrers was driven to Tyburn in his own landau drawn by six horses, wearing a suit of white and silver that he had been married in. Ferrers was hanged on 5 May at Tyburn gallows. Despite the legend, he was not hanged with a silk rope (King George III gave permission but one could not be found in time). He stood on the collapsible platform (a forerunner of the trap door) wearing a white cap and with his arms bound by a black sash. The 45 cm (18 in) drop, designed to break Ferrer's neck rather than strangle him, was too short, leaving his toes touching the boards; he took four minutes to die, even with the executioner and his assistant pulling on his legs to quicken his demise. Anatomists dissected his body at Surgeons' Hall then put it on public display for three days before it was buried under the belfry at St Pancras. He was reinterred at Staunton Harold on 3 June 1782. Ferrers left £1,000 each to his four daughters and £60 per year to his mistress, Margaret Clifford, and £1,300 for the children of his victim.

The execution of Earl Ferrers

Bathsheba Spooner

"In a little time I expect to be in bliss"

WHERE:
Worcester, Massachusetts, USA
WHEN:
Sunday 1 March 1778
THE AFTERMATH:
At their trial on 1 April 1778 all four conspirators pleaded not guilty and Bathsheba's lawyer tried to claim that she was insane. All were found guilty and sentenced to hang on 4 June 1778. The execution was delayed when Bathsheba claimed that she was pregnant. She was examined and found not to be with child. A second examination declared that she was indeed pregnant but the first midwives – staunch revolutionaries – insisted that their diagnosis was correct and on 2 July 1778 all four were hanged before a crowd of 5,000 people. Bathsheba was last to die and she called out, "I am ready. In a little time I expect to be in bliss." Her last request was a full autopsy, which showed "a perfectly developed male foetus aged between five and six months".

THE CRIME: Bathsheba Spooner is the holder of a number of criminal records: she was the first woman executed by Americans, hers was the last public hanging in the Commonwealth, the first capital case tried in American jurisdiction in Massachusetts and the first case of a capital offence under the new Constitution. She was also probably the most socially prominent American woman ever to have been executed. Beautiful, well educated and wealthy, she was the daughter of General Timothy Ruggles, a Chief Justice of the Massachusetts Court. In 1766, at the age of 18, she married Joshua Spooner, a wealthy retired merchant old enough to be her grandfather. The match was not a happy one but nor had her parents' been. One day she saw her mother serve her father his favourite dog for dinner, roasted. Her father also instilled in her his staunch royalist Tory views. In the early 1770s she took an interest in almost any man who passed by and cuckolded her husband many times.

At the start of the American Revolution she sent out her servants to lure soldiers back to her home for dinner and then her bed. In 1777 she began an affair with Ezra Ross, a young soldier with George Washington's army. At this time she decided to get rid of her husband. She had two reasons: he was too old to be any good in bed and he was a revolutionary whereas she was loyal to King George. On 8 February 1778 she saw two British soldiers Sergeant James Buchanan, 30, and Private William Brooks, 27, who had escaped from a prisoner of war camp. Using her feminine wiles, she persuaded the two to join Ezra Ross in killing her husband, for which they would be richly rewarded. On the night of 1 March 1778 the three men attacked Spooner outside his home, throttled him, then threw his unconscious body head first down a well. The corpse was soon discovered and Buchanan and Brooks were found a few days later wearing Spooner's clothes.

William Richardson

Richardson's alibi seemed solid until his companions recalled that he had visited the blacksmith alone

THE CRIME: William Richardson was the first murderer to be executed after being trapped by "scientific detection". In 1787 he murdered his 19-year-old girlfriend Elizabeth Hughan by cutting her throat. To add to the horror of the crime, she was seven months' pregnant at the time. Doctors ruled out suicide and concluded that since the cut was from the right to the left, the murderer must have been left-handed. Although it was midsummer and the ground hard, a trail of footprints was found in boggy ground near the cottage where Elizabeth lived with her parents. The tracks revealed that the person had been running and had at one point slipped and been immersed up to his knee. Blood was also found on a stile. Plaster casts of the footprints were taken, revealing that the shoes were shod with iron nails and had recently been repaired.

Police measured the footwear of all the men who attended the funeral; not only did Richardson's shoe match the impression but he was also found to be left-handed. His alibi seemed solid until his companions recalled that he had visited the blacksmith alone, was gone much longer than anticipated, and had returned with muddy stockings and a scratch on his cheek. A search of his cottage turned up the muddied stockings hidden in the thatch, and the clincher was that the mud on the stockings contained sand found only in the bog near Hughan's cottage.

WHERE:
Dumfries, Scotland
WHEN:
1787
THE AFTERMATH:
Richardson confessed and was hanged on 30 June 1787. His body was donated for medical research.

THE ANATOMIST OVERTAKEN by the WATCH ... CARRYING OFF Miff W— in a HAMPER

Burke and Hare drop their victim as they are confronted by a watchman.

Burke & Hare

"Burke's the murderer, Hare's the thief, And Knox the boy who buys the beef"

WHERE:
Log's Boarding House, Tanners Close
Edinburgh, Scotland
WHEN:
Monday 11 February 1828
THE AFTERMATH:
The trial opened on 24 December 1828 at the High Court of Judiciary in Edinburgh. Hare turned King's evidence. Burke stood trial with his girlfriend but the case against her was "not proven". Burke, on the other hand, was sentenced to death. In the death cell he charged people sixpence to sketch him. He was hanged on 28 January 1829 before a crowd of 25,000. Legend has it that Hare worked in a limekiln in the Midlands and when his workmates discovered his identity they blinded him.
A well-known 19th century verse

THE CRIME: William Burke and William Hare were both born in Ireland and moved to Scotland in search of work. Short and hefty, Burke began a relationship with a prostitute called Helen McDougal and they settled in the Beggar's Hotel in Edinburgh. In 1826 he met the tall, thin Hare and the two men moved to Log's Boarding House in Tanners Close. Another resident, known as Old Donald, died still owing rent and Hare realized that a medical school would be willing to pay for the body, since dissection of corpses was illegal and thus fresh flesh was hard to come by. Old Donald's coffin was filled with tan bark while his body was sold to anatomist Dr Robert Knox for £7 10s, £4 more than old Donald owed in rent.

Another old tenant was despatched by placing a pillow over his face. The next murder by Burke and Hare was on 11 February 1828 when the pair killed Abigail Simpson. Having plied her with whisky, Hare suffocated her and Burke held down her legs. Dr Knox bought the two corpses. The next victim was a prostitute, Mary Haldane.

On 9 April 1828 another prostitute, Mary Paterson, became their next victim. When they took the corpse to Knox he recognized Paterson because he had been one of her clients. If Knox realized how Burke and Hare came by their goods, he kept his own counsel. The killings came thick and fast, and included the slow-witted daughter of Mary Haldane who came to ask Hare where her mother was. Burke and Hare bought an old horse to help them transport the bodies but one day the horse refused to move while pulling a box containing corpses. They persuaded a porter to move the box on his barrow and Burke and Hare slit the throat of the horse. There is no record of how many people died at the hands of Burke and Hare but their last killing was on 31 October 1828. An old couple visited Log's Boarding House and discovered the corpse. They went to the police who found blood and old clothes belonging to victims.

about the body snatchers ran:
"Up the close and down the stair,
In the house with Burke and Hare.
Burke's the murderer, Hare's the thief,
And Knox the boy who buys the beef."

Antoine LeBlanc

LeBlanc was flayed and his skin made into purses, wallets and other knick-knacks

THE CRIME: Born in France, 31-year-old Antoine LeBlanc moved to Germany and then left for the New World. He arrived in New York on 26 April 1833 and moved to New Jersey where he was offered a job working on the farm of Judge Samuel Sayre and his wife Sarah. His job was to chop logs and look after the pigs. LeBlanc hated the fact that he was a lowly worker and had to sleep in a woodshed.

One night, after visiting a local bar, he told Samuel Sayre that there was a problem with the horses. The judge went out to the stable where LeBlanc hit him over the head with a shovel. He used the same ploy on Sarah Sayre and he buried their corpses under a pile of manure. LeBlanc discovered the Sayres' maid, Phoebe, asleep in her second floor bedroom and murdered her as well. Ransacking the house for valuables, he put everything he could carry into pillowcases and left the house on one of the Sayres' horses. Unbeknown to him, LeBlanc had overfilled the pillowcases and, as he galloped, part of his booty fell to the ground, leaving a trail. The next day Lewis Halsey, a friend of Judge Sayre, spotted some artefacts bearing the judge's monogram in the road. Believing that the house had been robbed, a posse went to the house and found the bodies. Sheriff George Ludlow set off in pursuit and found LeBlanc drinking in the Mosquito Tavern in Hackensack Meadows. The murderer tried to escape via the back door but was arrested.

WHERE:
217 South Street, Morristown, New Jersey, USA
WHEN:
10.30pm Saturday 11 May 1833
THE AFTERMATH:
The trial of Antoine LeBlanc, which opened on 13 August 1833, was a foregone conclusion. He was convicted after just 20 minutes of jury deliberation. He was hanged on the village green at 3pm on 6 September 1833, before a crowd of 12,000 people. The gallows shot him into the air rather than dropping him. His body was taken to a local doctor who, with a colleague, performed some very unusual experiments, including trying to reanimate him by hooking LeBlanc up to a battery. A death mask was made after his ears had been removed and LeBlanc was flayed and his skin made into purses, wallets and other knick-knacks, each coming with a personally signed letter of authenticity from Sheriff Ludlow. The Sayre home is now a restaurant and is said to be haunted by the ghost of the slain maid Phoebe.

119

James Cook

"The head was shaved and tarred, to preserve it from the action of the weather"

THE CRIME: A bookbinder by trade, 21-year-old James Cook owed money to John Paas who travelled up from London to Aylestone in Leicestershire to collect the outstanding sum. On 30 May 1832 a fire was spotted in Cook's workshop in Wellington Street but since he often had great fires for his trade no one took any notice. At 8pm that night Cook went to the Flying Horse pub where he drank and caused consternation when he produced a wallet full of money. At 10.30pm he returned to his workshop where he stayed until 4.30 the next morning. The following evening at 10pm the neighbours became concerned because the fire was still burning. They broke in and found human flesh burning in the grate.

Cook told them that it was horsemeat for his dog but when they found parts of John Paas's body and items of his clothing in the workshop, Cook was arrested. He had beaten Paas to death with an iron bar and then, after returning from the pub, had dismembered the body with a saw and meat cleaver. Freed on bail, Cook made a dash for freedom. In those days it was the responsibility of the victim's family to help with the search for criminals and Paas's family enlisted the help of two Bow Street Runners. Cook was arrested in Liverpool where he was about to board a ship bound for America. He was tried on 8 August and pleaded guilty. At 9.30am on 10 August 1832 Cook was executed in front of Leicester jail before 30,000 people.

James Cook

WHERE:
Wellington Street, Aylestone, Leicestershire, England
WHEN:
Wednesday 30 May 1832
THE AFTERMATH:
His corpse was then placed in a 10 m (33 ft) high gibbet in Saffron Lane near the Aylestone Tollgate. It was said that 20,000 people passed beneath. A contemporary report has it, "The head was shaved and tarred, to preserve it from the action of the weather, and the cap in which he had suffered was drawn over his face. On Saturday afternoon [11 August] his body, attired as at the time of his execution, having been firmly fixed in the irons necessary to keep the limbs together, was carried to the place of its intended suspension." James Cook thus became the last man to be gibbeted in Britain. However, the locals objected to the sightseers and after three days Cook's body was removed and buried. A replica gibbet is still on show at Guildhall, Leicester.

John Paas

120

John C. Colt

"Adams's severed skull was displayed in court"

THE CRIME: Brother of the inventor of the Colt revolving rifle and pistol, John Colt was a bookkeeper who wrote a book which he published himself. On 17 September 1841 the printer of the book, Samuel Adams, went to see Colt to collect monies owed to him. A week later, Adams's corpse was found in a packing crate in the hold of *Kalamazoo*, a ship about to leave New York. The crate, addressed to Colt, was destined for St Louis via New Orleans. Colt denied any knowledge of the crate but nevertheless was charged with murder. Police also found Adams's pocket watch hidden at Colt's home. John was the black sheep of the Colt family. In addition to brother Samuel, whose success with weaponry was well known, another brother, James, was a lawyer in St Louis – but John was famous only for gambling, forgery, burglary and womanizing. At the time of his arrest he was living with a pregnant woman posing as his wife, Caroline Henshaw.

After Colt's suicide, a fire broke out in the court rooms.

WHERE:
New York City, USA
WHEN:
Friday 17 September 1841
THE AFTERMATH:
The trial of John C. Colt began on 19 January 1842 in New York before judge William Kent. The first witness was Asa Wheeler who had an office next to Colt. He said that he had heard a loud bang and then a noise that sounded like swordplay on the afternoon of Adams's visit. He peered through the keyhole and saw a man leaning over a box. The next day he borrowed a passkey and went inside noting that the floor was freshly scrubbed clean. When Colt arrived at work, he told Wheeler that he had knocked over his pens and ink. A caretaker testified that he had seen Colt struggling down the stairs with a large box. A dustman said that Colt had paid him to take the box to the *Kalamazoo*. The packing crate and the canvas in which Adams's body had been wrapped were brought into court as evidence. Then his corpse was disinterred and his severed skull was displayed in court, so that doctors could declare that a hatchet, not a bullet or packing nail, had made the hole in its side. On 31 January, thousands of people waited outside the courthouse to hear the verdict, which was guilty. Colt appealed but he was turned down on 28 September and Judge Kent sentenced him to hang. Colt asked permission to marry his girlfriend and at noon on 18 November 1842, the day of his scheduled execution, Colt and Caroline Henshaw were married in his cell, attended by Samuel Colt and a few friends. At 3.55pm the warders returned to take Colt to the gallows but found his dead body instead. One of the wedding party had passed him a knife and Colt had stabbed himself in the heart.

Albert Tirrell

"Suicide is the natural death of the prostitute"

WHERE:
Boston, Massachusetts, USA
WHEN:
Monday 27 October 1845

THE AFTERMATH:
Tirrell went on the run on 28 October. He had been seen entering the brothel by a number of witnesses and was regarded as the prime suspect. He was arrested on 6 December in New Orleans, Louisiana, and sent back to Boston for trial. His parents hired Rufus Choate, a celebrated Boston lawyer. At the trial, which began on 26 March 1846, Choate said that witnesses had observed Tirrell enter but no one had actually seen him commit the murder. Choate added that Tirrell had no motive to kill Bickford and offered the jury two explanations for what happened. His first supposition was that Bickford had committed suicide – "What proof is there that she did not rise from her bed, set fire to the house, and in the frenzy of the moment, with giant strength, let out the stream of life... Suicide is the natural death of the prostitute".
When the ferocity of the attack rendered this explanation impossible, Choate turned to his second line of defence. Tirrell had a habit of sleepwalking and Choate claimed that Tirrell could have murdered Bickford while sleepwalking in a trance. At the time sleepwalking was a little understood condition. After less than two hours of deliberation, on 30 March 1846, the jury returned its verdict of not guilty. In January 1847 Choate used the same defence to have Tirrell acquitted of the charges of arson for setting fire to the brothel. These acquittals were the first in American history where sleepwalking was successfully used as a defence. Tirrell demanded that Choate refund half his legal fees since Tirrell's innocence had been so "obvious" in two trials. Choate refused.

THE CRIME: Albert Jackson Tirrell, 21, the son of a respectable family in Weymouth, Massachusetts, left his wife and two children in 1845 for Maria Ann Bickford, a stunningly beautiful woman who worked and lived in a Boston brothel where her customers were among the richest in the commonwealth. Bickford didn't give up her life of vice, much to Tirrell's consternation. It became too much for him and late on 27 October 1845, after her last client had left, Tirrell visited Bickford's room and, using a razor, slit her throat from ear to ear, so brutally that her head was nearly severed from her body. He also started three fires in the brothel, which woke Joel Lawrence, the owner, who discovered the body of Bickford and informed the police. A bloody razor lay near her body and remnants of Tirrell's clothing and his cane were left at the crime scene.

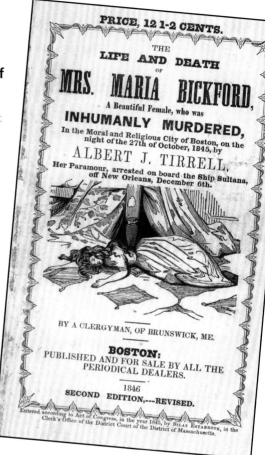

Publishers had a field day with graphic accounts of the murder.

John Tawell

"The suspected murderer...is in the garb of a Kwaker with a brown great coat on which reaches his feet"

THE CRIME: To outward appearances, 61-year-old Quaker John Tawell led a respectable life but appearances can be deceptive. Tawell was born in 1784 and was the second son of Thomas Tawell, a shopkeeper in Aldely, a village in Norfolk. When he was 22 Tawell seduced a servant-girl, whilst living in Whitechapel and later married her. He began work in a druggist's shop and attempted to forge a £10 note for which he received 14 years' transportation. In Australia Tawell got a job in a convict hospital and then as a clerk to Isaac Wood of the Sydney Academy, who was impressed enough to petition the governor for Tawell's pardon, granted in 1820. Tawell opened a druggist's shop and in three years was a success.

Back in England his wife and two sons died and he began an affair with a nurse, Sarah Lawrence, who bore him two children. In 1841 he married a Quaker widow, Mrs Cutforth, who had run a school in Clerkenwell, London. Tawell moved his lover, who had by now changed her name to Hart, to a small cottage in Salt Hill, near Slough and visited her in order to pay a weekly allowance of £1. On 1 January 1845, after Tawell's visit, his mistress was discovered on the floor writhing in agony and she died before help arrived. A neighbour, Mary Anne Ashley, spotted Tawell and rushed to Slough Station where the stationmaster, using the latest innovation, transmitted the following telegraph to Paddington Station: "A murder had just been committed at Salt Hill and the suspected murderer was seen to take a first class ticket to London by the train that left Slough at 7.42pm. He is in the garb of a Kwaker with a brown great coat on which reaches his feet. He is in the last compartment of the second first-class carriage." The misspelling of Quaker was deliberate since the telegraph at that time did not have a letter Q. Tawell was spotted by Sergeant Williams of the railway police, who followed him by bus and on foot to the Jerusalem Coffee House and then across London Bridge to a lodging house in Scott's Yard.

WHERE:
Jerusalem Coffee House, City of London, England
WHEN:
Thursday 2 January 1845
THE AFTERMATH:
The next day Tawell was arrested at the Jerusalem Coffee House, the first murderer caught by wireless telegraphy. At his trial it was revealed that he had bought two bottles of Scheele's prussic acid, normally used for the treatment of varicose veins and that Sarah had died from prussic acid poisoning. Tawell was publicly hanged at Aylesbury on 28 March, and the electro-magnetic telegraph used to make the historic capture was put on show for a shilling a look.

The trial of John Tawell

The mob gathers outside Horsemonger Lane Prison.

Frederick & Maria Manning

"I never liked him much and battered in his head"

WHERE:
3 Minver Place, Bermondsey, London, England.
WHEN:
Thursday 9 August 1849
THE AFTERMATH:
At their trial, which began on 25 October 1849, Frederick Manning laid the blame on his wife while she said that, as a foreign citizen, she was not subject to the jurisdiction of a British court. The judge, Mr Justice Creswell, dismissed the argument because of her marriage to a British subject. In the dock neither prisoner would look at the other. The trial was short. On 26 October both were sentenced to death. They kissed and made up 30 minutes before William Calcraft hanged the pair at Horsemonger Lane Prison on 13 November 1849 before an unruly crowd of 50,000. Among the spectators was Charles Dickens who wrote to *The Times* denouncing "the wickedness and levity of the immense crowd". Maria Manning was hanged in a black satin dress, a decision that caused that type of dress to go out of fashion for some years.

THE CRIME: Swiss-born Maria De Roux arrived in England in the 1840s and she met and married Frederick Manning, a former publican and thief, at St James's Church, Piccadilly, London, on 27 May 1847. They lived at Minver Place in Bermondsey on the proceeds of robberies perpetrated by Fredrick Manning. A regular visitor to Minver Place was an Irish docker named Patrick O'Connor. He had been Maria Manning's swain before her marriage and continued to court her. As well as his work at the docks, O'Connor made money as a moneylender. On 8 August 1849 O'Connor received a note from Maria inviting him to dine at her home the next day.

There Maria shot him and Frederick "found [him] moaning in the kitchen. I never liked him much, and battered in his head with a ripping chisel". They buried O'Connor in quicklime under the kitchen floor and then went to his home in Greenwood Street on the Mile End Road and stole £300 in cash, two gold watches and £4,000 in railway shares. When O'Connor failed to turn up to work, the police visited the Mannings but they feigned ignorance of his disappearance. Marie then left her husband and ran off to Edinburgh while he went to St Laurence on the island of Jersey. The corpse of O'Connor was found on 17 August 1849 and a hue and cry followed after which the Mannings were quickly arrested.

John White Webster

"That villain! I am a ruined man!"

THE CRIME: John Webster was a member of the American Academy of Arts and Sciences and Erving Professor of Chemistry and Mineralogy at Harvard. Despite his respected position, Webster lived way beyond his means and borrowed money from innumerable friends and colleagues including several thousand dollars from his fellow academic Dr George Parkman, who had made a large sum of money from real estate. Dr Parkman became annoyed at Webster's refusal to repay the money despite several reminders. On 23 November 1849 Dr Parkman disappeared. Originally, it was thought that he was a victim of a kidnapping and a reward was offered for his return. Local rivers were dredged and empty buildings searched for him. Then Webster went to Parkman's house at 8 Walnut Street and told the family that he had repaid $483, owing credence to a new theory that Parkman had been mugged and murdered.

However, Ephraim Littlefield, a janitor at the college had watched Parkman enter Webster's laboratory and then noticed that the wall behind the assay oven in Webster's laboratory was very hot. On 30 November and with his wife keeping guard, Littlefield broke into a privy adjoining Webster's lab and discovered part of a human leg and pelvis. He called the police who also found Dr Parkman's teeth inside the oven. When he was told what Littlefield had done, Webster cried, "That villain! I am a ruined man!" When Webster was arrested he tried to commit suicide by swallowing strychnine but still claimed to know nothing of the remains.

WHERE:
Harvard, Massachusetts, USA
WHEN:
Tuesday 23 November 1849
THE AFTERMATH:
Webster was tried in Boston on 19 March 1850 before Lemuel Shaw, the father-in-law of writer Herman Melville. Webster claimed that the teeth in the oven were those of a medical corpse and not Dr Parkman's. Such was the interest in the trial that a shift system was introduced in the public gallery and people changed seats every ten minutes. It was estimated that 60,000 people saw some part of the proceedings, which lasted 11 days. By law, Webster could not give evidence and his lawyer suggested several alternatives for how Parkman ended up in Wester's oven, to no avail. On 23 May, Webster confessed. Parkman had come to his room to demand repayment; Webster had lost his temper and killed him with a grapevine trunk before cutting up his body. Webster went to the gallows on 30 August 1850.

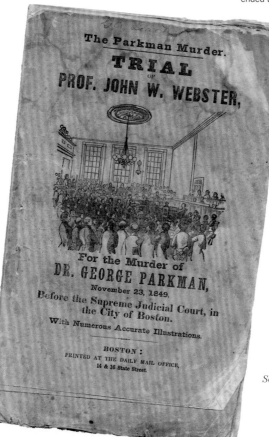

Several books recounting the details of the trial were published.

Catherine Wilson

The last woman to be publicly executed in London

WHERE:
Boston, Lincolnshire;
London, England
WHEN:
1853–1862
THE AFTERMATH:
As Catherine Wilson walked free
from the courtroom she was
immediately rearrested and charged
with the murder of Mrs Soames. This
time there was to be no escape and
on 20 October 1862 Wilson was
hanged at Newgate Prison before
20,000 people – the last woman to
be publicly executed in London.

THE CRIME: Catherine Wilson began work as housekeeper for Captain Peter Mawer at his home in Boston, Lincolnshire in 1853 when she was 31. Mawer grew fond of Wilson and told her that when he died he intended to leave something in his will for her. Not long afterwards Captain Mawer died of an overdose of the colchicum (a type of crocus that was curative in small doses but poisonous in large) that he was taking for his gout. Since it was well known that the captain was a martyr to his gout, no one attached any suspicion to his housekeeper. Wilson applied for a job in London and lodged with 48-year-old Maria Soames at her home in Bloomsbury. Wilson arrived with a man named Dixon and it is possible that she married him. Soon the couple fell behind with their rent and Catherine decided that the best way to deal with this unfortunate circumstance was to murder her landlady.

First, Dixon died under mysterious circumstances. An autopsy was carried out but the doctor missed the presence of colchicum. Four days later Mrs Soames, too, passed away. The autopsy again failed to reveal the presence of colchicum. Wilson then moved to Brixton and her wealthy friend Mrs Atkinson came to stay. On the fourth day of the visit Mr Atkinson received a telegram from Wilson informing him that his wife had died suddenly after being robbed of all her money. Next, Wilson began to work for a woman named Sarah Carnell and, tiring of using colchicum, she gave her sulphuric acid. Mrs Carnell spat it out and the liquid burned a hole in the sheets. Wilson fled but was arrested six weeks later for attempted murder and tried at the Old Bailey. She was acquitted when her lawyer persuaded the jury that a pharmacist had accidentally put the acid in the medicine bottle.

*The condemned cell in
Newgate Prison*

The execution of James P. Casey in San Francisco

James P. Casey

"My God! I did not intend to commit murder"

THE CRIME: James King, 34, had made and lost a fortune in the banking business in San Francisco in the 1850s. While making his money, King had noted that the industry was replete with crooks. His friends urged him to start a newspaper to reveal corruption and on 8 October 1855 he started the *Evening Bulletin*. When Charles Cora, a notorious gambler, murdered US Marshal William H. Richardson, and was arrested, King declared that if Cora was allowed to escape justice, the sheriff, David Scannell, must hang in his place.

Realizing that the public liked his exposés, King widened his targets. He revealed that James P. Casey, a city supervisor, had once been imprisoned in Sing Sing in New York. On 14 May 1856 Casey encountered King as the latter left the editorial offices of the *Bulletin*, on the west side of Montgomery Street, just north of Washington Street. Casey ordered King to draw his weapon but the newspaperman was unarmed and told Casey so. Casey pulled out a revolver and shot King. The journalist was taken to a room in the Montgomery Block (now the site of the Transamerica Pyramid), and treated by Dr R. Beverly Cole but he died on 20 May.

WHERE:
Montgomery Street, San Francisco, California, USA
WHEN:
Wednesday 14 May 1856
THE AFTERMATH:
As news of the shooting spread the 1851 Committee of Vigilance was formed at an old lodge room at Sacramento and Leidesdorff streets. On 20 May, following King's death, 3,500 members of the committee marched to the Broadway Jail where they demanded Casey be handed over. They later returned to the jail and took Charles Cora away. Both Casey and Cora were given lawyers to defend them; both were tried before a jury composed of members of the Committee of Vigilance and both were convicted. A large crowd filled Sacramento Street to watch the double hanging at 1.20pm on 22 May from a platform extended from the second storey windows of Fort Gunnybags. The noose was removed from Casey's neck and he was allowed to address the crowd, "Gentlemen, fellow citizens, I am not guilty of any crime. When I am dead... let no one dare traduce my character... I am guilty of no crime. I only acted as I was taught – to avenge an insult... Oh, God, have mercy on my soul! My God! I am not guilty of murder – I did not intend to commit murder." While all this was going on Cora waited patiently for Casey to finish and then both men were hanged simultaneously. Their bodies hung for an hour before they were cut down and given to the coroner.

127

Daniel E. Sickles, who had lost a leg at the Battle of Gettysburg.

WHERE:
Lafayette Square, Washington DC,
USA
WHEN:
Sunday 27 February 1859
THE AFTERMATH:
At the home of Attorney General Jeremiah Black on Franklin Square, Sickles gave himself up and confessed to the killing. While awaiting his trial Sickles was allowed to receive many visitors, so many that he used the head jailer's rooms to see them. Oddly, he was also allowed to keep his weapon while in prison. The president James Buchanan even sent Sickles a letter. Sickles hired several leading politicians to defend him, including Edwin M. Stanton, a future Secretary of War, and Chief Counsel James T. Brady. The trial opened on 4 April 1859. "You are here to fix the price of the marriage bed!" roared Associate Defence Attorney John Graham, in a speech so packed with quotations from Othello, Jewish history and Roman law that it lasted two days and later appeared in book form. Teresa's letter admitting her guilt was ruled inadmissible in court but Sickles leaked it to newspapers which printed it in full. Stanton argued that Teresa's infidelity had left Sickles temporarily insane with grief and therefore not responsible for his actions. For the first time in US history this defence succeeded — Sickles was acquitted and was even considered a public benefactor for rescuing other women from Key's beastly charms. Some time after the acquittal he admitted, "Of course I intended to kill him. He deserved it." As his biographer noted, Sickles "was always in some sort of crisis, be it financial, legislative, sexual, or homicidal, and these situations invariably galvanized him into action, not always wise." Sickles died on 3 May 1914, a few months short of his 95th birthday.

Daniel Sickles

"You have dishonoured my house. You must die!"

THE CRIME: A congressman from New York and later a Union general in the American Civil War, Daniel E. Sickles was also a rampant womanizer and his marriage to 17-year-old Teresa Bagioli in 1853 did nothing to deter his philandering ways. In fact, the New York State Assembly censured him for taking a prostitute, Fanny White, into its chambers. On 26 February 1859, Sickles, 39, discovered through a poison pen letter that his wife had been unfaithful, enjoying a year-long affair with "the handsomest man in all Washington society" Philip Barton Key. He was the US attorney for the District of Columbia and the son of Francis Scott Key, the composer of the *Star Spangled Banner*, the American national anthem. Sickles made Teresa write a full confession. On 27 February, Key was loitering near the Sickles residence on Lafayette Square in Washington DC when Sickles rushed out to confront him. Shouting, "Key, you scoundrel! You have dishonoured my house. You must die!" Sickles shot Key. Though wounded, Key struggled with Sickles who shot him again, then stood over his victim, reloaded and shot him a third time, at point blank range.

Constance Kent

"She bore no ill-will against the little boy"

THE CRIME: On 11 August 1853 Samuel Savile Kent, a widower with ten children, married Mary Drewe Pratt, governess to his family. By the summer of 1860 the couple had three children, a boy – (Francis) Savile Kent born on 9 August 1856 – and two girls. At 6am on 30 June the nursemaid Elizabeth Gough, 22, went to rouse Savile and saw that he was not in his cot. She presumed that his mother had taken him and it was an hour before anyone realized he was missing. He was found in a disused lavatory, a deep wound almost decapitating him.

WHERE:
Road Hill House, Road, Wiltshire, England
WHEN:
Friday 29 June 1860
THE AFTERMATH:
At the inquest a verdict of murder by "person or persons unknown" was recorded. Gough was arrested but let go because of lack of evidence. Inspector Jack Whicher, 45, of Scotland Yard was called in to investigate and on 20 July he arrested 16-year-old Constance Kent, the ninth child of the first marriage. One of her three nightdresses was missing and two friends testified that she had told them she was unhappy at home. But Constance was released and Gough rearrested on 24 September. It was rumoured that she and Samuel Kent were having an affair and, worried the boy waking would expose them, they had murdered him. The charges did not stick and on 18 April 1861 the Kent family moved to Wales while Constance moved to a finishing school in Dinan, France. She returned to England on 10 August 1863. On 25 April 1865 Constance of her own accord went to Bow Street Magistrates' Court and confessed. She was examined for her mental state and a doctor wrote, "She bore no ill-will against the little boy, except as one of the children of her stepmother." Found guilty of murder on 21 July, Constance Kent was sentenced to death but her sentence was commuted to life imprisonment on 27 July because of her youth.
YOU SHOULD KNOW:
She was released from prison on 18 July 1885, aged 41. She died on 10 April 1944, aged 100. Having lived to see her 100th birthday, she may have been the first convicted murderer to receive the birthday telegram from the monarch.

Constance Kent was sentenced to death, but the sentence was commuted to life imprisonment.

Franz Muller

The killer had taken the wrong hat – it was a mistake that was to cost him his life

WHERE:
On a train between Bow and Hackney
Wick, London, England
WHEN:
Saturday 9 July 1864
THE AFTERMATH:
When the police went to Muller's
home, he had already left for America
aboard the SS *Victoria*. Police caught
the faster *City of Manchester* and
were waiting for him when the ship
docked at New York. Muller was
wearing Mr Briggs's hat and was
carrying his gold watch when he was
arrested. Muller was tried at the Old
Bailey on 27 October 1864 before Mr
Baron Martin. The German Legal
Protection Society paid for Muller's
defence. The jury took just 15 minutes
to convict and Muller
was sentenced to
death. Despite a plea
for clemency from the
King of Prussia, Muller
was hanged outside
Newgate Prison on 14
November 1864 as a
large crowd watched.
The German
maintained his
innocence until a few
moments before the
trap door swung open,
when he confessed.

THE CRIME: The first railway murder was committed on a summer's day in 1864. Thomas Briggs, 70, the chief clerk of Robarts Bank in Lombard Street took the North London Railway Train from Fenchurch Street to Hackney Wick. Two passengers got into the first-class carriage at Hackney Wick and noticed blood on a seat. They alerted the police who found the bloodied body of Briggs on the line between Bow and Hackney Wick. He had been attacked on the train, beaten up, robbed of his gold watch (but the killer missed £5 in his pockets) and thrown off the train. He died later of his injuries. When the police searched the train compartment they found a bag and a walking stick belonging to Mr Briggs and a silk top hat that didn't. In his hurry the killer had taken the wrong hat – it was a mistake that was to cost him his life.

Headed by Dick Tanner, a founder member of the detective

force, the police also checked local jewellers and discovered that a gold chain on the dead man's watch had been swapped for a new one, in the Cheapside shop owned by a man called John Death, by a man with a foreign accent. Thanks to newspaper publicity a man named Jonathan Matthews came forward and said he had bought two hats like the one found in the carriage, one for himself and the other for 25-year-old Franz Muller, a German tailor, who lived in Bow.

*German tailor
Franz Muller*

Julia Bulette

She charged $1,000 for a night of passion

THE CRIME: Julia Bulette was born in 1832 in New Orleans (some sources state London) and arrived in Virginia City, Nevada, in 1859. At the time Virginia City was a shantytown, housing about 6,000 miners and very few women, so the enterprising Julia set herself up as a prostitute known as the Queen of Sporting Row. She began work before her cabin was finished and entertained her clients as other grateful men built the walls and roof around her.

Within a year she was a madam running six girls and opened a brothel that had daily fresh flowers delivered by Wells Fargo as well as the finest French wine and food. She charged $1,000 for a night of passion – an enormous sum at the time. She was appointed an honorary fire marshal, the only woman so honoured. Julia Bulette was probably the West's favourite prostitute – loved by rich and poor and often the subject of articles by a young cub reporter for the *Territorial Enterprise* who would go on to fame as the writer Mark Twain. During the American Civil War Julia raised money for the forerunner of the Red Cross and more than once turned her brothel into a hospital for the sick when an epidemic hit the town, even pawning her jewellery and furs to pay for much needed medicines. After the war, a different kind of person patronized Virginia City and Julia moved from being the centre of attention to an embarrassment to the place. On 20 January 1867 Julia Bulette was murdered, strangled in her bed at her home on D Street and most of her valuable possessions were stolen.

Julia Bulette, probably the West's favourite prostitute

WHERE:
D Street, Virginia City, Nevada, USA
WHEN:
Sunday 20 January 1867
THE AFTERMATH:
The miners – her original clients and supporters – were up in arms at Julia's death and rounded up 12 suspects all of whom, luckily for them, were able to prove their innocence. She was given what was virtually a state funeral with the fire brigade and a brass band leading the cortege. It was said that ladies closed their curtains lest they saw their husbands in the funeral procession. Some months later, John Millain was arrested while trying to rob another madam, Martha Camp, and many of Julia's possessions were found on him. He was tried on 2 July 1867 and quickly convicted. He was hanged on 24 April 1868, 1.6 km (1 mi) outside the city, such was the desire of so many people (3,000 or thereabouts) to witness justice.

Frances Kidder

The last public execution of a woman in Britain

WHERE:
Malling, Kent, England
WHEN:
Sunday 25 August 1867

THE AFTERMATH:
In the condemned cell Frances confessed the murder to the prison chaplain. She frequently became hysterical while awaiting her execution and, at noon on 2 April 1868 at Maidstone Prison, she had to be helped onto the gallows and held on the trapdoors by two warders. She prayed intently while the executioner William Calcraft strapped her wrists in front of her and put two leather straps around her body: one pinning her arms at elbow level and another around her legs to hold her long skirt down. He placed a white cotton hood over her head and adjusted the noose. Then he released the trap and some 2,000 people watched Frances drop 90 cm (3 ft) and struggle hard for two or three

THE CRIME: Frances Kidder, 25, was married to conman William Kidder but she deeply resented Louisa, William's daughter from a previous relationship. Frances constantly abused her and on more than one occasion threatened to kill her. On 25 August 1867 Frances drowned Louisa in a ditch. She must have struggled to hold the 11-year-old under, as the water was only just over 30 cm (12 in) deep. When Louisa's body was found in a nearby stream Frances claimed that they had fallen into the ditch together when they were frightened by passing horses, an excuse rightly rejected by the jury after just 12 minutes on 12 March 1868.

minutes. Her body was left hanging for an hour before being taken down and buried in an unmarked grave within the prison. William Kidder reputedly stood in the crowd and watched his wife hang. It was the last public execution of a woman in Britain.

Michael Barrett

"A great cry rose from the crowd as the culprit fell"

THE CRIME: The last person to be publicly hanged in Britain was an Irish terrorist who, 12 days before Christmas in 1867, tried to rescue two Fenian prisoners – Richard O'Sullivan Burke and one Casey – being held at Clerkenwell House of Detention in London by blowing a hole in the prison wall. The plotters parked a wagon packed with dynamite beside the prison and exploded it at 3.45pm. The explosion tore down the prison wall but it also devastated the block of houses opposite. The tenements were "stripped clearly of their frontages, left open like doll's houses with the kettles still on the hobs". Six people died immediately, another six later and 120 were injured. Most of the victims were women and children. Neither Burke nor Casey escaped.

Barrett was arrested when informers went to the police. He was taken into custody with a woman and four men, two of whom turned Queen's Evidence. Barrett spoke eloquently in his own defence but to no avail and he was found guilty of "Wilful Murder" and sentenced to death. Barrett claimed that he had been in Glasgow at the time of the explosion. In his prison cell, he wrote to a Glasgow newspaper thanking his supporters for "knowing me to be innocent of the crime for which I am called upon to suffer".

WHERE:
Clerkenwell House of Detention,
London, England
WHEN:
3.45pm Friday 13 December 1867
THE AFTERMATH:
On the day of his death – 26 May 1868 – Barrett wore a short red jacket and stripy grey trousers as he was led to the gallows outside Newgate. The crowd booed and hissed in equal measure but Barrett ignored them, listening instead to the priest who accompanied him. When someone in the crowd shouted, "Hats off" everyone obeyed. Barrett's last words were spoken to hangman William Calcraft, asking him to adjust the rope. The executioner complied and then immediately pulled the bolt, sending the Irishman to his death. *The Times* reported, "A great cry rose from the crowd as the culprit fell – a cry which was neither an exclamation nor a scream, but it partook in its sound of both". Barrett died instantly, no mean feat for Calcraft who often bungled his executions. *The Times* said, "In the presence of a vast concourse of spectators, Michael Barrett, the author of the Clerkenwell Explosion, was hanged in front of Newgate. In its circumstances there was very little to distinguish this from ordinary executions. The crowd was greater, perhaps, and better behaved; still, from the peculiar atrocity of the crime for which Barrett suffered, and from the fact of its being probably the last public execution in England, it deserves more than usual notice…" Another newspaper added, "He had gone to the scaffold with red hair and beard; when he was lifted off it, his hair, oddly, was said to have turned black."
YOU SHOULD KNOW:
Calcraft performed the last public executions in England, Scotland and the first private execution in England.

Police among the rubble of the Clerkenwell House of Detention

133

Priscilla Biggadike

"I can't live long in this state"

WHERE:
Stickney, Lincolnshire, England
WHEN:
6am Thursday 1 October 1868

THE AFTERMATH:
In a trial that lasted just seven hours, Priscila Biggadike was defended by Mr Lawrence. The jury did not leave their box before returning a verdict of guilty, with a recommendation for mercy, but the judge donned the black cap and said, "Priscilla Biggadike, although the evidence against you is only circumstantial, yet more satisfactory, and conclusive evidence I never heard in my life. You must now prepare for your impending fate, by attending to the religious instruction you will receive, to which if you had given heed before, you would never have stood in your present unhappy position. The sentence of the court is that you will be taken to the place from whence you came, and thence to the place of execution, there to be hanged by the neck until you be dead, and may the Lord have mercy upon your soul! Your body to be buried within the precincts of the prison." She was hanged at Lincoln Prison at 9am on 28 December 1868, the first private execution of a woman in England. Hangman Thomas Askern bungled it and she swung in agony for several minutes before death.

YOU SHOULD KNOW:
In 1882 Thomas Proctor died. On his deathbed, he confessed that he had put the arsenic in Richard Biggadike's tea.

THE CRIME: Priscilla Biggadike lived with her husband Richard, their three children and two lodgers: George Ironmonger, a 21-year-old fisherman, and 30-year-old Thomas Proctor, a rat-catcher. Their home was a small, two-roomed cottage containing just one bedroom and they all shared two beds, positioned just 38 cm (15 in) apart. Richard Biggadike left for work in the morning before the lodgers, which led to "an improper intimacy between Mrs Biggadike and one of the lodgers". That situation led to arguments between husband and wife. On 30 September 1868 Richard Biggadike returned home from work and his wife gave him a meal of hot cakes and mutton. Almost immediately Richard fell ill, being violently sick. He suffered 11 hours of agony – "I can't live long in this state" – before he expired at 6am the next day. The local doctor was called and he diagnosed food poisoning. Priscilla gave him some of the cake that her husband had eaten to prove that it was harmless.

An autopsy showed traces of arsenic in Richard Biggadike's body and his widow was arrested. She told police that she had found a suicide note in her husband's pocket but added that he must have asked someone else to write it because he was illiterate. However, when the police asked to see the note, she told them that she had burned it. Ten days later she said that she had seen her lodger Thomas Proctor, who may have been the father of her third child, putting a white powder into her husband's tea.

Alferd Packer

"There were seven Dimmycrats in Hinsdale County and you've et five of them!"

THE CRIME: One of the legends of American crime, Alferd Packer (his name is given as both Alferd – the result of a misspelled tattoo – and Alfred) was born in 1842 in Allegheny County, Pennsylvania and fought on the Union side in the American Civil War. He later became a prospector and on 9 February 1874 he and five others – Shannon Wilson Bell, James Humphrey, Frank "Reddy" Miller, George "California" Noon and Israel Swan – set off for Gunnison, Colorado despite a warning of impending bad weather. They were caught by snow in the Rocky Mountains. By his own account, Packer went to look for food and when he returned he claimed that he found Shannon Wilson Bell eating one of the other men.

When Bell saw Packer he tried to attack him with an axe so Packer shot him. On 16 April Packer finally returned to civilization and said that Bell had gone mad and killed all the others. Packer then admitted that the conditions had been so bad that when the oldest traveller, 65-year-old Israel Swan, died the others ate him. Four or five days later, James Humphrey died and "was also eaten". Frank Miller died in an accident and also ended up being eaten, as did California Noon. Packer then killed Bell in self-defence.

WHERE:
Rocky Mountains, Colorado, USA
WHEN:
February 1874
THE AFTERMATH:
On 5 August 1874 Packer confessed that he had killed the others and was jailed, but he escaped and went to ground. According to legend, the judge at his trial said, "Damn you, Alferd Packer! There were seven Dimmycrats in Hinsdale County and you've et five of them!" Contrary to many stories told years later, and even today, Packer was never charged with, tried for, or convicted of cannibalism, or crimes related to cannibalism. On 11 March 1883 he was unmasked while living as John Schwartze in Cheyenne, Wyoming. On 13 April he was found guilty of manslaughter and sentenced to death "until you are dead, dead, dead, and may God have mercy upon your soul". The verdict was overturned but on 8 June 1886 Packer was sentenced to 40 years in jail – then the longest custodial sentence in American history. Packer was paroled on 8 February 1901 and died six years later on 23 April 1907.
YOU SHOULD KNOW:
In 1968 University of Colorado students named their new café the Alferd G. Packer Memorial Grill with the slogan, "Have a friend for lunch!"

Alferd Packer was never charged with cannibalism.

William Fish

"I tried to abuse her and she was nearly dead"

WHERE:
Birley Street, Blackburn, England
WHEN:
Tuesday 28 March 1876
THE AFTERMATH:
Fish initially denied that he was responsible for the murder but later confessed. "I tried to abuse her and she was nearly dead. I then cut her throat with a razor... I then carried the body downstairs into the shop, cut off her head, arms and legs." Fish was hanged at Kirkdale Jail, Liverpool, on 14 August 1876, while Chief Constable Potts was ridiculed for his historic decision to allow dogs to do police work.
YOU SHOULD KNOW:
A popular riddle of the day ran "When was Mr Potts like the beggar Lazarus?" Answer: "When he was licked by dogs."

THE CRIME: The case of William Fish was the first recorded official use of dogs by police to capture a murderer. On 28 March 1876 seven-year-old Emily Agnes Holland went missing from Birley Street, Blackburn, after telling friends at St Alban's School that she was "going to fetch half an ounce of tobacco [from Cox's shop] for a man in the street".

Two days later, a child's naked torso was found by a labourer in Bastwell Field off Whalley Road, wrapped in two bloodstained copies of the *Preston Herald* – minus head, arms and legs. That afternoon a child's legs were discovered stuffed in a drain not far away in Lower Cunliffe, also wrapped in two copies of the *Preston Herald*. A post mortem revealed the child had been sexually assaulted, had bled to death from having her throat cut, and then had been dismembered. The post mortem also noted that the trunk had several different people's hair clippings stuck to it and so two local barbers came under suspicion: Denis Whitehead and father-of-three William Fish, who kept old newspapers. Fish was co-operative and allowed police to search his home three times. The third search revealed that four issues of the *Preston Herald*, corresponding with those used to wrap the torso and legs, were missing from his date-ordered stack of papers but Fish claimed he had use them to light the fire and there was insufficient evidence to charge him. Then Chief Constable Potts received an extraordinary offer from a painter named Peter Taylor, who owned a Springer spaniel and a half-breed bloodhound named Morgan, which he claimed could find Emily's missing remains. On 16 April – Easter Sunday – the dogs searched Bastwell and Lower Cunliffe but found nothing. Then they were taken to Fish's home at 3 Moss Street, where Morgan started barking in front of the bedroom fireplace. In a small recess in the chimney was a parcel containing fragments of human skull, hands and forearms, wrapped in a bloodstained copy of the *Manchester Courier*.

Charley Peace

"For that I don but never Intended"

THE CRIME: Born in Sheffield, England, Peace was the son of a circus-animal trainer. He was crippled aged 14, when his leg was damaged by red-hot steel which stunted his growth; he never grew taller than 1.62 m (5 ft 4 in). Five years later, on 26 October 1851, he began burgling. He was quickly caught but a testimonial from his ex-boss resulted in a sentence of only a month in jail. Out of prison Peace returned to burgling

Charley Peace was executed on 25 February 1879.

and on 20 October 1854 was sentenced at Doncaster Sessions to four years' penal servitude. Freed in 1858, Peace quickly resumed his nefarious activities and on 12 August 1859 was caught when he returned to the scene of a crime. This time he was sentenced to six years' penal servitude. Released, he once again began burgling and was caught in 1866 when trying to rob a house while drunk. At Manchester Assizes on 3 December 1866 he received eight years' penal servitude. He attempted to escape from Wakefield Prison and was recaptured in the prison governor's bedroom where he was waiting for a chance to break free. He was released in 1872.

At midnight on 1 August 1876 he shot and killed a policeman, Constable Cock, who was trying to arrest him for burglary at Whalley Range, Manchester. Two brothers stood trial for the murder – one was acquitted and one was sentenced to death but reprieved two days before his execution. On 29 November Peace murdered his former friend, a civil engineer called Arthur Dyson. He fled to his home as a hue and cry went up. He was trailed by the police but managed to give them the slip. Peace began disguising himself by dying his hair, shaving his beard and wearing glasses. Peace also wore a false arm to hide the fact that he was missing a finger. He continually moved around the country to avoid the police, finally moving to 25 Stangate Street, Lambeth in London, where he spent his nights burgling houses. Peace was finally caught at 2am on 10 October 1878 while burgling a house in St John's Park, Blackheath.

WHERE:
Banner Cross, Sheffield, England
WHEN:
Wednesday 29 November 1876
THE AFTERMATH:
The next day he appeared before the magistrate at Greenwich Police Court where, refusing to give a name, he was described as "a half-caste about 60 years of age, of repellent aspect". His mistress finally identified him and had the cheek to ask for the £100 reward (she didn't get it). On 4 February 1879 he was sentenced to death after the jury deliberated for ten minutes. Just before his execution Peace gave his wife a homemade funeral card, which read:
"In
Memory
of
Charles Peace
Who was executed in
Armley Prison
Tuesday February 25,
1879 Aged 47
For that I don but never
Intended."
YOU SHOULD KNOW:
Peace is mentioned in the Sherlock Holmes short story *The Adventure of the Illustrious Client.*

J. Milton Bowers

His fourth wife "fortunately survives him"

WHERE:
930 Market Street, San Francisco, California, USA
WHEN:
Tuesday 3 November 1885
THE AFTERMATH:
Bowers was released in August 1889 and married a fourth time. He returned to his practice and died at San Jose on 7 March 1904 of a stroke, the mystery of his third wife's death still unsolved. One obituary mentioned his propensity for marrying and finished by saying his fourth wife "fortunately survives him".

THE CRIME: Dr Milton Bowers was born in 1843 at Baltimore, Maryland, and was something of a ladies' man. Unfortunately, his ladies had a tendency to die prematurely. Of average height and sporting a beard and moustache, he was said to be pleasant looking rather than handsome and he claimed kinship to Robert E. Lee. He was also an abortionist. He married Fannie Hammond who died in Chicago in 1865. He married again and his second wife was a beautiful Jewish actress named Theresa Sherek whom he had met in Brooklyn. She died on 28 January 1881 of an "abscess of the liver" and six months later he married Cecilia Benhayon-Levy, against the wishes of her family. By 1885 he was practising medicine in San Francisco in a surgery in Geary Street. On 3 November that year the third Mrs Bowers fell ill and died, her body swollen. As she lay near death, he implored, "Baby's going, doctor – is there nothing we can do?" Her death was also ascribed to an "abscess of the liver".

An autopsy showed that she had died of phosphorus poisoning. Bowers was arrested and went on trial on 9 March 1886 and, after the longest trial in San Francisco history and a jury deliberation of just 35 minutes, was found guilty of first-degree murder. On 3 June Judge Murphy sentenced Bowers to be hanged. As Bowers waited to be put to death, Henry Benhayon, the brother of Cecilia Bowers, was found dead of cyanide poisoning in a rented room at 22 Geary Street on 23 October 1887. Next to him was a note in which he confessed to the murder of his sister. Doubts were raised as to whether the death really was a suicide and there was a suspicion that John Dimmig, the husband of Bowers's housekeeper, had been behind the death. Dimmig denied all knowledge but the police discovered that he had bought potassium cyanide and he went on trial on 14 December 1887. The jury could not reach a verdict in February 1888 and a second trial saw him acquitted.

William Kemmler

"Don't let them experiment on me more than they ought to"

THE CRIME: Born on 9 May 1860 William Kemmler achieved criminal notoriety by becoming the first person to die in the electric chair. Kemmler was an illiterate conman from Buffalo, New York, who, on 29 March 1889, murdered his mistress Tillie Ziegler with an axe in a drunken fit of jealousy. Found guilty, he was sentenced to death. The night before his execution Kemmler danced and sang to a banjo played by a fellow death-row inmate, but the following morning he begged the Deputy Sheriff Joseph Veiling: "I'll promise you that I won't make any trouble... Don't let them experiment on me more than they ought to." Veiling shaved Kemmler's crown then cut the back of his trousers, exposing Kemmler's spine for the second electrode. Kemmler entered the death chamber wearing yellow-patterned prison trousers, a dark grey sack jacket with matching waistcoat, a white linen shirt, highly polished black shoes and a bow tie which he self-consciously straightened. At 6.34am Warden Durston asked if he had any last words and he said: "Gentlemen, I wish you all good luck. I believe I'm going to a good place, and I'm ready to go. A great deal has been said about me that's untrue. I'm bad enough. It's cruel to make me out worse." Kemmler removed his jacket and sat in the chair but was asked to stand again because Durston suddenly realized he needed to cut another hole in the back of the shirt — Kemmler told him, "Take your time, Warden, and do it right. There's no rush. I don't want to take any chances on this thing you know." When the electrodes were securely attached Durston said, "God bless you, Kemmler," who replied, "Thank you." Durston then said, "Goodbye William," but there was no reply.

Durston rapped twice on the door, the executioner threw the switch and Kemmler's torso convulsed. His face and hands turned first red then

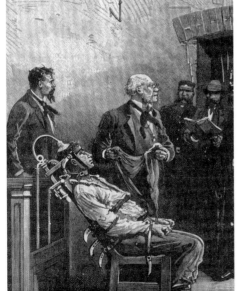

ashen – his staring eyes terrified the 25 witnesses. One of his fingers clenched so tight the nail cut into the flesh and blood started trickling down the arm of the chair. Fierce red spots appeared on his face. After 17 seconds Edward Spitzka, a celebrated anatomist, announced, "He's dead."

WHERE:
New York City, USA
WHEN:
Friday 29 March 1889

THE AFTERMATH:
The electricity was turned off and the body sagged forward. But as Durston started to remove the headpiece Kemmler's chest heaved, a gurgling sound came from his throat and foam bubbled out of his mouth. The switch was thrown again and the lifeless body sat up taut as the current surged back though it. This time smoke rose from the top of his head and drops of blood sparkled on his face, accompanied by a sizzling sound like meat frying in a pan. The smell of charred skin, singed hair, urine and faeces pervaded the room. At 6.51am Spitzka signalled Durston to turn the power off. Kemmler's second electrocution had lasted about a minute. Shocked witnesses agreed with Spitzka, "I've never seen anything so awful. I believe this will be the first and last execution of the kind." Though most of the press denounced electrocution as little more than torture, *The New York Times* said it would be absurd to go back to "the barbarism of hanging".

YOU SHOULD KNOW:
The world's first official electrocutioner was Edwin F. Davis, who went on to electrocute 240 others including the first woman, Martha Place.

William Kemmler became the first person to die in the electric chair at Auburn Penitentiary in 1890.

Florence Maybrick

"I am not guilty of this crime"

WHERE:
Battlecrease House, Aigburth,
Liverpool, England
WHEN:
Saturday 11 May 1889
THE AFTERMATH:
The death penalty was commuted to
life imprisonment and Florence was
released on 25 January 1904. She
moved back to America and died on
23 October 1941. Mr Justice Stephen
went mad and ended his days in an
asylum. In 1992 a story broke that a
diary, purportedly written by Jack the
Ripper, had surfaced in Liverpool. The
author of the diary was said to be
James Maybrick who had known of
Florence's infidelity and had taken
his revenge in Whitechapel, London
(see page 510).

*Florence Maybrick making
her statement at Liverpool
Crown Court.*

THE CRIME: On 27 July 1881 James Maybrick, a 50-year-old cotton merchant from Liverpool, married 18-year-old Florence Chandler, an American from Alabama. They lived in America for three years before relocating to England, settling in Liverpool. They had two children. James Maybrick's family disapproved of the match and he was a typical Victorian husband, domineering and short-tempered. He also fathered several illegitimate children. Florence found solace and companionship in the arms of Alfred Brierley, a friend of her husband. They quickly became lovers and in March 1889 spent a weekend together in London. When Florence returned to Liverpool, Maybrick was furious and not long after cut her out of his will. The couple bumped into Brierley at Aintree on Grand National Day and when they went home Maybrick blacked Florence's eye.

On 28 April Maybrick fell ill with vomiting and diarrhoea. Florence told the doctor that he had been taking a white powder. Thirteen days later, on 11 May, James Maybrick died. A love letter to Brierley had been intercepted by Alice Yapp, one of the family servants, and passed on to Maybrick's brother. An examination on 13 May found traces of arsenic in Maybrick's body and Florence was arrested the next day. Further investigation unearthed the fact that she had bought three dozen arsenical flypapers from chemists. At Liverpool on 31 July 1889 Florence went on trial, accused of murdering her husband. The various medical experts could not agree on the cause of death because Maybrick had been a hypochondriac who took many different drugs. Florence claimed she had used the arsenic as a cosmetic. The judge Mr Justice Stephen's summing-up was weighted against Florence because of her adultery and she was found guilty and sentenced to death. She said, "Although I have been found guilty, with the exception of the intimacy with Mr Brierley, I am not guilty of this crime."

Nathan Champion

"I wish there was someone here with me so we could watch all sides at once"

THE CRIME: Nathan D. Champion, known as Nate, was born a twin on 29 September 1857 near Round Rock, Texas, and was a rustler in Wyoming during the Johnson County War, a series of violent conflicts over land and cattle. The powerful cattlemen's association, the Wyoming Stock Growers Association (WSGA), hired killers from Texas to deal with Champion and his ilk. Fifty men known as Regulators were hired and they took two reporters along to ensure that they got a good spin on their antics. To prevent help being summoned, the vigilantes cut the telegraph lines. They headed to Champion's KC Ranch where he had three friends staying with him. Two – Ben Jones and Bill Walker – were captured as they went to the well for water and a third, Nick Ray, was shot and died a few hours later. The Regulators besieged the KC Ranch. Two people saw what was happening and rode to alert the sheriff Red Angus who got together a posse of 200 men and headed for the KC Ranch.

For several hours battle raged and Champion managed to kill four of the Regulators. During this time he kept a journal and addressed it to his friends, "Boys, I feel pretty lonesome just now. I wish there was someone here with me so we could watch all sides at once." The last entry read, "Well, they have just got through shelling the house like hell. I heard them splitting wood. I guess they are going to fire the house tonight. I think I will make a break when night comes, if alive. Shooting again. It's not night yet. The house is all fired. Goodbye, boys, if I never see you again."

The Regulators then set fire to the KC Ranch house, forcing Champion to leave. He ran out the back door, a knife in one hand, a gun in the other and his diary in his pocket. He was mown down by 28 bullets fired by four gunmen, making him the first person murdered by a band of hitmen.

WHERE:
KC Ranch, Wyoming, USA
WHEN:
Saturday 9 April 1892
THE AFTERMATH:
The Regulators stuck a note to Champion's bullet-riddled corpse bearing the legend, "Cattle Thieves Beware". They also removed pages from his diary that named names. One of the Regulators, Frank Canton, later became a US Marshal in Oklahoma Territory. From 1885 to 1909, 15 rustlers were killed by mobs.
YOU SHOULD KNOW:
Christopher Walken played Champion in Michael Cimino's mega-flop film *Heaven's Gate*.

Nathan Champion, left, with some of his gang of rustlers

Robert Buchanan

A cat was killed with morphine

WHERE:
New York City, USA
WHEN:
Friday 22 April 1892
THE AFTERMATH:
Buchanan's trial began on 20 March 1893 at New York before Judge E. C. Smyth. It was one of the first trials to be fought almost exclusively on forensic science testimony. During the proceedings, a cat was killed with morphine and then atropine dropped into its eyes. There were no pinpricks in its pupils. Buchanan's lawyer almost managed to undo a damning testimony from a medical expert but when Buchanan took the stand all hope was lost. The jury retired on 25 April and took more than 28 hours to return a guilty verdict. He died in the electric chair at Sing Sing on 2 July 1895.

THE CRIME: Born in Nova Scotia in 1862, Dr Robert Buchanan qualified to practise medicine at Edinburgh University in Scotland before crossing the Atlantic where he opened his practice at 267 Eleventh Street, New York in 1886. Despite spending virtually all of his spare time in bars and brothels he managed to maintain a successful practice. On 12 November 1890 he was divorced and 17 days later married Anna Sutherland who had been a successful madam and she became his receptionist. She was short, fat, had dyed orange hair and a large wart on the end of her nose. He persuaded her to leave her not inconsiderable fortune to him in her will. However, when patients learned of the former occupation of the second Mrs Buchanan and saw her vulgarity, they turned away from him leading to a sharp drop in his income.

On 21 April 1892 Dr Buchanan announced that he was going to be travelling alone to Scotland but, four days before his departure, he cancelled because his wife had suddenly fallen ill. Buchanan called two other doctors in to treat his wife but she died of a cerebral haemorrhage. Three weeks later Buchanan remarried his first wife, Helen, in Nova Scotia and also inherited $50,000 from his second wife. However, Buchanan's boasting and his interest in the case of Carlyle Harris, a medical student who poisoned his girlfriend with morphine, led to Ike White, a reporter from the *New York World*, investigating him. Buchanan had claimed that he could avoid the telltale signs of morphine poisoning (pinprick pupils) by using atropine, an alkaloid derived from belladonna. When Mrs Buchanan's body was exhumed on 22 May there were no pinpricks in her eyes. The police arrested the doctor.

Lizzie Borden

Lizzie Borden took an axe and gave her mother forty whacks

THE CRIME: Did she or didn't she? After almost 120 years the jury of history is still out. On a sweltering hot day – the temperature was more than 37°C (100°F) – wealthy 69-year-old banker Andrew Jackson Borden (born 13 September 1822) and his second wife Abby Durfee Gray, 64 (born 21 January 1828), were murdered in their home – he in the living room, she in the guest bedroom. The Bordens shared their home with his daughters Emma Lenora, 41, and Lizzie

Andrew, 32, and the servant Bridget Sullivan. At 11.10am Lizzie Borden screamed to the servant, "Come down quick! Father's dead! Somebody's come in and killed him!" He had been struck 11 times. Five minutes later, the body of Abby Borden was discovered. She had been struck 19 times and had probably been killed at 9.30am.

The day before she was murdered Abby Borden had claimed that someone was trying to poison her and her husband but no evidence was found during the autopsies, which began at 3pm. Emma Borden returned home four hours later from visiting friends. That night the sisters stayed in their rooms while Uncle John Morse, their visitor, slept in the room in which Abby had been murdered. During the police investigation a hatchet was found in the basement and was assumed to be the murder weapon. A second autopsy was performed on 6 August. The next day Lizzie was spotted burning a dress that, she claimed, was despoiled by paint. That action led to her arrest on 11 August for murder. On 2 December Lizzie was charged with three counts of murder – the murder of her father, the murder of her stepmother, and the murders of both of them. The trial began on 5 June 1893 and lasted 14 days. At 4.32pm on 20 June the jury returned a verdict of not guilty on all three charges.

WHERE:
92 Second Street, Fall River, Massachusetts, USA
WHEN:
Thursday 4 August 1892
THE AFTERMATH:
In August 1893 Lizzie and Emma bought a 13-room house at 306 French Street in Fall River's most fashionable area and renamed the house Maplecroft. In 1904 Lizzie began an intimate friendship with an actress called Nance O'Neil (1874–1965), which resulted in Emma leaving Maplecroft. On 1 June 1927 Lizzie died and Emma passed away nine days later. The sisters were buried with their father and stepmother and Alice Esther, another sister who had died on 10 March 1858, before her second birthday. The case is remembered in the (inaccurate) rhyme:
"Lizzie Borden took an axe
And gave her mother forty whacks.
And when she saw what she had done,
She gave her father forty-one."
YOU SHOULD KNOW:
The theories of whodunit are numerous: Lizzie did it because she hated her stepmother; Lizzie did it during an epileptic fit which left her with no memory of her actions; Lizzie did it, helped by the servant Bridget with whom she was having an affair; Emma did it because she thought her father was about to cut her and Lizzie out of his will; Emma did it with Lizzie's help; Bridget Sullivan did it because Mrs Borden asked her to wash the windows; a local developer, Dr Sewell W. Bowen, did it because Andrew Borden opposed his building plans.

Minnie Dean

"I believe this woman would have killed or abandoned this child"

WHERE:
Winton, Southland, New Zealand
WHEN:
Thursday 2 May 1895
THE AFTERMATH:
The trial for the murder of Dorothy Carter began at Invercargill on 18 June 1895. Defence lawyer A.C. Hanlon said that the death had been accidental but the judge summed up saying, "'It seems to me that the real honest issue is whether the accused is guilty of intentionally killing the child or is innocent altogether." On 21 June Dean was found guilty of murder and sentenced to death. She was hanged at Invercargill Jail on 12 August 1895 by the official executioner Tom Long. Minnie Dean thus became the only woman to be hanged for murder in New Zealand.
YOU SHOULD KNOW:
Charles Dean was also arrested but released without charge. He died in a house fire at Winton in 1908, aged 73.

THE CRIME: Born as Williamina McCulloch on 2 September 1844 in West Greenock, Scotland, Minnie Dean arrived in Invercargill, New Zealand in the early 1860s, a widow with two young daughters. On 19 June 1872 she married innkeeper Charles Dean at his home in Etal Creek, Southland. Etal Creek had once been a thriving community but by the time of the nuptials it was deserted and Charles Dean turned to framing to earn a living. By 1884 he was bankrupt. Four years earlier they had adopted five-year-old Margaret Cameron and in 1887 the family moved to The Larches, a large house at Winton about 1.5 km (1 mi) out of town.

The house burned down and Mr Dean built a two-roomed cottage with a lean-to. He began pig farming and she began baby farming – taking in unwanted babies for money. She advertised in the local paper, "Respectable Married Woman (comfortable home, country) Wants to Adopt an infant – Address, Childless, Times Office." To adopt a baby she took anywhere between £10 and £30, while fostering was charged at five to eight shillings a week.

Soon babies began to die at The Larches. On 29 October 1889 May Irene, six months old, died of convulsions after a three-day illness. In March 1891 six-week-old Bertha Currie died of inflammation of the heart valves and congestion of the lungs. The inquest reported that the house was overcrowded and Dean should take in fewer children but said that most of the babies were well looked after. Six weeks later, another baby died and Dean became concerned that she would be linked publicly with the baby farmers in Britain and Australia who had been convicted of murdering children for money.

Another young boy died in her care in 1894 and she buried him the back garden to avoid yet another inquest. The police put Dean under surveillance and prevented her from taking one baby, a detective writing, "I believe this woman would have killed or abandoned this child." On 30 April 1895 Jane Hornsby gave her one-month-old granddaughter, Eva, to Dean at Clarendon Station. On 2 May Dean boarded the train with the baby and a hatbox – when she got off she had only the hatbox with her.

After clothing belonging to Eva was found at The Larches, Dean was arrested and charged with infanticide. The police searched the garden at The Larches and found the bodies of two babies, Dorothy Edith Carter (who had died of a laudanum overdose) and Eva Hornsby (who died of asphyxiation), and the body of a 4-year-old boy. It was impossible to ascertain how he died. A coroner labelled Minnie Dean a murderer.

Adolph Louis Luetgert

Luertgert claimed that the bones belonged to animals

THE CRIME: A sausage-maker by trade, Adolph Luetgert (born in Gütersloh, Westphalia, Germany on 27 December 1845) was also a ladies' man. His reputation in that quarter almost equalled his reputation for making German sausage. He had several women on the go and even had a bed placed in his factory, A.L. Luetgert Sausage & Packing Company, so he did not have to be distracted from work for long. His long-suffering second wife Louisa Bicknese (born

12 January 1855) whom he had married on 18 January 1878, was aware of her husband's philandering. She ignored his philanderings when he was discreet but he became less discreet about his infidelities.

On 1 May 1897 Louisa disappeared. Luetgert told their two children, Louis (aged 11) and Elmer Paul (aged 5), that he had hired a private detective to find their mother but other relatives were dissatisfied and went to the police. They searched the factory and discovered, in one of the vats used to make sausages, bone, teeth and two engraved rings that had belonged to Louisa. Luertgert claimed that the bones belonged to animals but tests proved their provenance was human.

He was arrested and charged with his wife's murder. Several of his mistresses came forward to testify against him and their revelations made the story front-page news in Chicago. Luetgert continued to deny having anything to do with his wife's death but one lover said that he had spoken to her of crushing his wife. The police believed that the sausage-maker had stabbed Louisa to death and then put her body into a vat.

WHERE:
601–629 Diversey Boulevard, Chicago, Illinois, USA
WHEN:
Saturday 1 May 1897
THE AFTERMATH:
Luetgert went on trial in August 1897 but the jury was hung. A second trial was held in January 1898 and this time he was convicted and sentenced to life in jail. He died in Joliet Prison in July 1899, still maintaining his innocence.
YOU SHOULD KNOW:
Luetgert was a twin.

Adolph Luetgert at the time of his arrest

Roland Molineux

"We believe that the prosecution has failed to establish its charge"

WHERE:
61 West 86th Street,
New York City, USA
WHEN:
Wednesday 28 December 1898
THE AFTERMATH:
The second trial opened in October 1902 before Judge John D. Lambert. The time-lapse meant much evidence was unavailable and the jury acquitted Molinuex on 12 November after deliberating for just four minutes. Following his acquittal, Molinuex earned a living as a writer, having written one book *The Room With The Little Door* while incarcerated. He and Blanche Cheeseborough were divorced in 1903 and in 1913 he married Margaret Connell. Shortly, afterwards, he suffered a nervous breakdown. He was sent to the New York Hospital for the Insane at King's Park, Long Island where he died on 2 November 1917.

Roland Molineux preparing his poisoned medicines.

THE CRIME: The son of Edward Leslie Molineux, an American Civil War Union general and a big shot in the Republican Party, 30-year-old Roland Burnham Molineux was born into a wealthy and distinguished family. A handsome playboy, he was also an inveterate snob. A member of the elite Knickerbocker Athletic Club at Madison Avenue and 45th Street, he demanded that the club secretary bar anyone whose pedigree was not quite smart enough. In 1898 Molineux fell for the young and sexy opera singer Blanche Cheeseborough who, despite having only one eye, was regarded as a catch. He soon found himself competing for her affections with Henry C. Barnet, a successful New York City stockbroker. In November of that year Mr Barnet received in the post Kutnow Powder, a popular stomach remedy. Believing it was a reputable free sample, he took the powder. He fell violently ill and died on 10 November. The official cause of death: cardiac asthenia induced by diptheric poisoning. Less than three weeks later, on 29 November, Molineux married Blanche Cheeseborough.

In April 1897, Molineux lost a weightlifting competition to Harry Cornish, the Knickerbocker Athletic Club's 35-year-old athletic director. In December Molineux insisted that Mr Cornish be expelled from the club but the committee refused. On Christmas Eve 1898, a small, blue bottle of headache medicine, Bromo Seltzer, was delivered to Mr Cornish who passed it on to his landlady, Katharine J. Adams, when she suffered a headache on 28 December. She took the medicine and went into violent convulsions and died. An autopsy showed that she had died of mercury cyanide poisoning. A police investigation revealed forged letters to the drug companies supposedly written by Mr Barnet and Mr Cornish. The handwriting bore a remarkable similarity to Molineux's, so he was charged with the murder of Mrs Adams on 27 February 1899.

The trial began on 14 November 1899, with Judge John Goff on the bench. Prosecutor James W. Osborne produced more than a dozen witnesses to testify that the handwriting on the letters was Molineux's. The defence, led by George Gordon Battle and Bartow Weeks, called no witnesses and presented no evidence, merely stating, "We believe that the prosecution has failed to establish its charge and we rest the defence upon the People's case." Mr Osborne in his final summing-up unfortunately made a number of legal errors. On 11 February 1900 the jury returned a verdict of guilty and Molineux was sentenced to the electric chair. The appeal took 18 months to be heard, which time he spent in Sing Sing. On 15 October 1901 the verdict was overturned and a new trial ordered.

Albert T. Patrick

The forged cheque raised suspicions

THE CRIME: Millionaire businessman William Marsh Rice was born in Springfield, Massachusetts on 14 March 1816. He moved to Texas and made a fortune in cotton trading and land and railroad investments. He married twice but had no children and, by 1896, was living with his second wife in a mansion at Dunellen, New Jersey. She died in July of that year and he moved to New York but was shocked to find her will, made in Texas, left half of all their joint property to her relatives. He decided not to put the will into probate and in 1897 hired Charles F. Jones as his secretary and aide to help him. On 23 September 1900, William Rice was found dead in bed.

The year before New York City lawyer Albert T. Patrick had met Jones and persuaded him to join him in a nefarious act to defraud Rice. Patrick would write a letter in which Mr Rice would acknowledge his Texan home as his main residence thus validating his wife's will and Jones would arrange for him to sign it. Then, in June 1899, Patrick suggested Jones make up a new will in which half the estate was left to Patrick. Then greed got the better of Patrick. On 24 September, Jones wrote a $25,000 cheque on which Patrick forged Mr Rice's signature. Unfortunately, Jones had written "Abert T. Patrick" instead of "Albert T. Patrick" and it was queried by a bank clerk. The clerk telephoned Jones who assured him everything was fine but the clerk insisted on speaking to Mr Rice and was told the old man was dead. Mr Rice had been quickly cremated at Patrick's instruction but the forged cheque raised suspicions and on 4 October 1900 Patrick and Jones were arrested. Patrick had persuaded Jones to administer chloroform to Rice while he slept.

WHERE:
Madison Avenue, New York City, USA
WHEN:
Sunday 23 September 1900
THE AFTERMATH:
Jones turned state's evidence against Patrick. The two men were in adjoining cells and Patrick persuaded Jones that it would be best if he committed suicide and amazingly Jones did cut his own throat but survived. Patrick was tried before Judge John William Goff on 22 January 1902 and he represented himself. On 26 March 1902 he was found guilty and sentenced to death in the electric chair but launched several appeals. In 1906 his sentence was commuted to life in prison. Six years later, on 28 November 1912, he was pardoned and returned to the south to practise law. He died at Tulsa, Oklahoma, in 1940.

The fake will bearing the witness signatures of the two conspirators.

147

Nan Patterson

"False to her husband, false to her lover"

WHERE:
West Broadway and Franklin Street,
New York City, USA
WHEN:
Saturday 4 June 1904

THE AFTERMATH:
The jury having deliberated, the judge threatened anyone who spoke out of turn with contempt when the verdict was read. There was an air of disappointment when the foreman of the jury announced that they had not reached a decision and said "I am convinced that there is no hope of an agreement." After more conferring the jury foreman told the court that there was no hope of a verdict – they were voting eight to four for manslaughter in the first degree. On 13 May Patterson was finally freed. District Attorney Jerome said that it was a "miscarriage of justice of the most serious kind [attributable] to the attitude of the press of this city toward the accused woman." As soon as she was given her liberty Patterson and her sister went shopping on Sixth Avenue and posed for photographers.

YOU SHOULD KNOW:
After the collapse of the second trial, Patterson received numerous cards and letters, mostly from well-wishers. Armedi Beauparler's missive was not in that category. His read, "If the jury acquitted Nan, I would have shot her as she left the Tombs."

Dancer and actress Nan Patterson poses second from the right.

THE CRIME: Nan Patterson was a married, 19-year-old dancer and actress when, in 1902, she began an affair with the much older, equally married New York-based bookmaker Caesar Young. He paid for her to divorce her husband after which time she lived "on Young's bounty". Young promised to leave his wife for Patterson but never did. On 4 June 1904 Patterson and Mr Young were riding in a carriage down Broadway – he was on his way to the docks to meet his wife as he was going on a long overseas holiday with her. At some point in that journey Young was shot dead with a gun that belonged to Patterson. Police arrested Patterson and she was charged with the murder of Young.

Her first trial ended in a hung jury and she was tried again in the spring of 1905. The state alleged that Patterson killed Young because she was furious he would not leave his wife or that he had resisted her attempts at blackmail. The defence argued that the evidence showed that the bookmaker had committed suicide. During proceedings *The New York Times* suggested, none too subtly, that Patterson was innocent. On 2 May 1905 the prosecution took five hours to deliver its closing arguments. He argued that the bullet's trajectory made suicide difficult if not impossible. "Mr Young would not have held the weapon upside down when he fired the shot and sent the bullet through the apex of the left lung on its way to strike the fourth dorsal vertebra," he said. He tried to blacken Patterson's character, referring to the love letters sent by Young. "Did the defendant render them? No. Was that the conduct of a woman madly in love or of a mercenary creature who wanted to keep them in her possession for blackmail purposes?" he demanded. "And now as to the morning of the tragedy… The murder in her heart flamed into action, and she shot and killed. A little crack, a puff of smoke, and a dead man lay prostrate on this woman's lap. False to her husband, false to her lover, and false to her oath the defendant would have you believe by her story told at the previous trial that Young shot himself rather than be separated from her. A silly story – a lie she does not now dare attempt to support."

When the jury left for lunch they were "jostled by the crowd that packed the streets. All the way to the restaurant the jurymen heard yells of 'Free Nan Patterson! Set her free! Nan's all right! She's done nothing! You let her loose, that's the best you can do!'"

Harry Kendall Thaw

The Girl On The Red Velvet Swing

Millionaire Harry Thaw

THE CRIME: The heir to a multi-million dollar mine and railroad fortune, Harry Thaw (born 12 February 1871) had it all. He also had a nasty temper and a sharp tongue. A troublemaker from the age of three, according to his mother, he fared badly at school where teachers described him as "unintelligible". His wealth afforded him admission to the University of Pittsburgh to read law. His father died leaving him a trust fund with a monthly allowance of $200, which his mother raised to $80,000 a year. Thaw went to Harvard where he boasted that he studied "poker". His secondary disciplines were wine, women and going to cockfights. His life post-Harvard was one of debauchery and public outbursts of temper. He romanced showgirls from Broadway although there were rumours about his liking for sexual chastisement using dog leads. He became interested in a beautiful Pennsylvania-born model Evelyn Nesbit who appeared in the hit show *Florodora*.

She had been the beneficiary of the largesse of leading architect Stanford White who had designed mansions, clubs and Madison Square Garden. White was also a philanderer, something he kept from his wife. In his apartment he had installed a red velvet swing on which numerous young ladies were said to have swung. He taught the girls deportment, paid for their teeth to be fixed and they responded with their own gifts. One night White invited Evelyn to his apartment for dinner, which he had drugged and then raped her – until then she had been a virgin. When White's interest waned, Thaw's did not and he proposed to Evelyn. She hesitated, thinking Thaw would not want her when he discovered that she was a "fallen woman". Thaw took her to a remote farmhouse where he, too, raped her and then beat her with a dog lead. Eventually they married. On 25 June 1906 Mr and Mrs Thaw attended a production of *Mam'zelle Champagne* in the rooftop theatre of Madison Square Garden. Also in attendance was Stanford White and, during the finale, *I Could Love A Million Girls*, Thaw shot him in the face three times. The murder shocked the public and Evelyn became known as The Girl on the Velvet Swing. Thaw faced two trials – the first was a hung jury and at the second he was found not guilty by reason of insanity.

WHERE:
Madison Square Garden, Madison Avenue and 26th Street, New York City, USA

WHEN:
Monday 25 June 1906

THE AFTERMATH:
Thaw was sent to the Matteawan State Hospital for the Criminally Insane in Fishkill, New York. He was freed in 1913. In 1917 he was accused of sexually assaulting a teenage boy and again adjudged insane. He was released in 1924. Thaw died of a heart attack in Miami, Florida on 22 February 1947. He left $10,000 in his will to Evelyn Nesbit.

YOU SHOULD KNOW:
Thaw was expelled from Harvard for chasing a taxi driver through the streets of Cambridge with a shotgun, albeit an unloaded one.

Glenmore Inn at Big Moose Lake

Chester Gillette

"If I die, I hope then you can be happy"

THE CRIME:
Chester Gillette was born on 9 August 1883 in Montana and raised at Spokane, Washington. His parents were religious and joined the Salvation Army. Chester Gillette moved from job to job before finally settling at his uncle's Gillette Skirt Factory in Cortland, New York in 1905. One of his co-workers was Grace Brown, a farmer's daughter three years his junior, and in the spring of 1906 she told him that she was pregnant and expected him to do the decent thing.

Unbeknown to Grace, Gillette was seeing other women and marriage and a baby were not in his plans. She went to stay with her parents but the two corresponded. Her letters became desperate. One read in part, "If I could only die... if I die, I hope then you can be happy. I hope I can die... oh, please come and take me away." Gillette decided to do just that and booked a break in the country in the summer of that year. Grace expected him to propose or even to have a secret marriage planned. He booked them into the Glenmore Inn at the Adirondacks. He used a false name but one with the same initials – Carl Grahm of Albany – to match his expensive luggage. On the Wednesday Gillette hired a boat and took Grace rowing on Big Moose Lake.

Out of sight of land, he smashed her over the head with a tennis racquet and threw her overboard, leaving her to drown. Grace's body was discovered at the bottom of the lake the next day. Gillette was arrested on 13 July. He claimed that Grace had slipped and fallen and then said that she was depressed and had killed herself.

WHERE:
Big Moose Lake, Herkimer County, New York, USA

WHEN:
Wednesday 11 July 1906

THE AFTERMATH:
Chester Gillette's trial began on 12 November 1906 in the Herkimer County Courthouse. The defence finished their presentation on the evening of December 4 and the jury retired to consider its verdict. Six hours later, it was back. Gillette sent a telegram to his family, "I am convicted. Will write." Despite several appeals, he went to the electric chair at Auburn Prison, New York on the morning of 30 March 1908.

YOU SHOULD KNOW:
Gillette was the prototype for Clyde Griffiths in Theodore Dreiser's novel *An American Tragedy* which, in turn, became the movies *An American Tragedy* (1931) and the 1951 Academy Award-winning film *A Place in the Sun* starring Montgomery Clift and Elizabeth Taylor. The Brown family sued Paramount in 1934 over their depiction in the first film.

Countess Marie Tarnowska

"The whole pathway of my life is strewn with the bodies of those who have loved me most"

THE CRIME: Born in Russia in 1879, Marie Tarnowska attended a school in Kiev for the children of the nobility. At 13 she realized that she could use her beauty to manipulate men and three years later married Count Tarnowski and gave birth to three children. They became avid socialites but the count had a wandering eye so in revenge she slept with his brother. When she broke off the fling with the brother, he killed himself. Not long after, another lover killed himself when Tarnowska finished with him and took up with Alexis Bozevski of the Imperial Guard. He was violent and Tarnowska decided to get rid if him.

She invited him into her boudoir, knowing her husband was due to return any moment. When the count entered, Tarnowska began grappling with her lover and her husband assumed that his wife was being raped. He shot Bozevski who died not long after. In May 1903 Tarnowska hired a lawyer named Maximillian Prulikov and paid his fees in bed to arrange for her husband to be sent to Siberia. He failed and the count learned the truth about the "rape". He left his wife penniless. She persuaded Prulikov to leave his wife and children and travel around Europe with her, at his expense, naturally. When they returned to Russia she took the older and wealthy Count Paul Kamarovsky to her bed. The count told his new mistress that one of his friends Dr Nicholas Naumov was a misogynist. Marie Tarnowska was intrigued and began overtures towards the doctor that were so successful that he shot his own hand and allowed her to tattoo him with a dagger. She also enjoyed burning him with cigarettes during sex.

Fickle as ever, she decided that she wanted to be rid of both Count Paul Kamarovsky and Nicholas Naumov. She asked Naumov and the faithful lawyer Prulikov to kill Kamarovsky. She also arranged for Kamarovsky to take out a life insurance policy for £20,000 in which she was the sole beneficiary. She told Prulikov to wait with the police to arrest Naumov after the murder and ensured Naumov went through with it by having rampant sex with him just before. In Venice on 3 September 1907 Naumov shot Kamarovsky and then was arrested by the police and Prulikov as planned.

WHERE:
Lido, Venice, Italy
WHEN:
Tuesday 3 September 1907
THE AFTERMATH:
Tarnowksa's part in the conspiracy was soon revealed and she was arrested. Her trial began on 4 March 1910 and she was jailed for eight years, Prulikov for ten and Naumov just three. Tarnowska served two years before being freed in August 1912 through ill-health caused by the cocaine habit she acquired through a lover before the murder. She died in 1923.
YOU SHOULD KNOW:
Marie Tarnowska said "I am the most unfortunate woman in the world. I am a martyr to my own beauty. For any man to behold me is for him to love me. The whole pathway of my life is strewn with the bodies of those who have loved me most."

Marie Tarnowska

Oscar Slater

"You are convicting an innocent man"

WHERE:
15 Queen's Terrace, Glasgow, Scotland
WHEN:
Monday 21 December 1908
THE AFTERMATH:
Oscar Slater was reprieved and his sentence commuted to life imprisonment on 25 May 1909. He was sent to Peterhead Prison on 8 July 1909. In 1928 Slater was freed on appeal. He married in 1937 and died at Ayr in February 1948. In 1994 the truth was revealed. Miss Gilchrist had disinherited her relatives from her will. Two of them, Dr Francis Charteris and her nephew Wingate Burrell, had visited her and Burrell had beaten the old lady to death with a chair. The establishment covered up for the wealthy family and used Oscar Slater as a scapegoat.

THE CRIME: At 7pm four days before Christmas 1908, 81-year-old Marion Gilchrist sent Helen Lambie, her 21-year-old maid, to buy an evening newspaper. As Lambie returned to the luxury, seven-room, first-floor flat, Arthur Adams, who lived on the ground floor at number 14, stopped her. He said he had heard strange noises coming from Miss Gilchrist's home. Together they went up the stairs and entered the flat. As they did so a man came out of the spare bedroom "like greased lightning" and ran down the stairs, knocking over teenager Mary Barrowman in the street. In the dining-room was Miss Gilchrist, her head caved in by 60 or so blows. Despite the plethora of jewels in the flat, only one small piece was missing – a crescent-shaped diamond brooch.

The police had little to go on but on Boxing Day they were told that a man called Oscar Slater had been trying to pawn a crescent-shaped diamond brooch. The police went to Slater's home in St George's Road, Glasgow where he lived with his prostitute girlfriend but the couple had left for New York aboard the *Lusitania* that same day. Further investigation revealed that Slater had pawned a crescent-shaped diamond brooch but had done so on 18 November and that it had not been Miss Gilchrist's. However, Glasgow police did not let a complete lack of evidence deter them and in February 1909 they extradited Slater from America. Unfortunately for Slater, he was German, Jewish, lived off immoral earnings and preferred to gamble rather than work, all of which prejudiced the jury against him. On 3 May 1909 he went on trial at Edinburgh. The three witnesses Lambie, Adams and Barrowman said that they recognized Slater as the man seen running from the spare room – even though Barrowman was shown photographs of Slater before her identification, Adams was short-sighted and Lambie said the man was clean-shaven (Slater had a moustache). A 15-man jury deliberated for 70 minutes and found Slater guilty by a majority and he was sentenced to hang on 27 May 1909. He cried out, "You are convicting an innocent man."

Oscar Slater in London, following his release after 19 years in prison.

Dr Bennett Clarke Hyde

"Frances will know what to do"

THE CRIME: Bennett Clarke Hyde was born in 1872 in Cowper, Missouri, the son of a Baptist minister. He graduated in medicine at Kansas City, Missouri, and opened a practice there. In 1905 Hyde was appointed surgeon to the Kansas City Police Department but was sacked two years later for supposedly maltreating a patient. The same year he married Frances Swope in a secret ceremony on 21 June. She had a very rich uncle Colonel Thomas Hunton Swope, a childless bachelor who doted on his many nieces and nephews, some of whom lived with him in his mansion.

In September 1909 the colonel fell ill and Hyde arrived to take care of him. On 2 October he prescribed a pill for the old man who was by then 80 years old. The next day he died of "apoplexy", according to Hyde. A nurse who normally looked after Colonel Swope was suspicious but Hyde insisted on moving into Colonel Swope's mansion. Several family members also became sick and one, Chrisman Swope, died. Nine further people were treated by Hyde and died of typhoid fever. To cope with the sickness there were five nurses working in the mansion and they were afraid that Hyde's plan was to kill all the Swopes and keep the family money for himself.

They reported Hyde to the police who authorized autopsies on Colonel and Chrisman Swope. When both were found to have died of strychnine and cyanide poisoning, Hyde was taken into custody. On 15 February 1910 he was charged with murder. Mrs Hyde believed in her husband and used her own money to hire the best lawyers money could buy. His trial opened at Kansas City on 16 April 1910 before Judge Ralph S. Latshaw. The evidence against Hyde appeared compelling and convincing and on 16 May 1910 he was found guilty of murder. Two months later, on 5 July, Judge Latshaw passed a life sentence. But Hyde was undeterred. He said, "This case is not closed. My wife Frances will not forsake me. Yes, Frances will know what to do."

Mrs Hyde hired new lawyers to fight her husband's side and on 11 April 1911 the Supreme Court of Missouri overturned the conviction. A second attempt at justice ended in a mistrial when a juror fell ill. A third trial also ended without a verdict. In January 1917 the state attempted for a fourth time to successfully prosecute Hyde for murder. The case was dismissed when his lawyers pointed out that no one could be tried more than three times for the same offence under Missouri law.

Dr Bennett Clarke Hyde

WHERE:
Kansas City, Missouri, USA
WHEN:
Sunday 3 October 1909
THE AFTERMATH:
Hyde never practised medicine again. He lived off his wife's money.
YOU SHOULD KNOW:
Although publicly she supported her husband, in 1927 Frances left Hyde after she fell ill and he offered to care for her.

Dr Crippen and Ethel Le Neve in the dock charged with the murder of Mrs Crippen.

Dr Crippen

"I could see him smiling as he approached [the gallows]"

THE CRIME: The first murderer to be caught by wireless telegraphy, Hawley Harvey "Peter" Crippen was born in July 1862 in Coldwater, Michigan. After qualifying as a doctor at the Homeopathic Hospital in Cleveland he moved to New York where, on 2 December 1887, he married Charlotte Jane Bell, an Irish student nurse and had a son, Otto on 19 August 1889. On 24 January 1892 his wife, pregnant for the second time, suddenly and unexpectedly died, aged 33, of apoplexy at Salt Lake City, Utah. That same year he met and, on 1 September, married the 19-year-old, would-be music hall singer Cora Turner (real name Kunigunde Mackamotzki, stage name Belle Elmore who was born on 3 September 1873). Five years later the couple moved to London (he in April 1897 and her four months later) where Crippen opened an office selling patent medicines. The Crippens moved to Hilldrop Crescent on 21 September 1905. The marriage was stormy – Belle belittled her husband and brought home men for sex.

On 6 December 1906, Crippen began an affair with his secretary, Ethel Le Neve, more than 20 years his junior. Unable to stand Cora's behaviour any longer, Crippen poisoned her with hyoscine after a dinner party, which finished at 1.30am on Tuesday 1 February 1910. This is the only time hyoscine or, more correctly, hydrobromide of hyoscine, has been used to commit murder. Crippen buried the body in the cellar here and told his wife's friends that she had gone abroad. Later, he informed them she had died, on 23 March 1910, of pneumonia while travelling in California and had been cremated. Suspicious, the friends went to Inspector Walter Dew at Scotland Yard. At 10am on Friday 8 July 1910 Dew interviewed Crippen and his "housekeeper" Le Neve. Crippen said that his wife had left him for another man but he had been too embarrassed to admit this so he had said that she had died. Dew accepted the story but he did wonder why she had left much of her wardrobe behind and why Le Neve was wearing one of Mrs Crippen's brooches.

Thinking the jig was up, Crippen and Le Neve decided to flee the country. On the Monday morning Dew returned to Hilldrop Crescent and found the house deserted. A thorough police search uncovered

WHERE:
39 Hilldrop Crescent, Camden Road, London, England
WHEN:
1.30am, Tuesday 1 February 1910
THE AFTERMATH:
Dr Crippen was tried at the Old Bailey on 18 October, and four days later the jury took 27 minutes to convict him and he was sentenced to death; his petition for a reprieve was rejected by Winston Churchill. On 25 October, Le Neve was tried before the same judge, Lord Chief Justice Lord Alverstone, and acquitted. The night before his execution Crippen attempted to cheat the gallows by committing suicide but was foiled by a vigilant warder, who discovered that Crippen had removed an arm from his glasses, intending to cut himself with it and bleed to death. His last request, which was granted, was to die with a photo of Le Neve and letters from her in his coffin. John Ellis, a village barber who was an executioner in his spare time, hanged him in Pentonville Prison at 9am on 23 November 1910. In his memoirs, Ellis recalled, "I could see him smiling as he approached, and the smile never left his face up to the moment when I threw the white cap over it and blotted out God's light from his eyes forever." On the same day Ethel Le Neve, under the alias Miss Allen, boarded a ship for America. The Crippen house was destroyed in a German air raid on 8 September 1940. Ethel Le Neve died at Dulwich Hospital, London on 9 August 1967.

human remains in the cellar although, Mrs Crippen's head and limbs were never recovered. It was the first important case of Dr Bernard Spilsbury who was to become a legendary Home Office pathologist whose word (on more occasions than he would ever admit, wrong) could send a person to the gallows. Dew immediately issued descriptions of Crippen and Le Neve. The pair had fled to Antwerp in Belgium, where on 20 July they boarded the steamship SS *Montrose*, bound for Canada. Crippen had shaved off his moustache, Ethel had cropped her hair and bought boys' clothing, and they were posing as John Philo Robinson and his 16-year-old son, who was supposedly ill and travelling to Quebec for his health. Captain Henry Kendall, the 36-year-old skipper of the Montrose, recognized Crippen from a newspaper photograph and telegraphed the ship's owners, who in turn contacted Scotland Yard. Captain Kendall befriended the Robinsons and noted that Mr Robinson was reading *The Four Just Men*, the thriller by Edgar Wallace. On 23 July Dew set sail for Quebec on a faster ship, the SS *Laurentic*. At 9am on 31 July Dew, dressed as a pilot, boarded the *Montrose* from the pilot's launch and arrested Crippen and Le Neve, who fainted.

Thomas Jennings

"The circumstances of the...conviction were dramatic enough to furnish the 'big scene' in a sensational novel"

THE CRIME: The first murder in America solved by fingerprints occurred shortly after 2am on 19 September 1910 when Clarence B. Hiller and his wife were awoken by a strange noise. Mr Hiller got out of bed and, telling his wife to be quiet, went to investigate. At the top of the stairs he spotted a shadowy figure. He called out and rushed at the figure. Overbalancing, both men fell head first down the staircase. As they fell, two shots rang out and Mr Hiller was killed. The dark-clad figure fled into the night. Less than 1.5 km (1 mi) away, four off-duty policemen were waiting for a streetcar to take them home when they spotted a man acting suspiciously. They went to investigate and found a loaded pistol in his pocket and fresh bloodstains on his clothes. They immediately arrested the man and took him to the police station where he was identified as Thomas Jennings. At the station the police were told about the murder of Clarence B. Hiller. Investigating officers found four fingerprints in fresh paint, which matched Jennings's fingerprints with 33 points of identity, and Jennings's revolver cartridges were identical to three found beside Mr Hiller's body.

WHERE:
Chicago, Illinois, USA
WHEN:
Monday 19 September 1910
THE AFTERMATH:
Thomas Jennings went on trial charged with the murder of Clarence B. Hiller but the defendant's lawyers insisted that fingerprint evidence was not recognized by the laws of Illinois and should therefore be excluded from the proceedings. The judge disagreed and allowed the evidence. Jennings was found guilty and sentenced to death. His lawyers appealed again, objecting to the inclusion of the fingerprints. On 21 December 1911, after considerable legal wrangling, the Supreme Court of Illinois approved the legality of fingerprint evidence and the death sentence was upheld. *The Chicago Daily Tribune* stated: "The circumstances of the Negro's conviction were dramatic enough to furnish the 'big scene' in a sensational novel."

Stinie Morrison

"I decline such mercy!"

WHERE:
Clapham Common, London, England
WHEN:
Sunday 1 January 1911
THE AFTERMATH:
On 27 March 1911 the Court of Appeal upheld the death penalty due to be carried out at 9am on 20 April but Home Secretary Winston Churchill commuted the sentence to life in prison on 12 April. Morrison had a death wish and went on hunger strikes. He died on 24 January 1921 in Parkhurst Prison after being weakened by a lack of food.
YOU SHOULD KNOW:
The newspapers made great play of the "S" on Mr Beron's cheeks. They were said to stand for Spy but Mr Justice Darling said, "Anyone who sees the letter 'S' in either of these scratches has either better eyes or a more vivid imagination than I can possibly claim to possess."

A crowd gathers at Clapham Common where the body of Leon Beron was found.

THE CRIME: Leon Beron was born at Gulvaki, Poland on 17 April 1863 but his family left the following year and landed in Paris. In 1894 he moved to London where he bought nine ramshackle houses in Stepney in the East End. He rented them out for ten shillings a week and lived off the rental income. Despite his property portfolio Beron did not own a home and rented a room above a fruit shop at 133 Jubilee Street, Stepney, paying two shillings a week. Mr Beron was a man of habit – each day he spent one and sixpence on a meal at the Warsaw Kosher Restaurant at 32 Osborne Street, Whitechapel. He dressed smartly, a large gold watch and chain dangled from his waistcoat, and his beard was trimmed neatly. In December 1910 he met another Russian Jew, Stinie Morrison, who had come to England in 1898. Morrison was a convicted thief with five terms for burglary behind him and a penchant for using false names. He had been released on license from Dartmoor on 17 September 1910.

At 8.10am on New Year's Day 1911 PC Joseph Mumford discovered the body of Mr Beron, then 48, beneath some furze bushes on Clapham Common. There was a horseshoe-shaped wound on his head, he had been stabbed three times, his wallet emptied and his legs crossed, right over left. An "S" was apparently carved into each cheek "like the f holes on a violin". On 8 January Morrison was arrested as he ate breakfast at Cohen's Restaurant in Fieldgate Street. The police discovered that on the day of Mr Beron's murder, Morrison had left a pistol and more than 40 rounds of ammunition in the left luggage office of St Mary's Railway Station, Whitechapel. He had left his home to move in with Florrie Dellow, a 22-year-old prostitute from 116 York Road, Lambeth. He had informed his landlady, Mrs Zimmerman, that he was moving to Paris. Morrison claimed that he had not murdered Mr Beron and had spent the night at the Shoreditch Empire

watching Harry Champion and Harry Lauder. However, three hansom-cab drivers recognized his photograph in the newspapers and placed Morrison at the crime scene. His trial began at the Old Bailey at 10.30am on 6 March 1911 and the result, after nine days, was a guilty verdict. The jury had deliberated for only 35 minutes. When Mr Justice Darling passed the death sentence he finished with the words, "And may the Lord have mercy on your soul". Morrison yelled back, "I decline such mercy! I do not believe there is a God."

Fitzhugh Coyle Goldsborough

"I could have won against two bullets, but not against six"

THE CRIME: David Graham Phillips was born on 31 October 1867 in Madison, Indiana. After a career as a journalist, in 1901 he became a successful novelist with the publication of *The Great God Success*. His regimented attitude to work would have put modern writers to shame. Each day he worked at his desk until the early hours and then rose late. He wrote 6,000 words a day. He once said, "If I were to die tomorrow, I would be six years ahead of the game." Mr Phillips lived with his sister, Carolyn Frevert, in the National Arts Club on the south side of Gramercy Park in New York.

On 23 January 1911 he got up late as usual and got dressed in the affected style of a dandy, topped off with a black alpine hat. He set off for his club, the Princeton, to collect his post. He walked eastward on 21st Street when a man stood in front of him with a .32 calibre automatic pistol. The man fired six times and Mr Phillips slumped onto the railings outside the club, where florist John Jacoby caught him before he hit the ground.

The attacker cried out, "There you are! I guess that does for you" before pointing the gun at his own head, saying "I'll finish the job now" and killing himself. Newton James and Frank Davis, two members of the Princeton Club, and Mr Jacoby carried Mr Phillips inside where they put him on a sofa in the foyer. The novelist was taken to Bellevue Hospital. Examination revealed that one of the bullets had punctured a lung, another had missed the vital organs but the rest had hit the left forearm, both thighs and the right hip. An operation removed the bullet that remained in his body and doctors declared the prognosis good.

WHERE:
21st Street, New York City, USA
WHEN:
Monday 23 January 1911
THE AFTERMATH:
After the operation Mr Phillips told his sister that he had received anonymous threatening letters and telephone calls. One sent just before the shooting read, "This is your last day." The novelist's condition worsened on 24 January and he suffered internal haemorrhages in his stomach and lung. Just before he lapsed into a coma, he said, "I could have won against two bullets, but not against six." He died at 11.10pm. In the killer's pocket was an envelope which identified him as 31-year-old Fitzhugh Coyle Goldsborough, a paranoid, deranged music teacher and socialist, who had moved into the Rand School of Social Science on East 19th Street on 2 November 1910. It was thought that Goldsborough had taken grave offence at Margaret Severence, a character in one of the novelist's books *The Fashionable Adventures Of Joshua Craig*, and assumed it was a character assassination of his sister. However, Goldsborough's family blamed the murder and suicide on a bad case of the flu.
YOU SHOULD KNOW:
Goldsborough's younger brother had been committed to a lunatic asylum in Washington not long before the murder.

*Corrupt policeman,
Charles Becker*

Charles Becker

"The crookedest cop who ever stood behind a shield"

THE CRIME: We expect policemen to adhere to a higher standard than the rest of us and never more so was this true than in the earlier part of the last century. Charles Becker (born 26 July 1870) was a member of the New York Police Department – he was also corrupt but this did not stop his rise to become personal assistant to Commissioner Rhinelander Waldo in 1911. He used his position to extort money from politicians and gangsters to cover up their misdemeanours. Herman "Beansie" Rosenthal was a bookmaker and an ally of Becker. Together they owned the Hesper Club but, when Becker demanded an increase in his cut, Rosenthal balked. Becker took revenge by closing the club and putting his former partner under constant surveillance.

Eventually, it became too much for Rosenthal and he went to see District Attorney Charles Whitman who was determined to clean up the city in general and the police department in particular. Rosenthal also began speaking to reporters about the corruption in the police force and threatened to name names. On 15 July 1912 he was shot dead outside the Metropole Hotel by a number of gunmen. District Attorney Whitman offered immunity to anyone who would testify. When "Billiard Ball" Jack Rose (so-called because of his bald pate) was jailed and realized that Becker was not going to come to his rescue he agreed to testify. He said he had been asked by Becker to hire four men to kill Rosenthal. Becker was arrested on 29 July 1912 and went on trial on 7 October 1912 along with six other men. Becker was convicted on 30 October and sentenced to death. However, his appeal was successful because it was revealed that District Attorney Whitman had offered inducements to witnesses. The second trial opened on 2 May 1914 after the four gunmen had been put to death and "Billiard Ball" Jack Rose had been given immunity. Becker was again sentenced to death on 22 May.

WHERE:
Metropole Hotel, 147 West 43rd Street, New York City, USA
WHEN:
Monday 15 July 1912
THE AFTERMATH:
Charles Becker, "the crookedest cop who ever stood behind a shield", was electrocuted at Sing Sing at 5.53am on 30 July 1915. It took nine minutes and three separate bursts of electricity before Becker died, thanks to the incompetence of the electrocutioner. By this time Charles Whitman was New York's governor and unlikely to grant clemency. In a final irony, the hearse carrying Becker's remains broke down when its engine overheated.
YOU SHOULD KNOW:
Becker's widow had a silver plate attached to his coffin bearing the inscription, "Charles Becker, Murdered July 30 1915 by Governor Whitman".

Henriette Caillaux

"The gun went off accidentally"

THE CRIME: Henriette Raynouard was born in France in 1874 and began an affair with married former prime minister Joseph Caillaux. On 31 October 1911, when he had finally divorced his wife, they married. Three years later, in early 1914, the world was nearing the precipice that would lead to the First World War and tensions were high in many countries. Joseph Caillaux was appointed Minister of Finance but his was not a popular appointment and he was heavily criticized especially in *Le Figaro*, edited by Gaston Calmette. Calmette accused the politician of being a traitor and a womanizer. He published a letter, written in 1901, which seemed to infer a certain amount of hypocrisy by Caillaux when it came to a proposed new income tax bill. It looked as if the scandal could engulf Caillaux and forced his resignation from public life. On 16 March 1914 the newspaper published a letter from Caillaux to his former wife. It was too much for the current Madame Caillaux and, that afternoon, she ordered her chauffeur to drive her to the offices of *Le Figaro*. When she learned that the editor was not there she sat down to wait. When Calmette appeared at 6pm, he invited her into his office. She pulled out her Browning revolver and shot him four times in the chest. He died of his wounds at midnight in hospital at Neuilly. When the police arrived Caillaux told them that she would go to the police station in her own car, not theirs. They agreed.

WHERE:
26 Rue Druot, Paris, France
WHEN:
Monday 16 March 1914

THE AFTERMATH:
The case became a cause célèbre in France. Public opinion swung against Caillaux and then in her favour. By the time the case came to trial on 20 July the turmoil in Europe was even greater, following the assassination of Franz Ferdinand (see page 295). The leading lawyer Fernand-Gustave-Gaston Labori defended her and insisted that the crime was not premeditated and that as a woman Caillaux was unable to control her emotions in the way a man would. She said that "in the presence of the monster who had ruined our lives... the gun went off accidentally". On 28 July 1914 she was acquitted after the all-male jury deliberated for 55 minutes. She died in January 1943, never mentioning the case again.

YOU SHOULD KNOW:
The case did not affect the political career of Joseph Caillaux until he was charged with the very crime Calmette had accused him of – treason. He was sentenced to two years in jail.

The front cover of a Parisian journal shows an artist's impression of Madame Caillaux shooting Gaston Calmette.

Arthur Warren Waite

Mr Peck was given samples of typhoid, pneumonia and diphtheria in his desserts

WHERE:
435 Riverside Drive, New York City, USA
WHEN:
Sunday 30 January 1916
THE AFTERMATH:
Waite claimed to be insane at his trial, saying that he had been told to kill his in-laws by an Ancient Egyptian but that defence was disbelieved and he died in the electric chair at Sing Sing on 24 May 1917.
YOU SHOULD KNOW:
An autopsy on Waite revealed that he had slight meningitis on one side of the brain and an abnormally large heart.

THE CRIME: Arthur Warren Waite was a successful New York dentist, with a wealthy heiress wife Jane Peck, whom he had married in September 1915 but had known since childhood, and a Riverside Drive home on the Upper West Side. As well as his dentistry practice, Waite also worked as a bacteriologist at Cornell Medical School. In December 1915 his septuagenarian mother-in-law Hannah Peck came to stay for Christmas. During her stay she fell ill and died of pneumonia on 30 January 1916. John Peck was stricken with grief and he came to stay with his daughter and son-in-law. He, too, became sick and, after suffering various ailments, he died on 12 March. Waite arranged his father-in-law's funeral and rang an undertaker to sort out a cremation.

Things changed when the authorities demanded an autopsy. It revealed that the real cause of death was arsenic poisoning. Waite fled and attempted to kill himself with a drug overdose. When he recovered he was put on trial and confessed to both murders. He had killed Mrs Peck by putting germs from his research lab into her food after having tried various methods to kill her. These included taking her out in a car in the rain with all the windows open, putting glass in her marmalade and spraying her throat with cultures of anthrax, diphtheria and influenza. Mr Peck had been given samples of typhoid, pneumonia and diphtheria in his desserts before Waite used a massive dose of arsenic. His reason was simple – he wanted their money.

Arthur Waite at the courthouse in New York

Robert Franklin Stroud

"[Stroud] was a jerk. He was a guy that thrived on chaos"

THE CRIME: Robert Stroud – better known as the Bird Man of Alcatraz – was in prison for killing F.K. Van Dahmer in Juneau, Alaska when he committed his second murder. On 26 March 1916 he stabbed to death prison warder Andrew Turner in front of 1,200 witnesses in the mess hall after Warder Turner upbraided Stroud for a minor rule infraction. Stroud was tried and sentenced to die on 27 May but, after three trials and four years, his sentence was commuted to life imprisonment after his mother appealed to President Woodrow Wilson.

Stroud was to spend the rest of his life – 42 years –in solitary confinement. It was his feathered friends who helped him come to terms with the loneliness. In June 1920 he began by adopting three injured sparrows and eventually he was given an extra cell and plenty of equipment. He became an expert ornithologist. In 1933 he published an authoritative work on canary diseases and nine years later a book on all birds' maladies, entitled *Stroud's Digest On The Diseases Of Birds*. On 19 December 1942 he was moved from Leavenworth to the fortress island of Alcatraz where the conditions were harsher but he continued his interest in birds although he never actually kept any there. He went on to compile a history of the US Bureau of Prisons but the authorities refused to publish it.

A fictionalized film was made of Stroud's story starring Burt Lancaster in 1962. One of the killer's fellow inmates was asked if the cinematic portrayal was accurate. It wasn't, he said, Stroud "was a jerk. He was a guy that thrived on chaos."

Robert Stroud was the Bird Man of Alcatraz.

WHERE:
US Penitentiary Leavenworth, Kansas, USA
WHEN:
Sunday 26 March 1916
THE AFTERMATH:
In 1959 Robert Stroud was transferred to the Federal Medical Center at Springfield, Missouri where he died on 21 November 1963. Stroud was 73 and had spent 56 of those years behind bars.
YOU SHOULD KNOW:
From his cell Stroud ran a successful business selling patent medicines and appropriately caged birds. One of his customers was J. Edgar Hoover.

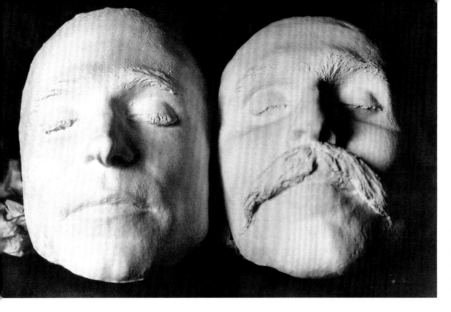

The death masks of Sacco and Vanzetti

Nicola Sacco & Bartolomeo Vanzetti

"Viva l'anarchia!"

THE CRIME: The Italian anarchists who became a cause célèbre when they were executed for murder in 1927, Ferdinando Nicola Sacco and Bartolomeo Vanzetti were both Italian immigrants who arrived in the United States in 1908. They did not meet till 1917, when they became involved in anarchist politics, joining the terrorist organization the Galleanists who would later be suspected of the September 1920 bombing of Wall Street, an atrocity that killed more than 30.

On the afternoon of 15 April 1920 the Slater-Morrill Shoe Company in South Braintree, Massachusetts was robbed of its $15,776.51 payroll. Paymaster Frederick Parmenter and security guard Alessandro Berardelli were both killed during the raid. On 5 May Sacco and Vanzetti were arrested as they collected a vehicle police thought was a getaway car. Two other anarchists escaped. Vanzetti, who was carrying a gun, was tried and convicted of a robbery at Bridgewater, Massachusetts in 1919. He was sentenced to 12 – 15 years in jail and was unhappy with his legal representation James Vahey, whom he claimed, "sold me for 30 golden money like Judas sold Jesus Christ".

Then Sacco and Vanzetti appeared in court at Dedham, Massachusetts where they were tried and convicted of the payroll murders. Vanzetti was found to be carrying a revolver, which the prosecution alleged that it had been taken from the murdered security guard. The anarchist claimed that he had the gun for protection. In apparent attempts to avoid deportation as anarchists, they lied to the police, and this would weigh heavily against them at their trial. In fact, it was to be a fatal error. There has much been much criticism of their trial. Many believe that Judge Webster Thayer was biased and determined to achieve guilty verdicts.

WHERE:
Pearl Street, South Braintree, Massachusetts, USA

WHEN:
3pm Thursday 15 April 1920

THE AFTERMATH:
After a number of appeals – the last on 8 April – failed Sacco and Vanzetti were electrocuted on 23 August 1927. Both men refused to receive the Last Rites. Sacco's final words were *"Viva l'anarchia!"* and *"Farewell, mia madre"*. Vanzetti shook hands with the prison warders, thanked them for their kindness, made a statement affirming his innocence, and said, "I wish to forgive some people for what they are now doing to me." On 23 August 1977, the 50th anniversary of their execution, Massachusetts Governor and future US Presidential candidate Michael Dukakis signed a proclamation, which declared, "Any stigma and disgrace should be forever removed from the names of Nicola Sacco and Bartolomeo Vanzetti. We are not here to say whether these men are guilty or innocent. We are here to say that the high standards of justice, which we in Massachusetts take such pride in, failed Sacco and Vanzetti."

YOU SHOULD KNOW:
The Galleanists' reputation for launching terrorist attacks meant that the courtroom at Dedham was fitted with cast-iron bombproof shutters.

Herbert Armstrong

"Scuse fingers"

THE CRIME: In early 1921 Katherine Armstrong, the wife of solicitor Major Herbert Armstrong, fell ill with vomiting, pains and muscular spasms but seemed to rally. On 16 February she was ill again after lunch and took to her bed, never to leave it. Two days later her arms and legs became paralysed. On the morning of 22 February she said to her nurse Eva Allen, "I'm not going to die, am I? Because I have everything to live for – my children and my husband." At 8am the major was summoned to his wife's bedside and was joined by family doctor Tom Hincks. Realizing that nothing could be done, the doctor drove the major into town and 15 minutes later Mrs Armstrong died. The burial took place on 25 February 1921. Dr Hincks continued to be puzzled by Mrs Armstrong's conflicting symptoms and wrote on her death certificate that she had died of heart disease arising from nephritis and gastritis.

No more was thought of the case until 26 October, when Armstrong invited rival solicitor Oswald Martin to tea and handed him a buttered scone with the words, "Scuse fingers." When he got home Martin was violently sick for five days, much to the puzzlement of Dr Hincks. Martin's father-in-law was the town's chief chemist and he told the doctor that Armstrong had been buying large quantities of arsenic from his shop. They had a sample of Martin's urine analyzed and it was found to contain arsenic. On 31 December Armstrong was arrested for the attempted murder of Oswald Martin. When he was searched he was found to have a packet of arsenic in his pocket and another packet in his desk drawer. When his wife's body was exhumed and found to contain the poison the charge was changed to one of murder.

WHERE:
Mayfield, Cusop, Hay-on-Wye, Wales
WHEN:
9.10am Wednesday 22 February 1922
THE AFTERMATH:
Pathologist Sir Bernard Spilsbury was the expert witness at Armstrong's trial, which opened on 3 April 1922. Armstrong claimed that he had bought the arsenic to kill dandelions. The jury did not believe him and he was sentenced to death, going to the gallows on 31 May 1922.
YOU SHOULD KNOW:
On 9 November 1920 – 109 days before Katherine Armstrong died – Harold Greenwood, another Welsh solicitor, had been acquitted of poisoning his wife. Coincidence or inspiration?

The body of Katherine Armstrong is exhumed.

Leopold & Loeb

"If I were not positive my glasses were at home, I would say those are mine"

WHERE:
South Side, Kenwood, Chicago, USA
WHEN:
Wednesday 21 May 1924

THE AFTERMATH:
Leopold and Loeb went on trial at the Criminal Court of Cook County on 21 July 1924 before Judge John R. Calverly, and Clarence Darrow defended them. Mr Darrow was unable to say that the Leopold and Loeb were homosexual lovers because of the social mores of the time and for fear of alienating the jury further. Leopold was also a paranoiac while Loeb was schizophrenic. The defence speech lasted for two days and saved his clients from the electric chair. They were both sentenced to life with 99 years for the kidnapping. On 28 January 1936 Loeb's throat was slashed from behind in the Joliet Prison shower. His murderer James E. Day claimed that Loeb had sexually assaulted him. Leopold was released from prison in 1958. He died of a diabetes-related heart attack on 29 August 1971.

YOU SHOULD KNOW:
Ed Lahey of the *Chicago Daily News* wrote of Loeb's murder, "Richard Loeb, despite his erudition, today ended his sentence with a proposition."

THE CRIME: Thrill killers Nathan Freudenthal Leopold, Jr, 19, and Richard A. Loeb, 18, killed because they could and because they thought that they were too intelligent to be caught. Both were German-Jewish and both believed in the Nietzschean philosophy of "superman". After carrying out some successful robberies they decided to commit the perfect murder.

In May 1924, while they were studying at the University of Chicago, they kidnapped 14-year-old Bobby Franks, hiring a car to transport away the youngster. He was gagged and his skull was bashed in with a heavy chisel four times. Young Bobby had his head held under the water in a swamp culvert at Wolf Lake in Hammond, Indiana and then the two teens poured hydrochloric acid to disfigure Bobby's face and forced his body into a drainpipe partially hidden by weeds on the Pennsylvania Railroad tracks near 118th Street. After the killing they retired to a restaurant for a hot-dog meal before going to Leopold's home and drinking whisky. They cleaned the car of bloodstains before telephoning Bobby's mother and telling her that he had been kidnapped and to expect a ransom demand and not to call the police. The note, signed George Johnson, duly arrived, demanding $10,000 and stating "Allow us to assure you that he is at present safe and well". Jacob Franks, a millionaire businessman, called the police the next day and was told that the body of a boy had been found. Unbeknown to the killers, Leopold had dropped his glasses by the culvert and it took the police just eight days to trace the spectacles to him. He said, "If I were not positive my glasses were at home, I would say those are mine." However, Leopold was unable to find his glasses at home and was arrested. Soon after Loeb was taken into custody, and police questioned the two until Loeb broke down and confessed. Leopold's confession was not long in following, although both claimed that the other had wielded the chisel.

The spectacles that eventually led to the arrest of Leopold and Loeb.

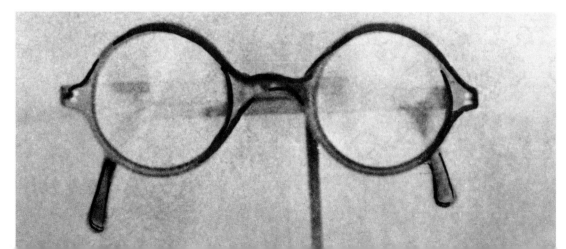

Martin J. Durkin

The first FBI Agent to be killed in the line of duty

THE CRIME: Martin James Durkin was a car thief by profession with links to the underworld. His modus operandi was to steal only top of the range models such as Pierce Arrows, Cadillacs and Packards. On 11 October 1925, when the FBI learned that Durkin was intending to hide a stolen car in a Chicago garage, they authorized 27-year-old Special Agent Edwin J. Shanahan, a five-year veteran of the force and native of Chicago, to capture him. Durkin was also wanted for the attempted murder of four policemen he had shot during previous attempts to arrest him. Special Agent Shanahan and policemen from the Windy City's police force lay in wait at the garage for Durkin to appear. He failed to turn up and it seemed as if the day had been wasted on misinformation. The police had left when Durkin rolled up in the car. Shanahan, who was alone at the time, stepped forward to arrest him but was unaware that Durkin had a revolver on the passenger seat. Durkin shot the G-man in the chest, killing him almost immediately. Edwin Shanahan thus became the first FBI agent to be killed in the line of duty.

WHERE:
Chicago, Illinois, USA
WHEN:
Sunday 11 October 1925
THE AFTERMATH:
On 2 November 1925 police arrived at Durkin's girlfriend's home to arrest him but Durkin murdered Sergeant Harry Gray as he attempted to apprehend him. Durkin was arrested on 20 January 1926 in a railroad carriage near St Louis, Missouri. Durkin was sentenced to 35 years in Joliet Prison for Shanahan's murder and received an additional 15 years on car theft charges. In 1946 he was taken to Leavenworth Federal Prison. Durkin was released from prison on 28 July 1954 and died in 1981.
YOU SHOULD KNOW:
It was not a federal offence to kill a Special Agent of the FBI until 1934, so Durkin was tried in state court for Shanahan's murder.

An artist's impression of one of Durkin's disguises.

165

Ruth Snyder & Judd Gray

"The Granite Woman and the Putty Man"

THE CRIME:
Ruth Snyder was a New York housewife in the 1920s. A former telephonist, she had married Albert Schneider who changed his name to Snyder at her insistence. She was unhappily married but her life changed in 1925 when she was 30 and met Henry Judd Gray, a corset salesman, 13 years older than her. They began an affair and spent much of their time in hotel rooms having sex. Gray was a weak character who referred to his lover as "Momsie".

In 1926 Snyder took out three insurance policies, worth $48,000, on her husband's life. She then decided that she would have to kill him and indeed Albert Snyder had some near escapes: twice he awoke to find the bedroom full of gas and on several occasions he was poisoned by his wife. However, he survived them all. In February 1927 Gray finally agreed to help his lover dispose of her husband.

It was the eighth attempt that finally did for Albert Snyder, on 20 March 1927. Albert was asleep in his bedroom when the couple crept in and Ruth hit him with a heavy sash weight. Albert was stunned and called out for his wife to help him. She responded by hitting him again before pushing a chloroform-soaked cloth onto his nose before the pair garrotted him with picture wire. Then Gray tied up his girlfriend so she could say that a burglar had attacked her.

Ruth Snyder was persistent in her attempts to murder her husband.

WHERE:
Queens Village, New York, USA

WHEN:
Sunday 20 March 1927

THE AFTERMATH:
The police found Gray's name in Sndyer's address book and when they questioned her, they told her that Gray had confessed to murder. She then admitted murder but said that the plot had been all Gray's idea. He, too, confessed but blamed her. The media had a field day, calling the couple "The Granite Woman and the Putty Man". The jury found both defendants guilty of first-degree murder. On 13 May 1927, the judge sentenced both to be executed. They went to the electric chair at Sing Sing on 12 January 1928. Just as Snyder was about to die, Tom Howard, a *Chicago Tribune* photographer working in cooperation with the *Tribune*-owned *New York Daily News* took a picture with a camera he had surreptitiously strapped to his leg.

YOU SHOULD KNOW:
The novel *Double Indemnity* by James M. Cain was inspired by the Snyder-Gray story.

Bath School Disaster

"Children were tossed high in the air; some were catapulted out of the building"

THE CRIME: Bath Township is a small community located 16 km (10 mi) northeast of Lansing, Michigan. In the late spring of 1927 it was the venue for three bombings, which killed 45 people and injured 58. Most of those who died were pupils aged between seven and 12 at Bath Consolidated School. It was the deadliest act of mass murder in an American school.

That morning school treasurer Andrew Philip Kehoe, who had money worries thanks to a property tax that led to foreclosure proceedings against his farm, murdered his 52-year-old tubercular wife, Ellen "Nellie" Price, by hitting her over the head. He then dumped her body in a wheelbarrow by the hen house. At 8.45am he set fire to his home, ensuring the animals were tethered so they would all burn to death. He had placed explosives at the farm to ensure maximum damage.

As firemen arrived at the farm the north wing of the school building was destroyed in an explosion at 9.45am. Kehoe had over the previous few months planted explosives in and around the school building. Teacher Bernice Sterling said, "After the first shock I thought for a moment I was blind. When it came the air seemed to be full of children and flying desks and books. Children were tossed high in the air; some were catapulted out of the building." People rushed towards the north wing to help as Kehoe drove up in his car at 10.15am. He had filled the car with metal tools, nails, rusty farm implements and explosives. He detonated the car, killing himself and the school superintendent, Emory E. Huyck, 33, and murdering and injuring several others. Thirteen ambulances were at the school by the afternoon to ferry the injured to hospital and remove the remains of the dead. Police found a wooden sign at Kehoe's farm bearing the legend, "Criminals are made, not born."

WHERE:
Bath Township, Michigan, USA
WHEN:
9.45am Wednesday 18 May 1927
THE AFTERMATH:
Search teams found another 227 kg (500 lb) of explosives hidden in the basement of the school's south wing. With it was a timer set for 9.45am but no one knows why it did not work.
YOU SHOULD KNOW:
When he was 14, Kehoe's stepmother accidentally set herself on fire. He watched her burn for several minutes before dousing the flames. She later died of her injuries.

The demolished north wing of Bath Consolidated School

Henry Colin Campbell

"If the defendant was conscious of the nature of his act he cannot be acquitted"

WHERE:
Cranford, New Jersey, USA
WHEN:
Saturday 23 February 1929
THE AFTERMATH:
The murder trial of Henry Colin Campbell began at Elizabeth, New Jersey on 9 June 1929 before Judge Clarence E. Case. Two court-appointed psychologists Dr Gus Payne and Dr Lawrence Collins had examined Campbell and said that he was fit to stand trial despite an addiction to morphine. Campbell did not deny that he had shot Mildred Mowry with the .38 automatic found in his home or that he had burned her body afterwards. His defence was based on a claim of amnesia and he said that he had no memory of having done so.
Prosecutor Abe J. David read Campbell's confession in which he said he had murdered Miss Mowry to cover up his bigamous marriage but also put into evidence 17 letters written by Campbell to his victim. They showed how he had manipulated her, playing on her loneliness, and when she finally discovered where he was he murdered her. Judge Case summed up, "If the defendant was conscious of the nature of his act he cannot be acquitted. The law does not recognize that form of insanity in which the faculties are so affected as to render a person suffering from it unable to control those urges." On 13 June the jury found Campbell guilty of murder and he was sentenced to death. On 17 April 1930 he was electrocuted.

THE CRIME: Henry Colin Campbell was a career criminal. On 23 February 1929 police found next to a motorway in Cranford, New Jersey, the burnt body of a woman who had been shot in the head. It was six weeks before the remains were identified as Mildred Mowry, a local woman, who had gone missing at the start of the month after joining a lonely hearts' agency. Investigators discovered that in August 1928 Mildred had married 60-year-old Dr Richard Campbell who had disappeared to California with her life savings of $1,000. Her increasingly desperate letters went unanswered probably because "Dr Richard Campbell" was not in the Golden State but much closer to home in Elizabeth, New Jersey, where he was living with his real wife, Rosalie, and his family, under his true name Henry Colin Campbell. When the lack of replies finally got to her, Mildred decided to look for her errant spouse. Then she vanished. The police finally tracked Cambell down on 11 April 1929 when he was arrested for murder.

Jewellery taken from the victim's body.

Fred Burke

Burke fired three times at the policeman who died later in hospital

THE CRIME: Born as Thomas Camp on a farm near Mapleton, Kansas on 29 May 1893, Fred Burke was an armed robber and contract killer and was a prime suspect for the St Valentine's Day Massacre (see page 328). He had his first clash with the law in 1910 when he was 17 and five years later he joined the Egan's Rats gang. He joined the US Army and served as a tank sergeant in France. When he returned to America Burke was arrested for land fraud and sentenced to a year in prison. On 3 July 1923 he and some gang members robbed $38,000 from the United Railways office. On 28 March 1927 he murdered three thugs who had killed his friend in what became known as the Milaflores Massacre.

Eleven days before Christmas 1929 Burke was involved in a car crash at St Joseph, Michigan, while drunk. The other driver George Kool, a farmer, demanded money to repair his bumper but when the police arrived Burke fled. Patrolman Charles Skelly jumped on the running board of Mr Kool's car and ordered him to follow Burke. Burke fired three times at the policeman who died later in hospital.

Burke fled south on Highway 12 where his car was later found in a ditch. Documents in the car identified the owner as "Fred Dane", an oilman. When the police raided Burke's bungalow they discovered a bulletproof vest, two sawn-off shotguns, two Thompson submachine guns – a 21AC model and a 21A – pistols, thousands of rounds of ammunition and stolen bank bonds. Burke was named as America's most wanted man and went on the run.

WHERE:
St Joseph, Michigan, USA
WHEN:
Saturday 14 December 1929
THE AFTERMATH:
Burke was arrested on 26 March 1931 at a farm near Green City, Missouri, after an amateur detective recognized him from a *True Detective Mysteries* magazine. Tried and convicted, he was sentenced to life in prison. He died aged 47 on 10 July 1940 in prison from heart disease.

Winnie Ruth Judd

"I've asked God many times to forgive me"

THE CRIME: Known as The Tiger Woman, Winnie Ruth Judd (born 29 January 1905) was convicted of the Phoenix Trunk Murders in 1931. She worked with her husband, Dr William Judd, in his medical centre in Phoenix, Arizona, where she became friends with Agnes Le Roi, 27, and Hedvig Samuelson who shared a flat. On 16 October 1931 there was a shooting at the flat and the next day Miss Le Roi did not turn up for work and Judd was late for work.

Later that day Judd telephoned a removals firm to arrange for a large trunk to be shipped. On 18 October she boarded a train bound for Los Angeles, accompanied by two trunks. As porters carried the trunks off the train at Union Central Station in Los Angeles, it was noticed that one was leaking a dark liquid. Judd was asked to explain but instead fled. When the trunks were opened they were found to contain the dismembered bodies of Agnes Le Roi and Hedvig Samuelson. Police found a letter from Judd to her husband. The letter detailed all sorts of sex orgies that had taken place in the Le Roi-Samuelson home, orgies that featured every kind of sexual coupling. On 23 October, after an appeal by her husband, Judd gave herself up to police.

WHERE:
Phoenix, Arizona, USA
WHEN:
Friday 16 October 1931
THE AFTERMATH:
Judd claimed that she had been visiting her friends when Miss Samuelson had pulled a gun. As she tried to disarm her, Judd shot both women. In fact, she had murdered them both in a fit of jealousy and then shot herself in the hand to substantiate her alibi about her story. She was taken back to Arizona where she stood trial. She was convicted and sentenced to death but that was commuted to life imprisonment on 24 April 1933 after psychiatrists said that she was mad. She stayed in the public eye because she escaped from prison seven times. Her last escape came in 1962 and she stayed on the run for seven years during which time she worked as a housekeeper in Concord, Massachusetts. Finally released in 22 December 1971, she died on 23 October 1998, aged 95.
YOU SHOULD KNOW:
She said, "I've asked God many times to forgive me."

Winnie Judd surrenders to the Los Angeles police.

Giuseppe Zangara

"I'm glad it was me instead of you"

THE CRIME: Sometimes people are just in the wrong place at the wrong time. Such was the case with Tony Cermak, the mayor of Chicago, Illinois, who was elected in 1931. An Austro-Hungarian immigrant, he arrived in America with his parents when he was around a year old. In 1902 he joined the Illinois state legislature and gradually rose up the political greasy pole until 1928 when he lost a race for the US Senate to Republican Otis F. Glenn. Three years later, he was running Chicago during the Great Depression, thanks in part to his wooing of the city's large immigrant population. On 6 April 1931, he beat the corrupt "Big Bill" Thompson to City Hall. Thompson had resorted to deliberately mispronouncing his rival's name. "He doesn't like my name... it's true I didn't come over on the *Mayflower*, but I came over as soon as I could," he responded.

Mayor Cermak's win ended the Republican stronghold in Chicago. His administration was beset by financial problems. On 15 February 1933 President-Elect Franklin D. Roosevelt was visiting Miami and was shaking hands with Mayor Cermak, also on a visit to Miami, when Giuseppe Zangara attempted to shoot him. Instead the bullets hit the mayor in the lung. As he was taken to hospital Mayor Cermak is supposed to have told the President-Elect, "I'm glad it was me instead of you" although the historical authenticity of this is doubted by many authorities.

WHERE:
Bayfront Park, Miami, Florida, USA
WHEN:
Wednesday 15 February 1933
THE AFTERMATH:
Mayor Cermak died of peritonitis on 6 March 1933. He was buried at the Bohemian National Cemetery in Chicago. Zangara pleaded guilty to murder and was sentenced to death. He then said, "You give me electric chair. I no afraid of that chair! You one of capitalists. You is crook man too. Put me in electric chair. I no care!" A fortnight after Mayor Cermak died Zangara was executed in the electric chair at Florida State Penitentiary in Raiford, Florida.
YOU SHOULD KNOW:
A plaque honouring the mayor stands at the murder site at Bayfront Park. It bears the legend, "I'm glad it was me instead of you."

*Giuseppe Zangara
in custody*

171

Brighton Trunk Murder

"The police? With my record?"

WHERE:
Basement Flat, 44 Park Crescent,
Brighton, England
WHEN:
Thursday 10 May 1934
THE AFTERMATH:
On 28 November 1976 Mancini
confessed to the *News of the World*
that he had murdered Violette Kaye.
They had fought, she attacked him
with the hammer, he wrested it from
her and struck her in the heat of the
moment. The identity of the woman in
the second trunk was never
established.

*Brighton murderer
Tony Mancini*

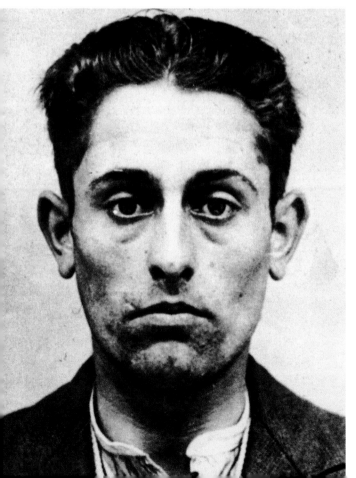

THE CRIME: Dancer turned prostitute Violette Kaye, 42, began a relationship with Tony Mancini, a waiter and petty thief 16 years her junior, whose real name was Cecil Lois England. She and Mancini lived together in a basement flat at 44 Park Crescent, Brighton. Mancini later claimed that she had stormed out after an argument on 10 May 1934, and had gone to work in Paris. However, on or about that day Violette was murdered and her body put into a trunk in the basement at 52 Kemp Street, Brighton, Mancini's new lodgings, along with the rest of Mancini's possessions on 14 May.

By coincidence, a trunk was deposited at Brighton station early in June and when it was opened on 17 June it was found to contain the torso of a woman, aged about 30, who was five months pregnant. Her legs were found the next day at the left luggage office at King's Cross station in London. Police began making house-to-house searches relating to the first trunk when they came across Violette. Painters had complained of the appalling smell emanating from number 52. The police broke into the basement and the trunk was opened on 15 July. Mancini was arrested two days later at Blackheath in southeast London. Violette's skull had been fractured and the Crown alleged that a hammer found at Park Crescent had been the murder weapon. The trial opened at Lewes Assizes on 10 December 1934 and J.D. Cassels, KC, and Quintin Hogg led for the prosecution. Norman Birkett, KC, and John Flowers, KC, defended Mancini who claimed he had come home from work at the Skylark Café to find his girlfriend dead "… she was on the bed… blood all over the sheets… I got frightened". Pathologist Dr Roche Lynch confirmed that there was morphine in Violette's body. Pathologist Sir Bernard Spilsbury admitted that a skull fracture from a fall would be indistinguishable from one from a blow. Birkett suggested that someone high on drink or drugs could have fallen down the steep stairs to the basement flat. Asked why he had not called the police when he found Violette, Mancini replied, "The police? With my record?" He suggested Violette might have been murdered by a client. After two and a half hours' deliberation the jury returned a verdict of not guilty.

Rattenbury & Stoner

"If I only thought it would help Stoner I would stay on"

Mr and Mrs Rattenbury and their son, John, accompanied by John's nanny.

THE CRIME: Randy woman marries a man 29 years older who drinks too much and she takes young lover. Young lover bashes in husband's head and both stand trial for murder. That was the scene that gripped puritanical, class-conscious Britain in the 1930s.

Yorkshire-born Francis Mawson Rattenbury was a distinguished architect who was living in Canada when, on 29 December 1923, he met Alma Pakenham, a divorcée with one son. They married in April 1925 and returned to England four years later. On 25 September 1934 they advertised in the *Bournemouth Daily Echo* for a "Daily willing lad, 14-18, for house-work; Scout-trained preferred". George Stoner applied for the job and began work. Two months later, on 22 November, he and Alma had sex for the first time.

Francis Rattenbury was reclusive, impotent and drank too much. Stoner became jealous if Alma showed any affection to her husband and finally he snapped. On 24 March 1935 Stoner attacked Rattenbury with a wooden mallet in the lounge. The blows were so savage that they removed the back of 67-year-old architect's head. Four days later he died.

Both Stoner and Alma were arrested – she was drunk at the time – and both confessed to the murder. However, when they went on trial at the Old Bailey on 27 May 1935 both pleaded not guilty. Alma was portrayed as an immoral woman who had "ensnared a hapless youth" while Stoner was apparently, "a poor lad cajoled into the vortex of this illicit love". Stoner refused to say anything at the trial other than answer to his name, while Alma put up a robust defence. On 31 May, after the jury deliberated for 50 minutes, Stoner was found guilty of murder and sentenced to death and Alma was released. As she left the Old Bailey, the crowd booed her.

On 4 June Alma Rattenbury took the train to Three Arches Railway Bridge in Christchurch where she stabbed herself six times in the breast with a knife. She left a note, "If I only thought it would help Stoner I would stay on. But it has been pointed out to me too vividly that I cannot help him. That is my death sentence."

WHERE:
Villa Madeira, 5 Manor Road, Bournemouth, England
WHEN:
10.30pm Sunday 24 March 1935
THE AFTERMATH:
After a more than 300,000-strong petition was signed, on 25 June 1935 Stoner was reprieved. He served just seven years in prison before being released in 1942. He served in the Army, fighting on D-Day. He died in Christchurch Hospital on 24 March 2000 aged 83, around 1 km (½ mi) from where Alma died and on the 65th anniversary of Francis's murder. Terence Rattigan's final play *Cause Célèbre* was based on the story. The figurative jury is still out as to who actually wielded the murder weapon that night. Was it Stoner violently jealous of his girlfriend's husband? Or was it the drug-addicted Alma who wanted to get rid of her husband?
YOU SHOULD KNOW:
On 28 September 1990 George Stoner, then 74, was convicted of a sex attack on a 12-year-old boy. He had sat naked in a public lavatory and lured the boy in, before kissing him and pulling his trousers down. The boy fled. Stoner was arrested wearing just a hat, socks and shoes. He was put on probation for two years.

Police hold back the crowds near Strangeways at the time of the execution.

Buck Ruxton

"This publicity is ruining my practice"

THE CRIME: The first murderer trapped by skull and portrait comparisons, Buck Ruxton was born on 21 March 1899 at Bombay as Bukhtyar Rustomji Ratanji Hakim. In 1930 he and his girlfriend Isabella Van Ess (she called herself Mrs Ruxton), 34, moved to 2 Dalton Square, Lancaster, England, where he began to practise as a doctor.

It was a fiery relationship and on more than one occasion the police were called. "We were the kind of people who could not lived with each other and could not live without each other," he said. On 14 September 1935 Isabella drove to Blackpool to look at the illuminations. She left at 11.30pm and was never seen alive again. At 6.30am the next day Ruxton visited his cleaner Agnes Oxley and told her that she did not need to visit the house that day. Ruxton told her and anyone who asked that Isabella and their children's nanny Mary Rogerson, 20, had gone to Edinburgh on holiday. At 11.30am he took the children to a friend's house who noticed that Ruxton's right hand was badly cut. He blamed it on a tin opener. He then asked one of his patients to scrub the staircase and bath at his house in preparation for decorators he said were arriving the next day. On 29 September the dismembered remains of two bodies were found in the River Linn at Gardenholme near Moffat, Scotland. One of the bodies was wrapped in a Lancaster edition of the *Sunday Graphic* and clothes were identified as belonging to the Ruxton household. Rumours began circulating about Ruxton's involvement and he complained to the Chief Constable of Lancaster, "This publicity is ruining my practice." On 13 October Ruxton was charged with murdering Mary Rogerson and on 5 November with Isabella's murder. His trial opened on 2 March 1936. All identifying characteristics had been removed from the bodies but, thanks to the masterful photographic reconstruction by Professor John Glaister, it was proved that the second body was Isabella. Ruxton was found guilty and hanged by Tom Pierrepoint at Strangeways on 12 May 1936.

WHERE:
2 Dalton Square, Lancaster, England
WHEN:
Sunday 15 September 1935
THE AFTERMATH:
It seemed likely that in a fit of jealousy Ruxton murdered Isabella when she returned from Blackpool. Mary saw what he had done so he strangled her, too. The bath in which Ruxton dismembered Isabella and Mary later became a horse trough for the mounted police at Preston.

Rainey Bethea

"I don't like to die with my shoes on"

THE CRIME: Rainey Bethea, 24, arrived in Owensboro, Kentucky in 1933 and soon got on the wrong side of the law. In April 1935 he stole two purses and was sentenced to a year in the state penitentiary. When he was released on 1 December 1935 he returned to Owensboro where a month later, on 6 January 1936, he was arrested for being drunk and disorderly. He was fined $100 but since he was earning just $7 a week he went to prison for three months instead and was released on 18 April.

On a summer's day two months later, Bethea drunkenly broke into the house of Lischia Rarick Edwards, a 70-year-old woman. When she awoke he raped and strangled her. He was caught because he left his prison ring at the scene. Bethea was arrested a week later as he boarded a river barge. The police saved Bethea from being lynched as feelings in Owensboro were running high. Bethea confessed but said that he did not know whether Lischia Edwards was live or dead when he raped her. This was a serious point as in Kentucky in 1936 it was not illegal to have sex with a corpse. The penalty for murder and robbery was death by the electric chair whereas for rape it was death by hanging. In the end Bethea was charged with only rape, not the other crimes. However, according to Kentucky State law, it was the job of the county sheriff to hang condemned criminals but in Owensboro the county sheriff was a woman. Florence Thompson had become sheriff on 13 April 1936 by default after her sheriff husband had died. Local man Arthur L. Hash offered his services. Unfortunately, even though it was sunrise, Hash turned up drunk and stumbled around the scaffold before finally locating the lever that sent Bethea to his doom.

WHERE:
322 East Fifth Street, Owensboro, Kentucky, USA
WHEN:
Sunday 7 June 1936
THE AFTERMATH:
At 5.32am on 14 August 1936 at Owensboro, Rainey Bethea became the last person to be publicly hanged in Kentucky (not America, as is often reported). He had removed his footwear before he ascended the 13 steps to the gallows, "I don't like to die with my shoes on," he said. An estimated 15,000 people turned up at sunrise to watch the farce, expecting to see Florence Thompson become America's first female executioner. Angry newspaper reporters who had invested heavily in the prospect misreported that Florence fainted on the scaffold. It took 15 minutes for Bethea to slowly strangle to death.

A crowd of around 15,000 watch the hanging of Rainey Bethea.

Theodore Edward Coneys

"A man would have to be a spider to stand it long up there"

WHERE:
3335 West Moncrieff Place, Denver, Colorado, USA
WHEN:
Friday 17 October 1941
THE AFTERMATH:
After Detective Fred Zarnow said, "A man would have to be a spider to stand it long up there", the local media dubbed Coneys the "Denver Spider Man of Moncrieff Place". Coneys was tried and convicted and sentenced to life at the Colorado State Penitentiary in Cañon City, Colorado. He was still there when he died on 16 May 1967.

THE CRIME: There is a celebrated story of Allied soldier Trooper Patrick Fowler spending the First World War hidden in a cupboard. Theodore Edward Coneys had a similar tale only he was not so heroic. He was born on 10 November 1882 at Petersburg, Illinois and was a sickly child who was not expected to reach adulthood. He did and became a bookkeeper for Denver Brass Works but, despite full-time employment, was homeless for much of his adult life.

In September 1941 he went to 3335 West Moncrieff Place, Denver, Colorado, the home of Philip Peters, a former friend, to ask to borrow some money. When he discovered that no one was home, he broke in. He hid in the attic, accessed through a small trapdoor, for five weeks undetected until 17 October 1941. That night 73-year-old Mr Peters found Coneys raiding his fridge and naturally took umbrage. Mr Peters struck Coneys with his walking stick and he hit back with an old gun that he had found about the house. Coneys broke the gun on Mr Peter's head and bludgeoned him to death with a heavy, iron stove-shaker. Coneys returned to his attic hideaway. That night Mr Peters's body was discovered by a neighbour.

The police searched the house but found nothing amiss. The doors and windows were locked, and it was assumed the trapdoor was too small for a man to climb through. Mrs Peters, who had been in hospital, returned to the house after her husband's death with a housekeeper. Not long after, both women began hearing strange noises and left, believing the property was haunted. On 30 July 1942 Coneys was caught when the police showed up at the house unexpectedly and spotted his legs disappearing through the trapdoor. He was hauled down and taken to the police station where he confessed to the murder of Philip Peters.

John Christie

10 Rillington Place was home to two stranglers operating independently of each other

THE CRIME: John Reginald Halliday Christie was born on Saturday 8 April 1899 at his parents' home, Black Boy House, near Halifax, England. On 10 May 1920 he married a typist, Ethel Waddington. He spent much of the next few years in and out of prison for theft and, on one occasion, for assault. In 1938 the Christies moved into the

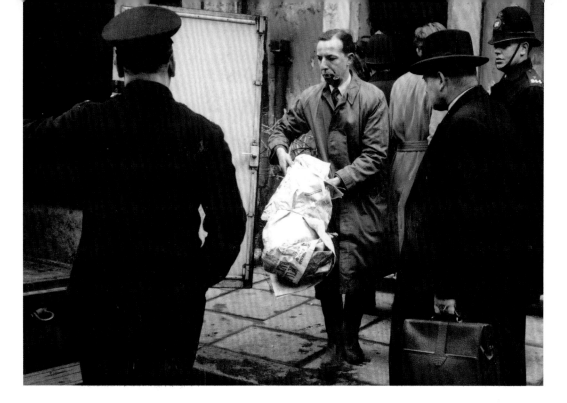

ground-floor flat of 10 Rillington Place in Notting Hill, London, where Christie found work as a clerk. In 1939, despite his criminal record, he became a war reserve policeman and won two commendations. At Easter 1948 an illiterate van driver, Timothy Evans, 23, and his pregnant wife, Beryl, moved into the upstairs flat. In 1949 Beryl found that she was pregnant again, but did not want a second child. She was offered an abortion by Christie. On 8 November Evans was told that the abortion had not been a success and that his wife had died. Christie said that he would dispose of the body and have baby Geraldine adopted but that Evans should leave London. He returned to Wales on 15 November but on 30 November went to the police. Evans told the police different stories and when the bodies of Beryl and Geraldine were discovered he signed a confession, admitting to both murders. Evans was tried at the Old Bailey between 11 and 13 January 1950, convicted and hanged by Albert Pierrepoint at Pentonville on 9 March 1950.

Three years later on 21 March 1953, Christie left Rillington Place. Three days later Beresford Brown, a new tenant, found six bodies in the garden, kitchen and under the sitting-room floor. They were identified as Ruth Fuerst, an Austrian nurse, missing since 1943; Muriel Eady, who had worked with Christie in 1944; Christie's wife, Ethel; and three prostitutes. All had been strangled. Christie was arrested on 31 March and went on trial at the Old Bailey on 22 June charged only with the murder of his wife. He was convicted and hanged at Pentonville on 15 July 1953 also by Albert Pierrepoint.

The bones of Christie's fifth victim are removed from 10 Rillington Place.

WHERE:
Ground Floor Flat, 10 Rillington Place, London, England
WHEN:
1943–1953
THE AFTERMATH:
After Christie went to his death, disquiet was raised over the conviction of Evans. On 18 October 1966 he was granted a posthumous pardon. In 1994, however, a book claimed that Evans was indeed guilty and that 10 Rillington Place was home to two stranglers, operating independently of each other. Rillington Place was renamed as Ruston Close after nearby Ruston Mews, which had taken its name from Ruston Parva, a village in Yorkshire. Ruston Close became a tourist attraction until the 1970s when it was torn down and rebuilt as Bartle Road, most likely after the nearby Bartle James Iron Works.

Patricia and Wayne Lonergan

Wayne Lonergan

The press labelled Lonergan a murderer

THE CRIME: On 23 October 1943 Patricia Lonergan, a 22-year-old socialite and brewery heiress to a $6 million fortune was found naked and dead in her apartment after going to a party. She had been struck with a candlestick and strangled. At the time of her death she was estranged from her husband Wayne Lonergan, a handsome, 1.82 m (6 ft) tall Royal Canadian Air Force aircraftman, three years her senior.

The police contacted his commanding officer and discovered that Lonergan had been on leave in New York during the weekend of his wife's death. He was discovered in Toronto and returned to New York voluntarily. He was interrogated for 84 hours and supposedly confessed to killing his wife during a quarrel. He also spoke of their sex life or lack of one, leading to speculation that Lonergan was homosexual. Unfortunately, much of the interview was leaked to the press, resulting in Lonergan being labelled a murderer before a court had had the chance to try him. At his trial in March 1944 doubt was cast on his confession and, although the police could prove that he was indeed in New York at the time of the killing, they could not prove he had been at the murder scene.

Assistant District Attorney Jacob Grumet testified that Lonergan confessed (the unsigned confession was repudiated by the defendant and his lawyers) to homosexual relations, both before and after his marriage. One of the men involved was said to have been William Burton, Patricia's father, who had set up the younger man in his own apartment and given him money to live on. When Mr Burton died in October 1940 Lonergan moved on to his daughter and they were married on 30 July 1941. Grumet also quoted Lonergan as saying that he derived "a certain amount" of satisfaction from his married life but that his separation from his wife was the result of "mutual boredom". One Manhattan psychiatrist spoke of Lonergan's "financial promiscuity, sexual promiscuity, emotional shallowness". Oddly, given the early press leaks, Judge James Garrett Wallace barred all spectators, except newspapermen, from the court. Lonergan was convicted of second-degree murder on 17 April 1944 and sentenced to 30 years to life in jail.

WHERE:
51st Street, New York City, USA
WHEN:
Saturday 23 October 1943
THE AFTERMATH:
After spending 22 years in Sing Sing, Lonergan was released on 2 December 1965 and deported to Canada.

Neville Heath

Her nipples had been bitten off and a poker had been forced up her vagina

THE CRIME: Born in Ilford, Essex on 6 June 1917 Neville George Clevely Heath joined the Rifle Battalion in 1934, transferring to the RAF two years later but was court-martialled for going AWOL and in September 1937 was dismissed. Not long after he was sent to borstal for housebreaking and forgery. An ignominious war followed and in 1946 he was back in England. On 16 June he moved into the Pembridge Court Hotel in Notting Hill Gate, London and called himself Lieutenant-Colonel Heath. On 20 June he went dancing at the Panama Club in South Kensington with Margery Aimeé Brownell Gardner, a 32-year-old wannabe actress who had left her husband and daughter in Sheffield to seek fame and fortune in London.

The next day at 2pm, her body was found naked on the bed in Heath's room, her wrists and ankles bound. Her nipples had been bitten off and a poker had been forced up her vagina. There were 17 mutilations on her corpse. Heath wrote to the police and told them that he had lent his room to Margery Gardner because she had wanted to have sex with someone and when he returned he found her dead. He moved to Bournemouth and on 23 June took a room at the Tollard Royal Hotel, using the name Group Captain Rupert Brooke. He dined with 21-year-old Doreen Marshall on 3 July 1946 – she was not seen alive again. "Brooke" told the police that he might be able to help with their inquiries into Miss Marshall's disappearance. At the police station he was recognized as Heath and arrested. The police searched his possessions and found a railway cloakroom ticket that lead them to an attaché case containing the whip that had done such damage to Margery Gardner. On 8 July the body of Doreen Marshall was found under a rhododendron bush in Branksome Dean Chine, Bournemouth. She was naked apart from her left shoe, one nipple had been bitten off and her body had been cut open from breastbone to pubis. Her vagina bore lacerations similar to Margery Gardner's.

WHERE:
Room 4, Pembridge Court Hotel, London, England
WHEN:
Friday 21 June 1946
THE AFTERMATH:
The trial of Neville Heath for the murder of Margery Gardner began at the Old Bailey on 24 September 1946. Although Heath pleaded not guilty, the question was one of his sanity at the time of the murders. He was found guilty and sane and sentenced to death. Albert Pierrepoint hanged him on 16 October 1946 at Pentonville Prison. He was 29 years old. Heath had asked Pierrepoint for a whisky, before adding, "Better make it a double."
YOU SHOULD KNOW:
It is thought that Margery Gardner was a masochist who enjoyed being stripped naked and whipped by a man. Unfortunately, in Heath, she picked the wrong man to indulge her passions.

Neville Heath is taken into custody by the police.

James Camb

If Miss Gibson had greeted Camb naked why were her pyjamas missing?

WHERE:
Off the coast of West Africa
WHEN:
2.58am Saturday 18 October 1947
THE AFTERMATH:
Camb was released on parole in September 1959 but in 1967 he was sentenced to two years' probation after molesting a 13-year-old girl. In 1971 he was returned to prison to serve out his life sentence for indecently assaulting minors. He was released in 1978 and died on 7 July 1979 of heart failure.
YOU SHOULD KNOW:
Although Camb did push Gay Gibson's body through the porthole, a questions remains as to whether he did murder her. A 1991 book suggested that she had died of heart failure while performing oral sex on Camb, not a conclusion that could be presented in the very different times of 1948.

The porthole from the Durban Castle *is carried into Winchester Assizes during the trial.*

THE CRIME: On 10 October 1947 the actress Eileen Isabella Ronnie "Gay" Gibson boarded the Southampton-bound liner *Durban Castle* at Cape Town. Most of the other passengers were older people. Eight days into the voyage, as the ship passed West Africa, it was noted that Miss Gibson was missing. Captain Arthur Patey of the *Durban Castle* put the vessel into reverse and a search began for the missing 21 year old. However, there was no sign. Her porthole in Cabin 126 on B deck was open and there were stains on her bedclothes.

The call button in the cabin had been pushed in the early hours of 18 October and when Frederick Steer, a member of the galley staff, responded deck steward James Camb, 31, answered the door. It was strictly forbidden for the crew to spend time with the passengers outside of work and Camb denied ever being in the cabin. When the ship's doctor examined Camb he noticed red scratches on the right side of the neck, shoulder and wrist, and Camb was put in the brig and handed over to the police at Southampton. Camb said that the red marks were a heat rash but admitted that he had been in the cabin and had had consensual intercourse with Miss Gibson, who was bored with spending time with the older passengers. However, during sex Miss Gibson, who had greeted him naked apart from a dressing gown, had suffered a seizure and Camb had tried to revive her. Believing her to be dead, he panicked and pushed her body through the porthole into the sea. At Winchester Assizes on 18 March 1948 Camb went on trial. According to the prosecution Camb had raped and strangled Miss Gibson and then thrown her body overboard. They asked, if Miss Gibson had greeted Camb naked, why were her pyjamas missing? If she agreed to sex, why was her diaphragm still in her suitcase? Since there was no body, much of the evidence was circumstantial – the stains on the sheets were inconclusive. At 7.10pm on 22 March after 45 minutes' deliberation the jury returned a guilty verdict and Camb was sentenced to death. He became the first British defendant convicted of murder without a body being found. The sentence was commuted to life imprisonment on 30 April 1948.

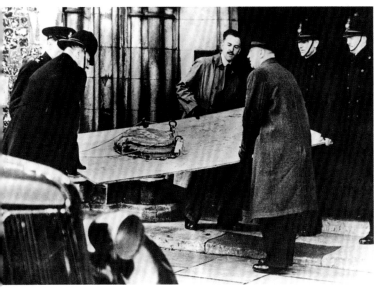

Donald Hume

"I watched the life run from him like water down a drain"

A piece of evidence in Donald Hume's trial is taken into the Old Bailey.

THE CRIME:
Brian Donald Hume was born in Swanage, Dorset, on 20 December 1919. He began joyriding and petty thieving and, during the Second World War, black marketeering. In 1942 Hume began a number of successful companies including a legitimate electrician's business.

In early 1949, Hume again met Stanley Setty, a flash, nattily dressed, 46-year-old Jewish spiv and car dealer. Their first meeting had been in December 1947. By day Hume would continue to work as an electrician and at night he worked for Setty, stealing cars to order. Setty would use logbooks from write-offs and match them to the cars brought to him by Hume. Hume also learned to fly a plane and smuggled anything and everything, including people. On 4 October 1949, when Hume returned to his Golders Green maisonette, Setty was sitting on the sofa. They began to argue and Hume pulled out an SS dagger and at 7.35pm stabbed Setty repeatedly. Hume was to say later, "I watched the life run from him like water down a drain." On 5 October he dismembered Setty with a hacksaw and a lino knife and made three separate packages, one each for the head, legs and torso. Hume flew over the Channel and threw out the head, legs, SS dagger, the hacksaw and lino knife. A second flight saw Hume dump the rest of Setty's body but the parcel floated up the Essex marshes where it was found on 21 October. Hume was traced and police found bloodstains at his home. He claimed three thugs had forced him to dispose of Setty's body and that defence earned him a not guilty of murder verdict at Court No 1 of the Old Bailey. Hume pleaded guilty to a lesser charge of accessory to murder and was sentenced to 12 years in prison.

WHERE:
620 Finchley Road, London, England
WHEN:
7.35pm Tuesday 4 October 1949
THE AFTERMATH:
Hume was released on 1 February 1958 and sold his confession to the *Sunday Pictorial* for £2,000. Due to the law of double jeopardy it was not possible to retry him for Setty's murder. He took to robbing banks and shooting cashiers in England and Switzerland. Caught in Switzerland, he was found guilty on 24 September 1959 and sentenced to hard labour for life. On 20 August 1976 the Swiss authorities released him. He was flown to England and examined by two psychiatrists. Hume was sent to Broadmoor, the hospital for the criminally insane. He was found dead in a field on 19 April 1988.

Yvonne Chevallier is congratulated by her lawyer as she is found not guilty.

Yvonne Chevallier

"My husband needs you urgently"

THE CRIME: Dr Pierre Chevallier was a member of the French cabinet when his 40-year-old wife, Yvonne, murdered him. They had met and married during his medical training and had two sons, Mathieu in 1940 and Thugal in 1945. By 1950 all the romance and affection had gone from their marriage. The Chevallier sons made friends with the three children of their neighbours, Jeanne and Leon Perreau. Leon Perreau was short, bald and portly while his wife was a glamorous redhead 15 years his junior. He ran a department shop in Orleans, which kept him away from his wife six days a week. It was not long before gossip began about Madame Perreau – it was said that she had a string of lovers. Dr Chevallier was soon counted among them. His wife was anxious about her husband, her looks and her family. She visited a doctor who prescribed her drugs to help but she became addicted to Maxiton, an amphetamine, and Veronal, a barbiturate.

In 1951 she received a poison pen letter informing her that her husband was keeping Jeanne Perreau's bed warm. She searched his wardrobe and found a love letter from Jeanne to her husband. It finished, "Without you life would have no beauty or meaning for me. Jeannette." Chevallier went to see Leon Perreau who told her that he knew his wife was sleeping with her husband but it did not bother him. On 11 August 1951 Dr Chevallier was sworn in as a government minister for education, youth and athletics. At home the Chevalliers argued and then she flung herself at him, begging him to end the affair. He refused. She ran from the room and fetched a gun she had recently bought and threatened to kill herself. He told her to do it. She fired but at him not herself. After the fourth shot 10-year-old Mathieu ran to his parents' bedroom to see what was happening. Chevallier took Mathieu downstairs and asked the family maid to look after him, before returning to the room where she pumped a fifth bullet into the back of her dying husband. She rang the police and said, "My husband needs you urgently."

WHERE:
Orleans, France
WHEN:
Saturday 11 August 1951
THE AFTERMATH:
When she came to trial (the location was moved from Orleans where Dr Chevallier had been a popular mayor to Rheims) on 5 November 1952, Yvonne claimed that it was a *crime passionel* but halting between firing the fourth and fifth rounds seemed to contradict this. In court Leon Perreau showed that he liked Dr Chevallier, "I got on with him very well." It was when Madame Perreau testified that the public opinion swung in favour of Chevallier and she was acquitted. The Catholic Church granted her absolution for the killing. She went to Africa to work with the poor and is believed to have died in the 1970s.

Derek Bentley & Christopher Craig

"Let him have it, Chris!"

THE CRIME: At 9.15pm on Sunday 2 November 1952 Derek Bentley, a youth with a low mental age, and Christopher Craig, a young thug, broke into Barlow & Parker's wholesale confectioners' warehouse in Croydon, Surrey. Bentley had a knife and Craig, whose elder brother was serving a 12-year sentence for armed robbery, a revolver. They were seen breaking and entering and the police were called.

When they arrived, the youths were trapped on the roof. Detective Constable Frederick Fairfax climbed up and arrested Bentley. The police claimed that Bentley, while in custody, shouted, "Let him have it, Chris!" and Craig fired a revolver, wounding Fairfax and shooting PC Sydney George Miles, 42, through the head.

WHERE:
Barlow & Parker's, 27–29 Tamworth Road, Croydon, Surrey, England

WHEN:
9.15pm Sunday 2 November 1952

THE AFTERMATH:
In a trial lasting two and a half days (9–11 December 1952) at the Old Bailey, before Lord Chief Justice Goddard, Bentley's mental state (he had a mental age of 11 and an IQ of 66) was not revealed. He was sentenced to death after the jury spent 75 minutes deliberating. The jury recommended mercy for Bentley, and Craig (who was under 18 at the time) was sentenced to be detained during Her Majesty's Pleasure. He was to serve ten and a half years (being released in May 1963 and marrying two years later). The Home Secretary, Sir David Maxwell Fyfe, refused to recommend that the Queen exercise the prerogative of mercy. Bentley was executed at Wandsworth Prison at 9am on Wednesday 28 January 1953 as an angry crowd waited outside. His older sister Iris began a campaign to clear his name. In 1966 Bentley's corpse was disinterred from the grounds of Wandsworth Prison and reburied in Croydon cemetery on Friday 4 March. Initially a headstone was not permitted but the government changed its mind in July 1994 and the tombstone bears the words "A victim of British justice". On 29 July 1993 the Home Secretary, Michael Howard, granted a partial pardon, which admitted it had been wrong to execute Bentley but maintained the guilty verdict. Five years later and a year after Iris's death, Derek Bentley's conviction was quashed on 30 July 1998. There is now some dispute as to whether anything at all was shouted by Craig, let alone the contentious words that sentenced Bentley to death. The Barlow & Parker factory was demolished in 1977 and replaced by houses.

Derek Bentley's conviction was quashed on 30 July 1998.

Barbara Graham

"Why do they torture me? I was ready to go at 10 o'clock"

WHERE:
1718 Parkside Avenue, Burbank, California, USA
WHEN:
Monday 9 March 1953
THE AFTERMATH:
On 3 June 1955 Graham was scheduled to die in the gas chamber at San Quentin at 10am, when there was a stay of execution until 10.45am. At 10.43am Graham was prepared for death only for another delay until 11.30am. Understandably, Graham was furious, "Why do they torture me? I was ready to go at 10 o'clock." At 11.28am she was again prepared for death and asked for a blindfold so she would not have to look at the witnesses. The executioner Joe Feretti told her, "Now take a deep breath and it won't bother you" to which she replied, "How in the hell would you know?" At 11.34am she spoke her last words just before she died. She was pronounced dead six minutes later. Santo and Perkins died in the gas chamber three hours later.
YOU SHOULD KNOW:
In 1958 Susan Hayward won an Oscar for playing Graham in the film *I Want to Live!*

THE CRIME: Barbara Elaine Wood was born in Oakland, California on 26 June 1923. She had an unhappy childhood and ran way from home when she was just nine. In 1939 she married for the first time but was divorced in 1941. She was sexually promiscuous and it wasn't long before she fell in love with a criminal element. A second marriage failed and in 1944 she was jailed for prostitution. By 1947 she was a drug-addicted prostitute and joined a gang of villains in San Francisco. She married for the third time in 1951 and in 1953 she met and married Henry Graham, by whom she had Tommy, her third child. On 9 March 1953 she and gang members Jack Santo, John True and Emmett Perkins, with whom she was having an affair, went to the Burbank home of elderly widow Mable Monohan, believing that she kept a large amount of money and jewellery on the premises. It was Graham's job to inveigle herself into Mrs Monohan's confidence and get into the house.

This she did by claiming her car had broken down and two members of the gang burst in and tied up Mrs Monohan. When the old lady cried out, according to True, Graham hit her over the head with a gun butt and then suffocated her. The gang left without their booty, which was not to be found in the house. The police quickly arrested the quartet. True gave evidence for the prosecution and was granted immunity from prosecution. The rest were all charged with murder. Graham bribed a policewoman to give her an alibi, which did not help her case at the trial. She said, "Oh, have you ever been desperate? Do you know what it means not to know what to do?"

Barbara Graham arrives at San Quentin the day before her walk to the gas chamber.

Pauline Parker & Juliet Hulme

"Mummy has been hurt – covered with blood"

THE CRIME: Pauline Yvonne Parker was born illegitimately on 26 May 1938 at Christchurch, New Zealand and was bored with her life at 31 Gloucester Street until she met Juliet Marion Hulme. Recently arrived from England, Hulme had been born in Blackheath, London on 28 October 1938. Her father was the physicist Dr Henry Hulme. The two girls became close friends but their friendship spilled over into physical passion and they consummated their affair and "enacted how the saints would make love". They "scribbled in exercise books effusions which they called novels, spent a good deal of time in each other's beds". Both sets of parents tried to break up the relationship seeing it as unhealthy.

Eventually, Hulme's father made plans to move to South Africa, having discovered his wife was having an affair. Parker wanted to accompany her friend but her mother, Honora, forbade it. The girls decided to kill 45-year-old Honora Parker. On 22 June they put half a brick into a stocking and in Victoria Park in Christchurch, Hulme dropped an ornamental stone so that Mrs Parker would bend over to pick it up and then Parker and Hulme repeatedly smashed the woman about the head with the brick. They ran to a teashop at 3.30pm where they said, "Please help us. Mummy has been hurt – covered with blood" before adding that Mrs Parker had fallen and banged her head and "it kept bumping and banging". When the police found the body it had 45 wounds on the head; they arrested the girls.

Parker, left, and Hulme leave the court after a preliminary hearing.

WHERE:
Victoria Park, Cashmere Hills, Christchurch, New Zealand
WHEN:
Tuesday 22 June 1954
THE AFTERMATH:
Pauline Parker had kept a diary of her affair and in it were references to "moidering" her mother. Parker and Hulme went on trial on 23 August 1954 for murder in Christchurch and were found guilty on 29 August. Both were sentenced to be detained at Her Majesty's Pleasure. They were each released in 1958. A condition of their release was that they were never to meet or contact each other again. Both moved to Great Britain. Parker became a devout Catholic, changed her name to Hilary Nathan and lived in the small village of Hoo near Strood, Kent where she ran a children's riding school. Hulme moved to the USA where she became a Mormon before settling in Portmahomack, Scotland, with her mother. She changed her name to Anne Perry and is a very successful crime novelist. Her first novel, *The Cater Street Hangman*, was published in 1979.

YOU SHOULD KNOW:
The story was made into the film *Heavenly Creatures* in 1994. Melanie Lynskey played Pauline and Kate Winslet Juliet.

Leslie Hylton

"My body belongs to him"

THE CRIME: Leslie George Hylton is the only Test cricketer to have been hanged for murder. A fast bowler, he was born on 29 March 1905 and made six appearances for the West Indies between 1935 and 1939 and helped to win against R.E.S. Wyatt's touring side in 1934–1935, taking 13 wickets in four Tests at an average of 19.3. In 1939 he was not included in the side to visit England under R.S. Grant and a public appeal raised £400 to pay for his fare. It turned out to be a waste of money He took just three wickets in two Tests. His top Test score was 19. He also played 40 first class matches for his native Jamaica, top scoring with 80 and taking 120 wickets.

In 1954 Hylton's wife Lurlene confessed to adultery with notorious womanizer Roy Francis. She said, "I'm in love with Roy. My body belongs to him," and pulled up her nightdress as if to prove it. Hylton shot her seven times then phoned the police. At his trial his counsel, his Jamaican cricket captain Noel "Crab" Nethersole, produced a letter Lurlene had written to Roy Francis. "My beloved," it said, "I'm realizing even more than I did before how much I love you. I am going to force my man's hand as soon as I can." Nethersole further claimed that Hylton was attempting to shoot himself but missed. It was an odd argument because Hylton had shot seven bullets into Lurlene which meant he had had to reload his revolver. The all-male jury still took 90 minutes to convict.

Leslie Hylton played cricket for the West Indies and his native Jamaica.

WHERE:
Jamaica
WHEN:
1954
THE AFTERMATH:
While in the death cell he was received into the Roman Catholic Church. Hylton was hanged at St Catherine's Prison, Jamaica on 17 May 1955.
YOU SHOULD KNOW:
Curiously, his obituary in *Wisden Cricketers' Almanack* makes no mention of the circumstances of his death, merely reporting that he died in Jamaica.

Serge Rubinstein

"Boy wizard of international finance"

THE CRIME: Serge Rubinstein was a womanizer, millionaire, conman and draft dodger. He was a crook – who called himself an international financier – and he got away with it because highly placed people were impressed by his spending and his patter. Born in St Petersburg, he claimed that his father had been a financial adviser to Rasputin (see page 296). After the Russian Revolution the family fled the country and arrived in Stockholm. A peripatetic existence followed and in Vienna his parents sent Rubinstein to see the psychologist Dr Alfred Adler who told him, "The way you are now, you'll be driven by ambition and desires." Rubinstein never went back.

By the time he was 23, he was the manager of the Banque Franco-Asiatique in Paris, which was the French financial agent for the Chinese government. A financial finagle in which he bought a million dollars worth of bonds for $25,000 led him to be labelled a "boy wizard of international finance". In 1935 he had to leave France after one scandal too many (he believed he was deported because he slept with the mistress of Premier Pierre Laval) and settled in the United States in 1938. He did not temper his behaviour and was charged with everything from swindling to violating the Mann Act (with a blonde on a Caribbean cruise) for which he was acquitted after paying double the legal fees.

In 1941 he married redheaded model Laurette Kilborn and then bought a mansion on Fifth Avenue in Manhattan. He conducted his business affairs from a suite of offices on Wall Street populated by innumerable beautiful secretaries. During the Second World War he was jailed for two years and fined $50,000 for draft evasion and his wife divorced him. Out of prison, he continued his womanizing ways, giving keys to his harem of lovelies. When he became fed up with them, he simply changed the locks.

On 26 January 1955 he dined with shop-worker Estelle Gardner at Nino's La Rue before retiring at 12.30am for a nightcap at his mansion. After an hour she left, as he was tired. Not too tired at 2.30am to call Pat Wray, another lover. She never arrived but his murderer did. That morning Rubinstein's English butler found his blue silk pyjama-clad master bound, gagged, strangled and quite dead.

WHERE:
814 Fifth Avenue,
New York City, USA
WHEN:
Thursday 27 January 1955
THE AFTERMATH:
The murder was never solved and one reporter quipped, referring to Rubinstein's lack of honesty, "They've narrowed the list of suspects down to ten thousand."

Rubinstein is pulled in for questioning.

Ruth Ellis

"I intended to kill him"

WHERE:
Magdala Tavern, 2a South Hill Park,
London, England
WHEN:
Easter Sunday 10 April 1955

THE AFTERMATH:
Ruth Ellis's trial opened at the Old Bailey on 20 June 1955. Ellis was asked what the purpose was of her visit to the pub, "I intended to kill him," she replied. It took the jury just 23 minutes to find her guilty on 21 June. On being sentenced to death Ellis simply said "Thanks". It was widely expected that she would be reprieved but Home Secretary Gwilym Lloyd George refused to sign the commutation orders. Ellis spent just 23 days in the condemned cell and was hangman Albert Pierrepoint's 16th female client. She wore her own clothes, apart from a compulsory pair of canvas knickers. Five minutes before the allotted time a telephone reprieve was received but a quick check revealed it to be a hoax call. In December 2003 an appeal by the Ellis family that the verdict should be set aside and replaced with one of manslaughter was turned down.

YOU SHOULD KNOW:
The last two women to hang in Britain (Ellis on 13 July 1955 and Styllou Christofi on 3 December 1954) both killed out of jealousy, both murdered their victims in the same road – South Hill Park Road, Hampstead and both were hanged by Albert Pierrepoint.
Ruth Ellis's original solicitor was Victor Mishcon who later represented Jeffrey Archer and Diana, Princess of Wales.

THE CRIME: Born in Rhyl, Wales on 9 October 1926 Ruth Ellis (née Neilson) was a good time girl, former model, club hostess and probably part-time prostitute. In 1953 while working as hostess of The Little Club in Knightsbridge, London she met a weak character by the name of David Blakely, a bisexual three years younger than her, and a racing driver.

Theirs was a stormy relationship peppered with violence and infidelities. In March 1955 she suffered a miscarriage (she already had two children) and Blakely tried to put some distance between himself and his naturally emotional girlfriend. This behaviour made her obsessively jealous and she became depressed. On Easter Sunday 1955 she armed herself with a Smith & Wesson .38 revolver and went to the Magdala Tavern in Hampstead where Blakely was drinking. As he left to walk to his car, Ellis shot him four times, wounding passer-by Gladys Yule in the process. She then calmly waited for the police to arrive. The murder would lead to her being the last woman in Britain to be hanged.

*Ruth Ellis with her doomed
lover, David Blakely*

John Gilbert Graham

"I wrapped about three or four feet of binding cord around the sack of dynamite"

THE CRIME: On the first day of November 1955 United Airlines Flight 629 took off from Stapleton Airport in Denver, Colorado bound for Alaska. Ten minutes later it exploded killing everyone – five crew and 39 passengers including an 18-month-old boy – on board. It quickly became apparent that the aircraft had been sabotaged. The wreckage was spread over 3 km (2 mi) and soldiers from the 168th Field Artillery of the National Guard were called in to protect the scene. Explosive material was found in the luggage of a passenger who had boarded when the plane refuelled at Denver.

Daisy King had been visiting her son and daughter-in-law before flying north. Just before she left, her son John "Jack" Gilbert Graham had insured her life for $37,500 although the policy was worthless because his mother hadn't countersigned it. When questioned by the police, he confessed to wrapping 6.3 kg (14 lb) of dynamite in a Christmas present for his mother. "I then wrapped about three or four feet of binding cord around the sack of dynamite to hold the dynamite sticks in place around the caps," he said. "The purpose of the two caps was in case one of the caps failed to function and ignite the dynamite... I placed the suitcase in the trunk of my car with another smaller suitcase...which my mother had packed to take with her on the trip." He seemed not to care that 44 innocent people were dead a month before Christmas, only that the world should know what a tough time he had had of it as a child. He was born on 23 January 1932, his father died when Graham was three and his mother was unable to cope and put the toddler into an orphanage. She later tried to make it up to him but he was having none of it and had become a juvenile delinquent. On 14 November 1955 Graham was arrested and charged with 44 counts of murder.

A coin operated insurance machine near the United Airline counter at Denver.

WHERE:
Airspace over Denver, Colorado, USA
WHEN:
7.03pm Tuesday 1 November 1955
THE AFTERMATH:
At his trial – the first to be televised – that began at 9.30am on 21 April 1956, Graham recanted his confession but he was found guilty after the jury deliberated for one hour and 12 minutes. He was sentenced to death. Prior to his execution, he was made to strip naked and given a pair of shorts because clothes retain the cyanide fumes. Graham was taken to the gas chamber of the Colorado State Penitentiary at Cañon City, Colorado on 11 January 1957. The cyanide tablets were dropped into the bucket of hydrochloric acid and a fog rose from it. At first Graham held his breath but he eventually had to breathe and he immediately gagged and his head shook from side to side. He let out an ear-piercing scream and his chest pushed against the leather straps. He became unconscious and was pronounced dead at 8.08pm.

Charlie Starkweather

"If I fry in the electric chair then Caril should be sitting on my lap"

WHERE:
924 Belmont Avenue, Lincoln, Nebraska, USA
WHEN:
Sunday 1 December 1957–Tuesday 28 January 1958
THE AFTERMATH:
Starkweather at first took the credit for all the killings but said that Fugate was involved. "If I fry in the electric chair," he told reporters, "then Caril should be sitting on my lap." She claimed that she only went along because he had threatened to kill her family (she said that she did not know that they were already dead). Charles Starkweather was executed in the electric chair at the Nebraska State Penitentiary on 25 June 1959. Caril Ann Fugate was sentenced to life in jail. She was paroled in June 1976.
YOU SHOULD KNOW:
The case inspired the films *Badlands* (1973) and *Natural Born Killers* (1994) and the Bruce Springsteen song *Nebraska*.

Charlie Starkweather is arrested after his killing spree.

THE CRIME: Charles Starkweather was born in Lincoln, Nebraska on 24 November 1938 and was nicknamed "Little Red" because of his lack of height (he was 1.6 m/5 ft 5 in tall), his red hair and bowlegged figure. He also had a minor speech impediment and was picked on at school because he wasn't terribly bright although that may have been due to his severe myopia. In 1956 he met 14-year-old Caril Ann Fugate and they began to go steady. He left school and found work in a warehouse but was not a good worker. His boss said, "Of all the employees in the warehouse, he was the dumbest man we had." Starkweather was thrown out of his home after Fugate crashed his car into another car and Charlie's father had to pay for the damages because he was the registered legal owner. Starkweather became a dustman.

On 1 December 1957 he killed petrol station worker Robert Colvert, 21, after he had refused to sell Starkweather a stuffed toy on credit. The next month he began his killing spree. He went to visit Fugate but she was not at home. As he waited for her to return, he sat playing with a .22 hunting rifle which annoyed her mother, Velda Bartlett. She told him to stop and he responded by shooting her dead. Next he shot and killed Marion Bartlett, Fugate's stepfather. When Fugate returned, she watched as Starkweather strangled and stabbed her two-year-old sister, Betty Jean. After Starkweather hid the bodies around the house, the couple stayed at the house for six days, sticking a notice that read "Stay a Way Every Body is sick with the Flue [sic]" on the front door.

Fugate's grandmother, Pansy Street, arrived but was fobbed off by Fugate. She became suspicious and rang the police. They did not arrive until 27 January by which time the killer couple had left. They drove to Bennet, Nebraska where they stopped at the farm of family friend August Meyer, 70. Starkweather shot him in the head. They abandoned their car and local teenagers Robert Jensen, 17, and Carol King, 16, offered Starkweather and Fugate a lift. Starkweather repaid their kindness by stealing the car and killing them both although he later claimed that Fugate had murdered and mutilated Miss King.

They next arrived at the home of rich businessman C. Lauer Ward, 47. The couple stabbed his wife Clara, 46, and maid Lillian Fencl, 51. When Mr Ward returned home from work that night, Starkweather shot him. They next shot travelling shoe-salesman Merle Collison, 37, in his car. Starkweather said that Fugate had killed Mr Collison after his gun had jammed. They were captured as they tried to escape.

Gunther Fritz Podola

"Police! Open this door!"

THE CRIME: Gunther Fritz Podola was born on 8 February 1929 in the Templehof area of Berlin, Germany. His father died on the Russian Front during the Second World War and Podola was an enthusiastic member of the Hitler Youth. Podola, a career criminal specializing in burglary and blackmail, was to find infamy as the only accused person in Britain to claim amnesia as a defence against a capital offence and the last person to be hanged in the UK for the murder of a policeman. On 21 May 1959, having been deported from Canada where he had been convicted of theft and burglary, he landed in England. He changed his name to Mike Colato because he thought it sounded like he was in the Mafia.

On 3 July 1959 he burgled the South Kensington flat of American model Verne Schiffman, stealing jewellery and furs worth $2,000. Hoping to increase his haul he tried to blackmail his victim by claiming to have embarrassing photos and tape recordings of her. Knowing she had nothing to hide she reported the phone call to the police who tapped her line and when Podola rang again on 13 July, they were able to trace the call to a public phone box inside South Kensington Underground Station. Two unarmed Detective Sergeants, John Sandford and Raymond Purdy, moved in and arrested him but moments later Podola twisted free and ran off. Chased, he was cornered in the hallway of a block of flats at 105 Onslow Square. While Sandford went to fetch the caretaker, Podola sat on a window ledge and suddenly produced a 9mm FB Radom V15 pistol. He shot DS Raymond Purdy, 43, through the heart and again escaped. When Purdy's belongings were returned to his widow she discovered Podola's address book which Purdy had taken when arresting Podola. This pointed the police towards the Claremont House Hotel, 95 Queens Gate, Kensington where Podola was staying in room 15. On 16 July armed police assembled outside the room and shouted, "Police! Open this door!" Hearing a click like the cocking of a gun, Sergeant Chambers charged the door and Podola, who was probably listening at the door, was floored, landing with his head in the fireplace. Despite this he continued struggling until he suddenly collapsed unconscious. He was hospitalized for four days as a result and claimed to have lost his memory of all events up to 17 July.

WHERE:
105 Onslow Square, London, England
WHEN:
Monday 13 July 1959
THE AFTERMATH:
He was tried at the Old Bailey on 19 July 1959 and even though it was proved that he had shot Purdy, if he genuinely couldn't recall doing so and was not mentally fit to stand trial, he would have had to have been acquitted. The jury rejected his defence of memory loss after 35 minutes' deliberation. Mr Justice Edmund Davies sentenced Podola to death. Podola's lawyer, Frederick Lawton, thought there were no grounds for appeal but the Home Secretary made legal history by sending the case to the Court of Criminal Appeal under section 19(a) of the Criminal Appeal Act 1907 as if it had been referred by the defence. On 15 October 1959 The Court of Criminal Appeal dismissed the appeal and on 2 November the Home Secretary insisted that the law should take its course. Harry Allen hanged Podola at 9.45am on 5 November 1959, the last person to be hanged for the murder of a policeman in Britain. Later that day, Podola was buried in the prison graveyard (grave 59). DS Purdy's widow, with three children to support, received an annual pension of £546.
YOU SHOULD KNOW:
Between 1900 and 1975, 33 men serving with London's Metropolitan Police were murdered on duty (see also page 201).

Gunther Podola on his way to a West London court where he was charged with the murder.

Raymond Finch & Carole Tregoff

"If you don't kill her, the doctor will; and if he doesn't, I will."

THE AFTERMATH:
Finch and Tregoff went on trial at the Los Angeles County Courthouse on 4 January 1960. John Cody testified that he had told Finch, "Killing your wife for money alone isn't worth it... Let her have every penny... Take Carole... up on a mountaintop and live off the wild. If the girl loves you, she's going to stick with you." He alleged that Tregoff had told him, "Jack, you can back out. But if you don't kill her, the doctor will; and if he doesn't, I will." Despite this apparently damning testimony the jury failed to reach a verdict and the trial collapsed on 12 March. A second trial between 27 June and 7 November 1960 also did not reach a verdict. On 3 January 1961 a third trial began and on 27 March resulted in guilty verdicts – he of first-degree murder, she of second-degree. Both were sentenced to life imprisonment. Tregoff was paroled in 1969 and changed her name to work in Pasadena. She still lives in the area. Her former lover was released in 1971 and he returned to medical practice. He died in 1995.

YOU SHOULD KNOW:
During their incarceration, Finch wrote often to Tregoff. She never replied.

Finch, centre, and his girlfriend, Carole Tregoff, consult their lawyer.

THE CRIME: Raymond Bernard Finch, 42, was a successful Californian doctor who was having an affair with 23-year-old ex-model Carole Tregoff. Rather than just carrying on their illicit passion, they decided that life would be simpler without the presence of his wife, Barbara. Finch was part owner of West Covina Medical Center and had married Barbara, his second wife, in 1951. Barbara turned a blind eye to Finch's indiscretions and agreed to separate but not to divorce. Unbeknown to his wife, Finch rented an apartment under a false name and installed his mistress, Tregoff, who was going through a divorce. In 1959 her divorce became legal and Finch wanted to marry her.

Under Californian law, Barbara was entitled to half Finch's $750,000 fortune and, if adultery could be proved, the court could award Barbara Finch all his estate plus alimony, which would have ruined Finch financially as well as socially. Finch and Tregoff decided to arrange for Barbara to be caught in a compromising position so that they could blackmail her. They hired ex-con John Cody to seduce her and then changed the deal to murder for the payment of $1,400. He did not go through with his part of the bargain so Finch and Tregoff decided to kill Barbara themselves.

At 10pm on 18 July they visited Barbara's home. Not long after they arrived Mrs Finch was found on the driveway of her home, a .38-calibre bullet in her back and her husband standing over with a gun in his hand. Finch and Tregoff were arrested. He claimed that his wife had produced the gun, they had struggled and he took the gun off her but as he threw it on to the ground it discharged the fatal shot.

Richard Hickok & Perry Smith

"I never believed for a minute he meant to carry it out. I thought it was just talk"

THE CRIME: The murder of the Clutter family was the inspiration for Truman Capote's bestselling 1966 book *In Cold Blood*.

1.62 m (5 ft 4 in) tall Perry Edward Smith (born in Huntington, Nevada on 27 October 1928) and 1.78 m (5 ft 10 in) tall, blond, muscular, chain-smoker Richard Hickok (born in Kansas City on 6 June 1931) had met in prison. On 15 November 1959 they visited River Valley Farm, Holcomb in Kansas, which belonged to Herbert Clutter. While in prison Hickok had been told by his cellmate Floyd Wells, a former employee at the farm, that Mr Clutter kept a safe at the farm that was said to contain $10,000. Later Wells told the authorities, "He said he and his friend Perry was gonna go out there and rob the place and was gonna kill all witnesses – the Clutters and anybody else that happened to be around. He described to me a dozen times how he was gonna do it, how him and Perry was gonna tie them people up and gun them down. I never believed for a minute he meant to carry it out. I thought it was just talk."

Perry was paroled on 6 June 1959 and Hickok on 13 August. Unfortunately, it wasn't "just talk" and the duo broke into the farmhouse but discovered that there was no safe and no $10,000, just a meagre "40 or 50 bucks". They tortured Mr Clutter to make him tell them where his money was but he insisted that he did not have any. Hickok and Perry murdered the four members of the Clutter family – Herbert, Bonnie, Nancy and Kenyon – with a shotgun from close range. They took the precaution of removing the spent cartridge shells from the murder scene. On 30 December 1959 Smith and Hickok were arrested in Las Vegas, Nevada.

Richard Hickok, above, and Perry Edward Smith, right, are taken to court.

WHERE:
River Valley Farm, Holcomb, Kansas, USA
WHEN:
Sunday 15 November 1959
THE AFTERMATH:
At the trial which began on 23 March 1960 after jury selection the previous day, Smith admitted the shooting of Herbert and Kenyon Clutter in the head with a shotgun at close range and cutting Herbert Clutter's throat. Hickok at first said that Smith had committed all the murders while Smith said that Hickok had murdered Bonnie and Nancy Clutter and then said that he had. Both men refused to testify in their own defence. Found guilty on 28 March after the jury deliberated for 40 minutes, they were sentenced to death. Truman Capote interviewed Smith on Death Row and the two men became firm friends. Smith and Hickock were hanged on 14 April 1965 at Lansing Prison (officially Kansas State Penitentiary), Kansas.
YOU SHOULD KNOW:
Awaiting trial Smith kept a diary in which he doodled while Hickok read novels by Irving Wallace and Harold Robbins. During a previous stint in jail, Smith had drawn such a terrific picture of Jesus that the prison chaplain had kept in the chapel for 22 years.

Uncut diamonds were scattered around Dieter von Schauroth's corpse.

Baron Dieter von Schauroth

"The second shot had been fired into the back of the neck as the body lay on the ground"

THE CRIME: This is a most unusual case in which the killer claimed that the victim had wanted, indeed begged, to be murdered. Baron Dieter von Schauroth was a 36-year-old farmer, well known on the Cape Town social scene where he lived with his 19-year-old wife Colleen in a flat in Mill Street, Gardens. The couple were seen at fashionable nightclubs on a regular basis. In 1960 von Schauroth had been forced to sell his flock of 4,000 karakul sheep to avert a financial crisis. On 24 March 1961 von Schauroth left home at 5.30pm on business in a car he had borrowed from his sister-in-law, telling his wife to be ready at 8pm to a promised trip to the cinema. She was never to see him alive again.

Just after 7.30 the next morning von Schauroth's body was discovered at the side of the Old Malmesbury Road, 24 km (15 mi) from Cape Town. There were two bullet wounds in the neck. A number of uncut diamonds were scattered around the corpse. The police found his car at Milnerton, 11 km (7 mi) north of Cape Town. There was no blood inside. Three days after the murder, the police arrested Martinus Rossouw, a flamboyant, 23-year-old railway fitter, nicknamed Killer, who had a penchant for dressing as a cowboy. At a hearing it was revealed that von Schauroth had insured his life for R360,000, paying all the premiums in cash. The trial of Marthinus Rossouw began in September 1961 at Cape Town Criminal Sessions before Judge-President Mr Justice Beyers. The defence counsel, Mr W.E. Cooper, said that Rossouw would admit killing the baron but under extenuating circumstances. He said that the baron was unhappy with his young wife and in financial difficulties. However, if he committed suicide, his insurance policies would be invalidated so the baron asked Rossouw to kill him. Rossouw claimed, "He often told me he was very unhappy because of his wife. He had found out she was going out with other men. I knew his wife before I got married. I used to go to nightclubs and saw her there in the company of men. I came to the conclusion she was not a decent girl." He said that Rossouw had given him a cheque for R2,300. That was the real motive said Mr van den Berg, the Attorney-General, and a ballistics expert added, "I cannot exclude the possibility that after one shot had been fired, the second shot had been fired into the back of the neck as the body lay on the ground." Rossouw had no explanation for the diamonds scattered about the body.

WHERE:
Old Malmesbury Road, near Cape Town, South Africa
WHEN:
Friday 24 March 1961
THE AFTERMATH:
On 27 September 1961, the jury retired to consider its verdict. After less than an hour, they returned a verdict of guilty. Marthinus Rossouw was hanged at Pretoria Central Prison on 20 June 1962.
YOU SHOULD KNOW:
As Rossouw walked to the gallows, he sang *Nearer My God to Thee*. Apart from one payment of R20,000 the insurance companies refused to pay out on von Schauroth's policies.

James Hanratty

"The DNA evidence establishes beyond doubt that James Hanratty was the murderer"

THE CRIME: At 9.30pm on Tuesday 22 August 1961 Michael John Gregsten, a 34-year-old, married father of two and a civil servant at the Langley Road Research Laboratory in Slough was canoodling in his grey 1956 Morris Minor in a cornfield off Marsh Lane in Dorney Reach, Buckinghamshire with his 22-year-old colleague and lover Valerie Storie when a man approached with a gun.

He told Gregsten to drive and, 48 km (30 mi) later, they stopped in a layby on the A6 in Bedfordshire known as Deadman's Hill. At 3am the man shot Gregsten and then raped Storie before shooting her five times and driving away in the stolen car, dumping it in Avondale Crescent, Ilford, Essex where it was found at 6.30am.

Storie survived her appalling injuries to describe her assailant and an identikit was issued. Two cartridge cases belonging to the gun were found in a room in the Vienna Hotel in Maida Vale, London. The occupant the night before the murder was 24-year-old petty crook James Hanratty, a man with four previous convictions, although none for violence or sexual assault. A man called Peter Alphon, another criminal, used the room the night after the crime. The gun was found under the back seat of a 36A London bus. On 9 October 1961 Hanratty was arrested in Blackpool and identified as the A6 killer. At first Hanratty claimed he had been in Liverpool then changed his story and said that he had been in Rhyl. Changing his alibi probably cost him his life. At 9.10pm on 17 February 1962, after what was then the longest murder trial of an individual in British criminal history, Hanratty was convicted. He was hanged at Bedford Prison at 8am on 4 April 1962.

WHERE:
A6 near Clophill, Bedfordshire, England
WHEN:
3am Wednesday 23 August 1961
THE AFTERMATH:
There was little confidence in the soundness of Hanratty's conviction and a public campaign to clear his name began involving, among others the pop star John Lennon, his wife Yoko Ono and campaigning journalist Paul Foot. On 12 May 1967 Peter Alphon confessed to the crime saying he had been paid to end the relationship between Gregsten and Storie. The Hanratty family continued to campaign for a pardon and their hopes were raised with the advent of DNA testing. On 22 March 2001, Hanratty's body was exhumed, a sample of his DNA taken and compared to that from the crime scene. The results were not what the Hanratty family and supporters were hoping for. The results showed there was a 2.5 million to one chance that the samples came from someone other than Hanratty. On 10 May 2002, Lord Woolf, the Lord Chief Justice, said: "In our judgment... the DNA evidence establishes beyond doubt that James Hanratty was the murderer."

James Hanratty, the A6 killer

Janice Wylie & Emily Hoffert

"The work of a maniac"

WHERE:
57 East 88th Street, Manhattan,
New York City, USA
WHEN:
Wednesday 28 August 1963
THE AFTERMATH:
On 26 January 1965 Richard Robles, a 22-year-old ex-convict and drug addict with a heroin habit, was arrested for the murders of Janice Wylie and Emily Hoffert. He had been burgling the apartment when his interest turned sexual. Then "I just went bananas", and beat the women unconscious before slashing and stabbing them to death. The charges against Whitmore were finally dropped and he was released on 10 April 1973. On 1 December 1965 Robles was convicted of the Career Girl Murders and in January 1966 sentenced to life imprisonment, but eligible for parole in 26 years. At a parole hearing on 5 November 1986 Robles, having proclaimed his innocence for 20 years, finally confessed. "I got in through a window. Miss Wylie was in the apartment. She was in bed... I tied her up... I wanted to have sex with her. I attempted to. She said 'No!' I stopped." Then Emily Hoffert came home. As he tied her up "She started telling me that she was going to tell the police on me," Robles said. "The thought entered my mind I have to kill... I killed... I was out of it." Robles remains incarcerated.
YOU SHOULD KNOW:
A book about the case, *Justice In The Back Room*, by Selwyn Raab of the *New York World-Telegram* and *Sun* was turned into a film starring Telly Savalas that later became the television show *Kojak*.

THE CRIME: On 28 August 1963 Dr Martin Luther King, Jr declared in Washington DC that he had a dream. On the same day *Newsweek* researcher Janice Wylie, 21, and teacher Emily Hoffert, 23, were murdered in their apartment on Manhattan's Upper East Side. Chief Medical Examiner Dr Milton Helpern described the murders as "the work of a maniac... both girls were stabbed repeatedly in the chest, abdomen and neck." The New York *Daily News* reported that "Emily had been the victim of multiple stab wounds and Janice had one huge slash across her abdomen." *Newsweek* offered a $10,000 reward for information leading to the arrest and conviction of the murderer.

The case lay dormant until 3.30am on 25 April 1964 when news agency AP released the following, "A 19-year-old Negro has admitted slaying Janice Wylie and Emily Hoeffert [sic] in their East Side apartment last August 28, Deputy Police Commissioner Walter Arm said early today." The item identified the confessor as George Whitmore, Jr, a 1.65 m (5 ft 5 in) tall, myopic, pockmarked black labourer with an IQ of just 60. The teenager had been arrested the day before as a rape suspect in Brownsville and, as he was being questioned, he confessed to the career girl slayings. Chief of Detectives Lawrence McKearney said that Whitmore had used a Coke bottle and three knifes to butcher the women. On 9 November 1964 Whitmore's trial for rape and assault began at the Brooklyn Criminal Court. During the trial it became clear that Whitmore had an alibi for the murders. However, he was convicted of the assault and was still in the frame for another murder, plus the Wylie-Hoffert killings. In 1966 he was sentenced to 5–10 years in Sing Sing prison.

From left to right: Janice Wylie, Emily Hoffert, George Whitmore and Richard Robles

Mississippi Civil Rights Murders

"We took care of your three friends tonight and you're next"

THE CRIME: In the summer of 1964 a Freedom School was being built on the site of the Mount Zion Union Methodist Church in Mississippi which had been firebombed by the Ku Klux Klan and James Earl Chaney, 21, Michael Henry Schwerner, 24, and Andrew Goodman, 20, were helping. They left the church when they were stopped and arrested by Deputy Sheriff Cecil Price for driving at more than 56 kph (35 mph). At 10.30pm Chaney was fined $20 for the traffic offence and the three men were ordered to leave Mississippi.

A mob was waiting for them and the three men were never seen alive again. At 2am the next day Buford Posey, a member of the National Association for the Advancement of Coloured People received a telephone call from Edgar Ray Killen, a Baptist preacher who doubled as chaplain for the local Ku Klux Klan. He said, "We took care of your three friends tonight and you're next." Mr Posey called the FBI. The bodies of the three were found in an earthen dam on Olen Burrage's Old Jolly Farm, Neshoba County, on 4 August 1964. All three had been shot. Their burnt-out blue Ford station wagon was dumped in the Bogue Chitto swamp. James Jordan, a member of the Klan, co-operated with the G-men believing that no jury could be found in the state that would convict those responsible for the murders.

Edgar Ray Killen sits in court 41 years after the murder.

WHERE:
Philadelphia, Mississippi, USA
WHEN:
Sunday 21 June 1964
THE AFTERMATH:
In November 1965 the FBI brought charges against 15 men, not of murder, but of conspiracy to deprive the victims of their civil rights. On 20 October 1967 James Jordan and Deputy Sheriff Price were among seven convicted and sentenced to four and six years respectively. Sheriff Lawrence Rainey and Edgar Ray Killen were among eight acquitted. The story did not end there. The story was made into the film *Mississippi Burning* in 1988. Deputy Sheriff Price died on 6 May 2001, aged 74.

Ironically, he died in the same hospital that carried out autopsies on the three civil rights workers he helped murder. Sheriff Rainey died on 8 November 2002, aged 79. On 6 January 2005, 11 days before his 80th birthday, Edgar Ray Killen was arrested on three charges of murder. On 21 June 2005 he was found guilty of manslaughter. Unrepentant, he labelled the three civil rights workers as communists who threatened Mississippi's way of life. He was sentenced to three terms of 20 years to be served consecutively. The earliest date Killen can be released is 22 January 2035 when he will be 110 years and five days old.

Gertrude, left, and her daughters Paula and Stephanie outside the courtroom in Indianapolis.

Gertrude Baniszewski

"I'm a prostitute and proud of it"

THE CRIME: Gertrude Nadine van Fossan was born on 19 September 1929, the third of six children. In 1945 she left school to marry John Baniszewski by whom she had four children. After ten years, the couple divorced, she married Edward Guthrie, divorced him, remarried John Baniszewski, divorced him again (in 1963) and lived with 23-year-old Dennis Lee Wright by whom she had a son before he left her.

In July 1965 Lester and Betty Likens, who worked in the circus, asked Baniszewski if she would look after their two daughters, Sylvia Marie, 16, and polio-stricken Jenny Faye, 15, for $20 a week. At first all went well but when $20 failed to materialize one week, Baniszewski beat the girls on their bare buttocks. The money arrived the next day. So began a regular pattern of abuse – physical and mental. In August Baniszewski encouraged her children to punch Sylvia and push her down stairs. She also accused Sylvia of being a prostitute. Sylvia and Jenny said that Baniszewski's daughters Paula and Stephanie were whores, which resulted in Sylvia being badly beaten by Baniszewski, Coy Hubbard, Stephanie's boyfriend, and several other classmates. That same month, Baniszewski forced Sylvia to strip naked in front of local boys and thrust a Coca Cola bottle into her vagina. The trauma of the incident left Sylvia incontinent so Baniszewski locked her in the cellar where she bathed her with scalding water and rubbed salt into her burns. For much of the time Sylvia was naked and starved and Baniszewski and her 12-year-old son John Jr made Sylvia eat her own faeces and drink her own urine.

Jenny wrote to her elder sister Dianna pleading for help but Dianna thought Jenny was making it up. However, after being refused admission to the house, Dianna rang social services but a social worker was fobbed off by a story that Sylvia had run away to become a prostitute. On 21 October Sylvia was taken from the cellar and tied to a bed. The next day, Baniszewski again shoved a Coke bottle up Sylvia's vagina and she and Ricky Hobbs inscribed the words, "I'm a prostitute and proud of it" on her stomach with a red-hot needle. Sylvia tried to escape but Baniszewski stopped her and pushed her back into the basement. Two days later, Coy Hubbard beat the girl unconscious with a broom handle. On the evening of 26 October Sylvia died. When the police arrived, Jenny Likens whispered to one, "Get me out of here and I'll tell you everything." The police arrested Gertrude, Paula, Stephanie and John Baniszewski, Richard Hobbs, and Coy Hubbard for murder. They also took into custody four local children for "injury to person".

WHERE:
3850 East New York Street, Indianapolis, Indiana, USA

WHEN:
Tuesday 26 October 1965

THE AFTERMATH:
An autopsy proved that Sylvia was still a virgin and death was caused by brain swelling, internal brain haemorrhaging and shock from severe and prolonged damage to her skin. On 19 May 1966 Baniszewski was found guilty of first-degree murder and was sentenced to life in jail without the possibility of parole. She appealed and at a second trial she was jailed for 18 years to life on 5 August 1971.

YOU SHOULD KNOW:
Despite pleas from the Likens family and a petition of more than 4,500 signatures Baniszewski was freed on parole on 4 December 1985. She sought to excuse her behaviour, "I'm not sure what role I had in it... because I was on drugs. I never really knew her... I take full responsibility for whatever happened to Sylvia." Baniszewski changed her name to Nadine van Fossan and died of lung cancer at Iowa on 16 June 1990. Jenny Likens Wade died in 2004, aged 54. Ricky Hobbs died of cancer when he was 21. Coy Hubbard has spent much of his life in and out of prison.

Richard Speck

"Born to raise hell"

THE CRIME: Richard Franklin Speck was born in Kirkwood, Illinois, on 6 December 1941. His father died when he was young and the boy did not like his new stepfather. He took to alcohol to numb his pains. When he was 19 Speck had a tattoo bearing the legend "Born to raise hell". He said, "I couldn't think of nothing to have on my arm, so I asked the tattooer if he had any ideas. He suggested all kinds of things, slogans and stuff and one of them was "Born to raise hell". That sounded kinda good, so I let him put that. Didn't mean anything special to me." In 1962 he married 15-year-old Shirley Annette Malone and they had one child.

Four years later, at 11pm on 13 July 1966, he broke into a dormitory of the South Chicago Community Hospital which housed young student nurses. He took nine hostage with a knife (and by some accounts a gun, too): Gloria Davy, Patricia Matusek, Nina Schmale, Pamela Wilkening, Suzanne Farris, Mary Ann Jordan, Merlita Gargullo, Valentina Pasion and Corazon Amurao. He tied all the women up with the bed sheets, telling them that he would not harm them. Corazon Amurao said that they should fight back but some believed he would rape them and that was preferable to more serious harm. One by one he took them from the room and strangled or stabbed them to death. Patricia Matusek was strangled; Nina Schmale was slashed on the neck and strangled; Pamela Wilkening was stabbed in the heart; Suzanne Farris was mutilated, stabbed nine times and strangled; Mary Ann Jordan was stabbed in the heart, neck and left eye; Merlita Gargullo was stabbed in the neck and Valentina Pasion was stabbed four times and strangled. Miss Amurao took the opportunity when Speck was out of the room to hide under a bed. Gloria Davy was the last to die – he raped her first for about 25 minutes and asked her "Would you mind putting your legs around my back?" before sodomizing her and killing her, leaving her naked body on a settee. In the early hours Miss Amurao left her hiding place and saw the carnage. She ran to the balcony screaming, "They're all dead! All my friends are dead!"

WHERE:
South Chicago Community Hospital Dormitory, 2319 East 100th Street, Chicago, Illinois, USA
WHEN:
Thursday 14 July 1966
THE AFTERMATH:
A fingerprint left at the scene was found to match Speck's. However, it was not until he was taken to hospital after a suicide attempt that he was finally recognized (by his tattoo) and arrested. He went on trial on 3 April 1967 at Peoria, Illinois. On 15 April, after a 49-minute deliberation, the jury found Speck guilty and recommended the death penalty. On 5 June Judge Herbert J. Paschen sentenced Speck to die in the electric chair. On 28 June 1971 the death sentence was overturned. On 21 November 1972 Speck was sentenced to 400–1,200 years in prison. Speck died of a heart attack at 6.05am on 5 December 1991, one day before his 50th birthday, at Silver Cross Hospital in Joliet.
YOU SHOULD KNOW:
Interviewed in prison, Speck had a message for Americans: "Just tell 'em to keep up their hatred for me. I know it keeps up their morale. And I don't know what I'd do without it." In 1996 a two-hour video shot eight years earlier at Stateville Prison showed prisoners taking drugs openly and Speck having oral sex with another prisoner. It also showed him sniffing cocaine, wearing silk knickers and showing off breasts grown by taking smuggled-in female hormone tablets. Speck said to camera, "If they only knew how much fun I was having, they'd turn me loose."

Evidence from the Speck murder trial is wheeled into the Peoria County courtroom.

Charles Whitman

"After my death I wish an autopsy on me to be performed to see if there is any mental disorder"

WHERE:
University of Texas, 1 University Station, Austin, Texas, USA
WHEN:
11.48am Monday 1 August 1966
THE AFTERMATH:
An autopsy, performed on Whitman, showed that he had a tumour the size of a walnut pressing on his brain which doctors believed may have caused the aggression.
YOU SHOULD KNOW:
The observation deck was closed for two years after the rampage. It reopened in 1968 but closed again in 1974 after a number of suicides. It reopened on 15 September 1999 but access is now strictly limited.

The bullet-hole through which Whitman carried out his shooting spree.

THE CRIME: Charles Joseph Whitman was born on 24 June 1941 in Lake Worth, Florida. Along with his two brothers, he served as altar boy at his local Sacred Heart Roman Catholic Church. He joined the US Marines Corps when he was 18, on 6 July 1959. On 15 September 1961 he enrolled on a mechanical engineering course at the University of Texas, thanks to a scholarship from the Marines. In December 1964 Whitman was honourably discharged from the Marines and returned to the University of Texas. In March 1966 he began acting oddly after his parents split up and his mother moved to Austin, Texas. On 29 March Whitman went to the campus counsellor to seek help for his unexplained violent losses of temper. He recommended Whitman see psychiatrist Maurice Dean Heatly. Whitman told him that he fantasized about shooting people from the top of a tall tower. Mr Heatly reported that Whitman had aggression issues but the student cancelled his next appointment because he wanted "to fight it out alone".

On 31 July he wrote a note, which said, "I am prepared to die. After my death I wish an autopsy on me to be performed to see if there is any mental disorder." He spent the next few hours with friends before going to his mother house just after midnight and stabbing her to death. He left a note saying: To Whom It May Concern: I have just taken my mother's life. I am very upset over having done it. However, I feel that if there is a heaven she is definitely there now... I am truly sorry... Let there be no doubt in your mind that I loved this woman with all my heart." Then he went home, 906 Jewell Street, and stabbed his wife, Kathleen Frances Leissner, three times in the heart as she slept. Later that day, he collected an arsenal of guns and went to the observation deck of the university. He hit the receptionist Edna Townsley in the face with a rifle butt. Just after he had pulled her body out of sight, a young couple, Cheryl Botts and Don Walden, entered. They saw a pool of blood on the floor but said nothing, smiled at Whitman, who returned the greeting, and left. Mike Gabour, 19, was not so lucky. Whitman shot him and his aunt and mother who were behind him. At 11.48am he climbed the tower and began shooting. Claire Wilson who was pregnant was shot in the stomach – she survived but the baby died. Thomas Eckman, 18, knelt beside his girlfriend to give first aid and was shot dead. Within 20 minutes, nine people were dead and eight wounded. The police tried using a light plane with a sniper aboard to take out Whitman but his marine training allowed him to drive the aircraft away. After 96 minutes three policemen burst into the tower and shot Whitman dead. He had killed 21 people and wounded 28 more.

The Braybrook Street Murders

"Harry Roberts, he's our man, he shoots policemen bang bang bang."

THE CRIME: On 12 August 1966 at 3.15pm three plainclothes policemen were on a routine patrol in Foxtrot 11, a police patrol Q car. They spotted a battered, blue Standard Vanguard Estate car (registration PGT 726) with no tax disc in Braybrook Street, near Wormwood Scrubs in London. The policemen were Detective Sergeant Christopher Head, aged 30, Temporary Detective Constable David Wombwell, 25, and their driver Police Constable Geoffrey Fox, 41.

The vehicle contained three criminals, John Witney, John Duddy and Harry Roberts. DS Head and TDC Wombwell walked towards the vehicle and asked Witney about the tax disc and discovered that he also had no MOT or insurance. As DS Head walked towards the passenger side of the vehicle Harry Roberts, in the passenger seat, pulled a 9mm Luger and shot TDC Wombwell in the left eye, killing him immediately.

DS Head ran back towards his vehicle, but Roberts pursued him and, after missing once, shot him in the head. John Duddy, the back-seat passenger, got out and grabbed a .38 Colt from a bag next to him, which also contained a third gun. He ran over to the Q car and shot out all the windows as PC Fox desperately tried to get away. PC Fox threw the car into gear but then ran over the prone body of DS Head, dying of his wounds, who became caught in the back wheels. Duddy then shot PC Fox in the head.

There several witnesses to the incident and Witney and Duddy were quickly arrested. Witney was identified by one boy because he bore an uncanny resemblance to the Manchester United footballer Bobby Charlton. Harry Roberts went on the run, aided by his knowledge of survival techniques learned in the army.

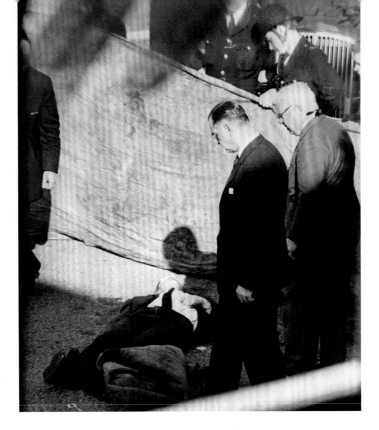

The body of one of the three officers in Braybrook Street

WHERE:
Braybrook Street, Hammersmith, London, England
WHEN:
3.15pm Friday 12 August 1966
THE AFTERMATH:
For three months, Roberts eluded capture before he was discovered and arrested on 15 November in a barn at Blount's Farm near Bishop's Stortford in Hertfordshire. At their trial, which began on 5 December 1966, all three men were found guilty of murder and the judge sentenced them to life with a recommendation they serve 30 years. Duddy died in Parkhurst Prison on the Isle of Wight on 8 February 1981; Witney was released in 1991 and was found beaten to death on 18 August 1999 at his home in Horfield, Bristol; Roberts is still behind bars, having made more than 20 attempts to escape. In the late 60s and early 70s Roberts's name would be chanted by football fans to taunt police: "Harry Roberts, he's our man, he shoots policemen bang bang bang."

Collins is surrounded by policemen as he is brought from the courthouse.

John Norman Collins

"If a person holds a gun on somebody – it's up to him to decide whether to take the other's life or not"

THE CRIME: The first of the Michigan, or Co-Ed, Murders happened on 10 July 1967 when bespectacled, 1.58 m (5 ft 2 in), 19-year-old Eastern Michigan University student Mary Fleszar was killed. Her body laid undiscovered for almost a month until 7 August when Russell Crisovan and Mark Lucas, both 15, found her remains while playing near an old farmhouse in a field in Superior Township, 3 km (2 mi) north of Ypsilanti. Mary was naked, prone, missing her feet, one forearm and hand and the fingers of the other hand were also gone. She had been stabbed about 40 times.

On 15 April 1969 Dawn Basom, 13, was found half-naked at the side of a country road in Ypsilanti. She had been raped, strangled with electrical flex and had her breasts almost cut off. Two months later, on 9 Jun the remains of Alice Kalom, 23, a student from Kalamazoo, were discovered near an abandoned barn on North Territorial Road. She had been raped, shot in the head and stabbed twice in the chest. She was barefoot. On 23 July Karen Sue Beineman, 18, went missing. She was found dead four days later, beaten, raped and strangled, her knickers stuffed into her mouth. Human hair was stuck to the underwear.

Police thought that the killer might return to the murder site and staked out the area. Sure enough a man turned up but poor weather made capture impossible. A description was circulated and campus policeman Larry Mathewson identified his friend John Norman Collins, who was questioned and released. Collins had been looking after the home of his uncle, David Leik, while he was on holiday. Police found bloodstains on the floor of Leik's basement, which was where Leik's wife cut their children's hair. Collins was re-arrested and charged with the murder of Karen Sue Beineman. His trial opened on 2 June 1970 at Washtenaw County Court in Ann Arbor. An expert stated that the hair found in the basement matched that found on Karen Sue Beineman's underwear.

WHERE:
Ypsilanti, Michigan, USA
WHEN:
Monday 10 July 1967
THE AFTERMATH:
On 19 August 1970 the jury unanimously found Collins guilty. On 23 August 1970, Collins was sentenced to life imprisonment with a minimum of 20 years to be served, with hard labour. Collins once said, "If a person holds a gun on somebody – it's up to him to decide whether to take the other's life or not."
YOU SHOULD KNOW:
In a bid to crack the case the police consulted Dutch psychic Peter Hurkos.

202

Mary Bell

"I know he's dead. I wanted to see him in his coffin"

THE CRIME: Mary Bell's name has entered the legal dictionary – a Mary Bell Order forbids publication of any information that could identify a child involved in legal proceedings – and is still a byword for childish wickedness. Mary Flora Bell was born in Newcastle upon Tyne, England on 26 May 1957, the illegitimate daughter of Betty Bell, a 17-year-old, mentally disturbed prostitute. On 11 May 1968 Bell, then ten, and her friend Norma Joyce Bell (no kin) were playing with her three-year-old cousin on a disused air raid shelter when he apparently fell and injured himself. The next day, three six-year-old girls complained after Bell had "squeezed their throats". On 15 May the police spoke to Mary and Norma Bell. On 25 May two boys found the body of four-year-old Martin George Brown in a derelict house. The next day, Bell tried to strangle Norma Bell and had to be slapped away by Norma's father. Later that day a nursery was broken into and vandalized. Four notes were found reading, "Fuch of, we murder, watch out, Fanny and Faggot", "WE did murder Martain brown, fuckof you Bastard", "I murder SO that I may come back" and "You are micey Becurse we murdered Martain Go Brown you Bete Look out THERE are Murders about By FANNYAND and auld Faggot you Srcews".

On 30 May Bell knocked on the door of the Brown family home and asked to see Martin. Mrs Brown said, "Martin is dead" to which Bell responded, "Oh I know he's dead. I wanted to see him in his coffin." Two months later, on 31 July, three-year-old Brian Howe disappeared. Bell told his sister Pat that he might be playing on some concrete blocks near waste ground. His body was found there at 11.10pm that night. He had been strangled, had cuts on his legs and a hole in his stomach. Twelve hundred local children were questioned and Norma Bell admitted that she had been there when Brian was killed and that Mary Bell had been responsible. Bell claimed that Norma Bell had strangled the toddler.

WHERE:
Scotswood, Newcastle upon Tyne, England
WHEN:
Saturday 25 May 1968

THE AFTERMATH:
Both girls went on trial on 5 December 1968 but while Norma was childlike, Mary Bell seemed to enjoy herself, parrying questions from barristers. A psychiatrist described her as "intelligent, manipulative, dangerous". Bell had told a WPC that she wanted to be a nurse so she could stick needles into people, "I like hurting people." Norma Bell was acquitted but on 17 December Bell was convicted of the "manslaughter due to diminished responsibility" of the two boys. She was sent to the Red Bank Special Unit from February 1969 until November 1973. She became masculine in appearance, causing her mother to say, "Jesus Christ, what next? You're a murderer and now you're a lesbian." In September 1977 she absconded from Moor Court Open Prison, lost her virginity and was recaptured after three days. She was released on 14 May 1980 and, unbelievably, was given a job in a children's nursery.

YOU SHOULD KNOW:
In 2002 Bell went to court to ask that her new identity and address be kept secret for life to protect her daughter who was born in 1984. She was granted the "Mary Bell Order" on 21 May 2003. Five years earlier, the journalist Gitta Sereny had paid Bell for her co-operation on *Cries Unheard*, a book about her life, which led many to believe that she should lose her anonymity. The sum paid to Bell is believed to have been around £16,000 and Bell and her 40-year-old boyfriend had used the money as a deposit on a small house on the south coast. When the location was discovered the police moved Bell and her daughter.

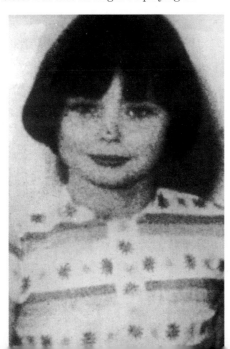

The seemingly angelic face of Mary Bell

Ramón Novarro

Tom Ferguson was shocked to find his brother and the actor naked on the bed having sex

WHERE:
3110 Laurel Canyon Boulevard, North Hollywood, California, USA
WHEN:
Wednesday 30 October 1968
THE AFTERMATH:
Thanks to forensic evidence and the 48-minute telephone call made by Tom Ferguson, the brothers were arrested two days later. They were tried in July 1969, convicted and sentenced to life imprisonment. The Fergusons were released in 1976.

THE CRIME: Movie star Ramón Novarro wasn't quite the devout celibate described in his early press cuttings. He had a penchant for rent boys and in the six months leading up to his death he had paid 140 prostitutes for their services. On Hallowe'en Eve 1968 he summoned two men to his home. At 5.30pm 23-year-old Paul Ferguson and his 17-year-old brother, Tom, arrived at Novarro's home where he welcomed them with drinks and sent out for cigarettes from the local newsagent shop. The three carried on boozing while Novarro recounted anecdotes about his career.

All the Fergusons were interested in was a stash of $5,000 in cash that Novarro supposedly kept in the house. Tom Ferguson, feeling woozy, went outside to get some fresh air while his brother stayed in the living room where Novarro serenaded him on the piano. After a while Novarro suggested they go somewhere more comfortable and led Paul Ferguson to the bedroom.

When Tom Ferguson returned to the house he went looking for his brother and was shocked to find him and the actor naked on the bed having sex. Tom Ferguson yelled at his brother to get out and the younger man staggered back to the living room where he rang his girlfriend. After about three quarters of an hour he heard Tom Ferguson calling for him. When Paul went to the bedroom he was greeted by the sight of a blood-soaked room and Novarro lying half on the bed. He had three large gashes on the back of his head. The Fergusons dragged the semi-conscious Novarro to the bathroom where they dunked him under the shower. They put him back on the bed. The ailing actor dragged himself to his feet only to be discovered by Paul Ferguson who began to thrash him, splitting his skull and face as he struck. Novarro collapsed onto the floor and there drowned in his own blood.

Tom Ferguson came up with the bright idea of making the murder look like a robbery so the two brothers trashed the old man's home. As a final touch Paul Ferguson placed the silver tip of the cane between Novarro's legs. In the house they found just $45.

An early studio photograph of Ramón Novarro. After the death of Rudolph Valentino, he became the screen's leading Latin actor and one of the great romantic lead actors of his time.

Hill-Robinson Murders

"Murder by omission"

THE CRIME: In 1957 Houston plastic surgeon John Robert Hill married Joan Robinson, the daughter of wealthy Texas oilman Ash Robinson. They led separate lives – he was busy with his practice and she was a keen equestrian. However, leading separate lives did not mean that Mrs Hill wanted her husband to share the beds of other ladies. On 3 December 1968 Hill filed for divorce but backed down when his wife contested the petition. However, according to a neighbour, in March 1969 Mrs Hill decided to instigate divorce proceedings.

Two days later, she fell ill and Hill broke a cardinal rule of medical practice by treating his wife himself. After some time at home he had her admitted to a hospital, in which he had a financial interest, where she died on 19 March of heart failure, aged 38. Her funeral was arranged without cause of death being properly established. Ash Robinson was unhappy and publicly accused Hill of allowing his daughter to die. In June 1969 Hill married divorcée and long-time lover Ann Kurth. Mr Robinson hired private detectives to follow him and badgered the district attorney to launch a murder case. Hill's response was to issue suit for libel and slander. Two grand juries were assembled and failed to indict Hill but in April 1970 a third did, charging him with "murder by omission".

Nine months after they married, Hill dumped the second Mrs Hill and she took revenge by claiming that he had admitted killing Joan Hill. The trial opened on 15 February 1971 at Houston before Judge Frederick Hooey. It collapsed on 26 February when Ann Kurth claimed that Hill had tried to inject her with a syringe and a mistrial was declared.

WHERE:
Sharpstown General Hospital, 6700 Bellaire Boulevard, Houston, Texas, USA
WHEN:
Wednesday 19 March 1969
THE AFTERMATH:
As the state decided whether to pursue Hill, fate took a hand. A retrial was set for November 1972. Hill was not to see the court. He had married for a third time but on 24 September 1972 a masked gunman shot Hill dead in his home in the exclusive Houston suburb of River Oaks. The gunman was later identified as Bobby Vandiver who was paid $5,000 for the killing. Vandiver alleged that Ash Robinson had hired him but before the truth could be ascertained, Vandiver was shot dead by a policeman while trying to escape. Mr Robinson denied any knowledge of Vandiver's accusations and when Hill's surviving wife, Connie, and son, Robert, launched a civil suit against him in 1977 for Hill's death it was thrown out of court. Mr Robinson died in 1985.

John Hill, seen here with his wife, Joan. They seemed the ideal couple, but that was not the case. Three years after her death, Hill was shot dead in his home by a masked intruder.

Manson Family Murders

"I'm the devil. I'm here to do the devil's business"

WHERE:
10050 Cielo Drive, Bel Air; 3301 Waverley Drive, Los Angeles, California, USA
WHEN:
Friday 8–Saturday 9 August 1969

THE AFTERMATH:
In mid August police raided the Family's Spahn Ranch and 26 arrests were made but all were released the next day. A lucky break finally led to the capture of the Family and they began to talk about the murders while in custody. On 1 December 1969 Watson, Krenwinkel and Kasabian were charged with murder. Later Manson, Atkins and Van Houten were similarly charged. Their trial began on 15 June 1970 and they were all sentenced to death on 19 April 1971. Before the sentences could be carried out the State of California abolished the death penalty and the punishments were commuted to life imprisonment. Doris Tate, Sharon's mother, attended parole hearings for Tex Watson and Susan Atkins. Watson, who has fathered three children since being incarcerated, was denied parole in 1985. Atkins, like Watson, claimed to have found God but Mrs Tate said to her: "You're an excellent actress – the greatest since Sarah Bernhardt." In 1990 Watson again applied for parole and again Mrs Tate turned up. Amazingly, one of those supporting his application was the daughter of Rosemary LaBianca. Doris Tate reminded the hearing of the words spoken by Watson as he entered her daughter's home: "I'm the devil. I'm here to do the devil's business." "As far as I am concerned, Mr Watson," she said, "you are still in business. What mercy, sir, did you show my daughter when she was begging for her life? For 21 years I have wanted to ask this prisoner 'Why?' He did not know my daughter. How can an individual, without any feelings, slice up this woman, eight-and-a-half months pregnant? What about my family? When will Sharon come up for parole? When will I come up for parole? Can you tell me that? Will the victims walk out of their graves if you get paroled?" Watson's application was denied. All the killers are still behind bars and the Tate family have devoted their time and energy to ensure that situation remains unchanged.

THE CRIME: On Friday 8 August 1969 the temperature in California reached 33°C (92°F). The heat wave had lasted for three days and the residents of Los Angeles were worried. At a house at 10050 Cielo Drive, rented by the film director Roman Polanksi, was his heavily pregnant wife actress Sharon Tate, her former boyfriend Jay Sebring, Polanski's friend Wojicieeh "Voytek" Frykowski and his girlfriend, coffee heiress Abigail Anne "Gibby" Folger. Around 6pm 16-year-old Debbie Tate rang and asked her sister if she could visit but Sharon put her off and also cancelled a dinner party invitation she had for that night. After dinner at a Mexican restaurant, the four returned to the house. Folger went to her bedroom, took the stimulant MDA and began to read. Frykowski also took the drug and listened to music in the living room. Sharon Tate lay on her bed in a bikini, chatting to Sebring. He drank beer and smoked a joint.

Outside the house were four black-clad members of Charles Manson's so-called "Family" of hippies and dropouts. They were former topless dancer, bar hustler and practising satanist Susan "Sadie" Atkins, Charles "Tex" Watson, former Sunday School teacher and insurance clerk Patricia "Katie" Krenwinkel, and Linda Drouin Kasabian who later became a prosecution witness.

After cutting the telephone lines, they first murdered 18-year-old Steven Parent, the caretaker. Watson levered open a window and climbed into the house, letting his accomplices in via the front door. Watson shook awake Frykowski, telling him: "I'm the devil. I'm here to do the devil's business." He then kicked Frykowski in the head. Atkins wandered around the house and saw Folger reading in bed. The coffee heiress looked up, smiled and waved. Atkins returned to the greeting and then found Sharon's room, before she went back to report to Watson. He gave Atkins a rope and she tied up Frykowski and then went to fetch Folger, Sharon and Sebring. Watson took another rope, tied Sebring's wrists and then put the rope around his neck before throwing the end over a ceiling beam. The other end he put around Sharon's neck. The four were ordered to lie face down and Sharon began to weep.

Sebring protested at the treatment of his former lover and was shot in the left armpit by Watson for his troubles. He then tied Folger's hands with a length of the rope that bound Sharon's neck. He tied it around Sebring's neck and, when he pulled it, Sharon and Folger had to stand on their toes to avoid being strangled. When Sebring moaned, Watson rushed to him and began to stab and kick him until he made no more noise. Frykowski made a dash for freedom but was caught on the lawn where he was stabbed 51 times and shot twice. Folger was stabbed 28 times, turning her nightie red. Her body was also discovered on the front lawn. Sharon pleaded for her life and that of her unborn baby. Susan Atkins screamed at her: "Look, bitch, I don't care about you! I don't care if you are going to have a baby! You had better be ready. You're going to die and I don't feel anything about it." Watson slashed his knife towards Sharon's face and Atkins began a stabbing frenzy. She took hold of Sharon's limp body, cradled it in her arms, put her hand onto Sharon's breast and then licked the blood from her fingers.

The four left but then remembered one of Manson's instructions. They drove back to the house and daubed the word "Pig" in Sharon's blood on the front door. Doctors estimated Sharon's baby, named Richard Paul on his gravestone, lived around 20 minutes after his mother's murder. Around 8.30am the next day housekeeper Winifred Chapman discovered the bodies. The police were alerted at 9.14am.

That night the four killers, plus Manson and Family member Leslie Sue Van Houten, set off to create more mayhem in Los Angeles. They butchered wealthy supermarket boss Leno LaBianca and his wife, Rosemary, at their home 3301 Waverley Drive, near Griffith Park. Despite finding "Death to Pigs" written in Mr LaBianca's blood at the scene, police didn't link the two sets of murders. They believed the Tate murders were related to the burgeoning drug culture and the LaBianca killings had been committed by copycats.

Charles Manson stares into the camera as he is brought into the Los Angeles City Jail.

Poisoner Graham Young

Graham Young

"When I get out, I'm going to kill one person for every year I've spent in this place"

THE CRIME: Graham Frederick Young was born in Neasden, London on 7 September 1947 and, whereas other teenagers might experiment with sex, drink or drugs, his favourite vice was poisons. When he was 14 he began poisoning his family and spent his pocket money on antimony and digitalis, claiming that they were needed for chemistry experiments at school. His family was constantly ill and on 21 April 1962 his stepmother Molly died from poisoning. His father, sister and a school friend, Christopher Williams, had also been poisoned and his Aunt Winnie became suspicious. Young even made himself ill on several occasions because he had forgotten which foods he had put poison in. Young was arrested on 23 May 1962 and admitted poisoning his father, sister and friend. He was not prosecuted for murder because the body of Molly Young had been cremated and so was not available for analysis. Young was sentenced to 15 years in Broadmoor, the youngest inmate since 1885, where he spent time learning more about poisons, before he was released on 4 February 1971. He told a nurse, "When I get out, I'm going to kill one person for every year I've spent in this place."

He got a job at John Hadland Ltd, a photographic supply store in Bovingdon, Hertfordshire. The company received references from Broadmoor but they were not told about his record of poisoning. Not long after Young started work, foreman Bob Egle, 59, fell ill and died on 7 July. Young had been in charge making the tea and added extra ingredients of antimony and thallium to the brew. The workers nicknamed the sickness that swept the factory the Bovingdon Bug.

Some months later, Fred Biggs, 60, another worker, fell ill and was admitted to the London National Hospital for Nervous Diseases where, after an agonizing few weeks, he died on 19 November. Around 70 people fell ill because of Young's meddling. In a bid either to get caught or to show off, Young went to the firm's doctor and asked if thallium had been considered as the reason for the sickness, mentioning that his hobby was studying poisons.

WHERE:
Bovingdon, Hertfordshire, England
WHEN:
Wednesday 7 July 1971
THE AFTERMATH:
On 21 November 1971 Young was arrested at Sheerness, Kent, where he was visiting his father and Aunt Winnie. In his pocket was thallium and the police discovered antimony, thallium and aconitine in his flat. They also found a diary in which he had entries detailing whom he had poisoned and with what dosages. He went on trial at St Albans Crown Court on 19 June 1972. After ten days, he was found guilty and was sentenced to life in jail. Young died of myocardial infarction in his cell at Parkhurst Prison on 1 August 1990, aged 42
YOU SHOULD KNOW:
In jail Young befriended Ian Brady (see page 388) who said, "It was hard not to have empathy for Graham Young."

Paul Knowles

"[I am] the only successful member of my family"

THE CRIME: Paul John Knowles was born in Orlando, Florida on 17 April 1946 and had his first brush with the law when he was 19 when he kidnapped a policeman who had stopped him for a traffic offence. He became a regular in prison before finally being released in May 1974. In the following six months Knowles was linked to the deaths of 18 people although he said he was responsible for 35. His first victim was 65-year-old Alice Curtis who died while he was burgling her home on 26 July. Knowles put a gag in her mouth and she choked to death. The next two to die were Lillian and Mylette Anderson, just 11 and seven years old. Knowles strangled them and threw them in a swamp. Knowles's victims were young and old, male and female and some who had befriended him. On 3 September he killed William Bates after drinking with him in Lima, Ohio. Knowles stole Bates's car, money and credit cards.

Twenty days later he met Ann Dawson and they travelled for six days together until Knowles murdered her. Her body has never been found. On 16 October he killed Karen Wine and her 16-year-old daughter, strangling them both with a nylon stocking after raping them. On 6 November he met Carswell Carr in a gay bar at Macon, Georgia and was invited to spend the night at the home Carr shared with his 15-year-old daughter Mandy. At the house an argument ensued and Knowles stabbed Carr who had a coronary. Knowles strangled Mandy and tried to have sex with her corpse. Knowles then met English journalist Sandy Fawkes in a Holiday Inn bar in Atlanta, Georgia. They ended up in bed. They spent six days together although there were things about Lester Daryl Golden, as he called himself, that worried Fawkes. They went their separate ways after a few days.

On 16 November State Trooper Charles Eugene Campbell, 35, pulled Knowles over in Perry, Florida but was kidnapped and forced into the backseat of his own patrol car. Knowles used the siren in the police car to stop businessman James E. Meyer, who was also forced into the car. Knowles tied both men to a tree before shooting them in the head.

WHERE:
Florida; Georgia, USA
WHEN:
Friday 26 July–Saturday 16 November 1974
THE AFTERMATH:
On 17 November Knowles drove through a police roadblock in Stockbridge, Georgia, but lost control of the car and hit a tree. He ran into the Henry County woods. Police captured Knowles who said he was "the only successful member of my family". On 18 December Knowles was transferred to a high-security prison in the back of a police car. While the car was driving on the I-20 close to Lee Road, Knowles used a paperclip to free himself from the handcuffs and made a lunge for Sheriff Earl Lee's gun. In the struggle, Georgia Bureau of Investigation agent Ron Angel shot Knowles three times.

Knowles arrives at the Baldwin County Courthouse.

Michael Skakel

A Season In Purgatory

THE CRIME: The night before Hallowe'en in 1975 Martha Moxley, a blonde, 15-year-old schoolgirl was murdered in the grounds of her family's home, 183 m (200 yd) from her front door. She was stabbed and beaten with a 6-iron golf club. The night of her death Martha had been having fun with a number of friends who included Thomas, 17, and Michael Skakel, 15, and the murder weapon had come from the home of the Skakels. The Skakel family was very wealthy and socially prominent in the area. The boys' aunt was Ethel Kennedy, the widow of Senator Robert F. Kennedy and former sister-in-law of President John F. Kennedy.

Martha was last seen some time between 9.30 and 11pm when she left the Skakel house. Sheila McGuire, a 15-year-old neighbour and classmate, discovered Martha's body, still wearing her blue ski parka and blue dungarees, at 12.15pm on Hallowe'en. Her underwear had been pulled down but there was no sign of sexual assault. Thomas Skakel had been pestering Martha to go out with him in the months leading up to her death. In 1976 the Skakels refused to co-operate further with the police, saying only that both sons were totally innocent of any crime.

This photograph of the Skakel family was exhibit No. 89 at Michael Skakel's trial. Michael sits second from the top.

WHERE:
38 Walsh Lane, Belle Haven, Greenwich, Connecticut, USA
WHEN:
Thursday 30 October 1975
THE AFTERMATH:
And there the case lay, unsolved for more than 20 years. In 1993 Dominick Dunne wrote *A Season In Purgatory*, a bestselling novel based on the murder. Five years later, former policeman Mark Fuhrman wrote *Murder in Greenwich* and named Michael Skakel as the prime suspect. In May 1998 a grand jury investigation was approved. More than 50 witnesses appeared before the hearings closed on 10 December 1999. At 9am on 19 January 2000 a warrant was issued for the arrest of Michael Skakel. At 3pm that day Skakel surrendered to Frank Garr of the State Prosecutors Office at the Greenwich Police Department and was charged with murder. His trial began at Norwalk on 4 May 2002. On 7 June 2002 Skakel was found guilty of murder. On 29 August he was sentenced to life imprisonment. The Connecticut State Supreme Court upheld his murder conviction on 14 January 2006.

John Shaw & Geoffrey Evans

"You have done a terrible, terrible thing, you wicked evil man"

THE CRIME: On 28 August 1976 Elizabeth Plunkett, a 22-year-old from Ringsend, County Dublin was kidnapped from a caravan park in Brittas Bay, County Wicklow, Ireland. Thirty-two days later, her decaying body was found off the Wicklow coast. Mary Duffy was a 25-year-old Castlebar shop assistant, waiting for her brother to give her a lift home when she disappeared. John Shaw and Geoffrey Evans, two Britons whose fantasy was to rape and murder a woman a week, had abducted both women. They were on the run from police in the UK, where they were accused of raping three girls.

They quickly fell into a life of crime and spent a short time in Mountjoy jail after being convicted of a series of burglaries carried out in County Wicklow. They took Miss Duffy to a caravan park in Connemara, County Galway where she was hit so hard that her dental fillings were knocked from her teeth. She was tied to a tree and raped repeatedly for some 36 hours before the two men smothered her with a cushion and dumped her remains in Lough Inagh, County Galway.

WHERE:
Brittas Bay, County Wicklow, Ireland
WHEN:
Saturday 28 August 1976
THE AFTERMATH:
As they planned their third victim in October 1976 the Gardaí arrested the two men. When he was arrested Shaw was shamed into confessing by a young detective, Gerry O'Carroll, who told him, "You have done a terrible, terrible thing, you wicked evil man. Did you ever believe when you were a little boy that you would stoop to what you've done? We're going to say a prayer together, you and I." In February 1978, Shaw was convicted of the murder of Mary Duffy and sentenced to life imprisonment, 14 years for rape and two years for false imprisonment. In December 1978 Evans was jailed for life for the murder of Mary Duffy plus 20 years for the rapes of Miss Duffy and Elizabeth Plunkett. In January 2009 Evans fell into a coma after a heart by-pass operation on 18 December 2008.

John Shaw with police officers

Charles Brooks, Jr

"I love you. Be strong"

WHERE:
Room 17, New Lincoln Motel, Tarrant County, Texas, USA
WHEN:
Tuesday 14 December 1976
THE AFTERMATH:
On 7 December 1982, after the Supreme Court of the United States rejected by six votes to three a petition to grant a stay of execution, Brooks became the first person ever to be executed by lethal injection. His last meal was T-bone steak with fries and tomato sauce and Worcestershire sauce, biscuits, peach cobbler and iced tea. Brooks was placed on a gurney and taken to the death chamber at the Huntsville Unit in Huntsville, Texas. His final statement was a prayer to Allah, as he had converted to Islam during his time in prison: "I, at this very moment, have absolutely no fear of what may happen to this body. My fear is for Allah, God only, who has at this moment the only power to determine if I should live or die... As a devout Muslim, I am taught and believe that this material life is only for the express purpose of preparing oneself for the real life that is to come... Since becoming Muslim, I have tried to live as Allah wanted me to live." The last words he spoke were to his girlfriend, Vanessa Sapp, who witnessed the execution, "I love you. Be strong." At 12.09am he was injected with a deadly combination of sedatives and drugs and pronounced dead seven minutes later.
YOU SHOULD KNOW:
Brooks was the first person executed in Texas after the reinstatement of capital punishment in 1974 and the sixth to die in the United States.

THE CRIME: Charles Brooks, Jr was born on 1 April 1942 into a wealthy family, which didn't stop him getting into trouble with the law. On 27 September 1962 he was sentenced to three years in prison for burglary at DeSoto Parish, Louisiana. He was paroled in 1963 but returned to jail in 1965. In 1968 he was sent to the United States Penitentiary, Leavenworth for three counts of illegal possession of firearms.

On 14 December 1976 Brooks and two friends Marlene Smith, a prostitute, thief, and heroin addict and her boyfriend Woody Loudres took heroin, drank, then decided to go shoplifting. When their car broke down, Brooks went to a car showroom and asked to test drive a car. He went out in a car with 26-year-old mechanic David Gregory who worked at the showroom, and on the journey the car stopped and Woody Loudres got in. The two men forced David Gregory into the boot before driving to a motel. Once inside, Mr Gegrory was tied to a chair and gagged with tape. Then he was shot once in the head. It was not long before both men were arrested although neither would admit who had fired the fatal shot. Lourdes was sentenced to 40 years in prison but Brooks was given the death sentence. He was sent to Death Row on 25 April 1978 and spent 1,697 days there.

Charlie Brooks awaits his fate in the cell in Huntsville.

David Lashley

"You are an appalling dangerous man"

THE CRIME: Blonde and beautiful heiress Janie Shepherd, a 24-year-old Australian, seemed to have it all. At 8.40pm on Friday 4 February 1977 she left 103 Clifton Hill, St John's Wood, London, the luxury home she shared with her cousin, Camilla Sampson, and Camilla's husband, Alastair, eager to start the weekend with boyfriend Roddy Kinkead-Weekes, a cricketer with the MCC, at his flat in Lennox Gardens, Knightsbridge. Janie stopped off at the Europa supermarket on Queensway to buy trout, chicory, tomatoes and yoghurt for their dinner. Then she disappeared.

The next day at 3.15am she was reported missing and on 8 February her dark blue Mini was found in Elgin Crescent, Notting Hill, covered in mud. It had been slashed inside with a knife and given two parking tickets. There were, however, few clues to be had from it. Police waited for a ransom demand but none came. Janie's mother and stepfather arrived from Australia two days later to conduct their own search but no clues surfaced and weeks went by. Police interviewed all known sex offenders in the locale. Janie's parents returned to Australia on 12 April and six days later two schoolboys found Janie's body in an area called Devil's Dyke on Nomansland Common, south of Harpenden in Hertfordshire. It was ten weeks and six days since her disappearance.

An autopsy showed that Janie had died from compression of the neck but the pathologist was unable to say whether it was manual or the result of a firm object being pressed against it. Oddly, when her body was found, it was clad in slightly different clothes from the ones she was wearing when she disappeared. Decomposition of the body made it difficult to ascertain whether she had been raped or sexually assaulted. The police took 825 statements but seemed no nearer to catching her killer when the coroner's jury returned a verdict of murder by person or persons unknown.

The mini belonging to Janie Shepherd was found four days after she disappeared.

WHERE:
Queensway, London, England
WHEN:
9pm Friday 4 February 1977
THE AFTERMATH:
The prime suspect in the case was a West Indian boxer called David Lashley. On 13 December 1977 he was jailed for 18 years for a number of crimes including attempted murder and two rapes (one of a young blonde woman). Shortly before Lashley was due to be released he told inmate Daniel Reece how he had waylaid Janie on Queensway before abducting, raping and murdering her. At 7am on 17 February 1989 Lashley was released from Frankland Prison and immediately arrested for the murder of Janie Shepherd. On 19 March 1990 after two and a quarter hours' deliberation the jury found Lashley guilty of murder and he was jailed for life. Mr Justice Alliott said, "You are such an appalling dangerous man that the real issue is whether the authorities can ever allow you your liberty in your natural lifetime."

Buddy Jacobson

Tupper's face was sliced with a knife

WHERE:
7F, 155 East 84th Street,
New York, USA
WHEN:
Sunday 6 August 1978
THE AFTERMATH:
Jacobson was charged with Tupper's murder; Giamo was released. Jacobson's trial began on 22 January 1980 and on 12 April 1980, after 11 weeks, Jacobson was found guilty of second-degree murder. While waiting to be sentenced, he escaped from the Brooklyn House of Detention and fled to California. He was rearrested after nearly six weeks on the run and offering to sell his story to George Carpozi, Jr of the New York Post for "big bucks". Jacobson was sentenced to a minimum of 25 years. He died of bone cancer early on 16 May 1989 at the Erie County Medical Center in Buffalo. He was 58 years old. He had been incarcerated at the maximum-security Attica Correctional Facility since 1984.

THE CRIME: The Carattini family was returning home to the Bronx after visiting relatives in Manhattan when they spotted some tricycles dumped in a vacant lot. Thinking that they would make good presents for their three children, they stopped. They saw two men in the vacant lot and noted down the registration number of the car one of the men was driving. They were disappointed to find the trikes were just junk but they saw a wooden crate burning and called the fire brigade. The crate contained the body of a badly beaten man whose face had been burned beyond recognition.

Later that day the police stopped a car driven by Howard "Buddy" Jacobson, a 47-year-old leading trainer of thoroughbred racehorses. His passenger was Salvatore Giamo, an illegal immigrant. Jacobson lived in an apartment in a townhouse he bought after his divorce on the Upper East Side with his model girlfriend Melanie Cain. They had started a modelling agency called My Fair Lady. Jack Tupper moved into apartment 7C, across the hall from Buddy Jacobson and Melanie Cain. He began an affair with Melanie Cain who tired of her much older lover's jealousy. She crossed the hallway and moved from Jacobson's bed to Tupper's. The couple moved into a suite at the Drake Hotel after the atmosphere at East 84th Street became too strained. They found an apartment to rent on 52nd Street and on 6 August Cain left Tupper in bed while she went to sign the lease. Tupper returned to the house on East 84th Street where Jacobson murdered him and then dumped his body in the lot where the Carattinis found it. Tupper's face was sliced with a knife, his head caved in, his body bludgeoned and he was shot eight times.

Jacobson is escorted by police as he is taken from the police station at Manhattan Beach.

Jim Jones

"A combination of Martin King, Angela Davis, Albert Einstein [and] Chairman Mao"

THE CRIME: In the 1950s Jim Jones began his People's Temple in his home state of Indiana. In 1960 Jones was appointed to a local government position in Indianapolis where he championed the rights of local blacks. With his wife, Jones adopted several children including one Native American and three Korean. In 1961 they became the first white couple to adopt a black child in Indiana. The following year Jones stopped off in Guyana during a trip to Brazil to find a new home for the People's Temple. He returned to Indiana in 1965 and predicted that the world would be devastated by a nuclear war on 15 July 1967. He moved the Temple to Redwood Valley, California for safety.

It was about this time that Jones began to reveal that his organization was very left wing: "If you're born in fascist America, then you're born in sin. If you're born in socialism, then you're not born in sin." He then began criticizing the Bible as a tool to subjugate women and black people. In 1975 the People's Temple moved to San Francisco. Leading political figures fêted Jones both publicly and privately. One descried him as "a combination of Martin King, Angela Davis, Albert Einstein [and] Chairman Mao." Despite being referred to as the Reverend Jim Jones, he was actually an atheist.

In 1974 he had began building Jonestown, a socialist paradise in Guyana. In that country relations became strained and in November 1978 Congressman Leo Ryan of South San Francisco led a deputation to address reported human rights' abuses in Jonestown. They arrived in Georgetown, Guyana, on 15 November, travelling to Jonestown two days later. The next day Temple member Don Sly attacked Congressman Ryan with a knife. Later that day, as Congressman Ryan and his party, along with 15 members of the Temple who wanted to return to America, tried to leave, Jones's cohorts attacked them, killing Mr Ryan and five others. The death of Congressman Ryan was the only time a member of Congress has been murdered in the course of his duty.

Bodies of cultists lie around the throne used by leader Jim Jones. The sign above the throne quotes a thought of philosopher George Santayana.

WHERE:
Jonestown; Port Kaituma Airstrip, Guyana
WHEN:
Saturday 18 November 1978
THE AFTERMATH:
Realizing that the world was about to fall on his head, Jones returned to the compound where more than 900 of his 1,000 or so followers, including 276 children, committed mass suicide by drinking grape Flavor Aid laced with cyanide. Jones died of a gunshot wound to the head. The commune of Jonestown was destroyed by fire in the mid 1980s.

Brenda Spencer

"I don't like Mondays"

Brenda Spencer is led from court after pleading guilty.

THE CRIME:

Brenda Ann Spencer was born on 3 April 1962. For Christmas 1978 her father, Wallace, had given her a. 22 rifle as a present. A month later, on Monday 29 January 1979, she achieved infamy when she began shooting at her school, Grover Cleveland Elementary, in San Diego from her home, located across the street. Spencer shot headmaster Burton Wragg, 53, as he was trying to protect the children. Head custodian Mike Suchar, 56, died as he tried to help Mr Wragg. In all, Spencer killed two and wounded eight children and a policeman. Twenty minutes after the shooting began, police surrounded the Spencer home and laid siege to it for more than six hours. When Brenda gave herself up, she was asked whom she wanted to shoot and replied, "I like red and blue jackets." When asked why, she said, "I don't like Mondays. This livens up the day… I had no reason for it, and it was just a lot of fun… It was just like shooting ducks in a pond… [The children] looked like a herd of cows standing around; it was really easy pickings."

WHERE:
Grover Cleveland Elementary School, San Diego, California, USA
WHEN:
Monday 29 January 1979
THE AFTERMATH:
Spencer, 16, pleaded guilty to two counts of murder and assault with a deadly weapon, and was sentenced to prison for 25 years to life. After being turned down for parole in 2005 she claimed that at the time of the shooting she had been drunk and on angel dust (PCP) and, also for the first time, that she had been sexually abused by her father. "I had to share my dad's bed till I was 14 years old," she alleged. Cleveland Elementary was closed in 1983 because it had too few pupils. A plaque in memory of the victims is at the site.
YOU SHOULD KNOW:
Spencer's comment "I don't like Mondays" inspired Bob Geldof to write the number one Boomtown Rats song of that name.

Charles V. Harrelson

"The most vicious, heartless, cold-blooded killer I have come across"

THE CRIME: Charles V. Harrelson was born on 23 July 1938 in Huntsville, Texas, the youngest of six children. He became a professional card player. In 1968 he was paid $2,000 to murder the Texas grain dealer Sam Degelia, Jr by shooting him in the head. The money came from Mr Degelia's partner Pete Scamardo. The jury was hung and it was not until 1974 that Harrelson was found guilty. He was sentenced to 15 years in prison. The murder cost him five years in Fort Leavenworth.

By 1979, Harrelson was back on the streets and Arab drug dealer Jimmy Chagra offered him $250,000 to kill 63-year-old Judge John Howland Wood. The jurist was known as "Maximum John" because of his policy of punishing guilty felons. Harrelson laid in wait outside the judge's home in San Antonio with a high-powered rifle. He fired one shot, hitting Justice Wood in the back. Chagra had been due to appear in court on the day the judge was murdered. Chagra had been told that he was certain to be sentenced to life in prison without the possibility of parole.

WHERE:
San Antonio, Texas, USA
WHEN:
Tuesday 29 May 1979
THE AFTERMATH:
Harrelson was caught and arrested after one of the biggest-ever FBI manhunts. Harrelson denied shooting the judge and said that he had claimed that he had shot him simply to collect the $250,000 on offer. As Judge William Session sentenced Harrelson to a double life term he described him as "the most vicious, heartless, cold-blooded killer I have come across". After the first murder Harrelson's ex-wife took their three sons to live in Ohio and did not tell them what their father had done until 1975. In 1996 Harrelson tried to escape from prison in Atlanta and was transferred to a high security jail. In 2003 Jimmy Chagra was released from prison and said that Harrelson was indeed innocent of the murder but he did not name the real killer. Charles Harrelson died aged 68 of a heart attack in the supermax prison in Florence, Colorado, on 15 March 2007.
YOU SHOULD KNOW:
Charles V. Harrelson's eldest son Woody grew up to become an actor and starred as Woody Boyd in the sitcom *Cheers*. He also played a serial killer in *Natural Born Killers* (1994).

Harrelson gives a interview from the Harris County Jail visitors' room.

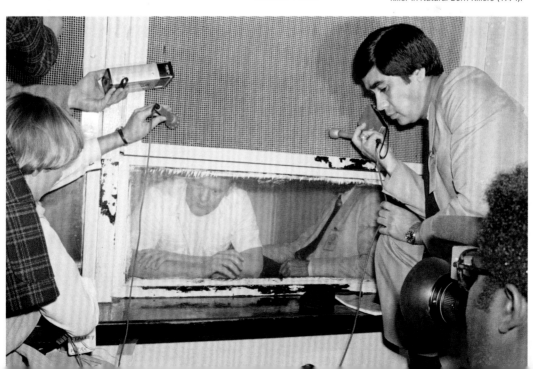

Paul Snider

Turn-offs: "Jealous people"

WHERE:
10881 Clarkson Road, Los Angeles, California, USA
WHEN:
Thursday 14 August 1980
THE AFTERMATH:
Dorothy Stratten's story was told in two films *Death of a Centerfold* (1981) and *Star 80* (1983) which starred Mariel Hemingway. The murder scene in the film was shot in the actual location that Dorothy Stratten died. Stratten's gravestone bears words from Mariel Hemingway's grandfather Ernest's book *A Farewell to Arms*. In a bizarre twist, Bogdanovich married Dorothy Stratten's younger sister, Louise, in 1988. They divorced in 2001.

THE CRIME: Dorothy Hoogstratten had it all – talent, beauty and a charming, trusting nature. It was that trusting nature which led to her ultimate downfall when her estranged husband murdered her. Born in a Salvation Army hostel in Vancouver, British Columbia, she was working in an ice-cream parlour when she met small-time pimp and hustler Paul Snider. He persuaded her to pose nude and, forging her mother's signature, sent the pictures to *Playboy*. The 1.75 m (5 ft 9 in) beauty impressed the magazine and in August 1979 she became their centrefold. On her Playmate data sheet she described one of her turn-offs as "jealous people". She also landed work as a bunny at the Los Angeles Playboy Club. In 1980 she was named *Playboy* Playmate of the Year. *Playboy* officials including Hugh Hefner advised Stratten (she dropped the Hoog) to sever her links with the paranoically jealous Snider but she had married him in June 1979 and believed he was in part responsible for her success. She landed bit part roles in a number of films: *Skatetown USA* (1979), *Americathon* (1979) and *Autumn Born* (1979).

In 1980 she was offered the starring role in a movie called *Galaxina* – it seemed that Stratten could become the first Playmate to achieve proper success. Finally, she gathered the courage to leave Snider and began an affair with the film director Peter Bogdanovich. Snider hired a private detective to follow his estranged wife. On 14 August 1980, 29-year-old Snider persuaded Stratten to return to their home in Los Angeles for one last time and, trustingly, she did so. Once inside Snider murdered 20-year-old Dorothy with a shotgun, blasting her face off before sodomizing her corpse. He then turned the shotgun on himself. Amazingly, the other people who lived in the house noticed Snider's bedroom door shut and, guessing that he wanted privacy, went about their business, unaware that two bloodied corpses lay just behind the door. Their bodies were not found until 11pm when the private detective hired by Snider let himself into the house.

Dorothy cuts her 20th birthday cake with the help of her husband, Paul Snider.

Sarai Ribicoff

"This is for real"

THE CRIME: Sarai Ribicoff was 23 years old, a Phi Beta Kappa Yale graduate, a reporter for *The Los Angeles Herald-Examiner* and the niece of Senator Abraham Ribicoff. She had much to live for when she went for dinner with John Shoven, a Stanford economics professor, in November 1980. They left Chez Helene Restaurant on Washington Boulevard, not far from her home, at about 10pm. They began walking to her car when they were accosted by two members of the Crips gang who had secreted themselves in the doorway of a local dress shop. One gang member, Frederick Thomas said, "This is for real" as he ordered them to hand over any valuables. Mr Shoven gave them his wallet, which contained $200, but Miss Ribicoff was pushed to the ground after saying that she did not have a purse with her.

Thomas tried to rip off her gold necklace as she was on her knees. He put his gun to her head and pulled the trigger, but it failed to go off. Thomas lowered his gun and shot Miss Ribicoff in the back before turning the weapon on Mr Shoven. He pulled the trigger but missed and managed to shoot himself in the wrist in the mêlée. Thomas and the other thug, Anthony LaQuin McAdoo, ran away after being chased by two knife-wielding chefs from a nearby restaurant. They went to an apartment at 919 5th Avenue at Broadway, where McAdoo's sister's cousin Maureen Young lived. They told her that a rival gang had shot Thomas in a drive-by shooting so she took him to Marina Mercy Hospital. McAdoo did not want to go with him but was persuaded into the car. In the car, McAdoo said, "The n****r must think I'm crazy. He shot the person and he wants me to take the gun and shoot the damn thing in the air." Thomas told him to "Shut your fucking mouth."

Frederick Thomas leaves court after his arraignment.

WHERE:
Chez Helene Restaurant, Washington Boulevard, Venice, California, USA
WHEN:
Wednesday 12 November 1980
THE AFTERMATH:
Thomas was arrested at the hospital but McAdoo stayed on the run until January 1981 when he surrendered. Originally, he agreed to testify against his former friend but then changed his mind after prison threats. When the trial finally started in November 1981, McAdoo did testify. Professor Shoven testified, "Sarai was pleading that she did not have a purse, which he seemed to want. He put a gun to her head and pulled the trigger... it did not go off... He then lowered the gun to her torso and shot her. He waved the gun at me and shot but missed." Thomas was found guilty of murder but on 22 December the jury could not decide on whether to sentence him to death so Superior Court Judge Laurence Rittenbrand declared a mistrial in the penalty phase of the trial. He was sentenced to life and McAdoo got 25 years as an accomplice.

YOU SHOULD KNOW:
Frederick Thomas had a long criminal record at the time of the murder for violence and possession of drugs. The first public defender assigned to the case had to refuse to take it because of a conflict of interest: he had dated the victim.

Bernard Welch leaves jail for the courtroom.

Bernard Charles Welch, Jr

"One of the most prolific burglars in the recent annals of American crime"

THE CRIME: Bernard Charles Welch, Jr was a career criminal who had been convicted of burglary several times in the 1970s. He was described by police spokesman Warren Carmichael as "one of the most prolific burglars in the recent annals of American crime". In 1974 he and another prisoner escaped from the Clinton Correctional Facility in upstate Dannemora, not long before Welch was due to be paroled. He spent five years on the run. He lived in Washington DC and, by day, he was an art collector and successful investor while, by night, he continued burgling. He lived in a $1 million home, which was filled with loot.

On 5 December 1980 he stepped up a league when he murdered cardiologist Dr Michael Halberstam, 48, at his home during a robbery that went wrong. Welch fired five shots, two of which hit the cardiologist in the chest. Dr Halberstam and his wife got into their car to drive to Sibley Hospital and saw Welch so Dr Halberstam ran him over. Welch was not badly injured but the doctor lost consciousness and drove into a tree. He was pronounced dead at the hospital.

WHERE:
Washington, DC, USA
WHEN:
Friday 5 December 1980
THE AFTERMATH:
Welch was tried in Federal Court, found guilty on 11 April 1981 and sentenced to 143 years in prison, making him eligible for parole in 2023. He was sent to the supermax prison in Marion, Illinois, where he befriended members of the Aryan Brotherhood. He then told the prison authorities about their plans resulting in a move into the witness protection programme and a transfer to a prison in Chicago. He escaped in May 1985 and stayed free for three months until he was arrested in Philadelphia while driving a stolen BMW with number plates that had been stolen from another car. He parked in another driver's slot and promptly fell asleep. When the other man arrived he called the police who arrested Welch. "I don't think it was Bernard Welch's finest hour," said Associate Deputy Attorney General Jay Stephens. Welch died in 1998 in prison.

John Lennon

"I just shot John Lennon"

THE CRIME: As one-quarter of the most successful pop group of all time, John Winston Lennon was responsible for great music and had a tongue that outraged as often as it pleased. In 1971 The Beatles were officially wound up and Lennon had a successful solo career with songs such as *Give Peace A Chance, Happy Christmas (War Is Over)* and *Imagine*. Then it all went silent for five years as he stayed at home to look after his new son, Sean, born in 1975. In 1980 Lennon decided to restart his musical career and began recording songs once again. He released an album *Double Fantasy*. On 8 November 1980 his song *(Just Like) Starting Over* entered the UK charts.

Exactly one month later, at 10.52pm, as he was returning home from a recording session with Yoko Ono, a man called out "Mr Lennon" and as Lennon turned, deranged loner Mark David Chapman shot him five times in his arm and back with a .38 revolver. Jose Perdomo, the senior doorman, shouted, "Do you know what you have just done?" Chapman replied calmly, "I just shot John Lennon." The ex-Beatle stumbled up the six steps to the building and collapsed in the vestibule from where he was taken by police car to Roosevelt Hospital on 9th Avenue and 58th Street. He was pronounced dead at 11.07pm, from major blood loss.

WHERE:
Section A, The Dakota, 1 West 72nd Street, New York City, USA
WHEN:
10.30pm Monday 8 December 1980
THE AFTERMATH:
Chapman had waited outside The Dakota all day and Lennon had even autographed a copy of *Double Fantasy* for him. The 25-year-old was obsessed with J.D. Salinger's novel *The Catcher In The Rye* and believed that the ex-Beatle had "sold out". After the shooting he calmly read the book. Beatles fans congregated on Central Park and a section was renamed Strawberry Fields on 21 March 1984. Lennon was cremated at Hartsdale Crematorium in New York State. Chapman was diagnosed as schizophrenic and sentenced to life imprisonment with a recommendation he serve 24 years before being eligible for parole. He is still incarcerated.

Fans of John Lennon hold a vigil after his murder on 8 December 1980.

Lawrencia Bembenek

"Run, Bambi, Run"

WHERE:
Milwaukee, Wisconsin, USA
WHEN:
Thursday 28 May 1981

THE AFTERMATH:
Bembenek appealed three times for a new trial but each time her petition was denied. On 15 July 1990 she escaped from prison, helped by her fiancé Nick Gugliatto, the brother of a fellow prisoner. They ran to Thunder Bay, Ontario, Canada, and spent three months free before they were caught. Her escape became the subject of a film with tagline "Run, Bambi, Run". On her return to prison she was given a new trial at which she pleaded no contest to second-degree murder and was sentenced to time served. She was released from prison in November 1992, having served a little over ten years.

YOU SHOULD KNOW:
In the time she has been out of prison Bembenek has been arrested on drugs charges, filed for bankruptcy, developed hepatitis C and become an alcoholic. In 2002 her leg was amputated below the knee after she fell or jumped from a second-storey window. In April 2008 Bembenek asked for her murder conviction to be quashed. Her appeal was denied in June 2008. She lives in the Pacific Northwest.

Bembenek answers questions at a press conference, flanked by her lawyers.

THE CRIME: Lawrencia Bembenek was born on 15 August 1958 and served with the Milwaukee Police Department before she was sacked in September 1980, after which she sued the force for sex discrimination. She got a job as a waitress at the Lake Geneva, Wisconsin Playboy club. Bembenek was married, on St Valentine's Day 1981, to Elfred "Fred" Schultz, a detective with the Milwaukee Police. He had been previously married to Christine, by whom he had two sons, Sean and Shannon, something that Bembenek found difficult to deal with. On 28 May 1981 Christine Schultz, 30, was shot to death in her Milwaukee home. Her sons, who were present for the crime, described the attacker as a man in a mask with black shoes and a green army jacket.

The first suspect was Fred Schultz who had, on 23 July 1975, accidentally shot and killed a fellow policeman but had been cleared of any wrongdoing. However, he had an alibi for the night his ex-wife was killed. The police then arrested Bembenek. They alleged that she wanted Christine Schultz dead so that her husband could stop paying her alimony ($363.50 plus $330 child support) and spend the money on Bembenek instead. The prosecution said that only Bembenek had the means, motive and opportunity, that she had financial problems and that the murder weapon was Bembenek's husband's off-duty pistol. Schultz's eldest son said that Bembenek was not the person he had seen kill his mother but Bembenek did not have an alibi for the time of the murder. On 24 June 1981 she was arrested for murder. In March 1982 she was found guilty and sentenced to life in Taycheedah Correctional Institution.

Vicki Morgan

"I killed someone. I did it with a baseball bat"

THE CRIME: Victoria Lynn Morgan was born on 9 August 1952 in Colorado Springs, Colorado, and at 16 gave birth to an illegitimate son. That year she married a 47-year-old man in a five-minute ceremony in Las Vegas. Like many beautiful young women, she went west in search of fame and fortune. She landed a job as an usher at Grauman's Chinese Theater in Hollywood and, while working there, met 54-year-old Alfred S. Bloomingdale, a close friend of Ronald and Nancy Reagan and a member of the celebrated New York department store family.

She became his mistress and lived a luxurious lifestyle, which he financed, spending a reported $1.5 million on her upkeep. Vicki did not keep her favours solely for her rich patron and bedded men, women and, by some accounts, Cary Grant and Princess Jawaher bint Saud, the lesbian daughter of King Faisal of Saudi Arabia as well. A friend said that she lived a life "of guilty compromise, a dishonourable truce between money and conscience". In 1982 Mr Bloomingdale was ill with terminal cancer and he agreed to give Vicki $18,000 each month. Before he died on 20 August his widow stopped the cheques so Vicki did the 20th century version of what many women scorned over the ages have done, she hired a lawyer. On her behalf, Marvin Mitchelson filed a $5 million dollar "palimony" suit against Mr Bloomingdale on 8 July 1982. The papers filed before the court case showed that Mr Bloomingdale had unorthodox sexual tastes, which Miss Morgan indulged. She later sacked Mr Mitchelson when she learned that he had dined at the White House with the president and first lady. She hired a new lawyer but her case was thrown out on 26 September when Judge Christian Markey declared her relationship with Mr Bloomingdale was based on "meretricious sexual services", in other words sex for hire, which was illegal in California. Immediately, Miss Morgan's monthly $18,000 cheques stopped. She began selling items bought for her by Mr Bloomingdale and threatened to write a tell-all book revealing the seamier side of high living among the rich and famous.

Without money, Vicky was forced to move from her luxury home in Los Angeles to a San Fernando Valley condominium. In June 1983 she rented a room to an acquaintance, 32-year-old homosexual Marvin Pancoast (born 13 November 1949) who had a history of mental problems. At 3.20am on 7 July he walked into North Hollywood police station and told the desk officer, Keith Wong, "I killed someone. I did it with a baseball bat."

Marvin Pancoast listens in court as he is accused of the killing.

WHERE:
4171-D Colfax Avenue, Studio City, California, USA
WHEN:
Thursday 7 July 1983
THE AFTERMATH:
At his trial Pancoast pleaded not guilty to murdering Vicki Morgan by reason of insanity but the jury rejected that and he was found guilty of murder. He was sentenced to 25 years to life. In November 1985 it was reported that Pancoast was suffering from Aids. He died of the disease on 4 December 1991.
YOU SHOULD KNOW:
Pornographer Larry Flynt offered to buy videotapes allegedly featuring important people in Washington DC having sex but Vicki Morgan's lawyer, who was selling them, claimed that they had been stolen.

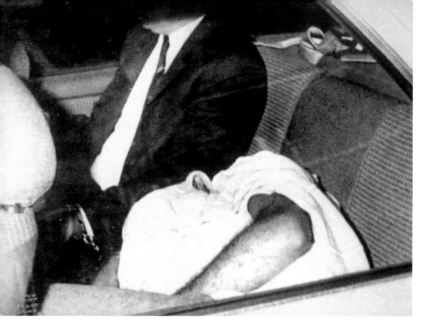

Pitchfork is driven from Leicestershire Magistrates Court after being charged.

Colin Pitchfork

"He would have been found guilty had it not been for DNA evidence"

THE CRIME: Colin Pitchfork was the first murderer to be captured using DNA evidence. On 21 November 1983 15-year-old Lynda Mann went to visit a friend but never returned. Her body was found the next day on a deserted footpath; she had been strangled and raped. The semen at the scene was from someone who belonged to a rare blood group. The police investigation centred on nearby Carlton Hayes Hospital, which housed a number of sex offenders but led nowhere. On 15 July 1986, another 15-year-old schoolgirl, Dawn Ashworth, was raped and murdered. Her body was found in woods near a footpath called Ten Pound Lane. Both girls had attended Lutterworth Grammar School.

Then the police got a breakthrough – or thought that they had. Richard Buckland, a 17-year-old kitchen porter from Narborough, confessed and was charged with murdering Dawn Ashworth. Because of the similarities with the Lynda Mann case, police assumed the same man had committed both crimes. Buckland's father, believing in his son's innocence, asked Professor Alec Jeffreys of Leicester University, who had perfected a system of identification based on DNA called genetic fingerprinting, to investigate. His conclusions were startling. Buckland had not killed either girl. His confession was completely fabricated. After serving three months in prison Buckland was released. Jeffreys said, "I have no doubt whatsoever that he would have been found guilty had it not been for DNA evidence. That was a remarkable occurrence."

Following Buckland's release, police decided to draw blood and saliva from every local male between the ages of 17 and 34 for DNA testing. Twenty-seven-year-old bakery worker Colin Pitchfork had previous convictions for exposing himself and feared the police might "fit him up" so he bullied co-worker Ian Kelly to act as a stand-in for him. Using a fake passport as proof of identity, Kelly took Pitchfork's blood test. On 1 August Kelly was drinking with three workmates and revealed what he had done. Six weeks later, after wrestling with her conscience, one of Kelly's workmates told the police what he had done. Pitchfork was arrested on 19 September 1987 and became the 4,583rd male in the investigation to be DNA tested. It proved his guilt.

WHERE:
Narborough, Leicestershire, England
WHEN:
Monday 21 November 1983
THE AFTERMATH:
Pitchfork, born in 1961, was jailed for life on 23 January 1988. He claimed that he had intended only to expose himself (something he claimed to have done to 1,000 women) but that it had turned to rape and, when he realized the girls could identify him, he murdered them.

James Huberty

"Society's had its chance. I'm going hunting. Hunting humans"

THE CRIME: James Oliver Huberty was 41 years old and a former welder from Canton, Ohio when he carried out one of the worst incidences of mass murder in American history. Huberty and his wife both had a history of violence: his wife threatened the mother of one of their daughter's friends with a 9mm pistol and later Huberty shot his Alsatian after an neighbour complained about the animal. Huberty found a job as an undertaker but was sacked because of his hostility to the bereaved. He had had to give up his job as a welder because a motorcycle accident had left him with a permanent twitch in his right arm. In January 1984 he began working as a security guard but was sacked from that a week before the murders.

On 18 July Huberty told his wife, "Society's had its chance. I'm going hunting. Hunting humans." With him, Huberty had a 9mm Uzi semi-automatic, a Winchester pump-action 12-gauge shotgun and a 9mm Browning HP. Arriving at McDonald's in San Ysidro, California he opened fire at 3.40pm and during the next 77 minutes he shot 21 people and wounded a further 19. He used up 257 rounds of ammunition before SWAT sniper Chuck Foster shot Huberty. The youngest victim was eight-month-old Carlos Reyes and the oldest Miguel Victoria-Ulloa who was 74.

James Huberty

WHERE:
460 West San Ysidro Boulevard, San Ysidro, San Diego, California, USA
WHEN:
3.40pm Wednesday 18 July 1984
THE AFTERMATH:
On 26 September 1984, McDonald's demolished the fast food store and donated the land to the city. In 1986 Etna Huberty, the widow of the killer, issued a lawsuit for $5 million against McDonald's and Babcock and Wilcox for whom Huberty had worked. She claimed that the former's food and the latter's work atmosphere had caused Huberty's unstable behaviour. The case was dismissed.
YOU SHOULD KNOW:
It may have been possible to avert the tragedy. Someone saw Huberty on San Ysidro Boulevard with two guns and rang the police. The telephonist gave the police patrol the wrong address.

Steven Benson

Benson put a bomb in the family car

WHERE:
13002 White Violet Drive, Port Royal,
Quail Creek, Naples, Florida, USA
WHEN:
9.18am Tuesday 9 July 1985
THE AFTERMATH:
Steven Benson was found guilty of
murder on 7 August 1986 and
sentenced to 50 years in prison.

THE CRIME: Steven Benson was born at Naples, Florida in 1951. His mother was tobacco heiress Margaret Benson of the Leaf Tobacco Company (not Benson & Hedges as is often reported). He lived a life of luxury with his mother and adopted brother Scott, who was really his nephew, Margaret's illegitimate grandson. However, Margaret Benson was tiring of her son's wayward behaviour and the lack of direction in his life and, when she learned he was dipping his fingers in the family till, she threatened to cut off his spending allowance.

Benson was not happy about this and on 9 July 1985 he put a bomb in the family car. A loud explosion shattered the smart district of Quail Creek, Naples. The family had all been in the car when Benson suddenly remembered that he had left something in the house and jumped out of the car to fetch it. A few seconds later, the car exploded killing Margaret and Scott Benson and burning Carol Lynn Benson Kendall (born 8 July 1944), a former Miss Florida runner-up, who was Steven's sister and Scott's real mother. Forensic examination revealed that the bomb consisted of two 10 x 25 cm (4 x 12 in) metal tubes packed with gunpowder. Further investigation showed a fingerprint on one of the bomb casings – it matched Steven Benson. At 10am on 22 August Benson was arrested and charged with two counts of murder and one of attempted murder.

Margaret Benson's home in Naples, Florida - the bombed car can be seen covered in plastic in the driveway.

Patrick Henry Sherrill

"Going postal"

THE CRIME:
Patrick Henry Sherrill was born on 13 November 1941 and 44 years later committed the worst massacre in postal history. Sherrill worked for the United States Postal Service but he was a terrible postman and on the verge of being sacked. One former colleague said, "He couldn't even find the WalMart and that's the biggest store in town." He was a social misfit with no friends at work or outside work – he lived alone in a house that didn't even have an extra chair for a visitor. He was nicknamed "Fat Pat" or "Crazy Pat" by the local children, the latter possibly because he had a habit of wandering the neighbourhood and staring in windows at people. He was also sensitive about his baldness. He had spent two years in the US Marines, leaving the service in 1966, and often boasted of his tour of duty in Vietnam although the records showed that he never left mainland America. Despite this he wore army fatigues every day.

At 7.05am on 20 August 1986 he arrived at work in his postman's uniform and in his mailbag were a .22 and two .45 calibre pistols. Silently Sherrill stalked through his workplace, shooting colleagues as he went. One woman screamed, "Get out of here, you crazy son of a bitch" so Sherrill shot her three times. Bill Bland, the supervisor who was going to sack Sherrill, was late in that day and so survived the massacre. The co-supervisor Rick Esser, 38, was the first to die. The one colleague that Sherrill' liked had been advised by him to take a day off so she, too, survived.

One of the bodies is taken from the post office in Edmund, Oklahoma.

WHERE:
US Post Office, 200 North Broadway, Edmond, Oklahoma, USA
WHEN:
7.05am Wednesday 20 August 1986
THE AFTERMATH:
In just 15 minutes and using 50 bullets Sherrill murdered 14 and wounded six more employees before committing suicide with a shot to the head.
YOU SHOULD KNOW:
The expression "going postal" is derived from the Sherrill case.

Robert Chambers

"You're the first man I've seen raped in Central Park"

WHERE:
Central Park at Fifth Avenue and
83rd Street, New York City, USA
WHEN:
Tuesday 26 August 1986
THE AFTERMATH:
Chambers was released on
14 February 2003. On 29 November
2004 he was charged with
possession of heroin and cocaine
and some motoring infractions. On
29 August 2005 he was sentenced to
90 days in prison and fined $200. On
22 October 2007 he and girlfriend
Shawn Kovell were arrested for
selling cocaine from their home. His
lawyer claimed that Chambers had
been an addict since he was 14 and
was using around a dozen bags of
heroin a day. On 2 September 2008
he was sentenced to 19 years in
prison for selling drugs.

THE CRIME: Tall (1.95 m/6 ft 5 in) and good-looking, Robert Chambers (born 25 September 1966) was used to New York women falling at his feet. A former altar boy, he won a scholarship to a prep school but suffered because he felt inadequate among his wealthier classmates and took to stealing and taking drugs. He spent one term at Boston University before being asked to leave over a stolen credit card. He was a regular at a bar called Dorrian's Red Hand at 1616 Second Avenue and 300 East 84th Street, Manhattan. He also had more brushes with the law for disorderly conduct, petty thefts and burglaries. He lived with his mother, Phyllis Shanley, a nurse. On the night of 25 August 1986 he was at Dorrian's Red Hand when his girlfriend Alex Kapp dumped him. Undeterred, Chambers left the bar that night with an ex, 18-year-old Jennifer Levin.

The next day Miss Levin's corpse was discovered behind the Metropolitan Museum of Art. Her bra and blouse had been pushed up about her neck and her skirt was around her waist. Her knickers were found 46 m (50 yd) away. Her body was covered in bites, cuts and bruises. An autopsy revealed that she had died of "asphyxia by strangulation". Bruises on her neck came from both her attacker's hands and her own as she attempted to pull his fingers away from her throat. Chambers was questioned as he had left the bar with Miss Levin and tried to pass off the scratches on his face and arms as being inflicted by his cat. After changing his tale several times, he settled on one where he went to the park with 1.63 m (5 ft 4 in) tall Miss Levin who had tied his hands with her knickers and then roughly manipulated his genitalia during sex, which caused him to push her off, and she fell awkwardly. Assistant District Attorney Saracco said to Chambers, "I've been in this business for a while, and you're the first man I've seen raped in Central Park." When his father came to visit, Chambers said, "That fucking bitch, why didn't she leave me alone?" Chambers was tried on two counts of second-degree murder. The jury failed to reach a decision for nine days and Chambers pleaded guilty to the lesser crime of manslaughter in the first degree and was jailed for 5–15 years.

Chambers ducks under the crime tape in Central Park near the spot where Jennifer Levin was killed.

Michael Ryan

"I wish I had stayed in bed"

THE CRIME: On 19 August 1987 Michael Ryan, then 27, armed with several weapons, including an AK-47 rifle and a Beretta pistol, shot and killed 16 people including his mother, and wounded 15 others, before shooting himself. The carnage began at 12.30pm when Ryan, clad in combat gear, abducted a nurse in Savernake Forest, near Marlborough, Wiltshire. Returning to his home in Hungerford, Ryan shot his pet labrador, Blackie, and set his house ablaze before shooting his neighbours. He walked around Hungerford firing indiscriminately at people and passing cars.

Remarkably, 77-year-old Dorothy Smith told Ryan off: "I said, 'You are frightening everybody to death. Stop it!' He had a funny sort of grin on his face. So I yelled out that he was a stupid bugger." Although people had called 999, the police refused to let most ambulance and fire crews into the vicinity, claiming it was too dangerous. One patrol car drove into Hungerford and as PC Roger Brereton pulled up, a warning came over his radio about a gunman on the rampage. Ryan unleashed 24 shots into the car, the policeman radioed for help and then died. Linda Bright and Hazel Haslett drove an ambulance which did get through but, as they reversed, they came under fire. Both women would get bravery awards.

By this time, a police helicopter was warning people to stay indoors. Those who heeded the advice could not believe that the police were allowing the killing to continue and that no armed officers had arrived on the scene. The first policeman with a gun arrived at 1.18pm but he went to Hungerford Common and waited there for other sharpshooters to arrive. Douglas Wainwright was shot while driving with his wife to visit their son, Trevor, a local policeman. By a terrible irony, it was PC Wainwright who had vetted Ryan when he wanted to modify his licence to cover the gun used in the Hungerford Massacre. Around 2.30pm, Ryan took refuge in the John O'Gaunt Secondary School where he was spotted at 5.25pm. The emergency services were allowed in, armed police surrounded the building and negotiations began.

Michael Ryan dressed in combat gear.

WHERE:
Hungerford, Berkshire, England
WHEN:
12.30pm Wednesday 19 August 1987
THE AFTERMATH:
At 6.52pm, Michael Ryan shot himself in the head, shattering his brain. The police took three hours to enter the building where they found Ryan's body in a classroom. He had said to one policeman, "I wish I had stayed in bed."

231

Simmons arrives at Arkansas State Hospital for psychiatric examination.

Ronald Gene Simmons

"In my particular case, anything short of death would be cruel and unusual punishment"

THE CRIME: Ronald Gene Simmons, Sr was born on 15 July 1940 and served in the US Army Air Force. Outwardly normal, in December 1987 he decided to kill his entire family. On the morning of 22 December he murdered his wife Rebecca and son Gene by shooting them with a .22 calibre pistol at the family home in Dover, Arkansas. He threw their corpses into a cesspit and waited for his other children to come home. When they arrived he told them that he had presents for them but wanted to hand them over one at a time. Seventeen-year-old Loretta was taken to another room where her father strangled her and pushed her head into a rainwater barrel. Simmons murdered the remaining children, Eddy, Marianne, and Becky in the same way.

At midday on Boxing Day the rest of the family arrived to celebrate the festive season. Simmons shot his son Billy and daughter-in-law Renata before strangling his grandson Trae. Simmons then shot his daughter Sheila, with whom he had been having an incestuous affair, and her husband Dennis McNulty. Simmons had fathered his own granddaughter by Sheila, Sylvia Gail, and she was strangled. Last to die was his grandson Michael, 21 months old. Simmons arranged the corpses neatly in the living room, covered with coats except for Sheila who had the best tablecloth draped over her. Simmons then went for a drink in a local bar before returning to his home where he sat watching television and drinking beer, surrounded by the remains of his family. The next day, he continued to relax with his feet up, television on and beer in hand. The Christmas holiday over, on 28 December he drove to Russellville where he murdered 24-year-old lawyer's receptionist Kathy Kendrick and then went to an oil company office and murdered J.D. Chaffin, 33, and wounded the owner, Rusty Taylor, 38. The gunman then wounded the manager of the Sinclair Mini-Mart, David Salyer, 38, and an employee, Roberta Woolery, 46, and then wounded Joyce Butts at the Woodline Motor Freight Company. He then calmly sat down and waited for the police.

WHERE:
Dover, Arkansas, USA
WHEN:
Tuesday 22–Saturday 26 December 1987
THE AFTERMATH:
Simmons was charged with 16 counts of murder, tried on 10 February 1989, found guilty, and sentenced to death. He refused to contest the sentence saying, "To those who oppose the death penalty in my particular case, anything short of death would be cruel and unusual punishment." On 31 May 1990, Arkansas Governor Bill Clinton signed Simmons's execution warrant. On 25 June Simmons died by lethal injection, the second to die by judicial execution that year.

John Albert Taylor

"Making peace with John allowed me to reclaim my life"

THE CRIME: John Albert Taylor was born on New Year's Day 1960. His father, Albert, either deserted or was thrown out and Taylor became a "whipping boy" for his mother and stepfather. He had seven sisters and stepsisters. One sister, Laurie Galli, said her brother raped her three times when she was a child. While a teenager, he spent three years in a sex-offenders programme at a Florida mental hospital and later spent ten years in a Florida prison on a burglary charge. It was said that he was a committed paedophile from the age of 17. In June 1989 he was visiting Laurie who lived in an apartment on Washington Terrace in Salt Lake City. Afterwards, he broke into the home of Sherron King. Mrs King was not at home but her 11-year-old daughter Charla Nicole was. She was one day short of her 12th birthday. He raped the child and then garrotted her with a telephone cord. He left her naked body on her mother's bed, the phone cord still around her neck. He was arrested two days after Charla's funeral when his fingerprints were matched to some found on the telephone in the King bedroom.

WHERE:
Washington Terrace, Salt Lake City, Utah, USA
WHEN:
June 1989
THE AFTERMATH:
Taylor was sentenced to death and was given the choice of a lethal injection or facing a firing squad. He opted for the latter because, he said, it would be costly and embarrassing for the state and because he was afraid of "flipping around like a fish out of water" if given an injection. He spent more than six years on Death Row before he was shot in Utah State Prison at 12.03am on 26 January 1996. He became a Catholic a week before his death. He is the last person to have been executed by firing squad in the United States. More than 150 television crews from around the world reported the execution. After eating a last meal of pizza "with everything" Taylor was dressed in dark a dark blue jumpsuit (so the blood wouldn't show) and placed into a steel chair adapted to collect blood and bodily fluids. A white circle was placed over his heart, and he was held in the chair by his arms, legs, chest, and head. In front of him were five identical .30-calibre deer rifles – four were loaded and one was blank so that each shooter – paid $300 – could believe that he had not fired the fatal shot.

YOU SHOULD KNOW:
Despite his large family, Taylor could not fill the five witness seats allocated to those closest to him. His victim's mother said, "Thanks to God for giving me the strength to get through the last six and a half years, and for helping me to forgive John Albert Taylor. I know many people cannot understand this, but making peace with John allowed me to reclaim my life and the wonderful memories I will always have of Charla."

The chair Taylor was strapped to when he faced the firing squad.

Menendez brothers

"They shot and killed my parents!"

WHERE:
722 Elm Drive, Beverly Hills,
California, USA
WHEN:
Sunday 20 August 1989
THE AFTERMATH:
In January 1997 Lyle married Anna
Erikkson. It lasted less than a year. In
June 1999 Erik married Tammi Ruth
Saccoman at Folsom State Prison.
Neither marriage has been
consummated. In 2005 Tammi
Menendez published a book *They
Said We'd Never Make It – My Life
With Erik Menendez*. Some reports
have it that the brothers have not
spoken to each other for more
than ten years.
YOU SHOULD KNOW:
In July 1988 Erik and Lyle began
breaking into the homes of their
parent's friends and stole more than
$100,000 in jewellery and money.
Jose Menendez paid restitution to
keep his sons out of prison.

THE CRIME: Of all the crimes in this book perhaps the worst is parenticide – the crime that Lyle and Erik Menendez committed in the summer of 1989. Cuban-born Jose Menendez married Kitty, who was three years older than him, and they had two sons Joseph Lyle (born 10 January 1968) and Erik Galen (born 27 November 1971). The Menendez brothers grew up in Princeton, New Jersey before relocating to California.

Jose and Kitty Menendez were watching a video of *The Spy Who Loved Me* in the den of their $4 million, 23-room Beverly Hills mansion when their sons burst in wielding shotguns. The first shots hit Mr Menendez in the arm and then one of the brothers shot him in the head. Mrs Menendez was shot in both legs and the left breast but began crawling away. They ran out of ammunition and left the house, reloading in the driveway. They returned and, as their mother was crawling towards them, they put the gun to her left cheek and pulled the trigger. The brothers left, changed their clothes and dumped their guns on Mulholland Drive. Then they went to a cinema to watch *Batman* to establish an alibi before returning to the house. At 11.47pm Lyle called 911 and cried, "They shot and killed my parents!" After their parents' deaths the brothers began spending lavishly; estimates put the figure at $1 million in six months. Lyle bought a Rolex and a Porsche Carrera and opened a restaurant while Erik hired a full-time tennis coach. Finally on 31 October, Erik confessed to his psychiatrist Jerome Oziel who went to the police. On 8 March 1990 the brothers were arrested.

On 8 December 1992 the Los Angeles County Grand Jury indicted the Menendez brothers on charges that they murdered their parents. They went on trial on 20 July 1993 and Erik's lawyer Leslie Abramson claimed that their parents had sexually abused the boys. She also claimed that during a family argument Kitty had pulled off Lyle's wig and the shock of seeing his bald brother made Erik take him into his confidence. The defence almost worked and the trial ended in two deadlocked juries on 25 January 1994. A second trial began on 11 October 1995 and saw both brothers convicted on 20 March 1996 of two counts of first-degree murder, plus conspiracy to commit murder. On 2 July 1996 Judge Stanley M. Weisberg sentenced Lyle and Erik Menendez to life in prison without the possibility of parole.

Lyle, left, and his brother Erik

Tracey Wigginton

"Need to feed"

Tracey Wigginton, the Lesbian Vampire Killer

THE CRIME: Tracey Avril Wigginton was born on 4 August 1965 and became known as the Lesbian Vampire Killer after she was accused of murder in 1989. She worked in a factory and was having an affair with Lisa Ptachinski (born 1 March 1965). In the autumn of 1989 Wigginton, Ptachinski and two other women, Kim Jervis and her lover Tracy Waugh went to Lewmors, a lesbian nightclub in Brisbane, where they got drunk on champagne.

Wigginton, a 1.78 m (5 ft 10 in) tall self-proclaimed vampire, announced that she had a "need to feed" and wanted to drink some human blood. Just before midnight the four women left the club in search of a victim for the overweight Wigginton. At Kangaroo Point they picked up 47-year-old Brisbane City Council worker Edward Clyde Baldock, a father of five, who had been drinking in the Caledonian Club. They lured him into their car, a green Holden Commodore, probably with the promise of sex, and then drove to a park on the banks of the Brisbane River. Once they arrived Wigginton stabbed Mr Baldock 15 times, with a ferocity that almost took off his head and then began to drink his blood. Rowers found Mr Baldock's body, naked apart from his socks, near the South Brisbane Rowing Club the next day at 6am. The women were caught when police found a Commonwealth Bank cashpoint card belonging to Wigginton in one of Mr Baldock's shoes. On 21 January 1991 the Supreme Court of Queensland sentenced Wigginton to life imprisonment. In February 1991 Ptaschinski also received a life term. Kim Jervis was sentenced to 18 years in jail for manslaughter, later reduced to 12 on appeal and Tracey Waugh was acquitted after her lawyer successfully argued that she had played no active role in the murder and had tried to stop Jervis from taking part.

WHERE:
Orleigh Park, Brisbane, Queensland, Australia

WHEN:
Saturday 21 October 1989

THE AFTERMATH:
In April 2008 Lisa Ptaschinski was given limited release from prison. A spokesman said, "Lisa Ptaschinski has had her application for resettlement leave approved by the Queensland Parole Board. Under the resettlement leave program, she is initially allowed a maximum of 12 hours of leave every two months for six months." The tattooed Wigginton remains behind bars.

Pamela Smart and her husband, Gregg, on their wedding day

WHERE:
4E Misty Morning Drive, Derry, New Hampshire, USA
WHEN:
8.30pm Tuesday 1 May 1990
THE AFTERMATH:
Smart was convicted on 22 March 1991 of being an accomplice to first-degree murder, conspiracy to commit murder and witness tampering, largely on the testimony of Flynn and secretly taped conversations that contradicted her claims. She was sentenced to life imprisonment without the possibility of parole. Smart claimed, and still claims, that she had nothing to do with Gregg's murder and that it was all Flynn's idea because she wanted to end their affair. "I have spent 10 years in prison for a crime I had no involvement in. I have been horribly punished for having an affair. The sentence I received is, in effect, a sentence of death." In October 1996 at the Bedford Hills Correctional Facility for Women in New York State, Smart was beaten up so badly by convicts Mona Graves and Ghania Miller that she suffered a fracture of her left eye socket and had to have a metal plate placed in the left side of her face. She now has no feeling there. The attack didn't stop her posing for raunchy pictures, which were published in the *National Enquirer* in 2003, an act that led to her being placed in solitary confinement. In an interview in 2000 she said, "I am very different from the media's portrayal of me. I am not a cold, uncaring individual." Flynn was sentenced to 28 years in prison for second-degree murder. He is incarcerated at the Maine State Prison in Warren and was turned down for parole on 12 February 2008. He has married while in prison.
YOU SHOULD KNOW:
Pamela Smart told her husband's killers to put her shih-tsu dog Halen in the basement, so it would not be traumatized and ordered them to use a gun, because a knife was too messy and might stain her white leather sofa.

Pamela Smart

"I am not a cold, uncaring individual"

THE CRIME: Pamela Ann Smart (née Wojas) is another woman who took a younger lover (in her case a 15-year-old schoolboy) who then killed his love rival. Born on 16 August 1967 in Coral Gables, Florida, blonde and beautiful Pamela married Gregg Smart (born 4 September 1965) on 7 May 1989 but less than a year later he was dead at the age of 24. Smart persuaded her boyfriend Billy Flynn and his three friends to kill Gregg, claiming that he was an abusive husband. She had seduced the boy after meeting him at Project Self-Esteem at Winnacunnet High School in Hampton, New Hampshire.

At 8.30pm on 1 May 1990 Gregg was shot in the head at his home after his wife had deliberately left the cellar door open for his killers to get inside. While Pete Randall held a knife to his throat, Gregg pleaded for his life. Flynn, after asking God to forgive him, shot him before the boys escaped in a car driven by Vance Lattime. Smart arrived home at 10.10pm in her 1987 silver Honda CRX and went inside to find her husband. She ran to the nearby condominiums to seek help shouting, "My husband's hurt! He's on the floor. I don't know what's wrong with him!" The neighbours called the police who found the body. Smart was arrested at 1.05pm on 1 August 1990. The arresting officer Detective Daniel Pelletier said, "I have some good news and I have some bad news. The good news is that we've solved the murder of your husband. The bad news is, you're under arrest".

Robert Thompson & Jon Venables

They sexually abused him before beating him to death using bricks and an iron bar

THE CRIME: Two days before St Valentine's Day 1993, Robert Thompson and Jon Venables, both just ten years old, abducted James Bulger, a month away from his third birthday, from Strand Shopping Centre in Bootle, Merseyside. James had been with his mother Denise and he wandered away from her as she shopped in a butcher's. Thompson and Venables who were playing truant from school had spent six hours trying to steal a child. When James left his mother's side at 3.40pm they pounced and left the shopping centre within two minutes. They took him 4 km (2.5 mi) to a railway line near Walton Lane police station and Anfield cemetery. There they sexually abused James and threw paint in his eyes before beating him to death using bricks and an iron bar. They pushed a battery up his back passage. After they had amused themselves, they placed his body on the track, covering it with bricks and bits of wood where it was cut in two by a passing train. James's body lay undiscovered until 14 February.

CCTV allowed the police to identify the two killers and they arrested Thompson and Venables and charged them with murder on 20 February. They were also charged with the attempted abduction of another child on the same day. Remarkably, 38 people had seen the evil duo with James Bulger but none had thought to intervene even though he was crying and some testified that they had seen a large wound on his head and saw him being kicked. The trial of Thompson and Venables opened on 1 November 1993 at Preston Crown Court. Twenty-three days later they became the youngest people to be convicted of murder in British criminal history. Venables cried in court but Thompson remained impassive. The judge, Sir Michael Morland, recommended that they serve a minimum of eight years but the Lord Chief Justice Taylor of Gosforth raised their minimum sentence to ten years. Home Secretary Michael Howard further increased their sentence to 15 years after a petition raised by James's parents collected 207,000 signatures.

WHERE:
Strand Shopping Centre, 73 The Hexagon, Bootle, Merseyside, England
WHEN:
Friday 12 February 1993
THE AFTERMATH:
Thompson and Venables went to the European Court of Human Rights in 1999 and were released on parole in June 2001 after serving eight years and four months. Their new identities were protected for life.

CCTV shots of James Bulger being led away by his abductors.

Edward Gingerich

"I'm the bad guy. My father will understand"

WHERE:
Frisbeetown Road, Rockdale
Township, Pennsylvania, USA
WHEN:
Thursday 18 March 1993
THE AFTERMATH:
When arrested by Pennsylvania State
Police Trooper Robert Rowles at a
dirt road intersection near his house,
Gingerich mumbled biblical passages
and made vague references to the
devil and said, "I'm the bad guy. My
father will understand." Trooper
Rowles told Gingerich to take off his
boots and coat and as he did so a
large piece of flesh fell to the ground.
The trial began on the morning of
24 March 1994 at the Crawford
County Courthouse in Meadville,
Pennsylvania. The jury found
Gingerich "guilty of involuntary
manslaughter but mentally ill". On
2 May 1994 he was sentenced to
imprisonment at the State
Correctional Institution in Cambridge
Springs, Pennsylvania for a minimum
term of two and a half years and a
maximum of five years. Gingerich
was released on 19 March 1998. He
moved to Harmony Haven, an Amish
mental health facility, in Evart,
Michigan, and then to 31426
Hogback Road, Cambridge Springs.
On 18 April 2007 he kidnapped his
daughter from a buggy and held her
for five days. On 5 December he was
sentenced to six months' probation
and fined $500 after pleading no
contest in October to interfering with
the custody of 17-year-old Mary.

THE CRIME: Edward Gingerich belonged to the strict religious sect the Amish – he is the only member ever convicted of murder. He chopped up his wife in front of their children.

The Amish, who have settlements in 22 states of America, eschew the modern world and preserve the simple outlook of their forebears. There is no such thing as an Amish divorce, and until 1993, there had never been an Amish murderer. Edward Gingerich arrived in Crawford County, Pennsylvania, 48 km (30 mi) south of the city of Erie, in 1983 with his family. He was 18 years old. By June 1985 Gingerich was working at the family sawmill on the corner of Frisbeetown Road. He became friends with Richard Zimmer, an Englishman – all non-Amish are known as English to the sect. He told Zimmer that he did not like the Amish ways and wanted to leave.

In 1985 Gingerich met Katie Shetler (born 17 March 1964), the daughter of a respected elder, and they began going out together. Under pressure from both families Gingerich proposed and on a rainy 2 December 1986 they married. They lived in her parents' basement until a home could be built. In the spring of 1987 Katie fell pregnant and on 20 September gave birth to a son, Dannie E., named after his paternal grandfather. Gingerich began spending more time alone, ignoring his new wife and family. In July 1988 he began to suffer from dizzy spells and sleeping a lot. Katie arranged an appointment for her husband with Dr Merritt W. Terrell, a medic favoured by the Amish. He diagnosed that Gingerich needed a toe pulling and a foot rub, gave him a jar of blackstrap molasses for purifying his blood and charged $25. Gingerich did not improve despite more visits and more molasses. On 21 March 1989 Katie gave birth to Enos and again Gingerich ignored her and their sons. On 3 December the sawmill, which was uninsured, burned to the ground. Gingerich was given permission to build a new mill. On 13 March 1990 Katie gave birth to daughter Mary. Gingerich refused to sleep with his wife again, fearful she would become pregnant and told her he wanted to leave the sect. In August Gingerich met born-again Christian David Lindsey who began to try and convert him. In November 1991 Gingerich and Katie moved into a new home. His health worsened and was further harmed by exposure to a solvent in his machine shop. Then his mental state became impaired but a visit to Dr Terrell resulted only in a shoulder rub, right-foot manipulation and another jar of blackstrap molasses. He began howling and racing around his living room on all fours.

In March 1992, Gingerich was finally sectioned. He was released on 3 April and attended psychiatric appointments but soon the insanity returned. Throughout 1992 his behaviour became more bizarre. He was taken to hospital where he told a doctor that he had "a bad case of liver cancer". Again he was sectioned but again let out, on 15 May, after ten days. Things worsened. On 17 March 1993 Gingerich was taken to Smicksburgh to see a special healer Jacob Troyer, a 46-year-old Amish. He told Katie, "Your husband has a mental problem. Take him to a hospital. I'm afraid of suicide… goodbye and good luck." The next day Gingerich remained in bed till 9am. He was taken to Dr Terrell who massaged his scalp and gave him "liver pills".

That day the Amish were celebrating a wedding but Katie refused to let her husband go. Around dusk the children played on the floor in the kitchen when Gingerich got up and punched his wife full in the face. He shouted at her, "I am the devil." She told Dannie to run and fetch Dan Gingerich, Edward's brother. The other two children remained. When Dannie arrived at his uncle's house he said that "Daddy isn't well" and Dan immediately set off. When he arrived Gingerich was astride Katie and punching her in the face. He stood up and smashed his right foot into her mouth and nose. Dan tried to stop his brother but then fled to the nearest house to seek more help. Dan went to an English house and dialled 911. Meanwhile, Gingerich put on his work boots and again smashed his wife in the face, crushing her head and causing her brains to begin oozing out. He then undressed her, grabbed a steak knife and slashed open her belly and through the 17 cm (7 in) cut removed her heart, lungs, spleen, liver, kidneys, ovaries and intestines, then stacked these in a neat pile beside her corpse. He then washed himself in the sink, threw his Bible into the fireplace and told the children to put on their coats on. "I'm taking you to Granddad's," he said, "then I'm coming back to burn down the house."

Gingerich was the only Amish ever convicted of murder.

Susan Smith

"I felt I had to end our lives to protect us from any grief or harm"

WHERE:
John D. Long Lake, Union, South Carolina, USA
WHEN:
Tuesday 25 October 1994
THE AFTERMATH:
Smith's trial began on 19 July 1995 at the Union County Courthouse. At 7.55pm on 22 July, after deliberating for two and a half hours, the jury returned a verdict of guilty of two counts of murder. At 4.45pm on 27 July Smith was sentenced to 30 years in prison. She will be eligible for parole on 4 November 2024.
YOU SHOULD KNOW:
Smith has had sex with at least two prison warders and in 2003 advertised on a dating website for convicts.

Police shot of Susan Smith

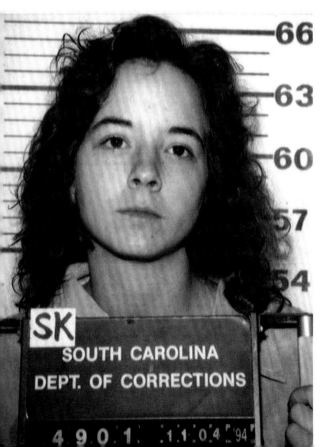

THE CRIME: Susan Leigh Vaughan was born on 26 September 1971 in Union, South Carolina. She married David Smith (born 27 July 1970) on 15 March 1991 and on 10 October that year she gave birth to Michael Daniel Smith and, a little under two years later, Alexander Tyler Smith followed. She worked at Conso Products, the largest employer in Union, South Carolina and, after splitting from her husband, began an affair with co-worker Tom Findlay, a 27-year-old rich bachelor who was the son of the owner of Conso Products. However, he did not want to raise her sons and wrote her several letters, one of which read, in part, "Susan, I could really fall for you. You have some endearing qualities about you, and I think that you are a terrific person. But like I have told you before, there are some things about you that aren't suited for me, and yes, I am speaking about your children." Eight days later, at 9.12pm on 25 October 1994 she told police that she had been carjacked by a black man and that he had driven away with her sons in her 1990 burgundy Mazda Protegé. She made tearful appeals on television for her sons to be returned. An appeal was also made on the internet asking for help. After nine days of police investigation Smith, then 23, confessed on 3 November. There had been no carjacking, no black man.

She had driven to John D. Long Lake, locked the car with her young sons inside and pushed the car into the water where both boys drowned. She wrote a detailed explanation for her actions: "I was very emotionally distraught. I didn't want to live anymore!... I felt I couldn't be a good mom anymore, but I didn't want my children to grow up without a mom. I felt I had to end our lives to protect us from any grief or harm... I was in love with someone very much, but he didn't love me and never would. I had a very difficult time accepting that... When I was at John D. Long Lake, I had never felt so scared and unsure as I did then. I wanted to end my life so bad... I... got out of the car and stood by the car a nervous wreck. I dropped to the lowest point when I allowed my children to go down that ramp into the water without me... I love my children with all my [heart]. That will never change... My children, Michael and Alex, are with our Heavenly Father now, and I know that they will never be hurt again. As a mom, that means more than words could ever say... I have put my total faith in God, and he will take care of me."

Timothy McVeigh

The sketch of the second man was an innocent bystander

THE CRIME: It was an ordinary spring day in Oklahoma City in 1995. People were going about their lawful business when suddenly a huge car bomb explosion wrecked the Alfred P. Murrah Federal Building and killed 168 people, including 19 children. Witnesses spoke of two men seen fleeing the scene and the FBI issued sketches of the two suspects. Around 120 km (75 mi) away, Timothy McVeigh was stopped for speeding and arrested when the policeman saw a gun in his car's glove box.

McVeigh is led away by FBI agents after being charged with the bombing.

The police were about to release McVeigh on bail when one of them noticed that he bore a resemblance to one of the men seen running away from the Oklahoma City bombing. The FBI announced they were looking for McVeigh's accomplice and on 21 April Terry Nichols surrendered. He looked nothing like the sketch of the second suspect. It turned out that the sketch of the second man was an innocent bystander. The forensic examiners managed to find intact the number plate of the vehicle used in the car bomb and traced it to McVeigh. He suffered from paranoia and had served in the first Gulf War where his hatred for America developed. It was exacerbated by what he saw as the authorities' heavyhandedness over the Waco Siege (see page 53). In September 1994 he began stockpiling the explosives he would use at Oklahoma City. He bought two tons of ammonium nitrate fertilizer, $2,775 worth of nitromethane car racing fuel and a 6-m (20-ft) long Ryder lorry which he drove to the Alfred P. Murrah Federal Building.

WHERE:
Alfred P. Murrah Federal Building, 200 NW 5th Street, Oklahoma City, USA
WHEN:
9.02am Wednesday 19 April 1995
THE AFTERMATH:
McVeigh was tried and on 14 August 1996 sentenced to death. In 1997 Nichols was sentenced to prison for life after being found guilty of voluntary manslaughter and conspiracy. In July 1999 McVeigh stopped all appeals against his death sentence. On 11 June 2001 McVeigh was put to death by lethal injection.
YOU SHOULD KNOW:
The US Government spent $82.5 million prosecuting the case against McVeigh and Nichols.

The Queen lays a wreath at the Dunblane Primary School.

Dunblane Massacre

Knockin' on Heaven's Door

THE CRIME: Thomas Hamilton was born as Thomas Watt in Glasgow on 10 May 1952, the son of Thomas Watt and Agnes Graham Hamilton. Shortly after his birth his parents separated and in 1955 they divorced. He and his mother moved to the home of his maternal grandparents in Cranhill, Glasgow. On 26 March 1956 they adopted him and his name was changed to Thomas Watt Hamilton. In 1963 he accompanied his adoptive parents when they moved to 11 Upper Bridge Street, Stirling. He grew up in the belief that his natural mother was his sister. In 1972 he opened Woodcraft, a shop at 49 Cowane Street, Stirling, which specialized in the sale of DIY goods. The shop closed in 1985 and Hamilton blamed the rumours about his pederasty for his business's failure. On 13 May 1974 Hamilton was sacked as a Scoutmaster after allegations that he had become too close to two Boy Scouts. He showed paedophile tendencies towards boys but had still been allowed to run 15 boys' clubs in Scotland between 1981 and March 1996. In 1987 Thomas Hamilton and his adoptive parents moved to 7 Kent Road, Stirling. In August of that year his adoptive mother died and in 1992 his adoptive father moved into sheltered housing, leaving Hamilton alone in the house. In 1991 he was sacked as a Scout leader.

Five years later, on 13 March 1996, the 43-year-old marched into the gymnasium of Dunblane Primary School – which had 640 pupils – armed with two 9mm Browning HP pistols and two Smith and Wesson .357 revolvers. With him, he had 743 bullets. He opened fire, killing 16 pupils (15 of them just five years old) and their teacher, Gwen Mayor, and injuring a dozen other children and two teachers, before turning one of his revolvers on himself.

WHERE:
Dunblane Primary School, Doune Road, Dunblane, Perthshire, Scotland
WHEN:
9.30am Wednesday 13 March 1996
THE AFTERMATH:
There is a memorial to the 17 victims in the local cemetery and a cenotaph in the cathedral. On 9 December 1996, a new version of Bob Dylan's *Knockin' on Heaven's Door* with lyrics by a Dunblane musician Ted Christopher was released by RCA Records in memory of the event. It featured the siblings of the dead children singing the chorus and Mark Knopfler on guitar. The Dunblane Centre, a £2 million youth centre and community sports hall built to commemorate the dead, was opened in September 2004.

"Sakakibara Seito"

"It is a thrill for me to commit murder"

THE CRIME: In February and March 1997 three young girls were attacked in Kobe, Japan. On 15 March ten-year-old Ayaka Yamashita was bludgeoned to death with a steel pipe in the same area. On 27 May 1997, some time before pupils were due to arrive at Tainohata Elementary School, the caretaker found the head of 11-year-old Jun Hase, who had been missing for three days, in front of the school gate. He had been decapitated with a handsaw and in his mouth was a note in red ink reading, "This is the beginning of the game... You police guys stop me if you can... I desperately want to see people die, it is a thrill for me to commit murder. A bloody judgement is needed for my years of great bitterness." It was signed The School Killer. Later the same day the rest of the boy was found under a house in the woods near the school. The killer also wrote a symbol similar to one used in San Francisco by the Zodiac (see page 536). Near most of the crime scenes were the mutilated bodies of cats.

On 6 June the newspaper *Kobe Shimbun* received a 1,400-word letter, purporting to be from the killer. It read in part, "I am putting my life at stake for the sake of this game. If I'm caught, I'll probably be hanged... police should be angrier and more tenacious in pursuing me... It's only when I kill that I am liberated from the constant hatred that I suffer and that I am able to attain peace. It is only when I give pain to people that I can ease my own pain." The letter was signed "Sakakibara Seito" with a PS, "From now on, if you... spoil my mood I will kill three vegetables a week... If you think I can only kill children you are greatly mistaken."

WHERE:
Kobe Japan.
WHEN:
Saturday 15 March–Tuesday
27 May 1997
THE AFTERMATH:
On 28 June 1997 a 14-year-old boy was arrested for the murders and assaults. He had begun mutilating animals when he was 12 (he would line up frogs and then cycle over them) and started carrying knives when in junior school. He had kept a diary detailing his exploits and in his bedroom police found thousands of comics and pornographic videos. Japanese law at the time meant that no one under 16 could be charged as an adult so he was sent to a reformatory for treatment. In 2003 he was pronounced cured and paroled on 10 March 2004, aged 21. His supervised parole ended on 31 December 2004 and he is now free, with a new identity.

Andrew Cunanan

"I take no joy in his death"

WHERE:
Casa Casuarina, 1116 Ocean Drive, Miami Beach, Florida, USA
WHEN:
Tuesday 15 July 1997
THE AFTERMATH:
On 23 July 1997, eight days after he murdered Versace, Cunanan shot himself in the head aboard a Miami houseboat moored at 5250 Collins Avenue, Indian Creek. The father of Jeff Trail said, "I take no joy in his death... Now nobody will be able to tell me why this happened."
YOU SHOULD KNOW:
Casa Casuarina, the site of Versace's murder, is now a members' only club.

THE CRIME: Andrew Phillip Cunanan was born into a middle-class family in San Diego, California on 31 August 1969. Gianni Versace was born at Reggio di Calabria, Italy on 2 December 1946. Both men were homosexuals and one was internationally famous while the other lived a good life, thanks to rich boyfriends and his own good looks. They met in October 1990 in a San Francisco restaurant and Cunanan realized what fun life could be like with the gay jet set. In 1992 to please his boyfriend Cunanan appeared in two gay porn films; the same year Versace bought the house where he would die for $2.9 million. Cunanan met Jeff Trail, a handsome sailor, and they became firm friends in late 1995 when Cunanan had left yet another older, wealthy boyfriend but Mr Trail could not be persuaded to jump into bed with Cunanan. In early 1997 Cunanan went to visit Mr Trail in Minneapolis where he was working. Returning to California, Cunanan worked as a transvestite prostitute to support himself.

On 26 April 1997 Cunanan returned to Minneapolis where, the next day at 9.55pm, he murdered Jeff Trail by smashing him over the head with a claw hammer. On 2 May he shot architect David Madson, another friend. Two days later, Cunanan killed property developer Lee Miglin, 72, in Chicago. On 9 May 1997 Cunanan murdered 45-year-old caretaker William Reese and stole his pick-up truck. He moved to Miami where he became a regular on the gay scene. On 15 July 1997 Cunanan murdered Versace as the fashion designer returned from breakfast at the News Café. The two men argued and then Cunanan pulled a heavy .40 calibre pistol from his backpack and shot Versace in the head. Versace fell to the ground and, to make sure that he was dead, Cunanan fired another bullet into the designer's skull.

Versace's blood stains the steps of his Miami Beach mansion.

Jack Kevorkian

"Dying is not a crime"

THE CRIME: Jack Kevorkian was born on 26 May 1928 in Pontiac, Michigan and in 1952 graduated from the University of Michigan Medical School. Kevorkian became a supporter of euthanasia and wrote articles for the German journal *Medicine and Law* extolling its virtues as he saw them. In 1987 he began to place advertisements in newspapers in Detroit offering "death counselling".

Beginning in 1990 and ending eight years later, Kevorkian helped more than 100 terminally ill people to die. They hooked themselves to a machine of Kevorkian's making, which he called a Thanatron, and it gave them a fatal dose of drugs. In 1991 the State of Michigan revoked Kevorkian's medical licence. Without a licence he was unable to get the necessary drugs for his Thanatron. After this he helped people to die using his Mercitron, basically a gas mask connected to a canister of carbon monoxide. He was tried several times for assisting in suicides but each time was acquitted. "Dying is not a crime," he said. On 17 September 1998 he made a videotape of the death of Thomas Youk, 52, who was suffering from motor neurone disease. On tape, Kevorkian injected Mr Youk with potassium chloride. Previously, Kevorkian had claimed that the patients had instigated their own deaths. He then dared the authorities to stop him. The tape was broadcast on the current affairs programme *60 Minutes* on 23 November 1998. The District Attorney called Kevorkian's bluff and on 26 March 1999 he was charged with first-degree murder and the delivery of a controlled substance to which he was not entitled (as his medical licence had been revoked).

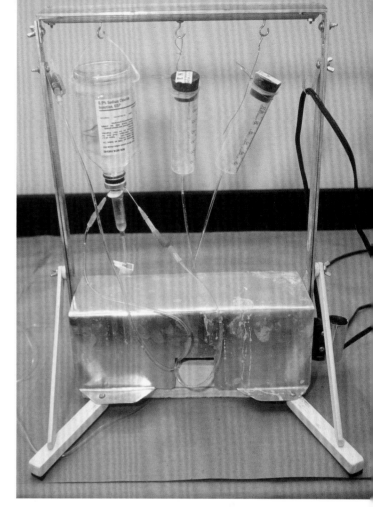

The euthanasia machine invented by Jack Kevorkian.

WHERE:
Oakland County, Michigan, USA
WHEN:
Thursday 17 September 1998
THE AFTERMATH:
Kevorkian represented himself at his trial and proved the truth of the maxim that a man who represents himself in court has a fool for a lawyer. He was convicted of second-degree murder and was sentenced to 10–25 years in prison. Judge Jessica Cooper told him, "You were not licensed to practise medicine when you committed this offence and you hadn't been licensed for eight years. And you had the audacity to go on national television, show the world what you did and dare the legal system to stop you. Well, sir, consider yourself stopped." Kevorkian was paroled on 1 June 2007.

Columbine Massacre

"The Trench Coat Mafia"

WHERE:
Columbine High School, 6201 South Pierce Street, Columbine, Jefferson County, Colorado, USA
WHEN:
11.19am Tuesday 20 April 1999
THE AFTERMATH:
A memorial to those who died was dedicated on 21 September 2007.

THE CRIME: Dylan Klebold (born 11 September 1981), 17, and Eric Harris (born 9 April 1981), 18, were pupils at Columbine High School. Both were outsiders and both had been bullied because of their general oddness. They wore long black coats, leading to their nickname "The Trench Coat Mafia". In 1997 Harris began posting death threats against the staff and other pupils at the school on his website. With his friend Klebold, he had practised exactly what they would do and kept a journal outlining their plans. They researched bomb-making on the internet and both enjoyed violent video games.

At 11.10am on 20 April (Hitler's birthday) 1999, they arrived at school in separate cars and planted two bombs in the canteen. They returned to the car park to wait for the explosions, timed for 11.17am. As that time came and went they realized their initial plan had failed. Donning their trench coats to hide their weapons, they returned to the school. Harris had a 9mm carbine rifle and a 12-guage pump sawn-off shotgun while Klebold was armed with a 9mm semi-automatic pistol and a 12-gauge pump sawn-off shotgun. At 11.19am two bombs, planted to create a diversion, exploded in a nearby field. It was the signal for the two to begin shooting.

Seventeen-year-old Rachel Scott (born 5 August 1981) was the first to die. Her friend Richard Castaldo, also 17, was wounded eight times. The rest of the school was unaware of the happenings, believing that the noise of the explosion was a prank by seniors awaiting graduation. Three more pupils were then shot. A group of pupils was eating lunch on the grass when Harris and Klebold opened fire on them. The pair entered the school, shooting as they went. A policeman arrived at 11.24am and a brief shoot-out ensued but the boys escaped. Stephanie Munson was shot in the ankle but managed to hop to safety.

Klebold and Harris then went to the library at 11.29am. Inside were 52 pupils, two librarians and two teachers. It was here the biggest carnage occurred – ten people were murdered and 12 more injured. Harris told them all to stand up whereupon Klebold shot a pupil. The two killers sat down to reload and spent the next 13 minutes taunting and shooting until at 11.42am they got bored. Then they wandered around the school for 20 minutes aimlessly shooting into classrooms and throwing bombs. Fortunately, no one else died and the pair returned to the library where they committed suicide – Klebold with a single shot to the head and Harris a single shot to the mouth – at 12.08pm. Thirteen innocent people died at Columbine High School.

CCTV cameras capture Dylan Klebold, right, and Eric Harris in the Columbine High School cafeteria during the shooting.

Katherine Knight

"I hope you are not going to kill Pricey and yourself"

*Knight stands alongside
victim John Price.*

THE CRIME: Katherine Mary Knight was born on 24 October 1955. She had six brothers and a twin sister. As she grew up, people knew not to cross her, fearful of her temper. Not terribly intelligent, she was a loner and a violent bully at school and was functionally illiterate. In 1974 she married David Kellett but the marriage got off to a bad start when she tried to strangle her husband on their wedding night because his sexual performance was not up to scratch. She took a job in a meatpacking factory. Two years later, her daughter, Melissa, was born and that year Knight was sectioned after she slashed a 16 year old in the face. After she was released, she left her baby on a railway track. Thankfully, it was saved by a local tramp. Then she stabbed a local policeman but escaped punishment because it was "just Katherine".

A second daughter, Natasha, was born in 1980 but Knight and Mr Kellett separated four years later. In 1987 she began an affair with David Saunders and a year later a child was born. It was another turbulent relationship: she stabbed Saunders with scissors, cut up all his clothes, vandalized his car and slashed the throat of his puppy. Knight was again sectioned. In May 1990 she started seeing alcoholic John Chillingworth, giving birth to his child the following year. In 1994 she met John Charles Thomas Price, a father of three known as Pricey. It was a tempestuous relationship, mainly due to Knight's instability and violent temper. On 28 February 2000 Pricey woke to find Knight standing over him with a knife in her hand. They were on the verge of splitting up but Knight demanded that he give his house to her. He refused and on 29 February took out an Apprehended Violence Order against Knight. That evening she took her children to dinner. As she left, her daughter Natasha said, "I hope you are not going to kill Pricey and yourself." That night, after watching *Star Trek*, she had sex with Pricey. Then she left the bedroom, went to the kitchen, picked up a knife and returned to the bedroom where she plunged the knife into his body 37 times. She then left and took $500 from a cashpoint at 2.30am before returning to the murder scene. Knight skinned Pricey and hung his hide on a meat hook in the living room. She then cut his head off and put the head in a crockpot on the oven. She cut meat from his buttocks and cooked it, preparing to serve it with vegetables and gravy to his children. She was arrested before she could serve the meal.

Jane Andrews

"Somebody is going to get hurt"

THE CRIME: Jane Andrews was born in the unglamorous town of Cleethorpes, Humberside, the daughter of a carpenter and a social worker. She wanted more, much more. Her first job was a designer for Marks & Spencer's children's clothes. When she was 21 she saw an advert for a job as a dresser to the Duchess of York in the magazine *The Lady*. Andrews applied and got the £18,000 a year position. In 1989 she married Christopher Dunn-Butler, a divorced, balding IBM executive, 20 years her senior. It lasted five years before the couple divorced – he accused her of infidelity. In 1995 she was in charge of the duchess's baggage when £250,000 worth of jewellery was stolen. Andrews had taken to imitating Sarah York, wearing similar clothes and styling her hair in the same way. She was devastated in 1996 when she lost her job in a cost-cutting exercise and began taking anti-depressants and seeing a therapist.

On New Year's Eve 1998 she met dashing bachelor Tom Cressman who had a taste for flashy sports cars. In October 1999 Andrews became PR manager for Claridge's hotel but her inexperience showed through and she left after just two months. She became a shop assistant but money worries meant that she relied on her wealthy boyfriend for help with her mortgage. He had his own demons – he often made cutting remarks about Andrews's appearance or opinions and had a taste for bondage, spanking and anal sex, which she indulged to please him. She was determined to marry him although he was said to have told friends, "She's a pair of old slippers I cannot throw away." The relationship became more tempestuous and Andrews bemoaned his lack of affection towards her. One day, she searched his computer and found messages to Deborah, another woman, albeit in Las Vegas. It sent her over the edge although she stayed in the relationship.

At home on 17 September 2000 they had a blazing row and at 11.35am Mr Cressman, a neighbour, rang 999 and told the operator, "Somebody is going to get hurt." The police did not attend. That night as her boyfriend slept Jane Andrews stripped naked and then smashed him in the head with a cricket bat before stabbing him in the chest with a 20 cm (8 in) knife. Andrews got in her car and in a layby on the A38 near Liskeard, Cornwall she took an overdose, in an apparent suicide bid.

Jane Andrews is rushed into court.

WHERE:
Maltings House, Bagley's Lane, Fulham, London, England
WHEN:
Sunday 17 September 2000
THE AFTERMATH:
Andrews was arrested three days later and went on trial at the Old Bailey on 23 April 2001. She attempted to traduce her dead lover's reputation, claiming that he forced her to have anal sex and that on the night he died he had twice tried to rape her anally. She told the jury, "He started hitting me and said I had ruined him. He said he was going to … kill me… I picked up the knife because I didn't want him anywhere near me. We came together and the next thing I knew he was on top of me. It must have gone into him. I crawled from underneath him and ran out of the room." On 16 May the jury convicted Andrews on a majority decision after 11 hours and 44 minutes' deliberation. She was sent to prison for life. She appealed her conviction, claiming her brother, Mark, had sexually abused her as a child. Her claims were rejected. Andrews is eligible for parole in 2012.
YOU SHOULD KNOW:
Many have wondered how Jane Andrews managed to buy a two-bedroom, second-floor flat in Prince of Wales Drive opposite Battersea Park and have around £50,000 in her bank account. An official at Buckingham Palace commented, "It was never proved legally, but we are convinced she stole a huge amount of money."

Michael McDermott

"Michael McDermott is owed no mercy by anyone"

WHERE:
Edgewater Technology, 20 Harvard Mill Square, Wakefield, Massachusetts, USA
WHEN:
Tuesday 26 December 2000

THE AFTERMATH:
When he came to trial in April 2002 McDermott announced that he had been born without a soul and that God had told him that he could earn one by going back in time to kill Nazis. McDermott testified that St Michael the Archangel had asked him to stop the Holocaust and claimed that he was in Purgatory. McDermott said he believed that he was killing Adolf Hitler and six Nazi generals when he killed his colleagues. "The whole idea was to prevent Nazi supremacy," said McDermott. "I would save tens of millions of people." However, prosecutor Thomas O'Reilly produced evidence that showed McDermott had researched on the internet how to fake mental illness and said that the real reason was that McDermott was furious that the company was intending to dock his wages to pay $5,500 in back taxes he owed to the Internal Revenue Service. After almost 16 hours of jury deliberations over three days, on 24 April 2002 McDermott was convicted on seven charges of first-degree murder and Judge R. Malcolm Graham sentenced him to seven consecutive life sentences without the possibility of parole. "Michael McDermott is owed no mercy by the court, by the families, by anyone," said Mr O'Reilly. "He deserves the ultimate punishment which is not allowed in Massachusetts."

THE CRIME: Software engineer Michael "Mucko" McDermott was born Michael McDermod Martinez on 4 September 1958. He was a strange-looking man: 1.82 m (6 ft 2 in) tall, overweight (he weighed more than 114 kg/250 lb) with a long bushy beard and shoulder-length hair that had the beginnings of a widow's peak. On Boxing Day 2000 he went into work at Edgewater Technology in Wakefield, Massachusetts,

where he earned $55,000 a year. He was armed with an AK-47 variant, a 12-gauge shotgun, and a .32 calibre pistol. There he brutally murdered seven colleagues. His victims ranged in age from 29 – Jennifer Bragg Capobianco from the marketing department and Craig Wood from personnel – to 58 – director of consulting Louis Javelle – and he shot them repeatedly in the back of the head. When the police arrived McDermott was sitting down calmly and informed them that he didn't speak German.

Michael McDermott is "helped" into court.

Bradley Murdoch

"Keep quiet or I'll shoot you"

WHERE:
Stuart Highway, near Barrow Creek,
Northern Territory, Australia
WHEN:
Saturday 14 July 2001
THE AFTERMATH:
Murdoch's murder trial began on
18 October 2005 before Chief Justice
Brian Ross Martin, QC, at the
Supreme Court of the Northern
Territory in Darwin. During the trial
Miss Lees admitted that she had had
sex with a man named Nick Riley in
Sydney, without Mr Falconio's
knowledge. Several authors have
attacked her credibility especially
after she confessed to using ecstasy
and marijuana and taking large sums
of money for media interviews.
However, the jury believed her and
on 13 December after deliberating
for eight hours they returned a
verdict of guilty. Murdoch was
sentenced to life imprisonment and
will not be eligible for parole until
2032. On 21 June 2007 the High
Court refused Murdoch special leave
to appeal. He has consistently
maintained his innocence.

*Joanne Lees and Peter Falconio
earlier in the Australian trip*

THE CRIME: This is another case of a murder where no body has ever been found. In 2001 Peter Marco Falconio (born Harrogate, North Yorkshire 20 September 1972) and girlfriend Joanne Lees (born 25 September 1973) decided to travel around Australia and bought an orange Volkswagen Kombi van for AUS$1,200 in which to travel. On 14 July 2001 they were on a road north of Alice Springs when a truck driver flagged them down. As they stopped, Mr Falconio got out of their vehicle to see what the problem was and Miss Lees heard a gunshot. The truck driver opened her door and dragged her out, handcuffing her. He told her, "Keep quiet or I'll shoot you". When Miss Lees asked he denied shooting Mr Falconio. Miss Lees managed to escape and hid in the bush for two hours until the man got tired of looking for her and drove off.

Mr Falconio's corpse has never been found, despite a thorough search by the police and expert Aborigine trackers. The police were no nearer to identifying the attacker until they arrested James Hepi, a 35-year-old Maori, on a drugs charge and, in exchange for a lighter sentence, he named Bradley John Murdoch (born 6 October 1958). Murdoch had been in trouble with the police before, beginning in 1980 when he received a suspended sentence following a conviction for causing death by dangerous driving. He was arrested in August 2002. Joanne Lees identified him as her attacker (although she has admitted that she had seen a photograph of Murdoch and an article linking him to the crime before the police interviewed her) and he was arraigned for trial. He was further linked to Miss Lees via DNA in blood found on her t-shirt.

Ian Huntley

"C ya around school"

Huntley was interviewed by the media and helped the police search for the missing girls before his arrest.

THE CRIME: It was at about 6.15pm on Saturday 3 August 2002 that Ian Huntley murdered best friends Holly Wells and Jessica Chapman, both ten years old. Just over an hour earlier, at 5.04pm, the two girls had been photographed at a family barbecue wearing their favourite Manchester United tops. The picture became an iconic image of the case. Police had investigated Huntley at least ten times for rape, underage sex, indecent assault and burglary before he began work as a school caretaker at Soham Village College on Monday 26

In February 1999 Huntley had met 22-year-old Maxine Carr at Hollywood nightclub in Grimsby, North Yorkshire. The couple moved to Soham and she landed a job as a teaching assistant at St Andrew's Primary School where she got to know Holly and Jessica. On the weekend of 3–4 August 2002, Carr visited her mother in Grimsby, leaving Huntley alone at home. It is believed that the two girls called round to see Carr who had recently lost her job at their school (they had sent her a card bearing the legend "C ya around school") or that they were enticed into the house by Huntley. He murdered both girls and then disposed of their bodies in a ditch 32 km (20 mi) away, near the perimeter fence of RAF Lakenham in Suffolk. Huntley had set the bodies on fire in a bid to destroy any evidence. The corpses were found on 17 August 2002.

WHERE:
5 College Close, Soham, Cambridgeshire, England
WHEN:
6.15pm Saturday 3 August 2002
THE AFTERMATH:
Huntley and Carr were arrested and their trial opened at the Old Bailey on 5 November 2003. He was faced with two murder charges while Carr, who had no knowledge of what her boyfriend had done, was charged with perverting the course of justice and assisting an offender. On 17 December Huntley was sentenced to life in prison. Carr was acquitted on the charge of assisting an offender but convicted of perverting the course of justice and sentenced to three and a half years in prison. She was released on 14 May 2004 after serving 21 months. Her identity and whereabouts are protected by a court order although this has not stopped the tabloid press writing stories – usually fictitious – about her. On 5 September 2006 prison warders were told to treat Huntley, who had attempted suicide three times in prison, as if he was a member of their own family, to make him feel wanted and valued. The caretaker's house has since been demolished.

Marc Cécillon

"Why did I shoot? It is a question I shall ask myself all my life"

WHERE:
Saint-Savin, France
WHEN:
Saturday 7 August 2004

THE AFTERMATH:
Cécillon, who had been known as "the calm man of rugby", was arrested and went on trial at the Court of Assizes at Isere, in Grenoble on 6 November 2006. Prosecutor Françoise Pavan-Dubois said that Cécillon had not acted on the spur of the moment but had planned to kill his wife. In court Cécillon said, "I wanted my wife to come back with me. I wanted the two of us to leave together. Why did I shoot? It is a question I shall ask myself all my life. I didn't plan anything. I wish I could understand." The defence claimed the killing was a crime of passion, committed under the influence of alcohol and that in addition Cécillon was depressed after his retirement from top-class sport. On 10 November 2006 the former rugby player was found guilty of murder, rather than the lesser charge of involuntary manslaughter. He was sentenced to 20 years in jail, five more years than the prosecution had demanded. On 3 December 2008 the sentence was reduced to 14 years on appeal.

YOU SHOULD KNOW:
Cécillon's male friends made excuses for him. Their wives were not so understanding. Pascale Tordo, the wife of retired rugby player Jean-François Tordo said, "'He was a drunk. He drank, he screwed and he always got away with it because he was Marc Cécillon. That's what 20 years of alcohol does to you – little by little it destroys you. Marc could not cope with his life. When you kill your wife, you are killing your life."

THE CRIME: Marc Cécillon was born on 30 July 1959 at Bourgoin-Jailleu and achieved two measures of fame. The first began in 1988 when he was selected to play rugby for France against Ireland. He went on to win 46 caps, his last in 1995 and he captained France on five occasions. He played in both the 1991 and 1995 World Cups. Nine years later, he achieved his second spell in the limelight when he murdered his wife Chantal. Cécillon and Chantal, 44, were invited to a garden party at the Flosailles villa of Christian and Babeth Beguy at Saint-Savin, near Bourgoin. Chantal arrived without her husband. There were rumours of infidelities on his part and even of an illegitimate son. It was 11pm when Cécillon finally turned up to the event, already drunk. He slapped Madame Beguy and, unsurprisingly, he was asked to leave. Perhaps equally unsurprisingly, Chantal refused to accompany him. Cécillon left the party alone and went to their home where he collected a .357 magnum. He returned to the event just before midnight where he shot his wife four times at point-blank range in the arm, chest and head in front of about 60 witnesses. It took about a dozen people to overpower the former rugby player. Alexandre, the Beguys' teenage son, threw a breezeblock, hitting Cécillon on the back but making no impression. When the police arrived, Cécillon was tied to a chair with electrical cord and was asking for Chantal.

Marc Cécillon, the "calm man of Rugby"

Seung-Hui Cho

"You caused me to do this"

THE CRIME:

After the Columbine Massacre (see page 246) America hoped that another similar shooting would never happen. On 16 April 2007 South Korean student Seung-Hui Cho proved them wrong. Diagnosed with depression and a severe form of an anxiety disorder, he was given treatment and allowed to attend school. Much of the work he submitted contained violence but no one thought to issue a warning. Seung-Hui Cho was born on 18 January 1984 and his family emigrated to America in September 1992, finally settling in western Fairfax County, Virginia. He was bullied at Westfield High School and rumours surfaced that he had compiled a hit list of fellow pupils he wanted to kill. In 1999 he had written in a school essay that he wanted to "repeat Columbine".

He enrolled on a business information technology degree course at Virginia Polytechnic Institute and State University (Virginia Tech) but then changed his course to English. He lived with five others in Suite 2121, Harper Hall on the campus. During his time there he was accused three times in late 2005 of stalking and was thrown out of a class for photographing the legs of female students under a table.

His killing spree began at 7.15am on 16 April 2007 when he shot Emily Jane Hilscher and Ryan "Stack" Clark, on the fourth floor of West Ambler Johnston Hall. Sometime before his next attack Cho sent a parcel of pictures, digital video files and documents to NBC *News*. Among his weapons were a .22 calibre Walther P22 semi-automatic pistol and a Glock 19 semiautomatic pistol. At 9.45am he walked into Norris Hall and in the space of nine minutes opened fire on dozens of people, killing 30 of them and wounding 25. As the police arrived Cho barricaded himself into Room 211 of Norris Hall and shot himself in the head. He was 23 years old.

A television screen shows the image of the mass murderer Seung-Hui Cho.

WHERE:
Virginia Polytechnic Institute and State University (Virginia Tech), Perry Street NW, Blacksburg, Virginia, USA
WHEN:
7.15am Monday 16 April 2007
YOU SHOULD KNOW:
Police found a note in Cho's room in which he blamed society and said, "You caused me to do this."

ROBBERIES

Colonel Blood

"It was a gallant attempt, however unsuccessful!"

WHERE:
Tower of London, England
WHEN:
7am Tuesday 9 May 1671
THE AFTERMATH:
Blood was taken to Court where on
12 May he was questioned by King
Charles, Prince Rupert, the Duke of
York, and other members of the royal
family. Remarkably, on 1 August the
king pardoned Blood and gave him
land in Ireland worth £500 a year. John
Wilmot, 2nd Earl of Rochester, wrote
in his *History Of Insipids*,
"Blood, that wears treason in his face,
Villain complete in parson's gown,
How much he is at court in grace
For stealing Ormond and the crown!
Since loyalty does no man good,
Let's steal the King, and outdo Blood!"
Blood died at 3pm on 24 August 1680
at his home in Bowling Alley, London.

THE CRIME: Thomas Blood was born in 1618 at County Meath, Ireland, the son of a blacksmith and grandson of an MP. During the Civil War he fought for the Royalists before changing sides to join Oliver Cromwell's Roundheads. At the cessation of hostilities, Cromwell made Blood a justice of the peace and awarded him land. However, when Charles II became king Blood fled to Ireland where he became a focal point for rebels. His plot to kidnap James Butler, 1st Duke of Ormonde and Lord Lieutenant of Ireland, was prevented the day before and Blood escaped to Holland. In 1670 he returned to England where he practised as a doctor or chemist in Romford Market in Essex. On the night of 6 December 1670 he attacked the Duke of Ormonde's coach in St James's Street, London, planning to take the duke to Tyburn (modern day Marble Arch) and hang him there but Ormonde managed to escape.

Blood then planned to snatch the Crown Jewels. In the spring of 1671 he visited the Tower disguised as a clergyman with a female accomplice pretending to be his wife. While admiring the Crown Jewels the "wife" pretended to be ill and was helped by the Assistant Keeper of the Jewel House, 77-year-old Talbot Edwards. Over the next few days Blood and his wife befriended the Edwardses, even inventing a nephew who could marry their daughter. On 9 May Blood brought his "nephew" and two friends to view the Jewels. Once inside, they attacked Edwards and bond and gagged him. Blood flattened St Edward's Crown and hid it under his cloak while his crony Captain Robert Perrot put the Sovereign's Orb down his trousers. A third man, Thomas Blood's son, filed the Sceptre with the Cross in two as Edwards struggled against his bindings, finally freeing himself to shout, "Treason! Murder! The crown is stolen!" As they fled to their waiting horses, they were captured and Blood declared, "It was a gallant attempt, however unsuccessful! It was for a crown!"

Irish adventurer Thomas Blood

Dick Turpin

"You have done wrong in shooting your landlord's cock"

Dick Turpin clears the Hornsey toll gate on his way to York.

THE CRIME: Dick Turpin was baptized on 21 September 1705 at Hempstead, Essex. He worked as a butcher but his stock was stolen from local farmers, an offence punishable by death. After one theft he ran into the depths of the Essex countryside and supported himself by robbing the smugglers who operated along the coast of East Anglia. He took up with a 20-strong gang, led by the blacksmith Samuel Gregory, which stole deer in the royal forest of Epping. On 11 January 1735 Turpin and five of the gang went to the house of Mr Saunders, a rich farmer at Charlton in Kent, at around 7pm. They burst in and discovered Saunders, with his wife and friends, playing at cards in the parlour. They told the company to stay still and they would come to no harm. They took a silver snuffbox and £100 of china. On 4 February they stole silver, china, money and threw a kettle of boiling water over Mr Lawrence, of Edgware, Middlesex, after getting drunk in a pub. One of the gang raped Mr Lawrence's maid. He then took up with Matthew King, "the Gentleman Highwayman". King was killed in a gun battle on 2 May 1737.

Two days later Turpin killed Thomas Morris, probably his first homicide. Morris was a servant of Henry Thomson, one of the keepers of Epping Forest and, during a routine walkabout of the forest Morris accidentally came across Turpin. Morris tried to arrest him but Turpin shot him. Turpin fled to Yorkshire with a £200 bounty on his head. Legend has it that Turpin rode the 240 km (150 mi) from London to York on his mare, Black Bess, in just 15 hours.

He assumed the name John Parmen and posed as a large-scale horse dealer. On 2 October 1738 he returned, drunk, to his lodgings and shot a gamecock belonging to John Robinson, his landlord. When a neighbour, Mr Hall, said, "You have done wrong in shooting your landlord's cock," Turpin threatened to shoot him as well. He was taken to the dungeons of York's Debtors' Prison where, on 6 February 1739, he wrote to his brother-in-law asking for help. However, these were days before the penny post and his brother-in-law refused to pay the sixpence delivery charge. That sixpence cost Dick Turpin his life. The letter was returned to the post office, which was run by John Smith. Smith recognized the handwriting and travelled to York where he identified Parmen as Dick Turpin and earned himself a £200 reward.

WHERE:
Green Dragon Inn, Welton, Yorkshire, England
WHEN:
Monday 2 October 1738
THE AFTERMATH:
On 22 March Turpin was tried and convicted at the Grand Jury House in York of two indictments of horse rustling. When news of Turpin's arraignment leaked, crowds flocked to see him and it was said that his jailer made £100 selling booze to visitors. On 7 April 1739 Turpin rode through the streets of York in an open cart, bowing to the crowds. Turpin was executed at Knavesmire, York (now the racecourse).
YOU SHOULD KNOW:
Historians have often argued that Turpin never actually made the 15-hour, 240-km (150-mi) ride on Black Bess to York to establish an alibi and that the incident is pure fiction. Numerous inns along the A1 claim that Turpin stopped there for food or a drink or to briefly stable his horse. The ride had been ascribed to the highwayman, John Nevison, known as Swift Nick or Swift Nicks. He was a highwayman in the time of King Charles II who, to establish an alibi, rode from Gad's Hill (near Rochester, Kent) to York – some 300 km (190 mi) – in about 15 hours.

Deacon Brodie

"A leap in the dark"

WHERE:
Chessel's Court, Edinburgh, Scotland
WHEN:
Saturday 8 March 1788
THE AFTERMATH:
On 12 March Brodie fled to London and then to Holland, from where he intended going to America but he was extradited back to Edinburgh, arriving on 17 July. Deacon Brodie and George Smith went on trial on 27 August 1788. Brown by this time was also a prosecution witness. Found guilty, they were hanged at the Tolbooth gallows on 1 October before 40,000 people. Brodie described his execution as "A leap in the dark." John Brown was eventually hanged in England for another crime and Andrew Ainslie was deported to Botany Bay, Australia.

YOU SHOULD KNOW:
The story of Deacon Brodie inspired Robert Louis Stevenson to write two plays and one novel on the case. The latter Longmans published as *The Strange Case Of Dr Jekyll And Mr Hyde* in January 1886, costing one shilling.

Scottish businessman and burglar William Brodie

THE CRIME: William "Deacon" Brodie was born at Brodie's Close, Lawnmarket, Edinburgh, the eldest of 11 children, on 28 September 1741. He was well educated and by the age of 22 was a Burgess, or freeman, of Edinburgh. In 1781 he became deacon (trade union leader) of the Incorporation of Wrights and succeeded his father on the town council where he served for six of the next seven years, until his death. He probably met Dr Samuel Johnson in this role and was certainly a friend of Robert Burns.

Something of a dandy, Brodie stood just 1.62 m (5 ft 4 in) tall but was always immaculate in his dress. However, the face of respectability by day, by night he was a masked thief and a leader of a gang of robbers. He also kept two mistresses, Jean Watt and Anne Grant, by whom he fathered five children in 13 years. Edinburgh shopkeepers hung their keys inside their shop doorways, making it easy for Brodie to make impressions of the keys in a small box filled with putty he carried with him. In August 1786 Brodie and his gang stole £800 from Royal Exchange bankers and robbed several goldsmiths on Parliament Close. At 1am 30 October 1787 the college mace was stolen from the university library. In 1788 a silk shop in the High Street was burgled and the Lord Advocate, Ilay Campbell of Succour, offered to pardon any gang members who turned king's evidence. The offer produced no results and in February 1788 Brodie was called to serve on a murder trial jury. On 8 March Brodie and his gang, John Brown, George Smith and Andrew Ainslie, attempted to rob the town's General Excise Office at Chessel's Court on the Canongate and a few days later Ainslie gave the authorities the names of the gang.

Sudden Solomon

"Scarcely paralleled in the history of human villainy"

THE CRIME: The first bank robbery in Australia was carried out by a Londoner with the unusual name of Sudden Solomon. He had been born George Blackston but often used the alternate spelling, Blaxton or the name William Blackstone. He was a criminal whose speciality was breaking into safes. One day in the early autumn of 1828 he realized that a drain cover in Lower George Street in Sydney led to a tunnel that went right under the foundations of the Bank of Australia. An idea immediately popped into his head and he recruited four others to help him with the plan. For nearly three weeks they dug a side tunnel until they estimated they were below the strong room. One of them, rejoicing in the name Skinny Charlie Farrell, managed to squeeze through a hole in the floor and passed through it £750 in English silver money, 2,000 Sovereigns, £14,500 in banknotes and 2,030 Spanish dollars, which were then legal tender in Australia. Before the robbers left, they destroyed scores of ledgers, bills and receipts, thus wiping out the debts of many customers. Mr Justice Dowling later described it as a plan of "cunning, contrivance and perseverance scarcely paralleled in the history of human villainy."

WHERE:
George Street (now Dalley Street), Sydney, New South Wales, Australia
WHEN:
Saturday 14 September 1828
THE AFTERMATH:
Within a year Sudden Solomon, now broke, was caught trying to rob a gambling den. He was sentenced to death but the sentence was commuted to 14 years on Norfolk Island –"a place of the extremest punishment short of death". After serving 18 months, Solomon was a broken man and offered to reveal all the details of the robbery for a pardon and free passage to England. He gave them Skinny Charlie Farrell's name, named Dingle as another robber and a fence called Woodward. The gang was quickly apprehended but, while waiting for a ship to take him back to England, Solomon ran out of money. To remedy his financial shortfall he decided to rob a small shop. He was caught and ended up back in prison with his own gang members. He was found dead in a swamp in 1844.

The Bank of Australia

Great Gold Robbery

"That means nothing, nothing at all"

WHERE:
London to Sussex railway line,
England
WHEN:
8.30pm Tuesday 15 May 1855

THE AFTERMATH:
The case may never have been solved if not for Agar's libido. He began the seduction of another thief's mistress and the thief framed Agar on forgery charges in August 1855. Agar was sentenced for penal transportation to Australia for life. Awaiting his fate, he wrote to his girlfriend, Fanny Kay, to tell her that she was owed £7,000 by William Pierce but she had received nothing. When Agar learned that he had been double-crossed he informed on his fellow thieves. William Pierce and James Burgess were arrested in London in November 1856 and William Tester, who had left England to work in Sweden, was captured when he returned to visit relatives. The trial of the four men began at the Old Bailey on 10 January 1857. Burgess and Tester were sentenced to penal transportation for 14 years; Pierce received two years and Agar went to Australia. He died there in 1881, having been told his name was legendary in London's underworld. "That means nothing," he replied, "nothing at all."

THE CRIME: On 15 May 1855, £14,000 of gold bars and coins was sent from London Bridge Station, bound for Paris via the South Eastern Railway. Also on board the train were the experienced thief, Edward Agar, and William Pierce, a former railway employee sacked for petty theft. Pierce wore a wig and false beard so that none of his former colleagues would recognize him.

The usual method of transporting gold was to place it in a heavy wooden box, bound with metal hoops. This was sealed by railway employees and then weighed. When it arrived at Boulogne it would be weighed again before being sent on to its final destination. On this day both men carried several satchels filled with lead shot to the exact weight of the gold shipment. They also carried instruments to break open the metal hoops and then reseal them. As soon as the train set off the two men made their way to the guard's van where the gold was stored. Waiting for them was James Burgess, a guard whom they had bribed. While Burgess kept watch, Agar broke into the boxes, removing the gold and replacing it with lead before resealing the hoops. When the train pulled into Redhill Station in Sussex, Agar took the opportunity to stretch his legs and to hand over two satchels of gold to William Tester, a corrupt railway official. When the train continued its journey Agar, Pierce and Burgess went to work on the remaining gold, swapping it for lead. The thieves had not brought enough lead shot to cover all the gold but took all the gold anyway. When the train pulled into Dover the thieves got off the train and waited for the porter to deliver their booty before returning to London. The "gold" was transferred to Boulogne where it was weighed and continued its journey to Paris where the theft was discovered the next day. The French police said that the theft had happened in England while the English police were convinced it had happened on the other side of the Channel. Meanwhile, Agar and Pierce began the task of melting down the gold and selling it. They then split their loot four ways.

The bullion box and the lead shot used in the robbery.

Edward Green

Green pointed his gun at the centre of the teenager's head

THE CRIME:
Edward Green was a 32-year-old postmaster with a drink habit and heavy debts when he staged America's first armed bank robbery. He had contemplated burning down the post office but changed his mind, fearful that innocent people would burn to death so instead he set fire to the building on the other side, hoping it would spread to the post office.

A few months later, on 15 December 1863, Green popped next door to his local bank to get change. At noon he returned to the bank to exchange a badly torn dollar note for a new one. There was only one bank clerk on duty, the president's 17-year-old son Frank E. Converse. Immediately formulating a plan as to how he could end his money worries, Green returned home, picked up his six-shooter gun and went back to the bank where he found Frank still on his own. Green lifted his gun and pointed it at the centre of the teenager's head, whereupon he fired at point-blank range, killing Frank outright. Green went to the bank's safe and helped himself to $5,000.

Postmaster Edward Green

WHERE:
Malden, Massachusetts, USA
WHEN:
Noon Tuesday 15 December 1863
THE AFTERMATH:
The case went unsolved for some time and no one suspected the postmaster next door. But then in January 1864 town folk noticed that Green had begun to pay off his debts and they wondered where the money had come from. He was arrested on 7 February 1864 and, when the police questioned him, Green broke down and confessed what he had done. He told them the rest of the money was hidden in an old boot and in the attic of the Volunteer Fire-Engine House. The press described Green as "rather short in stature". On 13 April 1866 at Middlesex County Jail, Edward Green, America's first armed bank robber, became America's first armed bank robber to be hanged.

Central Pacific Express Robbery

All 13 robbers rather foolishly began to spend recklessly

WHERE:
Verdi, Nevada, USA
WHEN:
Friday 4 November 1870
THE AFTERMATH:
Davis was released in 1876 after serving six years of his ten-year sentence. He met villains, Sam Bass and Joel Collins, and took up with them. Their first attempts at robbing stagecoaches were dismal failures – the first two refused to stop and the third earned them just a gold watch and $3. A fourth netted just $6. Davis then planned to rob a train and at Big Springs, Nebraska, on 18 September 1877 they robbed $60,000 from one. They split their booty and went their own way. Davis wasted his money in New Orleans, Louisiana and, by 1879 was back in Nevada robbing stagecoaches. That year, he was shot in the face by a Wells Fargo agent and disappeared. Some reports had him in Nicaragua in 1920 but they are unconfirmed.
YOU SHOULD KNOW:
Some authorities have Davis dying in a gunfight in 1874 and another man with the same name linking up with Sam Bass and Joel Collins.

THE CRIME: Born in 1845, "Big Jack" Davis arrived in Virginia City, Nevada in the 1860s hoping to make a living as a professional gambler. However, his luck was not in at the roulette wheels or in the poker hands so he turned to robbing stagecoaches to earn a living. In 1870 he met John T. Chapman, a former Sunday school superintendent, who hailed from Reno, Nevada, and they took to robbing trains. On 4 November Davis and six other men stopped and robbed the eastbound Central Pacific Express No 1 at Verdi, Nevada. They rode off in the direction of Virginia City where they divided up the spoils from the robbery – $41,600. Ten hours after Davis and his desperadoes had robbed the train, it was stopped again by six army deserters who promptly stole $4,490 that Davis's men had overlooked. All 13 robbers rather foolishly began to spend recklessly and they were soon captured by the authorities. They received sentences ranging from 10–15 years.

The point at which the Central Pacific Express was stopped on its way to Virginia City.

Theft of *Georgiana, Duchess of Devonshire*

"The Napoleon of the criminal world"

THE CRIME: Adam Worth, aka Henry Judson Raymond, was born in eastern Germany in about 1844 and moved with his parents to America when he was five years old. In 1861 he joined the Union Army where he perpetrated his first known crime – he deserted from one regiment to join another to gain a financial bonus. He even faked his own death at the second battle of Bull Run on 30 August 1862 and signed up again under a different name. After the war he moved to New York where he became a pickpocket, bank robber, forger and gambler. He was nicknamed Little Adam because of his lack of height. He worked for Fredericka Mandelbaum (see page 320). In late 1869 he moved to England with the proceeds of a $200,000 bank robbery he and his partner "Piano" Charley Bullard, a talented pianist and safe-cracker, had carried out on 20 November at the Boylston National Bank in Boston. With Irish barmaid, Kitty Flynn, the two men built up an international criminal industry.

Worth's earnings allowed him to have an apartment in Piccadilly, a mansion in Clapham, a string of racehorses and a steam yacht. On a foggy night in 1876 he broke into the Mayfair premises of Thomas Agnew & Sons, art dealers, and stole Thomas Gainsborough's portrait of Georgiana, duchess of Devonshire, which had been sold on 5 May 1876 for 10,100 guineas, then the highest price ever paid for a portrait at auction. It took Worth just five minutes to get in, grab the painting and get out. Worth stole the painting as a bargaining tool to free George Thompson, an accomplice, who had been jailed for cheque fraud. The plan came to nothing because by the time Worth had contacted the authorities Thompson had already been freed on a technicality. Mysteriously, Worth kept the painting for the next 24 years in a false-bottomed trunk.

WHERE:
Bond Street, London, England
WHEN:
Saturday 27 May 1876
THE AFTERMATH:
On 5 October 1892 Worth was arrested in the course of a robbery and on 20 March 1893 sentenced to seven years' hard labour in the Prison de Louvain, Liège, Belgium. Worth was released early through good behaviour. In poor health, he arranged for the painting to be returned to Thomas Agnew & Sons in return for $25,000 on 28 March 1901 in Chicago. Worth returned to London and on 8 January 1902, died at his home at 2 Park Village East, Camden, London.
YOU SHOULD KNOW:
Worth was the prototype for the evil Professor Moriarty in the Sherlock Holmes stories by Sir Arthur Conan Doyle. Sir Robert Anderson of Scotland Yard nicknamed Worth "the Napoleon of the criminal world".

Georgiana, Duchess of Devonshire,
by Thomas Gainsborough

Black Bart

"I've laboured long and hard for bread"

"Black Bart", the western outlaw

THE CRIME: Between 26 July 1875 and 3 November 1883 Black Bart, the pseudonym of Charles Earl Bolles (aka Charles Bolton aka Charles Boles) robbed 29 stagecoaches. John Shine drove the first stagecoach which was held up at Funk Hill on the Sonora–Milon Road, 6 km (4 mi) east of Copperopolis. Black Bart, wearing a mask made from a linen duster and a flour sack, jumped out in the front of the coach, levelled a shotgun at Shine and politely requested, "Please throw down the box,' adding less politely, "if he dares to shoot, give him a volley, boys." It was then that Shine noticed half a dozen rifles poking out of the brush. Bart took $60 in gold notes from the Wells Fargo express box and undetermined amount from the US Mail pouch. Shine drove off but soon returned to the scene to find that the six "rifle barrels" were just blackened sticks of wood.

For eight years the mysterious and polite Black Bart plagued Wells Fargo coaches using an unloaded shotgun, always on foot, and making a point of never robbing either the driver or passengers of their personal money. Between robberies he lived the high life as a mine owner and San Francisco dandy. His 29th and last robbery, on 3 November 1883, was at exactly the same place as his first but did not meet with the same success: he was wounded and later captured after Wells Fargo detectives James Hume and Henry Nicholson Morse identified a handkerchief Bart had dropped at the scene. When charged, he gave his name as T. Z. Spalding but his real name was found in a Bible given to him by his wife. The police report stated that Bart was "a person of great endurance. Exhibited genuine wit under most trying circumstances, and was extremely proper and polite in behaviour. Eschews profanity".

WHERE:
Funk Hill, Calaveras County, California, USA
WHEN:
Wednesday 3 November 1883
THE AFTERMATH:
On 16 November 1883 he was sentenced to six years in San Quentin and "seemed rather pleased with the sentence". He became a model prisoner and was released in January 1888. Asked by reporters if he was going back to his bad ways, he said, "No, gentlemen, I'm through with crime." In February 1888 he checked out of his San Francisco boarding-house and was never seen again.

YOU SHOULD KNOW:
After his fourth robbery (a stagecoach travelling from Point Arena to Duncan's Mills on 3 August 1877) Black Bart left this doggerel:
"I've laboured long and hard for bread
For honour and for riches
But on my corns too long you've tread
You fine haired sons of bitches."

Theft of the FA Cup

"At night it invited the envy of a burglar"

THE CRIME:
The FA Cup is the most prestigious club football competition in the world. Wanderers first won it at Kennington Oval on Saturday 16 March 1872 before a crowd of 2,000, beating Royal Engineers 1–0. It was the first of their five victories and Morton Peto Betts, playing under the pseudonym A.H. Chequer, scored their solitary goal. Twenty-three years later, on 20 April 1895, Aston Villa won the cup beating West Bromwich Albion at Crystal Palace in the first all-Midlands final. Villa won 1–0, with Bob Chatt scoring the fastest goal in FA Cup history, scored after just 30 seconds. The Football Association (FA) chose the design for the cup on 13 February 1872 from a submission by Messrs Martin, Hall & Company. It cost £20 and became known as "the little tin idol". Made of silver, it was inscribed with the legend, "The Football Association Challenge Cup". The cup was put on display in the window of a local football outfitter. It was left on show overnight and at 9pm on 11 September 1895 the shop was locked up.

That night someone broke in through the roof, pushed back the sliding window and removed the cup, helping themselves to a few shillings from the till as well. The local paper reported, "It stood there in the day for the admiration of the crowd, and it stayed there at night to invite the envy of a burglar."

£10 REWARD.

STOLEN!

From the Shop Window of W. Shillcock, Football Outfitter, Newtown Row, Birmingham, between the hour of 9-30 p.m. on Wednesday, the 11th September, and 7-30 a.m., on Thursday, the 12th inst., the

ENGLISH CUP,

the property of Aston Villa F.C. The premises were broken into between the hours named, and the Cup, together with cash in drawer, stolen.

The above Reward will be paid for the recovery of the Cup, or for information as may lead to the conviction of the thieves.

Information to be given to the Chief of Police, or to Mr. W. Shillcock, 73, Newtown Row.

The Birmingham police posted this notice after the theft.

WHERE:
William Shillcock Boot & Shoe Manufacturer, 73, Newton Row, Birmingham, England

WHEN:
Wednesday 11 September 1895

THE AFTERMATH:
William Shillcock, from whose shop the cup was stolen, offered a reward of £10 for its return, no questions asked. The FA had insured the trophy for £200 and Mr Shillcock had also taken out insurance but the trophy was priceless in sentimental terms. The police, under Inspector Dobbs, interviewed most of Birmingham's underworld but with no result. The FA fined Aston Villa £25 for negligence and used the money to buy a new cup from Messrs Vaughton's of Birmingham. The mystery went unsolved until 1958, when 81-year-old Harry Burge confessed that he stolen the cup while two confederates took boots and the money from the till. He said that they all retired to his home in Hospital Street where they melted down the cup and used the silver to make fake half-crowns. However, the police did not believe Burge, who had spent 46 of his 81 years behind bars and the case remains officially open.

Theft of the Irish Crown Jewels

"Spy. Informers beware. IRA never forgets"

The regalia of the Order of St Patrick was valued at £33,000 in 1907.

WHERE:
Bedford Tower, Dublin Castle, Ireland

WHEN:
Saturday 6 July 1907

THE AFTERMATH:
More than 100 years later, no one has ever been convicted, although Detective Chief Inspector Kane named a suspect but the Chief Commissioner of the Dublin Metropolitan Police refused to act on the information. On 23 October Vicars was suspended as Ulster King of Arms and Francis Bennett-Goldney and Shackleton were removed from their posts. On 6 January 1908 the Crown Jewels Commission (Ireland) was established but Vicars refused to participate. On 30 January Captain Nevile R. Wilkinson of the Coldstream Guards replaced Vicars as the new (and last) Ulster King of Arms. Vicars was told that Shackleton had stolen the jewels and indeed some historians have named him as the prime suspect although there is no definitive evidence. (Shackleton was not the suspect named by DCI Kane.)

YOU SHOULD KNOW:
Tragedy befell the Office of Arms. Pierce Gun Mahony, 36, was shot through the heart on 26 July 1914 in "a very peculiar shooting accident" near his home in Wicklow. The cause was given as his own shotgun discharging while climbing a fence but was it more than accident that blasted both barrels into his heart? Francis Bennett-Goldney became Tory MP for Canterbury in 1910. He was 53 when he died in France on 27 July 1918 in a motoring accident. Frank Shackleton went bankrupt, owing £84,441 12s 6d. He was convicted of fraud in 1913 and, following his release from prison in 1921, he took the name Mellor and died in 1941. In May 1920 Vicars was attacked in his home in County Kerry. Eleven months later, he was taken in his dressing gown from his bed by 30 men and murdered. His house was burned to the ground. A sign was placed around his neck: "Spy. Informers beware. IRA never forgets." Uncharacteristically, the IRA issued a statement saying they were not responsible for the crime.

THE CRIME: Thousands gathered in Dublin on 10 July 1907 to see the state visit of King Edward VII, Queen Alexandra and Princess Victoria. The king had arrived to visit the Irish International Exhibition in Herbert Park, which had been opened on 4 May by the Lord Lieutenant, Lord Aberdeen. Present at the opening had been the Ulster King of Arms (Sir Arthur Vicars, in his 14th year in the job), plus his staff from the Office of Arms: the Athlone Pursuivant (Francis Bennett-Goldney), the Dublin Herald (Francis Richard Shackleton, the younger brother of the explorer) as well as four Knights of St Patrick. The Cork Herald (Pierce Gun Mahony) was unable to be present. The regalia of the Order of St Patrick, otherwise known as the Irish Crown Jewels, was kept in the Office of Arms in the Bedford Tower in Dublin Castle. In 1907 these jewels were valued at £33,000. It was agreed that the jewels would be stored in a strong room on the ground floor of the Bedford Tower. It was only when construction was completed that it was discovered that the safe was too big to fit into the room so it was put in the library instead.

On 28 June 1907 Vicars spotted that the key to the front door to the Bedford Tower was missing and he had to be let in by a policeman. (The key reappeared on 8 July.) On 6 July a messenger from Messrs West and Son, jewellers, returned a gold and enamelled collar of the Order of St Patrick and Vicars gave the messenger the key to put the jewel in the safe. He discovered the safe was unlocked and the boxes containing the regalia of the Grand Master and of the Knights of the Order of St Patrick were empty. Superintendent John Lowe of the Detective Branch of the Dublin Metropolitan Police, Detective Officer Owen Kerr and Assistant Commissioner of the Dublin Metropolitan Police, William. V. Harrel, came to investigate the theft but, unable to cope, they called in Detective Chief Inspector John Kane of Scotland Yard. The safe had not been forced open and no duplicate keys had been used. A reward of £1,000 was offered for information leading to the recovery of the jewels and the capture of the thief or thieves.

Theft of the *Mona Lisa*

"To our astonished eyes the divine *Gioconda* appeared, intact and wonderfully preserved"

THE CRIME: Leonardo Da Vinci created the most famous painting in the world in the early 16th century. The *Mona Lisa*, or *La Gioconda*, measures just 76 x 53 cm (30 x 21 in) and is owned by the French government. In the summer of 1911, on a day when the museum was closed, it was stolen. The next day, Louis Béroud, an artist who copied works of art for tourists, arrived to paint the *Mona Lisa* but found an empty space where it had been. A guard thought that the painting was being photographed or having its frame fixed. It was not until 11am that the alarm was raised. The *Mona Lisa* was painted on wood not canvas so could not be rolled up and the police believed that the thief had waited in the museum overnight and then escaped during renovations and cleaning on the Monday. The police found a lefthand thumbprint but unfortunately in those days only the prints on the right hand were kept, so it was a dead end. The Louvre offered a reward of 25,000 francs; the newspaper *Le Matin* put up 5,000 francs, but both were topped by the magazine *L'Illustration* which offered 40,000 francs. Rumours circulated that an American millionaire had commissioned the theft or perhaps it was a German plot to discredit France.

On 10 December 1913 a moustachioed young man calling himself Vincenzo Leonard went to the offices of Alfredo Geri, an antique dealer on the Via Borgognissanti, Florence. The visitor said that he had the *Mona Lisa* and would be willing to hand it over for 500,000 lire and a promise it would stay in Italy. Geri and a friend Giovanne Poggi, Director of the Uffizi Gallery, went to the Hotel Tripoli, where the young man was staying, to view the painting. Geri later recalled, "The man opened a trunk full of wretched belongings. Then he took out an object wrapped in red cloth, and to our astonished eyes the divine *Gioconda* appeared, intact and wonderfully preserved." Leonard agreed to let the two men take the painting to the Uffizi to check its authenticity. Meantime, the head of Florence's police went to arrest the young man whose real name was Vincenzo Perugia.

WHERE:
Salon Carré, Palais Royal, Musée du Louvre, Paris, France
WHEN:
Monday 21 August 1911
THE AFTERMATH:
The painting was exhibited in Italy for two months before its return to France. On 4 January 1914 was unveiled at the Louvre. In June 1914 Perugia went on trial in Florence. He said that he had stolen the painting out of patriotic duty, a defence that endeared the public to him and he was sentenced to just one year and 15 days.
YOU SHOULD KNOW:
The only person arrested by French police in connection with the theft was the poet and art critic, Guillaume Apollinaire, on 7 September 1911. He implicated Pablo Picasso who was questioned. Both men were freed without charge.

The Mona Lisa *is carried back to the Louvre.*

Bonnot Gang

They were chased by two policemen, one on horseback and the other on a bicycle

WHERE:
Rue Ordener, Paris, France
WHEN:
8.25am Thursday 21 December 1911
THE AFTERMATH:
On 28 December 1911 the gang broke into a gun shop and on 2 January 1912 they murdered a wealthy Parisian and his maid, making off with 30,000 francs. On 25 March they robbed the Société Générale Bank at Chantilly, shooting three bank cashiers. They escaped in a stolen car and were chased by two policemen, one on horseback and the other on a bicycle. In March and April police began arresting gang members and by the end of April had 28 in custody. On 24 April, as they attempted to arrest Bonnot, he shot and killed one policeman and wounded another. Four days later, he was shot and killed as he tried to escape.
YOU SHOULD KNOW:
The leader of the gang was actually Octave Garnier (it was his idea to use cars to get away) but the press called it the Bonnot Gang after Bonnot turned up at the offices of the *Petit Parisien* newspaper to complain about their coverage of the gang.

THE CRIME: The Bonnot Gang (*La Bande à Bonnot*) was a group of anarchists who made history by using the first getaway car. They were active between 1911 and 1912. The first getaway car was a 1910 Delaunay-Belleville luxury limousine with green and black trim, registration number 783-X-3. It was stolen on 14 December 1911 by four of the gang – Jules Bonnot, Octave Garnier, Eugène Dieudonné and Raymond Callemin – who changed the plate to 668-X-8 and used it a week later to intercept Monsieur Caby, a bank messenger, en route to a branch of the Société Générale Bank in the Rue Ordener, in Paris. At 8.25am, Caby arrived by tram carrying a satchel and briefcase, to be met by a bank security guard. Octave Garnier and Raymond Callemin marched up to them and Callemin put a gun into the face of the guard who fled into the bank. Garnier grabbed the satchel but Caby would not let go and was dragged along the street until the robber fired three shots, two into the chest of the messenger. Bonnot drove the car parallel to the action and, as soon as Garnier and Callemin got aboard, he executed a screeching U-turn and sped away. The gangsters fired warning shots to anyone foolish enough to follow. They headed north and dumped the car on the beach near Dieppe Casino, leading French police to believe that they had left for England. The satchel contained 5,126 francs and the briefcase more than 130,000 francs-worth of useless cheques and bonds. Had they looked inside Caby's jacket, they would have found a wallet stuffed with 20,000 francs.

Some of the Bonnot Gang.
Top row, left to right: Carrouy, Dieudonné, Belonie, Callemin, Soudy, Rodriguez and Madge.
Middle row: Gaucy, Jourdan, Rimbauld and Kibaltchich.
Bottom row: Cherch, Gorodesky, Crozat of Fleury, Boe, Detweiller and Villemin-Schoofs.

Ray, Roy & Hugh D'Autremont

"They were clueless"

Hugh, Roy and Ray D'Autremont

THE CRIME: The last Wild West-style train robbery in America cost the lives of four men, the liberty of three more and launched a manhunt on a scale never before seen in the United States. It began with Southern Pacific Railroad's Train 13 from Seattle on its way to San Francisco, at Tunnel 13 just south of Ashland, under the Siskiyou Mountains that straddle the Oregon-California border. As the train entered the tunnel, two grease-faced, armed men jumped aboard the tender. At gunpoint, they ordered engineer Sydney Bates, 51, and fireman Marvin Seng, 23, to stop the train, leaving the engine, tender and mail car clear of the tunnel and all the other passenger-filled coaches inside. A third gang member attached and detonated dynamite to the side of the mail car but he miscalculated the explosion and destroyed the mail car and incinerated the mail clerk Edwin Daugherty. Investigators could only find his charred skull and a portion of vertebrae. The robbers panicked.

As brakeman Coyl Johnson, 37, ran to investigate he was shot three times, the third shot while he was lying on the ground still alive. Then they shot Marvin Seng twice and, finally, they shot Bates in the back of his head. After killing four men, the robbers fled empty handed. At the scene police found a detonator, a .45 Colt pistol, three sacks soaked in creosote (these were to drag along the ground to confuse sniffer dogs), a black travelling bag with a railroad shipping tag, a pair of greasy overalls and a pair of shoes. Despite many arrests the police got nowhere. Then they decided to request help from Dr Edward O. Heinrich, a master criminologist known as The Edison of Crime Detection. His investigations led to William Elliott, a known alias of a Roy D'Autremont. The three D'Autremont brothers were twins Ray and Roy, aged 23, and Hugh, aged 19. Their father was a barber while the boys tried their luck as lumberjacks. Two and half million wanted posters were distributed both in the United States and around the world. But it wasn't until 1927 that an American soldier stationed on Alcatraz Island (not a prison until 1933) recognized Hugh as James Price, a fellow soldier he had recently met in Manila. Hugh was quickly extradited and the twins located in Steubenville, Ohio where Ray's bleached hair failed to stop him being recognized from newly issued posters. Their trial was the last in the Jacksonville Court House built during the Oregon Gold Rush. The prosecution insisted on an all-male jury because it was frightened a woman's motherly instincts might cloud her judgement. One witness said, "They thought they'd get all this money and they didn't get anything. They were clueless."

WHERE:
Tunnel 13, Siskiyou Mountains, Oregon, USA
WHEN:
12.40pm Thursday 11 October 1923
THE AFTERMATH:
On 21 June 1927 Hugh was sentenced to life imprisonment. The twins confessed the next day and also received life sentences. Angry railwaymen never forgot and whenever a train passed on the line that skirted the southern perimeter of the Oregon State Prison the engineer would ring the warning bell reminding the brothers their release would not be a happy event. After 26 years of increasing mental deterioration Roy went berserk. It took six men 15 minutes to subdue him. He was given a prefrontal lobotomy in the same hospital that years later was filmed in *One Flew Over The Cuckoo's Nest*. He was paroled in March 1983 and died in June of that year. Hugh was paroled in 1958 but died three months later in San Francisco of stomach cancer. Ray was granted parole in 1961, aged 61, and died on 22 December 1984.

Thomas Holden, centre, hardly looks like one of the "Ten Most Wanted Fugitives".

Tough Tommy Holden

"A menace to every man, woman and child in America"

THE CRIME: Thomas James Holden was the first man to be listed on the FBI's "Ten Most Wanted Fugitives" list when it was released on 14 March 1950. Holden's career began in the 1920s, robbing banks and payrolls with his partner Frank Keating. They also held up mail trains. Two of their gang, Frank Weber and Charles Harmon, murdered a hostage during a bank robbery at Memonimie, Wisconsin and Holden and Keating were furious. Not long after, the bodies of Weber and Harmon were discovered in a ditch – Holden and Keating had executed both men.

In 1928 they robbed a train in Evergreen Park, Chicago, leading to them being nicknamed the Evergreen Bandits. Their luck was out as both were caught and sent to Leavenworth. They escaped in December 1931 using forged passes and fled to Kansas City where they joined the Barker-Karpis Gang (see page 36), robbing several banks. On 7 July 1932 Holden, Keating and Harvey Bailey were arrested on a golf course at Kansas City, Missouri. A fourth villain, Frank Nash, escaped because he was a poor player and had got left behind. Among the arresting officers was Special Agent Raymond Caffrey who would be killed aged 31 on 17 June 1933 in the Kansas City Massacre (see opposite). Holden was paroled from Leavenworth Prison on 28 November 1947 but could not keep out of trouble. On 5 June 1949 Holden was drinking with his family in Chicago when he and his wife fell into an argument. He shot her dead and then turned his gun on her two brothers, an action that led to his place in the FBI list. An FBI spokesman said that Holden was "a menace to every man, woman and child in America". He had fled Illinois, and was charged with unlawful flight across state lines on 4 November 1949. Holden adopted the name John McCullough and began working in Oregon as a plasterer. An local recognized Holden from his picture in a local newspaper and the FBI arrested him on 23 June 1951.

WHERE:
Evergreen Park, Chicago, Illinois, USA
WHEN:
1928
THE AFTERMATH:
Holden died in Illinois State Prison in 1953.

Pretty Boy Floyd

"A pretty boy with apple cheeks."

THE CRIME: Charles Floyd was born in rural Bartow County, Georgia, on 3 February 1904, the son of a farmer-bootlegger. In 1922 he tried to rob a post office but was caught and almost ended in jail, saved only by his father giving him an alibi. The next time he was not so lucky. On 11 September 1925 he stole $16,000 from a Kroger store in St Louis. It was from an eyewitness that day that he earned his "Pretty Boy" nickname. It was said that he was "a mere boy – a pretty boy with apple cheeks". Like Baby Face Nelson, Floyd hated his nickname. The haul also earned him his first spell in prison. On 19 December 1925 he began a five-year stretch at the Missouri State Penitentiary overlooking Jefferson City. On his release after three years, he moved in with Juanita Baird, the wife of a drug dealer, his own wife, Ruth Hargrove, having divorced him. The police began keeping the couple under surveillance and, to escape them, he moved to East Liverpool, Ohio. Between January and March 1930 Floyd and his gang committed a number of robberies there. On 8 March he was arrested after a gang member shot a policeman. Tried and convicted, he was sentenced to 15 years in prison but escaped from the bathroom of the bus taking him to jail. He returned to Kansas City where he was reunited with Juanita Baird and was joined by her sister, Rose, and a new confederate, William "Billy the Killer" Miller. Floyd and Miller killed the husbands of the Rose and Juanita, before travelling east to rob banks. On 16 April 1931 in Bowling Green, Ohio, a shop assistant recognized Floyd from a wanted poster and rang the police. A gun battle ensued on South Prospect Street and Patrolman Ralph Castner was shot, dying a week later. Miller was also killed and the two women arrested. Floyd escaped to Cookson Hills, Oklahoma. Floyd and his partner George Birdwell, robbed banks in Earlsboro, Konawa, Maud, Marble City, Morris, Shamrock, Tahlequah. On 12 December 1931 they robbed two banks in one day at Castle and Paden, Oklahoma. On 3 April 1932 he was shot during yet another gun battle. In the autumn of 1932 Floyd took up with Adam Richetti and they resumed their activities in May 1933. On 17 June, during an attempt to free gangster Frank "Gentleman" Nash, five men including FBI agent, Raymond Caffrey, were killed in what became known as the Kansas City Massacre. Floyd denied any involvement but the FBI claimed fingerprint evidence linked him to the crime scene. On 19 October 1934 Floyd was identified as one of the three robbers of the Tiltonsville Peoples Bank.

WHERE:
Castle and Paden, Oklahoma, USA
WHEN:
Saturday 12 December 1931
THE AFTERMATH:
On 22 October 1934 Floyd was killed in a shoot out with the FBI. He had been staying at the Conkle farm near Clarkson, Ohio, after Ellen Conkle took pity on him. As her brother, Stewart Dyke, prepared to drive Floyd to the bus garage, the police arrived.
YOU SHOULD KNOW:
In November 1929 Floyd's father died during an argument with his neighbour, James Mills. Floyd returned for the funeral and shortly afterwards Mr Mills disappeared.

Pretty Boy Floyd posing with Juanita Baird.

Babyface Nelson

"I'm gonna kill you sons of bitches!"

WHERE:
Grand Haven, Michigan, USA
WHEN:
Friday 18 August 1933
THE AFTERMATH:
Just four months after John Dillinger was shot to death, Nelson met his own end. On 27 November 1934 Nelson, his wife Helen Gillis, and John Paul Chase were driving in Barrington outside Chicago when they saw a police car coming towards them. Nelson had a pathological hatred of the police and federal agencies, even going so far as to compile a list of their unmarked car registration numbers. He recognized the car and gave chase, resulting in his car ending up in a ditch. Nelson came out of the ditch firing a Thompson sub-machine gun and shouting, "I'm gonna kill you sons of bitches!", fatally wounding Special Agent Herman Hollis, 31, and Inspector Samuel P. Cowley, 35. Nelson was hit 17 times but with the help of his wife and Chase, made a getaway in the FBI car. The next day the FBI found the bodies of their two agents and in a ditch in front of St Peter Catholic Cemetery in Skokie the corpse of Baby Face Nelson. His wife later said that he had died at precisely 8pm and she had wrapped a blanket around him because "Lester always hated to be cold." He was 25 years old.

THE CRIME: Despite his cutesy nickname there was nothing baby-like about Lester Gillis, who had a fearsome temper and propensity for violence, resulting in him killing more than a dozen policemen. Born in Chicago, Illinois, on 6 December 1908, he began his criminal career at an early age as a car thief and was arrested aged 13 and sent to a borstal. Two years later he was released on parole, but within five months he was returned on a similar charge. Like many criminals, Nelson was on the short side at 1.63 m (5ft 4in).

He was arrested for bank robbery in Chicago on 15 January 1931 and jailed for a year but escaped on 17 February 1932, after overpowering a guard. The following year, with safe-cracker Eddie Bentz, Nelson went to Grand Haven, Michigan on 18 August 1933 and robbed his first bank. The robbery was a disaster but most of those involved escaped. In 1934 Nelson joined John Dillinger's gang (see page 35). Following Dillinger's death, Nelson became Public Enemy Number One.

Babyface Nelson killed more than a dozen policemen.

Willie Sutton

"You can't rob a bank on charm and personality"

THE CRIME: Born on June 30, 1901, in Brooklyn, New York, Willie Sutton became famous for something he didn't say. When he wasn't robbing banks, he worked briefly as a clerk, a driller and a gardener. Well attired, he was the politest of bank robbers. One victim said witnessing one of Sutton's robberies was like being at the movies, except the usher had a gun. He usually carried either a pistol or a Thompson submachine gun. After all, as he said, "You can't rob a bank on charm and personality" but took pride in never using his weapon. He was nicknamed "Willie the Actor" or "Slick Willie". He robbed his first bank in 1927. On 5 June 1931 Sutton was jailed for 30 years on assault and robbery charges but on 11 December 1932 he escaped by scaling the prison wall on two joined-together 2.7-m (9-ft) long sections of ladder. On 15 February 1933 he and a friend tried to rob the Corn Exchange Bank and Trust Company in Philadelphia, Pennsylvania, but were put off by a nosy passerby.

Exactly eleven months later, on 15 January 1934, Sutton and two confederates broke into the bank though a skylight and robbed the bank after tying up the staff and security guard. He was arrested on 5 February and sentenced to 25–50 years in the Eastern State Penitentiary in Philadelphia. On 3 April 1945 Sutton made his fifth attempt to escape and did succeed in freeing himself, albeit temporarily – he was arrested the same day. Returned to prison, this time on a life tariff, he was transferred the Philadelphia County Prison, Homesburg, Pennsylvania. On 9 February 1947, during a snowstorm, he escaped dressed as a prison warder. On 20 March 1950 he was added to the FBI's list of "Ten Most Wanted Fugitives". On 18 February 1952 Arnold Schuster spotted Sutton on the New York subway and telephoned the police. The act cost the 24-year-old his life (see page 336) and Sutton was returned to jail. In his career he robbed probably 100 banks, netting $2 million.

Willie Sutton (centre) with the policemen who helped to capture him.

WHERE:
Philadelphia, Pennsylvania, USA
WHEN:
Monday 15 January 1934
THE AFTERMATH:
On Christmas Eve 1969 68-year-old Sutton, by now ill with emphysema, was released from Attica State Prison. The following year Sutton appeared in an advertisement for the New Britain, Connecticut Bank and Trust Company's new photo credit card. He said on the commercial, "Now when I say I'm Willie Sutton, people believe me." On 2 November 1980, Willie Sutton died in Spring Hill, Florida, at the age of 79. He was buried in the Sutton family plot at Holy Cross Cemetery in the Flatbush section of Brooklyn on 7 November.
YOU SHOULD KNOW:
When asked why he robbed banks, Sutton is said to have replied, "Because that's where the money is." In 1976 the words were used as the title of his second autobiography (*I, Willie Sutton* was published in 1952), *Where The Money Was: The Memoirs Of A Bank Robber.* He wrote, "I will now confess that I never said it. The credit belongs to enterprising reporter [Mitch Ohnstad] who apparently felt a need to fill out his copy. Why did I rob banks? Because I enjoyed it. I loved it. I was more alive when I was inside a bank, robbing it, than at any other time in my life. I enjoyed everything about it so much that one or two weeks later I'd be out looking for the next job. But to me the money was the chips, that's all."

Eight of the men involved in the robbery. From left: Michael Geagan, James Faherty, Thomas Richardson, Joseph McGinnis, Anthony Pino, Vincent Costa, Adolph Maffie and Henry Baker

1950 Brink's Robbery

"People need a few laughs these days"

THE CRIME: On a winter's day in 1950 the Brink's Building in Boston was robbed of $1,218,211.29 in cash, and over $1.5 million in cheques, money orders and other securities. The robbery was then the largest in the history of America. Anthony "Fats" Pino planned the heist and he hired Joseph "Big Joe" McGinnis, Stanley "Gus" Gusciora and Joseph "Specs" O'Keefe. The robbery took two years to plan and often the robbers would enter the building to sketch out the lay of the land. Pino then took on seven more men, including his brother-in-law, Vincent Costa, plus Michael Vincent "Vinnie" Geagan, Thomas Francis Richardson, Adolph "Jazz" Maffie, Henry Baker, James Faherty and Joseph "Barney" Banfield. They carried out a complete dress rehearsal in December 1949 and another on 16 January. Finally on 17 January everything was ready. They wore uniforms similar to Brink's staff plus rubber Halloween masks and overshoes. Pino and Banfield stayed in the getaway lorry while seven thieves entered the building. They bound and gagged five Brink's employees and in 35 minutes they were back outside again with their loot. They divided the money and then agreed not to touch it for six years until the statute of limitations expired.

WHERE:
165 Prince Street, Boston, Massachusetts, USA

WHEN:
6.55pm Tuesday 17 January 1950

THE AFTERMATH:
Brink's Incorporated offered a $100,000 reward for information leading to the arrest of the robbers and the recovery of the money. In June 1950 O'Keefe and Gusciora were arrested in Pennsylvania for a burglary. O'Keefe was sent down for three years in Bradford County Jail while Gusciora got 5–20 years in the Western State Penitentiary at Pittsburgh. When he was released O'Keefe was arrested on another burglary charge and bailed for $17,000. While free, on 18 May 1954, he kidnapped Vincent Costa, claiming he had never seen his share of the money. Pino hired Elmer "Trigger" Burke to kill O'Keefe. He shot O'Keefe on 16 June 1954 but the robber survived. In August 1954 O'Keefe was sentenced to 27 months in prison. The FBI continued to pressure him and he told them everything on 6 January 1956. Six days later the Feds apprehended Baker, Costa, Geagan, Maffie, McGinnis and Pino. On 16 May they arrested Faherty and

Richardson at Dorchester, Massachusetts. Banfield had died and Gusciora passed away on 9 July from a brain tumour and acute cerebral edema. The rest of the robbers came to trial on 6 August. O'Keefe was sentenced to four years and freed in 1960. The other eight men were sent to prison for life on 9 October 1956. When a film was made

Richardson and Maffie were invited to the set. Richardson said, "I'm glad they made something light out of it. People need a few laughs these days."

YOU SHOULD KNOW:
Only $58,000 of the $2.7 million was recovered. The robbers missed escaping prosecution by less than a week.

Theft of the Stone of Scone

"It's like the Loch Ness monster, it's certainly a puzzle and a mystery which is best not answered"

THE CRIME: It looks like any other bit of granite but the Stone of Scone, or Stone of Destiny, is an extremely important artefact in Scottish history. Measuring 66 cm by 40 cm by 27 cm (26 x 16 x 10.5 in) and weighing approximately 152 kg (336 lb), it is supposed to be the pillow stone used by Jacob in the Bible. It has been used in the coronation of the monarchs of Scotland, England, and, more recently, Britain. It is believed to have first been used at the coronation of Kenneth Mac Alpin, the first King of Scots, in around 847. Robert the Bruce gave a portion of the stone to Cormac McCarthy, king of Munster, Ireland, who installed it at Blarney Castle where it became the Blarney Stone. John Balliol was the last Scottish king to be crowned on the stone at Scone in 1292. In 1296 it was captured by Edward I and taken to Westminster Abbey where it was installed in St Edward's Chair, on which all subsequent English sovereigns, except Queen Mary II, have been crowned.

On Christmas Day 1950, four radical Scottish nationalist students from Glasgow University – Ian Hamilton, Gavin Vernon, Kay Matheson and Alan Stuart – took the Stone from Westminster Abbey, intending to return it to Scotland. As they stole it, they broke it into two. The larger part they left with gypsies in Kent for a few days while they attempted to take the smaller piece back to Scotland. They used a borrowed car and were helped by John Josselyn. Glasgow stonemason Robert Gray was given the Stone of Scone to repair by a Glaswegian politician. Repaired, the stone was left covered in a saltire at the altar in the ruins of Arbroath Abbey on 11 April 1951.

WHERE:
Westminster Abbey, London, England
WHEN:
Monday 25 December 1950
THE AFTERMATH:
The stone was returned to Westminster Abbey where it stayed until July 1996 when it was sent back to Scotland. The four students were not prosecuted.
YOU SHOULD KNOW:
Rumours persist that the stone is a fake and was either replaced to prevent Edward I having it or was copied by stonemason, Robert Gray, in 1951. Scottish First Minister Alex Salmond said, "It's like the Loch Ness monster, it's certainly a puzzle and a mystery which is best not definitively answered." Ian Hamilton, who stole it, believes that it is genuine. "Had it been a substitute for Edward to carry off it would have been produced when [Robert the Bruce] regained his kingdom. It wasn't."

St Edward's Chair in Westminster Abbey after the theft of the Stone of Scone.

Georges LeMay

LeMay directed everything via walkie-talkie from across the street

WHERE:
Montreal, Quebec, Canada
WHEN:
Saturday 1 July 1961
THE AFTERMATH:
The event was Canada's biggest robbery and the police had no clues. Although they suspected LeMay, there was no evidence to link him to the crime. On 5 January 1962 they raided his home and found $2,000 in American currency and three days later issued a warrant for his arrest. A fortnight later they discovered a yacht that LeMay had been using to sail from Montreal to Miami and also made four arrests, including Lise Lemieux who would become LeMay's second wife. In May 1965 the Royal Canadian Mounted Police broadcast LeMay's picture on a satellite television show and he was recognized by a boar repairer in Fort Lauderdale, Florida. LeMay surrendered without a fight and on 1 June 1965 he married Lise Lemieux which meant she could not be forced to testify against him. On 21 September LeMay escaped from the maximum security prison he was held in prior to extradition. He remained at large until 19 August 1966 when he was arrested in a Las Vegas casino. He was returned to Canada where, on 17 January 1969, he was jailed for eight years for the 1961 burglary. The money was never recovered. LeMay died in December 2006, a few days short of his 82nd birthday. However, his death was kept secret until September 2008.

THE CRIME: Georges LeMay was born in December 1924 and had intentions to become a Roman Catholic priest. However, while studying, he found that he liked women too much to be celibate and crime too much to be honest. During the week he would go to Montral nightclubs and try to pick up other men's girlfriends. Despite outward appearances as a playboy, he didn't smoke, drink or gamble much. His vices were fast cars, boats and planes. LeMay married for the first time on 19 May 1951 but on 4 January 1952 his wife, Huguette Daoust, disappeared under mysterious circumstances while they were on a second honeymoon. Despite a jury finding that she had met her death violently, LeMay was never charged with any crime. On 15 July 1957 he was charged with illegal possession of a gun and fined $25. On Canada Day 1961 LeMay and some cronies broke into the Bank of Nova Scotia in Montreal. LeMay organized the heist and directed everything via walkie-talkie from across the street. The gang broke into 377 safety deposit boxes, stealing in total $633,605.

Federal agents lead LeMay from the boat on which he was discovered.

The train stands by Bridego Bridge, the morning after the robbery.

WHERE:
Bridego Bridge, Ledburn, Buckinghamshire, England
WHEN:
3.03–3.27am Thursday 8 August 1963
THE AFTERMATH:
The insider who arranged which train to stop has never been identified. Only £343,448 of the stolen money was ever recovered. The trial of the 12 began on 20 January 1964. All were found guilty on 16 April and Tommy Wisbey, Bob Welch, Jim Hussey, Gordon Goody, Ronnie Biggs, Roy James and Charlie Wilson were all sentenced to 30 years' imprisonment; Roger Cordrey was given a 20-year sentence although it was reduced to 14 years on appeal; Brian Field and Leonard Field both received 25 years although that was reduced to five on appeal. On 12 August 1964 Charlie Wilson escaped from Winson Green Prison in Birmingham. He stayed on the run until 24 January 1968. On 23 April 1990 he was shot dead as he relaxed by his swimming pool in Marbella, Spain. On 8 July 1965 Ronnie Biggs escaped from Wandsworth Prison and remained free in Brazil until 7 May 2001 when, ill, he voluntarily returned to England. The last of the robbers to be captured, Bruce Reynolds, was arrested on 8 November 1968 and sent down for ten years. Buster Edwards escaped to Mexico but returned to England in 1966, homesick, and was jailed for 15 years for his troubles. Driver Jack Mills never recovered from the cosh on the head and died in 1970. Edwards, who on release ran a flower stall at Waterloo Station and was the subject of the 1988 film *Buster*, committed suicide on 29 November 1994.

Great Train Robbery

"It was a brilliantly planned operation"

THE CRIME: At 6.50pm on 7 August 1963 a Royal Mail train left Glasgow bound for London. On board were nearly 120 mailbags containing £2,631,784 in banknotes on their way to be destroyed. In the early hours of the next day the train was stopped at Seers Crossing and at Bridego Bridge it was robbed. "It was a brilliantly planned operation," said one senior policeman. The driver Jack Mills, 58, tried to stop the thieves and was hit over the head with an iron bar by one of the gang, Buster Edwards. The gang had hidden out at Leatherslade Farm in Oxfordshire but had been careless in cleaning up after themselves. They played *Monopoly* with real money and left several fingerprints, which came in useful when the police raided on 13 August. Roger Cordrey, who had arranged the signals that stopped the train, was the first to be arrested. Charlie Wilson was arrested on 22 August 1963. Eventually, 12 members of the 15-man gang were captured.

Illinois Enema Bandit

"Not sexually mature"

WHERE:
Champaign-Urbana, Illinois, USA
WHEN:
Saturday 3 May 1975
THE AFTERMATH:
Kenyon was released from prison and died in Chicago in 2004.
YOU SHOULD KNOW:
The story of the Illinois Enema Bandit was immortalized in a Frank Zappa song.

THE CRIME: Probably one of the most bizarre thieves of all time, Michael H. Kenyon was an armed robber who gave enemas to his victims. Born in 1943 at Elgin, Illinois, he was also known as the Champaign Enema Bandit and the Ski Masked Bandit. It is though that he as responsible for at least ten attacks between May 1965 and May 1975. One of his earliest attacks was on a March morning in 1966 at Champaign, Illinois, when, wearing a red argyle ski mask and carrying a gun, he climbed into a home through a window. He stole $70 from the wallets of two teenaged sisters – one was 16, the other 18 – and then tied them up with torn sheets. He then gave them both enemas.

In 1967 Kenyon graduated from University of Illinois at Urbana-Champaign with a degree in accountancy. Eight years later, on 3 May 1975, armed with a gun, he robbed and bound four women at the University of Illinois at Champaign-Urbana. He gave two enemas to one of the women and stole $120 from their apartments. Police arrested Kenyon in Palatine, Chicago, a short while after for a minor offence. At the time he was working as an accountant for the Illinois Department of Revenue. As the police questioned him, he suggested that they contact the Champaign police and he confessed to being the Illinois Enema Bandit. Under questioning by the Champaign police, he showed them the ski mask he wore to carry out the attacks and also his two shotguns and a pistol.

After a session with a psychiatrist, he was judged to be legally sane and stood trial on 1 December 1975. The next day Champaign Assistant State's Attorney Robert Steigmann said, "If he did not want to get caught, he would not be in court today." Kenyon pleaded guilty to six counts of armed robbery. His lawyer Ray Massucci said that Kenyon was "not sexually mature" and that his behaviour was the result of a "deep-seated neurosis". The judge imprisoned Kenyon for six concurrent terms of 6–12 years on 23 December.

Albert Spaggiari

"Without hatred, without violence, without weapons"

THE CRIME: While most of France was enjoying the long holiday weekend of 16–19 July 1976, a group of thieves was emptying several hundred safety deposit boxes in the vaults of the Société Générale bank in Nice. They contained about 50 million francs in cash, jewels and other valuables. The thieves had spent the previous two months building a 7.6-m (25-ft) long tunnel into the vaults. Once they had finished, they welded the vaults closed.

When the staff arrived for work on Tuesday 20 July 1976 they assumed that there had been a malfunction of the time locks. Only when the vaults were broken open did they realize that they had been robbed. On the wall was scrawled, "*Sans haine, sans violence et sans arme*" ("without hatred, without violence, without weapons"). The safety deposit boxes were strewn about the floor amid the remains of gourmet meals, oxy-acetylene torches and, in the tunnel, a pneumatic drill and a cable that they had cheekily plugged into the city's electric supply. When the story broke, the French were quietly amused by the gall and cunning of the robbers. The people whose property had been stolen were most unamused – especially when they learned that the vault had not been alarmed and that it was a short distance from Nice police headquarters, who had been unaware of what was happening under their noses. Much of the property in the vaults had been hidden from the taxman so was difficult for any insurance claim to be made.

WHERE:
Nice, France
WHEN:
Friday 16 July 1976
THE AFTERMATH:
In October 1976 the first arrest was made when a garage owner was caught with a bond that could be traced to the robbery. On 27 October 31 men suspected of being involved were arrested. Their leader was Albert Spaggiari (born at Laragne-Montéglin on 14 December 1932), a former member of the French Foreign Legion, paratrooper turned photographer and right-wing activist. The other gang members were Nice villains and ex-paras who had been associated with the pro-French Algeria movement, OAS, an anti-De Gaulle organization. On 10 March 1977 Spaggiari appeared in court but evaded the police and jumped out of the window onto the roof of a parked car before making his getaway. On 26 April 1978 he was sentenced to ten years' jail in absentia. On 8 June 1989 he died of throat cancer at Piedmont. The bulk of the loot was never recovered.
YOU SHOULD KNOW:
Just before his arrest, Spaggiari had been on a photographic jaunt to the Far East with the mayor of Nice, Jacques Médecin.

An artist's impression of the thieves at work in the vault.

Lufthansa Heist

No one was ever arrested for any of the murders associated with the robbery

WHERE:
John F. Kennedy International Airport, New York, USA
WHEN:
3.12am Monday 11 December 1978

THE AFTERMATH:
Instead of taking the van to a breaker's yard to be destroyed, Parnell Edwards, 31, decided to smoke a marijuana joint and left the van in a ditch before going home to get drunk and have something to eat. The van – complete with Edwards's fingerprints – was found within a week. To cover their tracks, DeSimone and Angelo Sepe shot Edwards dead in his home on 18 December 1978. His was the first death of those involved in the robbery. On 6 January 1979 Martin Krugman, 59, was killed. Eight days later, Tommy DeSimone, 28, was murdered. His girlfriend, Theresa Ferrara, 26, was murdered on 10 February and her body dismembered. The following month Louis Cafora and his wife, Joanna, were killed. On 16 May Joe Manri was discovered dead with a bullet to the back of his head. Paolo LiCastri, 44, was killed on 13 June and on 18 July 1984 Angelo Sepe, 43, and his girlfriend Joanna Lombardo, 19, were murdered in his basement apartment at 8861 on 20th Avenue in New Utrecht, Brooklyn. Louis Werner was the only person ever prosecuted for the Lufthansa heist.
No one was ever arrested for any of the murders associated with it. The authorities only ever recovered $20,000. Henry Hill, Peter Gruenwald, Bill Fischetti and Frank Menna all entered the Witness Protection Programme.

YOU SHOULD KNOW:
A semi-fictionalized account of the robbery is featured in the Martin Scorsese film *Goodfellas*.

Jimmy Burke is led away by police after being suspected of masterminding the heist.

THE CRIME: A fortnight before Christmas 1978 the then largest cash robbery on American soil happened, when around $5 million in money and $875,000 in jewels were stolen at JFK Airport. Once a month millions of dollars used by tourists and service personnel in West Germany were flown into the States by Lufthansa and stored in a vault at Kennedy Airport.

Louis Werner worked at the airport and was also an inveterate gambler who was in debt to bookie, Martin Krugman, to the tune of $20,000. Werner and his friend, Peter Gruenwald, had already been responsible for the theft of $22,000 in foreign currency from Lufthansa in 1976. Werner told Krugman about the money and he, in turn, told gangster Henry Hill who informed Jimmy Burke, an associate of the Lucchese crime family. Burke hired Tommy DeSimone, Joe Manri, Louis Cafora and Angelo Sepe and Sepe's ex-brother-in-law, Tony Rodriguez plus Paolo LiCastri, a member of the Gambino crime family. Parnell "Stacks" Edwards, a black wannabe gangster, was hired to get rid of the van they would use in the heist. Just after 3am on 11 December, security guard, Kelly Whalen, was attacked as he went to investigate a black Ford Econoline van parked near a loading bay. The robbers took Whalen's wallet and threatened to harm his family. Then the robbers went to the canteen where they held the rest of the employees at gunpoint while guard, Rudi Eirich, was made to open the vault. The gang of thieves took 40 bundles of loot in an operation that took 64 minutes to complete.

1981 Brink's Robbery

"The State simply isn't going to last 75 or even 50 years"

THE CRIME: The Black Liberation Army and 19 May Communists were responsible for a robbery that netted $1.6 million from a Brink's armoured van at a New York shopping centre. Just before 4pm Brink's security guards Peter Paige and Joe Trombino made their regular collection of money. As they loaded it into the van robbers surrounded them and one fired two shotgun blasts into the van's bulletproof windscreen, while another murdered Mr Paige and shot Mr Trombino.

The criminals took the money and fled the scene. The robbers swapped their vehicle for a U-Haul lorry but were spotted by an eyewitness who telephoned the authorities. All-points bulletins were issued and policemen Edward O'Grady, Waverly Brown, Brian Lennon and Artie Keenan stopped the U-Haul lorry at an entrance ramp to the New York State Thruway off New York State Route 59. The lorry was driven by Kathy Boudin who had dropped her son off with a babysitter prior to participating in the robbery. As she spoke to the police, six heavily armed men jumped from the back of the lorry and opened fire on the police. Officer Brown was shot and, as he lay on the floor, one of the robbers fired several bullets into him. Officer Keenan was shot in the leg and Officer O'Grady died 90 minutes later on a hospital operating table. Officer Lennon was trapped in his car but managed to fire his shotgun at the U-Haul lorry, which crashed into a police car. An off-duty prison warder arrested Boudin. Chris Dobbs, Samuel Brown and Judith Alice Clark were also taken into custody. Thieves Samuel Smith and Sekou Odinga were involved in a shootout with police which left Smith dead and Odinga captured. Three more were captured some months later. The last to be captured was Jeral Wayne Williams (aka Mutulu Shakur) who eluded police until 1986.

The police surround the Brinks armoured van.

WHERE:
Nanuet Mall, 75 West Route 59, Nanuet, New York, USA

WHEN:
3.55pm Tuesday 20 October 1981

THE AFTERMATH:
The first to be tried were Donald Weems (aka Kuwasi Balagoon) and 19 May Communists David Gilbert and Judith Alice Clark amid a heavy police presence. They represented themselves and were given three consecutive 25-year to life sentences. Weems said, "As to the 75 years in prison, I am not really worried because the State simply isn't going to last 75 or even 50 years." He died of Aids on 13 December 1986. Boudin was sentenced to 20 years to life. She was paroled in 2003. Samuel Brown was sentenced to 75 years to life. Williams was jailed for 60 years in 1988. In 2008 it was announced that the Nanuet Mall would be demolished.

YOU SHOULD KNOW:
Security guard Joe Trombino recovered from his injuries and returned to work for Brink's two years later. He was still working for the company when he was killed, aged 68, in the 9/11 terror attacks (see page 56). He was waiting in a Brink's van in the basement of the World Trade Center for three colleagues to return when the building was hit. His three colleagues all survived.

John Fleming, nicknamed "Goldfinger", was also accused of handling the stolen gold. He is depicted here arriving at Heathrow Airport after being expelled from the United States.

Brink's Mat Robbery

"Get on the floor or you're dead"

THE CRIME: Six thieves broke into the Brink's Mat warehouse at Heathrow Airport a month before Christmas 1983 and stole three tons of gold bullion (6,840 bars of it, packed into 76 cardboard boxes worth £26,369,777). Pointing a gun at guard Robin Riseley, a robber shouted, "Get on the floor or you're fucking dead." The robbers then cut the trousers off senior guard, Michael Scouse, and Robin Riseley before pouring watered-down petrol over them.

The raid was organized by Brian Robinson whose brother-in-law, Tony Black, was a security guard at the warehouse. The police quickly investigated the backgrounds of the security personnel and arrested Black, who confessed his role on Tuesday 6 December 1983. He received a sentence of six years on 17 February 1984 and served three. On 3 December 1984 Robinson, 41, and the gang leader Micky McAvoy, 33, were each sentenced to 25 years imprisonment at the Old Bailey for armed robbery. A third man, Tony White, 40, was cleared because of a lack of evidence. However, White, who was on the dole and living in a council house, quickly spent £400,000 buying and restoring homes in London and Kent. In 1997 he was jailed for his part in a drugs ring. Before he was sent down McAvoy gave part of his loot to an acquaintance called Brian Perry who, in turn, hired Kenneth Noye who had links to a genuine gold dealer in Bristol. Noye arranged for the gold to be melted down but, because there was so much gold, the money it raised (about £3 million) was noticed by the Treasury who alerted the police. Noye was put under surveillance on 26 January 1985. That month he discovered John Fordham, a 45-year-old undercover policeman in his garden at Hollywood Cottage, West Kingsdown, Kent, and stabbed him ten times. At the resulting trial, the jury found him not guilty on 12 December 1985 on the grounds of self-defence, despite there being no defensive wounds on DC Fordham's body. Noye was found guilty of conspiracy to handle the Brink's Mat gold, fined £700,000 and sentenced to four years in prison.

WHERE:
Unit 7, Heathrow International Trading Estate, Middlesex, England
WHEN:
6.25am Saturday 26 November 1983
THE AFTERMATH:
Noye was released from prison in May 1994. Two years later, at about 1.15pm on 19 May 1996, on the M25/M20 intersection at Swanley, in Kent, he killed Stephen Cameron, a small-time drug dealer who owed Noye money. Noye left England but in 1998 was arrested in Spain and deported back to England where he was jailed for life on 14 April 2000. None of the gold has been recovered. Some vanished completely and some probably reappeared in bank accounts in Luxembourg, Switzerland, the Cayman Islands, Miami and the Bahamas.

Candice Rose Martinez

"You have 40 seconds to put all your money in the box"

THE CRIME: It is usual when someone is robbing a bank that they concentrate on what they are doing. Not 19-year-old, Northern Virginia Community College student Candice Rose Martinez. When she took to stealing, she spoke continuously on her mobile while committing the robberies of four Wachovia Bank branches in Northern Virginia. It transpired that she was talking on the phone to her 19-year-old boyfriend, Dave Chatram Williams, who was also the getaway driver. The first robbery happened on 12 October 2005 and the last on 4 November 2005. In the first three heists Martinez walked into the bank chatting on her mobile and, when she got to the counter, gave a box to the cashiers. In the fourth robbery, she did not carry a box but showed a .38 calibre revolver and handed the cashier a note. On 22 October she gave the cashier an empty box with a typed note taped inside. It read, "You have 40 seconds to put all your money in the box, do not make any sudden moves." Martinez then told the cashier to put $100 and $50 notes in the box, saying, "I need you to empty all the drawers – you have three. You're taking too long, you have 40 seconds." Williams and Martinez were arrested on 14 and 15 November 2005, respectively. When police searched Martinez's Chantilly, Virginia, apartment, they found $3,500 in cash, a mobile phone box, a high school yearbook, a computer, some Louis Vuitton bags and a digital camera.

WHERE:
Northern Virginia, USA
WHEN:
Saturday 22 October 2005
THE AFTERMATH:
The four robberies resulted in a haul of $48,620, which the couple spent on a 1997 Acura Integra, two big-screen televisions and designer clothes and bags. On 13 December 2005 Martinez pleaded guilty in US District Court in Alexandria, Virginia, to two felony charges. On 3 March 2006 she was sentenced to 12 years in the Federal Bureau of Prisons, to be followed by five years on probation. District Judge Gerald Bruce Lee also fined Martinez $200 and ordered her to pay $43,850 in restitution. Williams, a former Wachovia employee, had also pleaded guilty and, a week earlier, was sentenced to 12 years in prison.

Surveillance footage of Candice Rose Martinez

ASSASSINATIONS

William the Silent

"My God, have pity on my soul"

WHERE:
Prinsenhof, Delft
WHEN:
Friday 10 July 1584
THE AFTERMATH:
Gérard was arrested while attempting to escape over a garden wall and imprisoned. He was tortured before his trial on 13 July. After being racked, his right arm was burned off with a red-hot iron. His body was then flayed with red-hot pincers, his abdomen sliced open and his bowels ripped out before his legs and remaining arm were hacked off. He is reported to have been alive until his heart was torn out and thrown in his face. It is said that Gérard remained silent throughout the ordeal. Dutch Catholics, happy in William's death, kept Gérard's head as a relic and sought to have him made a saint.

THE CRIME: William the Silent, the first head of state to be assassinated with a handgun, became Prince of Orange on 15 July 1544. In 1559, William was appointed *stadtholder* of the provinces of Holland, Zeeland, Utrecht and Burgundy. From August to October 1566, a wave of iconoclasm (*Beeldenstorm*) was rife throughout the Low Countries. In April 1567, William refused to appear before the committee investigating the *Beeldenstorm*. He was publicly outlawed and his property confiscated. However, William remained popular among the common people in no small thanks to a propaganda campaign, so William was reinstated as the *stadtholder* of Holland and Zeeland.

On 18 March 1582, after an al fresco lunch, 18-year-old Juan de Jáuregui, a Spaniard, shot William but the pistol had been loaded with too much gunpowder and it exploded, throwing de Jáuregui backwards and blowing off his thumb. The bullet entered William's face at an upward trajectory and somehow missed his teeth and tongue and exited through his cheek. William's aides immediately stabbed de Jáuregui to death. His body was decapitated and his torso cut into four and displayed on the Antwerp city walls. Later William said he had no recollection of being shot and had thought the roof had fallen on his head. Rumours immediately circulated Europe that William had died or was close to death and, indeed, he was not seen in public for many months. The politicians of Holland and Zeeland tried to pronounce William count of Holland and Zeeland, thus making him the official sovereign. Meanwhile 25-year-old Balthasar Gérard, a Catholic, was of the

William the Silent is fatally wounded by Balthasar Gérard.

opinion that William was a traitor to the Catholic faith so he decided to kill William. Pretending to be a French nobleman, Gérard inveigled himself into William's confidence. On 10 July 1584 he arranged a meeting at William's home in Delft to seek alms. After William had given him 12 crowns Gerard, instead of leaving, hid in a corridor near William's dining room. Later that day he shot him three times with a wheel-lock pistol. William's last words were, *"Mon Dieu, ayez pitié de mon âme; mon Dieu, ayez pitié de ce pauvre peuple."* ("My God, have pity on my soul; my God, have pity on this poor people.")

Spencer Perceval

"I am murdered"

Spencer Perceval is shot in the lobby of the House of Commons.

THE CRIME:
Spencer Perceval is the only British prime minister to have been assassinated. He became an MP on 9 May 1796. It was a year before he made his maiden speech. On 26 March 1807 the Duke of Portland appointed him Chancellor of the Exchequer. He moved into Number 10 two years later on 4 October 1809.

At 5pm on 11 May 1812, John Bellingham, a 42-year-old salesman from St Neots, Huntingdonshire, walked into the Palace of Westminster and sat near the fireplace in the lobby of the Commons. In a specially designed 23 cm (9 in) deep pocket in his coat he had a pistol, and a second gun was concealed about his person. Bellingham bore a grudge against the government. In 1804 he had travelled to Archangel in Russia, then an important trading post with Britain, but events conspired against him and he was accused, wrongly, of fraud. He spent five years trying to prove his innocence and was furious at what he saw as a lack of help from the British authorities.

The parliamentary business on 11 May 1812 was a discussion of embargoes on French trade so only about a tenth of the 658 honourable members were present. Perceval was supposed to be at the House at 4.30pm but was running late. Around the time that Bellingham was taking his seat in the lobby, Perceval was leaving Downing Street, having decided to walk to the House. As he arrived no one noticed John Bellingham as he stood up and slowly walked towards Perceval, withdrawing his pistol. He pointed the gun at the prime minister's chest and fired. Perceval cried out, "I am murdered", and fell to the floor. Perceval, 49, was carried to the Speaker's House where he was placed on a table but it soon became apparent that he was dead. Rather than trying to escape, Bellingham resumed his place by the fireside before he was taken into custody.

WHERE:
Lobby of the House of Commons, London, England
WHEN:
5.15pm Monday 11 May 1812
THE AFTERMATH:
The inquest into Perceval's death took place at 11am on 12 May 1812 at the Rose and Crown pub in Downing Street with a jury of 21 men. Bellingham was tried at the Old Bailey on 15 May 1812 and doorkeepers charged one guinea for admittance before realizing the huge demand for seats and raising the price to the three guineas. The first prosecution witness was William Smith, MP for Norwich and the grandfather of Florence Nightingale. The summing up by the judge, Lord Chief Justice Mansfield, was interrupted several times when he broke down in tears. The verdict returned was guilty and Bellingham was condemned to death, his plea of insanity being rejected. On a rainy 18 May at 8am William Brunskill hanged him at Newgate Prison, London. In the bowel of the scaffold Brunskill's assistants pulled on Bellingham's legs to hasten his death.

Richard Lawrence attempts to assassinate Andrew Jackson.

Andrew Jackson

"Let me alone! I know where this came from"

THE CRIME:

Richard Lawrence became the first known person to attempt to assassinate an American president.

Born in England around 1800, he worked as a house painter and it is believed that the fumes from the chemicals sent him mad. By the early 1830s he was out of work and so deranged that he believed that he was King Richard III of England. He also began to dress outrageously and told people that Andrew Jackson, the president of the United States, owed him a great deal of money from land stolen in 1802 and, once Jackson settled the account, he could take his place as Richard IIII. Lawrence also said that Jackson was responsible for the death of his father in 1823, this in spite of the fact that he had never set foot in the USA.

Lawrence plotted to kill Jackson; he bought two pistols and began to stalk the president. On 30 January 1835 Jackson was scheduled to attend the funeral of South Carolina congressman Warren Ransom Davis and this presented the perfect opportunity for Lawrence. Intending to shoot Jackson as he entered the service, Lawrence was too far away to get off a shot. Hiding behind a pillar on the east portico, he waited for the end of the service and, as the president walked by, aimed at the president's retreating back and fired, only for the pistol to misfire. He took out his second weapon but that, too, misfired. The rest of the congregation including Congressman Davy Crockett, wrestled Lawrence to the ground where, for good measure, Jackson hit him several times with his walking stick although he was prevented from administering too severe a beating. "Let me alone! Let me alone! I know where this came from," he screamed.

WHERE:
Rotunda of the Capitol, Washington DC, USA

WHEN:
Friday 30 January 1835

THE AFTERMATH:
The trial of Richard Lawrence opened on 11 April 1835 with the prosecution led by Francis Scott Key, composer of the American national anthem, *The Star Spangled Banner*. He spoke to the jury, "It is for me, gentlemen, to pass upon you, and not you upon me." The jury took just five minutes to find Lawrence not guilty by reason of insanity and he was sent to a mental hospital. Although it is generally accepted that Lawrence was a paranoid schizophrenic, Jackson was convinced that he was put up to the attempt by his Whig political foes. In 1855, Lawrence was moved to the new Government Hospital for the Insane in Washington DC, where he stayed until his death on 13 June 1861. (In 1981 John W. Hinckley, Jr would also be an inmate there, under its present name St Elizabeth's Hospital, after he tried to shoot President Reagan.)

Abraham Lincoln

"Sic semper tyrannis"

THE CRIME: The 16th and tallest – he was 1.93 m (6 ft 4 in) – president, Abraham Lincoln was elected on 6 November 1860, the first Republican president. On 11 February 1861 Lincoln left his home for the White House; a plot was hatched to kill Lincoln when the train stopped at the Calvert Street Depot in Baltimore, Maryland, on 23 February. Allan Pinkerton, who was assigned to protect Lincoln, discovered the plan and it was foiled. In his inauguration address, Lincoln said that he had no lawful right to interfere with slavery and nor did he intend to do so.

In September 1864, as the American Civil War was nearing its end, Samuel Arnold, Michael O'Laughlen, George Atzerodt, David Herold, Lewis Powell (aka Paine), John Surratt, Jr, and actor, John Wilkes Booth, formulated a plan to kidnap Lincoln and exchange him for Confederate prisoners of war. On 11 April 1865 Lincoln, in his last public speech, spoke outside the White House in favour of enfranchizing blacks. Booth became so enraged by the idea that he changed his mind about kidnapping Lincoln and decided to assassinate him instead. The president, Mrs Lincoln, Major Henry R. Rathbone and his fiancée Clara Harris were scheduled to attend a performance of the play, *Our American Cousin*, starring Laura Keene at Ford's Theatre on Good Friday 1865. President and Mrs Lincoln and their guests arrived at the theatre at 9pm and were taken to the presidential box (number 7). Around this time Booth arrived at the back of the theatre where he was known to the stage door staff.

Meanwhile, Lincoln's bodyguard, John F. Parker, was no longer in position, having left to get a drink. Booth quietly entered the box and shot Lincoln in the back of the head with a .44 calibre Deringer. Major Rathbone tried to stop Booth escaping but was stabbed in the arm for his troubles. Booth climbed onto the parapet to jump but was again grabbed by the major who was stabbed again. As Booth jumped, his spur caught on the Treasury flag and he fell awkwardly, breaking his left leg. He yelled out, "*Sic semper tyrannis*" ("Thus always to tyrants", the state motto of Virginia) before limping away. The mortally wounded president was taken to the William Petersen House at 516 10th Street. Lincoln never regained consciousness and was officially pronounced dead at 7.22:10am the following day. He was 56 years old.

WHERE:
Ford's Theatre, 511 10th Street, NW Washington DC, USA
WHEN:
10.15pm Friday 14 April 1865
THE AFTERMATH:
Booth and Herold fled to the home of Dr Samuel Mudd whom Booth knew. He put Booth's leg in splints. On 23 April Booth and Herold crossed the Potomac and then the Rappahannock and travelled to a barn belonging to Richard H. Garrett. On 26 April soldiers found them locked in the barn. Called upon to surrender, Herold gave himself up but Booth refused to leave the barn. The troops set the barn on fire and Sergeant Boston Corbett, a religious monomaniac, moved in close and shot Booth in the neck despite orders not to fire. Booth was carried to the porch of Garrett's house and lingered until around 7pm, when he died. His last words were, "Tell Mother – tell Mother – I died for my country." The other conspirators were arrested and tried by a military tribunal. On 5 July all the defendants were found guilty. Mary Surratt, Lewis Powell, David Herold and George Atzerodt were sentenced to death by hanging and went to the gallows in the Old Arsenal Penitentiary on 7 July. Samuel Mudd, Samuel Arnold and Michael O'Laughlen were sentenced to life in prison. John Surratt stayed in hiding in Canada, went to Europe and returned to America in December 1866. He became a teacher and died of pneumonia at 9pm on 21 April 1916.

John Wilkes Booth leans forward to shoot Abraham Lincoln at Ford's Theatre.

James Garfield

I am Going to the Lordy

WHERE:
Sixth Street Station, Washington DC, USA
WHEN:
9.30am Saturday 2 July 1881
THE AFTERMATH:
Guiteau's lawyers entered a plea of insanity but it was rejected and he was hanged on 30 June 1882 at the Washington Asylum and Jail. As he went to the gallows he recited a poem he had written while awaiting execution. It was called *I am Going to the Lordy*.

The gallows used to hang Charles Guiteau

THE CRIME: James Abram Garfield was the second US president to die by an assassin's bullet and his was also the second shortest time in office. A contented senator, Garfield found himself his party's nominee for president at the Republican National Convention and he reluctantly accepted. After his inauguration he spent much of the next few months being accosted by people wanting jobs. Bizarrely, in those days the president was responsible for the majority of the hirings in his administration, since everyone – from cabinet to clerks – was summarily sacked when the previous incumbent left office.

One of the people turned down for a job was a mentally unbalanced, 37-year-old religious fanatic called Charles Julius Guiteau. He believed that he had been responsible for Garfield's election and thought that an appointment as consul general in Paris would be a fitting reward for his efforts. He wrote a meandering letter to Garfield seeking his just desserts and then travelled to Washington DC. Despite the assassination of President Lincoln just 16 years previously, security at the White House was almost non-existent and Guiteau got to see the president. He handed him another copy of his letter, with "Paris consulship" written on the cover. Frustrated that he was not immediately appointed, Guiteau took to hanging around the White House before his odd behaviour finally got him banned. Guiteau became convinced that Garfield was personally blocking his appointment and he began to stalk the new chief executive. At 9.30am on 2 July 1881 Guiteau seized his opportunity and shot Garfield as he walked through the Sixth Street Station of the Baltimore and Potomac Railroad. One bullet went through the president's shoulder and exited his back while a second lodged in his chest. A policeman grabbed Guiteau, while the crowd wanted to lynch him. Garfield was taken to the White House to recover. Alexander Graham Bell invented a medical detector to try and find the bullet but the metal frame of the bed Garfield was laid on hampered his efforts. The president seemed to recover and was taken to Elberon, New Jersey to further recuperate. On 19 September 1881 at 10.35pm Garfield died of a massive heart attack, exactly two months after his 50th birthday. It is generally believed that if the medical attention he received had been competent, Garfield would have survived the shooting.

William McKinley

"I killed the president because he was the enemy of the good people"

THE CRIME: William McKinley, the 25th American president, was visiting the 1901 Pan-American Exposition in Buffalo, New York when he was shot by Leon Czolgosz, the son of Polish immigrant parents.

Unlike today's modern world, McKinley was patiently shaking hands with visitors to the exhibition with little or no protection around him. The people were happy to be able to get so close to their president but one of them had murder in mind. Czolgosz, an anarchist, his hand swathed in a fake bandage, waited for his turn to shake the presidential hand. When he reached the front of the line at 4.07pm he pulled out a .32 calibre Iver-Johnson and shot McKinley twice at point-blank range. Czolgosz had bought the gun four days earlier for $4.50.

The first bullet hit a button and was deflected but the second hit McKinley in the stomach, colon and kidney, and finally lodged in the muscles of his back. Doctors could not find the second bullet and hunted around inside the president for it, probably causing untold damage. One of the exhibits at the Pan-American exposition was a new X-ray machine but doctors were reluctant to use it to locate the bullet because they did not know if X-rays had any side effects. McKinley rallied and the medics believed that he would recover from his injuries. On the morning of 12 September he ate some solid food but that afternoon he suffered a relapse. He died two days later at 2.15am on 14 September 1901 of gangrene of the pancreas, although it is believed his death was as much to do with sloppy surgery as his wound. His last words were, "It is God's way. His will be done, not ours."

President William McKinley, left, at the Pan-American Exposition in 1901

WHERE:
Temple of Music, Pan-American Exposition, Buffalo, New York, USA
WHEN:
4.07pm Friday 6 September 1901
THE AFTERMATH:
Czolgosz was convicted and sentenced to death on 23 September in a trial that lasted 8 hours and 26 minutes from jury selection to verdict. Czolgosz was electrocuted by three jolts of 1700 volts each, on 29 October 1901, in Auburn prison, New York. His last words were, "I killed the president because he was the enemy of the good people – the good working people. I am not sorry for my crime." As the prison guards strapped him into the chair, however, he did say through clenched teeth, "I am sorry I could not see my father." Sulphuric acid was poured over his corpse to speed up decomposition. On 14 September 1901 Theodore Roosevelt was sworn in as president, the youngest man ever to hold the office. Within 36 hours of taking office, Roosevelt ordered the secret service to protect the president.

Theodore Roosevelt

"I have just been shot but it takes more than that to kill a Bull-Moose"

WHERE:
Hotel Gilpatrick, Kilbourn & North 3rd Street, Milwaukee, Wisconsin, USA
WHEN:
8pm Monday 14 October 1912
THE AFTERMATH:
At 12.30am on 15 October Roosevelt boarded a train for Chicago's Mercy Hospital where he stayed until 21 October, when he continued his campaigning. In the election Roosevelt came second, splitting the Republican vote and allowing Woodrow Wilson to become president. On 13 November 1912 Schrank was declared insane and sent to an asylum. On 15 September 1901, the day after President McKinley died, Schrank had had a dream in which, he said, the slain president's ghost appeared to him and accused Roosevelt of the murder. From then on, Schrank developed a passionate hatred for Roosevelt and when the former chief executive announced he was running for a third term Schrank's loathing festered even more. In 1912 McKinley again came to Schrank in a dream and told him to avenge his murder. Schrank followed Roosevelt's campaign for three weeks across eight states looking for a chance to kill him. Doctors decided that the bullet had penetrated Roosevelt too far to risk surgery and he carried the bullet until he died of natural causes at Oyster Bay, New York on 6 January 1919. When Schrank learned of his death he expressed sorrow. Schrank died on 15 September 1943 at Central State Hospital, Waupun, Wisconsin, 42 years to the day after his dream that led to the only assassination attempt to be made on a former president.

THE CRIME: The man who had appointed the Secret Service to protect the president following the assassination of William McKinley in 1901 (see page 293) was himself the subject of an attempt on his life. The assassination attempt did not occur until after he had left office albeit when Theodore Roosevelt was running for a third term (something that is now illegal) as the Progressive, or Bull-Moose, candidate.

On an autumnal day in 1912, 53-year-old Teddy Roosevelt was leaving the Hotel Gilpatrick in Milwaukee, Wisconsin, to give a campaign speech at the Auditorium when 36-year-old, Bavarian-born bar owner, John Nepomuk Schrank, shot him in the chest with a .38 Police Positive pistol from a distance of 2 m (6 ft), as the former president was getting into his car. The bullet pierced Roosevelt's overcoat, his metal spectacles case and his 50-page speech, folded double. Despite blood flowing from the wound, Roosevelt made his speech, which lasted for about 70 minutes. At times, only just above a whisper he told the crowd, "Friends, I shall have to ask you to be as quiet as possible. I do not know whether you fully understand that I have just been shot but it takes more than that to kill a Bull-Moose." As soon as he stopped speaking, he was rushed to Johnston's Emergency Hospital where doctors X-rayed him to assess the damage.

John Nepomuk Schrank shot Theodore Rooseevelt in the chest while Roosevelt was campaigning in Milwaukee.

Franz Ferdinand

"Sophie, Sophie! don't die! Live for our children!"

Archduke Franz Ferdinand and his wife Sophie are killed by Gavrilo Princip.

THE CRIME: On 30 January 1889, Franz Ferdinand Karl Ludwig Josef von Habsburg-Lothringen-Este became the heir presumptive to the Austro-Hungarian throne. In the years between 1903 and 1913 Serbia engaged in a number of disputes with its neighbours. It was against this volatile background that Franz Ferdinand, with his wife, Sophie, visited Bosnia at the invitation of General Oskar Potiorek, the governor of Bosnia.

The Serbian Black Hand, a terrorist group, decided to assassinate Franz Ferdinand and hired three 19-year-olds suffering from tuberculosis to kill the archduke. They were Gavrilo Princip, Nedeljko Cabrinovic and Trifko Grabez. Each of them was given a pistol, two bombs and a phial of cyanide with which to commit suicide after the event. On arrival in Bosnia-Herzegovina they were met by half a dozen more assassins: Vaso Cubrilovic, Veljko Cubrilovic, Danilo Ilic, Miško Jovanovic, Muhamed Mehmedbašic and Cvijetko Popovic. Seven of the would-be assassins mingled with the crowd as the royal couple travelled in a motorcade to the town hall. The first opportunity fell to Mehmedbašic but he lost his nerve and stood watching the motorcade pass safely by. The second assassin was Vaso Cubrilovic next to Mehmedbašic, armed with a revolver and a bomb. He, too, did nothing. Nedeljko Cabrinovic threw his bomb but the chauffeur saw it heading towards the car and accelerated. The bomb hit the roof of the vehicle and bounced off, exploding under the following car, wounding two of the occupants and 20 people in the crowd. Cabrinovic swallowed his cyanide pill and jumped into the Miljacka River. However, the poison did not work and he was dragged out and beaten up before the police arrested him.

Further down the route Princip heard the explosion and, believing that the assassination had been a success, went to a nearby café to celebrate. The motorcade made it safely to the town hall where Franz Ferdinand insisted on going to the hospital to see the injured. An aide advised against the visit, sensing that the danger had not passed. However, General Potiorek overruled him saying, "Do you think Sarajevo is full of assassins?" The general changed the route to the hospital but for some reason forgot to tell the driver who drove the planned route before Potiorek spotted his mistake and shouted, "This is the wrong way!" By coincidence, the car was in the street where Princip was in the café. As the driver began to reverse, Princip strode up and fired twice from less than a metre (3ft). The first bullet hit Franz Ferdinand in the throat and severed his jugular vein; the second hit Sophie in the abdomen. He called out, "Sophie, Sophie! don't die! Live for our children!" Sophie died 15 minutes after being shot, the archduke shortly afterwards.

WHERE:
Franz Joseph Street, Sarajevo, Bosnia
WHEN:
11.15am Sunday 28 June 1914
THE AFTERMATH:
Princip was arrested and along with Cabrinovic was tortured and gave the police the names of their fellow conspirators. They were all arrested and charged with treason and murder except Mehmedbašic who escaped to Serbia. On 28 July 1914 the Austro-Hungarian Empire declared war on Serbia. The arms race of the previous decade had precipitated treaties and alliances. In consequence, countries began by declaring war on one other so that by the second week of August 1914 most of Europe was involved in a bloody conflict that would cost millions of lives and last more than four years.

Rasputin

"Our objective has clearly been achieved"

THE CRIME: In 1903 Grigori Efimovich Rasputin arrived in St Petersburg, then the capital of the Russian Empire, and soon gained a reputation as a mystic with healing powers. In 1904 Tsarina Alexandra gave birth to a hæmophiliac son, Alexei, at Peterhof. In October 1912, the tsarina, desperately fearful that her son would die following an accident, asked a friend, Anna Vryrubova, to make contact with Rasputin whose reputation had reached royal circles. From his home in Siberia Rasputin prayed for the boy and Alexei recovered. Each time the boy fell ill, the tsarina contacted Rasputin and each time he "cured" the boy.

Thus Rasputin's influence at court grew. Rasputin claimed that the Russian armies would not be successful in the First World War

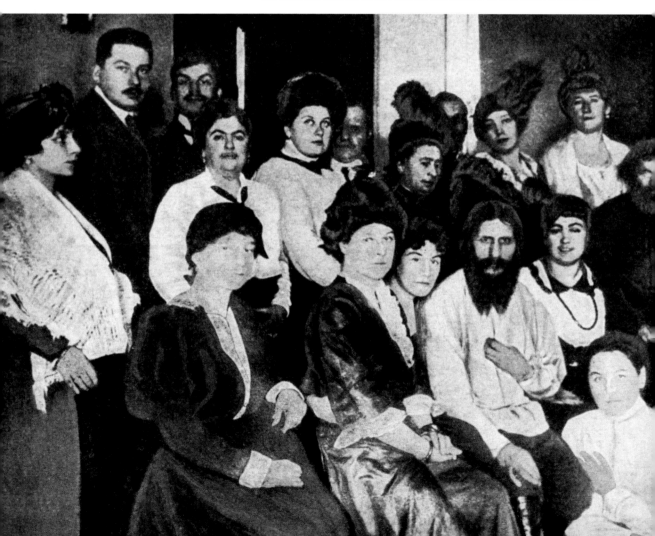

until Tsar Nicholas took command. While the tsar was away at the front, Rasputin's influence over Alexandra grew ever greater. It was a recipe for disaster.

On the night of 16 December a minor Russian royal, Prince Felix, collected Rasputin in a car from his home at 64 Gorokhovaya Street on the pretence that he was taking Rasputin to meet a beautiful Russian Romanov woman who was married to a homosexual transvestite, Yussopoff. Prince Felix took Rasputin to the basement of 94 Moika, his luxury home, where there were at least two women present. Also there were Lieutenant Oswald Rayner and Captain Stephen J. Alley, British soldiers attached to the Secret Intelligence Service Station in St Petersburg.

Rasputin was offered cakes and red wine liberally laced with cyanide but he refused them, so an attempt was made to beat him

to death. An autopsy of Rasputin's body shows that, among other injuries, his right eye was detached from its socket, his genitals had been crushed, there was a gaping wound in his back, and his right ear was almost ripped off. Assuming that Rasputin was dead, the assassins carried him outside. He groaned, indicating that he was alive, so was put into a sitting position against a snowdrift and was shot twice. The body was wrapped in a cloth and carried to a waiting car. As the assassins made for the car, Rasputin made a noise, alerting them to the fact that he was, astonishingly, still alive. He was placed on the ground and shot through the forehead, killing him instantly. The bullet that finished him off was reported to be a Webley .455 inch unjacketed round. Rasputin's body was taken to the icy River Neva and thrown in.

The only man present at the killing who owned a Webley was Oswald Rayner. Captain Stephen Alley wrote eight days after the murder, "Although matters here have not proceeded entirely to plan, our objective has clearly been achieved." At 8.40am on Monday 19 December Rasputin's body was retrieved. The corpse took two days to thaw sufficiently for a post mortem to be performed. The face was black and the eyes and nose swollen. The legs from the knees down were tied in a sack but the arms were free and were bent at the elbows as if clawing for air.

WHERE:
94 Moika, St Petersburg, Russia
WHEN:
Friday 16 December 1916
THE AFTERMATH:
No one was charged with the murder of Rasputin. Tsar Nicholas exiled Yussopoff to Kursk and co-conspirator Grand Duke Dmitri Pavlovich to Persia. The tsarina arranged for Rasputin's body to be buried in the ground of Tsarkoye Selo at 8.30am on 21 December 1916. Following the February Revolution, his body was dug up and burned in a nearby wood. Oswald Rayner burned all his papers before his death in Oxford from cancer on 6 March 1961.

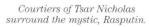

Courtiers of Tsar Nicholas surround the mystic, Rasputin.

Tsar Nicholas II & the Russian Imperial Family

"Now we must shoot you"

Tsar Nicholas II and his family photographed while they were held in custody.

THE CRIME: In February 1917 Russia suffered its first revolution of the year. On 2 March Tsar Nicholas abdicated. The following month, on the night of 16 April, the revolutionary Lenin arrived at the Finland Station in Petrograd from Switzerland, aboard a sealed train. The popularity of the Bolsheviks increased exponentially. The Provisional Government under Alexander Kerensky put the Romanovs under house arrest in the Alexander Palace at Tsarskoe Selo, 24 km (15 mi) south of Petrograd. In August, Nicholas and his family were evacuated to the Urals for their own safety. On 25 October 1917 Lenin led his Bolsheviks in an uprising against the Provisional Government. Many of the revolutionaries called for Nicholas to be put on trial.

At 8.40am on 30 April 1918 the tsar and tsarina and their third daughter, Maria, arrived in Ekaterinburg and were taken to the 21-room home of retired local engineer, Nikolai N. Ipatiev, which had been commandeered by the Bolsheviks and renamed the House of Special Purpose. Five rooms on the upper floor were converted into a prison and the windows painted white to prevent anyone seeing in or out. The downstairs became offices and rooms for the guards. At 11am on 23 May the rest of the children arrived at Ekaterinburg. At 2.33am on 17 July, Nicholas, 50, Alexandra, 46, Alexei, the 13-year-old tsarevich, their four daughters, Olga, 22, Tatiana, 21, Maria, 19, and Anastasia, 17, their doctor, Yevgeny Botkin, 53, and three servants, footman Alexei Trupp, 60, cook Ivan Kharitonov, 46, and Anna Demidova, 40, Alexandra's maid, were woken and taken into the basement. They were told that they would be moved and that they were to wait for cars. Nicholas, carrying the sleeping Alexei, asked for two chairs so that his wife and son could sit. The chairs were provided and then Yakov Yurovsky, a member of the secret police and the leader of the guards, returned with armed guards and told them, "Your relations have tried to save you. They have failed and now we must shoot you". The family and servants were executed on the orders of Lenin. The tsar said, "You know not what you do," before he was killed by a single shot to the head, while the tsarina had just time to make the sign of the cross before she too was felled by a single shot.

Emiliano Zapata

"Better to die on your feet than live on your knees!"

Emiliano Zapata and his staff

THE CRIME: Emiliano Zapata played a leading role in the civil wars that raged in Mexico between 1910 and his death in 1919. Born in San Miguel on 8 August 1879 (some sources say 1883), he began his revolutionary activities aged only 18 when he led a peasant's revolt against the owners of the hacienda where he had been raised. He was taken into custody and, not long after his release, joined the army.

On 18 November 1910 the Mexican Revolution began. In March 1911 Zapata joined the forces of Francisco Indalecio Madero in his battle against the dictatorial government of Porfirio Diaz but quickly came to the conclusion that Madero's revolutionary reforms were too timid and, when he came to power in October 1911, Zapata refused to support him. Zapata had impressed many with his call to arms, "*¡Es mejor morir de pie que vivir de rodillas!*" ("Better to die on your feet than live on your knees!"). When Zapata's men defeated the cruel and often drunk General Victoriano Huerta, he told the moderate revolutionaries that he would continue his own rebellion and Pancho Villa (see page 300) joined him.

The army of Zapata was responsible for a number of atrocities but they were as nothing compared to the horrors perpetrated by both sides during the wars in which almost one million Mexicans lost their lives. When Zapata's men occupied Mexico City in 1914 they did not pillage but "asked humbly for a little food, or approached passers-by to beg a peso". The revolutionary forces of Venustiano Carranza weakened Zapata and when Carranza became president in April 1915 he determined to wipe out all opposition. After an attempt to eliminate Zapata by force failed, he used subterfuge and General Jesus Guajardo, a Yaqi Indian, pretended that he and his men wanted to join Zapata.

Zapata agreed to meet Guajardo at the Hacienda de San Juan on 10 April 1919 to plot further action. Zapata arrived with 150 men but only ten went inside with him, the rest remaining outside to protect against attacks from government troops. Inside the building Guajardo's men formed a guard of honour and then a bugle sounded. On the third call the guard of honour turned their guns on Zapata and shot him dead along with his ten men. Zapata's men waiting outside fled.

WHERE:
Hacienda de San Juan, Chinameca, Ayala, Mexico
WHEN:
Thursday 10 April 1919
THE AFTERMATH:
For his treachery Guajardo was paid $10,000 and promoted to general. On 18 May 1920 Venustiano Carranza was assassinated. The Mexican Revolution finally ended on 1 December 1920.

Pancho Villa and his followers

Pancho Villa

"Don't let it end like this. Tell them I said something"

THE CRIME: The Mexican revolutionary was born as José Doroteo Arango Arámbula near San Juan del Río, Durango on 5 June 1878. Much of Villa's life story is disputed. It is said that when he was 16, he discovered that a local rancher had raped his 12-year-old sister. He sought the man out and shot him before stealing a horse and going on the run. He changed his name to Francisco Villa to avoid detection. He became a miner but the pay and conditions were so poor he took to robbing banks. When he started sharing the proceeds of his bounty with locals, he garnered a reputation as a Robin Hood figure.

The government of General Porfirio Diaz, in power since 1 December 1884, was unpopular, not least because of its punitive tax rates. In November 1910 the people rose up against Diaz, and Villa and his band of men helped the leader Francisco Madero to overthrow the government. The new order collapsed when Madero was assassinated on 18 February 1913. On that day, Pedro Lascurain became the head of state and ruled for less than one hour, the shortest rule on record. Lascurain was sworn in, appointed Victoriano Huerta as his successor and promptly resigned.

Villa was still in charge of his peasant army and ruled Chihuahua and northern Mexico. He refused to submit to Huerta who labelled him a traitor and signed his death warrant. Villa's reputation grew and he became a hero in the United States. He appeared as himself in films in 1912, 1913 and 1914. It did not harm his sex appeal either – it was said he married 26 times. However, Villa did not rule over a pleasant land. He had opponents or those who upset him summarily shot. As word reached north of the border, the people of the United States changed their opinion of him but his actions just enhanced his reputation with his own people. Eventually, his fellow revolutionaries forced him into retirement and he moved to Durango. On 20 July 1923, as he drove his huge 1919 Dodge from a bank in Parral, Chihuahua, he was assassinated for reasons that still remain mysterious. His last words were, "*No permitas que esto acabe así. Cuentales que he dicho algo.*" ("Don't let it end like this. Tell them I said something.") With him in the car were four bodyguards with two more on the running boards. All but one of the bodyguards died with him.

WHERE:
Parral, Chihuahua, Mexico
WHEN:
Friday 20 July 1923
THE AFTERMATH:
Mexican Congressman Jesus Salas Barrazas was believed to be behind the assassination and he was sentenced to 20 years in prison. However, he was freed after serving just a few months, supposedly because his life was in danger. In 1926 Villa's grave was robbed and his head was stolen. It is still missing.

King Alexander I of Yugoslavia

"I had the immediate impression that there was no hope"

THE CRIME: After the death of his father, Peter I, on 16 August 1921, Alexander I came to the throne as the King of Serbs, Croats and Slovenes. On 8 August 1928 the Serb leader Stjepan Radic died after being shot in the stomach in an assassination attempt in parliament. As a result, Alexander changed the name of the country to the Kingdom of Yugoslavia and on 6 January 1929 prorogued parliament and established himself as a dictator. In October he tried to ban the use of the Cyrillic alphabet and force his people to use the roman letters. Two years later, he proclaimed a new constitution but few of the terms were ever put into effect.

The Croats, especially, were unhappy with the proposals and with Alexander's reign and began plotting to assassinate him, aided secretly by Italy's Benito Mussolini. Because three of his relatives had died on a Tuesday, Alexander was superstitious about any public meeting on that day. Nevertheless, in 1934 he travelled to France abroad the cruiser *Dubrovnik* to try and forge an alliance with the country. On 9 October, a Tuesday, he was travelling through Marseilles with the aged French Foreign Minister Louis Barthou, General Alfonse Georges and Admiral Berthelot when Vlada Chernozamsky jumped out of the crowd onto the running board of the car and shot at the occupants. Alexander was hit twice and expired almost immediately. Then Chernozamsky turned his attentions to Barthou and shot him. He died an hour later, despite blood transfusions (in 1974 it was revealed that Barthou had, in fact, been killed by an overzealous policeman and not Chernozamsky). General Georges suffered only superficial injuries. A police sabre cut down Chernozamsky before he was attacked by the crowd and he was shot in the head by a policeman, dying a few minutes later, ten days before his 37th birthday.

Alexander's was the first assassination to be caught on film by newsreel cameras. Dr Henri, one of the first medics on the scene, recalled, "I had the immediate impression that there was no hope... We found two mortal wounds; the first bullet entered in the region of the liver, the second in the clavicle and came out of the shoulder. The king was in a state of coma from which he never recovered."

King Alexander I after being shot in Marseilles.

WHERE:
Place de la Bourse, Marseilles, France
WHEN:
4.05pm Tuesday 9 October 1934
THE AFTERMATH:
Alexander was buried in the Memorial Church of St George, which had been built by his father. His cousin Pavel succeeded him because Alexander's son, Peter II, was just 11 years old. Peter, who died in 1970 of cirrhosis of the liver, was the third and last king of Yugoslavia.

Huey Long

"God, don't let me die. I have so much to do"

*Mourners pass the open coffin
of Huey Long.*

THE CRIME: Senator and Governor of Louisiana, Huey Pierce Long elicited both love and hatred among the American people. In May 1915 he passed the Bar examination and built up a healthy practice, defending the poor against big companies. In 1918 he entered public service and his legal training allowed him to defend the measures that he had introduced. On 17 April 1928 Long was elected, with 96.14 per cent of the votes, to become governor of Louisiana. The poor, used to their opinions and needs being ignored, became Long's most vociferous supporters such was the novelty of a politician who appeared to keep his manifesto promises. Such was the opposition to him that one local council refused to accept the free textbooks that Long had offered saying that they did not want to take charity. Long also took to being accompanied by armed guards wherever he went. When his opponents prevented a scheme to build roads, Long stated that he would stand for the US Senate and use the vote as a mandate on his local initiatives. Long easily defeated the incumbent, Senator Joseph E. Ransdell. Long was nicknamed "Kingfish" after George "Kingfish" Stevens, a character on the radio comedy show *Amos 'n' Andy*.

From 1934–1935 Long was in charge of the legislature, judiciary, election officials and tax inspectors. In August 1935 he announced his candidacy for the presidency. On Sunday 8 September 1935 he went to the Louisiana State capitol for a special session of the legislature. At 9.22pm 28-year-old local doctor, Carl Austin Weiss, wearing a white linen suit, shot him with a Browning .32-calibre pistol. Long's bodyguards opened fire on Weiss who was shot 61 times, 30 times in the front, 29 in the back and twice in the head. Weiss was the son-in-law of Judge Benjamin Henry Pavy, who, it was claimed, had lost his job because of his opposition to Long. The Kingfish was reported as saying, "I wonder why he shot me." Long was admitted to the Our Lady of the Lake Sanatorium at 9.30am. An examination showed that he had a perforated abdomen; the bullet had entered his right side just below his ribs and exited through his back. He died, aged 42, two days later at 4.06am of internal bleeding. His last words were, "God, don't let me die. I have so much to do."

However, as with almost every assassination of a public figure, there is a question over what really happened. One belief is that Weiss punched Long and, in their overzealousness, the bodyguards opened fire and a stray bullet hit and killed Long.

Leon Trotsky

"Do not kill him! This man has a story to tell"

The scene of Ramón Mercader's assassination of Leon Trotsky.

THE CRIME: One of the leading forces in the Russian Revolution, Leon Trotsky was born as Lev Davidovich Bronstein on 26 October 1879 at Yanovka, Kherson Province, Russia.

After the 7 November 1918 revolution, Trotsky was second only to Lenin in the Bolshevik hierarchy. On 13 March 1918 he became commissar of war and head of the Red Army. In 1920–1921, Lenin and Trotsky's political and personal differences again came to the surface. Both were worried by the rise of bureaucracy and railed against it but one man, Joseph Stalin, the General Secretary of the Central Committee, encouraged its rise. Trotsky was on holiday in the Caucasus when he learned of Lenin's death on 21 January 1924. Stalin stage-managed Lenin's funeral and positioned himself as the true heir. On 31 January 1928, Trotsky was exiled to Alma Ata in Kazakhstan and in February 1929 was expelled from the Soviet Union. After travelling around Europe, he landed in Mexico at the invitation of the painter Diego Rivera, where he remained for the rest of his life. In 1939 Trotsky moved into Coyoacán, a suburb of Mexico City. Stalin announced that Trotsky had plotted to have him killed and ordered Trotsky's assassination.

At 4am on 24 May 1940, Stalinist agent Iosif Romualdovich Grigulevich, aided by 19 other men, attacked Trotsky's house riddling the building with hundreds of bullets. Although Trotsky survived, a bodyguard and an American visitor were killed. In the summer of that year Trotsky met a man calling himself Jacques Mornard, who was the lover of Sylvia Ageloff, one of Trotsky's followers. Mornard, whose real name was Ramón Mercader, claimed to be interested in Trotsky's political ideas and the two men had many long conversations. On 20 August 1940 Trotsky invited Mornard for tea and, because he was a guest, Trotsky's bodyguards did not search him nor did they think it odd that he was wearing a raincoat in the heat of summer. These were to be fatal mistakes. Without warning, Mornard pulled out an ice pick and thrust it into Trotsky's skull, his right shoulder and right knee. The attack was not immediately fatal and when Trotsky's bodyguards heard the commotion, they rushed to their boss's aid. Trotsky, still conscious, called out, "Do not kill him! This man has a story to tell." The former Soviet official was taken to hospital where he lingered for 26 hours before dying at 7.25pm, aged 61.

WHERE:
Coyoacán, Mexico City, Mexico
WHEN:
5.30pm Tuesday 20 August 1940
THE AFTERMATH:
Mercader's trial technically began on 22 August 1940, 48 hours after the arrest, in Mexico City. Three judges heard the case and there was no jury. On 16 April 1943 Mercader was convicted of murder and sentenced to 20 years in prison – 19 years and six months for premeditated murder and six months for illegally carrying a weapon. He was released from Mexico City's Palacio de Lecumberri prison on 6 May 1960 and moved to Havana. In 1961 he relocated to the Soviet Union where he became one of only 21 non-Soviet citizens to receive the Hero of the Soviet Union medal. He died in Havana on 18 October 1978 and is buried (under the name of Ramón Ivanovich López) in Kuntsevo Cemetery, Moscow.
YOU SHOULD KNOW:
Trotsky's books were banned in the Soviet Union until 1987 and have been published in Russian since 1989.

Adolf Hitler and Benito Mussolini visit Hitler's damaged headquarters in East Prussia.

Plot to Kill Hitler

"Long live sacred Germany"

THE CRIME: After D-Day in 1944 the number of Germans plotting against Hitler increased. Claus Philipp Maria Schenk Graf von Stauffenberg – a colonel – was the only officer among them and the only one with regular access to Hitler so he agreed to carry out Hitler's assassination, code-named Operation Valkyrie.

It was set for the Führer's briefing hut at the military high command in Rastenburg, East Prussia, called the Wolf's Lair. Stauffenberg put two small bombs – each weighing about 1 kg (2 lb) – in his briefcase. Each was equipped with a simple, soundless, chemical timer that could be set to explode after either a ten or 15 minute delay. When he arrived at 10.15am on 20 July, Stauffenberg discovered that Hitler's headquarters had been moved from the underground Führerbunker to the Lagebaracke, a hut made from wood, fibreglass and plaster with a reinforced concrete roof. Stauffenberg told Hitler's butler that he needed to use the bathroom and took his briefcase with him. He locked the door, opened his briefcase and began to prime the bombs. It was difficult because of the injuries he had suffered the previous year. He had lost his left eye, his right hand, and the fourth and fifth fingers of his left hand during a British strafing raid.

Stauffenberg had only managed to prime one bomb before he was called back into the room. He handed the other, unprimed bomb to his aide de camp. He put his case under the conference table not far from Hitler. The meeting went ahead 30 minutes earlier than planned at 12.30pm, because Mussolini was due to arrive at 3pm. After a few minutes, Stauffenberg excused himself saying that he had to make an urgent telephone call to Berlin. He waited in a nearby shelter for the explosion. The bomb went off at precisely 12.42pm and the hut was virtually destroyed. Hitler's stenographer, Heinrich Berger, was killed and every one of the other 23 men present injured. Hitler was saved because the heavy, solid oak conference table deflected the blast. Hitler suffered concussion, singed hair, cuts to his forehead, a bruised back, burned right calf and left hand and hurt eardrums but the main injury was to his dignity – the blast had ruined his new trousers.

WHERE:
Lagebaracke, Wolfschanze, near Rastenburg, East Prussia
WHEN:
12.42pm 20 July 1944
THE AFTERMATH:
Believing that Hitler was dead, Stauffenberg and his aide-de-camp, Leutnant Werner von Haeften arrived in Berlin at 4.30pm and began the second phase of the project: to organize the military coup against Nazi leaders. Propaganda minister Joseph Goebbels went on the radio at 6.30pm to announce that Hitler had survived an assassination attempt. Hitler himself later broadcast on state radio. Stauffenberg and two fellow officers were shot that night by a makeshift firing squad in the courtyard of the Bendlerblock, the army headquarters. His last words were, "Long live sacred Germany."
YOU SHOULD KNOW:
More than a thousand conspirators were condemned in show trials and executed.

Mahatma Gandhi

"The light has gone out of our lives"

THE CRIME: The Indian spiritual leader had faced many attempts on his life. The first came on 25 June 1934 as he was travelling to give a speech at the Corporation Auditorium in Pune. A bomb was thrown at the first car in his motorcade, injuring ten people when it exploded. Gandhi, in the second car, was unhurt.

Another attempt occurred in May 1944 as Gandhi was recuperating from malaria. A group of 20 young men, led by Nathuram Godse, protested against Gandhi. In the evening Godse rushed at Gandhi with a knife but was stopped by two aides, Mani Shankar Purohit and D. Billare Guruji. In September 1944 Nathuram Godse was found to be carrying a knife with which he intended to kill Gandhi. On 29 June 1946 a train carrying Gandhi was deliberately derailed near Pune. Again, he escaped unharmed. On 20 January 1948 a fifth attempt was made to kill him. A group of seven would-be assassins – Madanlal Kishanlal Pahwa, Shankar Kishtaiyya, Digambar Bagde, Vishnu Ramkrishna Karkare, Gopal Godse, Nathuram Godse and Narayan Dattatraya Apte – claimed that they wanted to take photographs but had no cameras with them. What they did have was a bomb which exploded harmlessly. Ten days later, as Gandhi was walking to pray, Nathuram Godse shot him dead in the garden of Birla House in Delhi. He fired three bullets from a Beretta into Gandhi's chest and stomach at point-blank range. There were no last words from Gandhi.

WHERE:
Birla House, Delhi, India
WHEN:
5.10pm Friday 30 January 1948
THE AFTERMATH:
Jawaharlal Nehru addressed the nation, "Friends and comrades, the light has gone out of our lives, and there is darkness everywhere, and I do not quite know what to tell you or how to say it. Our beloved leader, Bapu, as we called him, the father of the nation, is no more. Perhaps I am wrong to say that; nevertheless, we will not see him again, as we have seen him for these many years, we will not run to him for advice or seek solace from him, and that is a terrible blow, not only for me, but for millions and millions in this country." Gandhi was cremated and his ashes put into urns, which were sent across India for memorial services. A number of conspirators were arrested and Nathuram Godse and Narayan Apte were hanged at Ambala Jail on 15 November 1949. Pahwa, Gopal Godse and Kishtaiyya were sentenced to life imprisonment. Kishtaiyya later had his sentence overturned.

Mahatma Gandhi with his granddaughter

Harry S. Truman

"The patriot who never had doubts when his country called him"

WHERE:
Blair House, 1651–1653 Pennsylvania Avenue NW, Washington DC, USA
WHEN:
2.20pm Wednesday 1 November 1950

THE AFTERMATH:
Collazo's wife, Rosa, was arrested by the FBI on suspicion of conspiracy and spent eight months in federal prison. In 1952 Collazo was sentenced to death in the electric chair but his wife gathered a petition of 100,000 signatures opposing the penalty. Truman commuted the sentence to life imprisonment and Collazo was sent to the federal prison at Leavenworth, Kansas. Collazo said of Torresola's death, "It would not be justice to Griselio if we merely remembered him for his ability with weapons. We must remember the brave and expert guerilla of the mountains of Jayuya as the patriot who never had doubts when his country called him to completion of his duty." On 6 September 1979, President Jimmy Carter freed Collazo, after 29 years in jail. The Puerto Rican died of a stroke on 21 February 1994, a month after his 80th birthday.

YOU SHOULD KNOW:
Collazo and Torresola's guns are on display at the Harry S. Truman Library and Museum in Independence, Missouri. A plaque at Blair House commemorates Private Coffelt's actions.

Oscar Collazo lying wounded outside Blair House.

THE CRIME: In 1948 the American government launched Operation Bootstrap to improve the economy of Puerto Rico. In 1950 the Jayuya Uprising, led by the nationalist Blanca Canales in Puerto Rico, failed. Among those injured in the uprising was the sister of Griselio Torresola, a 25-year-old, New York-based member of the Puerto Rican Nationalist Party. Their brother Elio was arrested. In New York Torresola had befriended Oscar Collazo, another Puerto Rican nationalist, 11 years his senior. The two men decided to assassinate President Truman to bring the world's attention to Puerto Rico.

At 7.30pm on 31 October 1950 the two men arrived at Washington DC's Union Station and booked into the Harris Hotel separately, pretending not to know the other. The next day they set off for Blair House, where Truman lived for much of his presidency, because the White House was being redecorated. Torresola approached from the west while Collazo moved in from the east. Torresola walked up to a guardhouse and pulled open the door, firing four shots from his 9mm Luger semi-automatic pistol at Private Leslie Coffelt sitting inside. Three shots struck Coffelt in the chest and abdomen while the fourth missed. White House policeman Joseph Downs had just left the guardhouse after chatting with Private Coffelt. Downs was approaching the basement door when he heard shots but before he could pull his weapon Torresola shot him in the hip. The Puerto Rican let off two more shots at Downs, hitting him in the back and the neck before Downs managed to open the basement door and close it behind him.

Meanwhile, Collazo was in a fight with Secret Service Agents and White House policemen, firing his Walther P38 at them. Collazo was in the sights of policeman Donald Birdzell when Torresola shot the lawman in the left knee before reloading. Truman, asleep in his second floor bedroom, was woken by the gunfire and opened his window to see what was happening – just 10 m (31 ft) feet away from where Torresola stood reloading. Secret Service Agent Floyd Boring saw the president and told him to get away from the window, which he did. Then the mortally wounded Private Coffelt staggered from his guardhouse and shot Torresola in the head, killing him instantly. Private Coffelt died later that day, aged 40, from his wounds. Collazo was shot in the chest and arrested.

John F. Kennedy

"Mr President, you certainly can't say that Dallas doesn't love you"

THE CRIME: Undoubtedly the most written about assassination in history, John Fitzgerald Kennedy's death is still hotly debated more than 45 years later.

On 21 November 1963, facing a battle for re-election, a need to raise campaign funds and to mend fences with local Democrats, Kennedy and Vice-President Lyndon B. Johnson left for a three-day visit to Texas. At 11.47am on 22 November JFK's motorcade left for a 17-km (11 mi) journey to the Merchandise Mart where Kennedy was to address a lunch group. At 12.29pm the motorcade entered Dealey Plaza and, travelling at about 19 kph (12 mph) approached the Texas School Book Depository at 411 Elm Street. The motorcade moved down Elm Street and Nellie Connally, the governor's wife, said, "Mr President, you certainly can't say that Dallas doesn't love you." At 12.30pm, 24-year-old Lee Harvey Oswald, a former marine, shot Kennedy from the sixth floor window of the depository with a 6.5x52mm Italian Mannlicher-Carcano M91/38 bolt-action rifle with a six-round magazine.

The first bullet hit the president's upper back, penetrating his neck, and exiting his throat before entering Texas Governor John B. Connally's back, chest and right wrist. Nellie Connally cried out, "My God, they are going to kill us all!" A second bullet missed. As the motorcade passed the John Neely Bryan north pergola concrete structure, a third shot rang out and hit Kennedy in the head, smothering the inside of the car and a nearby motorcycle policeman with blood and brain matter. The First Lady shouted, "Jack! Jack! They've killed my husband! I have his brains in my hands!" Special Agent Clint Hill of the Secret Service, travelling on the car behind, ran and jumped onto the back of the presidential limousine where Mrs Kennedy had scrambled to try and retrieve a piece of the president's skull. Agent Hill pushed the First Lady back into the car and held on as the car sped to Parkland Memorial Hospital. At 1pm President Kennedy was officially pronounced dead. "We never had any hope of saving his life," one doctor said.

President Kennedy slumps forward as he is struck by a bullet.

WHERE:
Dealey Plaza, Dallas, Texas, USA
WHEN:
12.30pm Friday 22 November 1963
THE AFTERMATH:
Dallas police surrounded the Texas School Book Depository but Oswald was allowed to leave the scene of the crime after the building superintendent vouched for him. At 1.15pm Oswald shot Dallas policeman J.D. Tippit. There were 12 witnesses to the murder. Oswald walked briskly from the scene into a shoe shop and then a cinema, where he was arrested.
YOU SHOULD KNOW:
Vice-President Johnson took the oath of office at 2.38pm on board Air Force One just before it departed Love Field. The plane then flew back to Andrews Air Force Base carrying the new and the previous chief executive.

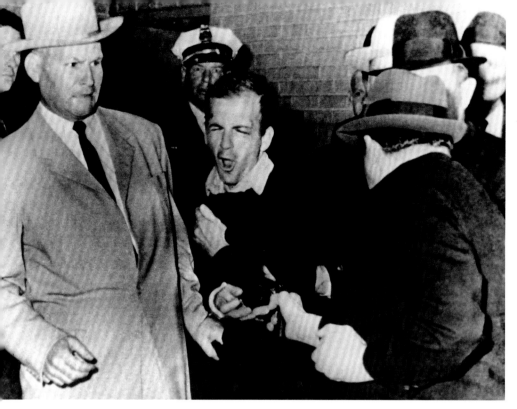

Lee Harvey Oswald & Jack Ruby

"You killed my president, you rat"

THE CRIME:
Before 22 November 1963 the name of Lee Harvey Oswald was unknown. Since that day it has become notorious as the assassin of the most charismatic American president of the 20th century (see page 307). However, Oswald was not to live to enjoy that infamy. At around 12.05am on Saturday 23 November Lee Harvey Oswald appeared before the press in the basement of City Hall at 2001 Commerce Street in Dallas. He denied all knowledge of the killing. At 1.30am he was formally arraigned with the murder of the president. At 10.25am the police again began to question Oswald. At 3.30pm Oswald received a visit from his brother, Robert.

At 4.35pm he appeared at the number two spot in a line-up alongside W.E. Perry (under number one), Richard L. Clark (three) and Don Ables (four), and was identified as Officer Tippit's killer by witness, Helen Markham. At 6pm, he faced more questions from the police. At 9.30am the next day, preparations were made to transport Oswald from his fifth floor cell to the local jail. At 11.15am the fateful journey began.

Six minutes later, as the handcuffed Lee Harvey Oswald was being led to a waiting vehicle, Jack Ruby, a 52-year-old local nightclub owner, shot him in the stomach with a Colt Cobra .38, shouting, "You killed my president, you rat". The assassination was watched on television by millions, the first time a murder was seen live. Oswald died without regaining consciousness. At 1.07pm – 47 hours and 53 minutes after JFK died – Oswald was pronounced dead at Parkland Memorial Hospital where his victim, the president, had been taken two days earlier.

Jack Ruby moves forward and fires at Lee Harvey Oswald at point-blank range.

WHERE:
2001 Commerce Street, Dallas, Texas, USA
WHEN:
11.21pm Sunday 24 November 1963
THE AFTERMATH:
Jack Ruby was arrested and charged with murder on 26 November 1963. On 14 March 1964, after a brief jury deliberation, he was convicted of murder with malice and sentenced to death. On 5 October 1966 the conviction and the death sentence were overturned. On 9 December 1966 Ruby was taken into hospital suffering from pneumonia. As preparations were being made for a second trial, Ruby died on 3 January 1967 of a pulmonary embolism at Parkland Memorial Hospital – which meant that the president, his assassin and the assassin's murderer all died in the same place.

Malcolm X

"Don't be messin' with my pockets"

THE CRIME: Malcolm X was born as Malcolm Little on 19 May 1925 at University Hospital, Omaha, Nebraska. Despite graduating top of his class, Little left school after a teacher he admired told him that studying to be a lawyer was "no realistic goal for a nigger". Little became a delinquent, was sent to borstal, then became a drug dealer and burglar and was sent to prison. Little became attracted to the Temple of Islam (later the Nation of Islam), a racist Muslim organization that referred to white people as "devils". It was after meeting Elijah Muhammad, a leader of the Nation of Islam, that Little took to calling himself Malcolm X.

After his conversion X worked hard proselytizing and from 1959 he began to appear on television as spokesman for the Nation of Islam. On 14 January 1958 X married Betty Jean Sanders in Lansing, Michigan. In August 1963 X criticized Martin Luther King's March on Washington, unable to comprehend why blacks were enthused at a protest "run by whites in front of a statue of a president who has been dead for a hundred years and who didn't like us when he was alive". On 8 March 1964 X announced that he had left the Nation of Islam and four days later founded Muslim Mosque, Inc. He converted to Sunni Islam and adopted a Muslim name, el-Hajj Malik el-Shabazz. The Nation of Islam regarded X as a traitor and tried to evict him from his home in Queens, New York, claiming that they had paid for the building. On 14 February 1965 the house was firebombed. X had just began his speech before a crowd of 400 on the first day of National Brotherhood Week when a man in the audience shouted, "Get your hand outta my pocket! Don't be messin' with my pockets!" As bodyguards moved in to quell the disturbance, X called out "Cool it there". A man rushed forward with a sawn-off shotgun and shot X in the chest. Two more men rushed the stage and fired pistols at X, who was hit by 16 bullets. The 39 year old was pronounced dead on arrival at 3.30pm at New York's Columbia Presbyterian Hospital.

WHERE:
Audubon Ballroom, Broadway and 165th Street, New York City, USA
WHEN:
3.10pm Sunday 21 February 1965
THE AFTERMATH:
On 27 February 1965 more than 1,500 people attended Malcolm X's funeral in Harlem at the Faith Temple Church of God in Christ (now Child's Memorial Temple Church of God in Christ). X was buried at the Ferncliff Cemetery in Hartsdale, New York. Three men were charged with the murder and convicted: Thomas Hagan (aka Thomas Hayer aka Talmadge Hayer), Norman 3X Butler (aka Muhammad Abd Al-Aziz) and Thomas 15X Johnson. On 30 April 1966 Hayer confessed to firing the shotgun but alleged that the two other accused were innocent. Instead, he said that Leon David and Wilbur McKinley were his accomplices. Norman 3X Butler was paroled in 1985, still a member of the Nation of Islam. Thomas 15X Johnson was paroled in 1987 and now calls himself Khalil Islam.
YOU SHOULD KNOW:
On 12 January 1995 X's daughter Qubilah Shabazz was arrested and indicted at Minneapolis with trying to hire an assassin to murder Nation of Islam founder Louis Farrakhan whom she blamed for the murder of her father. X's widow died in 1997 after she was badly burned at her home in a fire started by her grandson who was described at his trial as psychotic and schizophrenic.

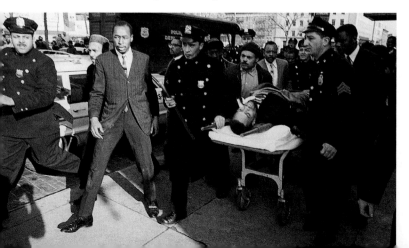

Malcolm X is rushed to hospital.

309

Martin Luther King

"Longevity has its place, but I'm not concerned about that now"

WHERE:
Lorraine Motel, 450 Mulberry Street,
Memphis, Tennessee, USA
WHEN:
6.01pm Thursday 4 April 1968

THE AFTERMATH:
James Earl Ray fled abroad and on 8 June 1968, 65 days after the assassination, he was arrested at Heathrow, London, trying to fly to Brussels. On 6 March 1969 Ray confessed to the assassination. The prosecution presented their evidence and the judge, W. Preston Battle, passed sentence. Then, three days later, Ray claimed that he had been pressurized into the guilty plea by his lawyer. The court refused to act after Judge Battle died on 31 March so Ray began telling anyone who would listen of his innocence. He gave dozens of interviews and wrote two books. He claimed that the real killer was a man called Raoul. Ray admitted buying the murder weapon and renting the room but only so that the mysterious Raoul could carry out the assassination. Ray died of kidney failure in prison on 23 April 1998, still protesting his innocence.

THE CRIME: Martin Luther King, Jr was born at Atlanta, Georgia, on 15 January 1929, as Michael Louis King. In 1947 he was ordained a minister and on 18 June 1953 he married a young concert singer named Coretta Scott and they had two sons and two daughters. In August 1957, Martin Luther King and 115 other black leaders founded the Southern Christian Leadership Conference. In September of the following year he narrowly escaped death in New York when a mad black woman stabbed him in the chest with a letter opener. The surgeon who operated said that if King had even sneezed he would have drowned in his own blood through a ruptured aorta.

On 28 August 1963, at the Lincoln monument in Washington DC, King made his most famous speech, Around 250,000 people – 60,000 of them white – were at the largest civil rights demonstration at which he proclaimed, "I have a dream." He travelled to Memphis in late March 1968 to help black dustmen who were striking for the right to form a trade union. On Wednesday 3 April 1968, at the Bishop Charles J. Mason Temple, King gave his last public speech. He said, "Like anybody, I would like to live a long life. Longevity has its place, but I'm not concerned about that now."

On 4 April racist criminal James Earl Ray booked into Room 5B on the second floor of the South Main Street doss house, which provided an unobstructed view of the Lorraine Motel where King was billeted. (Landlady Bessie Brewer later positively identified Ray, who had used the alias John Willard.) At 6.01pm King stood on the balcony outside Room 306 waiting for an aide to fetch him a coat.

King was shot in the throat and rushed to St Joseph's Hospital where he was pronounced dead at 7.05pm.

The rifle that James Earl Ray used is examined by the House Select Committee on Assassinations.

Robert F. Kennedy

"Now it's on to Chicago and let's win there"

THE CRIME: When his brother was elected president in 1961, Bobby Kennedy became Attorney General. Kennedy remained in his job under President Johnson for ten months but resigned to become senator from New York. On 16 March 1968 Kennedy announced his candidacy for the presidency. Bobby Kennedy spent the day of Tuesday 4 June 1968 relaxing and having fun with his family at the Malibu home of John Frankenheimer as he waited for the results of the California primary. Kennedy went to the Ambassador Hotel and at 11.40pm the news broke that Kennedy had unexpectedly won.

His party went down to the Embassy Ballroom where he made a brief speech thanking the campaign team, "We are a great country, an unselfish country, and a compassionate country, and I intend to make that my basis for running over the period of the next few month," ending with a V-sign and the words, "and now it's on to Chicago and let's win there." Kennedy's group headed towards the pantry. Assistant maître d'hôtel Karl Uecker moved in front of Kennedy and Thane Eugene Cesar, 26, a part-time bodyguard from Ace Security, was following. Kennedy shook hands with kitchen staff as he walked.

Suddenly a young man moved from the vicinity of the ice machine toward the steam table where Kennedy was shaking hands. The young man brushed past photographer Virginia Guy, his gun chipping one of her teeth. At 12.15am, he pulled an Iver-Johnson Cadet .22-calibre revolver from the waistband of his jeans, shouted, "Kennedy, you sonofabitch", and fired eight rounds. The shooter, Sirhan Sirhan, was grabbed and restrained by Uecker, the writer George Plimpton, the Olympic gold medalist decathlete, Rafer Johnson and the professional football player Rosey Grier. Kennedy and five other people were hit. The police arrived to take away Sirhan who claimed, "I did it for my country." Senator Robert Francis Kennedy died, aged 42, at 1.44am, a few minutes after being taken off a life-support machine.

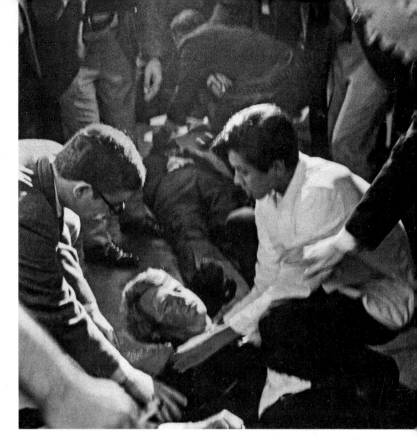

Robert Kennedy lies on the floor in the Ambassador Hotel after being shot by Sirhan Sirhan.

WHERE:
Ambassador Hotel, 3400 Wilshire Boulevard, Los Angeles, California, USA
WHEN:
12.15am Wednesday 5 June 1968
THE AFTERMATH:
On 3 March 1969 in a Los Angeles courtroom, Sirhan claimed that he had killed Kennedy "with 20 years of malice aforethought", although he has maintained since being arrested that he has no memory of the crime. Sirhan was convicted on 17 April 1969 and was sentenced to death six days later. He moved into death row in San Quentin on 23 May 1969. The sentence was commuted to life in prison on 17 June 1972.

Earl Mountbatten's body is taken away from the harbour at Mullaghmore.

Lord Mountbatten

"I put no bomb in the boat"

THE CRIME: Admiral of the Fleet, last Viceroy of India, Prince Philip's uncle and a rampant self-publicist, Louis Francis Albert Victor Nicholas, 1st Earl Mountbatten of Burma, KG, GCB, OM, GCSI, GCIE, GCVO, DSO, PC, was born at Frogmore House, Windsor, Berkshire in England, at 6am on 25 June 1900.

On 18 April 1955, he was appointed First Sea Lord. On 30 April 1959 he became Chief of the Defence Staff, a job he held for six years. Mountbatten spent much of his declining years ensuring the preservation of his own legacy.

Mountbatten usually holidayed at Classiebawn, his summer home in Mullaghmore, County Sligo, a small seaside village on the far north west coast of Ireland. In 1960 Mountbatten's estate manager, Patrick O'Grady, raised questions with the Gardai about the earl's safety. "While everything points to the fact that no attack of any kind on the earl, by subversive elements, was at any time contemplated" the reply went, "it would in my opinion be asking too much to say in effect that we can guarantee his safety while in this country." By 1971, 12 policemen were on duty "in case the IRA try to take me as a hostage". In 1974 Sir Robert Mark, the commissioner of the Metropolitan Police Force, said that he would prefer Mountbatten not to go to Ireland. That year 28 policemen were assigned to protect Mountbatten. As each year went by the danger for Mountbatten seemed to pass.

In 1979 he was nearly 80 years old and had not had any real power for 14 years. At 11.30am on 27 August 1979 Mountbatten and his party climbed aboard their 9-m (29-ft) long fishing boat *Shadow V*. Mountbatten was accompanied by his daughter, Patricia, son-in-law, Lord Brabourne, twin grandsons, Nicholas and Timothy, their grandmother, the 83-year-old Doreen, Dowager Baroness Brabourne, and a local boy, Paul Maxwell, a 15-year-old Protestant from County Fermanagh. The boat, steered by Mountbatten, raced to the first of the lobster pots, the point of the expedition. Before he could cut the engine, a 23-kg (50-lb) bomb blew the boat apart.

It appeared that the device had been activated remotely from the shore. Mountbatten died immediately, as did his grandson, Nicholas, and Paul Maxwell. Doreen Brabourne died of her injuries the following day.

WHERE:
On board *Shadow V*, Mullaghmore, Sligo, Republic of Ireland
WHERE:
Monday 27 August 1979
THE AFTERMATH:
At 9.40am on the day of the assassination police had stopped a car containing Thomas McMahon and Francie McGirl for a routine tax disk check. The driver, Francie McGirl of Ballinamore, County Leitrim, gave a false name to police. Shortly before noon, while both men were being questioned, *Shadow V* was ripped apart by an explosion activated by a timer. When McGirl said, "I put no bomb in the boat", the Irish police knew that they had caught the assassins. Thomas McMahon and Francie McGirl were tried for the murder. McMahon was convicted on 23 November 1979, McGirl acquitted. McMahon was released in 1998 under the terms of the Good Friday Agreement. McGirl died in a farming accident in 1995.

Ronald Reagan

"Honey, I forgot to duck"

THE CRIME: On 29 March 1981 a weird loner called John Hinckley arrived in Washington on a Greyhound bus and checked into room 312 of the Park Central Hotel on 18th and G streets. The next day, his 70th in office, Reagan arrived at the Washington Hilton hotel at 1.45pm to address 3,500 members of the American Federation of Labor and Congress of Industrial Organizations.

At 2.25pm Reagan left the building by a side entrance on T Street and waved to the small crowd outside. As he waved, Hinckley stepped forward and fired a Rohm RG-14 .22 calibre blue steel pistol six times in three seconds. The six bullets were Devastors, designed to explode on impact, although none of them did. The first round struck White House press secretary James Brady in the head; the second hit policeman, 47-year-old Thomas K. Delehanty in the back; the third missed its target and hit the window of a building across the road; the fourth hit Timothy J. McCarthy, 33, of the Secret Service in the abdomen as he courageously stood in front of Reagan; the fifth struck the bullet-proof glass of the presidential limousine and the sixth bounced off the side of the car and hit Reagan under his left arm. Agent Jerry Parr jumped on the president and pushed him to the ground while Agent Ray Shaddick pushed his colleague and the president into the car. Reagan winced in pain, "Jerry, you son of a bitch, I think you've broken one of my ribs." The president then began coughing up blood and the limousine screeched away from the White House and towards George Washington University Hospital. The car arrived at 2.35pm and Reagan, ever the showman, walked into the hospital but as soon as he was inside he collapsed. Parr and Shaddick carried him to Trauma Bay 5 where the medical staff cut off all the president's clothes. Reagan lay naked with blood pouring from his mouth, moaning that he could not breathe. A doctor cut a hole in Reagan's throat and put a breathing tube into his throat but it did not help. Reagan's blood pressure fell to 78 and he passed out. He came round to find Marisa Mize, a nurse, holding his hand. Nancy Reagan insisted on going to the hospital and, when she saw the president, he supposedly said, "Honey, I forgot to duck."

WHERE:
Washington Hilton Hotel, 1919 Connecticut Avenue NW, Washington DC, USA
WHEN:
2.25pm Monday 30 March 1981
THE AFTERMATH:
At 3.24pm Reagan was taken into theatre for surgery to remove the bullet. Dr Benjamin Aaron, chief of thoracic surgery, performed the operation. Dr Aaron found the bullet 3 cm (1 in) below the president's heart. Reagan's chest cavity was filled with blood and he had lost half of the blood in his body. Dr Aaron immediately decided to operate to repair the damaged lung. Hinckley had shot Reagan to impress the actress Jodie Foster, with whom he had become obsessed after seeing her in the 1976 film *Taxi Driver*. In his hotel room among other items was a note to Jodie Foster asking, "You are a virgin, aren't you?" On 21 June 1982, after a seven-week trial, Hinckley was found not guilty by reason of insanity and sent to St Elizabeth's Hospital, an asylum. On 17 December 2003 Judge Paul Friedman decided that Hinckley no longer posed a serious danger to himself or others and approved unsupervised visits to his parents in the Washington DC area.

Police and Secret Service agents dive in to capture Hinckley.

John Paul II

WHERE:
St Peter's Square, Rome, Italy
WHEN:
5.09pm Wednesday 13 May 1981
THE AFTERMATH:
In July 1981, Agca was sentenced to life imprisonment in Italy. Remarkably, the Holy Father forgave Mehmet Ali Agca. On 27 December 1983, he and Agca met and spoke privately at the prison where Agca was being held. The pope said, "What we talked about will have to remain a secret between him and me. I spoke to him as a brother whom I have pardoned and who has my complete trust." In June 2000, at the Pope's request, Agca was pardoned by president Carlo Azeglio Ciampi and extradited to Turkey. Five years later, in early February 2005, during the Pope's final illness, Agca sent a letter wishing him well.

"I spoke to him as a brother whom I have pardoned and who has my complete trust"

THE CRIME: The first non-Italian pope since Adrian VI in 1522, Karol Józef Wojtyla, John Paul II became one of the most beloved statesmen of the 20th century. Little did he know that a Turkish thug was intent on assassinating him.

In August 1980 Mehmet Ali Agca left Sofia in Bulgaria and began travelling across the Mediterranean region using a variety of aliases and forged travel documents. He left Milan and arrived in Rome by train on 10 May 1981. In the Italian capital Agca met three accomplices: a fellow Turk and two Bulgarians. The operation was commanded by Zilo Vassilev, the Bulgarian military attaché in Italy. On 13 May 1981 Agca and a back-up gunman Oral Çelik sat in St Peter's Square writing postcards and waiting for the Holy Father to arrive. They planned to shoot Papa Wojtyla and then set off a small bomb and, in the ensuing confusion, escape to the Bulgarian embassy. The Pope appeared in a white open-top jeep, among a crowd of 20,000 pilgrims. As John Paul passed, Agca fired several shots before the crowd grabbed him. Four bullets hit the Pope, two of them lodging in his lower intestine, the others hitting his left hand and right arm. Two bystanders were also hit.

Çelik panicked and fled without setting off his bomb or opening fire. The Holy Father was taken to the Agostino Gemelli University Polyclinic, where he underwent emergency surgery and blood transfusion.

Pope John Paul II collapses after being shot in St Peter's Square.

Benigno Aquino

"If they hit me in the head, I'm a goner anyway"

THE CRIME:

Benigno "Ninoy" Simeón Aquino, Jr was the charismatic, leading opposition politician during the presidency of Ferdinand Marcos in the Philippines. On 8 May 1980 Aquino travelled to America for treatment for his heart ailment. In the spring of 1983 Aquino decided to return home and ask Marcos to step down. Aquino left Logan International Airport, Boston on 13 August 1983, travelling under a false name. When he rang wife Cory, who was still in the United States, he learned that Marcos knew of his plans. Aquino muttered to one of his aides, "They're going to kill me at the airport and then kill the guy who did it." Prescient words, as it would turn out.

As his plane began its descent into Manila International Airport, Aquino placed a bulletproof vest under his white safari suit. He said to one journalist, "It's only good for the body, but if they hit me in the head, I'm a goner anyway." Awaiting Aquino were around 20,000 supporters and 2,000 security personnel, ostensibly to secure his safety. At midday on Sunday 21 August 1983, the aeroplane stopped at gate eight. As the "tube" reached the plane, five soldiers walked up to Aquino. They accompanied him along the tube. Within seconds of leaving the plane, and despite the apparent heavy security, Aquino was dead, a bullet in his head. A short distance away lay the bloodied corpse of a second man, clad in a white shirt and blue trousers. The government claimed that the dead man was the lone killer. He carried no identification and the only clue was the word "Rolly" on the waistband of his underpants. President Marcos said that the killer had been a professional assassin and had shot one bullet from a .357 Magnum into Aquino's head from a distance of just 45 cm (18 in).

A soldier drags Benigno Aquino Jr. to a military van moments after a flurry of bullets hit the opposition leader.

WHERE:
Manila International Airport, Philippines
WHEN:
Sunday 21 August 1983
THE AFTERMATH:
On 30 August 1983, the government announced that the killer was named Rolando Galman. It has never been officially established why, or even if, Galman had done it. In November 1985, to ease public concern with his regime, Marcos called an election, to be held in February 1986. Despite the Commission on Election calling the outcome for Marcos, Cory Aquino and her supporters refused to accept the result. Eventually Marcos and his wife, Imelda, were driven from the Philippines and Cory Aquino became president on 25 February. The Aquino administration was continually plagued by rumours of coup attempts. She retired in 1992.

Brighton Bomb

"I think that was an assassination attempt, don't you?"

WHERE:
Grand Hotel, 97–99 Kings Road, Brighton, West Sussex, England
WHEN:
2.54am Friday 12 October 1984

THE AFTERMATH:
Tory MP Anthony Berry was killed in the explosion, as were four others. Mrs Thatcher and her husband, Denis, spent the night at Lewes Police College. She was due to give a keynote speech at the conference that Friday and went ahead with it, to the delight of the party faithful. At 9.20am the conference opened and ten minutes later Mrs Thatcher walked onto the platform. Mrs Thatcher said, "The bomb attack… was an attempt not only to disrupt and terminate our conference. It was an attempt to cripple Her Majesty's democratically elected government." The IRA admitted responsibility saying, "Today we were unlucky but remember we only have to be lucky once; you will have to be lucky always." The police investigated the 800 people staying at the hotel and accounted for all but one – the carpenter Roy Walsh. The fingerprints he had left behind matched those of IRA member Patrick Magee. He was arrested and on 10 June 1986 sentenced to eight life terms with a recommendation that he serve at least 35 years before he became eligible for parole. In June 1999, he was released after serving just 13 years.

THE CRIME: Conservative Margaret Thatcher was the first woman to become British prime minister when she defeated the incumbent Labour leader James Callaghan on 3 May 1979. In autumn of 1984 the Conservatives arrived in Brighton on the south coast of England for their annual conference. On 19 September 1984 33-year-old Irish terrorist Patrick Magee booked into room 629 of the Grand Hotel using the name Roy Walsh. Over the next 24 days, although posing as a carpenter, he carried the tools of a very different trade into his room. He tore down a wall in the bathroom, planted 13 kg (30 lb) of gelignite in the space and rebuilt the wall – all without arousing the suspicion of the hotel staff.

On Thursday 11 October the Conservative Agents held their ball and Mrs Thatcher popped in before returning to her room at just after 11pm to work on her conference speech. At 2.54am Mrs Thatcher was in the sitting room of her suite on the first floor of the hotel when the bomb exploded. The bathroom was wrecked and although she may not have been killed she certainly would have been injured, had she been doing her ablutions. The bomb went off but the lights in the hotel stayed on and there was deathly silence. After a while, Mrs Thatcher said, "I think that was an assassination attempt, don't you?"

The front of the Grand Hotel in Brighton after the bomb attack

Olof Palme

"They can never nail me for it. The weapon is gone"

THE CRIME: Sven Olof Joachim Palme joined the Social Democratic Party in Sweden, becoming head of its youth section in 1955 when he was 28. Three years later he became an MP and in 1963 joined the cabinet for the first time. On 1 October 1969 he became prime minister but lost power in October 1976 when he tried to raise taxes to pay for welfare benefits. He was returned to office in 1982. He had many admirers but also a large number of enemies for his stance against American involvement in Vietnam, nuclear weapons and Franco; and for his support for sanctions against South Africa and the Palestinian Liberation Organization.

Four years later, on 28 February 1986, he and his wife, Lisbet, went to the cinema. They left to walk home. Palme did not have any bodyguards and freely walked the streets day and night. That night at 11.21pm, as he and Mrs Palme walked down Sveavägen in Stockholm, a gunman shot Palme in the back outside a pen shop. Mrs Palme was also shot but recovered. Two young women nearby rushed to help the stricken politician. The prime minister was taken to hospital but was pronounced dead at 12.06am on 1 March 1986.

WHERE:
Sveavägen, Stockholm, Sweden
WHEN:
11.21pm Friday 28 February 1986
THE AFTERMATH:
A reward worth $5 million was posted for information leading to the capture and conviction of Palme's killer but no one came forward. Various names, nearly all with right-wing connections, came into the frame for the killing. One of these people was mentioned, but not identified, by a policeman in his book about the case and then was himself murdered in North Carolina, America. In December 1988 an alcoholic petty crook called Christer Pettersson, aged 41, was arrested for the murder and picked out of a line-up by Mrs Palme. He was sentenced to life imprisonment but released in 1989 after his conviction was deemed unsafe. Despite his acquittal, Pettersson once confessed to shooting Palme. "Sure as hell it was me who shot [him], but they can never nail me for it. The weapon is gone," he told Swedish writer Gert Fylking in 2001. He later retracted the statement and said he was not involved in the killing. He died at the Karolinska University Hospital, Stockholm on 29 September 2004 of brain haemorrhaging and organ failure. The gun used in the murder was never found and officially the assassination remains unsolved.

Olof Palme addressing the UN General Assembly in 1985.

GANGSTER CRIMES, BOOTLEGGING & SMUGGLING

Fredericka Mandelbaum

"She was scheming and dishonest as the day is long"

WHERE:
Manhattan Savings Bank, Broadway and Bleecker Street, New York City, USA
WHEN:
Sunday 27 October 1878
THE AFTERMATH:
Scheduled to stand trial in December 1884, instead Mandelbaum fled to Canada, where she lived the remaining ten years of her life. Fredericka Mandelbaum died at her house in Hamilton, Ontario on 26 February 1894, surrounded by family and friends. She was buried in New York and, reported newspapers, several mourners had their pockets picked at her funeral.

THE CRIME: Born on 27 February 1818 (some sources say 1827) as Friederike Henriette Auguste Wiesener in Hanover, Prussia, she married Wolf Israel Mandelbaum and they moved to New York in 1850. They bought a dry goods store at 79 Clinton Street. In the following decade "Marm" Mandelbaum found her vocation as a fence and trainer of apprentice thieves. In 1867 she avoided prison when Moses Ehrich, a fellow fence, bribed the authorities. Her notoriety grew and George Washington Walling, the chief of New York City's police said that Mandelbaum had "no peer in the United States" as a receiver of stolen property. She paid fines for criminals who stole the items she fenced but she also never paid more than ten per cent of any item's worth to the thief. One thief, Banjo Pete Emerson, said, "She was scheming and dishonest as the day is long, but she could be like an angel to the worst devil as long as he played square with her."

In 1875 Wolf Mandelbaum died from tuberculosis. It seems that he had no part in his wife's criminal activities. In October 1878 Marm Mandelbaum was behind the Manhattan Savings Bank robbery, described by the *New York Times* as "one of the most daring and successful burglaries ever perpetrated". The thieves handcuffed the caretaker, forcing him to hand over the keys to the safe and to tell them the combination. They got away with around $2.7 million in cash and securities. Mandelbaum was arrested in July 1884, along with her eldest son Julius and her clerk Hermann Stoude, on charges of grand larceny. District Attorney Peter B. Olney determined to bring her down and could not be bribed. He hired the Pinkerton Agency rather than using the police to catch her. Mandelbaum spent one day behind bars before posting her bail of $21,000.

OLD MOTHER HUBBARD

BLACK LENA

KID GLOVE ROSIE

MARM MANDELBAUM

QUEEN LIZ

SOPHIE LYONS

MARM MANDELBAUM AND SOME OF HER CLIENTS

Marm Mandelbaum, successful female criminal and fence, with some of her clients.

Samuel Samuzzo "Samoots" Amatuna

Before Amatuna could say "I do" he slipped into unconsciousness

Samuel Amatuna's funeral drew thousands of spectators.

THE CRIME: Born in 1899, Amatuna began his career as a messenger for the Genna brothers. He progressed to become an enforcer and later bodyguard for "Bloody Angelo" Genna in 1920. He would beat up anyone who even criticized the brothers and was handy with both knives and guns. The Gennas ran the 19th Ward in Chicago – known as the Bloody 19th – and Amatuna ensured that everyone voted the way that the Gennas wanted.

John Powers had served the ward since 1888 but the Irish population had diminished, to be replaced by Sicilians and Italians. They put up Anthony D'Andrea as a candidate against Powers but the Irishman had been a devoted public servant and it was not just the Irish who wanted him to stay. Frank Lombardi was an enthusiastic supporter of Powers but in February 1916, while he was drinking in a bar on Taylor Street, the 17-year-old Amatuna gunned him down. Powers won the election but four years later, on 28 September 1920, Amatuna bombed the alderman's front porch. Powers was not deterred and surrounded himself with armed guards who accompanied him on the 1921 campaign trail. More bombs were set off in front of homes of both candidates and supporters. Powers won the election by 435 votes but Angelo Genna, Amatuna and Frank Gambino murdered Paul Labriola, a Powers supporter and court bailiff, on 9 March 1921. Amatuna also shot dead two more aides of Powers'.

Amatuna grew rich through his association with the Gennas and bought the Bluebird Café on Halstead Street. He never carried his guns inside and would entertain patrons nightly with his tenor voice. After the murder of Angelo Genna on 25 May 1925, Amatuna took over the presidency of the Unione Siciliane. On 13 November 1925, in preparation for a visit to see *Aida* with his girlfriend Rose Pecorara, Amatuna visited a barbers owned by Isadore Paul on Roosevelt Road, for a shave and a manicure. As a hot towel was placed over his face, Vincent "The Schemer" Drucci and Jim Doherty entered the shop and began firing, hitting Amatuna in the chest.

WHERE:
Taylor Street, Chicago, USA
WHEN:
Monday 21 February 1916
THE AFTERMATH:
Amatuna was taken to Jefferson Park Hospital where his last request was to be married to Rose. A priest was summoned and the ceremony began but, before Amatuna could say "I do", he slipped into unconsciousness. He died a short time after. He was just 26.

*Diamond Jim Colosimo and
Dale Winter*

Diamond Jim Colosimo

"Stick to the girls and gambling"

THE CRIME: Born in Calabria, Italy, Colosimo moved to America in 1895, arriving at the Levee district in Chicago. He quickly became the aide for corrupt politicians "Bathhouse" John Coughlin and Michael "Hinky Dink" Kenna, who made him manager of a poolroom and then a saloon. His job included collecting money from the sundry brothels, casinos and opium houses in the area. Victoria Moresco ran a brothel on Armour Avenue and she liked Colosimo so much that she married him in 1902.

Together they increased the number of brothels, going downmarket with girls charging $1 or $2 a trick. By 1903 Colosimo owned more than 100 bordellos where he took $1.20 for every $2 the whores earned, and he gave 20¢ to the two corrupt politicians for protection. Colosimo needed a regular supply of women and so became a white slaver, buying girls for $500 apiece. The passing of the Mann Act, or White Slavery Act, in 1910, halted this market. By this time Colosimo had a huge empire of prostitutes, saloonkeepers, union racketeers and casino employees. He hired musclemen to keep his employees in line and then hired Johnny Torrio (see page 324) to help him when the Black Hand Gang threatened him with extortion. With the younger man running things, Colosimo opened Colosimo's Café, which became the in place in Chicago. It had a full orchestra, a dance floor, top entertainers and great food, prepared by the finest chefs money could buy. In 1913 politicians cleaned up the Levee but Colosimo simply moved his brothels and casinos to other venues. When Big Bill Thompson, probably the most corrupt politician ever, was elected mayor in 1915, with Colosimo's help, business resumed in the Levee. Torrio

WHERE:
Colosimo's Café, 2126 South Wabash Avenue, Chicago, Illinois, USA
WHEN:
4pm Tuesday 11 May 1920
THE AFTERMATH:
There were rumours that Frankie Yale was the killer but, according to crime historian Jay Robert Nash, he had an alibi proving he was at a union meeting at the time of the killing. Johnny Torrio and Al Capone expanded Colosimo's empire and within five years bootlegging was providing them with an income of more than $50 million annually.

told Colosimo to prepare for Prohibition (the Volstead Act came into effect on 17 January 1920) but Colosimo was uninterested in illicit booze: "Stick to the girls and gambling," he said. Torrio decided that Colosimo's reign should come to an end. He told Colosimo that a shipment of whisky would arrive at the café at 4pm and that he should be on hand to take charge. Also in the café that day was Al Capone (see page 330) and as Colosimo entered the foyer Capone shot him in the head. Diamond Jim Colosimo was dead at 43.

Charles "The Ox" Reiser

Reiser murdered him but made the death look like suicide

THE CRIME: A safe-cracker by trade, Reiser was also a devoted family man. Using the name Charles Shopes, he was friendly and helpful. He used the money from robberies to buy a large apartment building in Chicago where he was known to be a good landlord. To the underworld and the police, however, Reiser was known to be a vicious thug. He was first arrested in 1902. While on bail, he killed the only witness to his crime and the case was dropped. Three years later, the same thing happened – he was arrested, the witness disappeared and the case was dropped. In 1907 he was convicted of assault with a deadly weapon and sentenced to 30 days in prison. In 1909 Reiser was arrested in Seattle, Washington and charged with burglary and murder. For a third time the witnesses in the case were killed.

In 1914 he met Dion O'Banion and became something of a mentor to the future leader of the Chicago North Side Gang. O'Banion began to go on jobs with Reiser. In 1919 May Mahoney, the wife of a criminal colleague of Reiser's, John Mahoney, threatened to go to the police. Reiser beat her to death at her home at 1137 West Washington Street, Chicago. In 1920 Clarence White, another crony of Reiser, was questioned by the police. The two men had stolen a safe belonging to Standard Oil and rifled its contents. To ensure that White did not betray him, Reiser murdered him but made the death look like suicide. In April 1921 the police arrested John Mahoney. He was caught in the act but not long after the police bailed him, pending further enquiries, he was found shot to death in an alley at 1814 South Peoria Street on 30 April 1921. Six months later, on 10 October 1921, Reiser was shot twice during a robbery attempt at a cold storage depot and was taken to the Alexian Brothers Hospital. On 21 October, he was found dead in bed after "a rattle of shots", with his second wife leaning over his body sobbing hysterically.

WHERE:
1814 South Peoria Street, Chicago, Illinois, USA
WHEN:
Saturday 30 April 1921
THE AFTERMATH:
Mrs Reiser was charged with her husband's murder but the case was dropped when a coroner's jury ruled his death a suicide despite the fact that he had ten separate bullet wounds and his right hand and left arm had been broken in the robbery.

Johnny Torrio

"This is for Deanie O'Banion, you dago bastard"

WHERE:
Schofield's Flower Shop, 738 North State Street, Chicago, Illinois, USA
WHEN:
Monday 10 November 1924
THE AFTERMATH:
Torrio lay near death for a week. Capone supplied an armed guard of 30 men outside Jackson Park Hospital to prevent another attempt. On 9 February 1925 Torrio was sentenced to nine months in prison for bootlegging. On his release he handed over the empire to his trusty lieutenant, Capone. On 22 April 1936 Torrio was arrested for income tax evasion and sentenced to two and half years. He was paroled on 14 April 1941. He died of a heart attack on 16 April 1957.

*Johnny Torrio leaves court
in Brooklyn.*

THE CRIME: Born in Osara, Italy, Torrio arrived in New York in 1884, aged two. He joined the James Street Gang but, since he was just 1.76 m (5 ft 6 in) tall, this was as much for protection as for villainy. He became a bouncer at Nigger Mike's on Pell Street. One of the roughest saloons in Manhattan, this was where Irving Berlin began as a singing waiter. In 1904, using money from robberies he had committed, Torrio opened a large pub at James and Walker streets and turned the upstairs into a brothel. The following year he was a high roller in the Five Points Gang. In 1908 during a gang war he opened the Harvard Inn with Frankie Yale in Brooklyn. In 1909 he sold his share in the Harvard Inn and moved to Chicago at the behest of Diamond Jim Colosimo (see page 322) where he became his right-hand man. He solved Colosimo's problem with the extortionist Black Hand Gang by shooting dead three members as they collected their money. In 1912 he married Anna Jacobs and created his headquarters at The Four Deuces, 2222 South Wabash Avenue, near Colosimo's Café. It was a bar on the ground floor and a brothel on the first and second floors. In 1919, after he learned of an attempt to be made on his life, Torrio sent for Al Capone (see page 330) to be his bodyguard. Torrio arranged for Colosimo's murder and took over his empire. He spent the next five years fighting off rival gangs. On 19 May 1924 Dion O'Banion set him up with the police on a bootlegging charge but Torrio had his revenge on 10 November 1924 by having three of his men murder O'Banion at his flower shop on North State Street. The killing set off a bloody warfare on the streets of Chicago and on 24 January 1925 an attempt was made on Torrio's life by Bugs Moran, Vincent Drucci, "Hymie" Weiss and Frank Gusenberg. He was shot several times and Moran stood over him as he lay on the ground, a gun in his hand, "This is for Deanie O'Banion, you dago bastard." When Moran pulled the trigger, the chamber was empty.

George "Bugs" Moran

"I don't want to be murdered beside the garbage cans in some Chicago alley"

THE CRIME: Born in Minnesota as Adelard Cunin, he moved to Chicago when he was a teenager and adopted the name George Moran so that he could join an Irish gang. His first arrest came on 17 September 1910 and they came thick and fast after that but he stayed out of jail until 31 May 1918 when he was sent to Joliet State Prison for armed robbery. He spent five years inside, gaining parole on 1 February 1923 and returned to his gang to find that Dion O'Banion had taken the reins. Moran worked with O'Banion, "Hymie" Weiss and Vincent "The Schemer" Drucci to run the North Side. Their men often invaded the territory on the South Side, ran by Al Capone and Johnny Torrio. Following O'Banion's murder, Moran became second-in-command to "Hymie" Weiss. They plotted their revenge and on 24 January 1925 Moran, Drucci, Gusenberg and Weiss tried to kill Torrio as he and his wife returned home to South Clyde Avenue from a shopping trip (see opposite).

On 13 June 1925 an attempt was made on the lives of Moran and Drucci. On 20 September 1926 Moran, Weiss and several cars of hoodlums drove slowly past Al Capone's Hawthorne Inn headquarters and sprayed the building with thousands of bullets. Capone lay under a table on the first floor. Remarkably, no one was killed in the attack. Capone gave orders to eliminate the North Side gang. On 11 October 1926 Weiss was machine gunned to death outside Holy Name Cathedral and Moran took over the gang. A policeman killed Drucci on 4 April 1927. For almost two years peace reigned between Moran and Capone and then Capone had several members of Moran's gang killed in the St Valentine's Day Massacre (see page 328).

Moran's power declined after that but he still ran the 42nd and 43rd Street wards in the 1930s. At 1am on 15 February 1936 Moran and his men executed "Machine Gun Jack" McGurn who was believed (wrongly) to be behind the 14 February carnage.

WHERE:
Hawthorne Inn, 4823 22nd Street, Cicero, Illinois, USA
WHEN:
Monday 20 September 1926
THE AFTERMATH:
By 1940 Moran's power was gone and he resorted to burglary to pay his bills. He said, "I hope when my time comes that I die decently in bed. I don't want to be murdered beside the garbage cans in some Chicago alley." In fact, he died at Fort Leavenworth Prison on 25 February 1957 while serving a sentence for robbery.

Bugs Moran, left, appearing in court.

Du Yuesheng

"You have my word"

WHERE:
Shanghai, China
WHEN:
1927
THE AFTERMATH:
In 1949 Chiang Kai-shek's Nationalist
government fled to Taiwan. Du left
China for Hong Kong where he
died in 1951.

THE CRIME: China's most notorious gangster operated out of Shanghai, where he became the leader of the *Qing Bang* (Green Gang), the most powerful secret society in the city. He rose through the ranks and worked closely with Huang Jinrong (1868–1953), nicknamed "Pockmarked Huang", who, as well as being a gangster, was the head of Chinese detectives in the French Concession's *Garde Municipale*. Du Yuesheng, usually known as "Big-Eared Du", was born in the village of Gaoqiao in the Pudong district in 1887 and later took on another title *Jung Shi* or "Boss of the Underworld". Du lived for many years in a three-storey mansion, which is now the Donghu Hotel on Donghu Lu. He kept a wife on each floor. One of his favourite phrases was, "You have my word."

W.H. Auden and Christopher Underwood, in their book *Journey to a War*, described Du in 1938: "Du himself was tall and thin, with a face that seemed hewn out of stone, a Chinese version of the Sphinx. Peculiarly and inexplicably terrifying were his feet, in their silk socks and smart pointed European boots, emerging from beneath the long silken gown. Perhaps the Sphinx, too, would be even more frightening if it wore a modern top-hat." With Du in command, the gang controlled prostitution, bathhouses, gambling dens and numerous protection rackets as well as dealing in opium. He also engaged the *Qing Bang* in politics, forming an alliance with Chiang Kai-shek against the communists and pro-communist unions in Shanghai. The resulting massacre of 5,000 people, known as the 1927 Shanghai Purge, ended the First United Front. For his help, Chiang appointed Du to the Board of Opium Suppression Bureau. He was also decorated with the Order of the Brilliant Jade. He led a charmed life, thanks, he believed, to the dried heads of monkeys that were always fixed to the back of his long gowns. For his financial help Du was permitted to run trade unions and deal in drugs. China was then quite segregated and Chiang was in nominal power only of the whole country so he had to rely on local gangsters to enforce his will.

When the Nationalists declared war on Japan in 1937, Du smuggled supplies from occupied Chinese territory. The relationship took a turn for the worse following the Second World War and the criminal activities of Du, his family and colleagues caused difficulties for the Kuomintang. When Chiang Ching-kuo, Chiang Kai-shek's son, began an anti-corruption campaign in Shanghai in the late 1940s, Du's people were among the first to be jailed. Like most gangsters, Du had information on his friends and enemies and his people were released after he threatened to make public crimes committed by Chiang Kai-shek's family.

Du Yuesheng dealt in the labyrinthine world of Chinese politics and crime.

Arnold Rothstein

"Look out for number one"

THE CRIME: Known as "Mr Big", Rothstein was born in New York City and soon rebelled against his Jewish background. He used his mathematical brain to win at gambling, running his own dice games. Described as the spiritual godfather of organized crime, most of the big names – Luciano, Lansky, Costello, Torrio – genuflected before Rothstein. By 1907 he was established as a bookmaker, turning a $10,000-a-week profit. He bestrode much of New York, having friends and acquaintances from both the law-abiding community and the underworld but always put himself first. "Look out for number one" was Rothstein's motto.

Arnold Rothstein

He was thought to be behind the Black Sox scandal of 1919 (see page 82) but whether he directly participated remains unclear. After that scandal Rothstein announced his retirement from gambling but kept his bookmakers for wealthy betters. He also used his financial clout to bankroll bootleggers, including Jack "Legs" Diamond, Waxey Gordon, Bill Dwyer and Frank Costello. He also began dealing in drugs and indulging in stock market fraud. He fenced stolen securities and sold worthless stocks. He worked from his office in midtown Manhattan in the afternoon before retiring to various haunts in the evening where he entertained friends. Rothstein did not drink, was rarely profane and had little of the flamboyance often associated with underworld characters.

Realizing that Prohibition would end some day, he made plans to diversify his empire. By 1928 he was running low on funds. From 8–10 September he lost $320,000 in a marathon poker game at the Park Central Hotel and then insisted that the game was fixed and refused to pay his debt. On 4 November 1928 he was shot in a room in the Park Central Hotel. The chief suspects were the men he owed money to from the poker game: "Nigger Nate" Raymond, Alvin "Titanic" Thompson and George "Hump" McManus.

WHERE:
Room 349, Park Central Hotel, 870 Seventh Avenue at West 56th Street, New York City, USA
WHEN:
Sunday 4 November 1928
THE AFTERMATH:
Rothstein was taken to the Stuyvesant Polyclinic Hospital where he died on 6 November without naming his killer. "Nigger Nate" Raymond and George "Hump" McManus were arrested for the murder. Raymond was released but McManus was indicted on 4 December 1928. He was acquitted when his lawyer pointed out a complete lack of evidence. Another suspect in the murder was Dutch Schultz (see page 331) who, it was said, saw an opportunity to increase his own empire with Rothstein out of the picture. Rothstein's empire was carved up among his subordinates.

The bloody aftermath of the St Valentine's Day Massacre

St Valentine's Day Massacre

"I'm not gonna talk – nobody shot me"

THE CRIME: The turf war in Chicago – known as the Chicago Beer Wars – between rival gangsters began with the murder of Charles Dean "Dion" O'Banion in November 1924. On 24 January 1925 an attempt was made on the life of Johnny Torrio (see page 324) and he retired to New York, allowing Al Capone to take over the South Side gang. The North Side gang was headed by Bugs Moran (see page 325). A meeting at the SMC Cartage Company between the two gangs was arranged by Moran (not Capone, as many versions of the story have it) for St Valentine's Day 1929. It is usually assumed that the North Side gang were there to collect a shipment of Old Log Cabin whiskey in a bootlegging deal but this has since been discovered to be untrue and was simply a guess made by a federal officer, who was later sacked.

Four men from the South Side gang – Fred Burke, John Scalise, Albert Anselmi and Joseph Lolordo – arrived in what looked like police cars and ordered the five members of the North Side gang present – Adam Meyer, Al Weinshank, James Clark (Moran's brother-in-law) and Frank and Pete Gusenberg – to line up against a wall inside. The men, thinking that these were policemen and they were going to be arrested, complied and stood quietly as the South Side gang members took out machine guns and murdered them all. The South Side gang then escaped by the simple ruse of two of the men, who were in police uniform, "arresting" the two men in plain clothes and escorting them to the waiting cars.

Bugs Moran escaped as he arrived late and, on seeing the "police cars", fled the scene. One of the Moran gang, Frank Gusenberg, survived. When the police asked who shot him, he replied, "I'm not gonna talk – nobody shot me."

WHERE:
SMC Cartage Company, 2122 North Clark Street, Chicago, Illinois, USA
WHEN:
10.30am Thursday 14 February 1929
THE AFTERMATH:
The massacre consolidated Al Capone's power base, although he was at the time far away at his Florida home. Bugs Moran lost the Chicago Beer Wars and his close ally, Joe Aiello, was murdered by Capone's gang on 23 October 1930 at 205 Kolmar Avenue, Chicago. Questioned by reporters Moran broke the code of silence, "Only Capone kills like that" while Capone commented, "The only man who kills like that is Bugs Moran." The SMC Cartage Company warehouse was demolished in 1977 and the site is now a car park for a nursing home.

Lucky Luciano

"I never abused anybody in my life"

THE CRIME: The founder of the Mafia in the United States was born Salvatore Lucania in Lercara Friddi, Sicily on 11 November 1897. The family arrived in America in 1906 and ten years later, in June 1916, Luciano was sentenced to a year in prison for opium trafficking. On his release he joined Giuseppe "Joe the Boss" Masseria's gang. A fight between Masseria's mob and a rival gang, led by Salvatore Maranzano, resulted in Luciano being stabbed with an ice pick, having his throat cut and being left for dead on Staten Island beach. Miraculously, Luciano survived and was given the nickname "Lucky".

On 15 April 1931 Luciano accompanied Masseria to lunch at Coney Island. He excused himself to visit the bathroom and while he was away Masseria was shot to death by a four-man team – Joe Adonis, Bugsy Siegel (see page 333), Albert Anastasia (see page 336) and Vito Genovese. Luciano rewarded Anastasia's loyalty by making him the head of Murder Inc's enforcement department. Luciano then learned that the Boss of Bosses Salvatore Maranzano wanted him, Al Capone and Genovese dead. Luciano struck first and on 10 September 1931 Maranzano was shot and stabbed to death in his Manhattan office. Luciano divided the city into separate areas, each controlled by a different family but all answerable to him. In 1936 Luciano was sentenced to 30–50 years in prison for extortion and direction of harlotry. During the Second World War, while incarcerated, Luciano helped the authorities although this was denied for political expediency. He was paroled after the war ended but as part of his parole Luciano, who never became a US citizen, was deported to Italy on 10 February 1946 aboard the Liberty Ship *Laura Keane*. In February 1947 he flew to Havana where he met many old cronies, including Meyer Lansky, Frank Costello (see page 337) and Bugsy Siegel. Luciano and Siegel fell out over the latter's involvement in Las Vegas and Luciano ordered his murder four months later. Luciano's presence in Havana became known and Cuban dictator Fulgencio Batista deported him to Italy where he was forbidden to leave Naples.

WHERE:
Eagle Building, 230 Park Avenue, New York City, USA
WHEN:
Thursday 10 September 1931
THE AFTERMATH:
Luciano spent his enforced retirement reading newspapers and going on long walks. He began giving interviews to journalists and contemplated writing his autobiography. He once said, "Anything I ever did in my life, I felt justified doing. I never abused anybody in my life. If people abuse me and I abuse them back – that ain't abuse." On 26 January 1962 he travelled to Capodichino Airport in Naples to meet a Hollywood producer with a view to a film being made of his life. As he went to greet the producer he suffered a heart attack and died instantly.

Lucky Luciano

Al Capone

"A. Capone, Antique Dealer"

THE AFTERMATH:
In prison Capone furnished his cell with a typewriter, rugs and a complete set of the *Encyclopedia Britannica*. His organization meanwhile flourished under the leadership of Frank Nitti. On 22 August 1934 he was transferred to Alcatraz but spent much of his sentence in hospital where he was suffering from syphilitic dementia. Capone was released on 16 November 1939 but his worst days were behind him because of the syphilis (caught by sleeping with the prostitutes he owned). Capone died of a heart attack on 25 January 1947, four days after suffering an apoplectic stroke. It was thought he had ordered the deaths of 500 men and 1,000 more died in the turf wars.

THE CRIME: Born in Brooklyn, Alphonse Capone began his career with two gangs, the Brooklyn Rippers and the Forty Thieves Juniors, before becoming a waiter-bouncer at Frankie Yale's Harvard Inn on Coney Island. It was while working here in the summer of 1917 that he received the injury that would lead to him being called "Scarface" (although never to his face). Frank Galluccio slashed Capone's face, avenging over familiarity with his sister.

Capone joined Johnny Torrio's gang and took over in January 1925 when Torrio retired. Capone called his organization The Outfit and they dominated bootlegging, prostitution, gambling and protection rackets in Chicago. By the end of the 20s Capone's annual income was said to be $100 million and he didn't pay a penny in income tax. He was listed in the Chicago telephone directory as "A. Capone, Antique Dealer 2200 South Wabash Avenue". On 20 September 1926 Dion O'Banion's mob tried to kill Capone by shooting up his Hawthorne Hotel headquarters. Capone paid for repairs to buildings and cars that were damaged nearby. Three years later he arranged to have his rival wiped out in the St Valentine's Day Massacre (see page 328). In May 1929 he was sentenced to a year in prison for gun possession. In 1931 he was charged with tax evasion for not declaring $215,000 back taxes on profits from gambling. Believing he could plea bargain his way out, Capone pleaded guilty but Judge James H. Wilkerson refused to make a deal. Capone changed his plea to not guilty and tried to bribe the jury. Judge Wilkerson changed the jury at the last moment and Capone was found guilty on five of the 23 charges, sending him to federal prison for ten years and the county jail for one. He was also fined $50,000 plus $30,000 in costs.

*A Miami Police Department
mugshot of Al Capone*

Dutch Schultz

"Mother is the best bet and don't let Satan draw you too fast"

THE CRIME: Dutch Schultz was born on 6 August 1902 (his grave states he was born in 1901) at 1690 Second Avenue, off 89th Street, in the Bronx, as Arthur Flegenheimer. He began his crime career in 1919, aged 17, when he was convicted of burglary and spent 15 months in borstal. It was to be the only sentence he served. In 1928 he became a partner in a Bronx bar during Prohibition and later became a bootlegger, supplying booze to upper Manhattan and the Bronx. At one time he was a partner with Jack "Legs" Diamond, Edward "Fats" McCarthy, and Vincent and Peter Coll.

It was said he made between $12 million and $15 million annually on protection rackets and union racketeering. He did not spend his money on flashy clothes. Lucky Luciano said of him, "One of the cheapest guys I ever knew… a guy with a couple of million bucks and he dressed like a pig." It was also said that he once kidnapped a rival called Joe Rock and hung him by his thumbs on a meat hook. Then he covered Rock's eyes with gauze that had been dipped in the discharge from a gonorrhoea infection. When the family paid the $35,000 ransom and Rock was returned to them, he was blind. Schultz trusted no one and had very few, if any, friends. In June 1931 he was arrested after shooting two undercover New York policemen, thinking they were his enemies the Coll brothers. On 19 December 1931 he ordered the killing of Jack "Legs" Diamond, "another punk with his hands in my pockets". In 1932 he had Vincent "Mad Dog" Coll murdered as he made a telephone call. On 25 January 1933 Schultz was indicted for evading $92,103.34 income tax. He went into hiding, finally surrendering on 28 November 1934. Two trials failed to convict him. He was fatally shot by Charles "The Bug" Workman in the back room of the Palace Chop House, a saloon in Newark, New Jersey on 23 October and died in hospital at 8.35pm the next day. He was 33. His last words were "Mother is the best bet and don't let Satan draw you too fast."

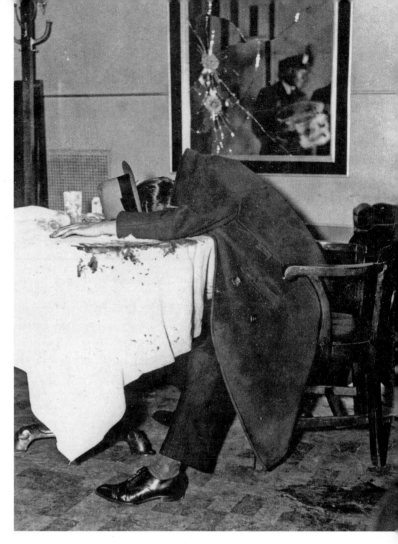

The bullet-ridden body of Dutch Schultz at the Palace Chop House.

WHERE:
Syracuse, New York, USA
WHEN:
Wednesday 25 January 1933
THE AFTERMATH:
Charles Workman was paroled, aged 54, on 10 March 1964, after spending 22 years and nine months in jail.

Machine Gun Kelly is escorted from the Memphis jail.

Machine Gun Kelly

"My people are good people even if I turned out to be an awful heel"

THE CRIME: George "Machine Gun" Kelly (née George Barnes, Jr) was a very bad man – his press agent said so and FBI chief J. Edgar Hoover helped by naming him Public Enemy Number One. Kelly's press agent was his second wife, Kathryn Shannon (whom he married in September 1930), and a reporter probably got closest to the truth when he wrote that Kelly was "a good-natured slob, a bootlegger who spilled more than he delivered".

Despite his name Kelly never even fired a shot at anyone, let alone killed anyone. When he met Kathryn he was a failed bootlegger and she was the one with the criminal connections. She bought him a machine gun for $250 as a present and made him practise shooting walnuts off fence posts. She would visit down market saloons and hand out spent cartridges saying, "Here, have a souvenir of my husband Machine Gun Kelly. He can't be here. He is away robbing banks." He did, in fact, rob a few financial institutions but his big moment came when, at his wife's insistence, with Albert Bates, he kidnapped millionaire oil tycoon Charley F. Urschel who was playing cards with a neighbouring couple. Kelly had not done much research and had no idea which of the men was Urschel so he took them both. In the getaway car he examined the wallets of both men and finally discovered which one was his intended target. He collected a ransom of $200,000 and then Kathryn insisted that they kill Urschel so that he couldn't later identify them but Kelly refused, saying it would be "bad for business". Unfortunately, Urschel was able to give the FBI so many clues that they were able to capture Kelly and Bates. Supposedly, when he was arrested on 26 September 1933 Kelly crouched in a corner with his hands above his head crying, "Don't shoot G-men... don't shoot." The story that this is where the nickname "G-men" for FBI agents came from is merely a legend, as Kelly was actually captured by three normal Memphis policemen. He once said of his family, "My people are good people even if I turned out to be an awful heel."

WHERE:
Oklahoma City, USA
WHEN:
11.15pm Saturday 22 July 1933
THE AFTERMATH:
Kelly, his wife and Bates were sentenced to life imprisonment on 12 October 1933. Kelly and Bates were sent to Alcatraz (where Bates died on 4 July 1948) before Kelly was moved to Fort Leavenworth. He died there of a heart attack on 18 July 1954, his 59th birthday. Kathryn Kelly was released in June 1958 and died in Oklahoma in 1984.

Bugsy Siegel

"We only kill each other"

THE CRIME: Benjamin – no one called him "Bugsy" to his face if they had sense – Siegel was born on 28 February 1906 in the Williamsburg district of Brooklyn, New York. He started his first protection racket before he was a teenager, charging local stallholders $5. He met and befriended Meyer Lansky and the pair formed a gang of car thieves and ran illegal gambling dens. Siegel began a semi-legitimate career as a taxi driver but used his position to work out rich pickings for burglary or robbery. In 1930, Lansky and Siegel joined forces with Lucky Luciano (see page 329) and Frank Costello (see page 337) and began bootlegging in New York, New Jersey and Philadelphia. On 22 November 1939, Thanksgiving, Siegel, his brother-in-law Whitey Krakower, Frank Carbo and Harry Segal killed gangster Harry "Big Greenie" Greenberg who, short of money, had written a letter asking for cash which was couched in such terms that it appeared a threat to go to the police if he did not receive $5,000. Greenberg was shot as he sat in the front seat of his new yellow Ford convertible reading a newspaper.

When four gangsters turned evidence, Siegel was arrested. To protect himself, Siegel murdered his brother-in-law as he sat on his stoop on Delancey Street enjoying the summer sunshine on 31 July 1940. On 16 August Siegel Carbo and Segal were indicted for Greenberg's murder. The case collapsed on 5 February 1942 when no witnesses could be found to the killing. In 1941 Siegel fell for the Alabama-born, good-time girl Virginia "Sugar" Hill. In 1945 he began work on the Pink Flamingo Hotel & Casino in Las Vegas. Many of the contractors ripped off Siegel, who had no previous experience in the construction business. Some would supply materials, steal them at night and then resell them to Siegel the next day. Costs mounted and Siegel became angry. An honest building tycoon, Del Webb, became worried when Siegel discovered more materials had gone missing. Siegel reassured him, "Don't worry, we only kill each other."

WHERE:
Delancey Street, New York City, USA
WHEN:
Wednesday 31 July 1940
THE AFTERMATH:
At a cost of $6 million the 105-room Pink Flamingo Hotel & Casino finally opened on Boxing Day 1946. The night was a disaster and the Flamingo promptly suffered huge losses. It was discovered that Siegel had himself been less than honest with the building costs of the Flamingo. On 20 June 1947, after a night out, he returned to Virginia Hill's home, 810 North Linden Drive in Beverly Hills, and sat in the living room, reading the previous day's *Los Angeles Times*. At 10.45pm a mob hit man (reportedly Eddie Cannizzaro) opened up with an M1 Carbine. Seven rounds were fired and one of the .30-calibre bullets hit the bridge of Siegel's nose, blowing his left eyeball out of its socket and 4 m (14 ft) across the room, where it was found intact. No one was ever charged with the murder.

The body of Bugsy Siegel

Mickey Cohen

"I have killed no man that didn't deserve killing"

WHERE:
Chicago, Illinois, USA
WHEN:
Tuesday 15 May 1945
THE AFTERMATH:
Cohen was released in 1972. He died of a heart attack in his sleep on 29 July 1976.

THE CRIME: Mickey Cohen – short, foul-mouthed, even fouler tempered – began his career as a boxer. On 15 May 1945 he murdered Chicago bookmaker, Max Shaman, before graduating to become the bodyguard of Bugsy Siegel (see page 333) and supposedly inherited Siegel's empire when he was murdered in June 1947. Following Siegel's death, Cohen walked brazenly into the lobby of the Roosevelt Hotel at 7000 Hollywood Boulevard in Hollywood and emptied the contents of two .45s into the ceiling, shouting for the killers to make themselves known. When only the police arrived, Cohen fled. Cohen had many of the neuroses typically associated with short men – he was 1.65 m (5 ft 5 in) – and he began to shoot his mouth off, bringing the activities of his friends and erstwhile colleagues to the awareness of the authorities.

Cohen presented himself to the press as a villain misunderstood by an underworld, led by Jack Dragna, that made several attempts on his life, including twice bombing his home on Moreno Avenue in Brentwood. On 6 February 1950 he was most upset that 40 of his $300 suits were shredded by one of the explosions which left him, his wife, their maid and dog unharmed. He hired Johnny Stompanato (see page 492) to be his bodyguard until he was killed in 1958. Ever the gentleman, Cohen sold Lana Turner's love letters to Stompanato to the press and had Stompanato buried in a cheap coffin. In Tinseltown Cohen ran a jeweller's and sidelined in gambling and sexual blackmail. In 1950 he appeared before the Kefauver Committee and when asked, "Is it not a fact that you live extravagantly… surrounded by violence?" Cohen replied, "Whaddya mean 'surrounded by violence'? People are shooting at me." As a result of his appearance on 20 June 1951 he was convicted of tax evasion and sent to prison for four years. On his release he became a minor celebrity and had fingers in many pies. He appeared on television and told interviewer Mike Wallace "I have killed no man that didn't deserve killing by the standards of our way of life." In 1961 Cohen was sent to Alcatraz for tax evasion where, in 1963, a fellow con tried to kill him by staving his head in with a lead pipe.

Cohen outside his exclusive Sunset Strip men's shop after he had to sell it to meet his bail.

Messina Brothers

"We Messinas are more powerful than the British Government"

THE CRIME: The five Messina brothers – Salvatore (born 20 August 1898), Alfredo (born 6 February 1901), Eugenio (born 1908), Carmelo (born 1915) and Attilio (born 1910) – came from a criminal background. Their Sicilian father, Giuseppe De Bono, was a white slaver in the early part of the last century. In 1934 Eugene Messina visited London to find out if it would be a suitable location for their nefarious activities. It was, and the family relocated to London, taking the name Messina. After the Second World War the five brothers carried on the family business, importing women from Belgium, France and Spain. To allow the women to work legally they were married to tramps that were paid and given a new suit to wear at the register office ceremony. By the late 1940s the Messinas ran 30 brothels in and around Bond Street. The women handed over 80 per cent of their earnings to the brothers. Attilio Messina said, "We Messinas are more powerful than the British Government. We do as we like in England." The brothers also paid off the police. Ostensibly, the family business was dealing in antiques, and exporting and importing diamonds. By the 1950s the police estimated that at least 200 of London's most expensive prostitutes were Messina girls.

It was a journalist who finally brought down the Messinas. Duncan Webb was the crime correspondent of *The People*. He began interviewing prostitutes, building up a dossier on the dealings of the Messinas. On 3 September 1950 *The People* published its exposé under the headline "Arrest These Four Men". The story featured interviews with more than 100 prostitutes along with names, photographs and dates – more than enough for the police to act.

Eugene Messina is led to court after his arrest in Belgium in 1955.

WHERE:
London, England
WHEN:
1945
THE AFTERMATH:
Eugene, Carmelo, Salvatore and Attilio left England. On 19 March 1951 Alfredo Messina was arrested and charged with living off the immoral earnings of his girlfriend, Hermione Hinden, and for attempting to bribe the policeman – Superintendent Guy Mahon – who arrested him. He was sent down for two years. On 31 August 1955 Eugene and Carmelo were arrested in Belgium as they were closing a deal with two Belgian girls and charged with procuring women for immoral purposes. Eugene received a seven-year sentence and Carmelo was acquitted of white slavery. He was banned from re-entering England but he did and was arrested on 3 October 1958. He was deported to Sicily in March 1959 after serving his sentence and he died there in the autumn of 1959. Attilio Messina was sentenced to four years in jail for procuring on 9 April 1959. Salvatore Messina was never caught.

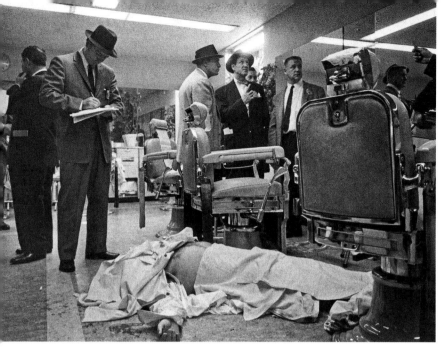

Albert Anastasia lies on the floor of the barber shop in the Park Central Hotel.

Albert Anastasia

"I can't stand squealers! Hit that guy!"

THE CRIME: The Lord High Executioner of Murder Inc, Albert Anastasia was born as Umberto Anastasio in Tropea, Italy on 26 September 1902. Arriving in New York in 1919, Anastasia, who was nicknamed The Mad Hatter, committed his first murder soon after. Anastasia and a friend, Joe Fiorino, robbed a jeweller in Brooklyn of $95. George Tirello, another docker, was asked if he could find out who had robbed the jeweller's. On 26 May 1920, he confronted them but they opened fire. Anastasia missed but Fiorino pumped three bullets into Tirello. On 26 May 1921 both men were sentenced to death in the electric chair. A crooked judge declared a mistrial and Anastasia walked free when four important witnesses were shot dead and a fifth confined to a mental asylum. Anastasia joined the gang lead by Giuseppe "Joe the Boss" Masseria and when he was murdered on 15 April 1931, Lucky Luciano rewarded Anastasia's loyalty by making him the head of Murder Inc's enforcement department.

Anastasia was never charged with murder – whenever a charge seemed likely, witnesses always disappeared or came down with a sudden case of amnesia. As a crime boss, Anastasia's brutality knew no bounds. In 1952 he ordered a 24-year-old Brooklyn tailor's assistant named Arnold Schuster to be killed. Unfortunately for Schuster, Anastasia had seen him on television talking about his role as a lead witness in fugitive bank robber Willie Sutton's arrest. Anastasia is said to have shouted at his aides, "I can't stand squealers! Hit that guy!" Schuster's murder on 8 March horrified other Mafia bosses because it brought more scrutiny on the organization and also broke a cardinal rule against killing outsiders. Arnold Schuster was found on the street where he lived, having been shot four times – once in each eye and twice in the groin. His killer was Frederick J. Tenuto, a career criminal on the FBI's "Most Wanted" list. Fearful that he would lead the authorities to him, Anastasia ordered Tenuto's own murder shortly afterwards. When Anastasia demanded a large slice of Meyer Lansky's Cuban gambling operation, he agreed to support Vito Genovese's plan to kill Anastasia.

WHERE:
45th Street, Brooklyn, New York City, USA
WHEN:
9.10pm Saturday 8 March 1952
THE AFTERMATH:
At 10.10am on 25 October 1957 Anastasia was murdered as he sat in the barber's at the Park Central Hotel at 870 Seventh Avenue at West 56th Street. One shot went into the back of Anastasia's head and lodged in the left side of his brain. Two more shots hit his left hand. Another bullet went into his back at a downward angle and penetrated a lung, a kidney and his spleen. The Anastasia murder remains officially unsolved. It is believed the killers were a three-man hit team selected by Joseph "Joe the Blonde" Biondo, who is thought to have chosen Stephen Armone, Arnold "Witty" Wittenberg and Stephen "Stevie Coogin" Grammauta, a convicted drug dealer and heroin smuggler.

Frank Costello

"The Prime Minister of the Underworld"

THE CRIME: Born as Francesco Castiglia in Lauropoli, near Cosenza in Calabria, southern Italy on 26 January 1891, Costello arrived in New York in 1895. On 25 April 1908 he was arrested on charges of assault and robbery. On 16 October 1912 he was again in court on the same indictment. Both times he walked free. He became a hired gun for Owney Madden's gang, The Gophers. On 12 March 1915 he was arrested for possession of a concealed weapon and sentenced to a year inside, of which he served ten months. With his partner Big Bill Dwyer, Costello ran the largest rum running operation in New York in the 1920s but was clever enough to create legitimate businesses, which he used to influence politicians. Costello became the de facto leader of the Tammany Hall political machine in 1928, following the murder of Arnold Rothstein (see page 327). Nine years later, he succeeded Lucky Luciano (see page 329) as the boss of New York's biggest Mafia family.

In 1929 he attended the crime bosses' meeting in Atlantic City and, when bootlegging ceased to be profitable, he moved into gambling with Meyer Lansky and their casinos in Havana, Cuba. Costello was seen as a master criminal who ruled a vast empire and was nicknamed the Prime Minister of the Underworld. Nevertheless, the media could find little evidence to confirm such popular suspicion. On 15 August 1952 he was sent to prison for contempt for refusing to answer a question before the Kefauver Committee investigating crime in interstate commerce. In April 1954 Costello was convicted of income tax evasion and in May 1956 began serving an 11-month prison sentence. On 2 May 1957 Costello survived a gang assassination attempt by Vincent "The Chin" Gigante, inspired by Vito Genovese. As Costello entered his home at 115 Central Park West Gigante shouted, "This is for you, Frank," before letting off a hail of bullets, one of which grazed Costello's head.

WHERE:
Washington DC, USA
WHEN:
Friday 15 August 1952
THE AFTERMATH:
Costello retired following the attempt on his life and Genovese took over control of the family. Costello died of a heart attack in New York on 18 February 1973. Gigante later became head of the Genovese crime family but in 1969 he began feigning insanity to avoid going to prison on racketeering charges. On 7 April 2003 in Federal District Court he pleaded guilty to obstruction of justice, revealing that his "insanity" was a fantasy to delay his racketeering trial. He died on 19 December 2005.

Frank Costello at his Kefauver Committee hearing.

Jack Spot & Billy Hill

"I should have shot Billy Hill"

WHERE:
Frith Street, London, England
WHEN:
Thursday 11 August 1955
THE AFTERMATH:
Jack Spot died on 12 March 1995, a forgotten man. He once said, "I made Billy Hill. Then he got over the top on me. I should have shot Billy Hill." Billy Hill died on 1 January 1984. Albert Dimes died aged 57 in November 1971 of cancer.

Jack "Spot" Corner shows off his scar, inflicted by Frankie Fraser and Robert Warren.

THE CRIME: Jack "Spot" Comer and Billy Hill – self-styled Boss of Britain's Underworld – came to prominence after the Second World War. Billy Hill was born on 8 December 1911. In 1926 he received two years' probation for breaking into a tobacconist. The following year he was sent to borstal for three years after burgling a house. Escaping on 18 September 1929, he broke into another house and attacked a maid. He was given nine months' hard labour and 12 strokes of the birch. By July 1947, when he replaced the fading Bill Black Mob, he was 36 and had spent 17 years behind bars. He told his gang not to carry guns and to use as little violence as possible. On 21 May 1952 his gang committed the Great Mail Bag Robbery. They stole £287,000. One thousand police were assigned to catch the crooks. On 21 September 1954 he was behind the theft of £45,000 in gold bullion. On 16 June 1955 he threw a party at Gennaro's Restaurant, Dean Street in Soho to mark the publication of his autobiography. The previous year Hill had been overseas and an interloper had tried to muscle in on his turf.

Jack Spot was born on 12 April 1912, the son of Polish immigrants. By the age of 16, he was calling himself King of Aldgate and went to work for a bookmaker. In 1936 he took part in the anti-fascist Battle of Cable Street. In 1937 he was sent to Wormwood Scrubs for GBH (grievous bodily harm). When Hill returned he decided to regain his throne. On 11 August 1955 there was a vicious knife fight in Frith Street, Soho, between Spot and Hill's friend Italian Albert Dimes. Spot chased Dimes into the Continental Fruit Store, slashing him with a knife. In the struggle the knife changed hands and Spot was cut. With both men bleeding heavily, Dimes escaped in a taxi but Spot collapsed in a barber's. Both men ended up in hospital and both were arrested. They were tried at the Old Bailey on 19 September 1955. It was a stalemate and the judge ordered the jury to find both men not guilty. At a second trial both men were acquitted; Spot mainly on the evidence of Reverend Basil Andrews, 88. It was later revealed that the clergyman had been a guest at the home of Jack and his wife Rita. On 6 October 1955 before they could be arrested for perverting the course of justice, they fled to Ireland. On 21 October Rita was arrested in Dublin and extradited to England where she was tried on 2 November. Found guilty, she was fined £50. On 2 May 1956 the couple was attacked as they walked home. Rita identified Billy Hill as the ringleader of the attackers. Two of the men – Mad Frankie Fraser and Robert Warren – were arrested and tried on 15 June 1956. Both were found guilty and they were sentenced to seven years. On 16 October 1956 three more of the men were jailed. Spot and Hill began to fade from the scene but their legacy lived on in two young men who at one time had worked for them both – Reginald and Ronald Kray (see page 342).

Sam Giancana

"I wasn't crazy. I was telling the truth"

THE CRIME: Sam Giancana was a vicious thug but a brave one nonetheless. He was a bagman for Al Capone (see page 330) and if any job was deemed dangerous, it was handed to "Momo" Giancana. He was a prime suspect in three murders before he turned 20. He avoided service in the Second World War after telling the draft board "I steal". It labelled him "a constitutional psychopath". Later he said, "They thought I was crazy. I wasn't crazy. I was telling the truth."

In the 1930s he was jailed for running a moonshine still. Inside he met a *capo* who told him that money was to be made in gambling. On his release, Giancana was instrumental in ensuring that the South Side gang ran all the gambling in Chicago. In the mid 1950s he became manager of operations and from 1957 until 1966 he was head of the Chicago mob. He was ruthless. In his nine years in control there were 79 mob murders. From 1966 until 1974 there were only 24. One of Giancana's girlfriends was Judith Campbell Exner who was also sharing a bed with President John F. Kennedy (see page 307). It was claimed that Giancana was involved in an attempt to assassinate Cuban dictator Fidel Castro. The attempt brought Giancana to public attention and on 1 June 1965 he was jailed for refusing to co-operate with a federal grand jury. On his release he went into self-imposed exile in Mexico.

Sam Giancana appears before the Senate Rackets Committee in 1959.

WHERE:
Chicago, Illinois, USA
WHEN:
1957–1966
THE AFTERMATH:
The FBI continued to investigate Sam Giancana when he retired and in July 1974 he was deported from Mexico and taken to Chicago, where he appeared before a grand jury investigating Syndicate gambling and the 1973 murder of Richard Cain, a policeman who turned to the dark side and became Giancana's bodyguard. After being unable to avoid the court, Giancana testified, much to the annoyance of his colleagues. On 19 June 1975, four days after his 67th birthday, as he cooked a plate of sausages and escarole at his home in Oak Park, Giancana was shot seven times at close range. He once said, "What's wrong with the Syndicate? Two or three of us get together on some deal and everybody says it's a bad thing, but those businessmen do it all the time and nobody squawks."

The trunks opened by French police at the Gard du Nord.

French Connection

Sonny "Cloudy" Grosso made the arrest of Tony Fuca while wearing a dinner jacket

THE CRIME: "The French Connection" refers to heroin that was smuggled from Turkey to France and then to the USA. In October 1961 New York Police detectives Eddie "Popeye" Egan and his partner Sonny "Cloudy" Grosso spotted a known villain, Patsy Fuca, a foot soldier in the Lucchese crime family, splashing a lot of cash at the Copacabana Club. This seemingly insignificant sighting led to hundreds of man-hours over four months spent by New York cops tailing American and French gangsters all over the city. The surveillance paid off and in February 1962 the police swooped, arresting most of the smugglers and recovered 50 kg (112 lb) of heroin. At the time it was the largest haul of heroin ever captured in America.

Fuca's uncle was *capo* Angelo Tumarino and he was the real target of the surveillance operation. Tumarino entrusted his nephew with arranging the drug shipments from Turkey via France. The police discovered the first 22 kg (50 lb) of the drug in Patsy Fuca's loft while the rest was found in the basement of a block of flats. One of the flats was occupied by Tony Fuca, Patsy's brother. The police discovered the whereabouts of the second stash after spending three weeks hiding in the basement to keep an eye on Tony Fuca. Sonny "Cloudy" Grosso made the arrest of Tony Fuca while wearing a dinner jacket – he had been to a friend's wedding.

WHERE:
New York City, USA
WHEN:
February 1962
THE AFTERMATH:
Patsy Fuca was arrested and sentenced to eight years in prison. The 1971 film starring Gene Hackman bore little resemblance to the actual events. The real crime had no shoot-outs, no deaths and no car chases. Eddie "Popeye" Egan and Sonny "Cloudy" Grosso had bit parts in the film. In 1972 all the heroin was stolen from a police locker and never recovered.

Richardson Brothers

"I started clubs where drinking was 24 hours. They were a bit illegal"

THE CRIME: The Richardson brothers – Charlie (born 18 January 1934) and Eddie (born 1936) – ran criminal activities in south London. They began the Peckford Scrap Metal Company in 1956 in Addington Square, but that was really a front for their crimes. The following year the Richardsons had five scrap yards in south London and savings of £20,000. "I started clubs where drinking was 24 hours. They were a bit illegal, given the licensing laws, but the police were on the payroll," Charlie revealed. He also knew how to create goodwill among the locals. "People would tell me of burglaries to their houses… we would know within hours who had done the job, give them a smack and tell them to fuck off to the West End to steal from rich people." The Richardsons created a number of "long firms" – buying goods and paying all bills on time to establish a line of good credit and then making a large order and disappearing without paying. They kept their employees in line with extreme violence, administered by the likes of Mad Frankie Fraser.

In 1959 Charlie was charged with receiving stolen sides of bacon and sent down for six months. In May 1960 he fled to Canada, after being charged with receiving stolen metals. He returned to England and, with witness intimidation, avoided prison. Eddie, in partnership with Fraser, ran a successful slot machine business off Tottenham Court Road and tried to distance himself from Charlie.

In 1966 the Richardson gang was arrested after a fight at Mr Smith's Nightclub in Catford at which a man was shot and killed. Eddie was shot in the buttocks and thigh, Fraser in the thigh. They were charged with murder and affray. Fraser was found not guilty but in a retrial Eddie was sentenced to five years' imprisonment.

Charlie, meanwhile, had sent Johnny Bradbury to South Africa to kill Thomas Waldeck, a business associate. On 29 June 1965 Waldeck was shot dead. Bradbury was arrested and sentenced to hang. He agreed to inform on Charlie in return for clemency. Charlie was arrested on 30 July 1966.

The trial – known as the Torture Trial – began on 4 April 1967. A number of victims of Richardson torture testified to their agonies. Jack Duval had been beaten with a golf clubs, Alfred Blore had to stand against a wall while kitchen knives were thrown at him; Benjamin Coulston had his teeth pulled with pliers (a particular favourite of Mad Frankie), and Lucien Harris had electrodes applied to his genitals. The Richardsons claimed that all the men were lying and there was even some attempt at jury nobbling. The jury eventually found both men guilty at 8.13pm on 7 June. Eddie was sentenced to ten years inside and his brother to 25 years.

WHERE:
Mr Smith's Nightclub, Catford, London, England
WHEN:
2am Tuesday 8 March 1966
THE AFTERMATH:
In May 1980 Charlie escaped from an open prison and stayed at large for some time. He was released in July 1984. Eddie was released in 1976. In October 1990 he was sentenced to 25 years in jail for drug smuggling. He was released after serving less than half the sentence.

The scrapyard in Camberwell, London, where victims and witnesses were tortured.

Kray Twins

"Society has earned a rest from your activities"

WHERE:
London, England
WHEN:
8.30pm Wednesday 9 March 1966;
Saturday 28 October 1967
THE AFTERMATH:
At 6am on 7 May 1968 Nipper Read
and his team arrested members of
the Krays' Firm. Both twins were in
bed with blonds – Reggie with a
woman and Ronnie a man. The trial
of the twins, brother Charlie and
seven of their men began at the Old
Bailey on 8 January 1969. On 5 March
1969 the Krays were found guilty on
all charges and sentenced to life
imprisonment with a
recommendation from the judge, Mr
Justice Melford Stevenson, that they
serve at least 30 years: "In my view
society has earned a rest from your
activities". Both twins, despite being
gay, married while incarcerated.
Ronnie died on 17 March 1995.
Reggie died on 1 October 2000.

*Reginald (left) and
Ronald Kray*

THE CRIME: Born on 24 October 1933, twins Reginald and Ronald
Kray were short, not especially bright, vicious thugs who terrorized
much of the East End of London in the 1950s and 1960s. They took a
percentage of other villains' jobs to finance their own lifestyle. On
16 July 1964 the *Daily Mirror* ran a story about "the picture we dare
not print". The picture showed Tory peer Robert Boothby on a settee
next to his lover Ronnie. Boothby sued for libel and won £40,000. It
was after this that a squad was formed by Detective Inspector
Leonard "Nipper" Read to bring down the Krays. On 9 March 1966
Ronnie shot George Cornell, a member of the south London
Richardson gang (see page 341) in the Blind Beggar pub. Kray and
his associate, Ian Barrie, walked into the pub and Kray fired three
shots but only one hit Cornell. Supposedly Ronnie had been enraged
when Cornell called him "a fat poof" but in 1989 he said that it was
because Cornell had threatened to kill him. Meanwhile, the twins had
arranged for Mad Axeman Frankie Mitchell to escape from prison on
12 December 1966. Holed up in a safe house, he became restless and
on 23 December 1966 Kray associate, Alfie Gerrard, shot him. In
October 1967 Reggie killed Jack "The Hat" McVitie. After a gun failed
to go off, he stabbed McVitie to death while Ronnie Hart and Tony
Lambrianou held McVitie. Reggie also killed Mad Teddy Smith, a gay
member of their gang who had helped with the Mitchell escape, when
he became an embarrassment. Ronnie murdered an unfaithful
prostitute boyfriend, and there were at least four other victims.

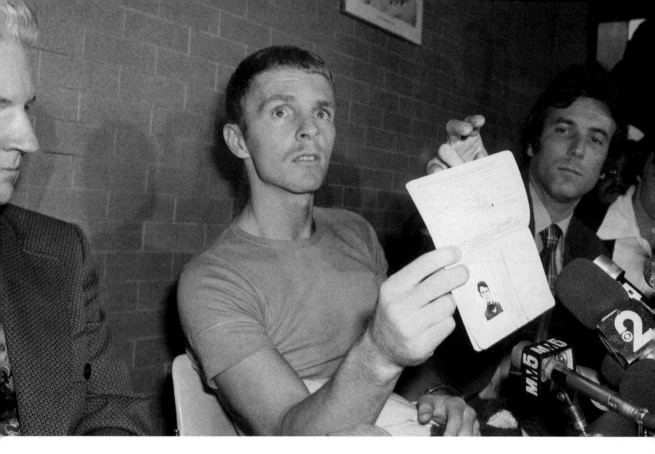

Billy Hayes

"I've always loved Turkey"

THE CRIME: Billy Hayes was born on 3 April 1947 in New York and, like many of his generation, he avoided the draft and took illegal drugs. He confessed to have illegally carried drugs between countries in Europe. As a 23-year-old, Roman Catholic student, he visited Istanbul where he smoked hashish regularly. On an autumnal day in 1970 he foolishly tried to smuggle 1.8 kg (4 lb) of the drug out of the country. At the time airlines had been on alert because of a PLO threat and the airport authorities searched all the passengers. When a guard felt a package under Hayes's shirt he assumed it was a bomb. He gingerly pulled up the shirt and saw the drugs. Arrested, Hayes was sentenced to four years and two months in a Turkish prison. In 1974 that sentence was increased to life. In July 1975 Hayes was transferred to Imrali Island Prison on the Bosporus. During a storm on 2 October 1975 he swam ashore and then made his way, first to Istanbul on 4–5 October then to Greece. On 20 October 1975 he was deported as a bad influence "upon the youth of Greece".

Billy Hayes at a press conference.

WHERE:
Yesilkoy International Airport, Istanbul, Turkey
WHEN:
Wednesday 7 October 1970
THE AFTERMATH:
Hayes arrived at Kennedy International Airport in New York on 24 October 1975. He wrote a book about his ordeal entitled *Midnight Express*, which was later filmed starring Brad Davis and directed by Alan Parker. The film is different from the true story in many respects, not least in that the Turkish guards never raped him nor did he kill any of them. "I loved the movie, but I wish they'd shown some good Turks. You don't see a single one in the movie, and there were a lot of them, even in the prison. It created this impression that all Turks are like the people in *Midnight Express*." In June 2007 Hayes returned to Turkey for the first time since his escape. "I've always loved Turkey," he said. "But it's been a strange psychological experience to come back."

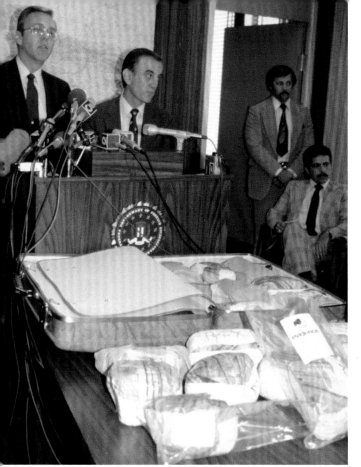

FBI agents show the cocaine found in DeLorean's possession.

John DeLorean

"Put the money into wine, women and song. They'll get the same return and have more fun"

THE CRIME: Tall (1.93 m/6 ft 4 in), handsome (after some plastic surgery), stylish, rich, successful in business – John Zachary DeLorean seemed to have it all. He had risen to become Executive Vice-President of General Motors before resigning on 2 April 1973 under mysterious circumstances. On 1 January 1974 he founded the John Z. DeLorean Corporation with offices at 100 West Long Lake, Detroit, Michigan. He hired himself out as a "consultant" to various companies, earning large sums of money for doing very little.

On 24 October 1975 the DeLorean Motor Company (DMC) was formed and at the end of that year DeLorean announced his plan to build the ultimate dream car. DeLorean's money men raised $6 million to finance a car. Not all the money was being spent on the car – DeLorean was paid a six-figure salary and he and his wife, Cristina Ferrare, lived in a luxury New York apartment. DeLorean was just about to sign a deal with the Puerto Rican government when he received a call from the British Government in the shape of the Northern Ireland Development Agency. The government was worried about the level of unemployment in the province – around 20 per cent – and was keen to encourage investment. The deal, worth £54 million, was signed on 3 August 1978. DeLorean hired Colin Chapman, the founder of Lotus Cars, to help with the design of the DeLorean-12. In autumn 1980 DeLorean went to see Humphrey Atkins, Secretary of State for Northern Ireland, and wangled another $33 million – DeLorean now had $120 million of British taxpayers' money and the taxpayer had not one car to show for it.

On 21 January 1981 the first DeLorean-12 moved off the production line, eight months late and $63 million over budget. To add to the difficulties, it was not a high-performance car and no one wanted to buy one. After questions were asked in the House of Commons, the government appointed Sir Kenneth Cork as a receiver for DMC. On 19 October 1982 the DMC factory in Belfast closed and the same day DeLorean was arrested and charged with conspiracy to buy and sell cocaine. DeLorean claimed that he had been entrapped by the FBI and, despite DeLorean being filmed in possession of a suitcase of cocaine, at 12.20pm on 16 August 1984 the jury found him not guilty.

WHERE:
100 West Long Lake, Detroit, Michigan, USA; The Cutts, Dunmurry, Belfast, Northern Ireland
WHEN:
1974–1984
THE AFTERMATH:
Six weeks after his acquittal, DeLorean's wife walked out on him and filed for divorce. The British taxpayer lost £85 million because of John DeLorean. He died on 19 March 2005, aged 80. Perhaps the final words should go to a Wall Street analyst who said, "When people ask my advice about investing in Mr DeLorean's ventures I tell them to put the money into wine, women and song... They'll get the same return and have more fun."

John Gotti

"They're telling me I'm too tough for the job"

THE CRIME: "The Teflon Don" was John Gotti's nickname for many years because it appeared that no charges would stick. In 1972 Manny Gambino, the nephew of Carlo Gambino, was kidnapped and murdered. The FBI arrested two of the kidnappers while Gambino put a contract out on the third, James McBratney. Gotti was one of a three-man team who killed McBratney for which he received a seven-year sentence. He was welcomed back into the fold on his release and soon promoted. Gotti believed that Aniello Dellacroce should be the head of the family instead of Paul Castellano but Dellacroce, dying of cancer, managed to keep the hotheaded Gotti in control. Gotti complained, "They're telling me I'm too tough for the job. Can you imagine what our thing is coming to?" On 18 March 1980 Gotti's neighbour, John Favara, accidentally killed Gotti's 12-year-old son Frank, running him over. On 28 July 1980, Favara was kidnapped as he left work. He was chainsawed to death and then his body was put in a car that was then crushed. An old-style gangster, Gotti became the head of the Gambino crime family in 1985 after Aniello Dellacroce and Paul Castellano were indicted. On 2 December Dellacroce died and a fortnight later Castellano and an aide were murdered outside a Manhattan steak house. Gotti was the new boss.

The FBI bugged his headquarters the Ravenite Social Club at 247 Mulberry Street. On 11 December 1990 they staged a raid and arrested Gotti, Salvatore "Sammy The Bull" Gravano, Frank Locascio and Thomas Gambino. Gotti was charged with 13 counts of murder (including Paul Castellano), conspiracy to commit murder, loansharking, racketeering, obstruction of justice, illegal gambling and tax evasion. On 2 April 1992, after 13 hours of deliberation, the jury found Gotti and LoCascio guilty on all 13 charges. On 23 June 1992 Gotti was sentenced to life imprisonment without possibility of parole.

WHERE:
Sparks Steak House, 210 East 46th Street, New York City, USA
WHEN:
Monday 16 December 1985
THE AFTERMATH:
John Gotti died of throat cancer at 12.45pm on 10 June 2002 at the United States Medical Center for Federal Prisoners in Springfield, Missouri.

John Gotti arrives at court to hear the verdict.

SERIAL KILLINGS

Thugs with one of their victims.

Behram Jemadar

"I may have strangled with my own hands about 125 men"

THE CRIME:

According to *The New Shorter Oxford English Dictionary* a thug is a member of a religious organization of professional robbers and assassins in India, and the word dates from the early 19th century. The cult began in about 700 and sacrificed people to the goddess Kali, wife of the god Shiva. Kali encouraged her followers to kill unbelievers and, with each murder, the follower's standing would be increased.

Kali would eat the human sacrifices until one day a follower saw her. She gave forth a tooth, a rib and a length of her sari, which became respectively a knife to dismember victims, a pickaxe to pluck out their eyes and a noose to strangle them. In southern India her followers were known as Phansigars (from the Hindustani phansi meaning "noose") and in northern India as Thugs (from the Sanskrti othag, meaning "to hide"). Both Muslims and Hindus joined the Thuggee cult.

Thugs usually kidnapped boys aged about ten to initiate them into the cult. Before each murder a group of thugs would pray before the statue of Kali. All the attacks took place in the winter and there was a strict protocol to be followed. They would only rob if the victim had been murdered in the approved fashion and they never killed women, boys under ten or anyone who was disabled.

The most infamous member of the Thuggee cult was Behram Jemadar, born about 1765 in India. He was said to have been the world's most prolific serial killer, dispatching 931 people between 1790 and 1840. He would sneak up behind them and strangle them with his *rumal* or ceremonial cloth. However, more recent research shows that far from offing nearly 1,000 people, he was actually only personally responsible for a quarter of that number. He did admit to being present when 931 people were murdered by the Thuggee cult but "I may have strangled with my own hands about 125 men, and I may have seen strangled 150 more." It is thought a gang of between 25 and 50 thugs were responsible for the mass murders.

WHERE:
India
WHEN:
700–1850
THE AFTERMATH:
The British Army in India began a crackdown on the cult and by the 1850s the Thugs had been all but suppressed. Behram was hanged in 1840.

Gilles de Rais

"The murder of children and sodomy"

THE CRIME: Born at Machécoul, Pays de Retz, on 10 September 1404, to French nobility, Gilles de Rais was a renaissance man – a brave soldier, a linguist and an arts patron. He was also a killer with a particular fascination for children. After the death of his parents, his cruel grandfather, Jean de Craon, raised the young Gilles. The old man arranged for de Rais to marry the boy's cousin, Catherine de Thouars of Brittany, the heiress to La Vendée and Poitou, but only after kidnapping her. The marriage made de Rais among the wealthiest of men in France. He joined the French army and fought alongside Joan of Arc, finally retiring in 1435. Bored with civilian life and freed from the tyranny of his grandfather after the old man's death in 1432, de Rais began to experiment with the occult. An extremely pretty boy by the name of Etienne Corrillaut, also known as Poitou, was taken to his castle at Machécoul and raped by de Rais. Just as the boy was about to be killed, a servant suggested keeping Poitou as a page and de Rais agreed. Poitou became one of his most devoted acolytes.

Boys would be lured to the castle where they would be fed and clothed. Then they would be taken to a special room where they would be hanged on a hook and raped. The boy would then be taken down, still alive, and comforted by de Rais before the process would be repeated again. De Rais either decapitated the child or had one of the servants do it. If his lust was not sated, de Rais would continue to abuse the headless corpse, cutting open the stomach and pulling out the entrails before masturbating over the bloody mess. Afterwards, he would retire to bed where he would stay for some time while his servants cleared up his mess, cremating the corpse in a special oven. Hundreds of children died this way. On 15 May 1440 after mass, de Rais kidnapped the priest, Jean le Ferron of the Church of Saint-Étienne-de-Mer-Morte. Violating ecclesiastical property was a capital offence and the Bishop of Nantes began an investigation, which concluded on 29 July. De Rais and his cohorts were arrested on 15 September.

WHERE:
Machécoul, Pays de Retz, France
WHEN:
1435–1440
THE AFTERMATH:
Gilles de Rais was charged with "the murder of children and sodomy, the invocation of demons, the offending of Divine Majesty and heresy". On 21 October he confessed and took the blame so that his companions might be freed but two days later Poitou and another aide, Henrie Griard, were condemned. Some of the more graphic passages were ordered by the judges to be stricken from the record. On 26 October 1440 de Rais, Griard and Poitou were hanged at Nantes.
YOU SHOULD KNOW:
Despite his depravity, de Rais was a devout Catholic who built several chapels and a cathedral for the church.

Gilles de Rais

GILLES DE LAVAL Seigneur
de Rets.

Countess Erszébet Báthory

"The female Dracula"

WHERE:
Cachtice Castle, Little Carpathians, near Trenčín, Hungary
WHEN:
1600
THE AFTERMATH:
It was in 1602 that rumours first began to spread about what was happening behind the walls of Cachtice Castle. However, it was not until 1610 that something was done. Erzsébet Báthory was never formally tried because it would have caused too much of a scandal. Juraj Thurzo, the Palatine of Hungary, went to the castle on 30 December 1610 and arrested Báthory and four of her servants. She was placed under house arrest but her servants were questioned on 2 January 1611 and then tried at Bytča on Monday 7 January. Dorkó, Jó and Újváry were found guilty and put to death. Dorkó and Jó had their fingernails ripped out before they were thrown into a fire alive, while Benická was beheaded before being thrown on the fire. Katarína Benická was sentenced to life imprisonment. The countess was not convicted of any crime but it was ordered that she be walled up in her own castle – all the doors and windows were bricked over, with just a small aperture for food to be given. On 21 August 1614 Erzsébet Báthory was found dead.

THE CRIME: "The female Dracula" was born into a wealthy Transylvanian family in Nyírbátor on 7 August 1560. Her uncle Stefan Báthory was the King of Poland. When she was four or five, Erzsébet suffered violent seizures and it is believed that these may have contributed to her later behaviour. On 8 May 1575 in Varannó she married Count Ferenc Nádasdy, not long after giving birth to a bastard child who was fathered by a peasant. As a wedding gift Nádasdy gave her his home Cachtice Castle, a country villa and 17 villages. The count was often away fighting in wars against the Ottomans so Erzsébet was often left alone. Bored, she took several lovers and also, thanks to her maid Dorothea "Dorkó" Szentes, began an interest in the occult. In 1585 she gave birth to a daughter, Anna, followed by Ursula, Andrew, Katherina and in 1598 her only surviving son, Paul. On 4 January 1604 her husband died aged 47 and the countess began inflicting torture on young girls. She was aided in her evil pursuits by Dorkó, Ilona Jó, Katarína Benická and János "Ficzkó" Újváry.

She had a blacksmith build a cylindrical cage with long metal spikes inside. A busty young girl would be chosen from among her seamstresses and forced to get into the cage, which would then be hoisted. Dorkó would stab the girl with red-hot pokers. As the unfortunate girl tried to escape being burned she would impale herself on the spikes, much to Erzsébet's sexual pleasure. With her husband out of the way, Erzsébet's behaviour knew no bounds and it is believed that up to 600 young women – many of them with large breasts – died at her hands. Another favourite pastime was to burn the girls' genitals with candles.

Erzsébet Báthory, "the female Dracula"

350

Gesina Gottfried

"I was born without a conscience"

THE CRIME: Born in Bremen, Germany, on 6 March 1785 as Gesche Margarethe Timm, Gesina was an attractive, blonde, blue-eyed, middle-class girl with a number of gentleman callers. In 1805 she married Johann Miltenberg, a successful businessman. In fact, the success was built on an edifice and the foundations were being eaten away by his drinking, much to his new wife's disgust. She knew that her mother used arsenic to kill rats so she tried some on her husband, putting it in his beer. He died on 1 October 1813, her first victim. Not wishing to be alone, she took a lover, a wealthy but shy man called Michael Christoph Gottfried. He was not keen to adopt a ready-made family and, fearing he would leave her, she killed her children: daughter Johanna died on 10 May 1815, followed eight days later by her other daughter, Adelheid and, on 22 September 1815, Heinrich, her son, died from poisoning. Gesina's parents did not approve of Michael Gottfried and made their feelings very clear. However, Gesina was not a woman to let parental disapproval stand in the way so she invited herself to dinner at their home – and promptly poisoned them: her mother, Gesche, died on 2 May 1815 and her father, Johann, on 28 June 1815. In the early summer of 1816 her alcoholic brother, Johann, arrived on leave from the army. Gesina was afraid that he might start asking awkward questions about the deaths of their parents so on 1 June 1816 she poisoned him, too. His death was ascribed to venereal disease.

All these deaths made Michael Gottfried even less keen on marriage so she began to poison him bit by bit while openly caring for him. Finally, in a delirium, he agreed to marry her. He signed over his worldly goods to her and on 5 July 1817, a few hours after the ceremony, he died in agony. She took a break from murdering for some years and even found a new fiancé, Paul Zimmermann. On 1 June 1823, he, too, died after he was poisoned. It seemed that virtually everyone who came into contact with Gesche Gottfried ended up dead. She poisoned her friend, Anna Lucia Meyerholz, on 21 March 1825 and another friend, Johann Mosees, nine months later. She landed a job as housekeeper to the Rumpff family after the bank foreclosed on her house in the Pelzerstrasse. Mr Rumpff worked as a wheelwright and on 22 December 1826 Gottfried murdered his wife, Wilhelmine, two days after she gave birth to a son. Death was put down to complications of childbirth. Gottfried continued to work in the house and gradually Rumpff began to feel ill. In the space of three days (13–15 May 1827) Gottfried murdered her friend Beta Schmidt and her daughter. Despite marrying wealthy men, Gottfried borrowed money. One of her creditors was Friedrich Kleine. He was murdered on 24 July 1827.

The poisoner Gesina Gottfried

WHERE:
Bremen, Germany
WHEN:
Friday 1 October 1813–24 July 1827
THE AFTERMATH:
Herr Rumpff waited until his housekeeper was out and went to the larder where he ate some uncontaminated food. Regaining some strength, he rummaged among the foodstuffs and found a joint of meat covered with a white powdery crust. He took it to the police who identified the powder as arsenic. Gesina Gottfried was arrested on 5 March 1828. She confessed to poisoning 30 people, 16 of whom died. Convicted, she was beheaded on 21 April 1831, the last person to be publicly executed in Bremen. She said, "I was born without a conscience, which allowed me to live without fear."
YOU SHOULD KNOW:
When those closest to her fell ill, it seemed that Gottfried was nursing them conscientiously, leading to her being nicknamed the "Angel of Bremen".

Hélène Jegado stands trial.

Hélène Jegado

"Death follows me wherever I go"

THE CRIME: Born in 1803 at Plouhinec, Morbihan, Brittany, Hélène Jegado was orphaned at seven and began working as a servant, albeit not a very good one. She often stole from her employers and was a bad cook. Her employers often had a bad habit of dying. When one died, Jegado would go into a convent until the fuss died down.

On 16 September 1850 she went to work for Théophile Bidard, a professor of law at the University of Rennes. After a short while, Rose Tessier, another servant, fell ill and died. Jegado appeared grief stricken and thus escaped any suspicion. Then Rosalie Sarrazin was hired and she became a close friend of Jegado, although Professor Bidard warned her not to become too close to the older woman. The two women stayed friends until Rosalie was promoted to work on the accounts and Jegado became jealous. Rosalie soon fell ill and died at 7am on 1 July 1851. Later that day, two doctors, Pinault and Boudin, concerned at the death, went to the office of the Procureur-General in the City of Rennes. An official and the two medical men went to Professor Bidard's home where Hélène Jegado greeted them and took them to the study where they were quickly joined by the professor. Jegado waited by the door. The Procureur said, "We have come on a rather painful mission. One of your servants died recently – it is suspected, of poisoning." "I am innocent!" The exclamation came from the servant. "Innocent of what?" asked the Procureur. "No one has accused you of anything!" The remark led to her arrest and an investigation revealed the trail of deaths in the houses in which she had worked over the previous 18 years. From 28 June until 3 October 1833 she had worked in a priest's house and seven people had died, including Jegado's sister, the priest and his father and mother. Between 1833 and 1841 Jegado's presence had been accompanied by 23 deaths, six illnesses, and numerous thefts. She said, "I'm afraid that people will accuse me of all those deaths. Death follows me wherever I go."

WHERE:
Rennes, France
WHEN:
1833 – Tuesday 1 July 1851
THE AFTERMATH:
Under examination by the Juge d'instruction at Rennes, Jegado denied all knowledge of the poison. "I don't know anything about arsenic – don't know what it is. No witness can say I ever had any." Hélène Jegado was charged with three murders, 11 thefts and three attempted murders. The trial began on 6 December 1851. After deliberating for 90 minutes the jury returned a guilty verdict. Jegado was guillotined in front of a large crowd on 26 February 1852.

William Palmer

"Are you sure it's safe?"

THE CRIME: It is thought that as many as 14 people met their deaths at the hands of The Rugeley Poisoner. Born on 6 August 1824, Palmer was spoiled by his mother after his father died when the boy was 13. Four years later Palmer was sacked from his first job for stealing. He spent the next five years as a doctor's apprentice during which time he fathered 14 illegitimate children and worked as an abortionist. He got a job at the Stafford Infirmary where he poisoned a man with strychnine to see its efficacy and then completed his studies in London. In 1846 he began to practise in Rugeley, Staffordshire and although he was quite successful he also gambled, a habit he could not break. He gambled away a £9,000 inheritance. In October 1847 at St Nicholas in Abbots, Bromley he married Anne Thornton, who had been born illegitimately, and fathered five children by her. Four died in infancy and it is a matter of debate whether he had a hand in their deaths.

In December 1848 his mother-in-law, Mary Thornton (who hated Palmer), came to visit and died a fortnight after, in January 1849. In May 1850 Palmer murdered Leonard Bladon, to whom he owed a considerable sum of money. Another creditor who was owed £800 also died. An uncle died after a heavy drinking session. By 1854 Palmer was heavily in debt and so insured his wife's life for £13,000. He paid the first premium and then she died in September of cholera, according to the death certificate. Later investigation revealed that antimony poisoning caused her death. Palmer insured his alcoholic brother, Walter, for £82,000 hoping he would die of the drink but years of drinking had strengthened his constitution so Palmer killed him with prussic acid in August 1855. To Palmer's annoyance, the insurance company refused to pay out. Palmer next killed John Parsons Cook after Polestar, a racehorse he owned, won several thousand pounds at Shrewsbury races. Cook died six days later on 19 November 1855 but his family insisted on his body being exhumed and examined. No evidence of poison was found but Palmer was arrested for murder on 15 December.

WHERE:
Rugeley, Staffordshire, England
WHEN:
1850–Monday 19 November 1855
THE AFTERMATH:
The bodies of Walter and Anne Palmer were exhumed but it was impossible to discover Walter's cause of death. William Palmer was the first Englishman convicted of a strychnine murder, albeit on mainly circumstantial evidence, and he was sentenced to death. He was hanged outside Stafford Prison on 14 June 1856. As he stepped onto the gallows, Palmer is said to have looked at the trapdoor and exclaimed, "Are you sure it's safe?"
YOU SHOULD KNOW:
Palmer was tried at the Old Bailey because of local prejudice, a decision that necessitated a change in the law (the Central Criminal Court Act 1856).

William Palmer

Mary Ann Cotton

"Gastric fever"

WHERE:
Northeast England
WHEN:
1860–1872
THE AFTERMATH:
Riley was shocked by the boy's
sudden death and went to the village
police to make a complaint. She was
arrested for Charles' murder
although the trial was delayed until
after the birth of her 12th child. Her
trial began on Wednesday 5 March
1873 and she claimed that Charles
had died from exposure to arsenic in
the wallpaper. After 90 minutes, the
jury found her guilty. She was hanged
at Durham County Jail on
24 March 1873.
YOU SHOULD KNOW:
Mary Ann Cotton left descendants.
One son was killed in a train crash
before the end of the First World War
and another was alive in 1950.

*A letter from the Governor
of Durham jail to the
Home Secretary confirming
Mary Ann Cotton's execution.*

THE CRIME: Mary Ann Cotton was born in Low Moorsley, County Durham in October 1832. An outgoing but religious child, she began working when she was 14, six years after her father had fallen to his death down a mineshaft. In July 1852 she married labourer William Mowbray and they made their marital home at Plymouth, Devon. In 1857 the couple returned to Durham with their one-year-old daughter Mary Ann. The mother revealed that they had had four more children but they all died young. Mary Ann then gave birth to Isabella in 1858, to Margaret in 1861 and John in 1863. On 24 June 1860, four-year-old Mary Ann died of "gastric fever". The child's death led to William Mowbray taking out life insurance on his own life and the lives of their children. In September 1864 John died after suffering diarrhoea. On 18 January 1865 William Mowbray lost his job and the same day came down with such a severe bout of diarrhoea that he died. The British and Prudential Insurance Company paid Mary Ann £35 on her husband's policy. In March 1865 Margaret died of "gastric fever". The insurance paid a further £30 on the deaths of the children.

Bundling up her remaining child, Mary Ann moved to Seaham Harbour where she fell in love with Joseph Nattrass but he was already married and refused to leave his wife. Mary Ann landed a job at the Sunderland Infirmary, where she fell for ex-patient George Ward, and they married in August 1865. Fourteen months later, he was dead from "fever". He left everything to his widow and she also received an insurance payout. At the end of 1866 she began working for a shipyard foreman John Robinson, whose wife had died not long earlier. His youngest child died shortly after and Mary Ann, who became pregnant, comforted him. She went to visit her mother who died on 9 June, nine days after Mary Ann's arrival. She ransacked her mother's house and took daughter Isabella back to the Robinson household. By the end of April, Isabella was dead from "gastric fever" and so were two of Robinson's children. In August 1867 Mary Ann married Robinson and in November Mary Isabella was born. She died four months later of "gastric fever". That year Mary Ann stole £50, ran up debts of £60 and insisted that James Robinson insure his life – he threw her out. She met widower Frederick Cotton, the brother of a friend, Margaret. In March 1870 Margaret died of "gastric fever" and not long after Mary Ann was pregnant with her 11th child. Frederick and Mary Ann married bigamously in September 1870. A son, Robert, was born early in 1871. On 19 September Frederick Cotton died, followed by Robert. She took up again with Joseph Nattrass – he died on 1 April 1872. She was offered a job as a nurse by a parish official, Thomas Riley, but her stepson Charles Edward Cotton was "in the way" and shortly after a workhouse rejected him, he died on 12 July 1872.

Lydia Sherman

"Queen Poisoner"

THE CRIME: Known as America's "Queen Poisoner", Lydia Sherman was born in 1825 as Lydia Danbury in New Brunswick, New Jersey, and became one of the greediest poisoners in American criminal history. In 1845, she married Edward Struck, a policeman, by whom she had six children. He was sacked from the New York Police Department for cowardice – he refused to break up a fight – and took to drinking and self-pity. He began to beat her up when he was drunk and she retaliated by putting arsenic in his soup. She insured her husband for $5,000 and then visited a chemist where she bought poison to kill rats. With her husband out of the way (he died on 26 May 1864, supposedly from alcoholism), she then insured the lives of her six children, aged from nine months to 18 years, before poisoning them as well.

The local township expressed its deep sympathy at such a tragedy and no one suspected the widow and mother was anything other than grieving. On 22 November 1868 she married Dennis Hurlbrut, a wealthy, elderly and, some said, senile farmer from New Haven, Connecticut. He promised to leave her all his money in his will. He died 14 months later and by 1870 she had spent all of his estate. In April 1870 she became housekeeper to Nelson Horatio Sherman, a rich widower and father of two who lived in Derby, Connecticut. The housekeeper eventually became the wife and showed her gratitude by poisoning first his baby son, Frank, and then his 14-year-old daughter, Addie. Lydia gave her husband poisoned hot chocolate and Nelson Sherman died on 12 May 1871. It was at this time that someone finally noticed. The local medic, Dr Beardsley, became suspicious and, after finding arsenic in Nelson Sherman's stomach, called for a second opinion and then a third. Realizing the jig was up, Lydia Sherman fled to New York.

Book released after the trial

WHERE:
Derby, Connecticut, USA
WHEN:
Friday 12 May 1871
THE AFTERMATH:
Dr Beardsley informed the police of his suspicions. The police in Connecticut ordered Lydia's extradition and she went on trial. Convicted of second-degree murder, she was sentenced to life in prison. In January 1873 she confessed to seven murders and said her victims were "better off dead". She died of cancer on 16 May 1878, incarcerated in Wethersfield Prison.

Thomas Neill Cream

"I'm Jack the…"

Dr Thomas Neill Cream

WHERE:
Chicago, Illinois, USA; Lambeth
Palace Road, London, England
WHEN:
1881–1892
THE AFTERMATH:
Cream was hanged on 15 November
1892 at Newgate Prison. As he stood
waiting to die, his last words, as the
trapdoor swung open, were
"I'm Jack the…"

THE CRIME: Born in Glasgow, Scotland, Thomas Neill Cream emigrated to Canada when he was four years old. Moving to America, he qualified as a doctor. In 1881 he was jailed for life in Chicago after having been convicted of killing Daniel Stott, his mistress's husband, with strychnine. Stott's gravestone inscription reads, "Daniel Stott Died June 12, 1881 Aged 61 Years Poisoned By His Wife & Dr Cream".

Life on that occasion meant ten years and, on his release, Cream moved to London and into Lambeth Palace Road. At night Cream would accost prostitutes and offer them his pills, which, he said, would improve their complexions. In fact, they were laced with strychnine and Cream returned to his home fantasizing about their death agonies. In October 1891 he murdered two women – Nellie Donworth, a 19-year-old prostitute, and Matilda Clover, a 27-year-old prostitute – and then had the audacity to complain to Scotland Yard that he was being followed and asked for a "reward" of £300,000 for naming the Lambeth Poisoner.

On 2 April 1892 he gave his poisonous pills to Lou Harvey but she only pretended to swallow them. Nine days later Cream met two more prostitutes, Alice Marsh, 21, and Emma Shrivell, 18, and gave them Guinness laced with strychnine. Both women died in agony. His downfall came about thanks to his boastfulness. He wrote to the police accusing two other doctors of murdering the prostitutes but in his letter revealed rather too much inside knowledge, including the fact that Matilda Clover's death was suspicious when publicly it had been announced as natural causes. When his home was searched the police found seven bottles of strychnine and equipment for making pills. The jury took just 12 minutes to find Cream guilty and he was sentenced to death.

Johann Otto Hoch

"I have done with...everybody"

THE CRIME: Johann Otto Hoch was born in 1855 (some sources say 1862) as John Schmidt in Horweiler, Germany. He moved to the United States in the early 1880s and began adopting a series of aliases as he worked in meatpacking plants in Chicago. He married Christine Ramb and had three children by her. He deserted them in 1887. Eight years later he married Maria Steimbucher who died four months later. He sold her property for $4,000. In November of the same year he married Mary Rankin and left her the next day, taking her money with him. In 1896 Hoch married four times and had another proposal rebuffed. Two of the wives died and Hoch was more than $2,000 richer by the end of the year. In January 1897 he married Julia Dose and vanished the same day but not before taking $700 with him.

Two years in prison for selling furniture that was not his did not deter Hoch and in 1900 he married Mary Schultz. Shortly after, the new Mrs Hoch, her 15-year-old daughter Nettie and $2,000 vanished. In November 1901 Hoch married Anna Goehrke and left her. On 8 April 1902 he married Mary Becker who died the following year. On 2 January 1904 Hoch walked up the aisle with Anna Hendrickson. He walked out on her 18 days later with $500 of her money. Eighteen months later he married Lena Hoch who died three weeks later leaving him $1,500 richer. On 20 October he married Caroline Streicher and left her eleven days later. On 16 November he rented a cottage in Chicago and spent $120 on furniture. On 5 December, he married Marie Walcker. As a wedding gift she sold her sweet shop for $75 and gave Hoch her life savings of $350. Fifteen days later, she fell ill and died on 12 January 1905. Three days later he married her estranged sister Amelia Fischer and she gave him another $750 before he upped and left. On 30 January he proposed to Katherine Kimmerle 20 minutes after taking a room in her house but she turned down his offer and, thanks to Amelia Fischer's persistence, Hoch was arrested. In his pocket was a fountain pen filled with 58 g (2 oz) of arsenic.

Johann Hoch (indicated by the arrow) at his arrest.

WHERE:
Chicago, Illinois, USA
WHEN:
1892–1905
THE AFTERMATH:
Following Hoch's arrest several of his dead wives were exhumed and arsenic was found in their bodies. On 19 May 1905 Hoch was found guilty of the murder of Marie Walcker and on 23 June sentenced to hang. He went to the gallows on 23 February 1906. Protesting his innocence, Hoch said, "I am done with this world. I have done with everybody."
YOU SHOULD KNOW:
Hoch had six pieces of advice for would-be Lotharios.
1. Nine out of every ten women can be won by flattery.
2. Never let a woman know her own shortcomings.
3. Always appear to a woman to be the anxious one.
4. Women like to be told pleasant things about themselves.
5. When you make love, be ardent and earnest.
6. The average man can fool the average woman if he will only let her have her own way at the start.

H.H. Holmes

He stole corpses, insured them, disfigured them and claimed the insurance

WHERE:
Sixty-Third Street and Wallace
Avenue, Chicago, Illinois, USA
WHEN:
1893
THE AFTERMATH:
The exact number of his victims is
unknown but the police believed that
he had killed 27. On 7 May 1896
Holmes was hanged at the
Philadelphia County Prison. The
hangman did not do the job properly
and Holmes took 15 minutes to die.
He asked to be buried in cement so
that his body could not be dissected.
YOU SHOULD KNOW:
A mysterious fire destroyed Holmes's
castle on 19 August 1895. The site
is now a post office.

THE CRIME: Born in Gilmanton, New Hampshire on 16 May 1860 as Herman Webster Mudgett, the man who became known as Dr Henry Howard Holmes was a serial killer with a tally of between 27 and over 100 victims. At Alton, New Hampshire on 8 July 1878 he married Clara A. Lovering. He was married bigamously on 28 January 1887 to Myrta Z. Belknap by whom he had a daughter, Lucy. Three years earlier he had graduated from the University of Michigan Medical School where he had stolen corpses, insured them, disfigured them and claimed the insurance. He turned to forging, horse theft and swindling as well as his "legitimate" business as a pharmacist in Chicago. He then got a job at Dr E.S. Holton's chemist on the corner of 63rd Street and Wallace Avenue in Englewood, Chicago. Dr Holton died of cancer not long after and Holmes murdered his widow.

Henry Howard Holmes was arrested and questioned about an insurance scam.

Across the road from the chemist, with the money he made from his various scams, Holmes built a large "castle" in 1892, one year before the city hosted the World's Fair. The ground floor was made up of shops while the first and second had about 100 windowless rooms. Holmes filled the rooms with lovers, clients and prospective victims, many of whom took out life insurance for which he would be the sole beneficiary. Some of the rooms were fitted with gas pipes so Holmes could poison the occupant at his whim – and he did, often. He liked to listen to their screams as they died.

On 9 January 1894 he married his third wife, Georgiana Yoke. The corpses of some of his victims were sold to medical schools. Others were cremated in the two giant furnaces in the basement while many were disposed of in vats of acid. Holmes also performed hundreds of illegal abortions, sometimes with a fatal outcome. After the World's Fair, Holmes moved to Fort Worth, Texas, and then to other states and Canada. He was arrested in Boston on 17 November 1894 when police discovered his involvement in a life insurance scam.

Joseph Vacher

"I committed the crimes in a moment of frenzy"

THE CRIME: Born on 16 November 1869, the last of 15 children of an illiterate farmer, Joseph Vacher was educated at a strict Catholic school. He was conscripted into the army and, when he was not promoted, he tried to cut his own throat. In 1893 he fell in love with a young serving wench named Louise. The love was unreciprocated, despite his best efforts, so he shot her four times. She survived and, in his desperation, Vacher tried to commit suicide but he, too, lived and he succeeded only in paralyzing one side of his face. He was sent to a mental hospital at Dole, Jura, but released after just a year. It was then that his murderous spree began. Between April 1894 and 1897 Vacher worked as a labourer and killed and mutilated one woman, five teenage girls and five teenage boys. The victims – mostly shepherds – were stabbed, raped, sodomized and often disembowelled. On 4 August 1897 he attacked a woman collecting pine cones in an Ardèche field but he underestimated her strength and determination and she screamed for help. Her husband and son came running at the noise and held Vacher until the police could arrive.

A newspaper of 1897 shows a graphic depiction of the murder of Louise Marcel.

WHERE:
Southeast France
WHEN:
1894–1897
THE AFTERMATH:
Vacher was sentenced to three months in prison for offending public decency. Then, although there was no evidence to link Vacher to the string of murders, he confessed, "I committed the crimes… I committed them all in a moment of frenzy." He claimed that he was mad, the result of a lick by a rabid dog when he was eight years old. Then Vacher changed his tale and said that he had been told by God to commit the murders. He was judged legally sane and was tried at the Cour d'Assises of Ain and sentenced to death on 28 October 1998. On New Year's Eve he was guillotined and the executioners had to drag him to the blade. He was 29 years old.

Amelia Dyer

"You'll know all mine by the tape around their necks"

A bag belonging to Amelia Dyer was found in the Thames with the body of a child inside.

THE CRIME: In 1895 Amelia Dyer, a 57-year-old ex-member of the Salvation Army, set herself up in Reading, England as a childminder, or what the Victorians called a baby farmer. She placed advertisements in local newspapers offering her services. In March the body of a child was found floating in the Thames, a ligature around the neck. The body had been wrapped in paper bearing an address in Reading – Amelia Dyer's address but when the police went to the house, it was empty.

In November 1895 25-year-old barmaid Evelina Marmon gave birth to an illegitimate daughter she named Doris in Cheltenham. No one knew who the father was. She advertised for someone to look after the child but, by coincidence, an ad next to hers read, "Married couple with no family would adopt healthy child, nice country home. Terms, £10." A Mrs Harding of Oxford Road, Reading, had placed it. Evelina wrote and received a reply from Mrs Harding, "I should be glad to have a dear little baby girl, one I could bring up and call my own. We are plain, homely people, in fairly good circumstances. I don't want a child for money's sake, but for company and home comfort. Myself and my husband are dearly fond of children. I have no child of my own. A child with me will have a good home and a mother's love." A week later, Evelina arrived to drop off Doris, leaving the baby, clothes and £10. Mrs Harding was in fact Amelia Dyer and Evelina never saw her daughter again. On 4 April 1896 Dyer was arrested and charged with murder, by which time at least six babies had met their end. She was sending little children to Jesus, she said, because He wanted them far more than their mothers did. All the babies had been strangled and wrapped in paper parcels. "You'll know all mine by the tape around their necks," she told police.

WHERE:
Reading, Berkshire, England
WHEN:
1895–1896
THE AFTERMATH:
Amelia Dyer appeared at the Old Bailey on 22 May 1896 and pleaded guilty to the murder of Doris Marmon. James Billington hanged her at Newgate Prison on 10 June 1896.
YOU SHOULD KNOW:
Two years after Amelia Dyer went to the gallows, another baby was discovered dead in a string parcel at Newton Abbot. She had been given to a Mrs Stewart to care for, for £12. Mrs Stewart was Polly, Amelia Dyer's daughter.

Herman Billick

"The Great Billick – Cardreader and Seer"

THE CRIME: In 1904 Herman Billick met a fellow expatriate Bohemian by the name of Martin Vzral. Vzral had worked in the milk trade and built up a considerable fortune of around $6,000. He also had a nice home on West 19th Street in Chicago that he shared with his wife and seven children. Billick's real name was Vajicek but he had changed it to the more pronounceable Billick. He had arrived in Chicago from Cleveland, Ohio, and was everything that Vzral was not – scheming, cheating and lazy. His business was very different – he was a magician and had cards printed "The Great Billick – Cardreader and Seer". He also sold love potions to his neighbours.

Billick decided to relieve Martin Vzral of his fortune and, one day, visited his milk depot where he suddenly began speaking in tongues before blurting out, "You have an enemy. He is trying to destroy you." As it happened, Vzral was caught up in rivalry with another milkman and Billick offered to cast a spell for him. Billick began to visit the Vzral home to work his magic and get some financial reward. On 27 March 1905 Martin Vzral died after a short illness punctuated by stomach pains. On 28 July his second daughter Mary died after suffering a similar complaint. She left $800 insurance money, which went to her mother, along with the $$2,000 left by Martin Vzral. In December another daughter, Tilly, died and her insurance policy was worth $600. In August 1906 Rose Vzral, 18, died after suffering stomach problems. She had been insured for $300. On 30 November 1906 Ella, 12 years old, died. Her life had been insured for $100.

WHERE:
West 19th Street, Chicago, Illinois, USA
WHEN:
Monday 27 March 1905–Friday 30 November 1906
THE AFTERMATH:
As locals gossiped, the police moved in and arrested Billick. A warrant was also issued for Mrs Vzral as an accomplice but she committed suicide by taking arsenic before the warrant could be executed. Billick was charged with six counts of murder after the bodies were exhumed and found to have been poisoned with arsenic. At his trial in July 1907 Billick confessed to swindling the Vzral family but denied involvement in their deaths. There was no evidence that Billick had ever possessed arsenic but the jury still found him guilty and sentenced him to death. His execution was stayed several times before it was commuted to life imprisonment. He was released in January 1917.

Herman Billick

Belle Gunness

"Triflers need not apply"

WHERE:
La Porte County, Indiana, USA
WHEN:
1906–1908
THE AFTERMATH:
Before he could arrive, the Gunness farm burned down on 28 April 1908. Four corpses were found – one without a head, later identified wrongly as Belle Gunness and her three children. The head was never found. On 23 May 1908 farmhand, Ray Lamphere, was indicted on four counts of murder and arson, but was only convicted on the arson charge. He died in prison. The authorities searched Belle's farm and found 13 bodies, all neatly chopped up and parcelled. The whereabouts of Belle Gunness remained a mystery.

Belle Gunness with her children

THE CRIME: Belle Gunness was born in Selbu, near Trondheim, Norway as Brynhild Paulsdatter Størseth on 11 November 1859. Her early life remains a mystery as she told many varying stories of her origins. In 1883 she arrived in America and the following year married Max Sorenson, a fellow Norwegian. They opened a sweetshop in Chicago but it was not a success and was razed in a mysterious fire a year later. Using the insurance money, they moved to Austin, Illinois, where they started a family. In 1898 their house burned down and they received another insurance payout and bought a farm. Her situation changed on 30 July 1900 when her husband died and Belle sold the farm for $100. She collected $8,500 in insurance money but her husband's family thought that Belle had murdered him. Using the insurance money, Belle bought a farm outside La Porte, Indiana, and moved in with her three daughters. On 1 April 1902 she married Peter Gunness, another Norwegian, and a week later his baby daughter died. In December Belle was widowed when an axe accidentally fell off a high shelf and embedded itself in Peter Gunness's head, killing him.

An investigation was dropped, probably because Belle was pregnant – a son, Philip, was born in 1903. In 1906 she began to advertise for gentlemen callers, "Personal – comely widow who owns a large farm in one of the finest districts in La Porte County, Indiana, desires to make the acquaintance of a gentleman equally well provided, with view of joining fortunes. No replies by letter considered unless sender is willing to follow answer with personal visit. Triflers need not apply."

Several men replied and Belle asked them for $5,000 to show their honest intentions. None of the suitors was ever seen again. In December 1907 Andrew Helgelien (some sources say Holdgren), a bachelor farmer from Aberdeen, South Dakota, wrote to her and in January 1908 they met after she wrote to him, "To the Dearest Friend in the World: No woman in the world is happier than I am. I know that you are now to come to me and be my own. I can tell from your letters that you are the man I want... My heart beats in wild rapture for you, My Andrew, I love you. Come prepared to stay forever." Andrew's brother contacted Belle but was told his brother was not with her so he decided to visit to see for himself.

Amy Archer-Gilligan

There were 48 deaths in a five-year period

THE CRIME: In 1901 Amy and James Archer opened Sister Amy's Nursing Home for the Elderly at Newington, Connecticut. Their chosen clientele was the wealthy and the Archers gained a reputation for the quality of their care, despite neither having any medical qualifications. In 1907 they moved to larger premises in Windsor, and opened the Archer Home for the Elderly and Infirm. In 1910 James Archer died and his widow carried on running the home alone until 1913 when she married Michael W. Gilligan, a wealthy widower. He died not long afterwards. Then strange happenings began at the home – inhabitants began dying despite being healthy. Franklin R. Andrews signed an agreement allowing Archer-Gilligan to take money from his account for his care and died on 30 May 1914. He had been in good heath. Residents had to pay $1,500 up front for a promised lifetime of care in the home but soon afterwards many of them died; the rate was estimated at ten deaths a year, six times greater than the average for the area. There were 48 deaths in a five-year period. Archer-Gilligan was hoping that the authorities would not notice, especially since her local doctor, Howard King, was signing the death certificates as natural causes. Among the victims Charles Smith was poisoned on 9 April 1914, Alice Gowdy in December 1914 and Maude Lynch died on 2 February 1916. Finally, the police did take notice and two bodies were exhumed, including that of Michael W. Gilligan. Both were found to contain very high levels of arsenic.

The prosecution showed that Amy Archer-Gilligan had bought large quantities of arsenic.

WHERE:
Windsor, Connecticut, USA
WHEN:
1911–1916
THE AFTERMATH:
Amy Archer-Gilligan was arrested and in June 1917 went on trial in Hartford, Connecticut. The prosecution showed that she had bought large quantities of arsenic, the poison found in the bodies of her victims. She claimed that she was devoted to her church and to the nursing profession. It cut no ice and she was convicted of five murders and sentenced to death. Her lawyer engineered a retrial in June 1919 and she was again convicted and sentenced to life imprisonment. She died aged 59 in 1928 while incarcerated in an insane asylum.

Some of the "Angel Makers" of Nagyrév.

Angel Makers of Nagyrév

"The Murder District"

THE CRIME:

Ninety-six km (60 mi) southeast of Budapest stands a little-known farming village called Nagyrév. It is near Tiszakurt and in the early part of the last century these two remote places were haunted by a band of serial killers.

WHERE:
Nagyrév, Hungary

WHEN:
1914–July 1929

THE AFTERMATH:
When Mrs Szabó was arrested she named her friend, Mrs Bukenoveski, who had poisoned her elderly mother and then thrown her in the Tisza River. Bukenoveski then pointed the finger at Mrs Fazekas who denied everything and was released. She returned to the village and warned the poisoners that the jig was up. Unbeknown to her, Mrs Fazekas was followed by the police who then proceeded to arrest 38 women. Twenty-six were tried at Szolnok and eight were sentenced to death: Susanna Olah, a septuagenarian called Lydia, Marie Kardos, Rosalie Sebestyen, Rosa Hoyba, Mrs Julius Csaba, Maria Varga and Julianne Lipke.

Seven were sentenced to life imprisonment and the rest to different jail terms. Mrs Julius Fazekas escaped justice by killing herself before she could be re-arrested.

Over a period of 15 years, they murdered around 300 people. The killings began during the First World War. With no hospital in Nagyrév, a midwife and abortionist, Mrs Julius Fazekas, met the medical needs of the village people, helped by her friend Susanna Olah. Most men in the village were away fighting but there was a prisoner of war camp nearby and many of the local women became involved with the prisoners. Numerous women took two or more lovers from the camp.

When their menfolk returned from the front, the women were not pleased that their sexual liberation had come to an end. Fazekas and Olah heard of the grumblings and began to sell arsenic, sourced from strips of flypaper, to the disgruntled women. In 1914 Peter Hegedus was the first victim. Around 50 women bought the poison and began calling themselves the "Angel Makers of Nagyrév". Some of the women were so enthusiastic that they killed children and relatives as well as husbands.

One woman, 45-year-old Marie Kardos, killed her husband, her lover and her 23-year-old disabled son – leading to the area becoming known as "The Murder District". The cousin of Mrs Fazekas signed the death certificates for all the victims. In July 1929 the killings stopped after Mrs Ladislaus Szabó poisoned the wine of a man who went to the police.

Henri-Desiré Landru

"A widower with a comfortable income and an affectionate nature"

THE CRIME: Bald and with a long red beard, Landru was an unlikely Bluebeard but he had something about him that attracted women. When he failed as a businessman (he was a building contractor, bicycle manufacturer and furniture remover) and as a petty crook (he spent seven terms in jail in 12 years for trifling offences such as the theft of a bicycle) he decided to capitalize on his other talent – seducing women.

In 1909 Landru began to romance elderly widows, holding out the promise of marriage, but when he had access to their bank accounts, he took their money and disappeared. When he became tired of fraud, having duped hundreds of lonely women (one, Madame Izoret, he took for 15,000 francs), he turned his hand to murder. He placed an advertisement in several newspapers, presenting himself as "a widower with a comfortable income and an affectionate nature". He was inundated with replies and details of the most interesting candidates he recorded in a notebook. In December 1914 he rented a villa at Vernouillet where he murdered four women. In December 1915 he rented the secluded Villa Ermitage in Gambais, a village southwest of Paris, to woo his victims. Between 1915 and 1919 he murdered 11 women. The first to die there was Madame Héon on 8 December 1915. The last victim was 36-year-old Marie-Thérèse Marchadier who disappeared on 15 January 1919. Relatives of the dead women began making enquiries to the mayor of Gambais and the trail led to Landru. Despite his prodigious use of aliases, he was arrested on his 50th birthday in 1919. The police found notebooks containing details of 283 women. Further examination of his villa revealed bones in the ashes of the oven and what appeared to be blood on a mattress. Closer examination showed them to be animal bones and sheep's blood. The police concentrated on the 283 names in the notebooks and began tracking down the women. Most were found and most confessed to having slept with Landru before he conned them. Eleven names were unaccounted for but the police could find no trace of their bodies.

WHERE:
Villa Ermitage, Gambais, France
WHEN:
Wednesday 8 December
1915–Wednesday 15 January 1919
THE AFTERMATH:
Landru went on trial on 7 November 1921 and was found guilty of 11 murders on 30 November. Protesting his innocence, he was guillotined at Versailles on 25 February 1922.

Henri-Desiré Landru pleads his case.

Fritz Haarmann

"The Butcher of Hanover"

WHERE:
8 Neuestrasse, Hanover, Germany
WHEN:
September 1918–June 1924
THE AFTERMATH:
Haarmann confessed to killing "30 or 40... I don't remember". He became known as "The Butcher of Hanover". He was tried on 4 December 1924 at the Hanover Assizes and convicted of 24 murders. He was guillotined on 15 April 1925 at Hanover jail. Grans was arrested on 8 July 1924, jailed for 12 years and died in 1980.
YOU SHOULD KNOW:
Haarmann told police, "I never intended to hurt those youngsters, but I knew that if I got going something would happen and that made me cry... I would throw myself on top of those boys and bite through the Adam's apple, throttling them at the same time. I'd make two cuts in the abdomen and put the intestines in a bucket, then soak up the blood and crush the bones until the shoulders broke. Now I could get the heart, lungs and kidneys and chop them up and put them in my bucket. I'd take the flesh off the bones and put it in my wax cloth bag. It would take me five or six trips to take everything and throw it down the toilet or into the river. I always hated doing this, but I couldn't help it — my passion was so much stronger than the horror of the cutting and chopping."

THE CRIME: Fritz Haarmann was born in Hanover, Germany, on 25 October 1879, the sixth child of an odd couple. His father was nicknamed Sulky Ollie and his mother was an invalid. A mummy's boy, he was sent to military school in 1895 but was discharged because of his epilepsy. Back in Hanover, he was sent to an asylum after being caught molesting small children but escaped after six months. In 1900 he rejoined the army to escape his pregnant girlfriend and was discharged in 1903. His father at first tried to have Haarmann declared insane and then financed him to open a fish and chip shop. He stole the takings and then in 1914 was caught burgling a warehouse and sentenced to five years in prison. He was paroled in 1918 and became simultaneously a smuggler and a police informant.

Near the end of the First World War Germany was in chaos and Haarmann used the confusion to pick up boys and teenagers. It was estimated that in 1923 more than 600 went missing. Haarmann was soon jailed for molesting a minor and on his release, in September 1919, he met and fell in love with 24-year-old Hans Grans, a gay pimp. They began to pick up and kill boys and young vagrants after sodomizing them. The bodies were then dismembered and sold to butchers as pork or beef. Some parts were thrown into the River Leine. Grans kept items of their clothing that he took a fancy to and sold the rest. One teenager was murdered because Grans liked his trousers. On 17 May 1924 a skull was found near the river, another five days later and two more in the river's sediment on 13 June. The police believed it was part of an elaborate, if macabre, practical joke but changed their minds on 24 July when children found a sack containing bones and another skull on the riverbank. The river was dragged and 500 more bones, belonging to 27 young men and boys, were found. Coincidentally, Haarmann was arrested on 22 June 1924 on a charge of indecency with 15-year-old Karl Fromm. When police searched his home at 8 Neuestrasse, they found bloodstains and clothes belonging to missing boys.

Fritz Haarman walks from the jail to the courthouse.

Albert Fish

"Grace sat in my lap and kissed me. I made up my mind to eat her"

THE CRIME: Albert Fish was born as Hamilton Fish in Washington DC on 19 May 1870. The Fish family was beset by insanity and bad luck. His father died when Fish was just five and he was taken to an orphanage from where he regularly ran away. When he was 12 years old, he began a relationship with a telegraph boy who introduced him to coprophagia. Fish also started visiting swimming pools to watch boys undress. In 1885 he began work as an apprentice painter and 13 years later married, fathering six children. Throughout his marriage he abused young boys usually under the age of six. In 1917 his wife left him.

His psychiatrist Dr Frederic Wertham said, "There was no known perversion which he did not practise and practise frequently." He self-flagellated, burned himself and stuck needles into his genitals. When he was arrested and X-rayed, police found 29 items in his body, some of which had been there so long that they had begun to rust. The police were aware of Fish through his habit of writing obscene replies to lonely hearts' advertisements and through some minor financial swindles that had seen him serve a number of short terms in prison.

On 3 June 1928 Fish, calling himself Frank Howard, arrived at the 406 West 15th Street, New York home of Edward Budd who wanted a job and "Howard" offered him a job on his fictional farm on Long Island. Then he remembered that his sister was holding a party and suggested that 12-year-old Grace Budd attend. The Budds allowed their daughter to go with Fish – it was the last time they ever saw her.

In November 1934, a letter was sent to Grace's parents: "Dear Mrs Budd… a friend of mine [worked] as a deck hand [and] sailed from San Francisco for Hong Kong, China. At that time there was famine in China. So great was the suffering among the very poor that all children under 12 were sold for food in order to keep others from starving. A boy or girl under 14 was not safe in the street. Part of the naked body of a boy or girl would be brought out and just what you wanted cut from it… On his return to N.Y. he stole two boys, one 7 and one 11. First he killed the 11-year-old boy, because he had the fattest ass and of course the most meat on it. At that time, I was living at 409 E 100 St. near–right side. He told me so often how good human flesh was I made up my mind to taste it. On Sunday June the 3, 1928 I called on you at 406 W 15 St. Grace sat in my lap and kissed me. I made up my mind to eat her… First I stripped her naked. How she did kick – bite and scratch. I choked her to death, then cut her in small pieces so I could take my meat to my rooms. Cook and eat it. How sweet and tender her little ass was roasted in the oven. It took me 9 days to eat her entire body." Fish later admitted that he had raped Grace. He was arrested after police traced the envelope.

Albert Fish

WHERE:
406 West 15th Street, New York City, USA
WHEN:
Sunday 3 June 1928
THE AFTERMATH:
Fish's trial opened on 11 March 1935 at White Plains, New York and lasted for ten days. Fish pleaded insanity and claimed to have heard voices from God ordering him to kill children. The jury found Fish guilty and he was sentenced to death.
YOU SHOULD KNOW:
Fish was executed at 11.06pm on 16 January 1936, in the electric chair at Sing Sing. He said that his death would be "the supreme thrill of my life". The chair is said to have short-circuited on the first attempt, caused by all the metal in Fish's body.

Bruno Lüdke

Lüdke had strangled or stabbed his victims before having sex with their corpses

WHERE:
Berlin, Germany
WHEN:
1928–1943
THE AFTERMATH:
Lüdke told his captors that because he was insane, under Nazi law he could not be indicted. Instead the Germans put him in a Viennese hospital where he was experimented on. On 8 April 1944 he died after being injected during one such "experiment".

THE CRIME: Born at Köpenick, Germany on 3 April 1908, the fourth of the six children of Otto and Emma, Lüdke was a teenage rapist, necrophiliac and murderer. His father, who suffered from throat cancer, died in 1937. The upheaval of the Second World War gave Lüdke the cover to carry out his fiendish work. In January 1939 the Third Chamber of the Erbgesundheitsgericht in Berlin ordered that Lüdke be sterilized because he was a suspected rapist but mainly because he was insane. After his sterilization, on 22 May 1940, he relocated to a small village outside Berlin where he carried on raping. On 29 January 1943 he was arrested, after the body of 51-year-old Frieda Rössner was found strangled near his home. Kriminalkommissar Franz interrogated Lüdke who confessed to the murder and admitted to 85 more, dating back to 1928. Lüdke had strangled or stabbed his victims before having sex with their corpses.

There is some debate as to whether Lüdke did, in fact, commit the murders since all of them had different *modus operandi*. No fingerprint evidence linked Lüdke to the murders and there was a belief that Kriminalkommissar Franz used Lüdke to clear up a number of his unsolved cases. Another investigator wondered how a mental defective like Lüdke could evade capture for 20 years and yet get caught stealing a chicken.

Peter Kürten

"I hope I hear my own blood gurgle"

THE CRIME: Born on 26 May 1883, the third of 13 children, in Cologne-Mulheim in Germany, Peter Kürten had an incestuous relationship with one of his sisters. Kürten's taste for sadism was awakened by the local dog catcher who taught the boy to masturbate the dogs and allowed him to watch while the dog catcher tortured them. In 1892 two friends of Kürten's drowned in the Rhine and it is likely that he was responsible for at least one, if not both, of the deaths. When he was 13, Kürten began practising bestiality and discovered he got pleasure from stabbing a sheep at the same time he was having sex with it. He was jailed for the first time when he was 15 – having been convicted of theft – the first of 17 sentences covering 27 years. In November 1899 Kürten claimed he committed his first murder, strangling a girl during sex, but no body was ever found. He spent most of the period between 1900 and 1904 behind bars. In 1905, having deserted from the army, he was jailed for seven years for theft. Released in 1912, he was convicted of a shooting in a restaurant and jailed again. On 25 May 1913 in Wolfsrasse, Cologne he murdered and sexually assaulted 13-year-old Christine Klein. Later that year, he was jailed for an unrelated offence. In 1921 he was released and met a woman who had shot a man who jilted her. This was the only human for whom Kürten felt normal affection. Even so, she did not agree to marry him until he threatened to murder her.

In 1925 they moved to Düsseldorf where Kürten began the reign of terror that led to him being dubbed the "Monster of Düsseldorf" attacking four women and starting 17 fires. In 1929 his reign began in earnest assaulting men, women and young girls. In the autumn and winter of that year Kürten attacked and raped ten women and girls. On 14 May 1930 he "rescued" an unemployed maid, Maria Budlick, 21, from the advances of another man at Düsseldorf station and took her home where he fed her. He then told her he was taking her to a hostel but as soon as they were alone he tried to have sex with her and strangle her. Asking her if she remembered where he lived, Maria said no so Kürten let her go. Reluctantly, she later led police to Kürten's home. Realizing he faced arrest, he confessed to his wife and on 24 May 1930 she went to the police. The reign of terror was over.

WHERE:
Grafenberger Wald, Düsseldorf, Germany
WHEN:
1899 – Wednesday 14 May 1930
THE AFTERMATH:
Peter Kürten's trial began on 13 April 1931 and a psychiatrist described Kürten as "the king of sexual perverts". The trial ended on 23 April and the jury took 90 minutes to find him guilty of nine murders. He was beheaded at 6am on 2 July 1931. He is reported to have said, "I hope I hear my own blood gurgle" as he was led to the guillotine.

Sketch by Kürten indicates where the body of one of his victims could be found.

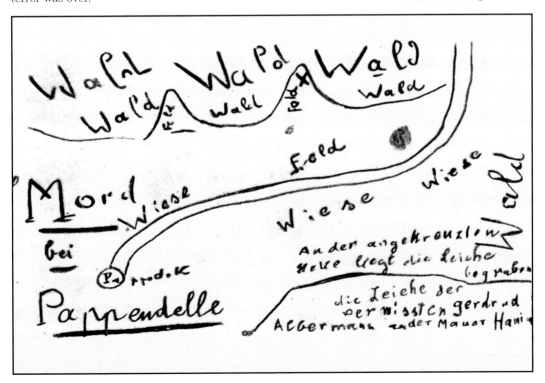

Marie Becker

"I can supply you with a powder that will leave no trace"

WHERE:
Liege, Belgium
WHEN:
1932–September 1936
THE AFTERMATH:
When digitalis was found in all the bodies, Becker was arrested and charged with murder. Found guilty, she was jailed for life.

THE CRIME: Marie Alexandrine Becker was born in 1877 and lived in Liege, Belgium. She married and fell into the stereotypical life of a bored, middle-aged woman in the town. Then one day in 1932, while she was visiting the local market, Lambert Beyer, the local Lothario, chatted her up as she bought vegetables. She was flattered by the attentions of the younger man and they began a passionate affair. Becker decided that, in order to be able to fulfil her dreams and desires, she would need to kill her husband. She made sure that the life insurance was up to date and then gave him a fatal dose of digitalis. Becker spent the insurance money on opening a smart dress shop. She spent all her spare time with her lover until he bored her and in November 1934 she poisoned Beyer with the same drug. He had left Becker money in his will and she had an income from the dress shop but it was not enough to finance her new life of nightclubs gigolos.

At the start of July 1935 Marie Castadot, an elderly friend, fell ill and Becker offered to nurse her. On 23 July Castadot died. Realizing that it was relatively easy to poison, Becker began killing friends and customers – all of whom left Becker a little something in their wills. It is thought that she killed 11 people before a friend

Marie Becker goes on trial in Liege, Belgium.

mentioned that she was being annoyed by her husband and wanted him to go away or die. Becker said, "If you really mean that, I can supply you with a powder that will leave no trace." On 2 October 1936 the police received an anonymous letter telling them that they should take a look at the widow Becker. She was arrested soon after, her house searched and the bodies of her husband, lover and some of her friends and customers were exhumed.

Joe Ball

"Joe...never hurt nobody unless he was driven to it"

THE CRIME: In the days of Prohibition, Joe Ball was a bootlegger but afterwards he became the landlord of The Sociable Inn on Highway 181 in Elmendorf, Texas. The bar had two selling main points – it had the sexiest waitresses in the area and a pool in the backyard in which five alligators lived. Ball would throw them meat or, occasionally, a live cat or dog for the entertainment of his patrons. Ball was born on 7 January 1896 and by the mid 1930s seemed to have a great life – booze, broads and bonhomie. He slept with most of his staff, which probably accounted for the fact that he had been married three times.

When his third wife disappeared in 1937, it was thought that she had left because she had discovered Ball's affair with 22-year-old Hazel "Schatzie" Brown, the latest barmaid to decorate the bar and Joe Ball's bed. Then Hazel vanished, too. Barmaids came and went and no one paid any mind, no one apart from Lee Miller, a Texas Ranger. He wondered why Hazel had told no one she was leaving town and why her bank account was untouched. Then a neighbour reported a terrible smell emanating from a rain barrel near The Sociable Inn.

The police visited the establishment and the proprietor told them that he had no idea where Hazel had gone and that the smell was coming from meat for the alligators. The policemen, John Gray and John Klevenhagen, returned the next day, 24 September 1938, and told Ball that they were taking him to San Antonio for questioning. He asked to shut the bar and walked to the till, pulled out a revolver and, after briefly waving it at the police, shot himself in the head.

A police officer loads alligators into a pickup truck so they can check the contents of their stomachs for human remains.

WHERE:
Elmendorf, Texas, USA
WHEN:
1937
THE AFTERMATH:
At first investigators believed that Joe Ball had killed all the missing barmaids and fed them to his pet alligators. Then police found the third Mrs Ball, alive and well. She had known of the killings and fled, not wanting to be the latest victim. She told police about handyman Clifford Wheeler, and he revealed the story. He took police to the remains of Hazel Brown and Minnie Gotthard, another waitress and Ball bedmate. It is believed that Ball killed up to twenty women but no remains of the rest were ever found. However, none of the rotting flesh in the alligator pond was found to be human. In 1939 Clifton Wheeler was sentenced to two years in prison. In 1957 another lover of Ball said, "[Joe] never put no people in that alligator tank. Joe wouldn't do a thing like that. He wasn't no horrible monster Joe was a sweet, kind, good man, and he never hurt nobody unless he was driven to it."
YOU SHOULD KNOW:
The Tobe Hooper film *Eaten Alive* was inspired by Joe Ball.

Seisaku Nakamura

Fumisada Nakamura took his own life in shame at what his son had done

WHERE:
Shizuoka Prefecture, Japan
WHEN:
1938–1942
THE AFTERMATH:
He was finally arrested on
12 October 1942 and charged with
nine murders, and confessed to two
more. On 11 November 1942 his
father, Fumisada Nakamura, took his
own life in shame at what his son
had done. Despite a plea by his
defence that he was insane,
Nakamura was tried, found guilty
and executed.

THE CRIME: Born profoundly deaf in 1924, Seisaku Nakamura was intelligent but his deafness meant that he had difficulty in communicating with people. His family were also ashamed of him because of the disability. Unable to talk to people, he buried himself in violent culture, spending much of his time watching films, especially enjoying those in which people died after being stabbed by Samurai swords.

He began to fantasize about re-enacting the scenes he watched. On 22 August 1938, when he was 14 years old, he attempted to rape two women but they fought back so he murdered them. Three years later, on 18 August 1941, he committed his third murder and two days later he killed three more people. On 27 September 1941 he murdered his brother, and severely injured his father, sister, sister-in-law and nephew. He kept his urges in check for a year but on 30 August 1942 he murdered a couple, their son and daughter and failed to rape a second daughter before fleeing the scene. As with many other war-time criminals, the chaos caused by the conflict prevented the authorities from stopping Nakamura and the news blackout halted the dissemination of information about his crimes.

Eugene Weidmann

"Remorse, what for? I didn't even know them"

THE CRIME: The last person publicly guillotined in France, Eugene Weidmann was born at Frankfurt-am-Main in Germany on 5 February 1908. A career criminal, he led a gang of teenage thieves before moving to Paris and progressing to more serious crimes, including six murders. He stole cars and, while on test drives, would shoot the owners in the back of the neck. He also strangled one victim. He was arrested on 8 December 1937 after a shoot-out at his home in St Cloud. When asked if he had any remorse for his victims, he replied, "Remorse, what for? I didn't even know them." He confessed to police that he and his confederates had planned to kidnap wealthy people and demand high ransoms.

Two of his accomplices were acquitted but Weidmann and Roger Million were convicted and sentenced to death. Million's sentence was later commuted but at 4.50am on 17 June 1939 Weidmann was beheaded in Rue Georges Clemenceau (in front of the Palais de

Justice), Versailles. The day before every vantage point overlooking the guillotine site was rented out at fantastic prices. From his cell Weidmann could hear the hammering of his guillotine being erected and the laughter of the revellers in cafés, waiting for the entertainment to begin. Even the morning drizzle didn't dampen the enthusiasm. The executioner Henri Desfourneaux, known for being very slow at the job, entered the record books as having officiated at the last public execution in France. It was also his only performance in front of a public audience. He was very nervous.

Dressed in black he set up the guillotine at 3am. Due to delays and miscalculations the decapitation took place in daylight rather than the break of dawn, which allowed photographers to take clear pictures. Weidmann was allowed a few puffs on a cigar and a mouthful of rum in his cell. The bascule, or see-saw plank to which the victim is strapped then tipped and loaded under the blade, had been badly adjusted and it took Desfourneaux three attempts to get Weidmann's neck into the crescent shaped head-holder correctly. Ultimately the assistant executioner had to pull Weidmann forward by his hair and ears. As the blade finally dropped it was accompanied by the eerie whistling sound that is heard at beheadings.

WHERE:
Paris, France
WHEN:
1937
THE AFTERMATH:
The photographs so shocked the public that, a week later, a statute was passed that all executions henceforth would be carried out in private.

Eugene Weidmann being taken to the guillotine. His shirt is pulled down so as not interfere with the blade.

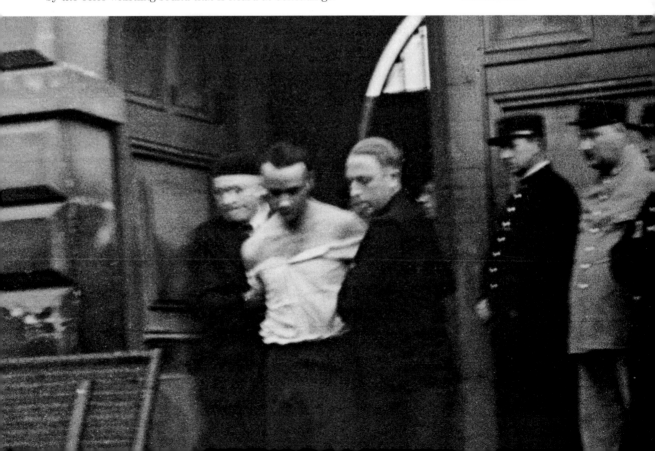

Leonarda Cianciulli

"I was able to make some most acceptable creamy soap"

WHERE:
Correggio, Reggio Emilia, Italy
WHEN:
1939–1940
THE AFTERMATH:
She was arrested after the sister-in-law of her last victim went to the police. Cianciulli readily confessed and was sentenced to 30 years in prison and three years in a criminal asylum. She died of cerebral apoplexy in a Pozzuoli asylum on 15 October 1970.

*Italian serial killer
Leonarda Cianciulli*

THE CRIME: Born on 14 November 1893 at Montella di Avellino, Italy Leonarda Cianciulli had an unhappy childhood. In 1914 she married Raffaele Pansardi, a clerk in the local register office. They made their marital home at Lariano in Alta Irpinia but in 1930 an earthquake destroyed it. They moved to Correggio, in the province of Reggio Emilia. Cianciulli fell pregnant 17 times, suffered three miscarriages and ten of her children died at an early age. The other four Cianciulli protected with the ferocity of a lioness. A gypsy fortune-teller had told her, "You will marry and have children, but all your children will die." She went to another gypsy who told her, "In your right hand I see prison, in your left a criminal asylum."

In 1939, as her eldest son Giuseppe was about to be conscripted, Cianciulli claimed to have been visited by the Virgin Mary who told her to sacrifice humans for her sons. Her first victim was Faustina Setti who was told that a husband had been found for her in Pola. Swearing her to secrecy, Cianciulli persuaded Signorina Setti to write some letters and postcards to her friends and relatives to be posted when she reached Pola. In them, she wrote of her good fortune. But the deluded woman never reached Pola. Cianciulli killed her with an axe and dragged the body into a closet, cut it into nine parts and gathered the blood in a basin. As she later told police, "I threw the pieces into a pot, added seven kilos of caustic soda, which I had bought to make soap, and stirred the whole mixture until the pieces dissolved in a thick, dark mush that I poured into several buckets and emptied in a nearby septic tank. As for the blood in the basin, I waited until it had coagulated, dried it in the oven, ground it and mixed it with flour, sugar, chocolate, milk and eggs, as well as a bit of margarine, kneading all the ingredients together. I made lots of crunchy tea cakes and served them to the ladies who came to visit, though Giuseppe and I also ate them." On 5 September 1940 Cianciulli murdered Francesca Soavi who was promised work at a Piacenza girls' school. She was also convinced to write postcards and then murdered. The third and final victim was Virginia Cacioppo, a 53-year-old former opera singer, who was murdered on 30 September 1940. "She ended up in the pot, like the other two; her flesh was fat and white, when it had melted I added a bottle of cologne, and after a long time on the boil I was able to make some most acceptable creamy soap. I gave bars to neighbours and acquaintances. The cakes, too, were better: that woman was really sweet."

Gordon Cummins

"A savage sexual maniac"

THE CRIME: In 1942 the streets of London were blacked out at night to stop lights giving the German bombers an easy target. It was against his backdrop that 28-year-old RAF aircraftsman Gordon Frederick Cummins took to the streets and began a killing campaign. The first victim was 40-year-old chemist's assistant Evelyn Hamilton whose body was found on 9 February 1942, in an air raid shelter in Montagu Place, Marylebone. She had been strangled and marks on her throat showed that her killer was left-handed. The next night Cummins murdered 35-year-old Evelyn Oatley (also known as Nita Ward), a former showgirl at the Windmill Theatre, at her flat on Wardour Street, Soho. Her throat was cut and she had been mutilated with a tin opener. More left-handed fingerprints were found. The third murder happened the next day, 11 February, when Margaret Florence "Pearl" Lowe, a 43-year-old prostitute, was killed in her flat on Gosfield Street, Marylebone. A silk stocking was tied around her neck and her body was mutilated with a razor blade, a knife and a candlestick. Pathologist Sir Bernard Spilsbury called her attacker "a savage sexual maniac". A few hours later police found a fourth victim – 32-year-old Doris Jouannet (also known as Doris Robson), who had been killed in the two-room flat in Paddington she shared with her husband. Her naked body had been mutilated.

On St Valentine's Day 1942 Cummins attacked Greta Hayward in a doorway near Piccadilly Circus but was disturbed and fled. In his hurry he left his gas mask behind. Cummins then attacked another prostitute, Kathleen King, also known as Mrs Mulcahy, at her flat near Paddington Station. She fought back and Cummins fled, this time leaving behind his RAF uniform belt. The gas mask had the serial number 525987, which was traced to Cummins, who was arrested on 16 February. When his billet in St John's Wood was searched, police found a number of items belonging to his victims.

WHERE:
Montagu Place, London, England
WHEN:
Sunday 9 – Friday 14 February 1942
THE AFTERMATH:
Gordon Cummins was tried at the Old Bailey on 27 April 1942 for the murder for Evelyn Hamilton. The trial was over in a day and the jury took just 30 minutes to return a verdict of guilty. Cummins was hanged at Wandsworth Prison, during an air raid, on 25 June 1942.

Gordon Cummins

Edward Leonski

"I killed! I killed!"

THE CRIME: Born in New York on 12 December 1917, Edward Joseph Leonski was raised in a family beset with alcoholism and mental instability. He joined the US Army in February 1941, nine months before Pearl Harbor. He was posted to Australia and on 2 February 1942 arrived in Melbourne.

His killing began shortly after – on 3 May 40-year-old Ivy Violet McLeod became his first victim. Her corpse was discovered in Albert Park, Melbourne. On 9 May Pauline Thompson, 31, went out on a date with an American GI. That night she was strangled. Nine days later Gladys Hosking, 40, was strangled while walking home from work at the Chemistry Library at Melbourne University. The police got nowhere with their investigation until an observant sentry remembered seeing a dishevelled man returning to camp late on the night of the Hosking murder. His description matched that of the man seen with Pauline Thompson on the night she died. The description matched that of 24-year-old Private Edward Leonski of the 52nd Signal Battalion and he was arrested.

WHERE:
Melbourne, Australia
WHEN:
May 1942
THE AFTERMATH:
Leonski had already said to a friend, "I'm a Dr Jekyll and Mr Hyde! I killed! I killed!" At his court martial on 17 July 1942 Leonski confessed and said he killed the women "to get their voices". He said that Pauline Thompson had sung to him as he walked her home and she had a beautiful voice, "I could feel myself going mad about it." On 1 November 1942 Leonski was sentenced to death. He was hanged at Pentridge Prison eight days later. In the hours before his death, Leonoski had been heard singing to himself in his cell.
YOU SHOULD KNOW:
Leonski was only the second American serviceman executed during the Second World War.

The angelic face of Edward Leonski

Marcel Petiot

"Gentlemen, I ask you not to look. This will not be very pretty"

THE CRIME: Born at Auxerre, France at 3am on 17 January 1897, Marcel André Henri Félix Petiot was a disruptive child with a streak of cruelty towards animals – he was seen blinding birds with needles. In January 1916 he was conscripted into the French army. He stole drugs to sell to addicts. Back in civvy street, he qualified as a doctor on 15 December 1921. He began to practise in Villeneuve-sur-Yonne and rose in the civic community to become the mayor on 25 July 1926, despite his kleptomania being well known. He took mistresses – one disappeared and one was found battered to death but no one moved against Petiot. In January 1933 Petiot opened a new practice at 66 Rue Caumartin in Paris where he dealt in drugs and performed illegal abortions as a sideline.

In 1940 the Germans occupied the French capital and Petiot moved to 21 Rue Le Sueur. Here he pretended to be a member of the French Resistance and offered to move wealthy French Jews to safety for 25,000 francs. Dozens took him up on this and were never seen again. Petiot told people to bring their belongings to his house after dark and there gave them an injection against a disease he claimed was endemic in the country he was sending them to. Leaving them, he watched their death throes through a small peephole in the wall. In March 1944 Petiot's neighbour Jacques Marcais complained of a foul-smelling smoke emanating from the doctor's house. When the police and fire brigade broke in on 11 March they found a human arm in a furnace plus piles of bones and bits of bodies in the cellar. In the garage, buried in quicklime, were scalps and jawbones. Petiot had left a note attached to the front door, saying he would be away for a month, and a warrant was issued for his arrest.

WHERE:
21 Rue Le Sueur, Paris, France
WHEN:
1944
THE AFTERMATH:
At his brother Maurice's house in Auxerre, Petiot had stashed 49 suitcases containing the possessions of his victims. They contained 115 shirts, 79 dresses and 66 pairs of shoes. Thanks to the confusion caused by the D-Day landings, Petiot remained at large until 2 November 1944. He confessed to killing 63 people but claimed that they were all Nazi collaborators. The suitcases told a different story. His trial opened on 18 March 1946. Marcel Petiot was found guilty of 27 murders at midnight on 5 April 1946. At 5.05am on 25 May 1946 he was guillotined. As he approached he said to the witnesses, "Gentlemen, I ask you not to look. This will not be very pretty." On 5 July 1952 an architect bought 21 Rue Le Sueur and gutted the property.

Dr Marcel Petiot on trial. Behind him are the suitcases, reported to belong to his victims.

Caroline Grills

"A killer who poisoned for sport, for fun"

WHERE:
Balmain, Sydney, New South Wales,
Australia
WHEN:
1947
THE AFTERMATH:
On 15 October 1953 she was found guilty of attempted murder and sentenced to death. The jury had taken 12 minutes to find her guilty of murder. Senior Crown Prosecutor Mick Rooney, QC, said that she was "a killer who poisoned for sport, for fun, for the kicks she got out of it, for the hell of it, for the thrill that she, and she alone, in the world knew the cause of the victims' suffering." Although the Court of Criminal Appeal dismissed her appeal in April 1954, her sentence was commuted to life imprisonment. She was admitted to the State Reformatory for Women where she was to stay for the next six and a half years. On 6 October 1960 she died of peritonitis at Prince Henry Hospital.
YOU SHOULD KNOW:
In prison she was nicknamed Aunt Thally by the other inmates.

THE CRIME: Murderers come in all shapes and sizes. Caroline Mickelson was born in 1888 in Balmain, Sydney, Australia and on 22 April 1908 she married labourer Richard William Grills, by whom she had five sons and a daughter. By the 1940s she was the proverbial little old lady, short and dumpy with thick-rimmed glasses. But in 1947 Caroline Grills began to kill people.

That year, her 87-year-old stepmother fell ill – the two women had never been close – and died. Shortly after, another octogenarian, Angelina Thomas, also became sick and died. Mary Anne Mickelson was the next, followed by John Lundberg, the brother-in-law of Mrs Grills's husband. He fell ill, his hair fell out and then in October 1948 he died. Caroline Grills cared for all the victims, taking great delight in sitting with them as they drank cups of tea she had prepared. Then John Lundberg's widow, Eveline, and daughter, Christine Downey, became very sick and their hair began to fall out. They began to recover when they stopped visiting the woman they called "Aunt Carrie". In 1953 Sydney was in the grip of thallium panic. Forty-six cases of poisoning involving the extremely toxic metal, normally used in rat poison and insecticides, had come to light.

The son-in-law of one of the intended victims became suspicious and, after visiting Grills, kept some of the tea she had prepared. He took it to the police who tested it and found it was laced with a potentially fatal dose of thallium. Police charged Grills with four murders and one attempted murder.

Thallium poisoner, Caroline Grills

John Haigh

"How can you prove murder if there is no body?"

THE CRIME: John George "Sonnie" Haigh was born, an only child, on 24 July 1909 and brought up in a religious atmosphere (both parents were members of the Plymouth Brethren) but as an adult he became lazy and indolent, relying on petty crime to finance his lifestyle. On 6 July 1934 he married Beatrice Hamer but left her when he was jailed for fraud on 22 November of that year. In 1944 he moved into the Onslow Court Hotel, Queens Gate, West London where he was a popular resident. He rented a basement workroom at 79 Gloucester Road where he worked on "inventions".

On 9 September 1944 he murdered Donald McSwann at 79 Gloucester Road and then extorted money from his victim's parents, before killing them on 2 July 1945. On 12 February 1948 he lured Dr Archie Henderson and his wife, Rosalie, to his "factory" (in reality a storeroom for Hurstlea Products, to which he had access) in Leopold Road, Crawley where he murdered them. He turned his attention to Olive Henrietta Helen Olivia Durand-Deacon, a wealthy 69-year-old widow who lived at the hotel. They discussed going into business together to manufacture fake fingernails and on 18 February 1949 they went to his "factory" where he shot her in the back of the head. As he had done with all his victims, Haigh put her body into a vat of sulphuric acid. Two days later, he expressed concern for Durand-Deacon and went to the police with another hotel resident, Constance Lane. Meanwhile, he pawned or sold her jewellery.

Suspicious of his glib manner, police searched his "factory" and found a cleaning docket for one of Mrs Durand-Deacon's coats. Her stolen jewellery was also traced. On 28 February Haigh was arrested at 4.15pm. He boasted, "Mrs Durand-Deacon no longer exists... I've destroyed her with acid... How can you prove murder if there is no body?" However, there is no need to produce a body to prove that a murder has been committed. In any case, Haigh was wrong. Pathologist Keith Simpson found several body parts among the sludge from the acid, including 11.4 kg (28 lb) of fat, a pelvis, an ankle, three gallstones and false teeth.

Professor Keith Simpson and his secretary Jean Scott-Dunn search for remains at Hurstlea Products.

WHERE:
79 Gloucester Road, London; Hurstlea Products, Leopold Road, Crawley, West Sussex, England
WHEN:
Sunday 9 September 1944 – Friday 18 February 1949
THE AFTERMATH:
Haigh's trial opened at Lewes Assizes on 18 July 1949. He pleaded insanity and claimed to have drunk his victims' blood. The jury did not believe him and took just 17 minutes to find him guilty. Albert Pierrepoint hanged Haigh at Wandsworth Prison on 10 August 1949.

Joseph Taborsky with his mother, Mabel

Joseph "Mad Dog" Taborsky

"I'm not even going to get a parking ticket"

THE CRIME: With his backward friend, Arthur Culombe, Joseph Taborsky robbed small shops, often killing their owners and whichever customers were unfortunate enough to be present at the time. He also raped numerous women and strangled six of them. Taborsky's reign of terror lasted just ten weeks. Taborsky is the only convict sent to death row not once, but twice, for different crimes.

At 14 Taborsky was sent to a borstal and grew to be 1.93 m (6 ft 4 in) tall. In 1950, on his 25th birthday, he murdered shop owner Louis Wolfson in West Hartford, Connecticut. His accomplice was his younger brother, Albert, who turned state's evidence and received a life sentence. Joseph was sentenced to death. He spent four years and four months on death row but was reprieved because the only witness – brother Albert – had been committed to an insane asylum. He left death row in early October 1955 and said, "You can't beat the law. From now on, I'm not even going to get a parking ticket."

He left the state for Brooklyn but often returned to visit his mother, Mabel. Taborsky then hooked up with Arthur Culombe and they began their crime spree. They committed several burglaries before becoming killers. At 6pm on 15 December 1956 Taborsky and Culombe robbed and shot Nickola Leone at his tailor shop on Zion Street in Hartford. An hour later they shot petrol station owner Edward Kurpewski, 30, in the back of the head after forcing him to kneel in the toilet. Daniel Janowski pulled into the garage at that time and was dragged out of the car by Taborsky, who shot him twice in the head.

Six days later the pair robbed the grocers belonging to 64-year-old Arthur Vinton and his wife, 62. On Boxing Day 1956 Samuel Cohn was found shot to death behind the counter of his East Hartford shop. The till was open and empty. Just after 7pm on 5 January 1957 the pair pistol-whipped shoe shop owner Frank Adinolfi after asking to see a pair of size 12 dress shoes. As Taborsky was raiding the till, a couple walked in. Bernard, 47, and Ruth Speyer, 45, were both shot behind the right ear. Mr Adinolfi lived and his statement about the large shoe size led police to check records for villains with big feet. The last killing came on 26 January 1957 when Taborsky and Culombe shot chemist John M. Rosenthal, 69, twice in the chest at his shop on Maple Avenue, Hartford shortly after 9pm.

WHERE:
Connecticut, USA
THE TIME AND PLACE:
1950–1957
THE AFTERMATH:
Taborsky and Culombe were arrested on 23 February 1957 and three days later Culombe confessed. Both men were sentenced to death on 27 June 1957. Culombe appealed and his sentence was commuted to life behind bars. On 17 May 1960 Taborsky, 35, ate a large banana split, drank a cherry soda and smoked cigarettes before being executed in the electric chair. That day Taborsky became the 73rd convict to die since Connecticut introduced capital punishment in 1894.
YOU SHOULD KNOW:
Taborsky donated his body to Yale Medical School.

Henry Lee Lucas

"I am not a serial killer"

THE CRIME: Most, but not all, serial killers act alone. When Henry Lee Lucas joined forces with Ottis Toole they became among the most deadly serial killers of all. They originally claimed to have murdered more than 600 people but then recanted their confessions. How many victims they actually killed is unknown. Lucas insisted, "I am not a serial killer." He was born the son of alcoholic bootleggers on 23 August 1936 in Blackburg, Virginia. His prostitute mother, Viola, detested him and made his childhood a misery. She even allowed him to play with a knife, which resulted in him losing an eye. At the behest of "Uncle Bernie", he began having sex with animals progressing, at 14, in March 1951 to trying to rape 17-year-old Laura Burnley but she fought him off so he killed her. He was jailed in June 1954 for burglary and released on 2 September 1959. On 11 January 1960 he murdered his 74-year-old mother and then raped her corpse. He was sent to a hospital for the criminally insane and released on 3 June 1970. He was back in jail from December 1971 to August 1975.

At the end of 1976 he met homosexual arsonist Toole, 29, who had a low IQ and they became lovers. Lucas moved in with Toole's family and took an interest in his mentally retarded, 10-year-old niece, Frieda Powell, who preferred to be called Becky. They began a sexual relationship. In January 1982 they ran away together to California and then to Texas before moving around the States. On 24 August they had an argument and 15-year-old Becky slapped Lucas's face. He stabbed her to death and cut up her body. Arrested on 11 June 1983, Lucas confessed to a litany of murders, implicating Toole who was then in a Florida jail. Many of their "victims" turned out to be alive and Lucas confessed to crimes in Spain and Japan even though it is thought he never left the USA.

WHERE:
Virginia; California; Texas, USA
WHEN:
1951–1982
THE AFTERMATH:
Lucas was sentenced to death for the murder of a female hitchhiker, nicknamed Orange Socks, those being the only items on her body when it was found at Williamson County, Texas, on Halloween 1979. However, Texas Attorney General Dan Morales believed it was "highly unlikely" that Lucas was involved in the murder. Toole's death sentence was commuted to life in prison and he died of liver failure on 15 September 1996. On 26 June 1998 Governor George W. Bush commuted Lucas's sentence to life imprisonment with no possibility of parole. Lucas died from heart failure on 13 March 2001.

Fantasist killer Henry Lee Lucas is arrested in Texas.

Delfina & María de Jesús González

"Bordello from hell"

WHERE:
San Francisco del Rincon, Mexico
WHEN:
1954–1964
THE AFTERMATH:
The sisters – known as *Las Poquianchis* – were finally arrested and stood trial in 1964. They were each sentenced to 40 years in prison. Delfina died while incarcerated but María was released and faded into obscurity.
YOU SHOULD KNOW:
A film entitled *Las Poquianchis*, starring Diana Bracho, Jorge Martinez de Hoyos, Tina Romero, Salvador Sanchez and Pilar Pellicer was released in 1977.

THE CRIME: Delfina (born 1909) and María de Jesús González (born 1924) were sisters who ran a brothel, Rancho El Ángel, near the town of San Francisco del Rincon, 300 km (200 mi) north of Mexico City. The sisters kidnapped girls to work in their establishment; many were runaway teenagers who were cajoled into the bordello with promises of money and safety. Once ensconced, they were drugged to keep them compliant. Clients also regularly raped them. When the girls lost their looks, became too difficult or customers no longer took an interest in them, the sisters murdered them. The sisters also murdered a number of customers who had come to the brothel with large sums of money.

The police were puzzled by the disappearance of so many girls but for a long time did not link them to the "bordello from hell". One day Josefina Gutiérrez, a woman well known in the world of drugs and prostitution, was arrested with a cargo of dozens of young girls. In custody, she confessed that the girls were bound for the Rancho El Ángel. The police raided the ranch but the González sisters had fled, leaving behind a number of drugged girls looked after by a cabal of thugs. They also found the bodies of 11 men, 80 women and several foetuses.

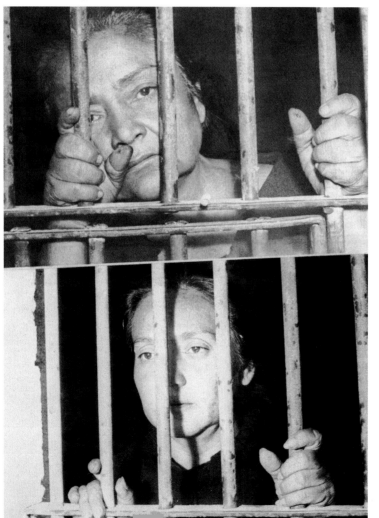

Delfina, top, and María de Jesús González look out from behind prison bars.

382

Peter Manuel

"Turn up the radio and I'll go quietly"

THE CRIME: Born in Manhattan, USA on 1 March 1927, Peter Manuel was a petty criminal who evolved into a serial killer before ending his life at the end of a rope at the age of 31. The family moved to Coventry, England in 1932 and then to Birkenshaw in Lanarkshire. Peter, the middle child, was soon in trouble. By the age of ten, he was known to police as a petty thief. The following year, he was put on probation for burgling a shop. He soon began to specialize in burglary and ended up in borstal. Freed, he took to roaming the fields where he stabbed any animal unfortunate enough to cross his path. After puberty, he began assaulting girls but was not arrested. He broke into a house and pulled down a woman's knickers before attacking her with a hammer. He committed the same outrage on a pregnant woman but did not rape her, either. Caught, he was sentenced to nine years in Peterhead Prison.

On 1 January 1956 he killed 17-year-old Anne Kneilands and left her half-naked body on a golf course in East Kilbride, Scotland. Eight months later on 17 September Manuel broke into the Watt household at 5 Fennsbank Avenue, Burnside, Rutherglen. He shot in the head disabled Marion Watt, 45, her 16-year-old daughter Vivienne and her aunt Margaret Brown, 41, and then helped himself to some food before leaving. Marion's husband, William, was charged with the murders and remanded at Barlinnie jail. Meantime, Manuel was imprisoned in the same jail for robbing a colliery and he wrote to Mr Watt's lawyer telling him that another prisoner had confessed to the murders. When he revealed that each woman had been shot twice – information not released to the public – William Watt was released. Manuel gained his freedom in November 1957.

On 28 December he murdered 17-year-old Isabelle Cooke on her way home to Carrick Drive, Mount Vernon, Glasgow. Just over a week later, on 6 January 1958, he broke into the home of Peter Smart at 38 Sheepburn Road, Uddingston. He shot Mr Smart, his wife, Doris, and their 11-year old son, Michael. Mrs Smart's clothes had been disturbed but she had not been sexually assaulted. Downstairs, Manuel helped himself to some food and fed the family cat. It was the local villains and landlords who turned Manuel in, disgusted by his actions.

Serial killer Peter Manuel

WHERE:
Glasgow, Scotland
WHEN:
1956–1958
THE AFTERMATH:
When the police arrested Manuel on 13 January 1958 he blamed another villain but confessed when his parents were brought to see him. On 12 May 1958 Manuel appeared at the North Court in Glasgow. The trial lasted 12 days and Manuel conducted his own defence. When the judge Lord Cameron summed up, he instructed the jury to find Manuel not guilty of the murder of Anne Kneilands and then praised Manuel's defence as "quite remarkable". The jury returned with seven guilty verdicts and Manuel was sentenced to death. As he awaited his execution, Manuel confessed to another nine murders and then swallowed disinfectant in a failed suicide bid. On 11 July he was hanged. His last words were: "Turn up the radio and I'll go quietly."
YOU SHOULD KNOW:
Manuel told police that he had thrown his guns – a Webley revolver and a Beretta automatic – into the River Clyde. The police used divers for the first time to retrieve the weapons.

A police officer examines the junk-littered kitchen at the home of Edward Gein.

Ed Gein

"Edward Gein had two faces. One he showed to his neighbours. The other he showed only to the dead"

THE CRIME: Edward Theodore Gein – the inspiration for *Psycho*, *The Texas Chain Saw Massacre* and Buffalo Bill in *The Silence of the Lambs* – lived with his father, George, brother, Henry, and overpowering mother, Augusta, on their farm in Plainville, Wisconsin. In 1914 Augusta Gein had moved her family onto a 79-hectare (195-acre) farm because she feared the "moral depravity" of the locals would affect her beloved sons – and they stayed in splendid isolation for 25 years. George Gein died on 1 April 1940. Henry Gein died in a brush fire on the farm on 16 May 1944, leaving Ed and Augusta together – they often shared a bed. Augusta died on 29 December 1945 and he kept her room exactly as she had left it (although he did not keep her corpse – that was a Hollywood invention).

Gein began to dig up dead people to study them and cut off, and kept, bits of their bodies. He liked to create "clothes" from their skin and would often wear them around his by now filthy home. In 1954 dead people no longer sated his lust and he began to murder to get fresh flesh. On 16 November 1957 Bernice Worden, a 58-year-old widow, disappeared from her hardware shop. Gein had been asking about her, which aroused the suspicion of the police.

When they went to question him, he was not at home so the police entered the property. They were horrified by what they saw at his farmhouse. There were parts from at least 15 bodies in his fridge, skulls decorated a bed, lampshades were made from human skin, a belt was studded with nipples, a patchwork shirt was made of human skin, there was a shoebox of human noses and female genitalia and on the kitchen stove was a heart in a pan. Also in the kitchen was a naked, headless female torso – later identified as Bernice Worden. Gein initially denied any knowledge of the happenings at his house, later confessing to 11 counts of grave robbery when he was arrested. He was committed to an institution for the criminally insane on 23 November 1957. Two days after his incarceration a local newspaper opined, "Edward Gein had two faces. One he showed to his neighbours. The other he showed only to the dead."

WHERE:
Plainville, Wisconsin, USA
WHEN:
Saturday 16 November 1957
THE AFTERMATH:
On 27 March 1958 his farm mysteriously burned down as it was being prepared for auction. Having been judged competent to stand trial, Gein finally had his day in court on 7 November 1968. A week later, on 14 November, Gein was found guilty of first-degree murder and returned to the institution. In February 1974 he was refused a hearing to show that he was sane, pending release from the institution. He died, still incarcerated, on 26 July 1984.

Eric Edgar Cooke

The Night Caller

THE CRIME: Like many serial killers, Eric Edgar Cooke (born 25 February 1931 at Victoria Park, Perth, Australia) was short. He began his career as a petty criminal. Cooke, married with seven children, decided to supplement his daily income as a forklift truck driver by becoming a nocturnal burglar, earning him the nickname "The Night Caller". He found that he liked the thrill of burglary but preferred to mix it with violence.

On 30 January 1959 he stabbed Pnena Berkman, a South Perth beautician. On 20 December he killed Jillian Brewster, 22. In the early hours of 27 January 1963 he shot a couple as they sat in their car at Cottlesloe. He then moved to Perth were he murdered three people: an accountant, 18-year-old student John Lindsay Sturkey and a retired grocer. A fortnight later there were two more murders and Brian William Robinson was charged with both, tried for one and hanged. On 16 February 1963 Cooke strangled a female social worker in West Perth. Perth became a city of fear, exacerbated on 10 August when 19-year-old Shirley McLeod was shot in the head while babysitting. The police discovered that the murder weapon was a .22 rifle and test-fired 60,000 guns looking for the murder weapon. By chance, a member of the public found such a weapon hidden in bushes in Mount Pleasant on 17 August. Police waited for someone to retrieve it and on 1 September Cooke showed up and was taken into custody.

WHERE:
Perth, Western Australia, Australia
WHEN:
1959–1963
THE AFTERMATH:
Cooke went on trial in the Perth Supreme Court on 25 November 1963 for the murder of John Sturkey. His defence claimed that he was schizophrenic and could not tell the difference between right and wrong. They claimed that he was beaten up by his father and was bullied at school because of a cleft palate and hare lip. The trial lasted three days and he was found guilty of murder and sentenced to death on 27 November. On 26 October 1964 he was hanged on the gallows at Fremantle Prison. Cooke's body was buried in an unmarked pauper's grave at Fremantle Cemetery on top of child-killer Martha Rendell, who was hanged in Fremantle Prison in 1909. Cooke was the last person to be legally hanged for wilful murder in Western Australia.
YOU SHOULD KNOW:
Cooke confessed to more than 200 thefts, five hit-and-run offences against young women, and two murders for which John Button and Darryl Raymond Beamish had been wrongly jailed. It was not until 2002 and April 2005 respectively that their convictions were quashed.

Eric Cooke points to the spot where he said he hit one of his victims, Rosemary Anderson.

385

William "the Mutilator" MacDonald

"The case of the walking corpse"

WHERE:
Sydney, Australia
WHEN:
1960–April 1963
THE AFTERMATH:
McCarthy went to the police who did not believe him so he went to the *Daily Mirror* who ran the story under the headline "The case of the walking corpse". MacDonald was arrested and went on trial in September 1963. He was found guilty but the jury rejected his claim of insanity and he was jailed for life.
YOU SHOULD KNOW:
In 2000 MacDonald refused to apply for parole. "I am institutionalized now. I have no desire to go and live on the outside. I wouldn't last five minutes. I am too old and besides, I have everything I could ever want where I am." That same year he gave an interview to a journalist and opined, "It's terrible out there. People aren't even safe in their own homes."

William MacDonald with Sydney detectives.

THE CRIME: Short (1.67 m/5 ft 6 in), thin and shy, William MacDonald was born in Liverpool, England, in 1924 as Allan Ginsberg. During the Second World War he served with the Lancashire Fusiliers where a corporal raped him in an air-raid shelter in 1943. The incident laid bare his latent homosexuality and he began a lifetime of "cottaging". In 1949 he emigrated to Canada and then six years later relocated to East Sydney, Australia, where he changed his name to William MacDonald.

He was soon arrested for chatting up a policeman in a public convenience and received a conditional discharge for two years. In 1960, outside the Roma Street Transit Centre in Brisbane, he met Amos Hurst, 55. The two men went drinking in a local pub before retiring to Hurst's home where MacDonald strangled him. His death was reported as accidental. In January 1961 MacDonald moved to Sydney where he became well known in the homosexual *milieu*. On 4 June 1961 police were called to Sydney Domain Baths where the naked corpse of Alfred Reginald Greenfield, 41, was found. He had been stabbed 30 times and his genitals had been cut off and thrown into Sydney Harbour. The press dubbed the killer the "Sydney Mutilator". MacDonald struck again, stabbing 55-year-old William Cobbin and removing his genitals. His remains were found in a public toilet at Moore Park. At 10.50pm on 31 March 1962 Frank Gladstone McLean was murdered in Bourke Lane, Darlinghurst and, he too, had his genitals sliced off. MacDonald put them in a plastic bag and took them with him.

MacDonald, using the name Alan Edward Brennan, was sacked from his post office job and fell out with his landlord. He bought a small shop in Burwood, New South Wales that came with accommodation. In November 1962 MacDonald met ex-con James Hackett, a thief and tramp, 42, in a wine bar in Pitt Street, Sydney. They returned to MacDonald's home where he stabbed Hackett in a homicidal frenzy but the knife was too blunt to remove the genitals. He put the corpse in the basement and concerned he would get caught, fled to Brisbane. The smell led to the police being called and a badly decomposed body was found. Everyone assumed it was Alan Brennan (MacDonald's alias). A memorial service was held and attended by several of his workmates. MacDonald was a free man but his urge to kill made him return to Sydney. On 22 April 1963 he bumped into an old friend, John McCarthy, on Pitt Street who told him what had happened and MacDonald fled to Melbourne.

Boston Strangler

There was not one iota of physical evidence to link DeSalvo to the killings

THE CRIME: The Boston Strangler is one of America's most famous killers – he is also a mystery. The first killing was that of divorcée Anna E. Slesers, 55, on 14 June 1962 on Gainsborough Street, Boston. She was strangled with the cord of her blue dressing gown and sexually assaulted. Two weeks later the oldest victim Mary Mullen, 85, died from a heart attack during an attack. On 30 June there was a double killing: Nina Nicols, 68, and Helen Blake, 65, were both sexually molested and strangled with their own nylon stockings. On 19 August Ida Irga, 75, became the fifth victim, followed the next day by Jane Sullivan, 67, who was found slumped over the bath. On 5 December Sophie Clark, 19, became the first black victim when she was strangled with her stockings and sexually assaulted.

On New Year's Eve Patricia Bissette, 23, was victim number eight. Unlike the other victims she was not left displayed nude but laid out on her bed with a blanket up to her chin. On 9 March 1963 Mary Brown, 69, was stabbed and beaten to death. On 6 May Beverly Samans, 23, was stabbed 22 times. On 8 September Evelyn Corbin, 58, was raped and strangled with her nylon stockings. The penultimate victim was Joann Graff, 23, who was murdered on 23 November.

The last and youngest victim was Mary Sullivan, 19, who was murdered on 4 January 1964. When her body was discovered, a broomstick was poking out of her vagina and a New Year card was wedged between the toes of her left foot. On 27 October another woman was attacked and this led to the identification of Albert DeSalvo, a 33-year-old rapist. However, the police did not regard DeSalvo as a suspect.

Eight of the Boston victims. Top, from left to right: Rachel Lazarus, Helen Blake, Ida Irga, J. Delaney. Bottom: Patricia Bissette, Daniela Saunders, Mary Sullivan and Israel Goldberg

WHERE:
Boston, Massachusetts, USA
WHEN:
Thursday 14 June 1962 – Saturday 4 January 1964
THE AFTERMATH:
It was not until 3 November 1965, when DeSalvo was held on a rape charge, that he gave a detailed confession to the Boston stranglings. However, there was not one iota of physical evidence to link DeSalvo to the killings. His lawyer F. Lee Bailey engineered that DeSalvo was tried not as the Boston Strangler but as The Green Man and The Measuring Man, identities under which he had committed earlier crimes. In 1967 DeSalvo was sentenced to life in prison. He was murdered in prison on 26 November 1973. Doubts exist as to whether DeSalvo was the Strangler and lawyers working on behalf of his family are attempting to prove his innocence.

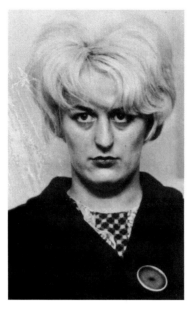

The iconic images of Ian Brady and Myra Hindley, issued at the time of their arrest.

Moors Murders

"It's the messiest yet. It normally only takes one blow"

THE CRIME: The most chilling murders of the 1960s still reverberate today. Myra Hindley and her boyfriend, Ian Brady, committed such vile acts that their names have become bywords for evil incarnate.

Hindley began work at Millwards, a chemical firm, on 16 January 1961 and at the office Christmas party on 22 December became involved with a colleague Ian Brady, a 23-year-old, illegitimate Scotsman with an interest in Nazism, Nietzsche and the Marquis de Sade. Hindley dyed her dark hair peroxide blonde to please her new boyfriend. Two years later, on 12 July 1963 Hindley lured 16-year-old Pauline Reade, whom she knew, into Brady's car and drove the teenager to Saddleworth Moor. Hindley told the innocent child that she had lost a glove and promised her records if she would help find it. Brady arrived on a motorbike and raped Pauline before cutting her throat. They buried her body on the moor. On 23 November 1963 they kidnapped and murdered 12-year-old John Kilbride and buried him on the moor too. On 16 June 1964, four days after his 12th birthday, they abducted Keith Bennett. He, too, was raped, murdered and buried on the moor. On 26 December 1964 they kidnapped 10-year-old Lesley Ann Downey. Brady took pornographic photographs of the little girl and then they taped themselves torturing her. Then Brady raped Lesley Ann and either he or Hindley strangled her to death.

The couple began to think they were invincible and boasted about their foul deeds to family and friends. They told Hindley's brother-in-law, David Smith, who did not believe them. On 6 October 1965 Hindley took Smith to their house at 16 Wardle Brook Avenue, Hattersley, and there he witnessed them butcher 17-year-old homosexual Edward Evans. Brady said, "It's done. It's the messiest yet. It normally only takes one blow." Smith went to the police and the pair was arrested. At their trial at Chester Assizes they tried to blame Smith but the evidence was overwhelming and both were convicted of murder on 6 May 1966 and sentenced to life imprisonment. The trial judge had ordered all women to leave the court while the Lesley Ann Downey tape was played.

WHERE:
Saddleworth Moor, off the A635, Oldham, Lancashire; 16 Wardle Brook Avenue, Hattersley, England

WHEN:
Friday 12 July 1963–Wednesday 6 October 1965

THE AFTERMATH:
Ian Brady has stated that he never wants to be released from prison. Myra Hindley had several lesbian affairs while incarcerated and mounted many bids for freedom. All were turned down. She died of a heart attack on 15 November 2002, aged 60. The bodies of Lesley Ann Downey and John Kilbride were recovered from Saddleworth Moor on 16 October and 21 October 1965 respectively. Pauline Reade's body was found on 1 July 1987. The body of Keith Bennett has never been found. In the autumn of 1987 16 Wardle Brook Avenue was demolished.

Jack the Stripper

Her knickers were in her mouth and her stockings around her ankles

THE CRIME: Jack the Stripper murdered six prostitutes from the Notting Hill–Bayswater area of west London. They were all between 1.52 and 1.6 m (5 ft and 5 ft 3 in) tall, they had all suffered from some form of venereal disease, they all disappeared between 11pm and 1am and their bodies were thought to have been dumped between 5am and 6am.

The first victim was 30-year-old Hannah Tailford whose naked body was found under a pontoon by Hammersmith Bridge by two brothers preparing for a weekend's sailing. Her knickers were in her mouth and her stockings around her ankles. At the autopsy it was discovered she was pregnant. Victim number two was Irene Lockwood, whose naked body was found at 8.30am on 8 April 1964 about 270 m (300 yd) from where Hannah Tailford's body had been found. She had appeared in porn films and, like Hannah Tailford, Lockwood was pregnant when she was murdered. On 24 April 1964 the body of convent-educated Helene Barthelemey, 22, was discovered in Brentford. She was naked and four of her front teeth were missing. There were traces of spray paint on her body and sperm in her throat. Victim number four was Mary Fleming, 30, on 14 July 1964. Her false teeth were missing; she had paint on her body and sperm in her mouth. Four months later, 21-year-old Margaret McGowan was found naked in a car parked near High Street Kensington Tube. Again there were traces of paint on her body and sperm in her mouth. The final victim was 27-year-old Bridie O'Hara, discovered on 16 February 1965 behind a shed on the Westpoint Trading Estate. Again there was sperm in her mouth and some of her teeth were missing.

Police discovered that paint flecks on the women's bodies matched those of a paint spraying shop on the Heron Factory Estate. It was likely that this was where the women had been kept prior to their corpses being dumped. It seemed that the women had all choked to death while performing fellatio on their killer.

WHERE:
London; Brentford, Middlesex, England

WHEN:
Sunday 2 February 1964 – Tuesday 16 February 1965

THE AFTERMATH:
John du Rose, in charge of the case, announced that 20 suspects had been whittled down to three. One of them, a married security guard from Putney committed suicide in June 1965, saying that he could not "stand the strain any longer". However, despite intensive searches of the man's home police found nothing to link him to any of the murders. Two unlikely suspects were the boxer Freddie Mills and Tommy Butler, the detective who investigated the Great Train Robbery (see page 279). However, there is no real evidence linking either Mills or Butler to the murders, which remain unsolved.

Westpoint Trading Estate, where the body of Bridie O'Hara was found.

TOWN OF RAMSGATE
CHARRINGTON

Edmund Kemper

"I just wondered how it would feel to shoot grandma"

WHERE:
California, USA
WHEN:
Thursday 27 August 1964–Friday
20 April 1973

THE AFTERMATH:
Kemper eventually telephoned the police to confess that he was the killer they were seeking but they refused to believe him and he had to persist before he was arrested. He was tried at Santa Cruz on 23 October 1973. On 8 November the six-man, six-woman jury deliberated for five hours before finding Kemper sane and guilty of eight counts of first-degree murder. Kemper told the judge that he wanted to be tortured to death. He was sent to Folsom Prison for life where he became a model prisoner, helping to read books on tape for the blind.

YOU SHOULD KNOW:
After killing his mother, Kemper cut out her vocal chords and tried to get rid of them in the waste disposal unit but they would not go down. He said, "That seemed appropriate as much as she'd bitched and screamed and yelled at me over so many years."

Edmund Kemper being escorted into court.

THE CRIME: Born in Burbank, California on 18 December 1948, as a young child Edmund Emil Kemper III tortured and killed animals. His mother was disturbed and made Kemper sleep in a locked cellar. His first killing occurred on 27 August 1964 when he visited his grandmother, Maude, 66, at her 7-hectare (17-acre) ranch in North Fork and shot her at her kitchen table. When his grandfather, Edmund I, 72, returned home, Kemper killed him as well. He telephoned his mother to tell her what he had done. He told police "I just wondered how it would feel to shoot grandma."

The 15-year-old was committed to Atascadero State Hospital but was released in 1969 despite the advice of his doctors who felt he still presented a danger. Despite having a near genius level IQ, Kemper worked at a series of menial jobs. By now Kemper stood 2 m (6 ft 9 in) and weighed more than 134 kg (294 lb). On 7 May 1972 Kemper murdered Anita Luchese and Mary Anne Pesce, two students at Fresno State College, Berkeley, after offering them a lift while they were hitchhiking. He stabbed them and took them back home where he had sex with their corpses. On 14 September he abducted 15-year-old Japanese schoolgirl, Aiko Koo, before suffocating her, having sex with her corpse, taking her home, decapitating her and having sex again with the headless body. He then cut her up and buried the body parts in the mountains near Boulder Creek.

Cynthia "Cindy" Schall was his fourth victim. He shot her on 8 January 1973, abused her corpse, cut her up in the shower and threw her off the cliffs at Carmel. There was another double killing on 5 February 1973 when he shot Rosalind Thorpe and Alice Liu but when he returned home, his mother was there so he had to decapitate them in the boot of his car. On Good Friday he murdered his mother and decapitated her. When her friend Sarah "Sally" Hallett came over for tea that day, he murdered her too before having sex with her corpse.

Patrick Kearney

"Trash bag murders"

THE CRIME: The killings began in 1965 and became known as the "trash bag murders" because the victims were often found in trash bags. Texan Patrick Wayne Kearney was 25 years old when he committed his first killing, a hitchhiker he murdered in Orange, California. Two years later, after more killings, Kearney relocated to Redondo Beach, near Los Angeles with his new boyfriend David Douglas Hill, whom he had met five years earlier. The pair had a tempestuous relationship and after an argument Kearney would get in his car and find a man to kill.

His victims, primarily gay, would be collected from gay bars or would be hitchhikers Kearney saw on the roadside. Kearney shot his victims without warning and then had sex with their corpses. The case officially began on 13 April 1975 when the body of 21-year-old Alberto Rivera was found near San Luis Capistrano. In the next seven months six more bodies were discovered in Los Angeles, Riverside, San Diego and Orange counties. All the victims were gay and all had been shot in the head and were found nude. The murders came to a conclusion on 13 March 1977. At 5.30pm that day 17-year-old John LaMay told his neighbour that he was going to Redondo Beach to meet "Dave", a man he had met at the gym. He arrived at Kearney's home and was invited in. Kearney shot LaMay in the back of the head and then hid the corpse in the desert. LaMay's mother called the police but they did not take the report seriously. Five days later, LaMay's dismembered corpse was found south of Corona. He had been drained of blood, washed and put into five industrial trash bags and then into an empty oil drum.

Wanted poster of the two killers, Patrick Kearney and David Hill.

WHERE:
California, USA
WHEN:
1965–Sunday 13 March 1977
THE AFTERMATH:
"Dave" was soon identified as David Hill and he and Kearney fled. They surrendered on 1 July 1977. Hill was cleared of involvement in his boyfriend's crimes and was released on 14 July. That day Kearney was charged with two murders and the next day he confessed to 28 more. On 21 December he was sentenced to life imprisonment after pleading guilty to three murders. In February 1978 he was charged with 18 more murders and pleaded guilty on 21 February. Kearney is in jail at California State Prison, Mule Creek.

Gilbert Paul Jordan

"I didn't give a damn who I was with... we're all dying sooner or later"

THE CRIME: Gilbert Paul Jordan was born as G.P. Elsie in Vancouver, Canada on 12 December 1931. By the time he was 16, he was an alcoholic (he drank more than three bottles of vodka a day – "Sober people wouldn't go out with me, so I didn't have much option. I didn't want to drink in my room all by myself") and high school dropout. By the time he left his teens, he had a criminal record for theft, assault, car theft and possession of heroin. He picked up 200 women a year for sex and would often pay prostitutes he picked up in the slums and bars of Vancouver's seedy Eastside.

In 1961 police found him with a five-year-old girl in his car but, although charged, he was never convicted of abduction. In December that year he threatened to jump off the Lion's Gate Bridge. In 1963 he was charged with theft and rape after luring two women into his car but was convicted only on the theft charge. In prison he learned hairdressing skills and opened Slocan Barber Shop, on Kingsway Avenue, Eastside. He invested his money in the stock market.

Soon the "Boozing Barber" progressed to murder. Elsie would pay women to drink or have sex with him in his barbers' shop or in a cheap hotel. He then offered more money if they drank straight liquor. When the women passed out, he forced alcohol down their throats, and raped them as they died. In 1965 he picked up English-born Ivy Rose "Doreen" Oswald, whose nude body was found in a Vancouver hotel room the next day. Her death was ruled accidental and would officially remain that way until 1987. A few days after the murder, Elsie changed his name to Jordan. As well as murdering at least ten women, Jordan also racked up convictions for indecent exposure and indecent assault in the early 1970s. In 1975 he was sentenced to 26 months for kidnapping a woman from a mental institution. Between July 1982 and June 1985 three alcoholic prostitutes died at his barbers' shop. On 11 October 1987 Jordan took prostitute Vanessa Lee Buckner, 27, to the downmarket Niagara Hotel in Vancouver. Her nude body was discovered the next morning after an anonymous call to police. The call was traced to Jordan's room at the nearby Marble Arch Hotel. In November, when Edna Shade died of alcohol poisoning, police followed Jordan. In the next 15 days, he attempted to poison four women but was disturbed each time by the police who finally arrested him as he tried to pour vodka down a prostitute's throat.

Cincinnati Strangler

**"Back in them days, the city was scared.
They needed an arrest. They got a scapegoat"**

THE CRIME: For 14 months in 1965 and 1966 the elderly women of Cincinnati were subjected to a reign of terror that left seven dead and one injured. The first attack occurred on 12 October when the Cincinnati Strangler beat and raped a 65-year-old woman but failed to strangle her with a plastic clothes line. Six weeks later, on 2 December, Emogene Harrington was murdered with a length of plastic clothes line in the basement of her apartment building. On 4 April 1966, the Monday before Easter, 58-year-old Lois Dant was raped and strangled in her first-floor Cincinnati apartment. On 10 June Jeannette Messer, 56, was discovered in a park, raped and strangled with a tie. On 12 October her daughter found 51-year-old Mrs Carl Hochhausler in the garage. She had been beaten, raped and strangled. On 20 October, 81-year-old Rose Winstsel was strangled with an electric cord in her home. On 9 December octogenarian Lula Kerrick was strangled, but not raped, in the lift of her apartment building.

WHERE:
Cincinnati, Ohio, USA
WHEN:
Tuesday 12 October 1965–Friday
9 December 1966
THE AFTERMATH:
In mid December 1966 former taxi driver Posteal Laskey was arrested and charged with the murder of a seventh victim, Barbara Rose Bowman, 31, whose body was found on 14 August 1966, near a taxi. She had been stabbed several times in the neck and her ankle broken. It was believed Laskey had run her down with the cab and then fled. He was convicted and sentenced to death in the electric chair, commuted to life imprisonment in 1972, but was never charged with the other murders. However, the police were confident of his guilt and, since the killings ended after his incarceration, they were almost certainly correct in that assumption. Naturally, his family disagreed. "Back in them days, the city was scared," said Laskey's brother, Russell. "They needed an arrest. They got a scapegoat." Laskey died, aged 69, on 29 May 2007 of natural causes at the Pickaway Correctional Institution in Orient in central Ohio. No one claimed his body and it was interred in a prison cemetery.

Was Posteal Laskey a scapegoat?

Fred and Rose West

"If attention is paid to what I think, you will never be released"

WHERE:
25 Midland Road; 25 Cromwell Street, Gloucester, England
WHEN:
August 1967–Friday 19 June 1987
THE AFTERMATH:
On 26 February 1994 Heather's remains were found. On 13 December the Wests were charged with murder. On 1 January 1995 Fred West hanged himself in his Winson Green Prison cell. On 22 November Rose West was found guilty of ten counts of murder and sentenced to life. Mr Justice Mantell said, "If attention is paid to what I think, you will never be released." On 7 October 1996 25 Cromwell Street was demolished. The following month, John West, Fred's brother, committed suicide while awaiting trial on rape charges.

THE CRIME: Fred West was born on 29 September 1941. He had a sexual relationship with his mother, beginning when he was 12. On 28 November 1958, at the age of 17, he suffered a bang on the head from a motorbike accident that left him comatose for eight days. On 9 November 1961 he appeared in court, accused of having sex with a 13-year-old girl, but the trial collapsed when his victim refused to give evidence. On 17 November 1962 West married prostitute Catherine "Rena" Costello who was pregnant by an Asian bus driver. Her daughter Charmaine was born on 22 March 1963. He began an affair with Anna McFall, a friend of his wife but when she wanted West to divorce Rena he murdered her in August 1967 and cut up her body. She was eight months' pregnant. On 6 January 1968 he murdered Mary Bastholm, 15, after abducting her in Gloucester. On 29 November 1968 he met Rosemary (Rose) Letts. It was her 15th birthday and he was pleased when she agreed to participate in his perverted sexual desires. She became a prostitute. On 17 October 1970 she gave birth to Heather.

On 4 December West was jailed for theft and motoring offences and was in prison until 24 June 1971. Just before West was released, Rose killed Charmaine at 25 Midland Road, Gloucester. Not long after, West murdered his wife. On 29 January 1972 West and Rose were married. In September they moved into 25 Cromwell Street. Over the next few years the Wests killed Lynda Gough (aged 21, in April 1973), Carol Ann Cooper (aged 15, on 10 November 1973), Lucy Partington (aged 21, abducted on 27 December 1973), Therese Siegenthaler (aged 21, in April 1974), Shirley Hubbard (aged 15, kidnapped on 14 November 1974), Juanita Mott (aged 19, in April 1975), prostitute Shirley Robinson (aged 18, and pregnant by West when she died in May 1978), Alison Chambers (aged 17, in August 1979) and, finally, on 19 June 1987 West murdered Heather. In May 1992 he raped a 13-year-old girl who told a friend. The police arrived on 6 August to search for evidence of child abuse. Both Wests were arrested but the case collapsed when their victim refused to testify. The search for Heather began and, on 25 February 1994, West was arrested for her murder. In custody he denied that Rose had anything to do with any of the murders.

Police search for evidence at 25 Cromwell Street.

Jerry Brudos

"The Lust Killer"

Jerry Brudos leaves Marion County Circuit Court after pleading guilty.

THE CRIME: Jerome Henry "Jerry" Brudos was born at Webster, South Dakota, on 31 January 1939, the youngest of four sons. His mother, who didn't want a baby boy, dressed him as a girl and constantly belittled him. From the age of five, he had a women's shoe fetish. He would become sexually aroused by women in high heels and was arrested when he was 17 after forcing a woman, at knifepoint, to take her clothes off while he took pictures. He was sentenced to nine months in a mental hospital. On his release, he joined the army in March 1959 but received a medical discharge on 15 October 1959.

He kept his oddness confined at home where he insisted his wife walk around naked except for a pair of high heels while he took pictures. He also wore her underwear. On 26 January 1968, 19-year-old Linda Slawson was selling encyclopedias in Portland, Oregon when she knocked on Brudos's door. He killed her and then cut off her left foot, which he kept in the freezer and took out to model the shoes he collected. He dumped her corpse in a nearby river. On 26 November 1968 he strangled Jan Whitney, 23, and then had sex with her corpse before cutting off her right breast and making a mould of it. He threw her corpse into the same river as Linda Slawson's body. On 27 March 1969 he killed 19-year-old Karen Sprinker in a Salem car park. On 21 April 1969 he attempted to kidnap Sharon Wood, 24, from a car park in Portland. She fought back and managed to escape. Two days later, Brudos claimed his last victim, 22-year-old Linda Salee. He kidnapped her from a supermarket by pretending to be a policeman. Brudos was arrested on 25 May 1969 when he approached girls on the campus of Oregon State University.

WHERE:
Portland, Oregon, USA
WHEN:
Friday 26 January 1968–Wednesday 23 April 1969
THE AFTERMATH:
On 27 June 1969 Brudos pleaded guilty to three counts of first-degree murder and was sentenced to life imprisonment. He died at Oregon State Penitentiary on 28 March 2006.
YOU SHOULD KNOW:
When Brudos was arrested, he was wearing women's knickers.

Gerald Eugene Stano

"I can't stand a bitchy chick"

THE CRIME: Born on 12 September 1951 in Schenectady, New York, as Paul Zeininger, Gerald Stano was given up for adoption when he was six months old. He was thought to be unadoptable for quite some time as he failed to respond to human contact and ate his own faeces. Nurse Norma Stano and her husband finally took pity on the boy and adopted him, renaming him Gerald Eugene Stano. Despite a loving family, young Gerald found it difficult to fit in and was often naughty. At school he was a below average student, except in music, and he stole money from his father to bribe his fellow pupils to let him win an athletics race.

Officially, his killings began in 1973 but it is believed that in 1969 he murdered several local girls but there was insufficient physical evidence to link him to the crimes and he was never charged. In 1973 he moved with his parents to Florida. He revealed that he killed because some women annoyed him and "I can't stand a bitchy chick." He picked up most of his victims as they hitchhiked or worked as prostitutes. They ranged in age from 12 to mid 50s. Like many psychopaths, Stano was outwardly charming and had no problem in persuading women to get into his car. His offer of drink or drugs also lulled them into a false sense of security. He was most active in 1976 and 1977 and most of the corpses were left in Pasco County. He often picked on women who wore blue but never killed when he was sober. After the murders he scrupulously cleaned his car of bloodstains and other incriminating marks. Stano was arrested on 1 April 1980, after attacking a prostitute at Daytona Beach, Florida.

The prison photo of Gerald Eugene Stano

WHERE:
Florida; New Jersey, USA
WHEN:
1969–Tuesday 1 April 1980
THE AFTERMATH:
In 1981 he was sentenced to three life terms for strangling and stabbing three women. A plea bargain kept him out of the electric chair. By the time of his 29th birthday he had confessed to 41 slayings. In January 1984 he was sentenced to death. On 18 May 1988, the day before he was due to be executed, he won an indefinite stay of appeal. That stay came to an end on 23 March 1998 when he died in Florida's electric chair.

Peter Sutcliffe

"I were just cleaning up the streets, our kid, just cleaning up the streets"

THE CRIME: For six years the north of England was terrorized by a vicious killer who stalked the back roads, killing women with a brutality unknown for many a year. In 1969 Peter Sutcliffe attacked a prostitute in revenge because he believed another whore had conned him out of £10. Working as a gravedigger in Bingley Cemetery in West Yorkshire, at the grave of Bronislaw Zapolski, he claimed to have first heard the "Voice of God" telling him to murder prostitutes. After being sacked for poor time-keeping, he began work as a lorry driver. Between 5 July 1975 (the assault of Anna Rogulskyj) and 17 November 1980 (the murder of Jacqueline Hill), he brutally murdered 13 women and attempted to murder seven more. Despite his "orders" from God, several of Sutcliffe's victims were not prostitutes.

His first murder occurred at 1.30am on 30 October 1975. The victim was Wilma McCann, a 28-year-old prostitute. Drunk and carrying a carton of curry and chips, she decided that she wanted a lift home to the Chapeltown area of Leeds rather than walking and began staggering in and out of traffic. Sutcliffe was also out drinking in Leeds that night and he saw Wilma McCann thumbing for a lift. When he stopped his lime-green Ford Capri GT, she got in and quickly asked him if he "wanted business". When Sutcliffe asked what she meant, she said, "Bloody hell, do I have to spell it out?" Wilma McCann's battered body was found at 7.41am the following morning by milkman Alan Routledge, and his ten-year-old brother, Paul. She was found lying on her back, her trousers down by her knees and her brassiere lifted to expose her breasts. Her strawberry blonde hair was matted with blood, and she had been stabbed in the lower abdomen, chest and neck.

For the next five years women in Yorkshire were afraid to venture out alone, for fear of the man they dubbed "the Yorkshire Ripper". On 26 June 1977, Sutcliffe murdered Jayne Macdonald, his first non-prostitute victim. On 2 January 1981 Sutcliffe picked up prostitute Olive Reivers but, thanks to the false number plate on his Rover, he was arrested. Telling police he needed to relieve himself he went behind an oil storage tank where he disposed of his ball pein hammer and knife. At the police station he dropped a second knife into a lavatory cistern. All the weapons were later recovered.

WHERE:
Bingley; Silsden; Keighley; Bradford; Halifax; Sheffield; Leeds; Huddersfield; Manchester, England
WHEN:
1969–Monday 17 November 1980
THE AFTERMATH:
His trial opened at the Central Criminal Court of the Old Bailey on 29 April 1981. He claimed to be suffering from paranoid schizophrenia. On 11 May 1981 he was found guilty of murder by a majority verdict of 10–2. Later Sutcliffe was asked by his brother to explain his actions. "I were just cleaning up the streets, our kid," he replied, "just cleaning up the streets."

Peter Sutcliffe on his wedding day in August 1974

Velma Margi Barfield

"Sorry for all the hurt that I have caused"

WHERE:
North Carolina, USA
WHEN:
1969–1978

THE AFTERMATH:
For her execution at 2am 2 November 1984 she wore her favourite pink floral-print pyjamas and blue slippers. The death gurney was rolled into her cell where matrons from another prison strapped her to it. The prison's own matrons had grown too fond of Barfield to assist in the execution. In the death chamber three syringes were attached to intravenous tubes through a curtain. Three executioners simultaneously pressed the syringe plungers but only two of them were connected to Barfield. This way each of the volunteer executioners could believe it wasn't him who killed her. Barfield said, "I want to say sorry for all the hurt that I have caused." Sodium thiopental was injected to induce a deep sleep, then doses of procuronium bromide, a muscle relaxant followed, stopping her breathing. She was pronounced dead at 2.15am. She attempted to donate her liver, kidneys and eyes for transplant and a team of doctors rushed her body to a local hospital. Ultimately bone, skin and eyes were used.

THE CRIME: Born on 29 October 1932, Velma Margi Barfield (née Bullard) was the first woman executed by lethal injection and the last woman executed in North Carolina. In 1963 she underwent a hysterectomy, which left her mentally scarred. In 1969 her husband Thomas Burke died in a suspicious house fire. She married Jennings Barfield in August 1970. He died, supposedly of a heart attack, on 21 March 1971, having threatened to divorce her because of her drug addiction. In the intervening years several of those closest to Barfield died unexpectedly. In 1978, aged 46 and working as a nurse's aide, Barfield was convicted of poisoning her fiancé by lacing his iced tea with ant and roach poison. She also admitted using arsenic to poison one husband, her mother and two invalids she had been attending. The motive for most of the killings was to stop the victims discovering she had stolen money from them to buy drugs.

The United States hadn't executed a woman for 22 years and Barfield was given the choice of dying in the gas chamber or by lethal injection, eventually choosing the latter as her "gateway to Heaven". During the lengthy appeal process that occupied six years on death row many people fought for her sentence to be commuted, including evangelist Billy Graham's wife and daughter. They claimed during her imprisonment Barfield had become a born-again Christian.

Velma Barfield awaits lethal injection at Central Prison in Raleigh, North Carolina.

Donald Harvey

"The next thing I knew, I'd smothered him"

Harvey looks over a list of his victims during an interview at the Warren Correctional Institution in Lebanon, Ohio

THE CRIME: Born at Butler County, Ohio on 15 April 1952, Donald Harvey was a hospital porter who called himself the "Angel of Death". He claimed to have murdered 87 people, although official estimates put the tally at slightly more than 50. In 1970 Harvey landed a job as a porter at the Marymount Hospital in London, Kentucky. During his ten-month employment he said that he killed a dozen people, some to alleviate their suffering and some because he was annoyed at them. One victim rubbed faeces into Harvey's face so he murdered him. "The next thing I knew, I'd smothered him. It was the last straw. I just lost it. I went in to help the man and he wants to rub that in my face." His next murder was that of an old lady whose oxygen mask he disconnected. Over the next 17 years Harvey murdered people at whatever hospital he was working. He used different methodology to keep his actions secret, preferring to use cyanide and arsenic but not averse to overdoses of insulin and morphine, suffocation, turning off respirators, insertion of a coat hanger into a catheter and injecting liquids contaminated with hepatitis B or HIV. Harvey murdered at the Cincinnati Veterans' Administration Medical Hospital and at Cincinnati's Drake Memorial Hospital where he had several homosexual affairs.

On 31 March 1971 he was arrested for burglary while drunk and babbled out a confession but the police found no evidence to charge him with anything other than the theft and he was fined. He suffered from depression and, in July 1972, admitted himself to the mental ward of the Veteran's Administration Medical Center in Lexington, Kentucky. He was released on 17 October 1972. He found a job at Cardinal Hill Hospital in Lexington and then another at Lexington's Good Samaritan Hospital. He said that he resisted the urge to kill there but in September 1975 he returned to Cincinnati, Ohio and the killing began in earnest. He was undiscovered until March 1987 when patient John Powell died and an autopsy found that his death was due to cyanide poisoning. Donald Harvey confessed to 33 murders on 11 August 1987.

WHERE:
Cincinnati, Ohio; Kentucky, USA
WHEN:
1970–1987
THE AFTERMATH:
On 19 August 1987 Harvey pleaded guilty to 24 murders and was sentenced to life for each killing and fined $270,000. On 7 September he was indicted in Kentucky and confessed to 12 murders. In November he received eight life terms plus 20 years. He is currently at the Warren Correctional Institution in Lebanon, Ohio.
YOU SHOULD KNOW:
Donald Harvey will not be eligible for parole until 2047 when he will be 95.

Dean Corll's home in the suburbs of Houston

Dean Corll

"I just killed a man..."

THE CRIME: Born in Fort Wayne, Indiana on Christmas Eve 1939, Dean Corll was America's worse serial killer until John Wayne Gacy (see opposite). He suffered from a heart condition but that did not stop him joining the army in 1964, when he first realized that he was homosexual. He was discharged after ten months.

His mother owned a sweet shop and Corll often gave sweets to his favourite young boys, earning him the nickname "The Candy Man". When the shop went bust Corll became an electrician at the Houston Lighting and Power Company. He befriended two young men, David Brooks and Elmer Wayne Henley, who became his partners in crime, sodomizing and murdering young boys. On 25 September 1970 Corll claimed his first known victim, hitchhiking, 18-year-old University of Texas student Jeffrey Konen. Most of Corll's victims were working-class boys from a section of Houston known as The Heights where running away was common and the police did not tend to investigate disappearances. Ten days before Christmas two teenage boys, Danny Yates, 15, and James Glass, 14, were lured to Corll's flat where he strangled them both. Another double murder occurred on 30 January 1971 when Corll killed brothers Donald, 17, and Jerry Waldrop, 13. Four more victims were despatched in 1971, including a former employee of the Corll sweet shop. The bloodlust continued into 1972. On 21 May he murdered Billy Baulch, 17, who had also worked for Corll. Billy's friend Johnny DeLome, 16, was killed the same day, shot in the head and then strangled by Henley. On 19 July 1973 Corll murdered Billy Baulch's younger brother Tony, 15. Corll's *modus operandi* was to give Brooks and Henley $200 to lure boys to his home where he gave them drink and drugs until they passed out. They were then stripped, strapped to a board and sodomized and tortured until they were murdered – sometimes days later. One investigator revealed that a victim had his "pubic hairs pulled out one by one, a glass rod shoved up his penis and a large bullet-like instrument pushed up his rectum".

WHERE:
Pasadena, Houston, Texas, USA
WHEN:
Friday 25 September 1970–Friday
3 August 1973
THE AFTERMATH:
The murders ended on 8 August 1973 when 17-year-old Henley telephoned the police to confess, "I just killed a man..." His victim was Corll whom he had shot six times in the head, back and shoulder. Police at first refused to believe Henley's story of serial killing but were convinced when he told them the names of boys who had disappeared and took them to Corll's boatyard where he had buried some victims. In August 1974 Henley was sentenced to life imprisonment but in December 1978 his conviction was overturned. He was retried in June 1979 and again sent down for life. Brooks received a life term in March 1975.

John Wayne Gacy

"John Wayne Gacy Meet Your Fate"

THE CRIME: Born on St Patrick's Day 1942 in Chicago, Illinois, John Wayne Gacy, Jr had a troubled childhood. After getting a business degree, he moved to Springfield, Illinois, where he met and, in September 1964, married Marlynn Myers. They relocated to Waterloo, Iowa where Gacy became manager of the local Kentucky Fried Chicken branch. At the end of 1968 Gacy was sent to the Iowa State Penitentiary for ten years for sodomizing two boys, aged 16 and 15. During his time inside his wife divorced him and he never saw her or his two children again.

Released, he worked a shoe salesman and then as a building contractor. In 1971 he bought a house in Norwood Park, a suburb of Chicago. The house had a 1.2-m (4-ft) deep crawl space under the floor. In June 1972 he married Carole Hoff, a mother of two, but on 22 June he was arrested after a young man said that Gacy had raped him. Carole Gacy noticed a smell coming from the crawl space but Gacy blamed it on a broken sewer pipe and put down lime to cover the odour. In 1975, Gacy began his own business, PDM Contractors, a building firm. The Gacys divorced in March 1976, around the time he found work performing as Pogo the Clown at charity functions. In December 1977 Gacy was accused of raping a 19-year-old young man but Gacy claimed that the teenager was a rent boy and the dispute was over his fee. On 13 December of the next year the police searched Gacy's home after Robert Piest, a 15-year-old schoolboy, went missing. One of the policemen had worked in a mortuary and recognized a familiar smell. In the crawl space under the house the police found the remains of seven boys and a further eight buried in the back garden. Gacy was found to have killed 33 boys and young men, but only 24 were ever identified. He had prowled the streets looking for victims, sometimes claiming he was a policeman, complete with flashing light on his car. Back at his home he would handcuff and torture the victims, putting their clothes in their mouths to stifle their screams, before killing them.

WHERE:
8213 West Summerdale Avenue, Norwood Park, Chicago, Illinois, USA
WHEN:
Monday 3 January 1972–Monday 11 December 1978
THE AFTERMATH:
On 6 February 1980 Gacy's trial began at the Cook County Criminal Courts Building in Chicago. He was found guilty on 13 March and sentenced to death. Gacy was executed by lethal injection at Stateville Correctional Center, Crest Hill, Illinois on 10 May 1994. His last meal was a dozen deep-fried shrimp, a bucket of original recipe chicken and fries from KFC, followed by fresh strawberries. Outside demonstrators chanted, "Justice, Justice, Not Too Late – John Wayne Gacy Meet Your Fate."
YOU SHOULD KNOW:
John Gacy was active in the local Democratic Party and on 6 May 1978 he met and was photographed with the First Lady, Rosalynn Carter. She gave him a signed photograph and he was given a badge by the Secret Service to show he had been given special clearance.

The body of a victim is removed from 8213 West Summerdale Avenue.

Charles Sobhraj

He hired a publicist and sold interviews

THE AFTERMATH:
He was arrested on 5 July 1976. In July 1978 Sobhraj was found guilty of culpable homicide after Leclerc testified against him. She was found guilty of drugging the students, jailed, paroled and died of ovarian cancer in April 1984. Sobhraj was given seven years' hard labour. He was tried for murder in 1982 and sentenced to life in jail. Remarkably, in March 1986 he threw a party to celebrate ten years in jail and managed again to drug his guards and escape. He was caught and returned to jail. On 17 February 1997 he was freed and returned to France where he hired a publicist and sold interviews. On 19 September 2003 he was arrested in Kathmandu in connection with two unsolved murders in Nepal in 1975. He was sentenced to life imprisonment on 12 August 2004.

French citizen, Charles Sobhraj, is taken to court in Kathmandu.

THE CRIME: Charles Sobhraj was born illegitimately in Saigon, Vietnam on 6 April 1944. His Indian father deserted the family and Sobhraj's mother took up with a Frenchman who moved them to Paris in 1953. The young Charles did not take to his new life and began to get involved in crime. He was not a particularly accomplished criminal and frequently ended up in prison. His first stint behind bars came in 1963. In 1970 he moved to Bombay and became a smuggler and black marketeer. Two years later, in September 1972, he bungled a burglary and fled to Kabul, Afghanistan where he was jailed for trying to avoid paying his hotel bill. He managed to escape from prison by drugging his guards. He fled Kabul by hijacking a car and forcing the owner, Habib, into the boot where he suffocated – it was Sobhraj's first killing. He moved to Teheran where he began stealing and ended up in an Iranian jail. Freed, he moved to Turkey in November 1973, where he hired his brother as his partner in crime and then to Greece where he was caught but escaped from jail. He moved back to India, then to Kashmir where he met Quebecoise Marie-Andrée Leclerc and they became a murderous robbing double act, first in Hong Kong then in Thailand.

They murdered several hippies who had come to the country for enlightenment and by 1976 Sobhraj was wanted for eight murders in Turkey, Thailand and India. He fled Bangkok with the help of a corrupt local official and, when police searched his apartment, they found documents relating to 20 victims. Back in Agra, India, in July 1976 he gave a group of 60 French engineering students a medicine to prevent dysentery. In fact, he intended to drug them into sleep and then steal their valuables. He miscalculated the dosage and some collapsed in the hotel lobby while others accused him of trying to poison them.

William Bonin

"I'm horny, let's do another one"

THE CRIME: Between 1972 and 1980 44 young men were murdered and raped, often strangled with their own t-shirts, by the Freeway Killer. In many of the cases the corpses had been mutilated with a knife. The police believed that more than one perpetrator was at large, committing the horrific murders. In 1974 14-year-old David McVicker attended a party and then decided to hitchhike home. He was picked up by another guest who drove him to a remote area where he stripped and raped him. The rapist did not kill the boy because he was worried that they had been seen together at the party. McVicker went to the police and they arrested William George Bonin (born in Connecticut 8 January 1947) who had been jailed in 1969 for messing around with boys. For the McVicker assault he was jailed for one to fifteen years. He was freed in October 1978 and the Freeway attacks resumed.

In April 1979 Bonin murdered hitchhikers Danny Jordan and Mark Proctor. On 28 May Bonin kidnapped 14-year-old hitchhiker Thomas Lundgren and then raped him before castrating and strangling the boy. Bonin's accomplice was a weird, 22-year-old factory worker called Vernon Butts who slept in a coffin and told everyone he was a wizard. In the next seven months seven more teenage boys died. On 1 January 1980 Bonin killed 16-year-old Michael McDonald and on 3 February in Hollywood Bonin garrotted 15-year-old Charles Miranda, leaving his naked body in an alley. Bonin was aided that time by a man called Gregory Miley. Bonin told him, "I'm horny, let's do another one." The two men then picked up and murdered 12-year-old James McCabe after raping him. He was the youngest victim. The last murder happened on 2 June 1980 when Bonin was helped by another accomplice, 18-year-old James Michael Munro. By now the police were frantically trying to catch someone and they remembered that David McVicker had told them that Bonin had said that he liked strangling hitchhikers. He was put under surveillance and on 11 June was arrested as he attacked a 15-year-old boy, known only as "Harold T.".

Bonin listens as the jury returns a guilty verdict.

WHERE:
California, USA
WHEN:
December 1972–Monday 2 June 1980
THE AFTERMATH:
Bonin confessed to the murders and on 25 July Vernon Butts was arrested. Gregory Miley was taken into custody on 22 August. On 11 January 1981 Vernon Butts hanged himself in his prison cell. On 4 November Bonin went on trial, Miley having agreed to testify against him. Miley and Munro were sentenced to 25 years to life and 15 years to life respectively for their roles. Bonin was convicted of all charges on 5 January 1982. On 23 February 1996 he was executed by lethal injection inside the gas chamber at San Quentin State Prison. It was the first execution by lethal injection in California. It took three minutes from the first injection for Bonin to be pronounced dead.

Randy Steven Kraft

"Passive, non-violent and hard working"

THE CRIME: Another serial killer whose reign of terror lasted a long time was Randy Kraft who was born on 19 March 1955. In 1969 Kraft disclosed that he was gay and was thrown out of the air force, officially on "medical" grounds.

Kraft, who lived with a male lover in Long Beach, was a computer specialist, earned a good salary and had a wide and varied social life, particularly

Randy Kraft listens to a testimony at a preliminary hearing.

enjoying a hand of bridge. But at night he prowled the motorways of California looking for young men. He chose hitchhikers, often military personnel, whom he picked up and offered beer and drugs. When his victims were incapacitated, Kraft sodomized them, tortured and castrated them before dumping their corpses by the side of the road.

He claimed his first victim, a 20-year-old marine named Edward Daniel Moore, in December 1972. Marine Moore had been raped, strangled and had traces of drugs in his system. There is speculation that the first victim was actually more than a year earlier on 20 September 1971, when 30-year-old gay barman Wayne Joseph Dukette was murdered. The police were at their wits' end because more than one serial killer was stalking the motorways (see William Bonin, page 403, and Patrick Kearney, see page 391). At just after 1am on 14 May 1983 Kraft was arrested on the San Diego Freeway when the police stopped him, thinking he was driving while drunk. In his passenger seat was Terry Lee Gambrel, a 25-year-old marine stationed at the nearby El Toro Marine Air Base, who appeared to be insensible but, on closer inspection, was revealed to be dead. The police searched Kraft's Long Beach home and found items belonging to his victims. They also discovered a coded list referring to his victims' names – the list had 67 names on it.

WHERE:
Southern California, USA
WHEN:
December 1972–14 May 1983
THE AFTERMATH:
Randy Kraft was held in custody for five years before he came to trial. At a hearing, Kraft's lawyer called him "passive, non-violent and hard working". On 12 May 1989 he was found guilty of 16 murders and nine charges of sexual mutilation and three of sodomy and, on 29 November, sentenced to death in the gas chamber at San Quentin. The California Supreme Court upheld the death sentence on 11 August 2000.

BTK Strangler

"Bind them, Torture them, Kill them"

THE CRIME: Dennis L. Rader was born on 9 March 1945. In 1966 he joined the US Army Air Force and served for four years in Turkey, Greece, Japan and South Korea. In 1971, after demob, he moved into 6220 North Independence Street in Park City, Kansas. That year, on 22 May, he married Paula Dietz, a secretary at the Veterans' Administration Hospital. In 1975 he had a son, followed three years later by a daughter.

Rader struck for the first time on 15 January 1974 when he murdered four members of the Otero family, Joseph and Julie and their son Joseph II (aged 9) and daughter Josephine (aged 11), at their home at 803 North Edgemoor Street. He also stole the family car. On 4 April Kathryn Bright, 21, was strangled at her home at 3217 East 13th Street and her brother shot – he survived. (Some dispute this was the work of Rader.) Six months later, a letter referring to the Otero murders was found in a library book. It was the first time that the murderer suggested that he should be called the BTK Strangler; BTK stood for "Bind them, Torture them, Kill them." On 17 March 1977 Shirley Vian Relford, 26, was strangled at her home at 1311 South Hydraulic Street. The killer locked her children in a bathroom before he murdered their mother. On 8 December Rader rang 911 after murdering Nancy Fox, 25, at her home at 843 South Pershing Street. Rader began taunting the police and media, sending them cryptic messages. On 15 August 1979 police broadcast the 911 call on radio and television and received more than 100 leads. On 27 April 1985 Marine Hedge disappeared from her home at 6254 North Independence Street, the same street that Rader lived on. Her body was discovered on 5 May near 53rd North Street and Webb Road. On 16 September 1986 Vicki Wegerle, 28, was strangled in her home at 2404 West 13th Street. On 1 February 1991 the remains of Dolores "Dee" Davis were discovered, 13 days after she was abducted. One message had been sent on a computer disk from a Lutheran church in Wichita. It was traced to dog catcher and church president, Rader, who was arrested on 25 February 2005.

WHERE:
Witchita, Kansas, USA
WHEN:
Tuesday 15 January 1974–Saturday 19 January 1991
THE AFTERMATH:
On 1 March 2005 Rader was charged with ten counts of first-degree murder. The next day, he was sacked for failing to turn up to work since 25 February. On 27 June Rader pleaded guilty to 10 counts of first-degree murder. On 18 August he was sentenced to ten consecutive life terms.
YOU SHOULD KNOW:
In March 2007 Rader's home was demolished, having been bought by the city from his ex-wife for $56,000.

A mask found with the body of Deloris Davis is shown in court.

Ted Bundy

"Give my love to my family and friends"

WHERE:
Seattle, Washington; Salt Lake City, Utah; Aspen, Colorado; Tallahassee, Florida, USA
WHEN:
Thursday 31 January 1974–Thursday 9 February 1978
THE AFTERMATH:
Bundy was arrested on 15 February 1978 and was sentenced to death. At 7.07am on 24 January 1989 he died in the electric chair in Florida. He had tried to save his life by offering to reveal where the graves of more victims were. His last words were, "Give my love to my family and friends."

THE CRIME: Theodore Robert Bundy was one of America's most notorious serial killers. Born on 24 November 1946, Bundy was dark-haired and handsome. He was also a psychopath, a peeping Tom, a compulsive masturbator and a cold-blooded killer. He began his criminal career in 1974 in Seattle, Washington.

On 31 January student Lynda Ann Healey disappeared. On 14 July Janice Ott, 23, and Denise Naslund, 19, vanished in separate incidents at Sammamish Park. Eyewitnesses told police that both girls had been seen with a handsome man with his arm in a sling. Their remains were found in September, along with those of a third victim, 3.2 km (2 mi) east of where they had disappeared. Over the next six months three more corpses were found. Then the killings stopped. In October 1974 young girls began to disappear in Salt Lake City, Utah but the police did not link the crimes to those in Seattle. Then on 8 November 1974 the killer made a mistake. Carol DaRonch escaped after a man pretended to be a policeman and tried to abduct her. She was able to give police a good description of her would-be killer, which matched the prime suspect in the Seattle slayings. On 12 January 1975 23-year-old nurse Caryn Campbell was murdered in Aspen, Colorado. Her naked body was not found until 17 February when the snow thawed.

On 16 August 1975 29-year-old Ted Bundy was arrested after he jumped a red light and police found tools in his boot that could be used for burglary or abduction. In December 1976 he was found guilty of aggravated assault in the DaRonch case. The police found it difficult to believe that the handsome, likeable Bundy was a depraved serial killer. As he prepared his own defence, Bundy escaped from jail twice but was recaptured. On 31 December 1977 he managed to escape again and began a six-week trail of havoc that led to Tallahassee, Florida where he attacked four sorority girls, one of whom, Lisa Levy, died after Bundy bit off her nipples. In February 1978 he attempted, but failed, to kidnap a 14-year-old girl. He did manage to take 12-year-old Kimberley Leach and murdered her on 9 February. He hid her body so that he could return to abuse it.

Dr Lovell J. Levine, a New York forensic odontologist, testifies that the teeth marks found on the buttock of one of the victims belong to Bundy.

David Berkowitz

"I am deeply hurt by your calling me a wemon [sic] hater. I am not. I am the 'Son of Sam'"

THE CRIME: The first attack happened on Christmas Eve 1975 when two girls were assaulted with a knife. The first murders occurred at 1.10am on 29 July 1976. Donna Lauria, 18, and Jody Valenti, 19, were in a car outside 2860 Buhre Avenue, Bronx, discussing a visit to a disco when a man approached and shot them, killing Donna and wounding Jody. At 1.30am on 23 October 1976 Carl Denaro, 20, and Rosemary Keenan, 18, were shot as they sat in a car at Flushing, Queens. At 12.40am on 27 November Joanne Lomino, 18, and Donna DeMasi, 16, were shot as they chatted outside Donna's home on 262nd Street, Queens. Joanne was left disabled. At 12.40am on 30 January 1977 Christine Freund, 26, and her fiancé John Diel, 30, were shot in their Pontiac Firebird in Queens. Freund died at 4.10am in St John's Hospital. At 7.30pm on 8 March 1977 Virginia Voskerichian became the next victim. She was shot in the head as she walked home from Barnard College, Columbia University. At 3am on 17 April 1977 Valentina Suriani, 18, and Alexander Esau, 20, were each shot twice as they kissed in Esau's car near the Hutchinson River in the Bronx area (a block away from where Donna Laurie had been shot).

The media and police believed that the killer was a misogynist and called him the .44 Calibre Killer after the type of gun he used. In the street near the shooting a policeman found a letter addressed to Captain Joseph Borrelli. It read, "…I am deeply hurt by your calling me a wemon [sic] hater. I am not. But I am a monster. I am the 'Son of Sam' … I'll be back, I'll be back! … Yours in murder – Mr Monster".

At 3.20am on 26 June 1977 Judy Placido, 17, and Salvatore Lupo, 20, were shot in a car outside 45–39 211th Street, Queens. The last attack occurred at 1.45am on 31 July 1977. Stacy Moskowitz and Bobby Violante were parked at Gravesend Bay in Brooklyn. Stacy died at 5.22pm on 1 August at the Coney Island Hospital. Bobby survived but was left blind after losing his left eye and 80 per cent of the sight in his right. A witness had seen the car that the killer escaped in and noticed that it had a parking ticket. There had been just four tickets issued that morning – one to David Berkowitz of 35 Pine Street, Yonkers. At 10.15pm on 10 August 1977 he was arrested.

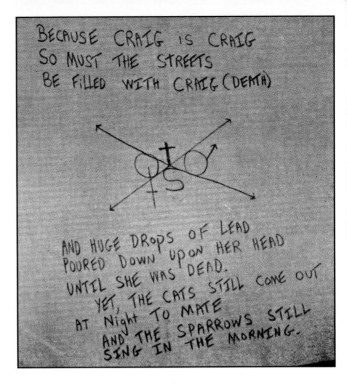

A note written by the "Son of Sam"

WHERE:
Bronx; Queens, New York, USA
WHEN:
Thursday 29 July 1976–Sunday 31 July 1977
THE AFTERMATH:
Arraigned on 23 August 1977, Berkowitz was sentenced to 365 years in prison. The name Sam came from the dog of a neighbour, Sam Carr, that Berkowitz claimed kept him up all night so he shot it.

The body of Cindy Lee Hudspeth was found in this car.

Hillside Strangler

"None of us are perfect"

THE CRIME: Black single mother and prostitute Yolanda Washington, 19, became the first victim of the Hillside Strangler on 18 October 1977. Thirteen days later, the body of 15-year-old prostitute Judith Ann Miller was discovered in a flowerbed at 2844 Alta Terrace Drive, La Crescenta in California. On 6 November Lissa Teresa Kastin, 21, a dancer and waitress, was found near Chevy Chase Country Club in Glendale. Like the previous two victims, she had been raped and strangled. Four days later prostitute Jill Barcomb, 18, was found nude and strangled at Franklin Canyon Drive and Mullholland Drive. On 17 November prostitute Kathleen Robinson, 17, was found dead. On 20 November the bodies of Sonja Johnson, 14, and Dolores Cepeda were found at Landa Street and Stadium Way. Later that same day, Kristina Weckler was found naked and strangled at Ranons Avenue and Wawona Street. On 23 November the decomposing body of scientologist and model Jane King, 28, was discovered near the Golden State Freeway. Six days later, the body of Lauren Wagner, 18, was found at 1200 Cliff Drive, strangled and with marks suggesting that she had been tortured. At the end of the month police decided that they were, in fact, seeking two perpetrators for the killings attributed to the man who had been dubbed "the Hillside Strangler". On 13 December police found the body of 17-year-old prostitute Kimberly Diane Martin. The last victim in Los Angeles was Cindy Lee Hudspeth, 20, a part-time waitress, who was found on 16 February 1978. The killings stopped as quickly as they had begun.

At 7pm on 11 January 1979 student Karen Mandic, 22, and her friend Diane Wilder, 27, arrived to house-sit at the home of an acquaintance, Kenneth Bianchi in Bellingham, Washington. At 11pm Karen's friend, Steve Hardwick, was concerned that she had not contacted him and rang the police. They interviewed Bianchi and then went to the house the women shared. Just after 4.30pm on 12 January the strangled corpses of the two women were found in Karen's car. Later that day, Bianchi was arrested. He insisted that the police had made a mistake but they charged him with two murders.

WHERE:
Glendale, California;
Bellingham, Washington, USA
WHEN:
Tuesday 18 October 1977–Thursday
11 January 1979
THE AFTERMATH:
On 21 March 1979, as he was being prepared for trial, Bianchi was hypnotized and became "Steve" a foul-mouthed braggart who boasted of the LA and Bellingham murders. He also claimed that he had a partner in crime, his cousin Angelo Buono, a petty criminal with an oversized ego. Bianchi had said, "[Angelo] may have been a criminal years ago… None of us are perfect." In October 1979 Bianchi pleaded guilty to the Bellingham killings. He was taken to Los Angeles where he pleaded guilty to five more murders. Meanwhile Buono was arrested and charged with ten murders. The trial began on 16 November 1981 and lasted 345 days, involving 392 witnesses and 56,000 pages of testimony. On 4 January 1984 they were both sentenced to life. On 21 September 2002 Buono died in prison of a heart attack.

Pedro Alonso López

"I like the girls in Ecuador. They are more gentle and trusting, more innocent"

THE CRIME: Pedro Alonso López was born on 8 October 1948 in Tolina, Colombia, the seventh of 13 children of a prostitute. The man who was to become known as "the Monster of the Andes" was eight years old in 1957 when he was thrown out of his home after his mother caught him fondling his younger sister. He lived on the streets foraging for food until he was abducted by a paedophile who constantly raped him. An American family spotted him on the streets of Bogotá and "adopted" him, enrolling him in a school for orphans but 12-year-old López ran away. Back on the streets, López became a petty thief and beggar. At 18 he was arrested for stealing cars and sentenced to seven years in prison. On his second day inside he was gang-raped by four other inmates and responded by killing three of them with a homemade blade. Two years was added to his sentence for the murders. By the time he was released in 1978, he was a very angry man with murder in his heart.

López held a particular hatred for women and in the next two years went on a murder spree, focusing his attention mainly on girls between eight and 12. He picked on girls from Indian tribes who were less likely to be missed than white children. He also covered his tracks by travelling widely, killing across the Andes in Colombia, Peru and Ecuador. López later confessed to murdering 100 Peruvian girls before the Ayachuco Indians caught him while he was trying to abduct a nine-year-old girl. The Ayachucos stripped and tortured López and were only stopped from burying him alive by the intervention of a female American missionary who persuaded them to hand him over to the authorities. Instead of trying him, they simply drove him to the Ecuadorian border and let him go. López resumed his killing in Ecuador and Colombia. Families reported missing children but the police did little or nothing, presuming the children had been abducted by slave traders. In April 1980 a flood in Ambato, Ecuador, uncovered the bodies of four children and finally the police began to take notice. Then Carvina Poveda saw López trying to kidnap her 12-year-old daughter, Maria, and screamed for help. The police arrested the serial killer but he refused to talk.

WHERE:
Colombia; Peru; Ecuador
WHEN:
1978–1980
THE AFTERMATH:
It was only when Father Cordoba Gudino pretended to be a fellow prisoner that López spoke of his crimes, much to the horror of the clergyman who asked to be relieved of the task. López admitted to killing 100 girls in Colombia, 110 in Ecuador and still more in Peru. "I like the girls in Ecuador. They are more gentle and trusting, more innocent. I lost my innocence at eight, so I decided to do the same to as many girls as I could." He also said he preferred to kill in daylight because he enjoyed seeing the fear in their eyes. At first police refused to believe him and it was only when he took them to the graves that they realized his tales were true. He is currently serving a life sentence.

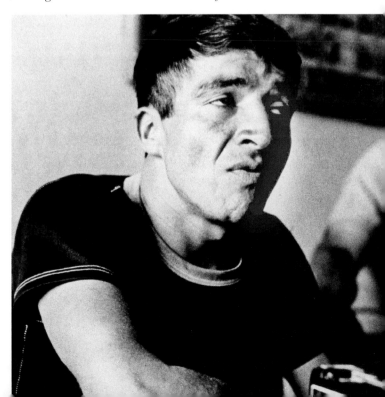

Pedro Alonso López, the "Monster of the Andes"

Theodore Kaczynski

Unabomber

WHERE:
Lincoln, Montana, USA
WHEN:
Thursday 25 May 1978–Monday
24 April 1995
THE AFTERMATH:
Kaczynski was arrested on 3 April
1996. To avoid the death penalty, he
pleaded guilty and was sentenced to
life in prison with no possibility of
parole. He is at United States
Penitentiary Administrative Maximum
Facility (ADX) in Florence, Colorado.

*Kaczynski shortly after he was
arrested.*

THE CRIME: Dr Theodore John Kaczynski was born in Chicago, Illinois on 22 May 1942. He graduated from Harvard in 1962 and earned a PhD in mathematics from the University of Michigan. In the autumn of 1967 he became an assistant professor at the University of California, Berkeley but left after just two years and, in 1971, moved to a remote cabin in Lincoln, Montana. Beginning in 1978 and ending with his arrest in 1995, Kaczynski sent 16 bombs to targets including universities and airlines, killing three people and injuring 23 more. He claimed that modern technology had impacted on the freedoms of mankind, making him less free. The FBI gave the then unknown bomber the code name UNABOM from UNiversity and Airline BOMber which led to the media nicknaming him the "Unabomber". The first bomb was sent on 25 May 1978 to Buckley Crist, a materials engineering professor at Northwestern University. The professor was suspicious and called the campus police. Officer Terry Marker opened the package, which exploded, injuring his left hand. On 15 November 1979 Kaczynski put a bomb in the cargo hold of American Airlines Flight 444, a Boeing 727 flying from Chicago to Washington DC. A faulty timer stopped the bomb exploding which would have brought down the aircraft. It was after this that the FBI became involved and a $1 million reward was offered. The first fatality was on 11 December 1985 when Hugh Scrutton, a 38-year-old computer shop owner was killed by a nail- and splinter-loaded bomb in his car park. On 24 April 1995, Kaczynski wrote to *The New York Times* promising "to desist from terrorism" if his thoughts (*Industrial Society And Its Future*) were published verbatim in that paper or *The Washington Post*. Kaczynski's manifesto was published in September and his estranged brother, David, recognized the handwriting and some of the phraseology and alerted the FBI.

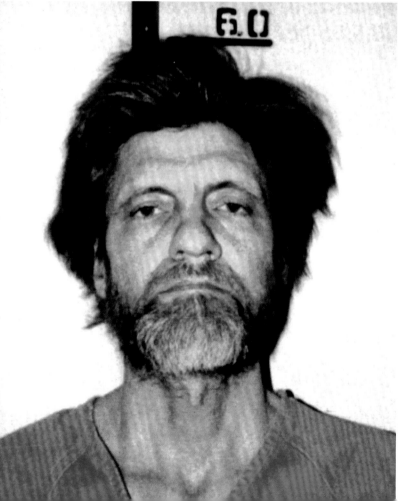

Andrei Chikatilo

"I know I have to be destroyed. I was a mistake of nature"

The smile of a serial killer.

THE CRIME: Born in Yablochnoye, Ukraine on 16 October 1936, Andrei Chikatilo had an elder brother, Stepan, whom he believed had been killed and eaten by the neighbours. In 1941 the Germans occupied his village when he no doubt witnessed atrocities. After he married and became a father, he landed a job as a school teacher in Novoshakhtinsk and began to abuse his pupils. He was sacked but no further action was taken against him.

In his early 40s, Chikatilo killed for the first time. He had moved to Shakhty, a small coal-mining town near Rostov-on-Don and on 22 December 1978 he kidnapped 9-year-old Lenochka Zakotnova, blindfolded her, attempted rape, stabbed her three times and then threw her into the Grushova River. Chikatilo was arrested but freed when his wife gave him an alibi. Aleksandr Kravchenko, a local rapist, was tried for the crime and executed. On 3 September 1981 Chikatilo killed 17-year-old Larisa Tkachenko, who was known to be free with her sexual favours. He filled her mouth with earth to stop her screaming. Chikatilo later said that he was excited by what he had done. His third victim was Lyuba Biryuk, in June 1982, and she was the first to suffer what became Chikatilo's motif – he gorged her eyes out. In 1983 he murdered six more times, including two young men.

The Soviet Union was always loath to publicize its troubles and to ask for help so the media were forbidden from writing about a serial killer being at large. This made it easier for Chikatilo to operate and in 1984 he murdered 15 times, eight in August alone. At the end of 1984 Chikatilo was arrested as he bothered some girls at a bus station but a mistake in forensics allowed him to go free and carry on butchering. Eight died in 1988 and nine in 1990 and on 6 November Chikatilo murdered 20-year-old Svetlana Korostik. He was stopped, sweating and with bloodstains on his clothes, leaving the crime scene. He was not searched – had the policeman done so he would have found Svetlana's breasts in Chikatilo's bag. Chikatilo – the Rostov Ripper – was finally arrested on 20 November after upsetting some children.

WHERE:
Rostov, Ukraine, USSR
WHEN:
Friday 22 December 1978–Tuesday 6 November 1990
THE AFTERMATH:
After nine days in custody Chikatilo confessed to 52 more murders. He was tried on 14 April 1992 and spent the time in an iron cage in the centre of the courtroom. He said, "When I used my knife, it brought psychological relief. I know I have to be destroyed. I was a mistake of nature." On 15 October he was found guilty of 52 murders and sentenced to death. On 14 February 1994 he was executed with a single shot to the back of the head.

The remains of one of Nilsen's victims are removed from his flat in Muswell Hill.

Dennis Nilsen

"Fifteen or sixteen"

THE CRIME: The first recognized homosexual serial murderer in Britain was born at 47 Academy Road, Fraserburgh, Aberdeenshire, Scotland on 23 November 1945. After an 11-year stint in the Army (1961–1972), he became a policeman with the Metropolitan Police Force and then worked for a security company before becoming a civil servant in 1974, working in a London labour exchange. The job gave Nilsen the perfect opportunity to meet lonely, disaffected and often homeless men. He also spent a lot of time in pubs chatting up men and then inviting them back to his home to carry on drinking or for sex.

His actions turned to murder on 30 December 1978 after he met 14-year-old Stephen Dean Holmes in a gay bar. They went back to Nilsen's house where he strangled Holmes with a tie and then drowned him in a bucket of water. Nilsen then bathed the corpse and went to bed with it. Thus began a pattern that would carry on for five years, until 26 January 1983 when he murdered Stephen Sinclair after meeting him in Oxford Street.

Nilsen murdered and attempted to murder 22 men. A biography of him claimed that Nilsen enjoyed the intimacy of gay sex but then did not want his lovers to leave, so murdered them – he killed for company. He burned the bodies in a large bonfire in his back garden. In November 1981 Nilsen moved to an attic flat in Muswell Hill where it was difficult to get rid of the remains of his victims. He took to flushing them down the lavatory. It was here that he murdered his last victim and put his remains down the drain, blocking it.

A man from Dynorod found a white sludge and left to return the next day. That night Nilsen walked to Muswell Hill Broadway and bought some fried chicken which he put down the drain, hoping to avert suspicion. The police were called and arrested Nilsen as he returned home from work. They found human remains scattered about his flat. When the police asked Nilsen how many bodies they were dealing with, he nonchalantly replied, "Fifteen or sixteen."

WHERE:
Garden Flat, 195 Melrose Avenue, Cricklewood;
Attic Flat, 23 Cranley Gardens, Muswell Hill, London, England
WHEN:
Saturday 30 December 1978–Wednesday 26 January 1983
THE AFTERMATH:
Nilsen went on trial at the Old Bailey in October 1983 and was sentenced to life in jail on 4 November.
YOU SHOULD KNOW:
Some of Nilsen's property ended up in Scotland Yard's Black Museum. The house in Cranley Gardens remained empty until 1984.

Wayne Williams

"Wiped out a generation of n****rs for good"

THE CRIME: The murders began at Atlanta in July 1979 when teenagers Edward Smith and Alfred Evans were killed. On 4 September a third teen, Milton Harvey, disappeared, followed on 21 October by nine-year-old Yusuf Bell, the son of Camille Belle, a civil rights leader. In March 1980 Angel Laner, 12, was raped and murdered – the first female victim – and in May Eric Middlebrooks was killed. On 9 June Christopher Richardson became the next victim. The death toll began to climb – all the victims were young and all were black.

Blacks began to fear that a racist was killing their children but this was soon discounted for two reasons. The area in which the children were taken was a heavily black one where any white face would stand out and serial killers tend to remain within their racial group – whites killing whites, blacks killing blacks, and so on. Then they believed that, because the victims were black, the police were not trying very hard to catch the perpetrator. By May 1981 the death toll had reached 21 with another child on the missing list. The investigation bill for the inquiry was $250,000 a month and President Reagan authorized a government grant of $1,500,000 to prevent Atlanta going bankrupt. On 22 May a young, black DJ named Wayne Bertram Williams (born 27 May 1958) was questioned after he was seen acting suspiciously near the Chattahoochee River. With no proof to link him to any of the murders, he was freed but put under surveillance. On 24 May the nude body of 27-year-old Nathaniel Cater was found in the river. A forensic test matched dog hairs on Nathaniel to those in Wayne Williams's car. When people came forward to claim that Williams had molested them, he was arrested on 21 June.

WHERE:
Atlanta, Georgia, USA

WHEN:
Saturday 21 July 1979–May 1981

THE AFTERMATH:
Wayne Williams went on trial on 6 January 1982 on two counts of murder. The evidence was mostly circumstantial but it was also noted that while Williams was in custody the Atlanta child killings ended. On 27 February 1982 Williams was found guilty and given two life sentences. Doubts exist as to the safety of Williams's conviction, especially when Charles T. Saunders of the Ku Klux Klan told the Georgia Bureau of Investigation that the killer "had wiped out a generation of n****rs for good". The parents of some victims do not believe that Williams was the murderer. Williams has continued to protest his innocence and his lawyers have demanded a new trial. Police refuse to reopen the case.

Williams shown talking to police outside his home.

Nikolai Dzhumagaliev

Metal Fang

WHERE:
Kazakhstan
WHEN:
1980
THE AFTERMATH:
In 1989 the authorities moved Dzhumagaliev to another hospital and he escaped. In a move reminiscent of the old Soviet policy of trying to censor bad news, the Kazakhstani government made no public mention of the jailbreak and it was not until August 1991 that he was recaptured at Fergana, Uzbekistan. He was released in January 1994 and remains at liberty.

Kazakhstani cannibal Nikolai Dzhumagaliev

THE CRIME: Nikolai Dzhumagaliev was nicknamed "Metal Fang" because of his metallic false teeth. Freed from a sentence for manslaughter, Dzhumagaliev found a job on an Alma-Ata building site in Kazakhstan. By day he laboured over bricks and mortar but by night he was a ladykiller, literally. Tall, handsome, well-mannered, smartly dressed Dzhumagaliev had one major flaw – he was a murderous cannibal. On his dates he would lead the woman to a remote spot where he would rape them before cutting up their corpses with a knife and an axe. Then he would start a fire and cook and eat the women. Having killed a woman, he would invite friends round to his home the following night for a roast dinner. He was captured after inviting two alcoholics to dine with him. They went to the police when they found a woman's head and intestines in Dzhumagaliev's kitchen. Dzhumagaliev was charged with seven murders but the court found that he was insane and he was sent to a mental institution in Tashkent.

Clifford Olson

"Beast of British Columbia"

THE CRIME: It was Christmas Day 1980 in Vancouver when the first mutilated body was found. She was identified as 12-year-old Christine Weller who had gone missing on 17 November. In the spring of 1981 the remains of 16-year-old Daryn Todd Johnsrude were found in some woods; his skull had been fractured. At about the same time 13-year-old Coleen Daignault disappeared on 16 April. On 19 May Sandra Wolfsteiner, 16, went hitchhiking and was never seen again. The next month, nine-year-old Susan Partington vanished after she spoke to a man in Surrey. Judy Kozma went missing early in July after she was picked up a by a man in New Westminster. At the end of the month her stabbed body was found in Lake Weaver along with that of Ray King who had vanished two days before Judy.

The police concentrated their efforts around Lake Weaver and their prime suspect was 42-year-old Clifford Raymond Olson (born 1 January 1940) who already had 94 convictions for offences ranging from fraud to rape. Olson was married with a baby son and lived near Vancouver. Despite being under police surveillance, he managed to evade them and went on holiday to America. On his return, the surveillance was abandoned. In July he murdered Louise Chartrand, Terri Lynn Carson and Sigrun Arnd, a German tourist. He was finally arrested on 12 August when he tried to abduct two girls. A search of his van revealed a notebook belonging to Judy Kozma.

Olson is escorted into court in Chilliwack, British Columbia.

WHERE:
Vancouver, British Columbia, Canada
WHEN:
Monday 17 November 1980–Thursday 30 July 1981
THE AFTERMATH:
In custody Olson demanded $10,000 for revealing where each body was buried, plus $30,000 for the three corpses that had already been discovered. The police refused to pay but the Attorney General overruled them and said that the money must be put in trust for Olson's son. Olson then offered to reveal the whereabouts of 20 bodies for $100,000. His offer was refused. He was tried before the Supreme Court of Canada in January 1982. On the third day (11 January), he changed his plea to guilty and was sentenced to 11 life terms to be served concurrently. He has since claimed to have committed anywhere from 80 to 200 murders. By his own admission, the self-proclaimed "Beast of British Columbia" is likely to kill again.

415

Genene Jones

"I'm the Death Nurse"

THE CRIME: Ex-beautician Genene Jones worked in the Paediatric Intensive Care Unit of the Bexar County Medical Center Hospital in San Antonio, Texas. Between May and December 1981 the children in the unit's care began dying at an alarming rate. Twenty died from heart attacks or uncontrollable bleeding and at the time of their deaths they were all in the care of Genene Jones, a licensed vocational nurse, working the 3pm to 11pm shift. She even joked, "They're going to start thinking I'm the Death Nurse." An inquiry comprising doctors from the USA and Canada was set up to look into the deaths and they spoke to all members of staff. They were surprised when one bluntly accused Genene Jones of killing the children. The inquiry's conclusion was that the hospital should sack Jones and the nurse who had accused her. The hospital, fearful of a lawsuit, demurred but pressure was put on Jones to resign, which she did in March 1982.

On 15 August 1982 Jones found a job working in a paediatric clinic in Kerrville, Texas run by Dr Kathleen Holland. Under Jones's care, several children fell ill with breathing difficulties. They all recovered and no one thought any more of the incident. On 17 September 14-month-old Chelsea McClellan was brought to the hospital by her parents for a routine injection against measles and mumps. Genene Jones gave the baby an injection and she went into seizure almost immediately. Chelsea died of a heart attack on the way to San Antonio for emergency treatment. As Jones administered treatment to other children at Kerrville, several became ill although none died. On 28 September Dr Holland sacked Jones. Finally, the medical authorities took notice and on 12 October convened a grand jury investigation. In February 1983 another grand jury was convened in San Antonio, to look into a total of 47 suspicious deaths at Bexar County Medical Center Hospital. On 25 May the grand jury returned indictments against 32-year-old Genene Jones and she was arrested and charged with murder after succinylcholine was found in Chelsea McClellan's corpse.

WHERE:
San Antonio, Texas, USA
WHEN:
May 1981–September 1982
THE AFTERMATH:
Awaiting trial, she said, "I always cry when babies die. You can almost explain away an adult death. When you look at an adult die, you can say they've had a full life. When a baby dies, they've been cheated." Genene Jones went on trial for the murder of Chelsea McClellan on 15 January 1984. Found guilty on 15 February, she was sentenced to 99 years in prison. A second trial on 24 October for administering drugs to a child saw her receive another 60 years.
YOU SHOULD KNOW:
Genene Jones was born on 13 July 1950 and immediately given up for adoption. Her adoptive father, Dick, was arrested in 1960 for theft of $1,500 and jewellery. He confessed but claimed it had been a practical joke and the charges were dropped. Genene Jones will be paroled in 2017.

*Genene Jones after a
pre-trial hearing*

Leonard Lake & Charles Ng

"They scream so loud I can't hear myself"

THE CRIME: Leonard Lake was born on 29 October 1945 in San Francisco, California. His mother encouraged him in an unusual hobby – photographing naked girls, including his sisters and cousins. He began having sex with one sister in return for protecting her from their violent little brother, Donald. In 1966 he joined the US Marines but was demobbed in 1971 after two years of psychiatric counselling. Back in civvy street, he moved to San Jose and got married but his propensity for photographing women in bondage scenes soon led to his divorce. In 1980 he received a year's probation for theft. In August 1981 he married again and moved to a communal ranch in Ukiah, California, a weird place that had medieval outfits and "unicorns" (surgically altered goats).

Soon after he met Charles Chitat Ng (pronounced Ing) a violent juvenile delinquent who had been born in Hong Kong on 24 December 1961. The FBI arrested both men in April 1982 for weapons violations. Lake fled but Ng spent 18 months in jail. On his release, the two men met again. Lake was living in seclusion near Wilseyville, a region 240 km (150 mi) east of San Francisco, where he had stockpiled illegal weapons and stolen video equipment. On Sunday 2 June 1985 Ng walked into South City lumberyard and stole a $75 vice, which he put in the boot of a nearby 1980 Honda Prelude (registration 838WFQ), before running away. When the police arrived the car was still there and at the wheel was a bearded man who said his name was Robin Stapley but he did not look like the photo on his driving licence. Arrested, he managed to take a cyanide pill and died on 6 June. He was identified as Leonard Lake. When police searched Lake's home they found that the video equipment had been used to make porn films showing women stripping before being raped and tortured. The two men in the films were Leonard Lake and Charles Ng. Twenty-one women were in the videos and six were found alive. The other 15, it was suspected, were murdered at the ranch. Ng told a friend, "You should hear the screams. Sometimes I have to gag them because they scream so loud I can't hear myself."

WHERE:
Wilseyville, Calaveras County,
California, USA
WHEN:
1981–1985
THE AFTERMATH:
A warrant was issued for the arrest of Ng for 12 murders: Kathleen Allen, her boyfriend Michael Carroll, Robin Scott Stapley, Randy Johnson, Charles Gunnar (Lake's best man), Donald Lake (Lake's brother), Paul Cosner, (the owner of the Honda Prelude), Brenda O'Connor, Lonnie Bond Sr, Lonnie Bond Jr, (Lake's neighbours) and Harvey, Deborah and Sean Dubs. Ng was arrested on 6 July 1985 as he shoplifted at The Bay department store in Calgary, Alberta, Canada. He was finally deported to America on 26 September 1991. In October 1998 after 13 years of delays and extended legal arguments, Ng's trial began. On 11 February 1999 after eight months the jury found Ng guilty of the murders of six men, three women and two baby boys. He was sentenced to death.

Leonard Lake plays with his pet dog, Cinder.

Altemio Sanchez

"He's the nicest person you'd ever want to meet"

WHERE:
Buffalo, New York, USA
WHEN:
1981–Friday 29 September 2006
THE AFTERMATH:
The police arrested Sanchez on
15 January 2007 and charged him with
murder. On 16 May Sanchez pleaded
guilty to three murders. He was
sentenced to 75 years in prison on
15 August 2007.
YOU SHOULD KNOW:
One of his neighbours, Jerry Donohue,
said, "The scary part is, he's the nicest
person you'd ever want to meet. This is
what's so upsetting. He never made
any sexual remarks about a woman,
never swore. You'd go to his parties
and have a beer or two with him."

*Sanchez is escorted to his
arraignment.*

THE CRIME: Altemio Sanchez's reign of terror lasted a quarter of a
century, during which time it is thought that he murdered three
women and raped around a dozen more in and around Buffalo, New
York. Born on 19 January 1958, in San Sebastian, Puerto Rico, one
of four children, he became known as the "Bike Path Rapist"
because he attacked many of his victims around remote bicycle lanes.

On 29 September 1990 he killed his first victim. Californian
Linda Yalem, 22, was a student at the State University at Buffalo
when Sanchez murdered her as she was jogging off the Ellicott
Creek bicycle path. It was more than two years before his second
murder. He strangled Majane Mazur, a 32-year-old prostitute, whose
body was found in a field near some railroad tracks in November
1992 and then, 14 years later, killed Joan Diver, a nurse and a
mother of four, on 29 September 2006. Two days later her corpse
was found on a cycle track in Newstead, New York. Miss Diver was
the only one of his victims that Sanchez did not rape. Sanchez, a
father of two young sons who lived on Allendale Street in
Cheektowaga, was caught only through a lucky break. In 1985
schizophrenic Anthony Capozzi was jailed for a rape committed by
Sanchez. It was 22 years before he would be released and that was
only when a policeman followed up a statement from a woman who
had been raped in 1981. Two years later, she saw her rapist and
noted his car registration number. When the police questioned the
owner, he was able to
provide an alibi. When
the police questioned
him again more than
20 years later he
confessed that he was
not driving the car
that day and had lent
it to his nephew –
Altemio Sanchez.

 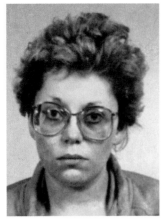  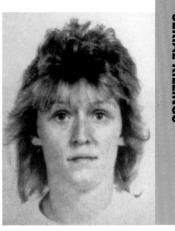

From left to right: Stefanija Mayer, Waltraud Wagner, Maria Gruber and Ilene Leidolf

Waltraud Wagner

"It's a small step from killing the terminally ill to the killing of insolent, burdensome patients"

THE CRIME: Lainz General Hospital is the biggest of its kind in Vienna and many of its patients are old or suffering from terminal illnesses. It would, therefore, not be too difficult for a determined killer to get away with murder. No one could imagine that in 1983 there were four killers at work at Lainz.

It would be six years and more than 40 deaths before the quartet, comprising leader Waltraud Wagner and her cohorts Maria Gruber, 19, Ilene Leidolf, 21, and 43-year-old grandmother Stephanija Mayer, was brought to justice. Wagner was 24 when she was asked by a 77-year-old patient to "end her suffering". Wagner was more than happy to oblige and found that she enjoyed having power over life and death. She recruited the others and they planned whom they were going to kill while they worked on the night shift. The foursome murdered their patients through drug overdoses and "oral hygiene treatment", where one nurse held the patient's head back while a second poured water down their throats until they drowned. It was an agonizing way to die and almost undetectable as murder. When examined, many elderly patients had fluid in their lungs.

At first the women euthanized (as they saw it) patients but that progressed to killing anyone who annoyed them by soiling the bed or asking for help. They were caught not through police work or a hospital investigation, but because of their own big mouths. One day the four were having drinks and boasting about what they had done when a doctor overheard them. He immediately went to the police and, after an investigation lasting six weeks, the women were arrested on 7 April 1989.

WHERE:
Pavilion 5, Lainz General Hospital, Vienna, Austria
WHEN:
1983–1989
THE AFTERMATH:
The women confessed to 49 murders with Wagner giving a "free bed with the good Lord" to 39 of them. One of the others believed that Wagner had actually murdered more than 200 in the previous two years. Awaiting trial, Wagner claimed that in fact the death toll was just ten and they were all mercy killings. The trial opened on 28 February 1991 and on 28 March all were found guilty. Wagner was convicted of 15 murders, 17 counts of attempted murder and two counts of assault. She was jailed for life. Leidolf was convicted of five murders and also received a life sentence. Gruber and Mayer were both jailed for 15 years for manslaughter and attempted murder. Ernst Kloyber, the state attorney, said, "It's a small step from killing the terminally ill to the killing of insolent, burdensome patients, and from there to that which was known under the Third Reich as euthanasia. It is a door that must never be opened again."
YOU SHOULD KNOW:
Wagner and Leidolf were paroled on 7 August 2008 and given new identities at taxpayers' expense. Gruber and Mayer had already been released and provided with new names.

Timothy W. Spencer

Southside Strangler

WHERE:
Richmond, Virginia, USA
WHEN:
Tuesday 24 January 1984–Tuesday
1 December 1987
THE AFTERMATH:
Spencer was arrested in January 1988
and charged with the murder of Susan
Tucker. DNA evidence also linked him
to the murders of Debbie Dudley Davis
and Susan Hellams although it was
insufficiently conclusive for the Diane
Cho killing. It also proved that he had
been responsible for the 1984 murder
of Carol Hamm. On 16 July 1988
Spencer was convicted of Susan
Tucker's murder and sentenced to life
imprisonment. A second trial began in
the Circuit Court of the City of
Richmond, Manchester Courthouse, on
17 January 1989. The jury convicted
Spencer of capital murder, rape,
sodomy and burglary on 12 May 1989.
He was executed in the electric chair
on 27 April 1994.
YOU SHOULD KNOW:
On 4 January 1989, Governor Gerald L.
Baliles granted David Vasquez an
absolute pardon. He received $117,000
compensation from the
Commonwealth of Virginia.

THE CRIME: Timothy Wilson Spencer was the first murderer to be convicted on DNA evidence in Virginia. His first killing was on 24 January 1984 when he raped and murdered Carol Hamm in her Arlington, Virginia home, a crime for which an innocent man, David Vasquez, spent five years behind bars. Vasquez was developmentally disabled and pleaded guilty to second-degree murder and burglary on 4 February 1985. He was sent to prison for 35 years. Two years later Spencer, who was born in 1962, began his reign of terror as the Southside Strangler. His first victim in September 1987 was 35-year-old Debbie Dudley Davis whom he raped and strangled with a sock, leaving her nude corpse on her bed at home.

A fortnight later, on the night of 2 October or early morning of 3 October, Dr Susan Elizabeth Hellams, a 32-year-old neurosurgeon at the Medical College of Virginia in Richmond, was raped, strangled and left in her own wardrobe. The killer gained access to the house by cutting out a large portion of a second-storey bedroom window screen. On 22 November 15-year-old schoolgirl Diane Cho was raped, strangled and left naked at her home 24 km (15 mi) south of Richmond in Chesterfield County. On 1 December the naked body of 44-year-old Susan M. Tucker was found in her Arlington townhouse. She had been raped and murdered by ligature strangulation.

Christopher Wilder

He persuaded two 15-year-old girls to pose nude for him.

THE CRIME: Born in Australia on 13 March 1945, Christopher Bernard Wilder began his criminal life while still in his teens. In 1963 he was put on probation for his part in a gang rape. Two years later, two teenage girls were murdered on Wanda Beach in Sydney and Wilder remains the prime suspect. In 1968 he married but his wife left him after a week. The following year he moved to America and into a mansion on Mission Hill Road, Boynton Beach, Florida where he made a fortune in the real estate business. From 1971 he was in and out of court on sex charges, including rape, but none ever stuck. In 1982 he travelled to Australia to visit his family and, while there, persuaded two 15-year-old girls to pose nude for him. Arrested, he was permitted to return to Florida before his trial. On 26 February 1984 Rosario Gonzalez, a model at the Miami Grand Prix, disappeared. On 5 March another model and Wilder's former girlfriend, Elizabeth Kenyon, went missing. Ten days later, Wilder went on the run. On 23 March the corpse of 21-year old Terry Ferguson was found at Canaveral Groves, five days after Wilder had abducted her from a shopping centre in Satellite Beach and murdered her. Three days earlier Wilder attempted to kidnap another girl but she fought back. On 21 March at Beaumont, Texas he asked 24-year-old Terry Walden to model for him but she turned him down. She disappeared on 23 March. Her body was found in a canal on 26 March, the same day that the body of 21-year-old Suzanne Logan was found in Oklahoma City. She had been raped, tortured and then stabbed to death. On 29 March 18-year-old Sheryl Bonaventura became Wilder's latest victim. She was shot and stabbed to death. On 1 April he murdered 17-year-old Michelle Korfman. He kidnapped 16-year-old Tina Marie Risico and, after photographing her, persuaded her to help him find other girls. She helped him kidnap 16-year-old Dawnette Wilt in Gary, Indiana whom he raped and stabbed but she survived. She also persuaded 33-year-old Beth Dodge to join them whereupon he shot the woman. He bought Risico a plane ticket for Los Angeles and headed for New Hampshire.

WHERE:
Florida; Texas; Oklahoma; Nevada; California; New York, USA
WHEN:
Sunday 26 February–Thursday 12 April 1984
THE AFTERMATH:
On Friday 13 April 1984, after he failed to kidnap another girl, Wilder was spotted by a police patrol in Colebrook, New Hampshire and in the ensuing fight was shot dead. His death was officially listed as a suicide.
YOU SHOULD KNOW:
Wilder left an estate worth $2 million.

Police mug shots of Wilder

Richard Ramírez

"I love all that blood"

THE AFTERMATH:
During his trial Ramírez sat either quietly or put his fingers to the sides of his head like horns and chanted, "Evil, evil…" On 20 September 1989 Ramírez was found guilty of 12 first-degree murders, one second-degree murder and 30 charges of rape and burglary. On 7 November he was sentenced to death. He told a fellow inmate, "I love all that blood." On 3 October 1996 Ramírez married Doreen Lioy, who had written him more than 70 letters while he was incarcerated.

YOU SHOULD KNOW:
During the trial, on 14 August 1989, juror Phyllis Singletary was murdered by her boyfriend, who later committed suicide. Some of the other jurors believed that Ramírez had somehow arranged her death, although it was later revealed to be unrelated.

THE CRIME: Richard Ramírez was a satanist who, between June 1984 and August 1985, murdered more than a dozen people. Ricardo Múñoz Ramírez was born in El Paso, Texas on 29 February 1960. Known as the "Night Stalker", he broke into houses through an open door or window. His first murder happened on 28 June 1984. After taking cocaine, Ramírez broke into the Glassell Park, Los Angeles home of 79-year-old Jennie Vincow. She was found the next morning stabbed to death, her head almost removed from her body and an autopsy revealed that she had been raped. The attacks continued and Los Angeles lived in fear. There were four attacks in March 1985. One old lady was attacked with a hammer with such ferocity that the hammer handle split. Often Ramírez would leave a lipstick-daubed pentagram at the scene. The violence reached a peak that summer.

The victims that survived described a tall thin man dressed in black with bad teeth and bad breath. As with so many criminals, it was luck that led to the capture of Ramírez. The FBI at Quantico were scouring a getaway car and discovered a fingerprint belonging to a petty crook on their files. His name was Richard Ramírez. The bureau issued a photograph of Ramírez which was published in the media. On 31 August 1985 Ramírez was recognized by the owners of a corner shop on whose news stand his face was pictured. He ran 3 km (2 mi) in 12 minutes and then attempted to steal Faustino Pinon's red Ford Mustang from his driveway. He did not know that Mr Pinon was working under the car and he stopped Ramírez driving away. Ramírez then tried to steal another car, was stopped and then attempted to flee. Locals chased him and one knocked him to the ground with a metal post before others sat on him until the police arrived.

Richard Ramírez at his trial

John Edward Robinson

The Slave Master

Kansas District Attorney, Paul Morrison, talks to the media following Robinson's court appearance.

THE CRIME: Born in Cicero, Illinois on 27 December 1943, John Edward Robinson was a conman and thief who worked his way up the criminal food chain to become a serial killer. In 1969 Robinson was convicted of theft and was sentenced to three years' probation. Between his first offence and 1991 he was convicted four times for embezzlement or theft. Paula Godfrey, an Olathe, Kansas teenager was supposedly offered a job by Robinson and she was never seen after September 1984. He was paid $2,500 by Don, his childless brother, to arrange an adoption. In January 1985 he met 19-year-old Lisa Stasi and her four-month-old baby, Tiffany. He told Stasi that he had a job for her but she would have to relocate to Texas. Two days after she left, Don Robinson was given a baby girl and a bill for $3,000. Lisa Stasi was never seen again. In 1987 Catherine Clampitt, 27, also was supposedly given a job by Robinson. She, too, disappeared in June 1987.

The FBI set a trap for Robinson and he was jailed but his conviction was overturned because of a procedural mistake by the bureau. However, he remained in jail until 1993 on a theft conviction. He was freed from prison on medical grounds, purchased a computer and began joining internet dating sites. Rather than romance, he targeted women for bondage sex – his user name was The Slave Master. In jail he had befriended a librarian, 49-year-old Beverly Bonner, and she left her husband for him. He murdered her soon after his release but kept on cashing her alimony cheques. He put her body in a chemical drum in a storage locker in Raymore, Missouri. Next to it, in similar containers, were the bodies of mother and daughter, 45-year-old Sheila Faith and 15-year-old Debbie who was wheelchair-bound. He banked the disability benefits sent for Debbie.

In late 1997 Robinson offered sexual submissive Izabela Lewicka, 21, a job with a caravan magazine he had started and a relationship as his slave. She signed a 115 clause contract, allowing Robinson control of every aspect of her life. In 1999, when he tired of her, she disappeared. Her body was later found in a barrel at Robinson's farm near La Cygne, Kansas.

Around the time Izabela vanished Robinson persuaded 27-year-old Suzette Trouten, a bored nurse by day and submissive slave by night, to come to Kansas where he would pay her $62,000 per year to look after his sick father. She left Robinson's name and phone number with her mother before she left for Kansas in February 1998. The police put John Robinson under surveillance and persuaded one woman who had violent sex with him to place a complaint against him.

WHERE:
Raymore, Missouri; La Cygne, Kansas, USA
WHEN:
September 1984–1999
THE AFTERMATH:
Robinson was arrested on 2 June 2000 at his caravan home, and accused of murdering three women. He was convicted at the Johnson County Court House in Olathe, Kansas in 2002 and sentenced to death in January 2003.

Thierry Paulin, the Monster of Montmartre

Thierry Paulin

Monster of Montmartre

THE CRIME: Born at Fort-de-France, Martinique on 28 November 1963, Thierry Paulin was abandoned by his father and raised by his paternal grandmother, a restaurateur who had little time for him. He was 10 years old before he moved back in with his mother who had remarried but he didn't get on in the new environment and soon went to live with his father in France. At school Paulin had few friends and did not do well. He became a paratrooper when he was 17 but did not fit in with his colleagues because of his colour and blatant homosexuality. He decided to exact revenge on society and, possibly, his grandmother.

In Paris there were a quarter of a million women aged 65 or over who lived alone, and it was this group that Paulin decided to attack. On 14 November 1982 he attacked an old lady with a knife in her grocery shop but she knew him and he was arrested. He was jailed for two years in June 1983 but the sentence was suspended. Leaving the army in 1984, he became a waiter at the Paradis Latin, a transvestite club. He met and began a relationship with French-Guyanese drug addict Jean-Thierry Mathurin, 19, and Paulin, too, began to take and sell drugs.

The attacks continued in earnest on 5 October 1984 when two old ladies – Germaine Petitot, 91, and Anna Barbier-Ponthus, 83 – were beaten in Paris. Barbier-Ponthus died of her injuries and the murderer also stole 300 francs from her. Over the next seven weeks, eight women were murdered, many in horrific circumstances. The attacker became known as the Monster of Montmartre and it was said that he would engage old ladies in conversation. If he disliked them, he would kill them.

More old ladies were murdered and the police collected fingerprints from 150,000 suspects. Paulin was not captured sooner because his prints had somehow vanished from the database. Paulin was jailed in 1986 for a year after beating up one of his drug dealers. Released, he killed 79-year-old Rachel Cohen on 25 November 1987 and the same day attacked 87-year-old Rose Finalteri. He left her for dead but, unfortunately for him, she survived and gave the police a description of Paulin. "*Il était un métis d'une vingtaine d'année coiffée à la Carl Lewis, avec une boucle d'oreille gauche,*" she said. ("He was mixed race in his 20s with hair like Carl Lewis and an earring in his left ear.") On 1 December Paulin was arrested.

WHERE:
Paris, France
WHEN:
Friday 5 October 1984–Wednesday 25 November 1987
THE AFTERMATH:
On 3 December Paulin confessed and implicated Mathurin. In prison he fell ill and was diagnosed with Aids. He died during the night of 16 April 1989, in the hospital wing of Fresnes Prison. Mathurin was tried for the first nine attacks and murders and was sentenced to life plus 18 years without parole.
YOU SHOULD KNOW:
Thierry Paulin was never convicted of the murders of which he was accused.

Frankford Slasher

"Maybe I killed her"

THE CRIME: This case remains unsolved 18 years after the last killing. Eight women were stabbed and sexually assaulted. The first to die was 52-year-old Helen Patent who lived in Parkland, Bucks County, Pennsylvania. She died on 19 August 1985. It was a week before she was found, naked from the waist down, with her legs open and her top pulled up to bare her breasts. Reports state that she was stabbed 47 times. Five months later, on 3 January 1986, Anna Carroll, 68, was killed. She lived on the 1400 block of Ritner Street and was discovered naked from the waist down, with a kitchen knife still in her. Susan Olszef, 64, was killed on Christmas Day 1986 at her home on Richmond Street. All three women had been regulars at the Golden Bar, or Goldie's, a bar that has now been demolished.

On 8 January 1987 Jeanne Durkin, a 28-year-old former go-go dancer and homeless woman who slept on the street near Goldie's, was murdered and left under a lorry. She had been sexually assaulted, stabbed 74 times and wrapped in an overcoat. Not long after, Catherine M. Jones, 29, was murdered. Some do not connect her to the slasher killings because she had no stab wounds and was not sexually assaulted. On 11 November 1988 Margaret Vaughan, 66, was found stabbed to death in the apartment building on Penn Street from which she had just been evicted.

Three months later, on 19 January 1989, Theresa Sciortino, 30, was discovered in her home on Arrott Street. She was naked apart from a pair of white socks and had been butchered. Several eyewitnesses placed Vaughn and Sciortino with a middle-aged white man. An identikit picture was drawn but no arrests were made. Early on 29 April 1990 Carol Dowd, a 46-year-old woman with a history of mental illness, was discovered stabbed three dozen times behind Newman's Seafood on Frankford Avenue. Her left nipple had been removed. The next day police questioned Leonard Christopher, who worked at Newman's. Two prostitutes placed Christopher at the scene of the crime, with a large utility knife tucked in his belt, at the time of the murders. He was arrested and charged with Carol Dowd's murder. His boss, Jaesa Phang, said that Christopher had said to her, "Maybe I killed her."

On 12 December 1990 Christopher was convicted. Many presumed that he had also committed the Frankford Slasher killings but one major fact seemed to dispute this – eyewitnesses had described a middle-aged white man and Leonard Christopher is black. On 6 September 1990 Michelle Dehner (aka Martin) was murdered in her Arrott Street apartment and, after that, the slasher killings stopped.

WHERE:
Frankford, Pennsylvania, USA
WHEN:
Monday 19 August 1985–Thursday 6 September 1990
THE AFTERMATH:
Who was the Frankford Slasher? And did Leonard Christopher really murder Carol Dowd? He said, "I was railroaded. I didn't kill Carol Dowd. I did not even know Carol Dowd. I was implicated by prostitutes... that the police put up."

Dorothea Puente

"I have not killed anyone"

WHERE:
1426 F Street, Sacramento,
California, USA
WHEN:
1985–1988
THE AFTERMATH:
On 12 November Puente fled but was
arrested in Los Angles at 10.40pm on
17 November in a downmarket motel.
She said, "I have not killed anyone. The
cheques I cashed, yes... I used to be a
very good person at one time."
Puente's trial began in February 1993
and lasted five months. One hundred
and fifty-three witnesses took the
stand and 3,100 pieces of evidence
were presented. The jury found Puente
guilty of murdering Dorothy Miller,
Benjamin Fink and Leona Carpenter
but could not reach a verdict on six
other charges so Superior Court Judge
Michael Virga declared a mistrial. On
10 December 1993 he sentenced
Puente to prison for life without the
possibility of parole.
YOU SHOULD KNOW:
In 2004 she wrote a recipe book,
Cooking With A Serial Killer.

Puente confers with her attorney in court.

THE CRIME: Dorothea Puente was born in San Bernardino County, California on 9 January 1929 as Dorothea Helen Gray and raised in an orphanage because both parents were alcoholics who died when she was young. In 1945 she married Fred McFaul and gave birth to two daughters but gave them both up. After just three years of marriage her husband left. An attempt at chequebook fraud resulted in a year in jail. When she was released Puente fell pregnant and gave up the resulting daughter for adoption. In 1952 she married Axel Johanson. Eight years later she was jailed for 90 days for running a brothel and then began working as a carer, looking after disabled and old people in private homes. In 1966 in Mexico City she married Roberto Puente who was 19 years younger than her, but the marriage ended after two years.

She then took charge of a three-storey, 16-bedroom care home at 2100 F Street in Sacramento, California. In 1976 she married an alcoholic named Pedro Montalvo but they soon split. Puente took to hanging around in pubs looking for old men, whose signatures she then forged to steal their pensions. Despite being arrested and charged, she continued to commit fraud while on bail. In 1981 she moved into an upstairs flat at 1426 F Street in downtown Sacramento. In April 1982 61-year-old Ruth Monroe began living with Puente but died not long after, although police adjudged her death a suicide. On 18 August 1982 Puente was jailed for five years for theft. Released after three, she moved back into 1426 F Street with Everson Gillmouth, her 77-year-old pen pal from prison.

In November 1985 Puente asked Ismael Florez to help with some DIY and gave him a car in return. She then asked him to build her a box 1.8 m by 90 cm by 60 cm (6 ft by 3 ft by 2 ft) to store "books and other

items". After telling him the box was full of junk, they dumped it in a river in Sutter County. When the box was found on 1 January 1986, it contained the badly decomposed body of an old man. That year she approached a social worker and told her that she was offering quality care for old people. The social worker sent 19 old men in two years but was surprised when she never heard from some of them again. After the neighbours complained about a weird small emanating from her garden, police arrived at 1426 F Street on 11 November 1988 and found a body buried in the garden.

Daniel Camargo Barbosa

"Because they cried"

THE CRIME: Colombia-born Daniel Camargo Barbosa's first offence occurred on 10 April 1964 when he learned that the woman he was in love with was not a virgin, so he raped her. Jailed, Camargo decided that any of his future victims would not live to tell their tale. On 3 May 1974 Camargo was arrested at Barranquilla, Colombia as he tried to bury the body of a nine-year-old girl he had raped and murdered. He was sentenced to 30 years' imprisonment, which was reduced to 25 on appeal. He was sent to the prison on the volcanic island of Gorgona on 24 December 1977. No one had ever escaped from the island until Camargo did, in a canoe in November 1984. The press reported that sharks had eaten Camargo but, unfortunately, he had lived and appeared in Ecuador, where he began a new career of rape and murder.

He was nicknamed the Beast of The Andes and, when he was arrested, confessed to the murder of 71 girls. In the port of Guayaquil, 55 young girls disappeared in the space of just 14 months. When the bodies of many victims were found, they had been brutalized with a blunt instrument and a machete. Sweet-wrappers were found at three of the murder scenes and police guessed that the killer was luring the children with sweets. In June 1988 the corpse of 12-year-old Gloria Andino was found on the edge of a mangrove swamp. Examination of the body led to the discovery of a sweet-wrapper in her hand. On the wrapper was a smudged fingerprint, which was identified as belonging to Camargo. A short time afterwards, a motorcycle policeman arrested a man behaving suspiciously in the vicinity of where Gloria Andino had lived. The man turned out to be Camargo and in his pocket was a picture of one of the missing girls.

WHERE:
Ecuador
WHEN:
1986–1988
THE AFTERMATH:
Camargo admitted to the killings and took the police to the graves of his last victims. He told police that he had indeed lured the children with sweets and pens and chose children, as he wanted virgins "because they cried". He was tried in September 1989 and sentenced to 16 years in jail, the maximum under Ecuadorian law. It has been reported that on 13 November 1994 another prisoner, the cousin of one of his victims, murdered Camargo in jail although this has not been confirmed.

Kenneth Erskine, Stockwell Strangler

"It says it will kill me if it gets me"

WHERE:
London, England
WHEN:
Wednesday 9 April–Thursday
24 July 1986
THE AFTERMATH:
Police questioned Erskine about the murders but he spent much of the time giggling, staring out of the window into the sky or masturbating. He told police a voice in his head told him to kill, "It tries to think for me. It says it will kill me if it gets me. It blanks things from my mind." Erskine went on trial at the Old Bailey on 12 January 1988, charged with seven murders. After 18 days, he was found guilty and told he would never be freed. On 23 February 1996 he saved the life of Yorkshire Ripper Peter Sutcliffe (see page 397) in Broadmoor when Paul Wilson tried to strangle Sutcliffe with the flex from a pair of headphones. On 30 November 2007 Erskine's sentence was changed to 40 years after psychiatrists diagnosed him as schizophrenic.
YOU SHOULD KNOW:
Erskine almost certainly murdered Wilfred Parkes, 81, on 2 June 1986 and 75-year-old Trevor Thomas in the bath of his home in Barton Court, Clapham on 12 July 1986. He has not been charged with either murder.

THE CRIME: In 1986 the elderly residents of a district of south London were terrorized by Kenneth Erskine, earning him the nickname the Stockwell Strangler. Born in 1962, West Indian Erskine struck for the first time on 9 April 1986, killing 78-year-old spinster Nancy Emms. She had been strangled and subjected to a horrific sexual assault before being laid out as if for burial at her unkempt basement flat in West Hill Road, Wandsworth. On 9 June 68-year-old Janet Cockett was discovered naked in her bed in her flat on the Overton Estate, Stockwell, having been strangled. A palm print and a smudged thumbprint were found at the flat. During the early hours of 27 June Erskine attempted to murder retired engineer Fred Prentice in his room in a council-run old people's home in Cedars Road, Clapham but was scared off when Mr Prentice managed to raise the alarm. The next night Erskine sodomized and murdered 84-year-old Valentine Gliem and 94-year-old Zbigniew Strabawa in their adjoining rooms at Somerville Hastings House, an old people's home in Stockwell Park Crescent. After the murders Erskine had a wash and a shave at the home. Ten days later, Erskine murdered and sexually abused William Carmen, 84, on the Marques estate in Islington, north London. Almost $500 was missing from the flat, the first time a robbery had taken place as well as murder and sexual assault. On 20 July, Erskine struck again, strangling William Downes, 74, at his home on the Overton Estate in Stockwell. This time the police found a clear set of palm prints. It took the police three months to link the prints to Erskine, despite his long criminal record. On 24 July Erskine struck again, killing 83-year-old widow Florence Tisdall at her home in Ranelagh Gardens, Putney. She had been strangled, sexually assaulted and her ribs broken when Erskine knelt on her chest. The police discovered that Erskine was on the dole and when he turned up to sign on at the Department of Social Security office in Southwark on 28 July, he was arrested without a struggle.

Kenneth Erskine, centre, is remanded in police custody.

Sara Aldrete

"He's dead! He's dead!"

THE CRIME: On 14 March 1987 four friends from the University of Texas arrived in Matomoros, a city 1000 km (621 mi) from Mexico City and 570 km (354 mi) from Houston. The quartet went on a bar crawl and during the outing 21-year-old Mark Kilroy disappeared. The Kilroy family hired an investigator to discover what had happened to their son but discovered nothing. Then, just as they were about to give up, they spoke to a policeman in the drugs squad that had recently raided Rancho Santa Elena where they had made several arrests. One of those in custody said that he had seen a "blond gringo" tied up in the back of a van at the ranch.

The police searched a shed at Rancho Santa Elena and found large amounts of cocaine and marijuana. The most disturbing thing in the shed was what appeared to be an altar covered with several bloodstains, human hair and brain matter and decorated with a goat's head. The ranch was home to a Satan-worshipping cult. Those arrested said that Mark Kilroy had been sacrificed to Satan to give the cult protection from the police. Every time that a large drug deal took place a young man or boy was sacrificed on the altar. Their hearts and brains were torn out and boiled for a cannibal stew before they were decapitated. At least 15 victims were found in a grave at the ranch. A godfather, Adolfo de Jesus Constanzo, and a high priestess, Sara María Aldrete, led the group and they had ordered the murders. Both had gone on the run by the time the police arrived.

Drug dealer and high priestess of the satanic cult Sara Aldrete

WHERE:
Matomoros, Mexico
WHEN:
Saturday 14 March 1987
THE AFTERMATH:
On 5 May 1989 Constanzo, Aldrete and other members of the cult were traced to an apartment block in Mexico City. The police laid siege until Aldrete screamed, "He's dead! He's dead!" In the apartment were three members of the cult but Constanzo and his gay lover were dead inside a walk-in wardrobe. Aldrete denied killing Constanzo and in August 1990 was acquitted of his murder. She was sentenced to six years in jail for criminal association. At a second hearing she was given a 62-year sentence for murder. Alvaro de Leo Valdez, a cult member, was convicted of Constanzo's murder and sentenced to life in jail.

429

*Courtroom sketch of
Karla Homolka*

WHERE:
Scarborough, Ontario, Canada
WHEN:
Monday 4 May 1987–Thursday
16 April 1992
THE AFTERMATH:
On 27 December 1992 Bernardo beat
up his wife with a torch. On 5 January
1993 she filed charges against him and
he was arrested. The police found a
mountain of evidence at the couple's
home. On 14 May 1993 Homolka
accepted a 12 year sentence plea
bargain to testify against her husband.
Legal arguments meant that
Bernardo's trial did not begin until May
1995. Bernardo claimed that while he
raped and tortured Leslie Mahaffy and
Kristen French, it was Homolka who
actually killed them. In 2004 the
Toronto Sun reported that Homolka
had had sex in prison with "a male
inmate she now wants to marry". It
also said that she was having a lesbian
affair with inmate Lynda Verronneau
who later wrote a book about
Homolka. On 1 September 1995,
Bernardo was convicted on all the
charges against him regarding the
kidnappings, rapes and murders of
Leslie Mahaffy and Kristen French. He
was sentenced to life in prison.
YOU SHOULD KNOW:
The six videotapes depicting the
torture and rape of Bernardo and
Homolka's victims were destroyed.
Homolka was released from Ste-Anne-
des-Plaines Prison on 4 July 2005. An
attempt to change her name to Emily
Chiara Tremblay was refused in the
summer of 2006. In February 2007 she
gave birth to a son and later that year
left Canada for the Antilles in the West
Indies where she now lives.

Paul Bernardo &
Karla Homolka

As she prepared for her wedding, she also prepared for him to rape her sister.

THE CRIME: Karla Leanne Homolka was born in Port Credit, Ontario,
Canada on 4 May 1970, the eldest of three girls. Blonde and beautiful, on
17 October 1987 she met Paul Bernardo, a handsome, sophisticated
professional accountant with money. Within an hour of meeting, they
were having sex. In 1989 Homolka was sacked from her job as a
veterinary assistant for stealing drugs. On Christmas Eve that year
Bernardo proposed in what Homolka said was "the most romantic
moment of my life". She vowed to do anything to keep him happy.
One problem arose: when they met Homolka was not a virgin, which
upset Bernardo. He persuaded Homolka that it was his right,
therefore, to take the virginity of her little sister, Tammy, 15, and that
he should be videoed in the act. In July 1990 Bernardo took Tammy
for a drink and later told Homolka that they "got drunk and began
making out." Homolka knew that her fiancée was chronically
unfaithful and was, in fact, the Scarborough Rapist who had attacked
12 young women since 4 May 1987. Still she loved him and as she
prepared her wedding, she also prepared for him to rape her sister.
Two days before Christmas 1990 Homolka and Bernardo spiked
Tammy's cocktail with sleeping tablets and then Homolka pressed a
Halothane-soaked rag against her sister's nose and mouth. They took
Tammy to the basement and filmed themselves raping her. While
unconscious, Tammy began being sick. A few hours later she was
pronounced dead at St Catharine's General Hospital. The cause of
death was choking on her vomit while drunk.

The couple moved into a house at 57 Bayview, Port Dalhousie
where Karla searched for a replacement for Tammy – and found one:
a girl who looked like Tammy. On Friday 7 June 1991 they drugged
the unwary teenager and raped her, taking her virginity, before
Bernardo sodomized her. The next morning she had no recollection of
what had happened. Eight days later, Bernardo met Leslie Mahaffy,
abducted her and took her back to the house where they repeatedly
raped her for 24 hours before killing her. Meanwhile, the teenager
they had drugged and raped returned regularly to the Bernardo home
where she gave oral sex to Bernardo. She thought that she was still a
virgin so refused to consent to full intercourse. On 30 November 1991
Terri Anderson, a pretty and vivacious 14-year-old, disappeared. On
16 April 1992 they kidnapped Kristen French from St Catharine's
Church car park. They spent three days torturing the girl and
captured it all on video. A fortnight after she was kidnapped, Kristen's
naked body was found in a ditch.

Richard Angelo

"I'm going to make you feel better"

THE CRIME: Richard Angelo worked the night shift (11pm–7am) as supervisor in the intensive-care unit at Good Samaritan Hospital in West Islip on Long Island in New York, beginning in April 1987. Most of his patients were old and frail and had heart or breathing problems, so it was not unexpected that many would die suddenly. On 11 October 1987 two patients died. Another almost passed away but 73-year-old Gerolamo Kucich managed to push the assistance button after Angelo gave him an injection, having told him "I'm going to make you feel better." A nurse took a urine sample and had it analysed. The urine contained Pavulon and Anectine, neither of which had been prescribed for Mr Kucich. Angelo's locker was searched on 13 November and police found a hypodermic syringe containing traces of Pavulon. When police arrived to arrest Angelo the next day he was not at home, but was attending a medical technicians' conference at Albany.

Hospital authorities found that there had been 37 Code Blue emergencies in a six-week period while Angelo was on duty and 25 patients died. Angelo was arrested on 15 November. He was 26 years old, single, collected rocks and had been in the Boy Scouts and a volunteer fireman. He had a desire to be needed, to be thought of as heroic. He intended to bring his patients to near death before reviving them, when all would praise his skills. Unfortunately, on several occasions he misjudged the dosage.

WHERE:
Good Samaritan Hospital, 1000 Montauk Highway, West Islip, Long Island, New York, USA
WHEN:
Wednesday 16 September–Sunday 11 October 1987
THE AFTERMATH:
Angelo confessed to his crimes. "I wanted to create a situation where I would cause the patient to have some respiratory distress or some problem, and through my intervention or suggested intervention or whatever, come out looking like I knew what I was doing. I had no confidence in myself. I felt very inadequate." Angelo was ultimately convicted of two counts of depraved-indifference murder, one count of second-degree manslaughter, one count of criminally negligent homicide and six counts of assault and was sentenced to 61 years to life.

Killer nurse Richard Angelo is lead away by police.

John Wayne Glover

"No more grannies"

WHERE:
Sydney, New South Wales, Australia
WHEN:
Wednesday 1 March 1989–Monday
19 March 1990
THE AFTERMATH:
John Wayne Glover, an English
immigrant who was born on
26 November 1932, went on trial on
18 November 1991 at the New South
Wales Supreme Court. He pleaded
not guilty by reason of insanity. After
two days Glover changed his plea to
guilty. On Friday 30 November 1991
he was found guilty and the judge
gave him six life sentences. On
9 September 2005 he hanged himself
in his cell at Lithgow Prison.
YOU SHOULD KNOW:
Glover worked as a salesman for a
company called Four'n'Twenty Pies.

*A police photograph of
John Glover*

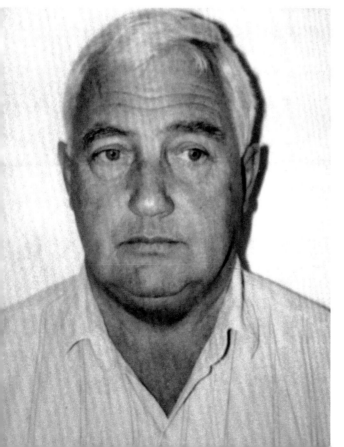

THE CRIME: Sydney Australia's Granny Killer committed his first murder on 1 March 1989 when he attacked 82-year-old Gwendoline Mitchelhill in the foyer of her block of flats in Military Road. He beat her around the head with a hammer and also broke several ribs. She died later that day of her injuries. Two months earlier 84-year-old Margaret Todhunter had been attacked on Hale Road, Mosman and had A$209 stolen. On 9 May the killer struck again and 84-year-old Lady Winifreda Ashton was found strangled with her tights and beaten with a hammer near her home on Raglan Street. The following month, on 6 June, 77-year-old Marjorie Moseley was sexually assaulted at the Wesley Gardens Retirement Home in Belrose. Eighteen days later at the Caroline Chisholm Nursing Home in Lane Cove the killer fondled the buttocks of one old lady and the breasts of another before escaping. On 8 August 1989 he attacked Effie Carnie on a back street in Lindfield and on 6 October, pretending to be a doctor, he groped the blind Phyllis McNeil at the Wybenia Nursing Home in Neutral Bay. Twelve days later he assaulted 86-year-old Doris Cox and on 2 November he murdered 85-year-old Margaret Pahud as she walked home from the shops.

A day later the Granny Killer struck again, murdering Olive Cleveland, strangling her with her tights just outside the Wesley Gardens Retirement Village. On 23 November he murdered 92-year-old Muriel Falconer in the hallway of her home in Muston Street. On 11 January 1990 82-year-old Daisy Roberts was indecently assaulted at the Greenwich Hospital in River Road, Greenwich. She cried for help and a nurse approached the assailant, who ran away. A sister managed to get his car registration number and the car was traced to pie-seller John Wayne Glover.

However, the police did not connect the assaults to the murders and, when they went to question Glover, found that he had attempted suicide on 19 January. At the hospital they were given a note written by Glover that contained the words, "No more grannies". Two weeks later the note was passed to the murder investigation team who finally realized that Glover was their man. Despite being put under surveillance Glover was able to kill his sixth victim. On 19 March 1990 he battered his platonic girlfriend, Joan Sinclair, and then attempted suicide by cutting his left wrist in her bath after downing Valium with a bottle of Vat 69.

Aileen Wuornos

"There's no sense in keeping me alive. This world doesn't mean anything to me"

THE CRIME: Aileen Pittman was born in Rochester, Michigan, on 29 February 1956. Her father was a child molester and on 18 March 1960 her maternal grandparents Lauri and Britta Wuornos legally adopted Aileen and her big brother, Keith. When she was six, Aileen's face was burned after she and Keith played with lighters. Aileen was later to tell the police that she had an incestuous relationship with Keith but it is impossible to verify since he died of throat cancer on 17 July 1976. On 23 March 1971 15-year-old Aileen gave birth to a son at a Detroit maternity home. On 7 July that year her grandmother died and Aileen became a prostitute. Over the next few years she was charged with various crimes, including disorderly conduct, drunk driving and assault.

On 20 May 1981 Wuornos was arrested at Edgewater, Florida, for armed robbery of a convenience store. Jailed on 4 May 1982, she was released on 30 June 1983. More arrests followed and on 4 January 1986 when she was arrested in Miami, police found a .22 pistol under the seat of her car. In 1987 she met and began an affair with lesbian Tyria Moore. They were together for four years. On 30 November 1989 Wuornos murdered five-times married, 51-year-old electrician Richard Mallory, after he picked her up as a prostitute. His corpse was found in the woods northwest of Daytona Beach, shot three times in the chest with a .22 pistol. On 1 June 1990 the remains of 43-year-old David Spears were found nude in the woods 64 km (40 mi) north of Tampa. He had been shot six times with a .22. Five days later Charles Carskaddon, 40, was found naked and dead. He had been shot nine times with a .22-calibre weapon. The police refused to believe that a serial killer was at large.

Peter Siems, a 65-year-old merchant seaman turned missionary, was reported missing on 22 June and his bloodstained car was found on 4 July. On 4 August Eugene Burress, 50, was discovered shot dead with a .22-calibre pistol. On 12 September former police chief Dick Humphreys, 56, was the next victim to be found. On 19 November 60-year-old Walter Antonio, a lorry driver and special policeman, was found naked apart from his socks. The police were given the names of Tyria Moore and Lee Blahovec as women having been seen with some of the victims. Blahovec also liked to call herself Lori Grody and Cammie Marsh Green and the police computer identified her as Aileen Wuornos. She was finally arrested on 9 January 1991 and a week later confessed to the murders.

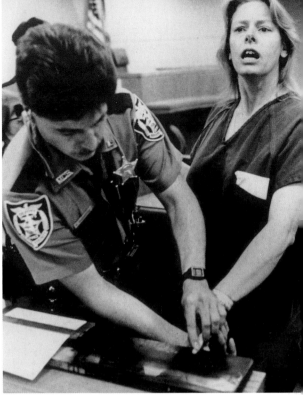

Wournos has her fingerprints taken after her arrest.

WHERE:
Florida, USA
WHEN:
1989–1990
THE AFTERMATH:
Wuornos went on trial on 13 January 1992 for the murder of Richard Mallory. She claimed that she had acted in self-defence when he tried to rape her. Found guilty, she screamed, "I was raped! I hope you get raped! Scumbags of America!" She was sentenced to death on 30 January. In April she pleaded guilty to the murders of Burress, Humphreys and Spears and received a second death sentence on 7 May 1992. On 20 July 2001 Wuornos admitted in court, "I killed those men in the first degree, robbed and killed them. I wanted to clear all the lies and let the truth come out." At 9.30am on 9 October 2002 she was injected with sodium pentothal. She died two minutes later. She had said, "There's no sense in keeping me alive. This world doesn't mean anything to me."

Rolling answers questions during his police interview.

Danny Rolling

Rolling murdered Christa Hoyt, cut her head off and put it on a nearby bookshelf

THE CRIME: Danny Harold Rolling was born in Shreveport, Louisiana, on 26 May 1954, the elder of two sons of James Rolling, a policeman, who often viciously punished the boy. James Rolling was also a sadist who would catch stray cats and then torture them. When Danny was nine his mother had a nervous breakdown. The trauma of that, added to his father's cruelty, led teachers to describe the boy as "suffering from an inferiority complex, with aggressive tendencies and poor impulse control". He turned to drink and, aged 13, was arrested by his father and left in jail for a fortnight. Four years later he joined the US Army Air Force but was discharged because of his drinking and drug use. In September 1974 he married 19-year-old O'Mather Halko but she left him in 1977, two years after the birth of their daughter.

Without the stabilizing influence of his wife, Rolling began a series of armed robberies. In the summer of 1979 he was jailed for robbing a convenience store. Paroled in 1984, he returned to Shreveport but soon began travelling. In July 1985 he robbed a shop in Clinton, Mississippi, and was sentenced to 15 years but served just three. On 6 November 1989 Rolling committed his first killings, slaughtering three members of the Grissom family: Tom and his 8-year-old grandson Sean had been stabbed repeatedly. Tom's 24-year-old daughter Julie, a petite brunette, was slashed and mutilated, her corpse covered in bite marks and then washed and posed sexually on her bed.

On 17 May 1990 Rolling shot his father in the head and stomach in an argument over whether the car window should be open or shut. His father survived the assault but Rolling fled to Gainesville, Florida, thinking he would be arrested. On 24 August Rolling murdered Sonja Larsen, 18, and Christina Powell, 17, in their home. One of the girls was sodomized and the other had her nipples cut off. On 27 August Rolling murdered 18-year-old Christa Hoyt and then cut her head off and put it on a nearby bookshelf. Her naked corpse was washed and posed as Julie Grissom's had been. The next day Tracy Paules and Manuel Taboada, both 23, were found dead in their apartment. Tracy had been sodomized and both had been stabbed several times. Rolling continued his burglary career until he was arrested on 1 September. A DNA swab linked him to the Gainesville killings.

WHERE:
Gainesville, Florida, USA

WHEN:
Monday 6 November 1989–Tuesday 28 August 1990

THE AFTERMATH:
In the autumn of 1991 Rolling was sentenced to three life terms plus 170 years in prison for the Tampa burglaries. On 15 February 1994 he pleaded guilty to all the charges. On April 20 1994, Rolling was sentenced to die. After a last meal of lobster tail, butterfly shrimp, baked potato and strawberry cheesecake, washed down with tea, Rolling was executed at 6.13pm on 25 October 2006.

YOU SHOULD KNOW:
1.85-m (6 ft 1-in) tall Rolling blamed his murderous rages on an alternate personality he called Gemini, who apparently loved to make people suffer.

Ivan Milat

"There is no reason to doubt the correctness of the verdict"

THE CRIME: The Backpacker Murders began in the autumn of 1992. On Sunday 20 September a decaying corpse was found in the Belangalo State Forest at an area called Executioner's Drop. The next day the remains of two British backpackers, Caroline Clarke and Joanne Walters, were found 30 m (97 ft) from the first body by PC Roger Gough and WPC Suzanne Roberts. The girls had disappeared from Sydney five months earlier. Joanne had been stabbed nine times and Caroline had been shot in the head several times. A year later, two more bodies were discovered and identified as Deborah Everist and James Gibson. The discovery puzzled police because Gibson's backpack and camera had been found at Galston Gorge, 90 km (60 mi) north.

On 1 November 1993 Sergeant Jeff Trichter found a skull, later identified as that of German tourist Simone Schmindl, who had last been seen hitch-hiking on 20 January 1991. The clothes at the scene did not belong to Simone Schmindl, but to another missing person, Anja Habschied. Habschied and her boyfriend, Gabor Neugebauer, were found in shallow graves on 3 November 1993. They had disappeared on Christmas Day 1991. Oddly, none of the victims had died the same way.

On 13 November 1993, Briton Paul Onions rang the New South Wales police to tell them his extraordinary story. On 25 January 1990 he had been hitch-hiking near Mittagong, New South Wales when a man who said his name was Bill picked him up. As they were driving, Bill pulled a gun and tried to shoot Onions but missed. Onions identified the man from police mugshots on 5 May 1994 as Ivan Milat, a convicted rapist. Seventeen days later, Milat was arrested by 50 policemen at his home at Cinnebar Street, Campbelltown, New South Wales. In his house was evidence linking him to the attacks. On 30 May he was charged with seven murders.

WHERE:
Berrima, New South Wales, Australia
WHEN:
January 1990–1994
THE AFTERMATH:
Milat's trial opened on 26 March 1996 and lasted four months, before the jury convicted him on 27 July. Milat was given seven life sentences, and six years for the attack on Paul Onions. In 1997 he tried to escape from Maitland Jail and was sent to a high security prison at Goulburn, New South Wales.
YOU SHOULD KNOW:
There are some who dispute Ivan Milat's guilt. However, in July 2001, Judge William Gummow refused an appeal by Milat. He said, "There is no reason to doubt the correctness of the decision by the New South Wales Criminal Court of Appeal."

Ivan Milat, right, with his brother Richard

Guy Georges

Beast of Bastille

WHERE:
Paris, France
WHEN:
Thursday 24 January 1991–Sunday
16 November 1997
THE AFTERMATH:
Georges's trial began on 19 March
2001 and he pleaded not guilty
before admitting his guilt. He
was jailed for life.
YOU SHOULD KNOW:
In December 2000 Georges tried to
escape from prison, along with three
other inmates, by sawing the bars
of his cell.

*Guy Georges at the start of
his trial in 2001*

THE CRIME: Guy Georges, the serial killer known as the Beast of Bastille, was born as Guy Rampillon at Vitry-le-François, France on 15 October 1962, the illegitimate son of an American GI. The Morin family, who had already taken on a dozen children, adopted Georges when he was six. At the age of 14 he tried to strangle his mentally handicapped, adoptive sister Linda and two years later attacked another sister, Christiane, with the result that he was returned to a special home.

On 6 February 1979 he began a series of assaults on strangers, beginning with a girl identified as Pascale C. She fought off his attempt to strangle her and Georges was arrested but freed a week later. He took to drink and in May 1980 attacked Jocelyne S. and Linda C. whom he stabbed in the cheek. He was sentenced to a year in prison and on his release became a rent boy in Paris. On 16 November 1981 he raped and stabbed Nathalie L., 18, in her home leaving her for dead but, luckily, she recovered. After a five-month jail term for theft, Georges attacked Violet K. in an underground car park of the 16th arrondissement on 7 June 1982. She survived and he was arrested and imprisoned, this time for 18 months. After an early release for good behaviour Georges raped Pascale N. in her car in February 1982. He was arrested the same evening and jailed for ten years. He did not serve the full sentence and towards the end of it was allowed out on day release, returning to jail at night.

On the evening of 24 January 1991 Georges killed for the first time, raping and then stabbing to death Pascale Escarfail, 19, whom he saw in the street and followed, attacking her in her home. He then returned to his jail cell for the night. Freed on 4 April 1992, he raped Eleonore D. eight days later, an assault that landed him another five-year prison sentence. He served just a year and on 7 January 1994 he murdered Catherine Rock, 27, in a garage after raping her. On 13 January he attacked radio host Annie L. on her front porch. On 8 November 1994 he murdered Elsa Benady and a month later, on 10 December, raped and murdered Dutch architect Agnes Nijkamp, 33. In June 1995 he raped Elisabeth O. and the next month he raped and murdered 27-year-old Helena Frinking as she returned from a party. On 25 August he attacked Melanie B. in the Marais district and he was identified but managed to escape. On 23 September 1997 he raped and murdered 19-year-old student Magalie Sirotti, followed by raping Leila T. on 28 October 1997. His last murder occurred on 16 November 1997 when he raped and cut the throat of Estelle Magd, 25. He was arrested on 27 March 1998 in Montmartre after his DNA was matched to that left at the scenes of four murders and one attempted rape.

Beverley Allitt

Despite the preponderance of fatalities and near-fatalities around Allitt, no one questioned her

Beverly Allitt holds a baby while on duty at the hospital.

THE CRIME: Since the days of Florence Nightingale, nurses have been regarded as angels of mercy. Sadly, that opinion is sometimes misplaced and never more so than in the case of Beverley Gail Allitt. Born on 4 October 1968, one of four children, Allitt became a State Enrolled Nurse and got a job at Grantham and Kesteven Hospital, Lincolnshire. No one noticed that she had a tendency to seek attention, was self-harming and constantly changing her doctor so her behaviour would not be noted.

On 21 February 1991 seven-month-old Liam Taylor was admitted with a chest infection. Allitt volunteered for extra night duty to care for the infant but that night the boy's condition worsened dramatically. He suffered a heart attack and had to be placed on a life-support machine. Liam's parents agreed to switch off the life-support machine and cause of death was recorded as heart failure. Allitt was never questioned about her role in Liam's death. A fortnight later, on 5 March 1991, Timothy Hardwick, an 11-year-old who suffered from cerebral palsy, was admitted following an epileptic fit. Allitt looked after him and he, too, died although no cause of death was established. On 8 March one-year-old Kayley Desmond had a heart attack in the same bed in which Liam Taylor had died – her nurse was Beverley Allitt. The resuscitation team were able to revive Kayley and she was transferred to another hospital in Nottingham where doctors discovered an unusual puncture hole under her armpit. There was no investigation. On 20 March Paul Crampton, five months old, was admitted because of a bronchial infection. Allitt looked after him and on three occasions he almost died before he was moved to another hospital. On 21 March, 5-year-old Bradley Gibson had two cardiac arrests as Allitt cared for him but he, too, survived after moving to another hospital.

Despite the preponderance of fatalities and near-fatalities around Allitt, no one questioned her. The next day, Yik Hung Chan, two, almost died because of Allitt's intervention. On 1 April Katie and Becky Phillips were admitted and Allitt took charge. After two days they were discharged and Becky died that night. Katie was re-admitted to Grantham and Kesteven as a precaution. When she was moved to another hospital, she was found to have five broken ribs and serious brain damage which left her partially paralysed and with sight and hearing damage. Four more victims followed, the last being 15-month-old Claire Peck who died on 22 April.

WHERE:
Ward 4, Grantham and Kesteven Hospital, Lincolnshire, England
WHEN:
Thursday 21 February–Monday 22 April 1991
THE AFTERMATH:
Allitt was arrested in November 1991. She went on trial on 15 February 1993 and on 23 May was found guilty and sentenced to 13 concurrent terms of life imprisonment. The judge recommended she serve at least 40 years, a tariff that was cut to 30 on 6 December 2007.
YOU SHOULD KNOW:
Sue Phillips, mother of Katie and Becky, was so grateful to Allitt for her care that she asked her to be Katie's godmother. In 1999 Lincolnshire Health Authority agreed to pay £2.125 million for treatment and equipment for the rest of Katie's life. It did not accept liability.

Dahmer is escorted to court.

Jeffrey Dahmer

"There was something missing in Jeff... We call it a conscience"

THE CRIME: One of America's most notorious homicidal cannibals, Jeffrey Dahmer was born on 21 May 1960 in West Allis, Wisconsin and grew up in a middle-class family. From an early age, he had an interest in cutting up animals and also knew that he was homosexual. He was bullied at school and took to drinking as solace. His father, Lionel, said, "There was something missing in Jeff... We call it a conscience."

His first victim was 19-year-old hitchhiker Stephen Hicks on 6 June 1978 near Akron, Ohio. They drank together, but when Hicks wanted to leave Dahmer smashed his head in with a barbell. He cut the body up and put it into five bin bags. As Dahmer was disposing of them a policeman stopped his car for a traffic violation. Dahmer would not kill again for nine years. He moved to Milwaukee to live with his grandmother.

Then in 1985 Dahmer began hanging out in bathhouses where he would take lovers to private cubicles and drug them. Dahmer wanted to be the active participant in sodomy, not the recipient. When his behaviour was discovered he was barred from gay hangouts and moved onto hotels. One day Dahmer took a lover to the Ambassador Hotel and, when he awoke, the man lying next to him was dead. Dahmer claimed to have no recollection of what he had done. It was the first of 16 murders. On 25 September 1988 his fifth victim escaped and Dahmer was sent to prison for molesting and taking photographs of a 13-year-old boy. On 30 May 1991 Konerak Sinthasomphone (the younger brother of the boy Dahmer had molested) was found on the street naked, bleeding from the anus and having taken drugs. Dahmer told the police that Konerak was his boyfriend and that they had had an argument. The police returned the boy to Dahmer who that night murdered him, keeping his skull as a souvenir. In that summer of 1991 Dahmer murdered almost one man a week. Dahmer's reign of terror ended on 22 July 1991 when his final victim, Tracy Edwards, escaped and ran handcuffed into the arms of police. Edwards told them Jeffrey Dahmer had imprisoned him and threatened to eat his heart.

WHERE:
Apartment 213, Oxford Apartments, 924 North 25th Street; Ambassador Hotel, Milwaukee, Wisconsin, USA

WHEN:
June 1978-Monday 22 July 1991

THE AFTERMATH:
In February 1992 Dahmer was sentenced to 957 years in prison. On 28 November 1994, at the Columbia Correctional Facility at Portage, Wisconsin, Christopher Scarver, a black, delusional schizophrenic who believed he was the son of God, caved in the heads of Dahmer and Jesse Anderson in the prison gym. Dahmer was pronounced dead at 9.11am. Ironically, Dahmer was killed with the same type of weapon he had used on his first victim. His body was cremated but his mother asked that his brain be studied. It was found to be normal. The home where Dahmer committed many of his murders has since been demolished.

Alexander Pichushkin

"A life without murder is like life without food"

THE CRIME: Alexander Yuryevich Pichushkin was born on 9 April 1974 in Mytishchi, Moscow Oblast. His father was not interested in the boy and walked out when he was still young. Pichushkin committed his first murder in 1992 when he was 18 years old, killing Sergei, the boyfriend of Olga, a neighbour he had fallen in love with. Police dismissed the murder as suicide. He began his murderous campaign in earnest in 2001 and, by the time he had finished, he was responsible for at least 48 deaths and possibly more than 60. Pichushkin, a supermarket worker who lived with his elderly mother, originally said that he wanted to kill 64 people, the number of squares on a chessboard. His main targets were old men with whom he played chess and shared a bottle of vodka or beer before hitting them on the head with a hammer. He then pushed the empty vodka bottle down their throats. "For me, life without murder is like life without food for you," he once said. "I felt like the father of all these people, since it was I who opened the door for them to another world." One victim, a woman, had stakes hammered into her skull. According to police, he would record each murder by marking it on a square of a chessboard, earning him the name, the Chessboard Killer.

WHERE:
Bitsevsky Park, Moscow, Russia
WHEN:
1992–2006
THE AFTERMATH:
Pichushkin was arrested on 15 June 2006 after police found a metro ticket in the pocket of his last victim, Marina Moskalyova, 36. He denied all knowledge of her until police showed him CCTV footage of the two of them together. Pichushkin told police that killing people was akin to a "perpetual orgasm". His trial began on 13 September 2007. He was convicted on 24 October 2007 of 48 murders and three attempted murders. From the glass cage in which he was held, he demanded another 11 murders be taken into account. The judge, Vladimir Usov, spent more than 60 minutes reading out the verdict before he sentenced Pichushkin to life imprisonment with the first 15 years to be spent in solitary confinement.

YOU SHOULD KNOW:
To get some of his victims away from busy public places, he offered to show them the grave of his dead dog. In February 2006 police shot an innocent man in the leg, thinking that he was the Chessboard Killer. They also detained a transvestite with a hammer in his purse, though he too was released.

Pichushkin in the bullet-proof glass defendants' cage of the Moscow City Court.

Christopher Mhlengwa Zikode

Zikode murdered her and then had sex with her corpse

WHERE:
Donnybrook, Kwazulu-Natal,
South Africa
WHEN:
1993–1995
THE AFTERMATH:
On 7 January 1997 a High Court
judge sentenced Zikode to 140 years
in prison, including five life
sentences.

THE CRIME: Having suffered the privations of apartheid for 42 years, South Africa had been through a tumultuous time. Just as the country seemed to be settling down, a serial killer began operating in Donnybrook, a town in rural Kwazulu-Natal, the seventh largest region in South Africa. Beginning in 1993, Christopher Mhlengwa Zikode, the Donnybrook Serial Killer, began his murderous campaign that left 18 dead over a period of two years. Zikode also attempted to murder another 11 people.

All his victims were aged between 20 and 30. He would select a victim and then break down their front door, shooting the man of the house in the head. He would then drag the woman to a nearby wood where he repeatedly raped her. The ordeal could last as long as five hours before he murdered her. If the woman resisted, Zikode murdered her and then had sex with her corpse. If the fancy took him, he would attack women as they went for a stroll. Remarkably, Zikode was just 21 years old when he was arrested in July 1995 for attempted murder. However, the police bailed him and he went on to commit five more crimes – two attempted murders and three burglaries with intent to rape and murder – before he was arrested again on 29 September 1995.

Kristen Gilbert

"I killed those guys"

THE CRIME: Kristen Gilbert was born on 13 November 1967 in Fall River, Massachusetts as Kristen Strickland. At school she was a typical teenage girl but as she got older she began to develop dishonest habits in her relationships, which were also tinged with violence. After school she went to Greenfield Community College, in Massachusetts. She began stealing and then denying it. She even told one victim that she had not stolen her blouse even though Gilbert was wearing it at the time. In 1988 she married Glen Gilbert and shortly after began work on Ward C of the Veteran's Affairs Medical Center in Northampton, Massachusetts. Her colleagues found her friendly and sociable and her bosses gave her

Kristen Gilbert was unrepentant about her killings.

WHERE:
Veteran's Affairs Medical Center, 421 North Main Street, Leeds, Northampton, Massachusetts, USA
WHEN:
1989–1996
THE AFTERMATH:
It was believed that Gilbert would dose the men with epinephrine so they would go into cardiac arrest, when her lover would be called. She would then impress him with her nursing skill. When she was suspended from the ward the death rate returned to normal levels. In mid 1996 James Perrault tired of the affair. Kristen Gilbert took an overdose and was admitted to the psychiatric ward. When some of the victims' bodies were exhumed, epinephrine was found in the body tissues. In 1998 Gilbert was charged with murder and Perrault testified against her. He claimed that she had told him, "You know I did it, I did it. You wanted to know, I killed those guys." On 14 March 2001 Gilbert was convicted of three counts of first-degree murder, one count of second-degree murder, and two counts of attempted murder. She was sentenced to life in prison without the chance for parole plus 20 years.

performance top marks. In 1990 she gave birth to her first son – life seemed great. When she returned to work on the 4pm to midnight shift, things began to go wrong. Patients began to die when Gilbert was on duty. She often gave her unqualified medical opinion, leading her colleagues to nickname her the Angel of Death. Many of the patients died of heart attacks, even when there was no history of cardiac problems. In 1993 Gilbert gave birth to her second son. Her home life changed and Glen told friends that he thought his wife was trying to poison him. She began an affair with James Perrault, a security guard at the hospital. In December 1994 she left her husband and sons to move in with Perrault. The death count on the hospital continued to rise. Her colleagues checked the stock room and found that there was a shortage of epinephrine (synthetic adrenaline), a drug that stimulates the heart. One day Gilbert asked her boss if she could leave work early if one of her patients died and was told that she could. Shortly afterwards, the patient died. In February 1995 an Aids sufferer had a relapse under Gilbert's care and her fellow nurses went to the hospital authorities. In Gilbert's seven years on the ward, 350 men had died.

An artist's impression of Dr Shipman in the dock at Preston Crown Court, watched by his wife Primrose, as the jury returns a guilty verdict.

Harold Shipman

Dr Death

WHERE:
Todmorden, West Yorkshire; Hyde, Cheshire, England
WHEN:
1975–1998
THE AFTERMATH:
Shipman was arrested on 7 September 1998 and the police began to look into 15 other deaths where Shipman had signed the death certificate. A trail of forged medical notes and the use of diamorphine was found in them all. On 5 October 1999 Shipman went on trial charged with the murders of Marie West, Irene Turner, Lizzie Adams, Jean Lilley, Ivy Lomas, Jermaine Ankrah, Muriel Grimshaw, Marie Quinn, Kathleen Wagstaff, Bianka Pomfret, Norah Nuttall, Pamela Hillier, Maureen Ward, Winifred Mellor, Joan Melia and Kathleen Grundy. Dubbed Dr Death by the media, on 31 January 2000, Shipman was found guilty of all 15 murders and sentenced to life imprisonment with a recommendation that he should

THE CRIME: On 1 October 1977 Dr Harold "Fred" Shipman began work at the Donneybrook Medical Practice, Hyde, Cheshire. The 31-year-old had begun practising as a family doctor three years earlier in Todmorden, West Yorkshire but after just a year of practice he was forced to enter rehab, after being caught forging prescriptions for pethidine for his own use. During the 1980s Shipman worked in and around Hyde before opening his own practice on Market Street in 1993. Shipman became a popular local figure.

Suspicions arose in March 1998 when Dr Linda Reynolds of the Brooke Surgery in Hyde was alerted by Deborah Massey, an undertaker, to the seeming high proportion of deaths among Shipman's patients, many of whom were cremated. Miss Massey thought that Shipman was killing those in his care – although she was unsure whether that was down to incompetence or malice. The police were informed but decided that there was a lack of evidence, dropping the case on 17 April 1998. Between then and his arrest, Shipman killed another three people, the last being Kathleen Grundy, a former Mayor of Hyde, who was found dead at her home on 24 June 1998. Shipman, the last person to see her alive, recorded her death as "old age". When Mrs Grundy's daughter discovered that her mother had left her entire £386,000 estate to Shipman she went to the police and an investigation began. Mrs Grundy's corpse was exhumed and an autopsy revealed traces of diamorphine.

never be released. The Shipman Inquiry believed that he had killed around 250 people although 459 people died under his care. On 13 January 2004, the day before his 58th birthday, Shipman hanged himself in his cell at Wakefield Prison.

Vincent Johnson

"I didn't see strangling her as something wrong"

THE CRIME: Born on 6 January 1969, Vincent Johnson was just 1.6 m (5 ft 3 in) tall. He was also a tramp and a crack addict. On 26 August 1999 someone – later dubbed the Brooklyn Strangler – began killing prostitutes in the Williamsburg and Bedford-Stuyvesant neighbourhoods of Brooklyn, New York. The first victim was Vivian Caraballo who was found in the lift room on the roof of 237 South Second Street in Williamsburg. Joann Feliciano, 35, was found strangled with trainer laces and speaker wire on 16 September 1999, on the roof of 171 South Fourth Street. Rhonda Tucker, 21, was discovered inside her apartment on Park Avenue in Bedford-Stuyvesant on 25 September 1999, strangled with the drawstring from her trousers. In early October the body of Katrina Niles, 34, was found in a Marcy Avenue apartment in Bedford-Stuyvesant, strangled with electrical cord and her throat slashed. In February 2000 firemen found the decomposed body of Laura G. Nusser, 43.

All the women were found nude or partly clothed and all were strangled with a ligature. The police leapt into action and arrested a tramp who was known to hang around with whores. However, a DNA test cleared him of any involvement. Not one to bear a grudge, he began hanging around the precinct house of the Brooklyn North Homicide Task Force. After a short time, he told the police of another tramp – a crack addict with a penchant for sadomasochistic sex. It was Vincent Johnson. When he was picked up by the police he refused to give a sample of his DNA and denied all knowledge of the murders. Fortunately, one of the Task Force had seen Johnson spit into a cup as he left the station after his first interrogation. A sample of the saliva was taken from the cup and sent for testing. It came back as a positive match for four victims. At 6.45pm on 4 August 2000 Johnson was arrested on the Manhattan side of the Williamsburg Bridge.

WHERE:
Brooklyn, New York, USA
WHEN:
Thursday 26 August 1999–February 2000
THE AFTERMATH:
On 5 August 2000, Johnson was charged with strangling five prostitutes: Patricia Sullivan, Rhonda Tucker, Joann Feliciano, Vivian Caraballo and Laura Nusser. He denied any involvement in the sixth death, that of Katrina Niles, although police believe he was the perpetrator. Johnson was charged under the so-called serial killer statute, a section of New York state law that provides for a maximum of the death penalty or life in prison without the possibility of parole if a defendant is convicted of killing two or more people in separate crimes over two years. Johnson blamed his mother for his murderous spree. "The thoughts of my childhood and foster care and mom came into my mind," he said of killing Patricia Sullivan, "I didn't see strangling her as doing something wrong at the time." His mother took just one day off work – a Thursday and Caraballo, Feliciano and Sullivan were killed on Thursdays. Johnson was jailed for life without parole.

Washington Sniper

"Dear Policeman: I am God"

WHERE:
Maryland; Virginia, USA
WHEN:
6.04pm Wednesday 2–5.59am Tuesday
22 October 2002

THE AFTERMATH:
On 24 October the Washington Sniper was discovered to be two men – John Allen Muhammad, 41, and Lee Boyd Malvo, 17. They were arrested after being found asleep in a blue 1990 Chevrolet Caprice sedan at a service station on the Interstate 70 near Myersville, Maryland. Ballistics tests proved that the Bushmaster XM-15 semiautomatic .223 calibre rifle found in the car was linked to the shootings. At their trials both were found guilty of murder. Muhammad was sentenced to death and Malvo life in prison without parole. The Virginia Supreme Court confirmed Muhammad's death penalty on 22 April 2005.

YOU SHOULD KNOW:
Some eyewitnesses described the shooter as "a crazy white guy armed with an AK-47, driving about in a boxy white van". The shooters were two black men in an old blue Chevrolet.

Lee Boyd Malvo in court

THE CRIME: During a three-week period in October 2002 ten people were killed and three seriously injured by a sniper in Maryland and Virginia. The first victim, James D. Martin, a 55-year-old program analyst, was killed at 6.04pm on 2 October 2002 in the car park of Shoppers Food Warehouse at 2201 Randolph Road, Wheaton, Maryland. The next morning four more people were murdered in the space of two hours and another was shot dead that evening in the District of Columbia. James L. "Sonny" Buchanan, 39, was shot about 7.40am while pushing a lawnmower behind a car showroom at 11411 Rockville Pike, White Flint. At 8.12am Premkumar Walekar, 54, a taxi driver, had just bought a lottery ticket, newspaper and chewing gum from a Mobil garage at Aspen Hill Road and Connecticut Avenue and was killed while filling his cab with petrol.

At 8.37am Sarah Ramos, 34, was shot while sitting on a bench in front of Crisp & Juicy Charbroiled Chicken restaurant at 3701 Rossmoor Boulevard, Silver Spring, Maryland and at 9.58am Lori Ann Lewis-Rivera, 25, a nanny, was gunned down while vacuuming her employers' maroon Dodge Caravan at the Shell garage on Knowles and Connecticut avenues, Kensington, Maryland. At 9.20pm Pascal Charlot, a 72-year-old retired carpenter, was shot on the corner of Georgia Avenue and Kalmia Road, NW Washington DC. At 2.30pm on 4 October, 43-year-old Caroline Seawell was shot in the car park of Michaels Craft Store at Spotsylvania Mall, Spotsylvania County, Virginia.

At 8.08am on 7 October 13-year-old schoolboy Iran Brown was shot in the chest after being dropped off at Benjamin Tasker Middle School, 4901 Collington Road, Bowie, Maryland. He survived. At the scene the police found the death card from a tarot pack on which had been written, "Dear Policeman: I am God". At 8.18pm on 9 October 53-year-old Dean Harold Meyers was shot in the head while buying petrol at the Sunoco gas station at 7203 Sudley Road in Prince William County, Virginia. At 9.30am on 11 October 53-year-old Kenneth Bridges was also buying petrol when he was shot dead at the Exxon garage at Route 1 and Market Street, Spotsylvania County. It was 9.15pm on 14 October when 47-year-old Linda Franklin, an FBI intelligence analyst, was shot dead at Seven Corners Shopping Center, Fairfax County, Virginia. On 19 October at 7.59pm Jeffrey Hopper, 37, was shot in the car park of Ponderosa Steakhouse, 809 England Street, Ashland, Virginia. At 5.59am on 22 October bus driver Conrad Johnson, 35, was killed as he stood on the top step of his bus at the junction of Grand Pre Road and Connecticut Avenue in Aspen Hill, Maryland.

Juana Barraza

"You'll know why I did it when you read my statement to police"

THE CRIME: Juana Barraza was born in 1957 in Mexico and worked as a female wrestler known as The Silent Lady but she had a sideline as a serial killer. The press nicknamed her *Mataviejitas* – The Old Lady Killer – and it is thought that she committed her first murder in around 1998, although the first murder ascribed to her by the police happened on 17 November 2003. It is not known how many old ladies she killed but estimates range from 24 to 49.

Mataviejitas would spot an old lady and then suggest that she did some work for the woman – cooking, cleaning, etc – but once she was over the threshold she either strangled or beat them before stealing a souvenir or two from the house. All the victims were 60 or over and the majority of them lived alone, making them easier prey. In some of the cases, the victim was also sexually abused. Despite the body count piling up, the police denied that a serial killer was at large up until the summer of 2005, when they launched a bizarre raid on Mexico City's transvestite prostitutes because they believed the killer was a man wearing women's clothes. On 25 January 2006 Barraza was arrested as she fled the scene in the Venustiano Carranza area of the capital, where she had strangled 82-year-old Ana María de los Reyes Alfaro with a stethoscope. According to the police, there was fingerprint evidence linking Barraza to at least 11 murders. She admitted that she had murdered Ana María de los Reyes Alfaro and three others but denied involvement in the other killings. She said to journalists, "You'll know why I did it when you read my statement to police."

Juana Barraza dressed in her wrestling costume as The Silent Lady.

WHERE:
Mexico City, Mexico
WHEN:
Monday 17 November
2003–Wednesday 25 January 2006
THE AFTERMATH:
Mexico City's chief prosecutor
Bernardo Bátiz called Barras "clever
and careful" with "a brilliant mind".
On 31 March 2008 she was found
guilty of 16 murders and sentenced
to 759 years in jail. She will be
eligible for parole in 2058.

Mohammed Bijeh was flogged before being publicly hanged.

WHERE:
Pakdasht, Iran
WHEN:
March–September 2004
THE AFTERMATH:
Bijeh was tried in camera where he gleefully confessed to murdering 16 boys aged between eight and 15. He said he wanted revenge on society because his stepmother had abused him as a child. Found guilty, he was sentenced to 100 lashes and then execution. A crowd of about 5,000 people gathered to watch the sentence being carried out at Pakdasht, south-east of Tehran on 16 March 2005. A succession of clerics administered the whipping and Bijeh collapsed twice although he did not cry out. Then Bijeh was hoisted 10 m (35 ft) in the air where he was slowly throttled to death. As Bijeh was being prepared for execution the 17-year-old brother of victim Rahim Younessi ran up and stabbed him before a mother in a black chador, Milad Kahani, put the blue nylon noose around his neck. Hanging by a crane does not involve a swift death, as the prisoner's neck is not broken. Ali Baghi was given a 15-year prison term and 100 lashes.
YOU SHOULD KNOW:
Police cars with loud speakers patrolled the area informing the locals where and when the execution was to be held.

Mohammed Bijeh

"I looked for my boy for nine months... all we got was a handful of bones"

THE CRIME: It would be wrong to assume that hard-line Islamic countries like Iran are not too troubled by serial killers. The press nicknamed Mohammed Bijeh the Tehran Desert Vampire. Born on 7 February 1975, he worked at a brick kiln. With his partner Ali Baghi (also known as Ali Gholampour) he would entice children into the desert south of Teheran on the pretext of hunting animals. Away from safety, he would knock the children out and sexually abuse them before burning or burying them in shallow graves. Afghan refugee Basre Shirzad whose son was one of Bijeh's victims commented, "I looked for my boy for nine months. After nine months all we got was a

all we got was a handful of bones." It is not known how many victims Bijeh really claimed but the official figures vary between 19 and 22.

Stephen Sakai

"I've had to sit there and listen to rie after rie"

THE CRIME:

Stephen Sakai was born in 1975 with the surname Sanders and grew up in Southeast Queens. Tall and well built, Sakai worked as a bouncer at Sunset Park strip bar Sweet Cherry and Opus 22 Café and Lounge at 559 West 22nd Street, New York.

In September 2005 he stabbed to death his ex-friend Wayne Tyson who was 56 and partially disabled. Two months later he shot fellow bouncer Edwin Mojica in the back of the head as he was putting the key in the door of his Williamsburg home. The two men had been feuding. Sakai was also annoyed with another bouncer, Irving Matos, and he was reported to have shot him in the back of the head as he sat on a settee. On 23 May 2006 he was on duty outside Opus 22 – famous for its Opus Bellini made with white peach purée and champagne – when violence erupted. When a drunken Gustavo Cuadros refused to leave Sakai began an argument with the man and then shot him once in the chest with a .45-calibre handgun. The 28-year-old man was pronounced dead at the scene. Sakai then shot Julian Cuadros, who was paralyzed from the neck down, and Jaison Correa as he ran away. Ian Davis was shot in the groin by Sakai.

WHERE:
559 West 22nd Street, New York City, USA
WHEN:
September 2005–Tuesday 23 May 2006
THE AFTERMATH:
Sakai's trial for the murders of Tyson, Mojica and Matos was one of the most bizarre in American jurisprudence. Despite being a black, native New Yorker he spoke at his trial in Brooklyn with an exaggerated fake Japanese accent – "Rast name, Sakai," he told the clerk of the court – and claimed to have regularly flown to the Far East for martial-arts tournaments despite never having had a passport. He also claimed to have been set up by a bent policeman. "Wayne Tyson was a good person. He was a friend of mine. He supported me when I needed him most. Irv Matos did the same. He referred to me as his rittle brother. These two people didn't die because there was someone running around killing. These two people died because they supported me, collecting evidence against a dirty cop, Christopher Bresrin [Breslin]. During this trial, I've had to sit there and listen to rie after rie." He also claimed the police had force-fed him poison, then injected drugs into his neck before forcing him to confess to the three killings. On 6 December 2007 Sakai was found guilty of two murders but cleared of the Matos murder because the jury didn't believe witness Daniel (Diggim) Fishback. On 2 January 2008 he was sentenced to 50 years to life. On 15 December 2008 he was sentenced to 90 years to life for the murder of Gustavo Cuadros and wounding his friends.

Baseline Killer

WHERE:
Baseline Road, Phoenix, Arizona, USA
WHEN:
Monday 7 November 2005–Thursday
29 June 2006
THE AFTERMATH:
On 7 December 2006 Phoenix police
announced that Goudeau was the
Baseline Killer. On 14 December 2007
he was jailed for 438 years for the
assault on the two sisters two years
earlier.

Police arrested Goudeau for sexually attacking two sisters – one was pregnant

THE CRIME: The Baseline Killer – so-called because he operated around Baseline Road, Phoenix, Arizona – killed nine people, sexually assaulted several more and committed armed robberies. The attacks began on 7 November 2005 when people were robbed at gunpoint inside Las Brasas, a Mexican restaurant, next door at Little Caesar's Pizza restaurant and later outside on the street. The thief stole $463. At 6.55pm on 12 December 2005 teacher and single mother of three Tina Washington, 39, was shot in the head on South 40th Street as she was on her way home from Cactus Preschool on 36th Street and Southern Avenue. The next day at 8pm a woman was robbed on East South Mountain Avenue. The

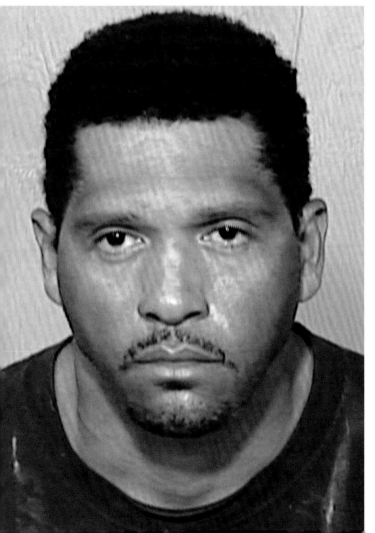

Mark Goudeau, aka the Baseline Killer

killer laid low for two months until 20 February 2006 when at 7.38pm the bodies of 38-year-old Romelia Vargas and 24-year-old Mirna Palma-Roman were found in their takeaway van parked at 91st Avenue and Lower Buckeye Road. Both had been shot to death. On 1 March there was another double murder. Liliana Sanchez-Cabrera and Chao Chou, who both worked at Yoshi's restaurant at 24th Street and Indian School Road, were shot in the head. On 29 March the badly decomposed body of Kristin Nicole Gibbons was found at 4102 North 24th Street. She, too, had been shot in the head. Sophia Nunez was murdered on 10 April 2006.

A man wearing a Hallowe'en mask raped a woman at gunpoint at 9pm on 1 May on North 32nd Street. Four days later the police made the unusual decision to release a list of 18 crimes that they believed to be the work of the Baseline Killer. The number rose at 8.30pm on 29 June when Carmen Miranda, 37, was murdered on East Thomas Road. She had been sitting in a car wash chatting on her mobile. On 4 September 2006 Phoenix police arrested Mark Goudeau for sexually attacking two sisters – one was pregnant – in September 2005. Goudeau was a 42-year-old construction worker with a record for aggravated assault and armed robbery.

Steve Wright

"This was a targeted campaign of murder"

THE CRIME: Nearly three decades after the Yorkshire Ripper (see page 397) terrorized women in the north of England, another serial killer began picking off prostitutes, this time in East Anglia. On 2 December 2006 the naked body of 25-year-old heroin addict Gemma Adams was found in Belstead Brook at Thorpe's Hill, near Hintlesham. On 8 December 19-year-old heroin and cocaine addict Tania Nicol's corpse was discovered in water at Copdock Mill just outside Ipswich. Nicol had been missing since 30 October. Two days later the naked body of Anneli Alderton was found in woods by the A14 in Nacton. A 24-year-old drug addict and mother of one, she had been strangled and was three months' pregnant. On 12 December, Suffolk police announced that the bodies of two more women had been found, later identified as 24-year-old drug addict and mother of three Paula Clennell, and 29-year-old heroin addict and mother of one Annette Nicholls. Their naked corpses were found in Nacton near the A1156 Levington turn-off.

WHERE:
Ipswich, Suffolk, England
WHEN:
Monday 30 October–Tuesday
12 December 2006
THE AFTERMATH:
The police launched Operation Sumac to find the killer or killers. A crank who frequently associated with the dead prostitutes was questioned and released without charge. At 5am on 19 December 2006 Steven Gerald James Wright, 48, was arrested at his home, 79, London Road, Ipswich, on suspicion of murder and charged two days later. Wright pleaded not guilty at his trial, which began on 14 January 2008 at Ipswich Crown Court. During the trial Wright admitted to having had sex with all five victims except Tania Nichols, which was how, his lawyer explained, his DNA was found on the victims. Wright's DNA had been added to the national database in 2001 after he was convicted of stealing £80 while working as a hotel barman. On 21 February 2008 he was found guilty of all five murders after eight hours of deliberation. Although the jury's verdicts were decisive, prosecutors admitted that they remained puzzled about the motive behind the killings. Wright was sentenced the next day to life imprisonment with a recommendation that he should never be freed. Mr Justice Gross said: "It is right you should spend your whole life in prison. This was a targeted campaign of murder. You killed them, stripped them and left them... why you did it may never be known."
YOU SHOULD KNOW:
Paula Clennell had been interviewed by local television about the murders and said that she was "a bit wary about getting into cars" but added, "I need the money."

KIDNAPPINGS

Chief Quanah, one of Cynthia Ann Parker's sons

Cynthia Ann Parker

"Me Cincee Ann"

THE CRIME: Cynthia Ann Parker had the unusual distinction in life of being kidnapped twice. Born in about 1825 in Crawford County, Illinois, Cynthia and her large family settled in east Texas in the 1830s and built Fort Parker on the headwaters of the Navasota River in Limestone County. On the morning of 19 May 1836 several hundred men from the Caddo, Comanche and Kiowa tribes attacked Fort Parker and captured five people, including Cynthia. The others were released but Cynthia stayed with the Comanche for almost 25 years and adopted their ways. She married the Comanche chief Peta Nocona and had two sons, Quanah Parker and Pecos, and a daughter, Topsannah.

On 18 December 1860 Texas Rangers, led by Lawrence Sullivan "Sul" Ross, captured Cynthia and her daughter at the Battle of Pease River at Mule Creek. Nocona was shot but managed to escape with his sons. Back at the Ranger's base Ross noticed that the woman his men had captured had blue eyes. The woman could not speak English and did not know her name but, when questioned, she told them of her capture as a child. The details matched what Ross knew of the Fort Parker Massacre of 1836. Ross sent the woman to Camp Cooper and a message to Colonel Isaac Parker, the uncle of a young girl kidnapped in the raid. When the colonel said that his niece's name was Cynthia Anne, the woman said, "Me Cincee Ann." On 8 April 1861 the Texas legislature made her cousins, Isaac Duke Parker and Benjamin F. Parker, Cynthia Anne's legal guardians and gave her a league of land and $100 a year for five years.

WHERE:
Fort Parker, Limestone County, Texas, USA
WHEN:
Thursday 19 May 1836
THE AFTERMATH:
Cynthia never enjoyed her return to "civilization" and attempted to escape several times. In 1863, her son Pecos died of smallpox and her daughter caught influenza and died, aged five, from pneumonia. Cynthia was heartbroken and refused to eat. She died in 1870 at the age of 45 and was buried in Fosterville Cemetery in Anderson County near Frankston. In 1910 her son, Quanah, moved her body to the Post Oak Cemetery near Cache, Oklahoma. She was later moved to Fort Sill, Oklahoma, and reburied beside Quanah who died on 23 February 1911.
YOU SHOULD KNOW:
The city of Crowell, Texas, holds an annual Cynthia Ann Parker Festival.

Charley Ross

"I don't expect to find Charley"

THE CRIME: Charley Ross, aged four, was the first American to be kidnapped for ransom. On 1 July 1874 Charley and his six-year-old brother, Walter, were playing outside their home when they were enticed into a horse-drawn carriage with the promise of firecrackers by two men. At 6pm their father, Christian Ross, came home from work and sat reading the newspaper for an hour before he became concerned at the fact that his two sons were not home. A search began for the boys and Walter was found crying on the corner of Palmer Street and Richmond Street in Kensington, 12 km (8 mi) from home. Of his brother there was no sign. The next day Walter was recovered enough to explain what had happened. The two men had taken the boys to a shop and Walter was given 25¢ to go inside and buy the firecrckers. When he came out, the carriage and his brother were gone.

The boys' mother Sarah was away recovering from illness in Atlantic City and did not know about the kidnapping until her husband advertised in newspapers, offering $300 for Charley's return. On 3 July Christian Ross received a letter from the kidnappers demanding a sum of money for Charley's release. Three days later another note arrived with a demand for $20,000. On 21 July New York police were told that William Mosher and Joseph Douglass were the kidnappers. The police continued to explore other avenues while looking for Mosher and Douglass, who had recently escaped from jail while awaiting trial for burglary. The next day the mayor of Philadelphia offered a $20,000 reward for the return of Charley or the arrest of his kidnappers. As with all such cases, the police were inundated with hundreds of replies from cranks and attacks were made on families who had children who looked like Charley. On 14 December Mosher and Douglass were shot during a burglary. Mosher was killed outright but Douglass lived long enough to admit the kidnapping but said that only Mosher knew where Charley was held.

A handbill distributed by The Pinkerton Detective Agency, offering a reward.

WHERE:
529 East Washington Lane, Philadelphia, Pennsylvania, USA
WHEN:
4pm–5pm Wednesday 1 July 1874
THE AFTERMATH:
William Westervelt, Mosher's brother-in-law, was charged in 1875 with writing the ransom notes and sentenced to seven years in prison and a $1 fine. Christian Ross spent the rest of his life looking for his son. He said, "This makes 573 boys I have been called to see... I don't expect to find Charley." He died in June 1897. Sarah Ross took over the search until her death on 13 December 1912. Walter died in 1943. The Ross home was demolished in 1926 and the Cliveden Presbyterian Church now stands on the site.

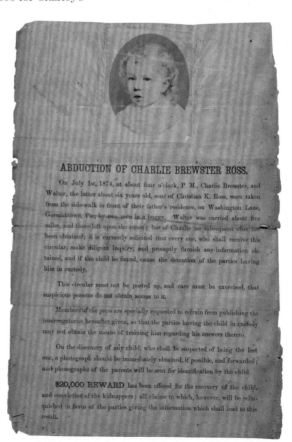

ABDUCTION OF CHARLIE BREWSTER ROSS.

On July 1st, 1874, at about four o'clock, P. M., Charlie Brewster, and Walter, the latter about six years old, sons of Christian K. Ross, were taken from the side-walk in front of their father's residence, on Washington Lane, Germantown, Pa., by two men in a buggy. Walter was carried about five miles, and there left upon the street; but of Charlie no subsequent clue has been obtained; it is earnestly solicited that every one, who shall receive this circular, make diligent inquiry, and promptly furnish any information obtained, and if the child be found, cause the detention of the parties having him in custody.

This circular must not be posted up, and care must be exercised, that suspicious persons do not obtain access to it.

Members of the press are specially requested to refrain from publishing the interrogatories hereafter given, so that the parties having the child in custody may not obtain the means of training him regarding his answers thereto.

On the discovery of any child, who shall be suspected of being the lost one, a photograph should be immediately obtained, if possible, and forwarded; and photographs of the parents will be sent for identification by the child.

$20,000 REWARD has been offered for the recovery of the child, and conviction of the kidnappers; all claims to which, however, will be relinquished in favor of the parties giving the information which shall lead to this result.

453

William Hickman

"Please Daddy, I want to come home this morning"

WHERE:
Mount Vernon Junior High School,
4066 West 17th Street, Los Angeles,
California, USA
WHEN:
Thursday 15 December 1927
THE AFTERMATH:
Found guilty of murder after the
court rejected the possibility he
might be insane, Hickman's hanging
at San Quentin Prison at 10.10am on
19 October 1928 was a terrifying
spectacle that caused three of the
witnesses to faint. Hickman fainted
as the trap door was opened,
causing him to fall horizontally
banging his head on the side of the
scaffold. At the end of the drop his
body jerked straight and began to
circle in a hideous death spiral. He
slowly strangled to death, his hands
twitching all the time.

THE CRIME: William Edward Hickman, the first ransom kidnapper in the United States to be executed, needed $1,500 to pay tuition fees at a school of divinity. He decided that kidnapping could raise the funds. He went to Mount Vernon Junior High School and told the headmaster that Californian banker Perry Parker was ill and he was there to collect his 12-year-old daughter, Marian. The next day Hickman sent a ransom demand via telegram of $1,500 in $20 gold certificates, signing himself The Fox. The kidnapper said that he would telephone with instructions but never did. Another ransom note arrived, "[You] gave me your word of hono[u]r… not to tip the police… you lied… you are insane to ignore my terms." It also included a note from Marian, "Please Daddy, I want to come home this morning. This is your last chance… come by yourself or you won't see me again." Another meeting was arranged at Manhattan Place Car Park, at 5th Avenue and South Manhattan Street in Los Angeles for 19 December and Mr Parker dropped off the ransom to a softly spoken man who had Marian next to him in the car.

Hickman drove up the street and pushed Marion out of the car. When her father ran to pick up his daughter, he found that Hickman had strangled the girl after which he had rouged her cheeks, cut off her arms and legs, slashed her body, removed her internal organs and wired her eyelids open. The missing legs and arms were discovered in Elysian Park, Los Angeles. They were wrapped in a towel, which had a laundry mark that led police to a young man called Evans. He turned out to be Hickman and had a record for forgery, received while working for Marian's father who'm he blamed for his downfall. Hickman escaped and fled to Washington and then Oregon but was finally captured at Pendleton, Oregon on 22 December. He was one of the first criminals to claim that he had been insane at the time of the crime. He told warders, "I always wanted to cut up a body. I used a pocket-knife, then drained each piece and washed them in the bathtub… then I went out to the cinema… I didn't like the pictures, they were too sad and made me cry."

Hickman enters his cell at San Quentin Prison shortly before his walk to the gallows.

Alexander Kutepov

Agents of Ogpu kidnapped Kutepov in Paris

THE CRIME: Alexander Kutepov was born on 16 September 1882 and, as a young officer, fought in the Russo-Japanese War of 1904 where he was wounded and won a medal. During the Great October Socialist Revolution he joined the Whites to fight against the Bolsheviks. He became the commander of the Kornilov Shock Regiment and in August 1918 he was appointed Governor General of the Black Sea region.

In January 1919 he became a lieutenant general of the White's I Army Corps. Kutepov brooked no dissent and often meted out the death penalty to looters and traitors. In November 1920 he and his troops were evacuated to Gallipoli and then, at the end of 1921, to Bulgaria. In 1923 he was expelled from Bulgaria and moved with his wife to Paris. In 1928 he became the leader of the Russian All-Military Union. On 26 January 1930 agents of Ogpu (the forerunner of the KGB) kidnapped Kutepov in Paris to take him back to Novorossisyk in the Soviet Union.

Alexander Kutepov

WHERE:
Paris, France
WHEN:
Sunday 26 January 1930
THE AFTERMATH:
It is unclear whether Kutepov died en route to the Soviet Union or whether he was killed upon arrival there. He was 47.

Charles Lindbergh, Jr

WANTED

INFORMATION AS TO THE WHEREABOUTS OF

CHAS. A. LINDBERGH, JR.

OF HOPEWELL, N. J.

SON OF COL. CHAS. A. LINDBERGH

World-Famous Aviator

This child was kidnaped from his home in Hopewell, N. J., between 8 and 10 p. m. on Tuesday, March 1, 1932.

DESCRIPTION:

Age, 20 months
Weight, 27 to 30 lbs.
Height, 29 inches

Hair, blond, curly
Eyes, dark blue
Complexion, light

Deep dimple in center of chin
Dressed in one-piece coverall night suit

ADDRESS ALL COMMUNICATIONS TO
COL. H. N. SCHWARZKOPF, TRENTON, N. J., or
COL. CHAS. A. LINDBERGH, HOPEWELL, N. J.

ALL COMMUNICATIONS WILL BE TREATED IN CONFIDENCE

COL. H. NORMAN SCHWARZKOPF
Supt. New Jersey State Police, Trenton, N. J.

March 11, 1932

"The biggest story since the Resurrection"

THE CRIME: The kidnapping of the Lindbergh baby – the son of Charles Lindbergh – caused a sensation. Journalist H.L. Mencken called it "the biggest story since the Resurrection".

The story began at 10pm on 1 March 1932 when the Lindberghs' nurse discovered that the 20-month-old boy was missing from his second-floor nursery. A badly spelled ransom note demanded $50,000 for his return and a crude ladder left outside showed how the kidnapper had made his entrance. Colonel H. Norman Schwarzkopf of the New Jersey State Police was put in charge of the case and a local teacher, Dr John F. Condon, offered his services to act as a mediator. Bizarrely, the Lindbergh family agreed to his help. Condon put an advert in the Bronx *Home News* and made contact with a member of the kidnap gang called John. The ransom demand was increased to $70,000 and Condon demanded proof that the boy was alive. On 15 March Charles's romper suit arrived in the post. The ransom drop was set for 2 April at St Raymond's Cemetery in the Bronx. Condon handed over $50,000 of the $70,000 and received details of the child's whereabouts, which proved to be false. Unsuccessful searches were made for young Charles Lindbergh. On 12 May 1932 the decomposing body of the baby was found 7 km (4.5 mi) from home. The skull was fractured, as were his left arm and left leg below the knee, and his internal organs were missing.

WHERE:
188 Lindbergh Road, Hopewell, New Jersey, USA

WHEN:
10pm Tuesday 1 March 1932

THE AFTERMATH:
On 15 September 1934 burglar and armed robber Bruno Richard Hauptmann spent a ransom bill at a Manhattan petrol station. The police found $14,000 of the ransom in Hauptmann's garage. He said that his friend Isidor Fisch had left him a shoebox when he returned to their native Germany where he later died. Fisch owed him money but Hauptmann forgot about the box until one day a leak made the box wet. Hauptmann opened it and saw the money. He took enough to cover the debt. The New York police arrested Hauptmann and proceeded to beat him up to force a confession. His trial opened on 2 January 1935 and on 13 February he was convicted. Hauptmann was executed in the electric chair on 3 April 1936. However, it is now likely that evidence was manufactured and Hauptmann was probably innocent of the crime.

Brooke Hart

"We didn't want to bother lugging him around the countryside so we bumped him off"

THE CRIME: Brooke Hart was born on 11 June 1911, the son of Alexander Hart, the wealthy owner of L. Hart & Son department store. A popular young man, he worked in the family business and was being groomed to take over from his father. On a November afternoon in 1933 he went to downtown San Jose to collect his Studebaker from a garage. As he got the car, Thomas Harold Thurmond and John Maurice Holmes kidnapped him. He was driven to what is now Milpitas, where the kidnappers changed cars and headed for the San Mateo-Hayward Bridge. At the bridge Hart was hit over the head with a concrete block and thrown into the San Francisco Bay. Since the tide was out and the water wasn't very deep, the kidnappers completed their murder by shooting Hart. At 9.30pm that night they contacted Hart's father to inform him of the kidnapping. At 10.30pm they called again and demanded a ransom of $40,000. More ransom demands, followed including ones that demanded that Alexander Hart drive to a location with the money, but Hart had never learned to drive.

WHERE:
Market Street, San Jose, California, USA
WHEN:
Thursday 9 November 1933
THE AFTERMATH:
At 8am on 15 November Thomas Thurmond was arrested at a payphone 137 m (150 yd) from the San Jose police station. At 3am he finally confessed to the kidnap and said that he had bound Brooke Hart with wire and thrown him off the San Mateo-Hayward Bridge on the night of the kidnapping. He revealed the name of his partner and at 3.30am John Holmes was arrested in his room at the California Hotel in San Jose. Thurmond told police, "We thought it would be easier with Hart out of the way. We didn't want to bother lugging him around the countryside and we didn't want to take the chance of his escaping... so we bumped him off."

The two men were indicted on 22 November and faced 20 years in prison and a $5,000 fine. Four days later, two duck hunters found the badly decomposed body of Brooke Hart south of the San Mateo-Hayward Bridge. His body had been severely damaged by crabs and eels. The face and hair had been eaten away and the hands and feet were destroyed. By 9pm the same day a crowd of 5,000 had gathered outside the San Jose jail where the kidnappers were held. At 11pm they broke into the jail and grabbed the two men. Thurmond was knocked unconscious and hanged from a tree in the local St James Park. Holmes continued to fight until the mob broke both his arms. Then he was stripped naked and lifted up while he kicked frantically into the air. The day after the lynching, Governor James Rolph expressed his approval of the double murder. "If anyone is arrested for this good job, I'll pardon them all. The aroused people of that fine city of San Jose were so enraged...it was only natural that, peaceful and law abiding as they are, they should rise and mete out swift justice to these two murderers and kidnappers."
YOU SHOULD KNOW:
After John Holmes and Harold Thurmond murdered Brooke Hart, Holmes took his wife to the cinema to watch Disney's *The Three Little Pigs*.

The angry mob watches as Thomas Thurmond is hanged.

Robert Greenlease Jr

"Bobby was struggling and kicking so I fired at close range"

WHERE:
Notre Dame De Sion School, 3823 Locust Street, Kansas City, Missouri, USA

WHEN:
10.55am Monday 28 September 1953

THE AFTERMATH:
Hall and Heady were charged on 30 October and pleaded guilty. On 19 November both were sentenced to death. Neither of their lawyers appealed and the pair died together in the gas chamber of the Jefferson City State Penitentiary on 18 December 1953. They sat side by side and were allowed to hold hands for a moment and kiss goodbye. She said, "Are you doing all right, honey?" He said, "Yes, mama." He was pronounced dead at 12.12am and she 20 seconds later.

YOU SHOULD KNOW:
Bonnie Heady is the only woman executed in America for kidnapping. Only half of the ransom was ever found and it is believed that corrupt members of the St Louis police department kept the rest. Two were charged but the money was never found.

THE CRIME: Bobby Greenlease was the six-year-old son of Kansas City millionaire Robert Cosgrove Greenlease, 71, who had made his money importing General Motors vehicles to the Great Plains. At 10.55am on an autumn day in 1953 Bobby was kidnapped from his exclusive prep school. A woman had visited the boy's school claiming to be his aunt and told Sister Morand that his mother had had a heart attack. At 6pm that day a ransom note was sent to the Greenlease home with a demand for $600,000 in $10 and $20 notes. The money – at the time the largest ransom demand in US history – was to be put into a duffel bag and left in a ditch between Kansas City and St Joseph, Missouri.

On 4 October the drop was made and the family waited for the safe return of Bobby. Under the terms of the Lindbergh Law the FBI could not become involved until seven days after the payment of the ransom and the Greelease family had asked Kansas City police to keep out of the matter. The police in St Louis observed no such caution and on 6 October raided the Town House Hotel after a tip-off at from a taxi driver about a man who was spending vast sums of money. They arrested 37-year-old drug addict Carl Austin Hall who had a gun with three missing bullets and $250,000 in cash on him. Hall was the son of a successful lawyer and had wasted a $200,000 inheritance before turning to crime. He confessed to the kidnapping and to murder: "Bobby was struggling and kicking so I took my revolver and fired at close range." Hall had buried Bobby near the porch of his house at 1201 South 38th Street in St Joseph, Missouri. Bobby's corpse was found at 8.40am on 7 October. Hall also gave up his partner, 41-year-old alcoholic, Bonnie Brown Heady, the widow of a bank robber. The couple were charged with federal kidnap after confessing that they had carried Bobby across state lines.

FBI agents move the body of Bobby Greenlease.

Graeme Thorne

"If you don't get the money, I'll feed the boy to the sharks"

Stephen Bradley leaves the police van on his way to court.

THE CRIME: This was Australia's first kidnapping. In 1960 travelling salesman Bazil Thorne, 37, paid £3 to enter the tenth lottery created by the New South Wales Government to raise money for the building of the Sydney Opera House. His ticket 3932 won the £100,000 prize on 1 June and his family details were splashed on Sydney newspapers' front pages. Bazil and Freda Thorne, their 8-year-old son Graeme and 3-year-old daughter Belinda lived in a two-bedroom, ground floor apartment at 79 Edward Street, Bondi. A family friend, Phyllis Smith, usually picked Graeme up at 8.30am to take him to school, The Scots College in Bellevue Hill. However, at 8.35am on 7 July 1960 the boy was not in his usual spot. Mrs Smith went to Edward Street and was told by Graeme's mother that he had left for school as usual. They checked with the school – again no sign – before alerting the police. At 9.40am the kidnapper rang the Thorne home's ex-directory number 307113 and Sergeant Larry O'Shea of Bondi police took his call. The kidnapper demanded £25,000 before 5pm or "If you don't get the money, I'll feed the boy to the sharks." He rang again at 9.47am and said that the money should be divided into two paper bags before hanging up. That was the last contact.

More than a month later, on 16 August, some children alerted their parents to a body that they had found in Grandview Grove, Seaforth in Sydney. Still in his school uniform, Graeme was covered in a blue tartan rug. His hands and feet were tied with rope and a silk scarf had been knotted tightly around the neck. An autopsy revealed that Graeme had either been asphyxiated or struck on the head or had died from a combination of both. It also revealed that he died within 24 hours of being snatched. The pathologist also found traces of pink mortar and of two plants, *Chamaecyparis pisifara* and *Cupressus glabra*. Witnesses had seen an iridescent blue 1955 Ford Customline double-parked near where Graeme was usually collected. A massive police search led, on 24 August, to electroplater Stephen Leslie Bradley, a 34-year-old Hungarian immigrant whose real name was Istavan Baranyay. He was helpful and friendly and explained that on 7 July he was moving house when Graeme was kidnapped. On 26 August his wife Magda booked a one-way passage to London for them and their three children. They sailed aboard the SS *Himalaya* on 26 September. Meantime, police examined Bradley's car and linked it with Graeme's kidnapping. On 10 October the *Himalaya* docked at Colombo, Ceylon and an immigration wrangle ensued because Australia had no extradition treaty with Ceylon. Finally, Bradley was flown back to Australia on 18 November.

WHERE:
O'Brien Street, Sydney, New South Wales, Australia

WHEN:
Thursday 7 July 1960

THE AFTERMATH:
Bradley confessed to the kidnapping but said Graeme had suffocated accidentally. Forensic experts disproved this and Bradley's trial began at the Sydney Central Criminal Court on 20 March 1961 and lasted nine days. Found guilty, he was sentenced to life imprisonment. Magda Bradley divorced her husband in 1965 and went to live in Europe. He died in prison on 6 October 1968, aged 42, while playing tennis with other prisoners. Bazil, Freda and Belinda Thorne moved out of Bondi into Rose Bay. Bazil died in 1978.

YOU SHOULD KNOW:
Since the Thorne case, lottery winners have had the chance to opt for no publicity.

Frank Sinatra, Snr hugs his son Frank Sinatra, Jr.

Frank W. Sinatra

"Dad, I'm sorry"

THE CRIME:
Franklin Wayne Emmanuel Sinatra was the only son of the legendary crooner Frank Sinatra, born to his first wife Nancy in 1944. He attempted to follow in the old man's footsteps and become a singer. In late 1963 Frank, Jr was booked to sing at Harrah's Lodge overlooking Lake Tahoe. On the evening of 8 December a blizzard was blowing and 19-year-old Frank, clad only in his underwear, was sitting in his room just 90 m (100 yd) from the casino. He and his friend, Joe Foss, aged 26, had just finished dinner before their first show. Two men burst into the room and held the two friends hostage at gunpoint. Foss was tied up and gagged while Frank was bundled into a 1963 white Chevrolet Impala and driven to a hideout at 8143 Mason Avenue in the San Fernando Valley. Foss managed to free himself and called hotel security who informed the police.

Sinatra rang his Rat Pack colleague Peter Lawford who contacted his brother-in-law Attorney General Bobby Kennedy, who offered FBI resources to be put at Sinatra's disposal. The first contact from the kidnappers came at 4.45pm on 9 December. Sinatra offered the kidnappers $1 million but they asked for only $240,000. Sinatra agreed to their demand and flew to Los Angeles where, with an FBI agent, he delivered the ransom. His son was released, after 54 hours in captivity, 3 km (2 mi) from his mother's Bel Air home at 700 Nimes Road. His first words back at home to his father were, "Dad, I'm sorry." Four days later, the kidnappers were arrested and most of the ransom money recovered. They were Barry Worthington Keenan and Joseph Clyde Amsler, both 23, who had taken Frank away and their accomplice, John Irwin, 42, who had placed the ransom calls. They were caught after Joe Amsler's brother, James, called the FBI.

WHERE:
Harrah's Lodge, 15 Highway 50, Stateline, Nevada, USA

WHEN:
9.30pm Sunday 8 December 1963

THE AFTERMATH:
In court in February 1964 Keenan claimed that Frank had been involved in his own kidnapping as a publicity stunt to bolster his singing career. The jury disbelieved that claim and all three kidnappers were found guilty. Keenan and Amsler were sentenced to life imprisonment plus 75 years while Irwin received a sentence of 16 years and eight months. Keenan served four and a half years, was released in 1968 and went on to become a successful estate agent. Amsler and Irwin served three and a half years.

YOU SHOULD KNOW:
In gratitude to the FBI, Frank Sinatra sent $2,000 gold watches to the agents who had helped free his son. They were returned with a note explaining that agents were not allowed to accept gifts for doing their jobs. Sinatra sent a similar watch to FBI chief J. Edgar Hoover. That gift was not returned.

Barbara Jane Mackle

"Kidnapped"

THE CRIME: Born in 1948, Barbara Jane Mackle was the daughter of Robert F. Mackle, a millionaire who, with his two brothers, owned the $65 million Deltona Corporation, one of the biggest home-building companies in America. The three were friends of Florida's Democratic Senator George Smathers and President-elect Richard Nixon (see page 98). Eight days before Christmas in 1968, Barbara, a student at Emory University, Atlanta, was suffering from flu and was staying with her mother, Jane, at the Rodeway Inn in Decatur, Georgia.

Gary Steven Krist, 23, knocked at the door and told them that one of Barbara's friends, Stewart Hunt Woodward, had been involved in a car crash. Inside the room he and his partner Ruth Eisemann-Schier, 26, who was disguised as a man, chloroformed, bound and gagged Jane, then pulled a gun on Barbara and forced her into their car. They drove for 32 km (20 mi) to a remote pine forest off South Berkeley Lake Road in Gwinnett County near Duluth where, at 8.30am, they buried their victim in a fibreglass-reinforced box . It had an air pump, water, food and a battery-powered lamp. The pair demanded $500,000 but the first ransom drop failed. Police found the kidnappers' abandoned blue Volvo containing documents identifying Krist and Eisemann-Schier, a collection of lacy panties and nude Polaroids of both kidnappers plus a picture of Barbara in the box holding a sign that read "Kidnapped". The second drop met with more success and on 20 December Krist rang the FBI to give a vague location for finding Barbara. More than 100 FBI agents began to search and found the girl unharmed, although dehydrated, stiff and 4.5 kg (10 lb) lighter after 83 hours underground. She was still wearing the red and white flannel nightie she had on when taken. She told the FBI agents who found her, "You are the handsomest men I've ever seen." Krist was quickly arrested on a boat he had hired with $480,000 of the ransom money, but Eisemann-Schier was at large for 79 days until 5 March 1969. She has the distinction of being the first woman on the FBI's "Ten Most Wanted" list.

A photograph, taken by the kidnappers, of Barbara Jane Mackle imprisoned in a box.

WHERE:
Rodeway Inn, Decatur, Georgia, USA
WHEN:
4am Tuesday 17 December 1968
THE AFTERMATH:
Krist was convicted and sentenced to life in prison in 1969, but was released on parole on 14 May 1979. In March 2006 Krist and his stepson were arrested for drug smuggling. On 16 May 2006 he pleaded guilty and on 19 January 2007 he was sentenced to more than five years in jail. Eisemann-Schier was convicted and sentenced to seven years in prison, paroled after serving four and deported to her native Honduras. She married Salvatore Randazzo and has four children. Barbara Jane Mackle wrote a book about her ordeal, *83 Hours 'Til Dawn*, which has been made into two films (*The Longest Night* in 1972 and *83 Hours 'Til Dawn* in 1990). Now happily married to Stewart Hunt Woodward with two children, she lives in Vero Beach, Florida and refuses all requests to talk about the kidnapping.
YOU SHOULD KNOW:
The box that Barbara was left in was 91cm wide, 1m deep and 2m long (3 ft x 3½ ft x 7 ft). The lid was fastened with fourteen screws. Krist had told Barbara the battery would last for 11 days. It failed after just three hours. Minus the cost of the boat he was arrested in, Krist made $761 from the crime.

Arthur & Nizamodeen Hosein

"You have a million by Wednesday night or we will kill her"

WHERE:
20 Arthur Road, Wimbledon, London, England
WHEN:
6pm Monday 29 December 1969
THE AFTERMATH:
During their trial at the Old Bailey on 14 September 1970 the brothers blamed each other, but neither confessed. Arthur was sentenced to life imprisonment and 25 years for kidnapping, 14 years for blackmail and 10 years for sending threatening letters. Nizamodeen received the same sentence, except for 10 years fewer on the kidnap charge. It was generally believed Mrs McKay had been drugged, shot, butchered and fed to the Hoseins' herd of Wessex Saddleback pigs. Both brothers were released after 20 years. It is not known where Arthur is but Nizamodeen returned to Trinidad on his release.

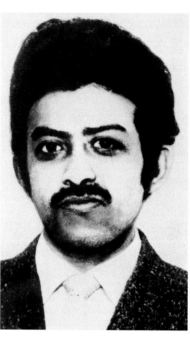

Nizamodeen Hosein, right, and Arthur Hosein, below.

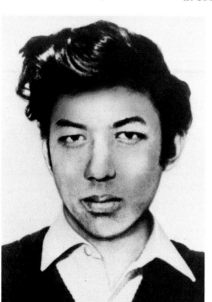

THE CRIME: At about 6pm on 29 December 1969 Trinidad-born Muslims Arthur Hosein, aged 34, and his younger brother Nizamodeen, aged 22, abducted Muriel McKay, 55, mistakenly believing she was Mrs Rupert Murdoch, the wife of the newspaper tycoon, in the first kidnap and ransom crime in Britain.

After an unsuccessful stint in the army, where he was court-martialled, Arthur Hosein became a tailor in Hackney before buying Rooks Farm, a remote, dilapidated pig farm at Stocking Pelham on the Essex–Hertfordshire border in 1967. He moved in during May 1968. Unable to make ends meet, he hatched the kidnap plot after seeing Rupert Murdoch being interviewed on television by David Frost. Arthur Hosein followed Murdoch's Rolls-Royce to Wimbledon, unaware that the car had been loaned to the tycoon's deputy chairman, Alick McKay, while the Murdochs were on holiday in Australia. Arthur Hosein abducted Muriel McKay and telephoned Alick McKay, "We are Mafia M3. We tried to get Rupert Murdoch's wife. We couldn't get her so we took yours instead. You have a million by Wednesday night or we will kill her." When DSC Smith, leading the inquiry, was asked if police were sure they were investigating a genuine ransom demand he replied, "How do we know? We've never had one before." Forty-one days later, police raided Rooks Farm and arrested the owner Arthur Hosein after his Volvo was seen repeatedly driving past the cases that held the ransom demand. His fingerprints were found on the ransom note. Mrs McKay's body was never found.

Steven Stayner

"I know my first name is Steven"

THE CRIME: Steven Gregory Stayner was born on 18 April 1965, the third of five children of Delbert and Kay Stayner in Merced, California. On 4 December 1972 Ervin Murphy, 31, and Kenneth Parnell, a 41-year-old with a criminal record for abusing children stretching back to 20 March 1951, approached Steven. Parnell told Steven that he was the priest at a local church and offered the boy a lift home. Instead of taking the child home, Parnell took him to a cabin strewn with toys.

That night Parnell made the boy give him oral sex for the first time. The paedophile told Steven that his parents did not want him any more and that he would be adopted and his new name would be Dennis Gregory Parnell. He was also ordered to call Parnell "Dad". A fortnight after the kidnapping, Parnell and Steven moved to Santa Rosa, California. They moved around California and the oral sex became sodomy. Parnell opened a shop selling bibles and other religious tracts but the business failed in June 1975. Parnell also babysat for Steven's friends. One day, Barbara, the mother of one of Steven's friends moved in with Parnell and Steven. Parnell invited the boy into bed with himself and Barbara, and Steven was forced to have sex with her. As Steven grew older Parnell had less sexual interest in him and began to look for a younger victim.

On 14 February 1980 Parnell and Sean Poorman kidnapped five-year-old Timmy White in Ukiah, California. Parnell did not touch Timmy that first night nor for the next two weeks. On 1 March Steven escaped with Timmy and hitchhiked into Ukiah. He told Timmy to walk into the police station but a policeman saw the two boys and stopped them leaving. Steven wrote a statement "My name is Steven Stainer [sic]. I am 14 years of age. I don't know my true birthdate but I use April 18 1965. I know my first name is Steven, I'm pretty sure my last is Stainer [sic] and if I have a middle name, I don't know it." Parnell was arrested on 2 March and tried for abducting Timmy on 8 June. He was convicted on 29 June and sentenced to seven years in jail. On 1 December he was tried for kidnapping Steven. On Christmas Eve he was convicted and sentenced to two years for kidnapping and five years for conspiracy. He was not tried on any counts of sexual assault. Ervin Murphy and Sean Poorman received lesser sentences.

WHERE:
Merced, California, USA
WHEN:
Monday 4 December 1972
THE AFTERMATH:
Steven married Jody Edmondson on 13 June 1985 and they had a son and daughter. He died at 5.35pm on 16 September 1989 after his motorbike crashed into a car. At the time he was not wearing a helmet and had been banned from driving. Timmy White, then 14, helped to carry Steven's coffin. On 3 January 2003 Parnell was arrested for trying to procure a young black boy for $500. Convicted on 9 February 2004, in April he was sentenced to 25 years to life. He died in Vacaville state prison hospital on 21 January 2008.
YOU SHOULD KNOW:
Steven's older brother is the convicted serial killer, Cary Stayner. He murdered four women in the same area where his brother was kidnapped, between February and July 1999. Convicted on 26 August 2002, he is currently on death row at San Quentin Penitentiary awaiting execution.

Timmy White and Steven Stayner at a press conference.

J. Paul Getty III

"This is Paul's ear. If we don't get some money within ten days, then the other ear will arrive"

THE CRIME: The grandson of oil billionaire J. Paul Getty was something of a loose cannon in the family. J. Paul Getty III lived life in the fast lane, forever getting into scrapes. After a night out with friends he was kidnapped in Rome in July 1973. He was driven 386 km (240 mi) south to Calabria where he was moved from safe house to safe house. On 12 July his mother, Gail, received a phone call from the kidnappers but they did not specify how much they wanted.

Because of his wild escapades the Getty family and much of the media believed the kidnap had been organized by Paul himself. On 18 July the kidnappers demanded 300 million lire ($500,000). The low amount solidified the belief that the kidnap was a hoax. J. Paul Getty said that to pay would put his other grandchildren at risk and "that acceding to the demands of criminals and terrorists merely guarantees the continuing increase and spread of lawlessness". J. Paul Getty II also refused to pay. On 24 July the demand went up to 10,000 million lire ($16.7 million). The police and the Getty family were still unsure as to the reality of the kidnap. On 15 August Getty sent J. Fletcher Chace, a trusted aide, to Rome to see if the kidnap was a hoax. When the kidnappers called, Chace offered them 53 million lire. The offer was rejected and the ransom went up to 3,000 million lire, accompanied by a threat of mutilation to Paul. On 10 November 1973 a package arrived at the offices of *Il Messagero*. It contained a lock of reddish hair and a human ear and a note, which read: "This is Paul's ear. If we don't get some money within ten days, then the other ear will arrive. In other words, he will arrive in little bits." The kidnappers asked for 1,700 million lire ($3.2 million). Two reporters from *Il Tempo* were sent Polaroids of Paul – he was missing his right ear. Even the mutilation did not galvanize the old man and he offered only 600 million lire ($1 million). Finally, he agreed to the ransom. He paid $2.2 million and loaned (at four per cent interest) his son $1 million to make up the rest. The money – 52,000 banknotes in three sacks – was handed over on 12 December.

J. Paul Getty III, his right ear missing, sits in a police station after being freed.

WHERE:
Piazza Farnese, Rome, Italy
WHEN:
3am Tuesday 10 July 1973
THE AFTERMATH:
Paul Getty III was released in Lagonero, southern Italy on 15 December 1973, shortly after the ransom was paid. However, his life was never the same. He became a drug addict and on 5 April 1981 overdosed on a cocktail of drink and drugs that left him permanently speechless, blind and paralyzed. He married Gisela Martine Zacher on 12 September 1974. Their son is the actor Balthazar Getty. Police arrested seven men and they were sent down for between four and ten years. Only $17,000 of the ransom was ever recovered.

Patricia Hearst

"The entire group is common criminals... and Miss Hearst is part of it"

THE CRIME: The granddaughter of newspaper tycoon William Randolph Hearst was kidnapped from the flat she shared with her fiancé, Steven Weed, by four masked members of the left-wing guerrilla group, the Symbionese Liberation Army (SLA) on 4 February 1974. The group, led by Donald DeFreeze, who had escaped from prison on 5 March 1973, wanted to overthrow the capitalist state and contained any number of losers and dropouts from every strata of society.

The SLA demanded that imprisoned members be freed in return for Hearst and, when that was refused, wanted the Hearst family to give $70 of food to every poor Californian, around $400 million in total. Hearst's father, Randolph Apperson Hearst, immediately gave $6 million of food to people living in the Bay area. On 3 April a tape recording was released in which Hearst announced that she had joined her captors and was now known as Tania. Twelve days later, at 9.40am, she took part in robbing the Sunset District branch of the Hibernia Bank in San Francisco. (The family of Patricia Tobin, one of her close friends, had founded the bank.) The SLA stole $10,960 and Hearst, wearing a beret, carried a sawn-off .30 calibre carbine. A warrant was issued for her arrest. Attorney General William Saxbe said, "The entire group is common criminals... and Miss Hearst is part of it." Another tape, released on 24 April, had Hearst calling her father a "pig". On 17 May the leadership of the SLA died in a shootout at 1466 East 54th Street in Los Angeles. Hearst was arrested on 18 September 1975 at 625 Morse Street in San Francisco. She told her lawyer to "Tell everybody that I'm smiling, that I feel free and strong and I send my greetings and love to all the sisters and brothers out there." Her trial began on 15 January 1976 and F. Lee Bailey defended her (see also Sam Sheppard and O.J. Simpson, page 536). On 20 March 1976 Hearst was convicted of bank robbery and sentenced to seven years in prison.

WHERE:
Apartment 4, 2603 Benvenue Street, Berkeley, California, USA
WHEN:
9pm Monday 4 February 1974
THE AFTERMATH:
On 1 February 1979 Hearst was released from prison, having served just 22 months after President Jimmy Carter commuted her sentence. In one of his odder decisions, President Bill Clinton pardoned her on 20 January 2001, his last day in office. Hearst married her bodyguard Bernard Shaw and has two children, Gillian and Lydia.

Patty Hearst joined her kidnappers' cause.

Princess Anne

"Not bloody likely"

WHERE:
The Mall, London, England
WHEN:
7.45pm Wednesday 20 March 1974
THE AFTERMATH:
On 22 May Ball, who was a 26-year-old schizophrenic, appeared in court charged with two counts of attempted murder, two of wounding and one of "attempting to steal and carry away Her Royal Highness Princess Anne". Ball was detained under the Mental Health Act. Inspector Beaton was awarded the George Cross; PC Hills the George Medal and Callender, McConnell and Russell the Queen's Gallantry Medal.

THE CRIME: On 20 March 1974 Princess Anne and husband Captain Mark Phillips were returning to Buckingham Palace after watching a charity film presentation when a car overtook their Rolls-Royce. It pulled in front forcing the royal vehicle to stop. The princess's bodyguard, Inspector James Beaton, pulled his Walther PPK automatic but the driver of the car Ian Ball had already drawn his .38 revolver and was pointing it at Alec Callender, the princess's chauffeur. He approached Anne's window and said, "I want you to come with me for a day or two, because I want two million. Will you get out of the car?" Anne replied, "Not bloody likely – and I haven't got two million." Ball shot twice at Inspector Beaton, hitting him in the shoulder. Then Callender grabbed Ball who responded by shooting him in the chest. Ball grabbed the princess's arm and told the policeman to "Drop that gun, or I'll shoot her." As Ball yanked at the princess, Captain Philips grabbed her round the waist, heaved her back into the car and he managed to close the door. Ball then shot Inspector Beaton in the stomach. PC Michael Hills, on duty at St James's Palace, rushed over and was also shot in the stomach. Passers by joined in the fracas. Journalist and writer Brian McConnell approached Ball "You can't do that, these are my friends. Don't be silly. Just give me the gun." Ball shot him in the chest. Ronald Russell, another passer by, punched Ball in the head and he aimed his gun at Mr Russell but missed. Ball made a run for it but was rugby-tackled by Detective Constable Peter Edmonds. In seven minutes 11 bullets were fired and four people injured.

Ian Ball's Ford Escort blocking Princess Anne's Rolls Royce.

Donald Neilson (aka The Black Panther)

Lesley was found naked and dead at the bottom of a sewer shaft

THE CRIME: Born on 1 August 1936, Donald Nappey served with the King's Own Yorkshire Infantry in Kenya during his National Service. He later said it was the best time of his life. On the birth of his daughter, Kathryn, in 1960, Nappey changed his name to Neilson to stop her being teased at school. When his joinery business failed, Neilson turned to crime and burgled more than 400 houses. The returns from burglary were not great so he took to robbing sub-post offices. On 15 February 1974 he murdered sub-postmaster Donald Skepper in Harrogate. On 6 September he shot dead Derek Astin and on 11 November he killed Sidney Grayland in the West Midlands.

Neilson's practice of wearing a black hood led to him being nicknamed The Black Panther. On 14 January 1975 he kidnapped 17-year-old heiress Lesley Whittle from her home in Highley, Shropshire. Neilson had planned her kidnap as early as May 1972 when he read an article in the *Daily Express* about the £82,500 she had inherited on the death of her father, George, who ran the Whittle coach business, one of Britain's biggest private coach firms. Neilson left detailed instructions for the Whittle family on a piece of Dymo tape that he left in the family's lounge. He demanded a £50,000 ransom.

Despite an intensive police search, the kidnapping ended in tragedy. On 7 March Lesley was found naked and dead at the bottom of an 18 m (60 ft) sewer shaft in Bathpool Country Park. She had been strangled using wire. On 11 December 1975 two policemen, Tony White and Stuart Mackenzie, spotted Neilson acting suspiciously outside a post office. They approached him and he pulled a sawn-off shotgun on them and ordered them to drive in their Panda car to Blidworth. Outside the Junction Fish and Chip Shop in Southwell Road the two policemen, helped by passer by Roy Morris, managed to disarm Neilson.

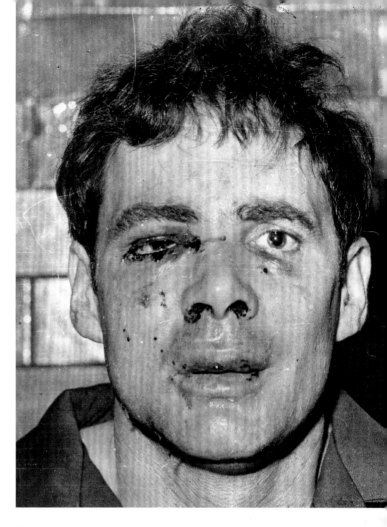

Donald Neilson, known as The Black Panther because of the hood he wore as a disguise.

WHERE:
Highley, Shropshire, England
WHEN:
Tuesday 14 January 1975
THE AFTERMATH:
Neilson's trial began at Oxford Crown Court on 14 June 1975. On 1 July 1976 he was sentenced to life imprisonment. He claimed that Lesley had died when she accidentally fell off the platform he had left her on. On 12 June 2008 Neilson was told that he must die in prison. Seventeen days later it was revealed that the multiple killer was suffering from motor neurone disease.

467

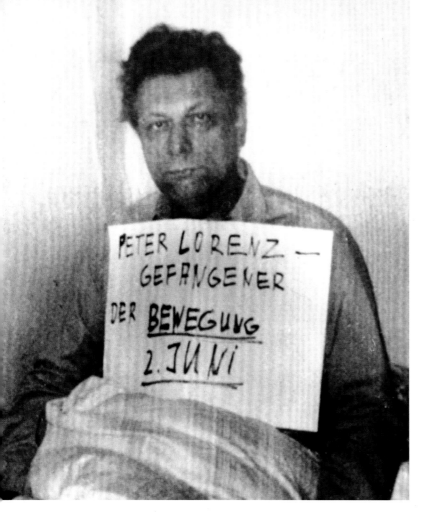

The photograph of Peter Lorenz issued by his kidnappers.

Peter Lorenz

"Peter Lorenz, prisoner of the 2 June Movement"

THE CRIME: Peter Lorenz was born on 22 December 1922. In 1969 he became the chairman of Berlin's Christian Democratic Union and, in 1975, his party's candidate for mayor of West Berlin. As he was leaving his home in the Zehlendorf district of the city three days before the elections, his Mercedes was blocked by a lorry and then rammed by a Fiat. Lorenz's driver, Werner Sowa, was beaten into unconsciousness and Lorenz bundled into another car by two armed men and a woman.

The incumbent mayor of West Berlin Klaus Schütz said that the election would go ahead as scheduled but that there would be no campaigning. The kidnappers issued a Polaroid picture of Lorenz the next day, with a sign around his neck reading, "Peter Lorenz, prisoner of the 2 June Movement". They demanded the release of six jailed terrorists – Horst Mahler, Verena Becker, Gabriele Kröcher-Tiedemann, Ingrid Siepmann, Rolf Heissler and Rolf Pohle – each of whom should be given $3,600 in cash and safe passage out of the country. With the demand was a message: "To our [Baader-Meinhof] comrades in jail. We would like to get more of you out, but at our present strength we're not in a position to do it." They also said that former mayor Heinrich Albertz must be on the flight to guarantee their safety. Albertz agreed but only in his role as a Protestant pastor, and as a former politician. However, Gabriele Kröcher-Tiedemann and Horst Mahler refused to leave prison. Helmut Schmidt, the German chancellor, intensified the hunt for the kidnappers and offered $18,000 for their capture. No arrests were made and after three days the six were freed and flown to Aden, South Yemen. On 4 March Albertz and the aeroplane crew returned to Frankfurt from Aden, having released Pohle, Becker, Heissler, Siepmann and Kröcher-Tiedemann (who had a change of heart and made the trip after all).

WHERE:
Zehlendorf, West Berlin, Germany
WHEN:
9am Thursday 27 February 1975
THE AFTERMATH:
Just before midnight on 4 March a car raced through Berlin's Wilmersdorf district stopping briefly to throw a blindfolded Lorenz from the back seat. He was given a 50 pfennig coin to call home and he rang his wife to say that he was safe. Although Lorenz won a plurality of the votes, Klaus Schütz, relying on a coalition of Social Democrats and Free Democrats, remained mayor. From 1982 to 1987 Lorenz was a parliamentary under-secretary of state in the federal government. He died on 6 December 1987.

Chowchilla School Bus Kidnapping

"I said to myself as soon as the bus stopped, 'What have I got myself into?'"

THE CRIME: No one had heard of Chowchilla until the summer of 1976 when America's largest mass kidnapping for ransom occurred there: a busload of children was kidnapped. Driver Ed Ray, a local farmer, stopped the school bus when he saw a white van apparently broken down. Then a man, carrying guns and with a nylon stocking stretched over his head, approached. The gunman told Mr Ray to move to the back of the bus. Two more masked men appeared from the broken-down van and got onto the bus. One of the men drove the school bus down Avenue 21, while a second watched Mr Ray and the 26 children, between the ages of six and 14. The third man drove the white van. After a short distance the children were transferred to two separate vans whose windows had been blacked out. At 4.15pm the two vans set off on what would be an 11-hour journey to Livermore, California, to a quarry fewer than 160 km (100 mi) from the site of their abduction. When they arrived, Mr Ray was told to take off his trousers and shoes and climb down a ladder sticking out of the ground into what appeared to be a cave. The cave turned out to be a Palo-Alto Transfer and Storage Company truck. The van was 7.6 m (25 ft) long and had bread, water, cereal, crisps, mattresses and a portable lavatory. The latter was too late for some of the children who had soiled themselves.

At 6pm worried parents alerted the police and the bus was found just after 8pm 15 km (9 mi) miles west of Chowchilla. The police search was called off when the area was hit by a freak storm. As night fell some of the older schoolgirls attempted to comfort the younger ones by having a singsong. Ed Ray and some of the teenage boys began to dig their way out of the tomb but it took them 16 hours. They walked to the guard's hut at the entrance to the quarry to alert the authorities. Meanwhile, the kidnappers had been unable to phone in their demands for a $5 million ransom to the Chowchilla police because the lines were always engaged with worried parents and journalists. The kidnappers had not thought their victims would escape and so had made little attempt to disassociate themselves from the vans or from the buried lorry.

WHERE:
Avenue 21, Chowchilla, Madera County, California, USA

WHEN:
Thursday 15 July 1976

THE AFTERMATH:
At 4am on 17 July the hostages were returned to their loved ones. Mr Ray was hypnotised and managed to recall the registration number of the first van and all but one digit of the second. Both vans were traced to a car dealer in Oakland, California. Police soon found the man who had bought the three vehicles, Mark Hall. Hall was 24-year-old Frederick Newhall Woods IV, the son of the quarry's owner. A number of the children remembered that the kidnappers had used the names Fred and James. This led to the brothers Richard Allen, 25, and James Schoenfeld, 23. Richard Schoenfeld surrendered on 23 July and James was arrested on 29 July. That same afternoon Fred Woods was arrested in Vancouver. James was to tell a local paper, "I said to myself as soon as the bus stopped, 'What have I got myself into?' Then you rationalize. You see them and you rationalize all your problems will be over in 24 hours." The three pleaded guilty on 25 July 1977 and agreed not to have a jury trial. On 15 December 1977, after 16 days of testimony, Judge Leo Deegan sentenced all three to life in prison – Woods and James Schoenfeld without possibility of parole. In 1981 they were told they might get parole and indeed the California Board on Parole Hearings deemed Richard Schoenfeld suitable for parole on 30 October 2008.

YOU SHOULD KNOW:
When the hostages were driven to the nearby Santa Rita Rehabilitation Center for medical checks and food, they were taken in a bus!

The kidnappers from left to right: James Schoenfeld, Fred Woods and Richard Schoenfeld

Joyce McKinney

"I loved Kirk so much I would have skied down Mount Everest in the nude with a carnation up my nose"

WHERE:
Banstead Road, Ewell, Surrey, England
WHEN:
Wednesday 14 September 1977
THE AFTERMATH:
In June 1984 McKinney was once again in court accused of continuing to harass Kirk Anderson. The case was dismissed. On 14 July 2004 she was arrested for communicating threats and cruelty to animals. In August 2008, calling herself Bernann McKinney, she was again in the news after she paid $50,000 to South Korean scientists to have her dead Pitbull dog, Booger, cloned. Five puppies were born on 28 July 2008.

Joyce McKinney is ushered into a police van in Epsom, Surrey.

THE CRIME: On 15 September 1977 Scotland Yard announced that Mormon missionary, Kirk Anderson, had disappeared in "most unusual circumstances". The day before, 21-year-old Anderson had received a telephone call from a man calling himself Bob Bosler. Anderson agreed to meet Bosler and his female friend at a church in East Ewell, Surrey. None of the trio had been seen since and the police were worried. The police in Salt Lake City, Utah, had advised their British counterparts that, prior to leaving for Britain, Anderson had been stalked by an obsessive woman.

Three days after disappearing, Kirk Anderson reappeared, claiming that he had been tied up and handcuffed, in a remote cottage in Okehampton on the edge of Dartmoor, Devon. Detective Chief Superintendent William Hucklesby asked the public for help in tracking down two Americans, 24-year-old Keith May (aka Bob Bosler) and 28-year-old Joyce McKinney. The Devon and Cornwall Police arrested the two within hours of Anderson's reappearance and found the cottage where he had been held. They examined the room where Anderson was kept and found an array of bondage items. DCS Hucklesby said, off the record, "I can't go into details but I'll tell you what; I've never been lucky enough to have something like this happen to me."

On 22 September McKinney, a former Miss Wyoming beauty queen, and May, an assistant architect, appeared in court charged with kidnapping and illegal possession of an imitation .38 revolver. Anderson admitted that he had asked McKinney for a back rub but said that did not mean he wanted sex. "My mom gives a pretty good back rub, but that does not mean I want to have sex with her." At a hearing on 30 November the court referred to a previous statement by McKinney in which she said that all the activity with Anderson was consensual and the bondage and oral sex was to help out with his difficulties. "Kirk cannot have an orgasm unless he is tied up," she said.

On 6 December 1977 she told the court, "I loved Kirk so much I would have skied down Mount Everest in the nude with a carnation up my nose." Magistrates released McKinney and May on £3,000 bail after three months in Holloway Prison. On 12 April both May and McKinney – heavily disguised and pretending to be members of a deaf and dumb acting troupe – jumped bail and fled to America on an Air Canada flight. After 13 months, the FBI found McKinney and she was found guilty of using forged passports and given three years' probation.

Aldo Moro

"Italy can survive the loss of Aldo Moro; it would not survive the introduction of torture"

THE CRIME: Aldo Moro was born at Maglie on 23 September 1916 and rose to become one of Italy's most influential politicians. He became leader of the Christian Democratic Party and was prime minister from 1963–68 and again from 1974–76. Two years later, he was expected to be named as the new Italian president.

On the morning of 16 March 1978 he was in his vehicle with five bodyguards on the way to meet prime minister Giulio Andreotti when the car was ambushed by 12 terrorists from the Red Brigades. More than 700 rounds were fired and all five bodyguards were murdered. Signor Moro was unharmed but was taken by the terrorists. They demanded the release of 14 Red Brigades members languishing in jail in return for Signor Moro. Instead of negotiating the Italian government assigned 21,000 soldiers and policemen to search for the kidnapped politician. They looked in vain and the government received photographs of Signor Moro in captivity and he was allowed to write letters to family, friends and to Pope Paul VI. In one he moaned that he felt "a little abandoned by all you".

Prime Minister Andreotti made many public speeches extolling a tough stance against terrorism. When a member of the security services suggested torturing prisoners to find Signor Moro's location, head of the police General Carlo Alberto Dalla Chiesa said, "Italy can survive the loss of Aldo Moro; it would not survive the introduction of torture."

On 15 April the Red Brigades announced that Aldo Moro had been sentenced to death. Three days later the terrorists released a photograph of Moro holding that day's newspaper to prove that he was still alive. On 5 May the terrorists said that unless their demands were met Signor Moro would be murdered within 48 hours. On 7 May he wrote to his wife for the last time. Two days later Signor Moro's corpse was discovered in the boot of a car riddled with 11 bullets. The car was parked in Via Caetani near the Christian Democratic Party's headquarters.

Aldo Moro's bullet-ridden body lies slumped in the back of a car.

WHERE:
Via Fani, Rome, Italy
WHEN:
Thursday 16 March 1978
THE AFTERMATH:
Eventually, in January 1983, 32 terrorists, including nine women, were convicted of various charges and sent to prison for life.

WHERE:
Sears, 3521 Hollywood Boulevard,
Hollywood Mall, Hollywood,
Florida, USA
WHEN:
Monday 27 July 1981
THE AFTERMATH:
The Walsh family attempted to sue
Sears but dropped the suit after the
store countersued. John Walsh helped
to found the National Center for
Missing and Exploited Children and
that led to his presenting *America's
Most Wanted*. On 25 July 2006
Congress passed the Adam Walsh
Child Protection and Safety Act, which
President George W. Bush signed into
law two days later on the South Lawn
of the White House. No one has ever
been convicted of the kidnap and
murder of Adam Walsh although serial
killer Ottis Toole (see page 381)
confessed. In September 1996, Toole
died in prison of cirrhosis of the liver
while serving a life sentence. Another
suspect in the case was Jeffrey
Dahmer (see page 438) although John
Walsh has said, "[There is] no
evidence linking my son's unsolved
kidnapping and slaying to serial killer
Jeffrey Dahmer." John walsh believes
that Otis Toole was the killer.

Adam Walsh

"[There is] no evidence linking my son's unsolved slaying to Jeffrey Dahmer"

THE CRIME: Adam Walsh was born on 14 November 1974, the son of John Walsh, future host of the television programme, *America's Most Wanted*. In the summer of 1981 Adam was visiting the Hollywood Mall in Hollywood, Florida with his mother, Revé. She left him with a group of older boys playing a video game at Sears and went to buy a lamp. When she returned to the video section, Adam had vanished. While she was gone, the boys had made a nuisance of themselves and were thrown out of the shop. Young Adam was also told to get out even though he did not actually know the others. An intercom announcement elicited no response. It is believed that when the boys left the mall Adam was left alone at the entrance. Someone kidnapped him from there. He was never seen alive again. Adam's head was found on 10 August 1981 in a canal at Vero Beach, Florida – the rest of his body was never recovered.

*John Walsh and his wife Revé
at the Missing Child Sub-
Committee Hearing.*

Polly Klaas

"[You] ain't got to show me no consideration or no respect"

THE CRIME: Polly Hannah Klaas was born on 3 January 1981 in Fairfax, California. On 1 October 1993 she invited two friends, Kate McLean and Gillian Pelham, over for a slumber party at her home in Petaluma, 64 km (40 mi) from San Francisco. At 10.30 that night Polly left her bedroom during a board game called Perfect Match to fetch some sleeping bags when a man later identified as Richard Allen Davis approached her with a knife. He said, "Don't scream or I'll cut your throats!" He tied up the two other girls, placed hoods over their heads and told them to count to 1,000. Polly was not so fortunate and he kidnapped her.

At 10.45pm Polly's mother Eve rang the police. At the time of the crime the California Highway Patrol already wanted Davis. As he escaped with Polly, policemen Michael Rankin and Thomas Howard found Davis, whose car had become stuck in mud. Unaware of the warrant issued by the California Highway Patrol, they helped him free his car and let him go. It is thought that Davis, who had convictions for robbery, burglary, assault, kidnapping and a long history of violence against females, immediately drove to a remote area, killed Polly and buried her in a shallow grave. On 19 October Davis was arrested for drink-driving but released after just five hours. On 28 November Polly's body was found. On 30 November the police again arrested Davis during a routine stop and search. He had left a palm print at the Klaas home and was charged with the kidnap. On 4 December Davis confessed to the kidnapping and took police to Cloverdale, California, where they found Polly's body. Davis claimed that he had strangled the girl with a piece of cloth from behind. As he confessed he began crying and was comforted by a policeman but Davis responded, "[You] ain't got to show me no consideration or no respect. I know I'm a piece of shit."

A reward poster posted on the internet shows a photograph of Polly Klaas and a sketch of her abductor.

WHERE:
Petaluma, California, USA
WHEN:
10.30pm Friday 1 October 1993
THE AFTERMATH:
Davis was charged with first-degree murder with special circumstances. On 18 June 1996 the jury convicted Davis of first-degree murder with special circumstances. Just before he was sentenced to death Davis claimed that he did not sexually assault Polly because she had said, "'Just don't do me like my Dad." Polly's father, Marc Klaas, denied any sexual impropriety with his daughter. On 23 July 2006 Davis attempted suicide in his death row cell on San Quentin. He remains on death row.
YOU SHOULD KNOW:
Actress Winona Ryder was raised in Petaluma and she offered a $200,000 reward for Polly's return. She later dedicated a film, *Little Women*, to memory of the victim.

Natascha Kampusch

"I did mourn him"

WHERE:
Heine-Strasse 60, Strasshof, Austria
WHEN:
Monday 2 March 1998

THE AFTERMATH:
Wolfgang Priklopil committed suicide the same day by jumping in front of a train at the Wien Nord station. Natascha said, "He was part of my life. That's why I did mourn him." She claimed to have had a nearly equal relationship with Priklopil whom she always called Wolfgang in interviews. "He was not my master... I was equally strong." She added that her captivity had had benefits: "I did not start smoking or drinking and I did not hang out in bad company." As compensation for her ordeal, Natascha was given Priklopil's house. An aide has said that Priklopil beat her regularly "so badly she could hardly walk". However, Natascha has refused to reveal whether Priklopil sexually abused her. "Everyone always wants to ask intimate questions that are nobody's business. The intimacy is mine alone." On 1 June 2008 she began to present her own television chat show.

YOU SHOULD KNOW:
During her time in captivity Natascha grew just 15 cm (6 in) and, when she escaped, she weighed the same as when she was kidnapped.

THE CRIME: In 1998 Wolfgang Priklopil (born 14 May 1962), a former engineer with Siemens, abducted 10-year-old Natascha Kampusch as she was on her way to school. He placed the girl in a 5 sq m (54 sq ft) nuclear bunker under his garage. The bunker was hidden behind a cupboard and was protected by a steel door. It was to be Natascha's home until 2006.

When she was first captured she attempted to raise an alert by throwing bottles at the walls. She spent the first six months of captivity in the garage before Priklopil allowed her into the house. He forced her to sleep in her cell and stay there while he was at work but the rest of the time she had limited freedom in his home. Priklopil encouraged the girl to read and to listen to classical music and documentaries on the radio. Numerous schoolbooks were later found in the garage. Priklopil took her shopping and on a skiing trip in the mountains near Vienna. Eventually he allowed Natascha into the garden without supervision. It was while she was there, cleaning his BMW, on 23 August 2006 that Priklopil received a call on his mobile and Natascha made good her escape. The police were called and the first policewoman to speak to the girl was astonished by her maturity and vocabulary.

Natascha Kampusch arrives at a civil court in Graz, Austria.

Joseph Fritzl

"Born to rape"

THE CRIME: Electrical engineer, Josef Fritzl ,was no ordinary father. He had been born an only child in Amstetten, Austria on 9 April 1935. In 1956 he married 17-year-old Rosemarie. In September 1967 he was sentenced to 18 months in prison for rape. When his daughter Elisabeth was just 11 years old he raped her for the first time. Five years later, when the girl was 16, she had tried to run away from home but he had foiled her plan. In the summer of 1984 she was 18 and again planning an escape, to work as a waitress in Linz. She liked to go out and visit clubs and flirt with boys. Her father was a strict disciplinarian – how strict she could have no idea. One day he told Elizabeth that he needed her help to carry a door down to the basement. Thus began a terror that would last 8,516 days – almost 25 years. Once in the basement, Fritzl handcuffed and drugged the terrified girl, attached her to a 1.5-m (5-ft) long dog lead and kept her locked in there until 2004.

In 1978 Fritzl had begun excavation (supposedly for a nuclear shelter) under his modest but comfortable three-storey home in Amstetten. He created a cellar beyond the basement that was protected by a steel and concrete door that weighed a third of a ton. In that cellar Elisabeth lived and became pregnant by her father eight times. As the brood increased, the prison also increased in size. Fritzl made his daughter carry out the work. Her reward was that he would rape her in one of the new rooms rather than in front of their children. If anyone asked what had become of Elisabeth, Fritzl would say that she had run off to join a cult. Fritz used his skill to install electronic locks on each of the rooms' doors, and locked the main door with a remote code. The basement contained a television, video, fridge, freezer, washing machine, hotplates and cramped bathroom facilities. It was also soundproofed. In 1984 Elisabeth miscarried a baby in the tenth week. In 1988 she gave birth to Kerstin. Stefan followed in 1990 and Lisa in August 1992. Fritz and Rosemarie adopted Lisa after Elisabeth supposedly gave her up on 19 May 1993. On 26 February 1994 Monika was born. Elisabeth next gave birth to twins, Alexander and Michael, in 1996 but Michael died three days later under mysterious circumstances. Fritzl cremated him in the household furnace, and he and Rosemarie raised Alexander upstairs. His last incestuous child was Felix born in December 2002. The torment came to an end on 19 April 2008 when Kerstin, now 19, fell ill and had to be taken to the Mostviertel-Amstetten State Hospital. A week later, Elisabeth, aged 42, but grey-haired, toothless and looking 20 years older left the cellar for the first time since 1984. The police were called and Elisabeth told all.

A photograph issued by the police department at the time of Joseph Fritzl's arrest.

WHERE:
40 Ybbsstrasse, Amstetten, Austria
WHEN:
Tuesday 28 August 1984
THE AFTERMATH:
On 14 November 2008 Fritzl was charged with the murder of his son Michael. His trial opened at Sankt Pölten, Austria on 16 March 2009. At first Fritzl pleaded guilty to four of six charges he faced but after he heard daughter Elisabeth's testimony he changed his plea to guilty on all charges. He was jailed for life on 19 March 2009. His cellar is to be filled in with concrete to stop it becoming a tourist attraction.
YOU SHOULD KNOW:
The cellar was 4.5 m x 4.5 m (15 ft x 15 ft) and the ceiling was 1.67 m (5 ft 6 in) high. As well as imprisoning his daughter and grandchildren, Fritzl also locked his mother away on the top floor of his house from 1959–1980.

OTHER MISDEEDS

Judas Iscariot

"Are you the King of the Jews?"

WHERE:
Gethsemane, Mount of Olives,
Jerusalem, Judea
WHEN:
Thursday 6 April 30
THE AFTERMATH:
Jesus was crucified on Friday 7 April
30 at Calvary (which means "place of
skulls") between two thieves. On His
cross was pinned a sign that read,
"This is Jesus, King of the Jews".
Having witnessed the result of his
betrayal, Judas hanged himself. Peter,
the Apostle who had denied Jesus
three times, became the first pope.

THE CRIME: Jesus Christ had been preaching His Gospel for three years around Judea and Galilee and upset the leaders of the Jewish establishment. On the Sunday before Passover Jesus made a triumphant entry into Jerusalem and then he went to the Great Temple where he threw out the money changers even though money-changing was legal. Afterwards the supreme court of priests and elders decided that Jesus had to be stopped. Jesus had gathered around Him 12 followers, known as Apostles and one of them, Judas Iscariot, was in charge of the finances. The high priests approached Judas and offered him 30 pieces of silver to betray Jesus. On the night of 6 April 30, the day before Passover, Jesus and His Apostles ate and then prayed in the garden of Gethsemane. Then Judas, Pharisees (adherents to traditional Judaism), high priests and elders approached Jesus and Judas kissed Him. Jesus was arrested and taken to the house of Caiaphas, the high priest, even though this action was illegal on several counts; the Sanhedrin (the supreme court of priests and elders) was not, under Jewish law, allowed to try people at night, during Passover or in a private house. Jesus was accused of blasphemy and high treason (against the authority of Rome).

Unfortunately, no witnesses could be found to testify to these crimes. Around 8am the next day Jesus was taken to Pontius Pilate, the governor of Judea who asked, "Are you the King of the Jews?" to which Jesus replied, "You say that I am." Pilate washed his hands of Jesus, sending Him to Herod Antipas, the ruler of Galilee. However, when Jesus appeared before Herod, He refused to answer any questions and was sent back to Pilate who found no evidence of guilt. Nevertheless, he ordered Jesus to be scourged and then freed. The Jews refused to accept what they saw as a lenient sentence. It was the tradition to free a prisoner during Passover and Pilate gave the crowd a choice – Jesus or the seditious murderer, Barrabas. The crowd called for Barrabas to be freed and Pilate handed Jesus over to the Romans.

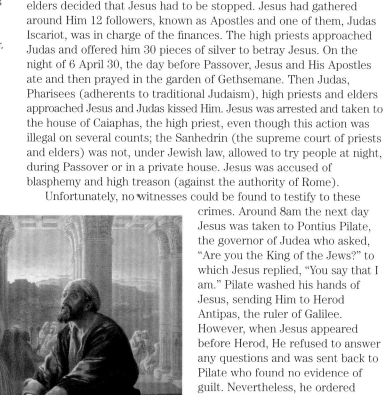

Judas and the 30 pieces of silver, given to him for betraying Christ.

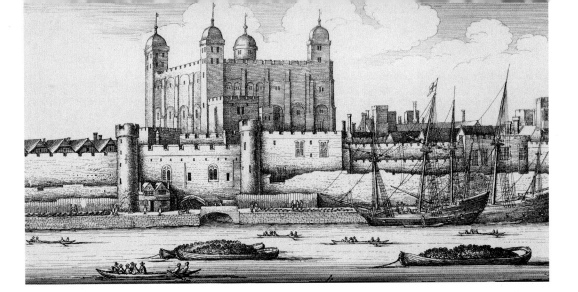

An engraving of the Tower of London in the 17th century

Ranulf Flambard

Ranulf was the first prisoner in the newly built Tower of London

THE CRIME: Ranulf Flambard was born at Bayeux in Normandy about 1060; his father was a priest. He moved to England and joined the court of William the Conqueror. Ranulf was a skilled financier and, although he enjoyed William's favour, the nobility disliked him. They gave him the nickname "Flambard" which means "incendiary". When William died on 9 September 1087 Ranulf became chaplain and treasurer to his son William (II) Rufus. Ranulf encouraged the public to support William and his vices and mad schemes. In 1089 Ranulf was put in charge of Canterbury and in September 1093 he became a judge.

The following year William Rufus summoned 20,000 men to Hastings to join an expedition to fight his brother, Robert Curthose, in Normandy. Ranulf also went to Hastings and there he took from each man the ten shillings that their villages had given them for their keep. While William Rufus was in Normandy Ranulf ran the country. He oversaw the building of the first stone bridge in London and the king's hall at Westminster. On 5 June 1099 he became the Bishop of Durham. When William Rufus died under mysterious circumstances in the New Forest on 2 August 1100, Ranulf fell from favour. Henry I had him imprisoned in the Tower of London on 15 August 1100 for treason. Ranulf was the first prisoner in the newly built Tower, then comprising only the square keep now known as the White Tower. On 2 February 1101 after 171 days of captivity, Ranulf became the first person to escape from the Tower of London. Friends sent in a cask of wine and Ranulf allowed his jailers to share it with him. When they were lying in a drunken stupor, Ranulf broke open the cask and found a rope concealed within. He used it to climb down to the ground where his friends were waiting with horses.

WHERE:
Tower of London, London, England
WHEN:
Wednesday 15 August 1100
THE AFTERMATH:
Ranulf fled to Normandy with his elderly mother, where he became an advisor to Robert, Duke of Normandy. Ranulf later made peace with Henry and returned to England in 1106. As a penance Ranulf completed the magnificent nave of Durham Cathedral. Ranulf died on 5 September 1128.

Everyday life in Plymouth

Mary Latham and James Britton

"Take heed of evil company"

THE CRIME: In the days before the United States of America came into being there was a different morality in place. In 1641 Massachusetts, basing its laws on the Ten Commandments, made adultery a capital offence.

Mary Latham was 18-years-old, well brought up, and her only crime was to fall in love with the wrong man at the wrong time in the wrong place. Latham fell in love but her affections were not returned and she determined to marry the first man who came along. Unfortunately, he was three times her age, "had neither honesty nor ability" and the match was not a happy one. Mary soon began to entertain "divers young men", both married and unmarried, who "solicited her chastity." One of her paramours was James Britton, a 30-year-old professor and playboy, who had recently arrived from England. The two were at a party one day when, having had a lot to drink, they sneaked away to have sex. After he had sex with Mary, Britton fell ill with "a deadly palsy and a fearful horror of conscience" and, believing that it was a punishment from God, confessed his "sin".

Both he and Mary were arrested the next day. She admitted that Britton had tried to have sex with her but said that he did not succeed. However, they had been seen having sex and when confronted, Mary confessed. Adding to her poor behaviour, it was reported that "she did frequently abuse her husband, setting a knife to his breast and threatening to kill him, calling him old rogue and cuckold, and said she would make him wear horns as big as a bull". The magistrates decided that there was not enough evidence against her to convict but the jury found against her and Mary confessed to sex with 12 men (five of them married). Five of her lovers were arrested, the rest having fled but since their accuser was herself now a felon the case against them was dropped.

WHERE:
Plymouth Colony, Massachusetts, America

WHEN:
Tuesday 21 March 1643

THE AFTERMATH:
Both Mary Latham and James Britton were sentenced to death – the only couple to be hanged in America for adultery. Mary "had deep apprehension of the foulness of her sin, and... was willing to die in satisfaction to justice". Britton "was very much cast down for his sins, but was loath to die, and petitioned the general court for his life, but they would not grant it". On 21 March 1643 they went to their deaths "both... very penitently, especially the woman, who... gave good exhortation to all young maids to be obedient to their parents, and to take heed of evil company".

Salem Witch Trials

"I know not what a witch is"

THE CRIME: One of the most shameful incidents in American history resulted in 14 women, six men and two dogs being executed. Of the 20 human executions, 19 people were hanged and one pressed to death. The witch trials in Salem were not the first in America – in 1648 a witch was hanged in Charleston and another in 1655 in Boston.

One day in the house of the Reverend Samuel Parris, ten girls aged nine to 17 listened to the tales of his West Indian slave, Tituba, who told them of voodoo, black magic and sorcery. Later, Elizabeth, the nine-year-old daughter of the clergyman, awoke after having a nightmare. A doctor examined her and insisted that she had been bewitched. Soon some of the other girls who had heard Tituba's tales began to exhibit signs of being possessed by evil. Three women were arrested – Tituba, Sarah Good and Sarah Osborne – and charged. A further 175–200 people were imprisoned, at least five of whom died in jail. The first to be hanged (on 10 June 1962) was 60-year-old Bridget Bishop, a thrice-married woman known for her outrageous dress sense. Bridget denied all charges of witchcraft, saying, "I know not what a witch is." Sarah Osborne died in prison on 10 May 1692 before she could be tried. On 1 March 1692 Sarah Good was tried and she was hanged on 19 July. On 24 March 1692 Dorothy – sometimes called Dorcas – Good was arrested and apparently confessed to being a witch, despite being only four years old. She was kept in chains in prison for eight months until she was released on 10 December for a bond of £50.

On 19 September 1692 Giles Corey, 80, became the only man ever to be pressed to death in America. He was accused of witchery but refused to enter a plea at his trial. He was dragged into a field opposite the jail where he was spread-eagled naked, his ankles and wrists tied to stakes, and a rough wooden board the size of a door placed over him. As more stones were added he said only "More weight", so that he might die sooner. His ribs cracked, his intestines burst and lungs were crushed. *In extremis* Corey's tongue involuntarily protruded from his mouth; the sheriff used his cane to push it back. Corey suffered for two days before dying. Pressing (*peine forte et dure*) had been illegal in Massachusetts since 1641 (51 years before Corey's death), although it was not abolished in England until 1827.

WHERE:
Salem, Massachusetts, America
WHEN:
Friday 10 June 1692
THE AFTERMATH:
The paranoia about witches disappeared almost a quickly as it arrived and the townspeople decided that the young accusers had been mistaken. No punishment was administered to them. Legend has it that the ghost of Giles Corey appears in Salem prior to a disaster occurring in the town. In 1956 the Massachusetts General Court exonerated Bridget Bishop.

The execution of Bridget Bishop

481

Louis Aimé Augustin Le Prince

It seems likely that Le Prince was murdered for his invention

WHERE:
Dijon Station, Dijon, France
WHEN:
2.42pm Friday 16 September 1890
THE AFTERMATH:
There were various theories as to what had happened to Le Prince. In 1928 one author posited that Le Prince had committed suicide because he was on the verge of bankruptcy and arranged for neither his body nor his luggage ever to be found. Le Prince's widow believed that he had been murdered and in 1900 his son Adolph Le Prince also died under mysterious circumstances after losing a lawsuit against Thomas Edison. Another theory, aired in 1985, had Le Prince disappearing voluntarily because of his family's shame over his homosexuality. In this theory Le Prince died in obscurity in Chicago in 1898. Another has a suicidal Le Prince being murdered by his brother. In 2003 a photograph of a drowning victim was discovered in the Parisian police archives and the man look very much like Le Prince. It seems likely that Le Prince was murdered for his invention and his body and luggage were thrown from the train as it passed over a river. However Le Prince died it was the Lumiere brothers, and not he, who got the credit for inventing the cinematic film.

THE CRIME: Born at Metz, France on 28 August 1842, Le Prince is regarded by many as the true father of the cinematic film. He moved to Leeds in northern England in 1866. In 1881 he emigrated to the States to work and became an agent for a number of French artists. He patented in 1888 in America a combined camera-projector. On 14 October of the same year in Roundhay, Leeds, he filmed Roundhay Garden Scene and Leeds Bridge, using his single-lens camera and paper supplied by George "Kodak" Eastman. His films were shown privately but never publicly. In 1889 Le Prince took dual French-American citizenship so that he could work in New York. In September 1890 he planned to exhibit the fruits of his work and research at Jurnel Mansion in New York. However, he disappeared before he could make the presentation. On a Friday in September 1890 he boarded a train at Dijon for a journey to Paris. From the French capital he was due to return to London. However, when the train pulled into Paris there was no sign of Le Prince or his luggage. A search of the track gave no clues.

Louis Aimé Augustin Le Prince was a pioneer of cinematography.

Opera singer Enrico Caruso

Enrico Caruso

"Italian pervert"

THE CRIME: Italian singer extraordinaire Enrico Caruso was born on 25 February 1873 in Naples, Italy. Caruso was a tenor celebrated for his strong, romantic voice. He was able to captivate audiences with his depth of feeling and musical range. He is recognized to have been the first person to understand the value of the phonograph as a means of recording voices and made a lot of money from his records. He smoked two packets of strong Egyptian cigarettes a day but protected his voice by wearing fillets of anchovies around his neck. He once said, "I am a great singer because I have always remained a bachelor. No man can sing unless he smiles and I should never smile if I were married." When he was 45, however, Caruso married Dorothy Benjamin, 20 years his junior, and they were devoted to each other for the rest of their lives.

On 16 November 1906 Caruso was arrested for indecent assault in the monkey house of the Central Park Zoo in New York. He was accused of pinching the backside of a strange woman described as "pretty and plump". The newspapers labelled the singer an "Italian pervert" and he was shunned by polite society.

WHERE:
Monkey House, Central Park Zoo, New York City, USA
WHEN:
Friday 16 November 1906
THE AFTERMATH:
At his trial a white-veiled mystery figure claimed that Caruso had fondled her at the Metropolitan Opera House. A deputy police commissioner claimed that he had a dossier of women who claimed that they had been groped by the singer. Caruso was found guilty and fined $10 despite the arresting policeman's reputation for filing trumped-up charges. It did not go unnoticed that he had been the best man at the wedding of the Monkey House victim – 30-year-old Hannah Graham from the Bronx – who had refused to testify. Caruso claimed that his rivals in the operatic world had framed him. Nonetheless, he would not perform for some time, fearful of being hounded further by the press. When he did return to the New York stage he was greeted with a standing ovation. He died on 2 August 1921.

The lynching of Leo Frank

Murder of Mary Phagan & the Lynching of Leo Frank

"That negro hire doun here"

THE CRIME: At around noon on 26 April 1913, a public holiday known as Confederate Memorial Day, 14-year-old Mary Phagan went to the National Pencil Factory in Atlanta, Georgia, where she worked to collect her $1.20 wages before going to watch the parade. Also working that day was the manager Leo Frank, a 29-year-old, married, Jewish, university graduate. At 3am the next day, Mary Phagan's body was found in the basement by the black night watchman, Newt Lee. She had been strangled and beaten but not sexually assaulted. Next to her body was a note that read in part, "That negro hire doun here". Lee and Frank were both arrested and charged with her murder. The case against Frank was dependant on the testimony of a 29-year-old, black factory janitor called James Conley. He accused Frank of sexually abusing the factory girls.

The trial, which began on 28 July 1913, was anti-Semitic and for the first time in America, a white man was convicted on the word of a black man. According to Georgia law, Frank gave a statement in which he refuted all the allegations against him – cross-examination of the four-hour statement was not allowed. Such was the hostility surrounding the trial, that the judge ruled that Frank and his lawyers not be present in court when the verdict was read in case Frank was found not guilty and the courtroom erupted. The jury found him guilty and Frank was sentenced to death. Public opinion rallied to his aid and 20 June 1915, John M. Slaton, the governor of Georgia, commuted the sentence to life imprisonment. On 17 August 1915, a gang calling themselves The Knights of Mary Phagan broke into the jail and kidnapped Frank, taking him to Marietta, 386 km (240 mi) away, where he was lynched. The mob featured several prominent citizens including Joseph Mackey Brown, the ex-governor of the state, Judge Newt Morris, a doctor, three lawyers, and the former sheriff of Cobb County. Frank asked that he be allowed to write a note to his wife, that his wedding ring be returned to her and that his lower body be covered before he was hanged since he was clad in only a nightshirt.

WHERE:
National Pencil Factory, Forsythe Street, Atlanta, Georgia; Marietta, Georgia, USA
WHEN:
Saturday 26 April 1913; Tuesday 17 August 1915
THE AFTERMATH:
On 11 March 1986 Leo Frank was pardoned for the crime he did not commit.

Mata Hari

"I have never loved any but officers"

THE CRIME: The myths around Mata Hari are multifarious and mostly wrong. Her scandalous life with men began at the age of 16, when she had sex with 51-year-old Wybrandus Haanstra, the headmaster of her school. She married Rudolf MacLeod, a syphilitic soldier 20 years her senior, on 11 July 1895. She was to later write, "Those who are not officers… do not interest me… I have never loved any but officers." Standing 1.80 m (5 ft 11 in) tall, she was certainly in a position to look down on privates!

Dancer but no spy, Mata Hari

In 1898 she made her stage debut and her marriage began to deteriorate, as her husband accused her of infidelity. On 27 August 1902 she filed for divorce and three months later returned to Amsterdam. In 1903 she arrived in Paris where she became a prostitute, developed a series of "sacred dances", and appeared almost naked in theatres. As her fame grew she adopted the name Mata Hari and made her debut under that name on 13 March 1905. On 26 April 1906 she was divorced. When the First World War started she attempted to return to Paris but found herself stranded in Berlin without money. In the autumn of 1915 a German consul visited and offered her 20,000 francs to become a spy and gave her the codename H21. She took the money but had no intention of spying for Germany. She returned to Paris but, unbeknown to her, her movements were monitored by British counter intelligence and French police. They discovered that she was promiscuous and liked the finer things in life but uncovered no evidence of espionage. Mata Hari met Georges Ladoux, head of the French secret service, who wanted to recruit her to spy for France but she was more interested in earning money than learning secrets. In December 1916 in Spain she was asked to spy for the Russians. On 13 February 1917 Mata Hari was arrested as she breakfasted in Room 131 of the Elysée Palace Hotel. She was sent to the filthy, rat- and flea-infested Saint-Lazare prison in Paris as prisoner 72144625.

WHERE:
France, Holland, Spain, England
WHEN:
1915–1917
THE AFTERMATH:
Mata Hari's trial began at 1pm on 24 July 1917 at the Palace of Justice. She was accused of causing the deaths of 50,000 French soldiers. On 25 July she was found guilty and sentenced to death and her property sold to offset the cost of the trial. At 6.15am on 15 October 1917 Mata Hari was executed at Vincennes. She refused to be tied to a stake as 12 soldiers took aim and fired before Sergeant-Major Petoy administered the *coup de grâce*. Four days later Georges Ladoux, the man who had done so much to bring about her downfall, was arrested as a German spy.

Papillon

He was sentenced to eight more years in solitary confinement

WHERE:
Devil's Island, French Guiana
WHEN:
1944
THE AFTERMATH:
Charrière travelled to Georgetown and then on to Venezuela, where he was jailed near El Dorado. Finally on 18 October 1945 he was granted his freedom. He stayed in the country and became a celebrity chef. He published his autobiography in 1969 and Steve McQueen took the lead role when it was filmed in 1973. Henri Charrière's book sold more than a million copies in France alone. He died of throat cancer in Madrid on 29 July 1973.

THE CRIME: Henri Charrière was born at Ardèche, France, on 16 November 1906. In 1923 he joined the French navy for his military service and served for two years. On demob he became a criminal and was nicknamed Papillon, because he had tattoos of butterflies on his chest. On 26 October 1931 he was sentenced to hard labour for life in the penal colony of French Guiana for the murder of pimp Roland le Petit, a crime he denied committing. Charrière was sent to St Laurent-du-Maroni prison. Just over two years later, on 29 November 1933, he escaped from the hospital at St Laurent with two fellow cons, Clousiot and Maturette. As they escaped, the residents of a leper colony, a British family and several others helped them. They made it to Colombia but poor weather stopped them leaving and they were caught and imprisoned again in French Guiana in 1934. The three men were sentenced to two years' solitary confinement – nicknamed the "Devourer of Men" – as punishment. They were released on 26 June 1936 but Clousiot was broken by the ordeal and died a few days later.

Determined to escape again, Charrière plan was foiled and he murdered an inmate who informed on him. He was sentenced to eight more years in solitary confinement but was released after 19 months. Charrière next feigned madness and when he "recovered" he asked to be transferred to the seemingly inescapable Devil's Island. Charrière decided to escape by throwing himself into the sea and using a bag of coconuts as a raft. He studied the waves and noted that the seventh wave was stronger and bigger than the rest and might be enough to push him away from Devil's Island. Charrière persuaded a prisoner called Sylvain to accompany him and they jumped off a cliff with their bags of coconuts. For four days and three nights they drifted until they spotted land. Sylvain let go off his bag and was pulled under by quicksand, just 300 m (300 yd) from shore. Charrière allowed the tide to take him to the shore.

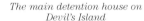

The main detention house on Devil's Island

Philby, Burgess, Maclean & Blunt

"I have no reason to conclude that Mr Philby has betrayed the interests of this country"

Kim Philby jokes with newsmen at his mother's London home during a 1955 press conference.

THE CRIME: In 1929 Kim Philby went up to Trinity College, Cambridge to read history and economics, followed a year later by Guy Burgess and in 1931 by Donald Maclean. Maclean wrote an article calling capitalism a "crack-brained criminal mess", yet in 1935 joined the Foreign Office. Burgess became personal assistant to a Tory MP and later worked for the BBC. In 1935 he recruited Anthony Blunt, a fellow homosexual, to their espionage network. Philby became a spy in 1934 and while covering the Spanish Civil War for *The Times*, ironically escaped death when a Russian-made shell hit his car. In January 1939 Burgess began working for MI6 and in August 1940 he hired Philby. In 1939 Blunt had joined MI5. In 1944 the bisexual Maclean worked in the British embassy in Washington DC.

In August 1945 a Russian defector offered to name three moles inside the British establishment – the man sent to arrange his defection was Kim Philby. The defector was also asked to find the traitor known as Homer but Philby already knew his identity – Maclean. On Friday 25 May 1951 – Maclean's 38th birthday – Foreign Secretary Herbert Morrison authorized the interrogation of Maclean on the following Monday.

Burgess and Maclean fled England at 11pm that night although there is still a mystery as to why Burgess went. Philby told him not to and it threw suspicion on others, including Philby himself. Philby was tried secretly in June 1952 but the evidence against him was circumstantial. On 7 November 1955 Foreign Secretary Harold Macmillan said in the Commons, "I have no reason to conclude that Mr Philby has at any time betrayed the interests of this country." Unbelievably, Philby continued to work for MI6 until 1962 when the CIA provided definite evidence of his treachery. In January 1963 he, too, fled east.

WHERE:
London, England
WHEN:
1934–1963
THE AFTERMATH:
In 1956 Burgess and Maclean were paraded by the Soviets. Neither man was happy behind the Iron Curtain. Burgess died a hopeless alcoholic on 30 August 1963 and Maclean died on 6 March 1983. Philby was happy – he became a senior KGB officer and married Donald Maclean's ex-wife. He died on 11 May 1988. In April 1964 Blunt (Sir Anthony from May 1956) confessed his treachery but was allowed to keep his job as Surveyor of the Queen's Pictures for 15 more years until his public exposure in November 1979, when he was stripped of his knighthood. He died in March 1983.

A prison officer checks on a prisoner through a peep-hole in a cell door in Dartmoor Prison.

Ruby Sparks

"I signed it so the screws would know it was me who had escaped"

THE CRIME: John Wilson, aka Charles Sparks, aka Alfred Watson, was a career burglar who was sent to borstal at an early age and in the leitmotif that would be the hallmark of his life, he escaped. He was nicknamed Ruby after breaking into the Park Lane home of an Indian Maharajah and stealing $40,000 worth of uncut rubies. Ruby was, on this occasion, no bright Sparks – he gave the rubies away, thinking they were not real.

On 27 May 1927 he was sentenced to three years' penal servitude in the tough Strangeways Prison for a smash and grab robbery in Birmingham on 20 November 1924, during which a woman died. A warder told Sparks, "Nobody has ever escaped from here." A fortnight later, Spark became the first man to escape. He paid $400 in bribes and bought mailbag thread and a knife. Then Sparks made a dummy from a blanket, stool and chamber pot. He was wearing a suit he had had made himself from a blanket because his clothes had been taken from him and he simply used his knife to saw through the cell bars. He left a signed poem on his bed:

> The Cage is Empty
> The Bird is Flown
> I've gone to a Place
> Where I'm better Known

He later said, "I signed it so the screws would know it was me who had escaped and not Shakespeare." In May 1930 he was sentenced to five years for a series of car thefts. On 30 June he tried unsuccessfully to escape from Wandsworth Prison. By 1939 he was in Dartmoor Prison. He became the first successful escapee from the bleak prison, which he did on 10 January 1940 with Alec Marsh and Dick Nolan. Unable to steal the five keys he needed to escape, Sparks mentally photographed them and spent a year making them from metal he stole from the machine shop. He became known as "Public Enemy Number One" and spent 170 days on the run.

WHERE:
Strangeways Prison, Manchester; Dartmoor Prison, Devon, England
WHEN:
1927–1940
THE AFTERMATH:
On his retirement Sparks wrote his autobiography, *Burglar To The Nobility*.

Helen Duncan

"I didn't do anything"

THE CRIME: Born in Scotland on 25 November 1897, Helen Duncan was a tomboy who was nicknamed "Hellish Nell" when she was a young girl. Even her mother said that one day she would be burned as a witch. In 1916 Helen married Henry Duncan, an invalided soldier she had "first met in her dreams". They had six children and Henry spent much of his time helping his wife's spiritualism business rather than concentrating on his career as a cabinet maker. Helen claimed that she was helped by her spirit guide Albert Stewart, a sarcastic Scotsman who had emigrated to Australia. Helen became a very popular medium, especially when she manifested ectoplasm from her mouth and nose. Even when this was shown to be a trick (she had swallowed cheesecloth), her popularity did not wane. In 1933 she was fined £10 for fraudulently procuring money from the public yet still she was still as popular as ever. By 1944 she was an obese, hard-drinking, chain-smoking star who swore like a fishwife.

On 25 November 1941, a German U-boat sank HMS *Barham* in the Mediterranean, killing 868 men. By this time Helen and her husband had moved to Portsmouth and at one of her séances there a dead sailor, wearing an HMS *Barham* cap, materialized for his mother. This was a shock for the mother because the Admiralty had kept secret the fate of the ship to confound the Germans and uphold morale. The next day the mother telephoned the Admiralty for confirmation. Two officers interviewed her and wanted to know the source of her information. On 19 January 1944 Helen Duncan was arrested along with three members of her audience during a séance. She was originally charged under Section 4 of the Vagrancy Act (1824) but when the case came to court on 23 March she was prosecuted under Section 4 of the 1735 Witchcraft Act which was not repealed until 1951. The case caused a sensation and Helen even offered to perform a séance in court to prove her powers. On 3 April 1944 she was found guilty and jailed for nine months. When the sentence was passed, she said, "I didn't do anything" and promptly collapsed.

WHERE:
Court 4, Old Bailey, London, England
WHEN:
10.30am Monday 3 April 1944
THE AFTERMATH:
When she was released from Holloway Prison on 22 September 1944, Duncan returned to mediumship. She died on 6 December 1956, a few days after police raided another of her séances.

Helen Duncan supposedly producing ectoplasm in the 1930s.

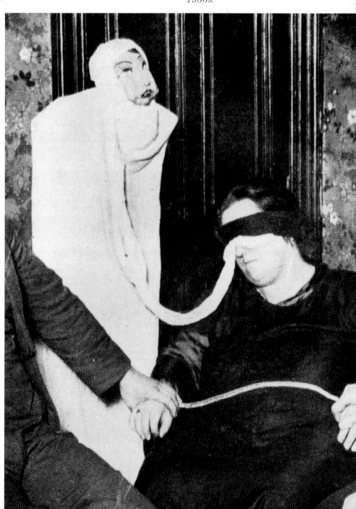

Julius and Ethel Rosenberg

Albert Einstein and Pope Pius XII urged the death sentence be set aside

WHERE:
Sing Sing Prison, Ossining, New York, USA

THE TIME:
Friday 19 June 1953

THE AFTERMATH:
For two years lawyers fought to have the sentence commuted or to gain a new trial and thousands of people in America and overseas pleaded for clemency for the Rosenbergs. They wrote to each other from their prison cells and the letters were published in a book. Albert Einstein, the president of France and HH Pope Pius XII all urged the death sentence be set aside. The Supreme Court refused three times to review the case and on 19 June 1953 the court voted 6-3 to vacate the stay of execution. Later that day, the Rosenbergs were electrocuted at Sing Sing prison in New York. FBI documents later revealed that Hoover had recommended clemency for Ethel but not Julius. In September 2008 evidence emerged that the conviction of Ethel Rosenberg was based on perjured testimony.

Ethel and Julius Rosenberg in a police van in New York shortly before their execution.

THE CRIME: The so-called Atom Bomb spies, Julius and Ethel Rosenberg, were electrocuted for supposedly passing secrets to the Soviet Union. Both were born on the Lower East Side of New York, the children of Jewish immigrants, Ethel Greenglass on 28 September 1915 and Julius on 12 May 1918. They married on 18 June 1939 and had two sons, Michael Allen and Robert Harry. Julius worked as an engineer for the army from 1940 until February 1945 but was sacked for lying about his membership of the Communist Party. Between 1945 and 1950 he organized three small businesses, two of them machine shops run by his wife's brothers Bernard and David Greenglass.

On 17 July 1950 J. Edgar Hoover personally announced Julius's arrest on charges of selling secret information about American atomic research. In January 1950 Alger Hiss had been convicted of perjury for denying his involvement in spying. The following month, Klaus Fuchs was arrested and, in March 1950, sentenced to 14 years in prison for spying. His courier Harry Gold named David Greenglass as someone who had given him secret information. Greenglass was arrested on 15 June 1950 and he in turn said that Julius Rosenberg had recruited him in 1944. On 11 August Ethel was arrested and, a week later, Morton Sobell, a schoolmate of Julius. The trial of the Rosenberg Spy Ring began on 6 March 1951 in New York. The lead witnesses against the Rosenbergs were David Greenglass and his wife Ruth. The decision of the Rosenbergs to testify turned out to be unhelpful as Ethel incriminated herself. Despite the fact that the entire government case was based on the testimony of David (he had pleaded guilty in October 1950) and Ruth Greenglass, all four defendants were convicted on 29 March 1951. On 5 April Judge Irving R. Kaufman passed sentence. David Greenglass received 15 years in prison; Morton Sobell was sent down for 30 years and the Rosenbergs were sentenced to die on 21 May 1951.

George Blake

"I did what I did for ideological reasons, never for money"

THE CRIME: Born in Rotterdam, Holland on 11 November 1922, George Blake was named for King George V. At the outbreak of the Second World War he worked for Dutch resistance for a time before relocating to England where he joined the Royal Navy and was assigned to the Dutch section of MI6.

After the end of hostilities he was sent to Hamburg where he recruited former German soldiers and sailors for MI6. In October 1948 he was sent to head up a new MI6 station in Seoul, Korea. He was captured at the start of the Korean War in June 1950. In jail he told his captors that he wanted to contact the Soviet embassy in Pyongyang, North Korea. It was the time he became a spy for the Soviet Union. "I did what I did for ideological reasons," he said, "never for money." He was released in 1953 and moved back to London where he worked in MI6's Y section. His first betrayal occurred in October of that year when he gave away "a list of top secret technical operations carried out by MI6 against Soviet targets". In 1955 he went to Berlin and, ostensibly working for MI6, was in fact in the pay of the KGB. In 1961 he was recalled to London and accused of being a Soviet spy after a defector revealed his identity. Blake confessed, was tried for treason in May 1961 and sentenced to 42 years in prison "a year for each agent betrayed".

George Blake with his mother, who visited him in Russia.

WHERE:
London, England
WHEN:
October 1953
THE AFTERMATH:
On 22 October 1966 Blake escaped from Wormwood Scrubs with the aid of IRA man Sean Bourke. The Irishman and two others smuggled Blake to East Germany. Rumours have long persisted that the KGB financed the escape, enlisting the help of the IRA. In 1990 Blake admitted that he was disillusioned by the demise of communism and longed for the old days of totalitarianism. According to reports from Moscow, Blake is still an active member of the Russian Secret Service.

Lana Turner appears on the verge of collapse as she testifies.

Johnny Stompanato

"I'm deathly afraid of him"

THE CRIME: Glamorous Lana Turner appeared in films and gossip columns, married seven times and had one child, a daughter, Cheryl Crane, on 25 July 1943. Lana's choice of men was not always wise and in the late 1950s she took up with small-time hoodlum Johnny Stompanato. He had first contacted Lana in April 1957 during the making of *The Lady Takes A Flyer*, calling himself John Steele. She finally agreed to have a drink with him and they began an affair and by the time Lana discovered his true identity he had charmed her. On 18 September 1957 Lana flew to England to film *Another Time, Another Place* but she was lonely and the weather depressed her. She paid for Stompanato to visit her. He visited the set and warned Lana's co-star Sean Connery to "stay away from the kid" which resulted in the burly Scotsman punching him. In retaliation, Stomanato attacked Lana so she arranged for him to be deported soon afterwards.

When they were both back in America, Stompanato often laid hands on Lana with the result that she was in fear for her life. Cheryl told her mother to leave the thug but Lana replied, "I'm deathly afraid of him." Things came to a head on a friday when Stompanato and Turner had a furious argument in the bedroom of her Beverly Hills mansion. Fearing her mother's life was in danger, Cheryl picked up a 20-cm (8-in) kitchen knife and, when Stompanato opened the bedroom door, either she accidentally stabbed him or he walked onto the weapon.

When the police arrived two hours later they arrested 14-year-old Cheryl. Stories have long persisted that it was, in fact, Lana herself who plunged the knife into her lover's stomach. In her autobiography, written while her mother was still alive, Cheryl sticks to the story that she was the killer. Johnny Stompanato's family believed that Lana had killed him and sued her for $1 million but accepted $20,000.

WHERE:
730 North Bedford Drive, Beverly Hills, California, USA
WHEN:
Friday 4 April 1958
THE AFTERMATH:
An inquest on 11 April 1958 found Cheryl Crane guilty of justifiable homicide. She appeared before a closed juvenile hearing on 24 April and was made a ward of court. On 11 March 1960 she was sent to El Retiro, a reformatory for problematic girls. On 11 June 1961 Cheryl was arrested with two other girls during a "wild drinking party" and the police noted that Cheryl was dressed in "mannish clothes". In April 1970, police found three half-grown cannabis plants in the back seat of her car but charges were dropped through lack of evidence. In 1988, Cheryl published her autobiography, the first public mention by her of the killing. She lives in Palm Springs, California, with her lesbian lover and works as an estate agent. Lana Turner died a little after 10pm on 29 June 1995 at her home, Suite 2006, 2170 Century Park East, Century City, California.

John & Clarence Anglin & Frank Lee Morris

They created life-like dummies to leave in their beds when they escaped

THE CRIME: Frank Lee Morris was born at Washington DC on 1 September 1926. He was a career criminal, beginning his nefarious activities when he was just 13 years old. On 20 January 1960 he was sent to Alcatraz and immediately began planning his escape. Brothers John and Clarence Anglin and Allen West joined him in his plan. The Anglins had been sent to the Rock for bank robbery. John William Anglin was born at Donalsonville, Georgia on 2 May 1930 and arrived at Alcatraz on 21 October 1960. His brother Clarence was born a year later on 11 May 1931 and he arrived on the Rock on 10 January 1961. Allen West was born at New York on 10 September 1926. A car thief, he was sent to Alcatraz in 1957.

For two years the men plotted and planned. They created a 5 x 4-m (16 x 14 ft) raft and life-like dummies to leave in their beds when they escaped. They took turns to dig behind the 15 x 22-cm (6 x 9-in) ventilation holes in their cells, while one man kept watch. On the night of 11 June 1962, without West who had been slow to dig in his cell, they made their break for freedom. They went down the tunnels they had made and onto the roof of Alcatraz. They climbed down and set sail into the bay on their raft.

WHERE:
Alcatraz Prison, San Francisco, California, USA
WHEN:
Tuesday 11 June 1962
THE AFTERMATH:
The FBI began one of the biggest manhunts since the Lindbergh kidnapping (see page 456) but only found parts of the raft and a waterproof bag containing the Anglins' letters. The official verdict was that the men drowned in their attempt. On 17 July 1962 a Norwegian freighter spotted a body floating face down 32 km (20 mi) northwest of the Golden Gate Bridge but did not report the sighting for three months. The FBI pointed to the fact that the men were habitual criminals and yet were never again arrested. They closed the case officially on 31 December 1979. The Anglin family believe that the brothers died and another, Alfred, was electrocuted while trying to escape from Kilby Prison in Montgomery, Alabama, in 1964. Allen West left Alcatraz on 6 February 1963 when the prison closed. He was released in 1967 but was arrested again in 1968. In January 1969 he was jailed for life. On 30 October 1972 he stabbed a black prisoner to death. He died in jail of acute peritonitis on 21 December 1978. The story was made into a film, *Escape from Alcatraz*, starring Clint Eastwood as Frank Morris. Allen West's name was changed to Charley Butts in the film.

Mug shots of the three escapees. From top to bottom: Clarence Anglin, Frank Lee Morris and John William Anglin

Profumo Scandal

"Well he would, wouldn't he?"

WHERE:
Taplow, Berkshire; London, England
WHEN:
1961–1963
THE AFTERMATH:
Profumo left public life immediately and devoted the next 40 years to doing good works. He died aged 91 at midnight on 10 March 2006 in the Chelsea and Westminister Hospital. Harold Macmillan resigned as prime minister on 18 October 1963, citing ill health and Lord Home took over. He led the Conservatives to a heavy defeat in the 1964 General Election. The Denning Report into the affair was published on 25 September 1963. Christine Keeler was sentenced to nine months in prison on 6 December 1963 for perjury at the trial of Lucky Gordon. She was released in June 1964. She has married twice but lives in poverty in London. Mandy Rice-Davies became a cabaret singer. On 29 January 1963 Eugene Ivanov returned to the Soviet Union. He died on 17 January 1994.

Christine Keeler outside the Old Bailey

THE CRIME: On 8 July 1961 Minister of War, John Profumo, 46, encountered a naked, wet and embarrassed Christine Keeler, a 19-year-old good-time girl, at a cottage on the Cliveden estate of Lord Astor. Keeler's friend, Stephen Ward, had a standing invitation to use the swimming pool. The next day another pool party was organized and this time Ward's friend the Soviet Naval attaché Eugene Ivanov, 35, turned up and he and Profumo competed for Keeler's attention. By Sunday Keeler's phone number was in Profumo's pocket but she spent that night in bed with Ivanov. Profumo first slept with Keeler on 16 July 1961. He was to later claim that they had only had sex on three occasions. Profumo gave Keeler a number of presents including a Flaminaire cigarette lighter and £20 "for your mother" – a polite way of paying for her services. Keeler later summed up the liaison as "a very well-mannered screw of convenience; only in other people's minds, much later, was it 'An Affair.'" Profumo ended the brief fling in December.

Keeler took up with an unstable West Indian drug dealer called Lucky Gordon but left him for another volatile man, Johnny Edgecombe. When Edgecombe showed up at Ward's home in the early afternoon of 14 December 1962, Keeler and her friend Mandy Rice-Davies refused to let him in. He fired several shots at the door. Edgecombe was later arrested at his Brentford flat.

On 15 March 1963 the *Daily Express* published a front-page story revealing that Profumo had wanted to resign "for personal reasons" but had been persuaded to stay on by Prime Minister Harold Macmillan. The story was not true but also on the front page was a report about the disappearance of Christine Keeler – it was a subtle way of linking the War Minister to the call girl. On 22 March Profumo made a personal statement in the chamber of the House. He claimed that "There was no impropriety whatsoever in my acquaintanceship with Miss Keeler". It was a lie that was to do for his political career. The rumours would not go away and, while on holiday, he confessed the truth to his wife, who stood by him, and to the Conservative Party, which did not. Profumo confessed that he had misled the House and resigned on 5 June. The matter did not end there for Stephen Ward. As the scandal broke, his wealthy, powerful and influential friends deserted him and on 8 June 1963 he was arrested at Watford and charged with living off immoral earnings. His trial began at the Old Bailey on 22 July. When called to the witness stand the next day Mandy Rice-Davies said that she had an affair with Lord Astor but when the barrister said that the peer denied it, she retorted, "Well he would, wouldn't he?" Before a verdict could be reached, Stephen Ward took an overdose of Nembutal. On 31 July the jury returned a guilty verdict. Ward died on 3 August.

Stockholm Syndrome

"The party has just begun"

THE CRIME: The term "Stockholm Syndrome" is derived from the taking of four hostages during a robbery at the Sveriges Kreditbank, Stockholm in 1973. Criminologist and psychologist Nils Bejerot coined the term, which refers to the behaviour of kidnap victims who become sympathetic to their captor.

Not long after the bank opened for business on 23 August, 32-year-old Jan Erik Olsson walked in and raked the place with machine gun fire, announcing, "The party has just begun." The police were rapidly on the scene and two policemen entered the bank. Olsson shot one and the other was forced to sit on a chair and "sing something". He chose *Lonesome Cowboy*.

Olsson then took four bank employees – three women and one man – hostage in the vault. Olsson demanded three million kronor and the freeing of prisoner Clark Olofsson, who had six more years to serve and who had tried to escape just two weeks previously. He also wanted a fast car, two guns, bulletproof vests and a helmet. Clark Olofsson was brought to the bank where he took part in the negotiations.

Kristin Enmark, one of the hostages, said that she felt safe with the two criminals but feared the situation would worsen if the police attempted to rescue her and the other three clerks. The police negotiators agreed to the demand of a car but refused to allow Olsson and Olofsson to leave in it if they tried to take the hostages. Olsson rang Prime Minister Olof Palme (see page 317) and threatened to kill the hostages if his demands were not met. The next day, Enmark rang Mr Palme and said that she was upset by his attitude and asked that the robbers be allowed to leave. On the evening of 28 August the police used tear gas to end the siege after 131 hours.

The four bank clerks taken hostage during the robbery at the Kreditbank, Stockholm.

WHERE:
Sveriges Kreditbank, Norrmalmstorg Square, Stockholm, Sweden
WHEN:
10.15am Thursday 23 August 1973
THE AFTERMATH:
Jan Erik Olsson was sentenced to ten years in prison for his part in the robbery. Clark Olofsson was returned to jail after also being convicted but he claimed that he had tried to help the situation and his conviction was quashed. He later became friends with Kristin Enmark. Jan Erik Olsson married one of the women who wrote him fan letters while he was in prison.
YOU SHOULD KNOW:
Released from prison, Jan Erik Olsson continued to commit crimes. Finally, racked by guilt, on 2 May 2006 he gave himself up, only to be told that the police were no longer interested and were not planning to prosecute.

Lord Lucan

"I've just escaped from being murdered"

THE CRIME: John Bingham, 7th Earl of Lucan, was a dashing figure – he once auditioned to be James Bond. In November 1974 he murdered Sandra Rivett, his children's nanny, who had begun work for the family less than three months earlier on 26 August, mistaking her for his estranged wife. Lucan, a gambler nicknamed Lucky, had been increasingly angry with his wife and had told several friends at the Clermont Club that he wanted to murder her.

Knowing that Thursday was the nanny's night off, Lucan let himself into the house and removed the light bulb from the kitchen staircase so his victim would not see him. Just before 9pm a woman came down the stairs to make some tea and Lucan struck her over the head with a 60-cm (2-ft) piece of lead piping. Unfortunately, the intended victim was not the Countess of Lucan, but 29-year-old Sandra Rivett who had changed her day off. Hearing a commotion, Lady Lucan came downstairs and was attacked by Lucan. She managed to grab him between the legs and he stopped the assault. Incredibly, he apologized to the woman he had just tried to murder and began to tend her wounds. When he went upstairs to fetch a towel to stem the bleeding, Lady Lucan made her escape. She ran to the nearby Plumber's Arms and burst into the saloon bar at 9.50pm screaming, "Help me, help me, help me! I've just escaped from being murdered. My children, my children! He's murdered my nanny, he's murdered my nanny."

Lucan fled to the Sussex home of his friends, Ian and Susan Maxwell-Scott, and was given a drink by Mrs Maxwell-Scott. Lucan rang his mother and then wrote two letters to his brother-in-law, Bill Shand Kydd. At 1am, after another Scotch and water, he left and disappeared. Lucan's car was discovered in Norman Road, Newhaven two days later. Of the missing earl, there was no trace. So began the biggest manhunt in British history, spanning several continents.

WHERE:
46 Lower Belgrave Street, London England

THE TIME AND PLACE:
Thursday 7 November 1974

THE AFTERMATH:
In June 1975 the inquest jury named Lucan as Sandra Rivett's killer. In 2005 the respected author John Pearson propounded the theory that Lucan had been smuggled out of the country to Switzerland. The shadowy figure that had helped Lucan to escape became fearful that the earl would return to England and begin a custody battle for his children. If this happened several members of Lucan's social circle could be implicated in the events of 7 November and their aftermath. With no other choice, Lucan was murdered and his corpse buried in Switzerland.

YOU SHOULD KNOW:
In January 1985 a second Lucan nanny was killed. Christabel Martin began working for the Lucans in January 1973 and returned after Sandra Rivett's murder. In October 1985 her husband, Nicholas Boyce, was convicted of her manslaughter after the jury heard that he had strangled and then dismembered her, before roasting and boiling her corpse which he then dumped in more than 100 plastic bags around London in skips and dumps. He had encased her skull in concrete and, while out walking with their 3-year-old son Boyce, threw it over Hungerford Bridge.

Lord Lucan with his bride Veronica at their wedding in 1963.

Claudine Longet & Spider Sabich

"I've always known she shot Spider Sabich and meant to do it"

THE CRIME: Claudine Georgette Longet was born at Paris, France on 29 January 1942 and became a popular singer during the 1960s, no doubt helped by her marriage to Andy Williams on 15 December 1961. They had three children and divorced in January 1975.

In 1972 Longet took up with Olympic skier Vladimir "Spider" Sabich, nearly four years her junior, following her separation from Williams and she and her three children moved in with the handsome sportsman. After a time, Sabich began to tire of life with Longet and told friends he wanted to separate. However, he did not ask her to move out because he adored her children. On 21 March 1976 the couple was together at his house in Aspen when Sabich went to take a shower. He was undressed down to his blue thermal underwear when Longet shot him. He bled to death on the way to Aspen Valley Hospital. When the police arrested her, she told them that the gun had gone off accidentally as Sabich was showing her how to use it.

An autopsy showed that the skier was bent over with his back to her and no nearer than 2 m (6 ft) away when he was killed. However, Longet stuck to her story that it was all a tragic accident when she came to trial. Williams publicly supported his ex-wife throughout the trial in January 1977. The Aspen police had made two mistakes when prosecuting the case. They had taken a blood sample from Longet – which showed cocaine in her system – and taken her diary in which she recounted bitter arguments with Sabich. However, both these actions were carried out without a warrant, which rendered them inadmissible in court. The weapon was also unaccounted for for three days as a policeman kept it in the glove compartment of his car. Longet threw herself on the jury's mercy saying that they should not find her guilty because her children needed her. The jury listened and on 14 January 1977, after 40 minutes' deliberation, acquitted her of felony manslaughter but convicted her of criminal negligence, a misdemeanour. Judge George E. Lohr sentenced her to spend 30 days in jail and pay a $250 fine and even let Longet choose when she served her sentence.

WHERE:
Starwood, Aspen, Colorado, USA
WHEN:
Sunday 21 March 1976
THE AFTERMATH:
Longet went on holiday with her lawyer Ron Austin who left his wife and children for her. They later married. Longet never performed again. She was sued by the Sabich family for $1.3 million but settled out of court for a large sum and a promise never to write or tell her story. Prosecutor Frank Tucker said, "I've always known she shot Spider Sabich and meant to do it."
YOU SHOULD KNOW:
Mick Jagger wrote a song about the case, entitled *Claudine*, but it was edited from the 1980 Rolling Stones album *Emotional Rescue*.

Andy Williams escorts Claudine Longet down the steps of the courthouse in Aspen.

Roman Polanski

"It's an unpleasant memory... [but] I can live with it"

WHERE:
12850 Mullholland Drive, Los Angeles, California, USA
WHEN:
Thursday 10 March 1977

THE AFTERMATH:
On 1 February 1978 Polanski fled to London and the next day to France, where he has remained ever since because he has French citizenship (he was born in Paris) and because that country does not extradite its own citizens. In 2003 Samantha Geimer said, "Straight up, what he did to me was wrong. But I wish he would return to America so the whole ordeal can be put to rest for both of us. I'm sure if he could go back, he wouldn't do it again. He made a terrible mistake but he's paid for it." Five years later, she added, "I think he's sorry, I think he knows it was wrong. I don't think he's a danger to society. I don't think he needs to be locked up forever and no one has ever come out ever – besides me – and accused him of anything. It was 30 years ago now. It's an unpleasant memory... [but] I can live with it."

Roman Polanski is sentenced to 90 days for unlawful sexual intercourse.

THE CRIME: In 1977 Roman Polanski was a successful film director, living in America. He suggested that he photograph "sexy, pert and thoroughly human" teenage girls for *Vogue Hommes*. A friend passed him the number of Samantha Jane Geimer (then known as Samantha Gailey), the 13-year-old sister of his current girlfriend.

After a brief meeting in February 1977 Polanski took the girl to the hills in San Fernando where he photographed her in various outfits and topless. At 4pm on 10 March 1977 Polanski returned for a second shoot and then drove Samantha to the Mullholland Drive home of the actress Jacqueline Bisset for more photographs. On the journey Samantha told Polanski that she loved champagne and Quaaludes and that she had lost her virginity aged eight. Polanski took some pictures by Bisset's swimming pool. Realizing that he needed more shots, Polanski moved to the home of Jack Nicholson, also on Mullholland Drive. Both Nicholson and his then girlfriend, Anjelica Huston, were away from home. Polanski took more pictures of the teenager and according to him she was happy to be seen naked. He then took more photographs in Nicholson's Jacuzzi and then went for a swim after which Samantha told him that her asthma was giving her problems. They went into Nicholson's television room where they had sex.

The next day the Los Angeles police arrested Polanski for rape. Polanski was initially charged with furnishing a controlled substance – methaqualone – to a minor, committing a lewd or lascivious act upon a child under 14, perversion, sodomy, engaging in unlawful sexual intercourse with a minor and rape by use of drugs. His lawyer plea-bargained to the lesser charge of engaging in unlawful sexual intercourse with a minor after Polanski pleaded guilty on 9 August 1977 – the ninth anniversary of the death of his second wife Sharon Tate (see page 208).

Did he or didn't he?
Claus von Bülow poses by the
fireplace in his living-room.

Claus von Bülow

"We know, and he knows, that he tried to murder our mother"

THE CRIME: Socialite Claus von Bülow lived a charmed life until he was 50 years old. He went to Trinity, Cambridge, was personal assistant to J. Paul Getty and on 6 June 1966 he married Martha Crawford, known to all as Sunny. A daughter, Cosima, was born in April 1967. They became well-known jet setters, supposedly happily married, living in style at Clarendon Court, a 20-room mansion that was used as a set in the film *High Society* (1956).

However, behind closed doors Sunny was depressive and diabetic and, according to some, suicidal. In 1980 she suddenly lapsed into a coma in the bathroom at home on Rhode Island. The police became suspicious and investigated. A black bag was found in a bathroom containing an insulin-encrusted syringe. On 6 July 1981 von Bülow was indicted by a Rhode Island grand jury for the attempted murder of his wife. He was arraigned on 13 July. The police claimed that he wanted to get rid of Sunny so that the way would be clear for him to marry his long-term girlfriend Alexandra Isles, the former television soap actor.

WHERE:
Clarendon Court, Bellevue Avenue, Newport, Rhode Island, USA
WHEN:
Sunday 21 December 1980
THE AFTERMATH:
On 16 March 1982 von Bülow was found guilty after the jury had deliberated for six days and he was sentenced to 30 years in prison. He appealed the sentence and in 1984 hired Alan Dershowitz, a law professor at Harvard, as his lawyer. The verdict was overturned because the syringe had been found during an illegal search and a second trial ordered. On 10 June 1985 von Bülow was cleared of all charges. The Crawford family still believed that von Bülow was guilty and Cosima von Bülow was disinherited by her grandmother for supporting her father. Two children, Ala and Alexander from Sunny's first marriage, sued von Bülow for $56 million. Von Bülow agreed to give up his claim to Sunny's $75 million estate if Cosima was reinherited. The case was filmed as *Reversal Of Fortune* (1990) starring Jeremy Irons and Glenn Close. Von Bülow lives in London. Alexander said, "We know, and he knows, that he tried to murder our mother." Sunny remained in an irreversible coma for almost 28 years, cared for at the private Mary Manning Walsh Nursing Home in New York City. She died on 6 December 2008.

Heidi Fleiss awaits the verdict.

Heidi Fleiss

"I am going to prison, and for what? Sex. That's it"

THE CRIME: Heidi Lynne Fleiss seemed like so many other Jewish American Princesses but, unbeknown to many, she was the teenage lover of crooked financier Bernie Cornfeld (see page 93), almost 40 years her senior, and developed a taste for older men. Her next lover was film producer Ivan Nagj and he introduced her to 60-year-old Elizabeth Adams, aka Madam Alex, a notorious purveyor of prostitutes to the rich and shameless. It was not long before Heidi was working for Madam Alex. Fleiss then took over as top dog in the escort business but soon began boasting of her activities, which forced the Los Angeles police department to act.

Her world came crashing down on 9 June 1993 when she was arrested at her Benedict Canyon home for running a high-priced call girl service. Four undercover policemen pretending to be Japanese businessmen had trapped Fleiss. On 9 August 1993 Fleiss was charged on five counts of pandering (procuring prostitutes) and one count of selling cocaine. On 28 July 1994 a federal grand jury added further charges of conspiracy, tax fraud and money laundering. Fleiss said, "I am going to prison, and for what? Sex. That's it. I would never hurt another human being. I'm a vegetarian because I can't even think of hurting animals." On 2 December 1994 Heidi was sentenced to three years in prison and a $1,500 fine. In August 1995 the grand jury convicted her of eight counts of conspiracy, tax evasion and money laundering and she was sentenced to 300 hours of community service, a $400 fine and three years and one month in prison. Just before she was due to start her federal prison sentence Heidi tested positive for drugs and was sent to rehab until her transfer to the federal prison at Dublin, California, in September 1996. She recalled, "It was a lesbian hell. Prison was a journey I had to take. I came away with a lot of things I was lacking: wisdom, compassion, honesty." She was released in November 1998 and sent to a halfway house in Los Angeles. She was finally released in September 1999.

WHERE:
1270 Tower Grove Drive, Los Angeles, California, USA
WHEN:
Wednesday 9 June 1993
THE AFTERMATH:
After prison Heidi Fleiss filed for bankruptcy with debts of $269,000. She also had plastic surgery on her face and breasts. In 2001 Fleiss and her friend and former co-worker Victoria Sellers, daughter of Peter, hosted and produced an instructional DVD titled *Sex Tips with Heidi Fleiss and Victoria Sellers*. Fleiss moved to Pahrump, Nevada, where on 1 July 2007 she opened a laundrette called Dirty Laundry after her plans for a brothel hit a snag. On 7 February 2008 Fleiss was arrested in Nye County, Pahrump for illegal possession of prescription drugs, drink-driving and driving without a licence.

Tonya Harding & Nancy Kerrigan

"Why me? Why me? Why now?"

THE CRIME: Brunette Nancy Kerrigan, 24, and blonde Tonya Harding, 23, both had high hopes for the 1994 Lillehammer Winter Olympics. On 6 January Nancy Kerrigan was practising before about 200 people at the ice rink at Cobo Hall in Detroit. As she left the rink Kerrigan stopped to talk to journalist Dana Scarton of the *Pittsburgh Post-Gazette*. No one noticed the black-clad figure hovering in the background who rushed forward and hit the back of the skater's legs with a 53-cm (21-in) retractable baton. She fell to the ground crying, "Why me? Why me? Why now? Help me! It hurts so bad. Please help me."

When she was examined, it was discovered that the attack had failed. The thug had hit just too high to fracture the leg but he had still done enough damage to rule her out of competitive skating. The United States Figure Skating Association wanted Kerrigan on the plane to Lillehammer and said that, as long as she was fit, she would be included in the team.

A few days later, the police received a tip-off that a woman had heard a tape of three people from Portland, Oregon – Tonya Harding's hometown – discussing an attack on Kerrigan. One of them was Jeff Gillooly, Harding's ex-husband with whom she still lived; another was Shawn Eckhardt, her bodyguard. The FBI placed Eckhardt under surveillance and he obligingly lead them to Derrick Smith, the driver of the getaway car and then to Smith's nephew, Shane Stant, the man who had wielded the baton.

The FBI quickly discovered that none of the men had the intelligence to arrange the plot and the evidence for that quickly pointed to Jeff Gillooly. At first he denied any involvement in the attack but then broke down and confessed. He believed that, with Kerrigan out of the picture, Tonya Harding's chances would be improved. Harding professed ignorance but her estranged husband claimed that, far from knowing nothing of the plot, Harding had actively encouraged it. Desperate to compete in the Olympics, Harding then admitted that she had learned about the planned attack but had done nothing with the information. On 26 February 1994 both women competed for the gold medal. Harding finished eighth and Kerrigan finished second to Oksana Baiul, the Ukrainian.

WHERE:
Cobo Hall, 600 Civic Center Drive, Detroit, Michigan, USA
WHEN:
2.35pm Thursday 6 January 1994
THE AFTERMATH:
On 1 February 1994, Jeff Gillooly agreed to testify against his ex-wife. On 16 March 1994 Harding pleaded guilty to a felony count of conspiring to hinder prosecution. She was sentenced to three years' supervised probation, a $100,000 fine and forced to resign from the United States Figure Skating Association. She was also told to create a $50,000 fund for the Special Olympics, reimburse the District Attorney's Office to the tune of $10,000, serve 500 hours' community service and undergo psychiatric evaluation and treatment. In September 1994 *Penthouse* published stills from a sex tape of Harding and Gillooly. In a celebrity boxing match for Fox TV in 2002 she beat Paula Jones, the woman who accused Bill Clinton of sexual harassment. In 2003 Harding became a professional boxer. Nancy Kerrigan is married to her agent and they have three children.

Tonya Harding, left, and Nancy Kerrigan during a training session for the 1994 Winter Olympics.

Grave robbing

Charlie Chaplin and Alistair Cooke

WHERE:
Vevey Cemetery, Etienne Buenzod,
Switzerland (Chaplin); New York City,
USA (Cooke)
WHEN:
Wednesday 1 March 1978 (Chaplin);
March 2004 (Cooke)
THE AFTERMATH:
In December 1978 Roman Wardas
and Gantscho Ganev were found
guilty of stealing Chaplin's coffin and
extortion. Wardas was sentenced to
four and a half years' hard labour.
Ganev received an 18-month
suspended sentence. A simple cross
marks the spot in the field where
Charlie Chaplin's coffin was found.
On 27 June 2008 Michael
Mastromarino, a drug addict and
former oral surgeon from New
Jersey, was jailed in New York's
Supreme Court for between 18 and
54 years for his part in the bone-
stealing scandal. Mr Cooke's
daughter, the Reverend Susan
Kittredge, said, "I hope the people
responsible for these desecrations
get their come-uppance."

*Charlie Chaplin's coffin was
found after 11 weeks.*

THE CRIME: The Little Tramp – Sir Charlie Chaplin – one of the
world's greatest cinematic comedians died in his sleep on Christmas
Day 1977 at his Swiss home. When he died he made his wife, Oona,
the richest widow in the world. His funeral was held in the Anglican
Church at Vevey on 27 December. On 1 March 1978 Roman Wardas,
a 24-year-old Pole, and Gantscho Ganev, a 38-year-old Bulgarian,
both car mechanics, stole his body from its grave in Vevey
Cemetery, Etienne Buenzod. A ransom note for 600,000 Swiss
francs was delivered but not paid. On 17 May the body was
recovered from a cornfield near Noville and reburied in a vault of
concrete, 1.8 m (6 ft) thick.

Born on 20 November 1908, Alistair Cooke was most famous for
his long-running radio show *Letter From America* which ran for
58 years until 2 March 2004 when, aged 95, Cooke announced his
retirement. He died 28 days later at his home in New York City. His
body was cremated and his ashes scattered by his family in Central
Park. On 22 December 2005 the New York Daily News reported that
body snatchers working for Biomedical Tissue Services of Fort Lee,
New Jersey had removed bones from Mr Cooke and many other
people prior to their cremation. They were using the bones for
grafts. To ensure that the bones of Mr Cooke were suitable, the
thieves doctored his death certificate, changing his age from 95 to
85 and altering his cause of death.

Children who disappear

April Fabb, Genette Tate, Martin Allen, Ben Needham, Madeleine McCann and others

THE CRIME: It is every parent's worse nightmare but each year children go missing. Thankfully, they are usually found safe and sound but for some parents the nightmare never ends.

At Easter 1969 April Fabb, 13 years old, set off on her bicycle to deliver a birthday present to a relative in Metton, Norfolk. She stopped to talk to some friends before cycling on. Nine minutes later, she disappeared. Her bicycle was found in a field close to her home.

Nine years later, on a summer's afternoon in 1978 Genette Tate (born 5 May 1965), also 13 years old, set off on her newspaper round. She was last seen at 3.30pm and, just a few minutes later, her bike was found in a country lane, newspapers strewn all around but of Genette there was no sign.

Martin Allen, 15, vanished on Bonfire Night 1979 from King's Cross Station in London after saying goodbye to a friend, Ian Fletcher. He was seen with a man in a denim suit. Martin's brother Kevin said, "He might be alive but I hope to God he is dead – because whoever's keeping him, Martin can't be enjoying it."

Ben Needham (born 29 October 1989) disappeared on the Greek island of Kos on 24 July 1991 where he was living with his mother, Kerry. His mother and grandparents were redecorating a farmhouse and Ben was just a few metres from them when he was taken.

The highest profile disappeared child of recent years has been Madeleine McCann (born 2003) who disappeared while on holiday with her parents and siblings in Praia da Luz, Portugal on 3 May 2007. Madeleine and her siblings were left alone in their holiday apartment at 8.30pm while her parents Gerry and Kate went to a tapas bar with friends. The McCanns noticed their daughter was missing at around 10pm. For a time the McCanns were named as official suspects by the Portuguese police.

Gerry and Kate McCann show a picture of three-year-old Madeleine at a press conference in Amsterdam.

WHERE:
Metton, Norfolk, England (Fabb); Aylesbeare, Devon, England (Tate); London, England (Allen); Kos, Greece (Needham); Praia da Luz, Portugal (McCann).

WHEN:
Tuesday 8 April 1969 (Fabb); 3.30pm Saturday 19 August 1978 (Tate); 3.50pm Monday 5 November 1979 (Allen); Wednesday 24 July 1991 (Needham); Thursday 3 May 2007 (McCann)

THE AFTERMATH:
The Norfolk police sent their file on April Fabb to their Devonshire counterparts when Genette Tate went missing. The Devon police interviewed more than 9,000 in the hunt for Genette Tate, spending over £1 million in the first year alone. John Tate, Genette's father, founded International Find A Child to raise public awareness of missing children. A suspect in the Tate case was Robert Black, a convicted child killer, but he denied any involvement. No trace has ever been found of Martin Allen. Kerry Needham married and has a daughter but hopes that whoever took Ben has cared for him. On 21 July 2008 the status of suspect – arguido – was lifted on the McCanns. April Fabb, Genette Tate, Martin Allen, Ben Needham and Madeleine McCann remain missing.

503

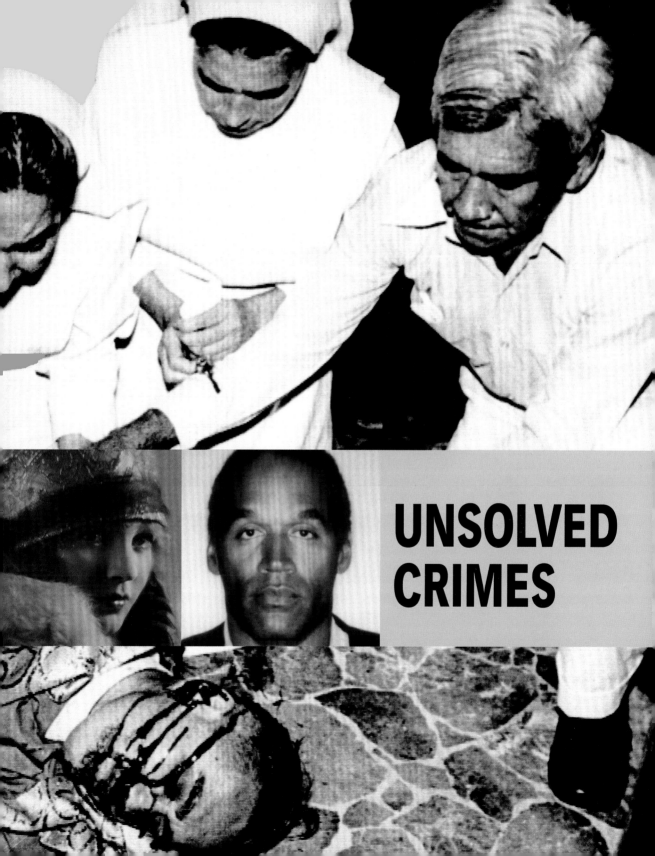

UNSOLVED CRIMES

Harvey Burdell

A prison doctor believed the pregnancy was nothing more than a well-placed cushion

WHERE:
31 Bond Street, New York City, USA
WHEN:
Friday 30 January 1857
THE AFTERMATH:
The authorities were suspicious of Cunningham despite the acquittal and staked out 31 Bond Street, where she still lived. On 27 July 1857 the police stopped a nun with a basket at the door. Inside the basket was a baby, which Cunningham had paid $1,000 to adopt. Cunningham confessed that she had never been pregnant and never been married to Burdell but her acquittal for his murder made it virtually impossible for her to be brought to justice. She left New York for California and spent her days running a vineyard.
YOU SHOULD KNOW:
Supposedly, the mother of the baby in the basket rented it to P.T. Barnum for $25 a week for public display.

THE CRIME: Dentist Harvey Burdell was a wealthy man who owned a mansion in New York. He had been born at Herkimer, New York, in 1811 and moved to New York City after qualifying as a dentist. He rented out parts of his home and his tenants included Emma Augusta Hempstead Cunningham (1816–1887) and John J. Eckel. Reportedly, Cunningham was sexually active with both Burdell and Eckel. Despite his social standing, Burdell was not the most honest of men and had been accused of embezzlement, welshing on his debts and in 1835 had demanded $20,000 from his fiancée's father to go through with the wedding. The furious father threw Burdell out of the house and cancelled the nuptials.

On the morning of 30 January 1857 Dr Burdell's servants found his body in his home office. He had been stabbed 15 times and strangled. An investigation revealed that the attacker had been left-handed. Emma Cunningham was left-handed and she was arrested and charged with the dentist's murder. About 8,000 people attended the funeral and Cunningham melodramatically flung herself on Burdell's coffin during the ceremony. In prison awaiting trial Cunningham suddenly claimed to be Burdell's wife, and also to be pregnant by him. She produced a marriage certificate "proving" that they had married on 28 October 1856. Eckel resembled Burdell and the police suspected that he had impersonated the dentist at the wedding ceremony. If acquitted, Cunningham would be entitled to Burdell's estate worth $100,000. The trial began on 6 May 1857 and Cunningham testified that she had had a happy, if brief, marriage. The witnesses were divided – some painted a different picture featuring violence and some a portrait of domestic harmony. As the trial progressed Cunningham's baby bump increased in size but a prison doctor told the prosecutor that he believed the pregnancy was nothing more than a well-placed cushion, having been refused permission to physically examine her. Burdell's reputation for dishonesty counted against him and on 9 May 1857 the jury acquitted Emma Cunningham.

Harvey Burdell

Madeleine Smith

"Not proven"

THE CRIME: Madeleine Hamilton Smith was part of a well-to-do Glaswegian family – her father, James, was a wealthy architect. In March 1855, aged 19, she met Jersey-born clerk Pierre Emile L'Angelier, a man almost 12 years her senior, and they fell madly in love. Via Madeleine's servant Christina Haggart they exchanged passionate love letters but found it difficult to engineer meetings because of their different social standings. Madeleine burnt Pierre's letters but he kept the 198 epistles she sent to him. Eventually they arranged to spend time at her father's country house Rowaleyn at Row on the River Clyde and there they finally went to bed together on 6 May 1856.

In their letters she referred to L'Angelier as her "beloved husband" and signed them "Mimi L'Angelier". When they returned home it again proved difficult to meet and they had to communicate via the basement window of her bedroom in her home at 7 Blythswood Square. When James Smith found out about the affair he forbade Madeleine to see her lover and told her that he had plans for her marriage that did not include a shipping clerk. Madeleine told L'Angelier that the affair was over and asked him to return her letters but instead he threatened to send them to her father. Madeleine pleaded with him not to do that. In February 1857 L'Angelier fell ill and died on 23 March. A post mortem was carried out and cause of death was established as arsenic poisoning. When the letters were discovered Madeleine was arrested on 31 March and charged with her lover's murder. She admitted buying arsenic but said that it was to kill rats. She later said it was for cosmetic reasons. Madeleine went on trial on 30 June 1857. The prosecution alleged that she had poisoned L'Angelier with the arsenic mixed in a chocolate drink. The defence claimed that L'Angelier ate arsenic regularly and that he was a blackmailer and a seducer of young girls. On 9 July 1857 the jury returned the peculiarly Scottish verdict of "Not proven" – in essence "We know you did it but it has not been proven so go away and don't do it again."

Scottish gentlewoman Madeleine Smith

WHERE:
11 Franklin Place, Glasgow, Scotland
WHEN:
Monday 23 March 1857
THE AFTERMATH:
James Smith died in 1862. After the court case, Madeleine moved to London and then to America. She married twice (firstly on 4 July 1861 to George Wardle [died 1910] by whom she had two children) and died as Lena Sheehy on 12 April 1928 aged 93.

Benjamin Nathan

New York's "most famous mystery murder"

WHERE:
12 West 23rd Street, New
York City, USA
WHEN:
Friday 29 July 1870
THE AFTERMATH:
The mayor of New York offered a large
reward for information leading to the
capture of the perpetrator or
perpetrators. Others came forward to
add to the fund which, together with
contributions from the Nathan family,
finally reached a total of $47,000. The
New York Stock Exchange where
Nathan had worked also offered a
reward, this time $10,000. The media,
especially the Jewish press, ran many
stories on the case hoping it would
lead to an arrest. Frederick and
Washington Nathan were investigated
and cleared of any involvement in their
father's death. Some imprisoned
members of the underworld gave
names of suspects they believed were
involved but when the police checked
out the tales they turned out to be
false accusations. Benjamin Nathan
was buried on 1 August 1870, the day
the inquest into his death opened. The
case described by Chief Byrnes of the
New York Police Department as the
city's "most famous mystery murder"
was never solved.

THE CRIME: Benjamin Nathan was 57 years old and a prominent Jewish businessman in New York when he met his death. On 28 July 1870 he and two of his four sons, Frederick, 25, and Washington, 23, returned from their summer house to the family home at West 23rd Street in New York. The next day was the anniversary of Nathan's mother's death and he wanted to visit the Nineteenth Street synagogue in commemoration.

However, his house was full of decorators and so the housekeeper Anne Kelly made up a room for the master in the front parlour on the second floor and for the sons on the third floor of the Victorian mansion. Just before 6am the next day the neighbourhood was woken by the shouts of Frederick and Washington Nathan. Washington's socks and nightgown were covered in blood when he had gone into his father's room to waken him and found the old man beaten to death.

Patrolman John Mangam of the 29th Street Precinct was on his beat when he saw the two distraught sons. The police found the room awash with blood and a 45-cm (18-in) long iron bar nearby, which had been used to smash in Benjamin Nathan's head. There were 12 separate blows to the body. It seemed initially that robbery was the motive for the crime as a safe and a small cash box in the room were both open.

Adelaide Bartlett:

"Now she's acquitted, she should tell us, in the interests of science, how she did it"

THE CRIME: Adelaide Blanche de la Tremouille was born in Orleans, France, illegitimately on 19 December 1855. She married wealthy grocer Edwin Bartlett, ten years her senior, on 6 April 1875. Their marriage was reasonably happy although Edwin believed that every man should have two wives – one for companionship and the other for sex. Adelaide was to be the wife for companionship but she claimed Edwin did not seek a second wife for sex. In 1885 they met Reverend George Dyson. He was a 27-year-old Wesleyan minister and a friend to both, who had long conversations with Edwin about sex, marriage and relationships. During one chat Edwin told the Reverend Mr Dyson that in the event that Edwin died he would like to "give"

Adelaide to the clergyman. In the months leading up to his death Edwin took vicarious pleasure watching his wife and Dyson kissing. The clergyman also wrote poems to Adelaide calling her "My Birdie".

In August 1885 Edwin and Adelaide moved to two rooms in Pimlico, London but they no longer shared a bed. Edwin was suffering several unpleasant illnesses, including halitosis caused by rotting teeth and tapeworms. He also believed that he had syphilis and took mercury to cure it. In December 1885 he fell ill with gastritis and a dentist removed his rotten teeth. Edwin's health improved but he remained depressed.

On 1 January 1886 Edwin was found dead in bed. According to the post mortem he had swallowed chloroform. When the police learned of her relationship with George Dyson, Adelaide was arrested and charged with Edwin's murder. The trial of Adelaide began at the Old Bailey on 12 April 1886. The case was prosecuted by the Attorney General Sir Charles Russell and Edward Clarke, QC, defended Adelaide. It was revealed in court that on 28 December 1885, at Adelaide's urging, Dyson had bought four small bottles of chloroform but Adelaide claimed that these were to dampen Edwin's suddenly rediscovered ardour. However, it was a mystery how a whole bottle of chloroform had found its way into Edwin's stomach without burning his throat or mouth and without any screams of agony being heard. The jury returned a verdict of not guilty on 17 April.

WHERE:
85 Claverton Street, London, England
WHEN:
Friday 1 January 1886
THE AFTERMATH:
Sir James Paget, surgeon to Queen Victoria, commented, "Now she's acquitted, she should tell us, in the interests of science, how she did it."

An artist's impression of Bartlett's court case

Jack the Ripper

"I'll soon get my doss money, see what a jolly bonnet I have now"

WHERE:
London, England
WHEN:
Friday 31 August–Friday
9 November 1888
THE AFTERMATH:
More than 120 years later, we are no
nearer to knowing his true identity.
YOU SHOULD KNOW:
The name "Jack the Ripper"
was almost certainly invented
by a journalist.

THE CRIME: The unknown killer struck five times and theories about his identity abound: he was either a cricketer (Montague John Druitt), a prince (Albert Victor, Duke of Clarence), a cotton merchant (James Maybrick), a Jewish slaughterman (unnamed), a confidence trickster (Michael Ostrog), a former lover (Joseph Barnett), a directory compiler (Thomas Cutbush), a hairdresser (Aaron Kosminksi), one of three surgeons (Sir William Withey Gull, Oswald Puckeridge or Vassily Konovalov), a killer (James Kelly), a plumber (Frederick Deeming), a poisoner (Dr Thomas Neill Cream), a cobbler (John Pizer aka "Leather Apron"), a painter (Walter Sickert), a quack doctor (Francis Tumblety), a philanthropist (Dr Thomas Barnardo), a shopkeeper (Edward Buchan), a military historian (Sir George Arthur), one of four doctors ("Dr Stanley", Dr Cohn, Frederick Chapman or John Hewitt), Cambridge University fellow (James Kenneth Stephen), a journalist and sacked doctor (Robert Donston Stephenson), an insurance salesman (G. Wentworth Bell Smith), a coroner (Dr William Wynn Westcott), a butcher (Jacobs), a sawdust seller (William Henry Bury), a former soldier (William Grant Grainger), a vagrant (Alfred Gray), a traveller (Frank Edwards), a barber (Severin Klosowski aka George Chapman), a hairdresser (Charles Ludwig), a landlord (John McCarthy) and even a woman (Olga Tchkersoff).

The first victim, Polly Nichols, was last seen alive, drunk, at 2.30am on 31 August 1888 on the corner of Osborne Street and Whitechapel High Street. She had been turned away from a doss house because she didn't have the requisite 4d. She told the landlord, "I'll soon get my doss money, see what a jolly bonnet I have now." At 3.45am her corpse was discovered. Victim number two, eight days later, was "Dark Annie" Chapman. Discovered shortly before 6am in the rear yard of 29 Hanbury Street, her dress was pulled up over her knees and her intestines lay over her left shoulder. Her throat was cut deep to the spine and there were two cuts on the left side of the spine. On 30 September the Ripper struck twice and "Long Liz" Stride and Catherine Eddowes died. Eddowes had been disembowelled and a piece of her ear, her left kidney and part of her entrails were missing. The final victim was Mary Kelly, the youngest and the only one to die indoors. She was mutilated beyond recognition.

A very graphic front page from a popular newspaper of the time

Axeman of New Orleans

The Axeman attacked the sleeping couple with an axe before slitting their throats with a razor

THE CRIME: During a 16-month period the residents of New Orleans lived in fear of attack from a maniac with an axe. On the night of 23 May 1918 someone broke into the grocery store home of Joseph and Catherine Maggio on the corner of Upperline Street and Magnolia Street and attacked the sleeping couple with an axe before slitting their throats with a razor. Joseph Maggio's brother Andrew was arrested but released a few days later. In 1911 three Italian grocers had been murdered with an axe and the police believed that the same fiend was at work again.

On 28 June grocer Louis Besumer and his girlfriend, Anna Harriet Lowe, were attacked with an axe at their shop on Dorgenois Street. They both survived the attack but Lowe died on 5 August. Before she died she said that it was in fact Besumer who had attacked her. He was arrested the same day. The night of his arrest the pregnant wife of Edward Scheider was attacked with an axe. Fortunately, she survived the onslaught and a week later gave birth to a baby girl. On 10 August the Axeman murdered barber Joseph Romano. In all cases the attacker gained access to homes by removing a panel in the back door with a chisel.

On 10 March 1919 Charles Cortimiglia was attacked in his bedroom. The Axeman was disturbed by the screams of Rose Cortimiglia and he turned his attentions to her, striking her once and killing her two-year-old daughter, Mary. For some reason, Rose accused members of the Jordano family who lived across the street of the attack and Frank Jordano and his father, Iorlando, were arrested. Despite little evidence the Jordanos went on trial on 21 May and were convicted five days later. Frank was sentenced to death and Iorlando to life imprisonment. In April Louis Besumer had been acquitted of the murder of his girlfriend.

On 10 August the Axeman attacked Steve Boca and on 2 September pharmacist William Carlson saw a chisel being put through the door to his home and fired at the door, scaring off the Axeman. The next night Sarah Laumann, 19, was attacked as she slept but she survived. The last attack came on 27 October when Mike Pepitone was struck 18 times in the head and died the following day.

WHERE:
New Orleans, Louisiana, USA
WHEN:
Thursday 23 May 1918–Monday 27 October 1919
THE AFTERMATH:
On 7 December 1920 Rose Cortimiglia, by now suffering from smallpox and deserted by her husband, withdrew her allegation, saving Frank Jordano from the gallows. On 2 December 1920 Joseph Mumfre was shot dead in Los Angeles by the widow of Mike Pepitone, the last victim. She said that Mumfre was the Axeman. She served three years of a ten-year sentence. The Axeman was never identified.

In 1919 Joseph John Davilla wrote the song "The Mysterious Axman's Jazz (Don't Scare Me Papa)". Published by New Orleans based World's Music Publishing Company, the cover depicted a family playing music with frightened looks on their faces.

Joseph Bowne Elwell

"The evidence is entirely devoid of any fact that would justify accusing any man or woman"

WHERE:
244 West 70th Street,
New York City, USA
WHEN:
8.35am Friday 11 June 1920
THE AFTERMATH:
Police believed that the killer was probably a man, it being thought that the .45 too heavy a gun for a woman to handle. The murder weapon and the killer were never found. District Attorney Edward Swann said, "The evidence is entirely devoid of any fact that would justify accusing any man or woman."

244 West 70th Street where Elwell was found.

THE CRIME: Joseph Elwell began his working life as a hardware salesman before his talent for bridge made him rich and famous. His book *Elwell on Bridge* was the definitive work on the game. He was regarded as a handsome catch, with a fine head of dark hair and sparkling teeth. On 26 May 1900 he married Helen Derby but, as he became more successful, he began to womanize and his wife left him. On 10 June 1920, 47-year-old Elwell went to the Ritz Hotel in New York to eat dinner with friends and then his party went to watch the Midnight Frolic show at the New Amsterdam Roof Theatre. By 2.30am the next day Elwell was on his way home alone in a taxi. He stopped to buy the *Morning Telegraph* newspaper and when he got home made several phone calls, the last at 6.09am.

At 8.35am Elwell's Swedish housekeeper Marie Larsen arrived to begin work and in an armchair in the living room saw a bald, toothless old man in red silk pyjamas dying from a .45-calibre bullet wound to the head. It turned out that the man was not a stranger but Elwell who kept his youthful appearance by wearing wigs (he owned 40) and false teeth, and through regular trips to the plastic surgeon. Mrs Larsen ran into the street to summon help. Elwell was admitted to Flower Hospital on East 64th Street at 9.19am and died within the hour, without regaining consciousness.

In Elwell's four-storey brownstone mansion was a collection of lingerie and a detailed list of more than 50 women, dubbed by the press the "Love List". The senior detectives in the New York Police Department took charge of the case and interviewed Elwell's entire harem of women but no action was taken against any of them. No fingerprints were found in the house apart from those of Elwell and Mrs Larsen. Money and jewellery were still in Elwell's house, ruling out robbery as a motive for the murder.

Victor Grayson

"Don't let anyone drink my whisky. I shall be back in a few minutes"

THE CRIME: Firebrand orator Albert Victor Grayson was born in Liverpool, England on 5 September 1881 and was elected MP for Colne Valley in July 1907 by 153 votes. Despite standing for the Independent Labour Party, he was not welcomed by the party hierarchy. In the House he attacked the Liberal Government and said, "I look forward to the day when the government bench will be occupied by socialists sent there by an indignant people." He supported the Irish nationalists. In 1908 he easily won a poll to find the most popular Yorkshire MP. In November that year, the Serjeant-at-Arms threw him out of the House of Commons for refusing to obey the Speaker.

In 1910 Grayson lost his seat and took to the bottle. On 7 November 1912 he married actress Ruth Nightingale. In 1913 he suffered a nervous breakdown. Unlike most left-wingers, Grayson spoke out in favour of the First World War. He was declared bankrupt on 26 August 1914 with debts of £496 3s. He later enlisted in the New Zealand Army and was wounded on 12 October 1917. His wife died in childbirth on 4 December 1918. The next year Grayson launched a bitter attack on Lloyd George and the selling of political honours. He also threatened to publicly name the middleman Maundy Gregory (see page 80) whom he knew was spying on him.

In September 1920 Grayson was attacked on The Strand, London and left with stitches in his head and a broken arm. At the end of the month Grayson was drinking with friends at the Georgian Restaurant in Chandos Place, London when he received a message from the receptionist that his luggage had been sent to the Queen's Hotel in Leicester Square by mistake. Grayson said, "Don't let anyone drink my whisky. I shall be back in a few minutes." He was never seen again.

Victor Grayson as a young man

WHERE:
Georgian Restaurant, Chandos Place, London, England
WHEN:
6pm Tuesday 28 September 1920
THE AFTERMATH:
It was not until 1927 that the public was aware that Grayson disappeared. His family made an appeal via the BBC in 1934 but received no response. His sister Annie made another appeal in September 1942, again with no response. Rumours abounded that Grayson had been murdered on the orders of Maundy Gregory but nothing has been proved.

The remains of a victim are examined.

Cleveland Torso Murderer

"There's a man down there – and he hasn't got any head!"

THE CRIME: The Cleveland Torso Murderer (also known as the Mad Butcher of Kingsbury Run) was a serial killer who struck between 1935 and 1938 in the Cleveland, Pittsburgh, and Youngstown areas of Ohio. He killed a dozen but some believe that there may have been as many as 40 victims. The victims were usually homeless, working-class people whose names were never known. Only two or three were ever identified for certain. The murderer cut the heads off his victims while they were still alive and usually dismembered them, and poured oil or acid over the corpses. Most of the male victims were castrated.

The first victim, an unidentified man, was found on 23 September 1935 in the Jackass Hill area of Kingsbury Run by two small boys who cried, "There's a man down there – and he... hasn't got any head!" The second victim was found on the same day about 9 m (30 ft) from victim number one. He was identified as Edward W. Andrassy, 28. On 26 January 1936 Florence Genevieve Polillo was found at 2315 East 20th Street in downtown Cleveland. Five months later, on 5 June, a male known as the "tattooed man" was discovered in Kingsbury Run. He had six tattoos, including one with the initials "W.C.G." and another with the names "Helen and Paul". His underwear bore the initials "J.D." but despite a great investigation the victim was never identified.

On 22 July another unknown male victim was discovered in the Big Creek area of Brooklyn, west of Cleveland, the only victim found on the West Side. Then another unidentified man, the fourth, was found dead on 10 September at Kingsbury Run. The first unidentified woman, nicknamed "The Lady of the Lake", was discovered on 23 February 1937 near Euclid Beach on the shore of Lake Erie. On 6 June another woman was found beneath the Lorain-Carnegie Bridge. She was believed to be Rose Wallace who had vanished ten months earlier. Exactly a month later, a man was found dead in the Cuyahoga River in the Cleveland Flats. The venue was the same for the next female victim, found on 8 April 1938. On 16 August another female and a male were discovered at the East 9th Street Lakeshore Dump.

WHERE:
Ohio, USA
WHEN:
Monday 23 September 1935–Tuesday
16 August 1938
THE AFTERMATH:
There were three suspects for the murders but nothing more than circumstantial evidence was ever available and no prosecution was ever brought despite the best efforts of one detective called Eliot Ness.

514

Edward Hall
& Eleanor Mills

"She's a liar, she's a liar"

THE CRIME: Edward Wheeler Hall was the chubby, balding, 41-year-old Episcopal minister of the Church of St John the Evangelist in New Brunswick, New Jersey. He was having an affair with the married lead soprano of his choir Eleanor Mills, 34, the wife of the church sexton. Both lovers left their homes at 7.30pm on 14 September 1922 – Mrs Mills from 49 Carmen Street, Reverend Hall from 23 Nichol Avenue – for an assignation. Two days later Raymond Schneider, 23, and his girlfriend Pearl Bahmer, 15, came across two people they initially thought were having sex under a crab-apple tree. Then they noticed that both had been shot in the head and the woman's throat was cut from ear to ear and her tongue had been removed. Scattered around were love letters, written by Mrs Mills to the clergyman. Letters written by the Reverend Hall to Mrs Mills were later sold to newspapers by James Mills, the 45-year-old cuckolded husband, for $500. Frances Hall, the reverend's wife, was phenomenally wealthy and had even paid for an operation for Mrs Mills – unaware of her husband's betrayal.

    The police were no nearer solving the case when Jane Gibson, aka Easton, came forward to say that she had seen the murders. Known as the "Pig Woman" because she was a hog farmer, she said that she had been riding her mule Jenny in search of poachers when she witnessed the crime. However, on 27 November 1922 a grand jury failed to indict anyone for the killings. The case rested until 28 July 1926 when the police arrested Frances Hall. On 3 November 1926 Mrs Hall and her brothers Henry and Willie went on trial in Somerville, New Jersey, for double murder. A star – if somewhat dramatic – witness was the Pig Woman who, suffering from cancer, was wheeled into court in a bed whence she gave her evidence. Despite her illness and a passage of four years, the Pig Woman gave detailed testimony, all the time her mother chanting, "She's a liar, she's a liar." However, her memory was called into question as, when asked about her numerous husbands, the Pig Woman could not even remember all their names. After deliberating for four and a half hours, the jury returned not guilty verdicts for all three defendants on 3 December 1926.

WHERE:
De Russey's Lane, Franklin Township, New Brunswick, New Jersey, USA
WHEN:
Thursday 14 September 1922
THE AFTERMATH:
Mrs Hall continued to attend her husband's church. She never remarried and died in December 1942. Her brother Willie died the same month and Henry died on 3 December 1939. The Pig Woman lived until 7 February 1930.

A detective examining the clothing of the murder victims.

William Desmond Taylor

"Dey've killt Massa!"

WHERE:
404-B South Alvarado Street, Los Angeles, California, USA

WHEN:
8.15pm Wednesday 1 February 1922

THE AFTERMATH:
Film director King Vidor took a close interest in the murder in 1966 and spent a year investigating the crime. He concluded that the murder was committed in a fit of jealousy by Charlotte Shelby.

YOU SHOULD KNOW:
Despite his public reputation as a ladies' man, Taylor was also said to have had male lovers.

An autographed photograph of Mary Miles Minter

THE CRIME: Irish-born Hollywood director William Desmond Taylor escorted numerous film stars, including Mabel Normand and Mary Miles Minter. By 1922 Taylor was head director at Famous Players-Lasky, a Paramount subsidiary. On the evening of 1 February 1922 Mabel Normand visited Taylor. His butler, Henry Peavey, a black man who spoke for some reason in a falsetto, gave Taylor and Normand drinks and left them at 6.30pm. One hour and 15 minutes later, Normand was driven away by her chauffeur. At approximately 8.15pm a sound like a car backfiring was heard.

At 7:30 next morning Henry Peavey arrived and found Taylor lying on the floor, a dried streak of blood at a corner of his mouth and two .38-calibre bullets in his body. Peavey ran into the street shouting, according to the *Los Angeles Examiner*, "Dey've kilt Massa! Dey've Kilt Massa!" Mabel Normand alerted the studio who sent executives over to carry out a damage-limitation exercise. Eventually the police were called when neighbours tired of Peavey's hysterics.

Mary Miles Minter was a beautiful blonde ingénue, being groomed to replace Mary Pickford. Her mother, Charlotte Shelby, disapproved of her daughter's relationship with William Taylor so much that she had threatened him. Discovered in Taylor's bedroom was a love note with a letterhead in the shape of a butterfly. On the wings and body of the butterfly was written MMM. The note read: "Dearest – I love you – I love you – I love you – – –" Then followed a sequence of ten kisses in the shape of Xs. The love note was signed "Yours always! Mary".

Mary admitted, "I did love William Desmond Taylor. I loved him deeply and tenderly, with all the admiration a young girl gives a man like Mr Taylor." Her mother confessed to owning a .38-calibre pistol, but insisted she obtained it for protection against burglars, not to use against Taylor. In fact, Mrs Shelby insisted, she had no objection to her daughter's infatuation for the director. The murder ended Taylor's life and Mary Miles Minter's career. The public tarred her with guilt by association.

Dot King

"Darling Dottie, I want to...kiss your pretty pink toes"

THE CRIME: Blonde, blue-eyed, sexy and petite Dorothy Keenan left home, a slum in New York, in 1915 when she was 19 years old. Like many attractive teenagers, she became a model and worked for a dress shop on Fifth Avenue. Under the name Dot King she was soon noticed by New York's playboys and began to be seen regularly on the arms of some of Manhattan's most eligible men at the hottest nightspots. Upon the advent of Prohibition in January 1920 she became the hostess of a speakeasy and soon saw her name in the press, usually accompanied by the nickname the "Broadway Butterfly". Sugar daddies paid for her outfits and one – Dot claimed that she only knew him as Mr Marshall – paid for her apartment at 144 West 57th Street, near Carnegie Hall. Other beaux presented her with jewellery said to be worth $30,000. A gigolo called Alberto Santos Guimares befriended Dot and then moved in with her. Twice a week Mr Marshall spent the night with Dot and on those nights Guimares found an alternative berth. Dot paid for the gigolo's clothes and sent some of the money given to her by Mr Marshall to her mother. However, unbeknown to Dot, Guimares was also romancing rich socialite Aurelia Dreyfus. In 1922 he beat up Dot for the first time and then made a regular habit of it. Her friends begged her to leave him but she replied, "Someday Alberto will marry me." It was not to be.

On 15 March 1923 Dot was found dead in bed. Her face was scratched and her mouth burned by chloroform. Her apartment had been robbed and police found love letters from Mr Marshall, one of which read in part, "Darling Dottie, I want to see you, o so much! And to kiss your pretty pink toes." Mr Marshall turned out to be John Kearsley Mitchell, the married son-in-law of a multi-millionaire. He was arrested but was later released without charge. Guimares was questioned but he told police that he had been with Aurelia Dreyfus at the time of Dot King's murder and was released.

Dot King, the Broadway Butterfly

WHERE:
144 West 57th Street, New York City, USA
WHEN:
Thursday 15 March 1923
THE AFTERMATH:
In 1924 Amelia Dreyfus mysteriously fell to her death from a Washington DC hotel balcony. In her effects was an affidavit swearing Guimares had not been with her the night of Dot's death and that she had committed perjury. Guimares was not charged and he died in 1953, aged 63.

The mysterious Alfred "Jake" Lingle

Jake Lingle

"I'll catch up with you and it won't be long either"

THE CRIME: Alfred "Jake" Lingle was born on 26 July 1891 and joined the *Chicago Tribune* in 1912 as a copyboy, earning $12 a week. He progressed up the ranks to become a cub reporter but never made it to full reporter. The problem Jake Lingle had was that he could not write. He would go out on a story and gather the facts before turning them over to a rewrite man who would polish his words into a readable story. Consequently Lingle, who by then was earning $65 a week, never got to see his name in print in his newspaper.

However, unlike most journalists Lingle was very rich. He also considered himself to be a friend of Al Capone (see page 330). Capone gave Lingle a belt buckle with the letters AJL spelt out in diamonds. Lingle had a wide range of contacts but no one wondered how he could afford to travel in a chauffeured limousine or place $1,000 bets at the race course. He was living in a hotel while his wife and two children stayed at the family home. He also bought a holiday home in Long Beach, Indiana for $16,000, paying $10,000 of the asking price in cash.

In 1924 Lingle and two other reporters had been arrested in possession of illegal alcohol but the case against him mysteriously disappeared. Such was his influence that no casino could open without his say so. In late May 1930 former state senator John J. "Boss" McLaughlin opened a casino at 606 West Madison Avenue and was raided the first night because he hadn't sought permission. McLaughlin rang Lingle to threaten him: "I'll catch up with you and it won't be long either."

Just before noon on 9 June 1930, Lingle left his hotel and went to the bank where he deposited $1,200, before heading for the office. At 1.15pm he set off for Illinois Central Station to catch the train to the race course. He bought a *Racing Form* and entered the subway, his eyes on the paper and a cigar clenched between his teeth. As he walked, oblivious to the hundreds of people milling around, someone walked up behind Lingle and put a snub-nosed .38 to the back of his head and pulled the trigger. Lingle was dead before he hit the floor.

WHERE:
Illinois Central Station, Randolph Avenue and Madison Avenue, Chicago, Illinois, USA

WHEN:
Monday 9 June 1930

THE AFTERMATH:
At first the *Tribune* ran tributes to its man and offered a reward, then slowly the real story unravelled. Lingle had been using his press contacts to help organized crime and been richly rewarded for his efforts. On 1 July 1930 Frank Foster was arrested and charged with Lingle's murder. However, on 16 March 1931 Al Capone arranged for Leo Vincent Brothers to go on trial for the killing and on 2 April Brothers was convicted and sentenced to 14 years. He served eight and was released in 1940. He died in 1950.

Judge Crater

"The missingest man in New York"

THE CRIME: Born on 5 January 1889, Joseph Force Crater's childhood ambition was to be a judge. Having qualified at Columbia Law School in 1916 he joined a Manhattan law firm where his colleagues believed he was on his way to a seat on the United States Supreme Court. Crater worked on all the cases that other lawyers shunned, writing intricate briefs. On 16 March 1917 he married Stella Wheeler whose divorce he had negotiated exactly a week earlier. In 1920 he became secretary to Judge Robert Wagner of the New York Supreme Court. By 1927 Crater was earning $75,000 a year and he bought a luxury flat at 40 Fifth Avenue and a summer estate at Belgrade Lakes, Maine. Although a womanizer, Crater had a main girlfriend, an ex-model called Constance Marcus for whom he had acted in her divorce. He paid part of her rent and gave her money to run a dress shop.

To finance his lifestyle Crater became involved in dodgy deals. In 1930 he lobbied to replace the retiring New York Supreme Court Justice Joseph M. Proskauer, despite the fact that he would have to take a 75 per cent drop in salary. He used every contact he had, including his mistress, and Governor Franklin D. Roosevelt appointed Crater on 8 April. Crater looked forward to the November election and confirmation of the 14-year post with a possible eye on the United States Supreme Court. Political opponents began digging into some of the deals brokered by Crater. He and his wife travelled to their summer home in June. He then returned to New York on 1 August to meet his mentor Robert Wagner.

Back in Maine, he received a phone call on 3 August and told his wife he had to return to Manhattan but promised to be back in time for her birthday on 9 August. By 11am on 6 August he was working hard in his office. He sent a minion to the bank for $5,150. At lunchtime he left the office, with the money and bundles of important files. At 8pm he went to Billy Haas's restaurant at 332 West 45th Street for dinner. At 9.15pm he jumped in a taxi for a trip to the theatre. Judge Crater was never seen again. His disappearance, one of the most famous in American history, earned him the title "The missingest man in New York".

WHERE:
332 West 45th Street, New York City, USA
WHEN:
9.15pm Wednesday 6 August 1930
THE AFTERMATH:
The City of New York offered a $5,000 reward for information. Judge Crater was declared legally dead on 6 July 1939. In 1985 the New York Police Department officially closed the case. In 2005 a woman died, leaving a note claiming that her late husband, a policeman, and his cab-driving brother-in-law were responsible for Crater's death and his corpse was buried on Coney Island beneath what is now the New York Aquarium.
YOU SHOULD KNOW:
Crater had two vices – fashion and women – and although one was obvious, he took pains to keep his extra-marital life a secret.

"Lucky" Blacklet, the old prospector that led the reporters on a futile search, holds up a picture of Judge Crater.

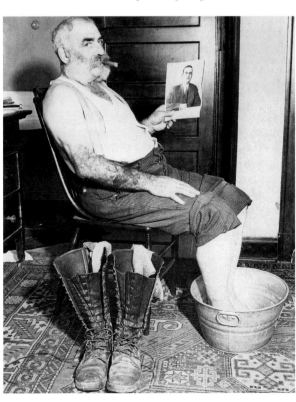

Thelma Todd

"I suggest the possibility strongly exists this was a monoxide murder!"

WHERE:
17531 Posetano Road, Pacific Palisades, California, USA
WHEN:
10.30am Monday 16 December 1935
THE AFTERMATH:
On 21 December 1935 the LAPD formally dropped their investigation into Thelma's death. They agreed with the county autopsy surgeon's report and coroner's jury verdict that the actress died "apparently accidentally". It seems likely that after Luciano dropped her off at the Café, two men grabbed Thelma and put her in her car, switched on the ignition and closed the garage door.

Thelma Todd in her heyday as a Hollywood star.

THE CRIME: Blonde Thelma Todd won the Miss Massachusetts beauty contest in 1925, which led to a call from Hollywood, and Thelma made her film début in *Fascinating Youth* in 1926. That led to a highly successful movie career, working as a foil for virtually every comedian in film. By 1934, divorced from her husband, she opened Thelma Todd's Sidewalk Café at 17575 Pacific Coast Highway, north of Santa Monica, with producer and director Roland West. That year she began an affair with gangster "Lucky" Luciano (see page 329) who "arranged" for her to become hooked on diet pills. Luciano began pressing Thelma to let him use a room at the Sidewalk Café as a gambling den but she refused. On 14 December 1935 Thelma attended a party at the Café Trocadero in Hollywood. Before she left at 2.45am, a waiter told Thelma that a man was waiting to see her. He was an acolyte of Lucky Luciano and Thelma refused his "invitation". Thelma was taken to the Sidewalk Café by her chauffeur Ernest Peters, arriving at 3.30am. Another car pulled up and Thelma got in, next to Luciano.

At 10.30am on 16 December Thelma's body was found by her maid, May Whitehead, slumped on the front seat of her Packard convertible in her garage, the sliding doors slightly opened. According to Dr A.F. Wagner, Los Angeles County's autopsy surgeon, Thelma Todd had died of carbon monoxide poisoning. The coroner's jury returned a verdict of suicide but that was overturned and a grand jury hearing was ordered. The jury foreman George Rochester, said: "I and other members of the jury believe a plot is afoot to show that Thelma Todd had a suicide complex, even though she had youth, health, wealth, fame, admiration, love, and happy prospects. It looks as if they are trying to build up this case as a suicide, but in the actual evidence, I have found nothing to support this theory definitely. I suggest the possibility strongly exists this was a monoxide murder!"

King Ananda of Siam

All three were strapped to crosses and machine-gunned to death

THE CRIME: On the evening of 8 June 1946 King Rama VIII Ananda Mahidol, the 20-year-old monarch of Siam, called the court physician, complaining of feeling unwell. He had spent most of his life in Switzerland and found the heat and humidity of what is now Thailand oppressing. The doctor prescribed sleeping pills and castor oil. At 6am Princess Mahidol, his mother, woke the king and brought him water, milk and brandy to wash down the castor oil. He felt much better and at 8.30am a page, But Pathamasarin, gave the monarch a newspaper and some orange juice. His other page, Chit Singhaseni, was off duty. The king returned to bed. At 9am the king's brother Prince Bhoomipol visited but reported that the king was dozing. At 9.20am a shot was heard and the king's mother, brother, nanny and doctor rushed to his bedroom to find him lying dead in bed, a bullet hole over his right eyebrow. The king's Colt .45 was near his left hand. The first thought of those in the palace was suicide and Prime Minister Pridi announced that the death had been an accident.

WHERE:
Barompiman Hall, Grand Palace, Bangkok, Thailand
WHEN:
9.20am Sunday 9 June 1946
THE AFTERMATH:
Prime Minister Pridi announced an enquiry into the king's death but many believed that he had had a hand in the fatality. On 7 November 1947 he was deposed in a coup and fled to Singapore. The new regime named Pridi and Lieutenant Vacharachai as the prime suspects in what was now called a murder. Senator Chaleo Patoomros, the king's secretary, and pages But

Pathamasarin and Chit Singhaseni were arrested and charged with conspiracy to murder the king. Their trial opened on 28 September 1948 with all three pleading not guilty. The trial lasted until 9 May 1951. On 27 September the court delivered its verdict – the king had been assassinated. Chaleo Patoomros and But Pathamasarin were acquitted but Chit Singhaseni was found guilty of aiding the unknown assassin and sentenced to death. Chit appealed his sentence and the prosecution appealed the acquittals. The appeal court confirmed Chit's sentence but also instituted guilty verdicts against

The cremation site of the body of King Ananda Mahidol of Siam

the other two. At 4am on 17 February 1955 all three were strapped to crosses and machine-gunned to death. Was the king murdered or did he commit suicide? The truth is still not known.

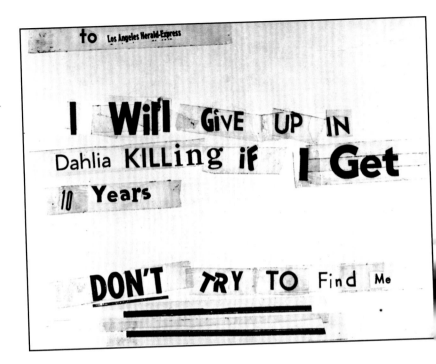

This threatening letter assembled from newspaper stories, was sent to the Los Angeles Herald-Express.

Elizabeth Short

"I want the cops to chase me some more"

THE CRIME: It is unlikely that anyone would now know the name of Elizabeth Short, if not for the appalling circumstances of her death. Born in poverty in Hyde Park, Massachusetts on 29 July 1924, she moved to Santa Barbara where she was noticed because of her habit of always wearing black and was nicknamed the Black Dahlia. Promises of a screen career never developed and she became a prostitute. In December 1946 she became a lesbian for a brief period but decided that she wanted to find a man, settle down and raise a family. Then she told her friend she had fallen for a man she called only "Red".

On the morning of 15 January 1947 Betty Bersinger and her three-year-old daughter were out for an early morning stroll when they came across the bisected torso of a naked woman. When the police examined the remains of the woman they noted that the face had been slashed and the mouth cut on each side so that it resembled a huge grin. The breasts, thighs and arms had all been cut and rope burns were apparent on her wrists and ankles. There were cigarette burns all over the body and the letters BD had been carved into one thigh. The lower half of the body was in a recumbent position. Elizabeth Short's body had been drained of blood, washed and then dumped where it was found.

Sam Sheppard

"Killer" Sheppard

THE CRIME: Sam Sheppard was a neurosurgeon at Bay View Hospital, a medical establishment he owned with his father and two brothers. Unknown to his wife Marilyn, for 15 months Sheppard had been having an affair with Susan Hayes, 21, a colleague. The Sheppards had been high school sweethearts and had married in 1945. On 3 July 1954 they invited friends to dinner at their home overlooking Lake Erie for an Independence Day party. The dinner party broke up not long after midnight and Marilyn, who was four months pregnant, went straight to bed while Sheppard remained downstairs and fell asleep on a settee. He woke up when he heard screams and ran up the stairs where he saw his wife lying on the bed. A bushy-haired intruder ran past him knocking him over. Sheppard chased the intruder and they fought by the lakeside. Sheppard was knocked out. When he came to, after two hours, and went back into the house he found his wife dead, her head caved in by 27 blows.

Rumours began to circulate that Sheppard was responsible for his wife's death and he was arrested on 30 July. He went on trial – then the longest-running in American history – on 18 October and at 4.25pm on 21 December he was convicted of second-degree murder, despite the murder weapon not being found and there being no physical evidence to link Sheppard to the crime. As with many cases, it was the character of the accused that did for him rather than any evidence. Sheppard spent 12 years in prison until he won a retrial on 6 June 1966. At his second trial, which began on 24 October 1966, F. Lee Bailey represented Sheppard and had the earlier verdict overturned, freeing the doctor on 16 November.

WHERE:
28944, Lake Road, Bay Village, Ohio, USA
WHEN:
Sunday 4 July 1954
THE AFTERMATH:
Sam Sheppard found it difficult to come to terms with life outside prison and was not helped by the whispering campaign by people who still thought he was responsible for Marilyn's death. He became a professional wrestler (under the name "Killer" Sheppard) and married twice more but divorced twice. He turned to drugs and alcohol for solace and died on 6 April 1970, aged 46, of liver disease. In 1997 Sam Sheppard's body was exhumed and a sample of DNA taken, which finally exonerated him of murdering his wife. In November 2001 a book on the case named Richard Eberling, the family handyman, as the "bushy-haired intruder" who murdered Mrs Sheppard. Eberling died in 1998 while in prison for the rape and murder of a 90-year-old lady.
YOU SHOULD KNOW:
The Sheppard case was the inspiration for the television series *The Fugitive* starring David Janssen as a man wrongly accused of murdering his wife.

Dr Lester Adelson examines x-rays of Marilyn Sheppard's body.

Lake Bodom Murders

Nils Gustafsson went on trial more than 45 years after the murders

WHERE:
Lake Bodom, Finland
WHEN:
Saturday 4 June 1960

THE AFTERMATH:
On the 12th anniversary of the slayings a man committed suicide and left a note claiming he was the killer. He had been working in a soft drinks kiosk near the lake on the day of the murders and had sold lemonade to the victims. A police investigation cleared him of any involvement. In March 2004 the police arrested Nils Gustafsson and accused him of being the killer of his friends. In 2005 the Finnish National Bureau of Investigation declared the case solved. Gustafsson, they said, was suddenly gripped by a terrible jealousy for his new girlfriend, Maila Irmeli Björklund and, after bludgeoning her, he stabbed her several times post mortem. The others were not attacked with such severity. The trial of Nils Gustafsson began on 4 August 2005 – more than 45 years after the murders. The prosecution called for a mandatory life sentence for the three murders, citing new DNA evidence. The defence suggested that Gustafsson's wounds were too severe for him to have been able to carry out one murder let alone three. He was acquitted of all charges on 7 October 2005 and awarded 44,900 euros compensation for mental suffering during his incarceration. So, as Nils Gustafsson did not kill his friends, who did? The year before the trial a doctor who worked at a nearby hospital named a suspect in a book. Professor Jorma Palo had been on duty in June 1960 when German-born Hans Assmann wandered into the hospital seeking treatment for some unexplained wounds. Assman was allegedly an East German spy and Palo claimed that the German was able to escape detection because of a diplomatic cover-up. He also claimed that before his death in 1997 Assman confessed that he was the murderer. The Finnish Government has denied that Assman was ever a serious suspect.

THE CRIME: In June 1960 four Finnish teenagers – Maila Irmeli Björklund, 15, Anja Tuulikki Mäki, 15, Seppo Antero Boisman, 18, and Nils Wilhelm Gustafsson, 18 – went camping on the shores of Lake Bodom, a small lake by the city of Espoo about 20 km (13 mi) west of Helsinki. Some time between 4am and 6am on 4 June 1960 three of the teenagers were stabbed and beaten to death. The only one to survive was Nils Gustafsson who was concussed and suffered a fractured jaw and face. The case remains unsolved.

Nils Gustafsson at his trial

Bible John Murders

"My father says these places are dens of iniquity"

THE CRIME: In a 20-month period in Glasgow, Scotland an unknown killer, who was given the nickname Bible John because he liked to quote from the Holy Book, murdered three women. The only link between the victims seemed to be a love of dancing. Patricia Docker, 25, a separated mother of a four-year-old son, became the first victim. She had been strangled and was found near a garage in Carmichael Lane on 22 February 1968. On the night of her death she had been to the Majestic Ballroom in Hope Street. Police believed she had met a man there and left with him but refused to have sex with him because she was menstruating. In frustration, he killed her. A year and a half later, on 16 August 1969, mother of three Jemima McDonald was found at 23 Mackeith Street, a short distance from where she lived, and she, too, had been strangled. Police investigated and discovered that she had been at the Barrowlands Ballroom at midnight and had been seen with a man aged around 35.

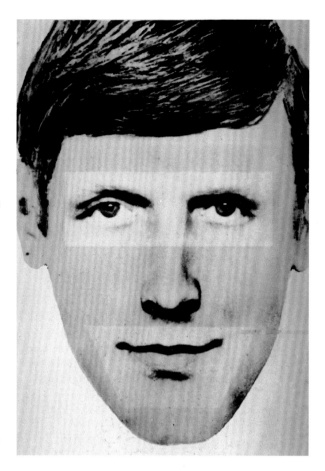

The photofit of "Bible John"

On 30 October 1969 Helen Puttock, a 29-year-old mother of two, her sister Jeannie and two friends, Marion Cadder and Jean O'Donnell, went dancing at the Barrowlands Ballroom. Helen's husband babysat the children. Jeannie was chatted up by a man called John and spent the rest of the evening with him. Helen was approached by a man, also called John. They talked about a number of subjects and he mentioned the Bible several times. "My father says these places are dens of iniquity," he said, adding he disapproved of married women going out dancing. When the ballroom closed at 11.30pm the two couples left the club together. "Bible John" called a taxi and got in with the two women while the other John made his own way home. After dropping Jeannie off, the taxi left Helen and "Bible John" at Earl Street. Her body was found outside a tenement block at 7am the next day by a man walking his dog. Jeannie was interviewed by the police and was able to give a detailed description of "Bible John". Newspapers printed a photofit with appeals and Scotland's biggest manhunt began.

WHERE:
Glasgow, Scotland
WHEN:
Thursday 22 February 1968–Thursday 30 October 1969
THE AFTERMATH:
In 1995 Donald Simpson wrote a book, naming furniture salesman John Irvine McInnes as Bible John. The police had questioned McInnes at the time of the killings but took no further action. He died in 1980. In 1996 McInnes's body was exhumed and his DNA compared to stains left on the third victim and his teeth compared to bite marks on her body. The investigation took five months but the evidence was inconclusive and the Bible John murders remain unsolved.

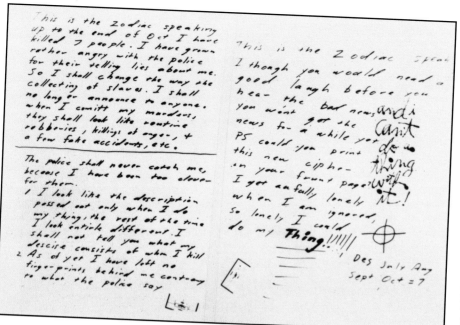

The Zodiac Killer sent letters and cryptograms to newspapers.

Zodiac Killer

"Vallejo/12-20-68/7-4-69/Sept 27-69-6:30/by knife"

THE CRIME: The Zodiac Killer – the way the killer signed himself in letters to San Francisco newspapers from 7 August 1969 – struck for the first time at 11pm on 20 December 1968. David Arthur Faraday, 17, and Betty Lou Jensen, 16, were shot on Lake Herman Road in Vallejo, California as they sat in his mother's Rambler station wagon. On 4 July 1969 Michael Renault Mageau, 19, and Darlene Elizabeth Ferrin, 22, were shot in the car park of the Blue Rock Springs Golf Course on the outskirts of Vallejo. Darlene died but Michael survived, despite being shot in the face, neck and chest. At 12.40am a man rang the Vallejo Police Department and boasted of the attack and also claimed credit for the Faraday-Jensen murders.

On 1 August three letters arrived at the offices of the *Vallejo Times-Herald*, the *San Francisco Chronicle* and the *San Francisco Examiner*, all nearly identical and all claiming credit for both sets of murders. On 27 September, as they picnicked at Lake Berryessa in Napa County, Bryan Calvin Hartnell, 20, and Cecelia Ann Shepard, 22, were both stabbed. Bryan lived but Cecelia died two days after the attack. He told the police that their attacker had been wearing a hood with a zodiac symbol on it. The killer had also written on Hartnell's car door "Vallejo/12-20-68/7-4-69/Sept 27-69-6:30/by knife". At 9.55pm on 11 October taxi driver Paul Lee Stine, 29, was shot and killed on Cherry Street at Presidio Heights in San Francisco. This was the closest Zodiac came to being caught, as three teenagers witnessed the murder and called the police. The police were told the suspect was black so when Officers Don Fouke and Eric Zelms saw a white man near the scene they let him go. Zodiac claimed to have killed 37 people but police believe that there were only seven victims. During 1970 Zodiac wrote to newspapers many times including cryptic clues, astrological signs and ciphers. No more was heard until 1974 when the *San Francisco Chronicle* received further letters from the Zodiac Killer.

WHERE:
San Francisco, California, USA
WHEN:
11pm Friday 20 December 1968–9.55pm Saturday 11 October 1969
THE AFTERMATH:
The San Francisco Police Department investigated an estimated 2,500 suspects over a period of years. Only one, Arthur Leigh Allen, was ever seriously considered. However, after his death on 26 August 1992, his DNA was compared to that taken from the letters written by Zodiac. There was no match. The case remains open.

Alphabet Murders

All three victims had been strangled and subjected to a sexual assault

THE CRIME: The Alphabet Murders began on 16 November 1971 when 11-year-old Carmen Colon disappeared. Her body was found two days later in Churchville, 19 km (12 mi) from where she was last seen. Almost a year and a half passed before the next murder. At 5.15pm on 2 April 1973 Wanda Walkowicz, also 11, vanished from Rochester as she went to the grocery store for her mother. She bought several items and was on her way home when she was abducted. At 10.15am the next day a New York State Trooper, while on patrol, found Wanda's body at a rest area off State Route 104 in Webster, New York, 11 km (7 mi) from her home. Seven months later, on 26 November 1973, Michelle Maenza, ten, disappeared. Her remains were discovered two days later in Macedon, Wayne County, 24 km (15 mi) from Rochester. All three victims had been strangled and subjected to a sexual assault.

The case became known as the Alphabet Murders because each of the three girls' first names and surnames began with the same letter and their corpses were found in locations that began with the same letter as their names – Colon in Churchville, Walkowicz in Webster and Maenza in Macedon. All three victims came from poor Roman Catholic families in Rochester and all were reportedly in trouble at school at the time of their deaths.

WHERE:
Rochester, New York, USA
WHEN:
Tuesday 16 November 1971–Monday 26 November 1973
THE AFTERMATH:
The police questioned hundreds of people but came up with no substantial leads. One potential suspect committed suicide six weeks after the last murder but he was cleared through DNA in 2007. Another suspect was Kenneth Bianchi who, with his cousin Angelo Buono, perpetrated the Hillside Strangler murders in Los Angeles in 1977 and 1978 (see page 408). There is no evidence, however, linking him to the case. According to the New York State Police these cases have not been officially connected, however, all three remain open. A film loosely based on the case, *The Alphabet Killer*, was released in 2008.

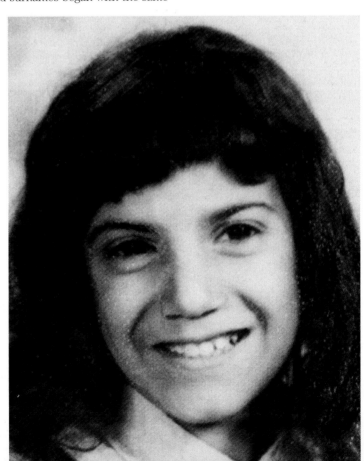

Eleven-year-old Carmen Colon who was raped and murdered in Churchville, New York.

D.B. Cooper

"I have a bomb in my briefcase. You are being hijacked."

WHERE:
Sky over Portland, Oregon, USA
WHEN:
Wednesday 24 November 1971
THE AFTERMATH:
More than 35 years after the event the police are no nearer to identifying the hijacker or explaining what happened to the bulk of the money. The FBI interviewed a man named D.B. Cooper who had no link with the crime but the initials D.B., rather than Dan, continue to be used to refer to the hijacker. The FBI, which has codenamed the case Norjak, believes that Cooper did not survive the parachute jump. On 10 February 1980 Brian Ingram, eight, found $5,880 in decaying $20 notes on the banks of the Columbia River, 8 km (5 mi) northwest of Vancouver, Washington. It was part of Cooper's hoard and 15 of the notes were auctioned in Dallas on 13 June 2008, raising $37,000.

The badly decomposed $20 dollar notes found near the Columbia River.

THE CRIME: On the day before Thanksgiving in 1971 a man calling himself Dan Cooper boarded a Boeing 727-100, Northwest Orient (now Northwest Airlines) Flight 305, at Portland International Airport in Oregon, bound for Seattle, Washington. He was in his mid 40s, about 1.82 m (6 ft) tall, and wearing a black raincoat, loafers, a dark suit, a white shirt, a black tie, black sunglasses and a mother-of-pearl tie pin. He sat in seat 18C, for which he had paid $18.52, and not long after take-off passed a note to air hostess Florence Schaffner. Assuming he was passing her his telephone number, she put the note into her pocket without looking at it. Cooper said, "Miss, you'd better look at that note. I have a bomb." With trembling hands she unfurled the note, which read, "I have a bomb in my briefcase. I will use it if necessary. I want you to sit next to me. You are being hijacked." The note also demanded $200,000 in used $20 notes and four parachutes.

The FBI decided to accede to Cooper's demands. While the authorities were busy on the ground, Cooper relaxed and drank bourbon and soda. Air hostess Tina Mucklow later commented that the hijacker "seemed rather nice". At 5.24pm the plane landed at Seattle-Tacoma International Airport near Seattle, Washington. The four parachutes and the money were delivered to Cooper who released all 36 passengers and air hostess Florence Schaffner, as he had promised. The plane was refuelled and, having checked the parachutes and money, Cooper told the crew to take off at 7.40pm and head for Mexico City but then decided on Reno, Nevada as the destination. At 8.13pm, during a heavy rainstorm, Cooper lowered the aft stairs and jumped from the plane over southwestern Washington. He would never be seen again. At 10.15pm the Boeing landed at Reno and the FBI recovered two of the four parachutes.

Jimmy Hoffa

"Hoffa is a very evil influence on the United States"

THE CRIME: James Riddle Hoffa was the vitriolic head of the powerful Teamsters Union in America. He was also in the pay of organized crime. In 1931 Hoffa began organizing a union among workers of a grocer's. He won his men a 40 per cent pay rise and earned himself a full-time job with the International Brotherhood of Teamsters. However, the only money Hoffa then earned was a percentage of the subs from members he had personally recruited. In days when employers would think nothing of settling industrial disputes with violence Hoffa encouraged his members to fight fire with fire. As times changed and employers became more enlightened Hoffa began to intimidate other union leaders and in 1946 was investigated for extortion. On 4 October 1957 he was elected head of the Teamsters after his predecessor, Dave Beck, was jailed for bribery. By 1964 virtually every lorry driver was a member of the Teamsters. It was rumoured that Hoffa was stealing a portion of the union funds for himself and his criminal friends.

The government stepped in and in August 1964 Hoffa was jailed for 13 years for jury tampering, conspiracy, and mail and wire fraud. Former Attorney General Bobby Kennedy had said, "Hoffa is a very evil influence on the United States and something has got to be done about it." Hoffa was freed on 23 December 1971 after President Richard Nixon commuted his sentence. As part of his freedom Hoffa was banned from union activities until 6 March 1980. Despite this, Hoffa began moving to regain control. Others preferred that he remained "retired", including New Jersey union leader Anthony "Tony Pro" Provenzano, who also happened to be a member of the Genovese crime family. The Mafia preferred to work with Hoffa's successor Frank Fitzsimmons. On 30 July 1975 Hoffa arranged to meet Provenzano and another mobster, Anthony "Tony Jack" Giacalone, at a restaurant. When his guests did not show, Hoffa made two calls from a pay phone in the restaurant. He was never seen again.

Jimmy Hoffa in front of the Teamsters offices

WHERE:
Car park of Machus Red Fox Restaurant, 6676 Telegraph Road, Bloomfield Township, Michigan, USA
WHEN:
3.45pm Wednesday 30 July 1975
THE AFTERMATH:
The next day Hoffa's green 1974 Pontiac Grand Ville was found unlocked in the restaurant car park. Questioned by police, Provenzano and Giacalone swore they knew nothing about a meeting with Hoffa. Hoffa had been seen that day in the back of a maroon Mercury belonging to Joe Giacalone, the son of Anthony, and in 2001 a DNA match was made to Hoffa with a hair found in the car. Joe Giacalone claimed that he had lent the car to a friend. Hoffa was legally declared dead in 1982. Machus Red Fox Restaurant closed in 1996.
YOU SHOULD KNOW:
Hoffa's son, James P., is president of the Teamsters while his daughter, Barbara, is a judge.

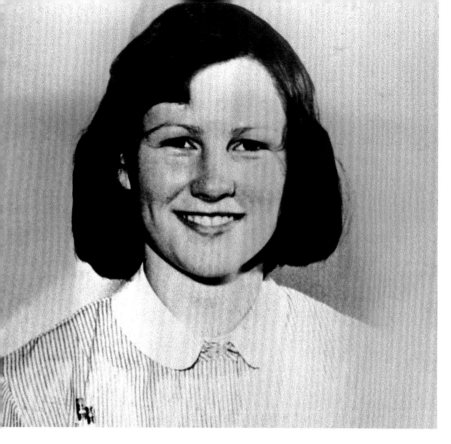

Helen Smith

"If I was to say Helen Smith's death was an accident, I would be a liar"

THE CRIME: Helen Linda Smith was born on 3 January 1956, the daughter of a former policeman. Having failed the exams needed to become a police officer, Helen chose nursing and landed a job at St George's Hospital in Tooting, south London. She transferred to St James's Hospital in Leeds in 1977. On 5 December 1978 she flew to Jeddah to begin work at the new Bakhsh Hospital. On 19 May 1979 she attended a party for diver Tim Hayter at the sixth-floor home of Bakhsh's senior surgeon Dr Richard Shackelton Arnot and his wife Penny at which alcohol was illegally served. There were 11 people present and Helen arrived at 9.45pm.

At some point between then and early the next morning Helen Smith and another guest, a tugboat captain named Johannes Otten, 35, fell to their deaths. The body of Johannes Otten was impaled on railings while Helen's was found on the marble floor nearby. Or at least that was the official story. When Helen's father, Ron, saw her body in the morgue he was shocked to find that there appeared to be no broken bones or anything to suggest that she had fallen any distance, let alone from a sixth-floor balcony. Her right side and inner thighs were badly bruised and there was a deep indent in the middle of her forehead. As he was leaving the Bakhsh Hospital the next day, Mr Smith was approached by friends of his daughter who told him that she had been murdered.

WHERE:
Jeddah, Saudi Arabia
WHEN:
Sunday 20 May 1979
THE AFTERMATH:
Richard and Penny Arnot were both arrested and sentenced on 24 March 1980. Richard received a year in prison and 30 lashes while Penny was sentenced to 80 lashes. Helen Smith's body was flown back to England in June 1980. An autopsy was performed on 16 December. Home Office pathologist Dr Michael Green said, "If I was to say Helen Smith's death was an accident, I would be a liar." A second autopsy found an injury to the left side of the scalp that would have knocked Helen unconscious, if not killed her. Far from death resulting from falling from a great height, Helen Smith had been beaten in the face several times, had received a potentially fatal blow to the head and had been raped. An inquest into Helen's death opened in Leeds on 18 November 1982. At 6.47pm on 9 December 1982 the jury returned a majority open verdict.

Helen Smith in her nurse's uniform

Oscar Romero

"If they have killed him for doing what he did, then I too have to walk the same path"

THE CRIME: Archbishop Romero, more properly Oscar Arnulfo Romero y Galdámez, was born in Ciudad Barrios, El Salvador on 15 August 1917 and joined the seminary of the Claretian Order when he was 13. When he was 24 he moved to the national seminary run by Jesuits in the capital, San Salvador. He was ordained on 4 April 1942 and worked as a parish priest from 1944 until 1966. In 1970 he became auxiliary bishop to the Archbishop of San Salvador Luis Chávez y González and five years later, in December 1975, became bishop of Santiago de María. On 23 February 1977 he was consecrated Archbishop of San Salvador. On 12 March Father Rutilio Grande, a social reformer and a close friend of Archbishop Romero, was assassinated as he made his way to celebrate mass.

Until his friend's death Archbishop Romero had been a conservative man, unwilling to upset the status quo. The death opened his eyes to social inequalities and spurred him on to become a reformer. "If they have killed him for doing what he did," he said, "then I too have to walk the same path." The archbishop criticized the El Salvador government and the endemic corruption it created. He also spoke out against the torture and assassination of political enemies. In 1979 he was nominated for a Nobel Peace Prize. In February 1980 he had an audience with Pope John Paul II to express his concern about the happenings in El Salvador. The terror had increased, following the coup that deposed President Carlos Romero in 1979. In the 12 years that followed as many as 80,000 people died at the hands of death squads. The archbishop asked President Jimmy Carter to halt American aid to El Salvador but Carter ignored him. On 24 March 1980 the archbishop celebrated mass at La Divina Providencia, a small hospital chapel near his cathedral, when a group of men in combat fatigues burst in and shot him to death.

WHERE:
La Divina Providencia, San Salvador, El Salvador
WHEN:
Monday 24 March 1980
THE AFTERMATH:
Archbishop Romero's funeral on 30 March 1980 was attended by more than a quarter of a million people. During the ceremony the government let off bombs and, in the confusion, murdered around 50 mourners. In 1993 a United Nations report identified Major Robert D'Aubuisson (who had died of cancer on 20 February 1992, aged 38) as the man who had ordered the killing. In 1997 Archbishop Romero was proposed for beatification, the first step on the road to sainthood.

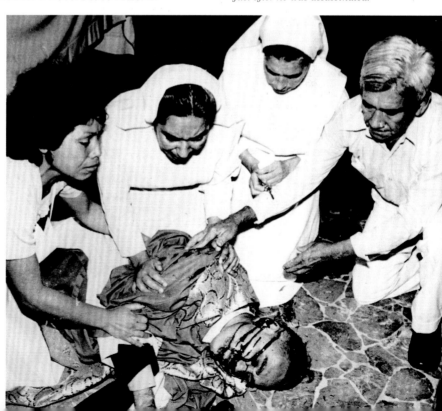

Onlookers crouch around the bullet-ridden body of Oscar Romero, just after he was assassinated.

Roberto Calvi

"If the whole thing comes out it will be enough to start World War III"

WHERE:
Blackfriars Bridge, London, England
WHEN:
7.30am Friday 18 June 1982
THE AFTERMATH:
A second hearing in July 1983 changed the suicide verdict to an open one. In July 1991 a Mafia informer claimed that Calvi had been murdered when the Cosa Nostra lost money in Banco Ambrosiano's collapse. In December 1998 Calvi's body was exhumed and an independent forensic report stated that he had been murdered, an opinion shared by the Calvi family. In September 2003 the City of London Police Force reopened the case. On 5 October 2005 five men, including Calvi's ex-bodyguard and chauffeur, went on trial in Rome, accused of his murder. All were acquitted on 6 June 2007.

THE CRIME: The body of Roberto Calvi, the 62-year-old chairman of the Banco Ambrosiano, who had gone missing from his London home the day before, was spotted hanging from scaffolding under Blackfriars Bridge on 18 June 1982. In his pockets were stones, a forged passport and £15,000 in sterling, Swiss francs and Italian lire. The inquest on 23 July returned a suicide verdict. The Home Office pathologist Professor Keith Simpson testified that Calvi had not been drugged or manhandled before death.

Calvi was known as "God's banker" because the Vatican was the fourth largest shareholder in the Banco Ambrosiano. In the late 1970s Calvi began lending money to foreign companies that existed only on paper and were, in fact, owned by Calvi, who then proceeded to buy shares in Banco Ambrosiano thus gaining a shareholding in the bank bought with the bank's own money. Michele Sindona, a Sicilian entrepreneur, met Calvi and used his web of international bank branches to funnel his own less than honestly acquired money. Two more men became involved in Calvi's web – Bishop Paul Marcinkus, the head of the Vatican Bank and Pope John Paul II's bodyguard, and Licio Gelli, the head of the Masonic lodge P2. Marcinkus had written promissory notes guaranteeing some of the fake companies set up by Calvi and Gelli had invited Calvi into P2, thus guaranteeing his loyalty. When Gelli's premises were raided on 17 March 1981, police found a membership list for P2, which contained the names of 962 public figures, including magistrates, police chiefs, cabinet members and Roberto Calvi. On 6 May 1981 Calvi was arrested. Found guilty of various frauds, on 20 July he was sentenced to a four-year prison term and fined 16 billion lire. He was freed on bail and spent the next 11 months trying to cover his tracks. On 31 May 1982 the Bank of Italy wrote to Calvi and his fellow directors, demanding a complete account of all the Banco Ambrosiano's foreign lending. On 10 June 1982 Calvi fled to Britain on a forged passport and moved into a serviced apartment in Chelsea Cloisters, Sloane Avenue in London. He said, "If the whole thing comes out it will be enough to start World War III." On 17 June 1982 Calvi disappeared from his home.

"God's Banker" Roberto Calvi

Shergar

"It was several minutes before the horse, which was in agony, slowly bled to death"

THE CRIME: On 3 June 1981 Shergar, ridden by 19-year-old Walter Swinburn, won the Derby by a record ten lengths. The horse's odds were 11/10 on. That November the thoroughbred was retired to stud at Ballmany Stud, near Newbridge in Ireland, one of two farms owned by the Aga Khan.

After producing 35 foals, Shergar was kidnapped just after 8.30pm on a cold February night by eight masked men bearing machine guns. Three of the men knocked at the house of Jim Fitzgerald, the 53-year-old head groom of the stud. Bernard Fitzgerald, the 21-year-old son of Jim, opened the door and had a machine gun thrust into his face. The men forced their way into the living room where Mrs Fitzgerald was with six members of her family.

Her husband came running when he heard the commotion. The masked men threatened to kill all the family unless Jim Fitzgerald did as he was told. Mrs Fitzgerald was locked in a room with her five sons and two daughters while Mr Fitzgerald was forced to go outside and identify Shergar's stable. The gunmen loaded the stallion into a horse box and forced Jim Fitzgerald to lie face down, head covered, in one of the other vehicles. Four hours later, he was freed about 11 km (7 mi) from the stud.

The jockey, Walter Swinburn, riding Shergar at Ascot racecourse.

WHERE:
Ballmany Stud, near Newbridge, County Kildare, Republic of Ireland
WHEN:
Tuesday 8 February 1983
THE AFTERMATH:
Two days after the kidnapping, a ransom demand for £2 million was made. The kidnappers mistakenly believed that the Aga Khan owned Shergar outright, rather than just a share in him along with 34 other owners. It was feared that if a ransom was paid every valuable horse in Britain and Ireland would be targeted. Several IRA strongholds were raided by police looking for the horse, uncovering arms dumps but no racehorses. Four days later, it is believed that the Army Council of the IRA realized that their victim was worthless and ordered him to be put down. Then two members of the IRA went into a stable and machine-gunned Shergar to death. A source told a Sunday newspaper, "There was blood everywhere and the horse even slipped on its own blood... It was several minutes before the horse, which was in agony, slowly bled to death."

Colonial Parkway Killer

Robin's belt was undone and her bra was around her neck

WHERE:
Colonial Parkway, Virginia, USA
WHEN:
Sunday 12 October 1986
THE AFTERMATH:
Police have no real idea who the
Colonial Parkway Killer is, although
some have suggested that he (or
they) are law officials.

THE CRIME: The Colonial Parkway Killer struck for the first time on 12 October 1986. His first two victims were a lesbian couple, stockbroker and former sailor Cathleen Marian Thomas, 27, and student Rebecca Ann Dowski, 21. Their corpses were discovered by a jogger on the back seat of their Honda Civic, which had been shoved down an embankment of the York River, 11 km (7 mi) east of Williamsburg and about 1.6 km (1 mi) from Cheatham Annex, near an area popular with gay courting couples. It is believed that they preferred to park on the Colonial Parkway for privacy. They

had been strangled, tied up and had their throats slashed but there was no evidence of sexual assault. Robbery was not a motive as their handbags and purses were still in the car. Their bodies had been doused with diesel, although not set alight.

Just under a year later, in September 1987, David Lee Knobling, 20, and Robin M. Edwards, 14, were found murdered in the Ragged Island Wildlife Refuge, at the foot of the James River Bridge on the south shore of the James River, in Isle of Wight County, near Smithfield, Virginia. They had last been seen on 19 September 1987. Robin's belt was undone and her bra was around her neck. David's black Ford pick-up was spotted two days later. The radio was on, the driver's side window was half down, the keys were in the ignition and David's wallet was on the dashboard. Their bodies were found about 3 km (2 mi) from the truck. Police think that the pair was marched through the woods for 2 km (1.5 mi) before they were summarily executed and then dumped into the river.

The next murders occurred seven months later on 9 April 1988. Cassandra Lee Hailey, 18, and Richard Keith Call were reported missing after their first date together. On 10 April Call's red Toyota Celica was discovered empty on the Colonial Parkway at 9am but no trace of either person has ever been found. The couple's clothing, including underwear, was on the back seat of the car.

On 5 September 1989 Anna Marie Phelps, 18, and Daniel Lauer, 21, went missing. A hunter found their skeletal remains near Interstate 64 between Williamsburg and Richmond the following month. Both had been stabbed.

The leafy surrounds of the Colonial Parkway, near Williamsburg

Nicole Brown Simpson & Ronald Goldman

"[Nicole] was virtually decapitated. Her jugular was all but completely severed"

WHERE:
875 South Bundy Drive, Brentwood, California, USA
WHEN:
9.45pm–10.45pm Sunday 12 June 1994
THE AFTERMATH:
At 11.45pm Simpson had flown to Chicago to attend a business conference. Police searched Simpson's estate at 360 North Rockingham Avenue and Detective Mark Fuhrman found a bloody right hand glove, which matched one found near the two corpses. Unfortunately the police had not waited for a search warrant. Simpson was arrested at his home on 17 June 1994 after a slow-motion chase which began at 5.51pm and was watched live on television by millions, ending at 7.57pm. "The trial of the century" began before Judge Lance Ito on 24 January 1995 with Simpson defended by the so-called Dream Team of Johnnie Cochran, Robert Shapiro and F. Lee Bailey, among others. During the trial Detective Fuhrman was accused of being a racist who had framed Simpson and Simpson refused to don the bloodstained gloves. At 10am on 3 October 1995 Simpson was acquitted of both murders much to the shock of many. The jury had taken just five hours and four minutes to deliberate. On 5 February 1997 at a civil hearing Simpson was found liable for both deaths and ordered to pay the Goldman family $19.5 million. He never paid a cent.
YOU SHOULD KNOW:
On 13 September 2007 in Las Vegas Simpson and a group of men retrieved sporting memorabilia they claimed had been stolen from them. On 3 October 2008 Simpson was found guilty of 12 charges of armed robbery and kidnapping regarding the incident. On 5 December he was jailed for up to 33 years by Las Vegas district court Judge Jackie Glass who said the evidence against him was overwhelming. "You went to the room, you took guns... you used

THE CRIME: O.J. Simpson was a popular American football player who, on his retirement in 1978, became a popular actor and a spokesman for various organizations. Having divorced his first wife by whom he had three children, Simpson married Nicole Brown, 12 years his junior, on 2 February 1985 and had two more children.

During and after their separation Nicole had made at least 20 calls to the police in fear of her life. At 4.30pm on 12 June Nicole, 35, attended a dance recital at her daughter Sydney's school before going for dinner at 6.30pm at a Brentwood trattoria called Mezzaluna, where 25-year-old Ron Goldman was a waiter. Nicole's mother left a pair of prescription sunglasses there and Goldman offered to return them.

At 9.45pm he went home to change clothes before heading over to Nicole's home where they were both brutally butchered. A neighbour discovered the two bloody corpses at 12.10am on 13 June. One forensic examiner said, "[Nicole] was virtually decapitated. Her jugular was all but completely severed by a gash inflicted from the left side of her neck to her right ear." Goldman's throat was slashed and he was stabbed 19 times in the torso.

force, you took property... and in this state that amounts to robbery with a deadly weapon," she said. Simpson said, "I didn't mean to hurt anybody and I didn't mean to steal from anybody. I did not know that I was doing anything illegal... I thought that I was confronting friends and retrieving my property." Outside

court Ron Goldman's father said, "There's never closure. Ron is always gone. What we have is satisfaction that this monster is where he belongs: behind bars."

Tupac Shakur

"All the n**rs who change the world die in violence. They don't die in regular ways"**

THE CRIME: Born on 16 June 1971, Tupac Amaru Shakur was the son of a Black Panther Party member who was jailed for terrorism while pregnant with him in Brooklyn, New York. He was named after Túpac Amaru, the Incan revolutionary who was sentenced to death by the Spanish. Shakur was raised in Oakland, California. In 1991 he came to public attention with the group Digital Underground and his solo album *2Pacalypse Now,* and went on to become a top-selling recording artist. He was criticised for the references throughout his tracks to sexual violence and killing policemen. He was also a promising actor; his first acting role was that of the character Bishop in *Juice* (1992). The following year he starred opposite Janet Jackson as Lucky in *Poetic Justice.* In 1994 he was sentenced to 15 days in jail for assault and battery. That year he appeared in *Above The Rim.*

On 29 April 1995 Shakur married Keisha Morris but the marriage was annulled the following year. That year he was accused of sexually assaulting a female fan but he was released after eight months, pending an appeal. His last films were *Bullet, Gridlock'd* and *Gang Related,* released in 1997.

On 7 September 1996 Shakur watched the Mike Tyson–Bruce Seldon fight in Las Vegas, Nevada. Afterwards he was driving with Death Row Records chief executive Marion "Suge" Knight to a party, when he was shot four times. He was taken to University Medical Center hospital where his right lung was removed, but doctors could do no more and, after six days in a coma, he died at 4.03pm on Friday 13 September. Earlier that year he had told an interviewer: "All good n****rs, all the n****rs who change the world, die in violence. They don't die in regular ways."

WHERE:
Flamingo Road, Las Vegas, Nevada, USA
WHEN:
Saturday 7 September 1996
THE AFTERMATH:
The murder was put down to rivalry between East and West Coast rappers. On Sunday 9 March 1997 rapper and former drug dealer, Notorious B.I.G., attended the 11th annual Soul Train Music awards. As he was leaving for an after-show party at the Petersen Automotive Museum in Los Angeles he, too, was shot in a drive-by shooting. He died at 1.15am the next day. Many believed his death was retribution for the murder of Tupac Shakur. Both murders are unsolved.

Gangster rapper Tupac Shakur lives on through this mural.

WHERE:
755 (now 749) 15th Street, Boulder,
Colorado, USA
WHEN:
Thursday 26 December 1996
THE AFTERMATH:
In December 2003 a DNA sample was
recovered from JonBenet's underwear
but no match was found. Police later
revealed that 38 registered sex
offenders were living within a 3 km
(2 mi) radius of the Ramsey house. On
16 August 2006 a 41-year-old

*John and Patsy Ramsey
hold a flyer offering $100,000
for information.*

JonBenet Ramsey

John found his daughter's corpse covered by a white blanket

THE CRIME: JonBenet Ramsey was born on 6 August 1990 in Atlanta, Georgia. Her parents began entering her into beauty contests, her mother, Patsy, having been Miss West Virginia 1977. JonBenet won several of the competitions she entered. On Boxing Day 1996 Patsy discovered her daughter was missing and found a two and a half-page ransom note demanding $118,000 for the six-year-old's safe return. Patsy called the police at 5.52am and summoned family and friends to her side, despite instructions not to in the ransom note. The police examined the Ramsey's

house but found no signs of a break-in although a basement window had been broken before Christmas and left unrepaired. JonBenet's father John arranged for the ransom and then was asked by the police to conduct a search of his house to see if he noticed anything suspicious. They began in the bathroom in the basement and then moved on to another room before entering the wine cellar where John found his daughter's corpse covered by a white blanket. The police immediately suspected the Ramseys of murdering their daughter. The autopsy revealed that the little girl had been garrotted with a cord and the broken handle of a paintbrush and that she had also suffered a skull fracture. The bristles of the paintbrush were found in Patsy's belongings but the final part of the broken paintbrush was never found.

paedophile, John Mark Karr, was arrested in Bangkok in connection with the case. He claimed to have been with JonBenet when she died and said her death was an accident. However, his DNA did not match that at the crime scene and on 28 August it was announced that no charges would be brought against Karr.

YOU SHOULD KNOW:
On 9 July 2008 the Boulder District Attorney's Office exonerated the Ramsey family of any involvement in JonBenet's death. It was rather too late for Patsy Ramsey – she had died aged 49 of ovarian cancer on 24 June 2006.

Anne Pressly

Pressly was unconscious and bleeding from a head wound

THE CRIME: Born in South Carolina on 28 August 1982, blonde, beautiful Anne Pressly moved with her family to Little Rock, Arkansas when she was in secondary school. She was educated at Rhodes College in Memphis, Tennessee but returned to Little Rock and, in 2004, landed a job as an on-air reporter and presenter for the local television station KATV, an ABC network affiliate station. She had conducted interviews with a number of high-profile personalities during her time at the station.

Anne Pressly bore a slight resemblance to the rabidly right-wing commentator Ann Coulter which led to her being hired to play a Coulter-type character in Oliver Stone's film *W*, which was filmed in Shreveport, Louisiana. On the night before she died Anne had eaten at a restaurant with her friend Mallory Hardin, a reporter at KARK-TV, before going to see *W* with other friends.

Anne's mother Patti Cannady would give her a daily wake-up call for her breakfast show *Daybreak*. However, her mother discovered Pressly in her bed at 4.30am half an hour before she was due on air on 20 October 2008. Pressly was unconscious and bleeding from a head wound. Initial reports stated that she had been stabbed but this was later revised to state that she had been hit repeatedly in the face, head and neck with a blunt instrument. Her handbag was missing. The attack occurred between 10.30pm on Sunday and 4.30am the following morning.

WHERE:
Club Road, Little Rock, Arkansas, USA
WHEN:
Monday 20 October 2008
THE AFTERMATH:
Doctors were hopeful that Anne would recover from the beating as the swelling in her brain had decreased and they reduced the painkillers. However, on Saturday 25 October she took a turn for the worse and died, aged just 26, at St Vincent Infirmary Medical Center. KATV set up a reward fund for information leading to the arrest and conviction of Pressly's killer. Within 24 hours, the total donations had reached $30,000. The police discounted the theory that Anne had been targeted because of her media profile. They believed that she was the victim of a random burglary that had gone horribly wrong. On 26 November police arrested Curtis Lavelle Vance, 28, at a home in Little Rock.